International Management

Culture, Strategy, and Behavior

Tenth Edition

Jonathan P. Doh
Villanova University

Fred Luthans
University of Nebraska–Lincoln

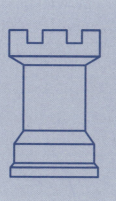

Mc
Graw
Hill
Education

INTERNATIONAL MANAGEMENT: CULTURE, STRATEGY, AND BEHAVIOR, TENTH EDITION

Published by McGraw-Hill Education, 2 Penn Plaza, New York, NY 10121. Copyright © 2018 by McGraw-Hill Education. All rights reserved. Printed in the United States of America. Previous editions © 2015, 2012, and 2009. No part of this publication may be reproduced or distributed in any form or by any means, or stored in a database or retrieval system, without the prior written consent of McGraw-Hill Education, including, but not limited to, in any network or other electronic storage or transmission, or broadcast for distance learning.

Some ancillaries, including electronic and print components, may not be available to customers outside the United States.

This book is printed on acid-free paper.

1 2 3 4 5 6 7 8 9 LWI 21 20 19 18 17

ISBN 978-1-259-70507-6
MHID 1-259-70507-2

Chief Product Officer, SVP Products & Markets: *G. Scott Virkler*
Vice President, General Manager, Products & Markets: *Michael Ryan*
Vice President, Content Design & Delivery: *Betsy Whalen*
Managing Director: *Susan Gouijnstook*
Director, Product Development: *Meghan Campbell*
Director, Management/OB: *Michael Ablassmeir*
Director of Digital Content: *Kristy Dekat*
Product Developer: *Laura Hurst Spell*
Marketing Manager: *Debbie Clare*
Marketing Coordinator: *Brittany Bernholdt*
Digital Product Analyst: *Sankha Basu*
Director, Program Management: *Linda Avenarius*
Program Manager: *Mark Christianson*
Content Project Managers: *Danielle Clement/Karen Jozefowicz*
Buyer: *Jennifer Pickel*
Design: *Jessica Serd*
Content Licensing Specialists: *Shannon Manderscheid/Lori Hancock*
Cover Image: *© Glow Images/Rodrigo A Torress*
Compositor: *SPi Global*
Printer: *LSC Communications*

All credits appearing on page or at the end of the book are considered to be an extension of the copyright page.

Library of Congress Cataloging-in-Publication Data

Names: Luthans, Fred, author. | Doh, Jonathan P., author.
Title: International management : culture, strategy, and behavior / Fred
    Luthans, University of Nebraska-Lincoln, Jonathan P. Doh, Villanova
    University.
Description: Tenth Edition. | Dubuque: McGraw-Hill Education, [2018] |
    Revised edition of the authors' International management, [2015]
Identifiers: LCCN 2016055609| ISBN 9781259705076 (alk. paper) | ISBN
    1259705072 (alk. paper)
Subjects: LCSH: International business enterprises—Management. |
    International business enterprises—Management—Case studies.
Classification: LCC HD62.4 .H63 2018 | DDC 658/.049—dc23 LC record
available at https://lccn.loc.gov/2016055609

The Internet addresses listed in the text were accurate at the time of publication. The inclusion of a website does not indicate an endorsement by the authors or McGraw-Hill Education, and McGraw-Hill Education does not guarantee the accuracy of the information presented at these sites.

mheducation.com/highered

Dedicated in Memory of

Rafael Lucea,
A Passionate Advocate for Global Business Education and Experience.

Preface

Changes in the global business environment continue unabated and at an accelerated pace. Many surprising and difficult-to-predict developments have rocked global peace and economic security. Terrorism, mass migration, the United Kingdom's exit from the European Union, and the rise of anti-immigration political movements in Europe, the United States, and elsewhere have called into question assumptions about the direction of the global political economy. In addition, rapid advances in social media have not only accelerated globalization but also provided a means for those who seek political and economic changes to organize and influence their leaders for more responsible governance, or, in some cases, advance a more narrow ideological agenda (see opening articles in Chapters 1 and 2). In addition, concerns about climate change and other environmental issues have prompted companies, in conjunction with governments and nongovernmental organizations, to consider alternate approaches to business and governance (see Chapter 3 opening article).

Some of these developments have challenged longstanding beliefs about the power and benefits of globalization and economic integration, but they also underscore the interconnected nature of global economies. Although many countries and regions around the world are closely linked, important differences in institutional and cultural environments persist, and some of these differences have become even more pronounced in recent years. The challenges for international management reflect this dynamism and the increasing unpredictability of global economic and political events. Continued growth of the emerging markets is reshaping the global balance of economic power, even though differences exist between and among regions and countries. Although many emerging markets continued to experience growth during a period when developed countries' economies stagnated or declined, others, like Russia and Brazil, have faced major setbacks. Further, some developed economies, such as Greece, Italy, Spain, and Portugal, continue to face formidable challenges that stem from the European debt crisis that began in 2009. Low or negative interest rates reflect a "new normal" of slower-than-average growth among many global economies.

The global political and security environment remains unpredictable and volatile, with ongoing conflicts in the Middle East and Africa and continuing tensions in Iran, North Korea, Iraq, and Afghanistan and elsewhere. Another crisis stemming from conflict in Syria and elsewhere has resulted in mass migration—and broad dislocations—across North Africa and Southern, even Northern, Europe (see Chapters 1 and 2 for further discussion). On the economic front, the global trade and integration agenda seems stalled, largely due to domestic political pressures in Europe and North America. Although the Trans-Pacific Partnership (TPP), a proposed free-trade agreement including 12 countries in the Americas and Asia, was concluded, its ratification in the United States is uncertain. Similarly, the fate of the Transatlantic Trade and Investment Partnership, which was still under negotiation at the time of this writing, is also unclear.

As noted above, the advent of social networking has transformed the way citizens interact; how businesses market, promote, and distribute their products globally; and how civil society expresses its concerns that governments provide greater freedoms and accountability. Concurrently, companies, individuals, and even students can now engage in broad "mass" collaboration through digital, online technology for the development of new and innovative systems, products, and ideas. Both social networking and mass collaboration bring new power and influence to individuals across borders and transform the nature of their relationships with global organizations. Although globalization and technology continue to link nations, businesses, and individuals, these linkages also highlight the importance of understanding different cultures, national systems, and corporate management practices around the world. The world is now interconnected geographically, but also electronically and psychologically; as such, nearly all businesses have been touched in some way by globalization. Yet, as cultural, political, and economic differences persist, astute international managers must be in a position to adapt and adjust to the vagaries of different contexts and environments.

In this new tenth edition of *International Management,* we have retained the strong and effective foundations gained from research and practice over the past decades while incorporating the important latest research and contemporary insights that have changed the context and environment for international management. Several trends have emerged that pose both challenges and opportunities for international managers.

First, more nationalistically oriented governments and/or political movements have emerged in many regions of the world, challenging previous assumptions about the benefits and inevitability of globalization and integration. Second, while emerging markets continue to rise in importance, some—such as China and India—have fared much better economically than others—such as Brazil and Russia. Third, aging populations and concerns about migration have challenged many developed country governments as they wrestle with these dual pressures. Fourth, social media and other forms of electronic connectivity continue to facilitate international business of all sorts; however, these connection go only so far, with many barriers and limitations imposed by governments.

Although we have extensive new, evidence-based material in this edition, we continue to strive to make the book even more user-friendly and applicable to practice. We continue to take a balanced approach in the tenth edition of *International Management: Culture, Strategy, and Behavior.* Whereas other texts stress culture, strategy, or behavior, our emphasis on all three critical dimensions—and the interactions among them—has been a primary reason why the previous editions have been the market-leading international management text. Specifically, this edition has the following chapter distribution: environment (three chapters), culture (four chapters), strategy (four chapters), and organizational behavior/human resource management (three chapters). Because the context of international management changes rapidly, all the chapters have been updated and improved. New real-world examples and research results are integrated throughout the book, accentuating the experiential relevance of the straightforward content. As always, we emphasize a balance of research and application.

For the new tenth edition we have incorporated important new content in the areas of the emergence and role of social media as a means of transacting business and mobilizing social movements, the global pressures around migration, the role of the "sharing" economy as represented by companies such as Uber, and other important global themes. We have incorporated the latest research and practical insights on pressure for MNCs to adopt more sustainable practices, and the strategies many companies are using to differentiate their products through such "green" management practices. We have updated discussion of a range of contemporary topics, including continued exploration of the role of the comprehensive GLOBE study on cross-cultural leadership.

A continuing and relevant end-of-chapter feature in this edition is the "Internet Exercise." The purpose of each exercise is to encourage students to use the Internet to find information from the websites of prominent MNCs to answer relevant questions about the chapter topic. An end-of-book feature is a series of Skill-Building and Experiential Exercises for aspiring international managers. These in-class exercises represent the various parts of the text (culture, strategy, and behavior) and provide hands-on experience.

We have extended from the ninth edition of *International Management* the chapter-opening discussions called "The World of International Management" (WIM), based on very recent, relevant news stories to grab readers' interest and attention. Many of these opening articles are new to this edition and all have been updated. These timely opening discussions transition the reader into the chapter topic. At the end of each chapter, there is a pedagogical feature that revisits the chapter's subject matter: "The World of International Management—Revisited." Here we pose several discussion questions based on the topic of the opening feature in light of the student's entire reading of the chapter. Answering these questions requires readers to reconsider and to draw from the chapter material. Suggested answers to these "WIM—Revisited" discussion questions appear in the completely updated Instructor's Manual, where we also provide some multiple-choice and true-false questions that draw directly from the chapters' World of International Management topic matter for instructors who want to include this material in their tests.

The use and application of cases are further enhanced in this edition. All cases have been updated and several new ones have been added. The short within-chapter country case illustrations—"In the International Spotlight"—can be read and discussed in class. These have all been revised and three have been added—Cuba, Greece, and Nigeria. In addition, we have added an additional exercise, "You Be the International Management Consultant," that presents a challenge or dilemma facing a company in the subject country of the "Spotlight." Students are invited to respond to a question related to this challenge. The revised or newly added "Integrative Cases" positioned at the end of each main part of the text were created exclusively for this edition and provide opportunities for reading and analysis outside of class. Review questions provided for each case are intended to facilitate lively and productive written analysis or in-class discussion. Our "Brief Integrative Cases" typically explore a specific situation or challenge facing an individual or team. Our longer and more detailed "In-Depth Integrative Cases" provide a broader discussion of the challenges facing a company. These two formats allow maximum flexibility so that instructors can use the cases in a tailored and customized fashion. Accompanying many of the in-depth cases are short exercises that can be used in class to reinforce both the substantive topic and students' skills in negotiation, presentation, and analysis. The cases have been extensively updated and several are new to this edition. Cases concerning the controversies over drug pricing, TOMS shoes, Russell Athletics/Fruit of the Loom, Euro Disneyland and Disney Asia, Google in China, IKEA, HSBC, Nike, Walmart, Tata, Danone, Chiquita, Coca-Cola, and others are unique to this book and specific to this edition. Of course, instructors also have access to Create (www.mcgraw-hill-create.com), McGraw-Hill's extensive content database, which includes thousands of cases from major sources such as Harvard Business School, Ivey, Darden, and NACRA case databases.

Along with the new or updated "International Management in Action" boxed application examples within each chapter and other pedagogical features at the end of each chapter (i.e., "Key Terms," "Review and Discussion Questions," "The World of International Management—Revisited," and "Internet Exercise"), the end-of-part brief and in-depth cases and the end-of-book skill-building exercises and simulations in the Connect resources complete the package.

International Management is generally recognized to be the first "mainstream" text of its kind. Strategy casebooks and specialized books in organizational behavior, human resources, and, of course, international business, finance, marketing, and economics preceded it, but there were no international management texts before this one, and it remains the market leader. We have had sustainability because of the effort and care put into the revisions. We hope you agree that this tenth edition continues the tradition and remains the "world-class" text for the study of international management.

McGraw-Hill Connect®: connect.mheducation.com

Continually evolving, McGraw-Hill Connect® has been redesigned to provide the only true adaptive learning experience delivered within a simple and easy-to-navigate environment, placing students at the very center.

- Performance Analytics—Now available for both instructors and students, easy-to-decipher data illuminate course performance. Students always know how they're doing in class, while instructors can view student and section performance at a glance.
- Personalized Learning—Squeezing the most out of study time, the adaptive engine within Connect creates a highly personalized learning path for each student by identifying areas of weakness and providing learning resources to assist in the moment of need.

This seamless integration of reading, practice, and assessment ensures that the focus is on the most important content for that individual.

Instructor Library   The Connect Management Instructor Library is your repository for additional resources to improve student engagement in and out of class. You can select and use any asset that enhances your lecture.

To help instructors teach international management, this text is accompanied by a revised and expanded Instructor's Resource Manual, Test Bank, and PowerPoint slides, all of which are in the Connect Library.

Acknowledgments

We would like to acknowledge those who have helped to make this book a reality. We will never forget the legacy of international management education in general and for this text in particular provided by our departed colleague Richard M. Hodgetts. Special thanks also go to our growing number of colleagues throughout the world who have given us many ideas and inspired us to think internationally. Closer to home, Jonathan Doh would like to thank the Villanova School of Business and its leadership, especially Provost Pat Maggitti, Interim Dean Daniel Wright, Dean Joyce Russell, Interim Vice Dean Wen Mao, and Herb Rammrath, who generously endowed the Chair in International Business Jonathan now holds. Also, for this new tenth edition we would like to thank Ben Littell, who did comprehensive research, graphical design, and writing to update chapter material and cases. Specifically, Ben researched and drafted chapter opening World of International Management features, developed a number of original graphics, and provided extensive research assistance for other revisions to the book. Allison Meade researched and drafted the Chapter 4 World of International Management feature on "Culture Clashes in Cross-Border Mergers and Acquisitions." Fred Luthans would like to give special recognition to two international management scholars: Henry H. Albers, former Chair of the Management Department at the University of Nebraska and former Dean at the University of Petroleum and Minerals, Saudi Arabia, to whom previous editions of this book were dedicated; and Sang M. Lee, former Chair of the Management Department at Nebraska, founding and current president of the Pan Pacific Business Association, and close colleague on many ventures around the world over the past 30 years.

In addition, we would like to acknowledge the help that we received from the many reviewers from around the globe, whose feedback guided us in preparing the tenth edition of the text. These include

Joseph S. Anderson, Northern Arizona University

Chi Anyansi-Archibong, North Carolina A&T State University

Koren Borges, University of North Florida

Lauryn De George, University of Central Florida

Jae Jung, University of Missouri at Kansas City

Manjula S. Salimath, University of North Texas

Our thanks, too, to the reviewers of previous editions of the text:

Thomas M. Abbott, Post University

Yohannan T. Abraham, Southwest Missouri State University

Janet S. Adams, Kennesaw State University

Irfan Ahmed, Sam Houston State University

Chi Anyansi-Archibong, North Carolina A&T State University

Kibok Baik, James Madison University

R. B. Barton, Murray State University

Lawrence A. Beer, Arizona State University

Koren Borges, University of North Florida

Tope A. Bello, East Carolina University

Mauritz Blonder, Hofstra University

Gunther S. Boroschek, University of Massachusetts–Boston

Charles M. Byles, Virginia Commonwealth University

Constance Campbell, Georgia Southern University

Scott Kenneth Campbell, Georgia College & State University

M. Suzanne Clinton, University of Central Oklahoma

Helen Deresky, SUNY Plattsburgh

Dr. Dharma deSilva, Center for International Business Advancement (CIBA)

David Elloy, Gonzaga University

Val Finnigan, Leeds Metropolitan University

David M. Flynn, Hofstra University

Jan Flynn, Georgia College and State University

Joseph Richard Goldman, University of Minnesota

James Gran, Buena Vista University

Robert T. Green, University of Texas at Austin

Annette Gunter, University of Central Oklahoma

Jerry Haar, Florida International University–Miami

Jean M. Hanebury, Salisbury State University

Richard C. Hoffman, Salisbury State University

Johan Hough, University of South Africa

Julie Huang, Rio Hondo College

Mohd Nazari Ismail, University of Malaya

Steve Jenner, California State University–Dominguez Hills

James P. Johnson, Rollins College

Marjorie Jones, Nova Southeastern University

Jae C. Jung, University of Missouri–Kansas City

Ann Langlois, Palm Beach Atlantic University

Robert Kuhne, Hofstra University

Christine Lentz, Rider University

Ben Lever III, College of Charleston

Robert C. Maddox, University of Tennessee

Curtis Matherne III, East Tennessee State University

Douglas M. McCabe, Georgetown University

Jeanne M. McNett, Assumption College

Lauryn Migenes, University of Central Florida

Alan N. Miller, University of Nevada, Las Vegas

Ray Montagno, Ball State University

Rebecca J. Morris, University of Nebraska–Omaha

Ernst W. Neuland, University of Pretoria

William Newburry, Rutgers Business School

Yongsun Paik, Loyola Marymount University

Valerie S. Perotti, Rochester Institute of Technology

Richard B. Peterson, University of Washington

Suzanne J. Peterson, University of Nebraska–Lincoln

Joseph A. Petrick, Wright State University

Juan F. Ramirez, Nova Southeastern University

Richard David Ramsey, Southeastern Louisiana University

Owen Sevier, University of Central Oklahoma

Mansour Sharif-Zadeh, California State Polytechnic University–Pomona

Emeric Solymossy, Western Illinois University.

Jane H. Standford, Texas A&M University–Kingsville

Dale V. Steinmann, San Francisco State University

Randall Stross, San Jose State University

George Sutija, Florida International University

Deanna Teel, Houston Community College

David Turnipseed, University of South Alabama–Mobile

Katheryn H. Ward, Chicago State University

Li Weixing, University of Nebraska–Lincoln

Aimee Wheaton, Regis College

Marion M. White, James Madison University

Timothy Wilkinson, University of Akron

George Yacus, Old Dominion University

Corinne Young, University of Tampa

Zhe Zhang, University of Central Florida–Orlando

Anatoly Zhuplev, Loyola Marymount University

Finally, thanks to the team at McGraw-Hill who worked on this book: Susan Gouijnstook, Managing Director; Anke Weekes, Executive Brand Manager; Laura Hurst Spell, Senior Product Developer; Erin Guendelsberger, Development Editor; Michael Gedatus, Marketing Manager; and Danielle Clement, Content Project Manager. Last but by no means least, we greatly appreciate the love and support provided by our families.

Fred Luthans and Jonathan P. Doh

Luthans DoH

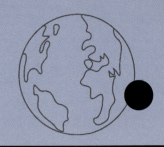

The tenth edition of *International Management: Culture, Strategy, and Behavior* is still setting the standard. Authors Jonathan Doh and Fred Luthans have taken care to retain the effective foundation gained from research and practice over the past decades. At the same time, they have fully incorporated important new and emerging developments that have changed what international managers are currently facing and likely to face in the coming years.

New and Enhanced Themes

- Thoroughly revised and updated chapters to reflect the most critical issues for international managers.
- Greater attention to demographic trends and human mobility, underscoring the importance of aging work forces, migration, culture, and global talent management.
- Focus on global sustainability and sustainable management practices and their impact on international management.
- New or revised opening World of International Management (WIM) features written by the authors on current international management challenges; these mini-cases were prepared expressly for this edition and are not available elsewhere.
- Discussions of the rise of global terrorism, the migrant crisis, the growing role of social media in international transactions, and many other contemporary topics presented in the opening chapter and throughout the book.
- New and updated discussions of major issues in global ethics, sustainability, and insights from project GLOBE and other cutting-edge research.
- Greater emphasis on major emerging regions, economic challenges in major countries such as Brazil and Russia, and specific case illustrations on how companies are managing these challenges.

Thoroughly Revised and Updated Chapter Content

- New or revised opening WIM discussions on topics including the global influences of social media using the case of Snapchat; the role of social networking in political change in the Middle East; sustainability as a global competitive advantage using examples of Patagonia, Tesla, and Nestlé; and cultural challenges in global mergers and acquisitions. Others address the competitive dynamics between Apple and Xiaomi and Amazon and Alibaba, the emergence of Haier as the largest global appliance company, Netflix's challenges in China and Russia, and many others. These features were written expressly for this edition and are not available elsewhere.
- Updated and strengthened emphasis on ethics, social responsibility, and sustainability.
- Extensive coverage of Project GLOBE, its relationship to other cultural frameworks, and its application to international management practice (Chapters 4, 13).
- Revised or new "In the International Spotlight" inserts that profile the key economic and political issues relevant to managers in specific countries.
- Greater coverage of the challenges and opportunities for international strategy targeted to the developing "base of the pyramid" economies (Chapter 8 and Tata cases).

x

Thoroughly Updated and/or New Cases, Inserts, and Exercises

- Completely new "In the International Spotlight" country profiles at the end of every chapter including the addition of profiles on Cuba, Greece, and Nigeria.
- "You Be the International Management Consultant" exercises presenting an actual company's challenge in that country and inviting students to recommend a course of action.
- New "International Management in Action" features, including discussions on timely topics such as the rise of Bitcoin, the Volkswagen emissions scandal, and the political risks facing Uber, to name a few.
- Thoroughly updated cases (not available elsewhere): TOMS shoes, Russell Athletics/Fruit of the Loom, Euro Disneyland and Disney Asia, Google in China, IKEA, HSBC, Nike, Walmart, Tata, Danone, Chiquita, Coca-Cola, and others are unique to this book and specific to this edition.
- Brand new end-of-part cases developed exclusively for this edition (not available elsewhere): *TOMS Puts Its Right Foot Forward*; *The Ethics of Global Drug Pricing*.
- Brand new "World of International Management" chapter opening discussions, including topics such as Netflix's expansion to emerging markets, the merger of ABInBev and SABMiller, the battle brewing between Apple's iPhone and Chinese cell phone startups, the impact of Russian sanctions on international businesses, and the growth of Chinese brand Haier, to name a few.
- New and revised graphics throughout.
- Timely updates throughout, based on the latest research, including an extended discussion of the GLOBE project, the continued impact of global terrorism on international business, and the push towards a sustainable future, to name a few.

Totally Revised Instructor and Student Support

The following instructor and student support materials can be found in Connect® at connect.mheducation.com for the Tenth Edition.

- The Instructor's Manual offers a summary of Learning Objectives and a teaching outline with lecture notes and teaching tips, as well as suggested answers to questions found throughout and at the conclusion of each chapter. Suggested answers are also provided for all the cases found in the book.
- The test bank is offered in both Word and EZ Test formats and offers over 1,000 test items consisting of true/false, multiple choice, and essay. Answers are provided for all test bank questions.

LEARNSMART®

SMARTBOOK®

- PowerPoint Presentations consisting of 30 slides per chapter give instructors talking points, feature exhibits from the text, and are summarized with a review and discussion slide.
- **LearnSmart®:** The Tenth Edition of *International Management* is available with LearnSmart, the most widely used adaptive learning resource, which is proven to improve grades. To improve your understanding of this subject and improve your grades, go to McGraw-Hill Connect® at connect.mheducation.com and find out more about LearnSmart. By helping students focus on the most important information they need to learn, LearnSmart personalizes the learning experience so they can study as efficiently as possible.
- **SmartBook®:** An extension of LearnSmart, SmartBook is an adaptive eBook that helps students focus their study time more effectively. As students read, SmartBook assesses comprehension and dynamically highlights where they need to study more.
- **Create:** Instructors can now tailor their teaching resources to match the way they teach! With McGraw-Hill Create, create.mheducation.com, instructors can easily rearrange chapters, combine material from other content sources, and quickly upload and integrate their own content, like course syllabi or teaching notes. Find the right content in Create by searching through thousands of leading McGraw-Hill textbooks. Arrange the material to fit your teaching style. Order a Create book and receive a complimentary print review copy in 3–5 business days or a complimentary electronic review copy (echo) via e-mail within one hour. Go to create.mheducation.com today and register.

McGraw-Hill Campus™

McGraw-Hill Campus is a new one-stop teaching and learning experience available to users of any learning management system.

This institutional service allows faculty and students to enjoy single sign-on (SSO) access to all McGraw-Hill Higher Education materials, including the award-winning McGraw-Hill Connect platform, from directly within the institution's website. With McGraw-Hill Campus, faculty receive instant access to teaching materials (e.g., eTextbooks, test banks, PowerPoint slides, learning objectives, etc.), allowing them to browse, search, and use any instructor ancillary content in our vast library at no additional cost to instructor or students. In addition, students enjoy SSO access to a variety of free content and subscription-based products (e.g., McGraw-Hill Connect). With McGraw-Hill Campus enabled, faculty and students will never need to create another account to access McGraw-Hill products and services. Learn more at **www.mhcampus.com.**

Assurance of Learning Ready

Many educational institutions today focus on the notion of *assurance of learning*, an important element of some accreditation standards. *International Management* is designed specifically to support instructors' assurance of learning initiatives with a simple yet powerful solution. Each test bank question for *International Management* maps to a specific chapter learning objective listed in the text. Instructors can use our test bank software, EZ Test and EZ Test Online, to easily query for learning objectives that directly relate to the learning outcomes for their course. Instructors can then use the reporting features of EZ Test to aggregate student results in similar fashion, making the collection and presentation of assurance of learning data simple and easy.

AACSB Tagging

McGraw-Hill Education is a proud corporate member of AACSB International. Understanding the importance and value of AACSB accreditation, *International Management* recognizes the curriculum guidelines detailed in the AACSB standards for business accreditation by connecting selected questions in the text and the test bank to the six general knowledge and skill guidelines in the AACSB standards. The statements contained in *International Management* are provided only as a guide for the users of this textbook. The AACSB leaves content coverage and assessment within the purview of individual schools, the mission of the school, and the faculty. While the *International Management* teaching package makes no claim of any specific AACSB qualification or evaluation, we have within *International Management* labeled selected questions according to the six general knowledge and skills areas.

About the Authors

JONATHAN P. DOH is the Herbert G. Rammrath Chair in International Business, founding Director of the Center for Global Leadership, and Professor of Management at the Villanova School of Business, ranked in 2016 as the #1 undergraduate program in the United States by *Bloomberg Businessweek*. He is also an occasional executive educator for the Wharton School of Business. Jonathan teaches, does research, and serves as an executive instructor and consultant in the areas of international strategy and corporate responsibility. Previously, he was on the faculty of American and Georgetown Universities and a trade official with the U.S. government. Jonathan is author or co-author of more than 70 refereed articles published in leading international business and management journals, more than 30 chapters in scholarly edited volumes, and more than 90 conference papers. Recent articles have appeared in journals such as *Academy of Management Review*, *California Management Review*, *Journal of International Business Studies*, *Journal of Management*, *Journal of Management Studies*, *Journal of World Business*, *Organization Science*, *Sloan Management Review*, and *Strategic Management Journal*. He is co-editor and contributing author of *Globalization and NGOs* (Praeger, 2003) and *Handbook on Responsible Leadership and Governance in Global Business* (Elgar, 2005) and co-author of the previous edition of *International Management: Culture, Strategy, and Behavior* (9th ed., McGraw-Hill/Irwin, 2015), the best-selling international management text. His current research focus is on strategy for and in emerging markets, global corporate responsibility, and offshore outsourcing of services. His most recent scholarly books are *Multinationals and Development* (with Alan Rugman, Yale University Press, 2008), *NGOs and Corporations: Conflict and Collaboration* (with Michael Yaziji, Cambridge University Press, 2009) and *Aligning for Advantage: Competitive Strategy for the Social and Political Arenas* (with Tom Lawton and Tazeeb Rajwani, Oxford University Press, 2014). He has been an associate, consulting, or senior editor for numerous journals, and is currently the editor-in-chief of *Journal of World Business*. Jonathan has also developed more than a dozen original cases and simulations published in books, journals, and case databases and used at many leading global universities. He has been a consultant or executive instructor for ABB, Anglo American, Bodycote, Bosch, China Minsheng Bank, Hana Financial, HSBC, Ingersoll Rand, Medtronic, Shanghai Municipal Government, Siam Cement, the World Economic Forum, among others. He is an external adviser to the Global Energy Resource Group of Deloitte Touche. Jonathan is part of the Executive Committee of the Academy of Management Organizations and Natural Environment Division, a role that culminated in service as chair of the division in 2016. He was ranked among the top 15 most prolific international business scholars in the world for the period 2001–2009 (Lahiri and Kumar, 2012) and in 2015 was elected a fellow of the Academy of International Business. He is a frequent keynote speaker to academic and professional groups in Europe, Asia, and Latin America. He holds a PhD in strategic and international management from George Washington University.

FRED LUTHANS is University and the George Holmes Distinguished Professor of Management, Emeritus at the University of Nebraska–Lincoln. He is also a Senior Research Scientist for HUMANeX Ventures Inc. He received his BA, MBA, and PhD from the University of Iowa, where he received the Distinguished Alumni Award in 2002. While serving as an officer in the U.S. Army from 1965–1967, he taught leadership at the U.S. Military Academy at West Point. He has been a visiting scholar at a number of colleges and universities and has lectured in numerous European and Pacific Rim countries. He has taught international management as a visiting faculty member at the universities of Bangkok, Hawaii, Henley in England, Norwegian Management School, Monash in Australia, Macau, Chemnitz in Germany, and Tirana in Albania. A past president of the Academy of Management, in 1997 he received the Academy's Distinguished Educator Award. In 2000 he became an inaugural member of the Academy's Hall of Fame for being one of the "Top Five" all-time published authors in the prestigious Academy journals. For many years he was co-editor-in-chief of the *Journal of World Business* and editor of *Organizational Dynamics* and is currently co-editor of *Journal of Leadership and Organizational Studies*. The author of numerous books, his seminal *Organizational Behavior* is now in its 13th edition and the 2007 groundbreaking book *Psychological Capital* (Oxford University Press) with Carolyn Youssef and Bruce Avolio came out in a new version in 2015. He is one of very few management scholars who is a Fellow of the Academy of Management, the Decision Sciences Institute, and the Pan Pacific Business Association. He received the Global Leadership Award from the Pan Pacific Association and has been a member of its Executive Committee since it was founded over 30 years ago. This committee helps to organize the annual meeting held in Pacific Rim countries. He has been involved with some of the first empirical studies on motivation and behavioral management techniques and the analysis of managerial activities in Russia; these articles were published in the *Academy of Management Journal, Journal of International Business Studies, Journal of World Business*, and *European Management Journal*. Since the very beginning of the transition to market economies after the fall of communism in Eastern Europe, he has been actively involved in management education programs sponsored by the U.S. Agency for International Development in Albania and Macedonia, and in U.S. Information Agency programs involving the Central Asian countries of Kazakhstan, Kyrgyzstan, and Tajikistan. Professor Luthans's recent international research involves his construct of positive psychological capital (PsyCap). For example, he and colleagues have published their research demonstrating the impact of Chinese workers' PsyCap on their performance in the *International Journal of Human Resource Management* and *Management and Organization Review*. He is applying his positive approach to positive organizational behavior (POB), PsyCap, and authentic leadership to effective global management and has been the keynote at programs in China (numerous times), Malaysia, South Korea, Indonesia, Philippines, Singapore, Taiwan, Japan, Vietnam, Costa Rica, Mexico, Chile, Fiji, Germany, France, England, Spain, Norway, Finland, Denmark, Netherlands, Italy, Russia, Macedonia, Albania, Morocco, South Africa, New Zealand, and Australia.

Brief Contents

Organizational Behavior and Human Resource Management   <u>Part Four</u>

Table of Contents

Part Two   The Role of Culture

Part Three   **International Strategic Management**

**Organizational Behavior and Human
Resource Management**   **Part Four**

PART ONE

Chapter 1

GLOBALIZATION AND INTERNATIONAL LINKAGES

OBJECTIVES OF THE CHAPTER

Globalization is one of the most profound forces in our contemporary economic environment, although support for free trade and open borders is not universal. The practical impact of globalization can be felt on all aspects of society, and effective management of organizations in an increasingly complex global environment is crucial for success. In nearly every country, increasing numbers of large, medium, and even small corporations are engaging in international activities, and a growing percentage of company revenue is derived from overseas markets. Yet, continued economic and political uncertainties in many world regions, the rise of more nationalistic political movements, and continued concerns about the impact of immigration have caused some to question the current system for regulating and overseeing international trade, investments, migration, and financial flows. Nonetheless, international management—the process of applying management concepts and techniques in a multinational environment—continues to retain importance.

Although globalization and international linkages have been part of history for centuries (see the International Management in Action box "Tracing the Roots of Modern Globalization" later in the chapter), the principal focus of this opening chapter is to examine the process of globalization in the contemporary world. The rapid integration of countries, advances in information technology, and the explosion in electronic communication have created a new, more integrated world and true global competition. Yet, the complexities of doing business in distinct markets persist. Since the environment of international management is all-encompassing, this chapter is mostly concerned with the economic dimensions, while the following two chapters are focused on the political, legal, and technological dimensions and ethical and social dimensions, respectively. The specific objectives of this chapter are

1. **ASSESS** the implications of globalization for countries, industries, firms, and communities.

2. **REVIEW** the major trends in global and regional integration.

3. **EXAMINE** the changing balance of global economic power and trade and investment flows among countries.

4. **ANALYZE** the major economic systems and recent developments among countries that reflect those systems.

The World of *International Management*

An Interconnected World

Only 23 years old, Evan Spiegel faced a major business decision: whether or not to accept a US$3 billion offer from Facebook's Mark Zuckerberg for his social media start-up Snapchat. Taking the deal would make Spiegel one of the youngest self-made billionaires in history.

Just two years prior, Spiegel was a typical college junior at Stanford University, living in a fraternity house and working towards graduation. As a product-design student with a knack for computers, Spiegel was keenly aware that popular social media applications, such as Twitter and Facebook, record a digital "paper trail" of their users. Content uploaded to these social media sites, such as text, comments, and photos, are kept indefinitely on servers. For young college graduates trying to enter the workforce, this log of past activity has the potential to be particularly harmful; employers are often able to see this information by simply searching for a job applicant's name online. Spiegel, however, had a clever solution: create a social networking application that would allow users to create and share content that "self-destructs" immediately after viewing. For a school project, Spiegel and co-founder Bobby Murphy programmed and developed the application, and the social media application Snapchat was born.[1]

Around the same time, Facebook executives were actively looking to expand their product line. Having just survived a rocky IPO and finally emerging as a profitable enterprise, Facebook began purchasing several social media applications, including Instagram and WhatsApp in 2012 and 2014, respectively, for several billion dollars each. By mid-2013, Facebook's Mark Zuckerberg had taken notice of the rapidly expanding Snapchat; to Zuckerberg, the appeal of Snapchat seemed to align with that of the typical Facebook user. In an attempt to grab market share from the Snapchat user base, Facebook first introduced a copycat application, called Poke. Though heavily promoted, Poke quickly flopped. Snapchat, meanwhile, continued to grow exponentially. By the beginning of 2014, Snapchat had over 30 million active users and 400 million "snaps" were being received daily.[2]

Sensing defeat, Zuckerberg approached Spiegel with a lucrative offer: US$3 billion for the application. At that time,

Snapchat had not made a single dollar in revenue. In a controversial and unexpected move, 23-year-old Spiegel gave Zuckerberg a firm answer: "No." If Spiegel turned down a US$3 billion offer for a single application, just how valuable is social media to the global community?

Social Media Has Changed How We Connect

Though the market value of social media applications, such as Snapchat, are yet to be determined, one thing is certain: We currently live in a world interconnected by social media. Through online networking, the way we connect with others has drastically changed. The volume of content being created and shared is staggering, with virtually anyone on the globe only a few clicks away. In fact, the average number of links separating any two random people on Facebook is now only 4.74.[3] Statistics from some of the most used social networking applications underscore how social media has connected people across the globe:

Facebook

If Facebook were a country, it would be the **largest**.

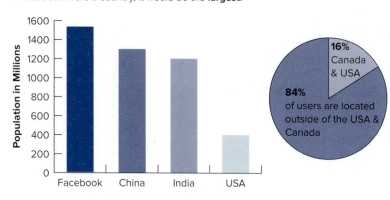

900 million users, or about **90%** of the daily users, access Facebook through their mobile devices. Globally, the average user has 338 "friends":

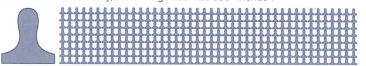

Source: Original graphic by Ben Littell under supervision of Professor Jonathan Doh, based on information from Facebook.com & Smith, Aaron, "6 New Facts About Facebook," Pew Research Center, February 3, 2014. http://www.pewresearch.org.

Instagram

- Over 300 million people create content on Instagram every month.
- Over 70 percent of Instagram users are from outside the United States.
- 70 million new photos are uploaded and shared every day.[4]

Snapchat

- Snapchat reached 100 million active members in less than four years.[5]
- 60 percent of 13–34 year olds in the United States are on Snapchat.
- More than 5 billion videos are viewed on Snapchat every day.
- Over 60 percent of Snapchat users create and share original content everyday.[6]

Certainly, social networks are a part of many people's lives. Yet, has the virtual world of social media networks made a permanent impact in the world of international business?

Social Media Has Changed Global Business Strategy

General Electric (GE), a company with a long-standing legacy in multiple industries, and one of the most recognizable brands on the planet, has strategically leveraged social media to improve its long-term image. By interacting daily with customers across a variety of social networks, the 100-year-old company aims to transform the way that its brand is perceived while simultaneously building a new generation of consumers. A section of GE's website, called the "Social Hub," serves as a central spot for this social media activity, compiling its pictures and videos posted to Facebook, Twitter, and Google+ into one location online.

Since 2015, GE has strategically leveraged social media as an advertising tool. Geo-filters, which are graphic advertisements that Snapchat users can add to their "snaps" depending on their geographic location, have been utilized by GE on multiple occasions. Advertising through these filters provides GE with an opportunity to increase brand awareness with a younger, more tech-savvy generation while simultaneously linking their brand to specific events and locations. GE's first Snapchat geo-filter, which was released for the summer solstice, was shared by nearly 5 million users.[7]

Through its "Ecomagination" program, GE utilizes social media to crowdsource sustainable solutions to current environmental issues. A central component of the program is the Open Innovation Challenges, in which teams work together to solve a specific problem specified by GE. Intellectual property rights are shared by GE and the participants, and winners receive funding to co-develop their ideas with GE scientists.

Social Media Has Changed How We Do Business Globally

In his book *Socialnomics: How Social Media Transforms the Way We Live and Do Business*, Erik Qualman writes, "Social media platforms like Facebook, YouTube, and Twitter are fundamentally changing the way businesses and consumers behave, connecting hundreds of millions of people to each other via instant communication." In essence, social media is reshaping how "consumers and companies communicate and interact with each other."[8]

Social media has changed how consumers search for products and services. Qualman gives the example of a woman who wants to take a vacation to South America, but she is not sure which country she wants to visit. In the past, she would have typed in "South American vacation" to Google, which would have brought her to travel websites such as TripAdvisor. After hours of research, she would have picked a destination. Then, after more research, she would pick a place to stay. With social media, this woman's vacation planning becomes streamlined. When she types "South American vacation" into a social network, she finds that five of her friends have taken a trip to South America in the last year. She notices that two of her friends highly recommended their vacations to Chile with GoAhead Tours. She clicks on a link to GoAhead Tours and books her vacation. In a social network, online word of mouth among friends carries great weight for consumers. With the data available from their friends about products and services, consumers know what they want without traditional marketing campaigns.[9]

This trend means that marketers must be responsive to social networks. For example, an organization that gives travel tours has a group on Facebook. A marketer at that organization could create a Facebook application that allows its group members to select "places I'd like to visit." Let's say that 25 percent of group members who use the application choose Victoria Falls as a place they would like to visit. The organization could develop a tour to Victoria Falls, and then could send a message to all of its Facebook group members to notify them about this new tour. In this way, a social network

serves as an inexpensive, effective means of marketing directly to a business's target audience.

Social Media Has Impacted International Diplomacy

The United Nations (U.N.) has increasingly embraced social media as a tool to increase diplomacy and understanding worldwide. The U.N. maintains official accounts on Facebook, Twitter, YouTube, Flickr, Google+, Tumblr, Instagram, and LinkedIn, and, as of 2016, boasts over 2 million followers on its primary Facebook page. As part of its "2015: Time for Global Action" campaign, the U.N. utilized various social media platforms to spread its action plan and its new sustainable development goals worldwide. The hashtag "#action15" was used to link activities across various networks, while Twitter and Facebook served as primary platforms for disseminating information to its global audience (refer to Chapter 3, Table 3-3, for a further discussion of the U.N.'s 2015 sustainable development goals).[10]

In another pioneering move, the U.S. government sent an unconventional delegation to Moscow that included the creator of Twitter, the chief executive of eBay, and the actor Ashton Kutcher. One of the delegation's goals was "to persuade Russia's thriving online social networks to take up social causes like fighting corruption or human trafficking," according to Jared Cohen, who served on former-Secretary of State Hillary Clinton's policy planning staff. In Russia, the average adult spends 10.4 hours a month on social networking sites, based on comScore market research. This act of diplomacy by Washington underscores how important social networks have become in our world today, a world in which Twitter has helped mobilize people to fight for freedom from corruption.

Social media networks have accelerated technological integration among the nations of the world. People across the globe are now linked more closely than ever before. This social phenomenon has implications for businesses as corporations can now leverage networks such as Facebook to achieve greater success. Understanding the global impact of social media is key to understanding our global society today.

Social networks have rapidly diffused from the United States and Europe to every region of the world, underscoring the inexorable nature of globalization. As individuals who share interests and preferences link up, they are afforded opportunities to connect in ways that were unimaginable just a decade ago. Facebook, Twitter, LinkedIn, and others are all providing communication platforms for individuals and groups in disparate—and even isolated—locations around the world. Such networks also offer myriad business opportunities for companies large and small to identify and target discrete groups of consumers or other business partners. These networks are revolutionizing the nature of management—including international management—by allowing producers and consumers to interact directly without the usual intermediaries. Networks and the individuals who make them up are bringing populations of the world closer together and further accelerating the already rapid pace of globalization and integration.

As evidenced by Evan Speigel's rejection of a US$3 billion offer for his social networking application Snapchat, social media is, in many ways, invaluable to the global community. The pace of interconnectivity across the globe continues to increase with the new communication tools that social networking provides. Social media has altered the way that we interact with each other, and businesses, like

GE, have gained real advantages by leveraging online networks. In this chapter, we examine the globalization phenomenon, the growing integration among countries and regions, the changing balance of global economic power, and examples of different economic systems. As you read this chapter, keep in mind that although there are periodic setbacks, globalization continues to move at a rapid pace and that all nations, including the United States, as well as individual companies and their managers, are going to have to keep a close watch on the current environment if they hope to be competitive in the years ahead.

■ Introduction

Management is the process of completing activities with and through other people. **International management** is the process of applying management concepts and techniques in a multinational environment and adapting management practices to different economic, political, and cultural contexts. Many managers practice some level of international management in today's increasingly diverse organizations. International management is distinct from other forms of management in that knowledge and insights about global issues and specific cultures are a requisite for success. Today more firms than ever are earning some of their revenue from international operations, even nascent organizations, as illustrated in The World of International Management chapter opening.

Many of these companies are multinational corporations (MNCs). An **MNC** is a firm that has operations in more than one country, international sales, and a mix of nationalities among managers and owners. In recent years such well-known American MNCs as Apple, Chevron, Johnson & Johnson, Coca-Cola, Ford Motor Company, ExxonMobil, Caterpillar, Walmart, Microsoft, and Google have all earned more annual revenue in the international arena than they have in the United States. Table 1–1 lists

management
Process of completing activities efficiently and effectively with and through other people.

international management
Process of applying management concepts and techniques in a multinational environment and adapting management practices to different economic, political, and cultural environments.

MNC
A firm having operations in more than one country, international sales, and a nationality mix of managers and owners.

Table 1–1
The World's Top Nonfinancial MNCs, Ranked by Foreign Assets, 2015
(in millions of dollars)

Rank	Company Name	Home Economy	Foreign Assets	Total Assets	Foreign Sales	Total Sales
1	Royal Dutch/Shell Plc	United Kingdom	$288,283	$340,157	$169,737	$264,960
2	Toyota Motor Corporation	Japan	273,280	422,176	165,195	236,797
3	General Electric	United States	257,742	492,692	64,146	117,385
4	Total SA	France	236,719	244,856	123,995	159,162
5	British Petroleum Company Plc	United Kingdom	216,698	261,832	145,640	222,894
6	Exxon Mobil Corporation	United States	193,493	336,758	167,304	259,488
7	Chevron Corporation	United States	191,933	266,103	48,183	129,648
8	Volkswagen Group	Germany	181,826	416,596	189,817	236,702
9	Vodafone Group Plc	United Kingdom	166,967	192,310	52,150	61,466
10	Apple Computer Inc.	United States	143,652	290,479	151,983	233,715

Source: UNCTAD, *World Investment Report 2016* (June 21, 2016), Annex Table 24, http://unctad.org/en/Pages/DIAE/World%20Investment%20Report/Annex-Tables.aspx.

the world's top nonfinancial companies ranked by foreign assets through 2015. General Electric, headquartered in the United States, for example, now has more than 50% of its assets located outside of its home market.

In addition, companies from developing economies, such as India, Brazil, and China, are providing formidable competition to their North American, European, and Japanese counterparts. Names like Cemex, Embraer, Haier, Lenovo, LG Electronics, Wipro, Telefonica, Santander, Reliance, Samsung, Grupo Televisa, Airtel, Tata, and Infosys are becoming well-known global brands. Globalization and the rise of emerging markets' MNCs have brought prosperity to many previously underdeveloped parts of the world, notably the emerging markets of Asia. Since 2009, sales of automobiles in China have exceeded those in the United States. Boosted by tax breaks, vehicle sales in China reached a record 24.6 million units in 2015, according to the China Association of Automobile Manufacturers, far ahead of the 17.5 million cars and light trucks sold in the U.S.[11] Moreover, a number of emerging market auto companies are becoming global players through their exporting, foreign investment, and international acquisitions, including the purchase of Volvo by Chinese automaker Geely and Tata's acquisition of Jaguar-Land Rover (see the In-Depth Integrative Case at the end of Part Three).

In a striking move, Cisco Systems, one of the world's largest producers of network equipment, such as routers, announced it would establish a "Globalization Center East" in Bangalore, India. This center includes all the corporate and operational functions of U.S. headquarters, which have been mirrored in India. Under this plan, which includes an investment of over $1.1 billion, one-fifth of Cisco's senior management will move to Bangalore.[12,13]

In March 2014, Procter and Gamble celebrated the grand opening of their Singapore Innovation Center (SgIC), which will function as the primary research and development center for P&G's hair, skin, and home care products. According to P&G, the SgIC will contain more than 250 research laboratories and 500 researchers, focusing on more than 18 different fields of study. The Asian market, with nearly two billion customers and 25 different brands, is particularly important for P&G's future growth plans.[14] Similarly, Unilever has opened R&D centers in Bangalore, India, and Shanghai, China. The Shanghai Center is one of Unilever's largest R&D buildings, covering some 30,000 square meters and housing more than 450 professionals from 22 nationalities.[15] Citing the massive growth in the health care market in Asia, General Electric moved its X-ray business headquarters to China in 2011, and vice chairman John Rice relocated to Hong Kong.[16,17]

Accenture, another American archetype, had about 336,000 employees globally in 2015, with about 237,000 of those employees located outside of the United States. Originally focused on IT services within the United States, Accenture has quickly transformed into one of the largest consulting firms worldwide. The company's operations in India now employ nearly 150,000 people, twice as many as in the United States.[18] With offices in 200 cities across 55 countries, Accenture has focused on providing services for both developed and growing markets.[19] In 2015, Accenture drew 47 percent of its revenue from outsourcing.[20]

These trends reflect the reality that firms are finding they must develop international management expertise, especially expertise relevant to the increasingly important developing and emerging markets of the world. Managers from today's MNCs must learn to work effectively with those from many different countries. Moreover, more and more small and medium-sized businesses will find that they are being affected by internationalization. Many of these companies will be doing business abroad, and those that do not will find themselves doing business with MNCs operating locally. And increasingly, the MNCs are coming from the developing world as previously domestic-oriented companies from countries like China and India expand abroad through acquisitions or other means. Table 1–2 lists the world's top nonfinancial companies from developing countries ranked by foreign assets in 2014.

Table 1–2
The World's Top Nonfinancial TNCs from Developing and Transitioning Economies, Ranked by Foreign Assets, 2014
(in millions of dollars)

Rank	Company Name	Home Economy	Foreign Assets	Total Assets	Foreign Sales	Total Sales
1	Hutchison Whampoa Limited	Hong Kong/China	$91,055	$113,909	$ 27,043	$ 35,098
2	Hon Hai Precision Industries	Taiwan	73,010	77,803	138,023	139,018
3	China National Offshore Oil Group	China	71,090	182,282	26,084	99,557
4	Samsung Electronics Co., Ltd.	South Korea	56,164	211,205	176,534	196,263
5	Vale SA	Brazil	55,448	116,598	31,667	37,608
6	Petronas – Petroliam Nasional Bhd	Malaysia	45,572	153,770	76,726	100,602
7	China Ocean Shipping (Group) Company	China	44,805	57,875	18,075	27,483
8	America Movil SAB De CV	Mexico	41,627	86,795	41,547	63,793
9	Lukoil OAO	Russian Federation	32,907	111,800	119,932	144,167
10	Tata Motors Ltd.	India	30,214	38,235	37,201	43,044

Source: UNCTAD, *World Investment Report 2016* (June 21, 2016), Annex Table 25, http://unctad.org/en/Pages/DIAE/World%20Investment%20Report/Annex-Tables.aspx.

■ Globalization and Internationalization

International business is not a new phenomenon; however, the volume of international trade has increased dramatically over the last decade. Today, every nation and an increasing number of companies buy and sell goods in the international marketplace. A number of developments around the world have helped fuel this activity.

Globalization, Antiglobalization, and Global Pressures for Change

Globalization can be defined as the process of social, political, economic, cultural, and technological integration among countries around the world. Globalization is distinct from internationalization in that internationalization is the process of a business crossing national and cultural borders, while globalization is the vision of creating one world unit, a single market entity. Evidence of globalization can be seen in increased levels of trade, capital flows, and migration. Globalization has been facilitated by technological advances in transnational communications, transport, and travel. Thomas Friedman, in his book *The World Is Flat*, identified 10 "flatteners" that have hastened the globalization trend, including the fall of the Berlin Wall, **offshoring**, and **outsourcing**, which have combined to dramatically intensify the effects of increasing global linkages.[21] Hence, in recent years, globalization has accelerated, creating both opportunities and challenges to global business and international management.

On the positive side, global trade and investment continue to grow, bringing wealth, jobs, and technology to many regions around the world. While some emerging countries have not benefited from globalization and integration, the emergence of MNCs from developing countries reflects the increasing inclusion of all regions of the world in the benefits of globalization. Yet, as the pace of global integration quickens, so have the cries against globalization and the emergence of new concerns over mounting global pressures.[22] These pressures can be seen in protests at the meetings of the World Trade

globalization
The process of social, political, economic, cultural, and technological integration among countries around the world.

offshoring
The process by which companies undertake some activities at offshore locations instead of in their countries of origin.

outsourcing
The subcontracting or contracting out of activities to endogenous organizations that had previously been performed by the firm.

Tracing the Roots of Modern Globalization

Globalization is often presented as a new phenomenon associated with the post–World War II period. In fact, globalization is not new. Rather, its roots extend back to ancient times. Globalization emerged from long-standing patterns of transcontinental trade that developed over many centuries. The act of barter is the forerunner of modern international trade. During different periods of time, nearly every civilization contributed to the expansion of trade.

Middle Eastern Intercontinental Trade

In ancient Egypt, the King's Highway or Royal Road stretched across the Sinai into Jordan and Syria and into the Euphrates Valley. These early merchants practiced their trade following one of the earliest codes of commercial integrity: *Do not move the scales, do not change the weights, and do not diminish parts of the bushel.* Land bridges later extended to the Phoenicians, the first middlemen of global trade. Over 2,000 years ago, traders in silk and other rare valued goods moved east out of the Nile basin to Baghdad and Kashmir and linked the ancient empires of China, India, Persia, and Rome. At its height, the Silk Road extended over 4,000 miles, providing a transcontinental conduit for the dissemination of art, religion, technology, ideas, and culture. Commercial caravans crossing land routes in Arabian areas were forced to pay tribute—a forerunner of custom duties—to those who controlled such territories. In his youth, the Prophet Muhammad traveled with traders, and prior to his religious enlightenment the founder of Islam himself was a trader. Accordingly, the Qur'an instructs followers to respect private property, business agreements, and trade.

Trans-Saharan Cross-Continental Trade

Early tribes inhabiting the triad cities of Mauritania, in ancient West Africa below the Sahara, embraced caravan trade with the Berbers of North Africa. Gold from the sub-Saharan area was exchanged for something even more prized—salt, a precious substance needed for retaining body moisture, preserving meat, and flavoring food. Single caravans, stretching five miles and including nearly 2,500 camels, earned their reputation as ships of the desert as they ferried gold powder, slaves, ivory, animal hides, and ostrich feathers to the northeast and returned with salt, wool, gunpowder, porcelain pottery, silk, dates, millet, wheat, and barley from the East.

China as an Ancient Global Trading Initiator

In 1421, a fleet of over 3,750 vessels set sail from China to cultivate trade around the world for the emperor. The voyage reflected the emperor's desire to collect tribute in exchange for trading privileges with China and China's protection. The Chinese, like modern-day multinationals, sought to extend their economic reach while recognizing principles of economic equity and fair trade. In the course of their global trading, the Chinese introduced uniform container measurements to enable merchants to transact business using common weight and dimension measurement systems. Like the early Egyptians and later the Romans, they used coinage as an intermediary form of value exchange or specie, thus eliminating complicated barter transactions.

European Trade Imperative

The concept of the alphabet came to the Greeks via trade with the Phoenicians. During the time of Alexander the Great, transcontinental trade was extended into Afghanistan and India. With the rise of the Roman Empire, global trade routes stretched from the Middle East through central Europe, Gaul, and across the English Channel. In 1215 King John of England signed the Magna Carta, which stressed the importance of cross-border trade. By the time of Marco Polo's writing of *The Description of the World,* at the end of the 13th century, the Silk Road from China to the city-states of Italy was a well-traveled commercial highway. His tales, chronicled journeys with his merchant uncles, gave Europeans a taste for the exotic, further stimulating the consumer appetite that propelled trade and globalization. Around 1340, Francisco Balducci Pegolotti, a Florentine mercantile agent, authored *Practica Della Mercatura (Practice of Marketing),* the first widely distributed reference on international business and a precursor to today's textbooks. The search for trading routes contributed to the Age of Discovery and encouraged Christopher Columbus to sail west in 1492.

Globalization in U.S. History

The Declaration of Independence, which set out grievances against the English crown upon which a new nation was founded, cites the desire to "establish Commerce" as a chief rationale for establishing an independent state. The king of England was admonished "for cutting off our trade with all parts of the world" in one of the earliest antiprotectionist free-trade statements from the New World.

Globalization, begun as trade between and across territorial borders in ancient times, was historically and is even today the key driver of world economic development. The first paths in the creation of civilization were made in the footsteps of trade. In fact, the word meaning "footsteps" in the old Anglo-Saxon language is *trada,* from which the modern English word *trade* is derived. Contemporary globalization is a new branch of a very old tree whose roots were planted in antiquity.

Source: Thomas Cahill, *Sailing the Wine Dark Sea: Why Greeks Matter* (New York: Doubleday, 2003), pp. 10, 56–57; Charles W. L. Hill, *International Business,* 4th ed. (New York: McGraw-Hill Irwin, 2003), p. 100; Nefertiti website, http://nefertiti.iweland.com/trade/internal_trade.htm, 2003 (ancient Egypt: domestic trade); Gavin Menzies, *1421: The Year China Discovered America* (New York: William Morrow/HarperCollins, 2003), pp. 26–27; Milton Viorst, *The Great Documents of Western Civilization* (New York: Barnes & Noble Books, 1994), p. 115 (Magna Carta) and p. 168 (Declaration of Independence).

Organization (WTO), International Monetary Fund (IMF), and other global bodies and in the growing calls by developing countries to make the global trading system more responsive to their economic and social needs. These groups are especially concerned about rising inequities between incomes, and nongovernmental organizations (NGOs) have become more active in expressing concerns about the potential shortcomings of economic globalization.[23] In addition, candidates in various election campaigns around the world often find themselves pressured to criticize globalization, including migration of people, for contributing to lost jobs and general economic insecurity even though these problems are obviously the result of a range of factors of which globalization is just one.

Who benefits from globalization? Proponents believe that everyone benefits from globalization, as evidenced in lower prices, greater availability of goods, better jobs, and access to technology. Theoretically, individuals in established markets will strive for better education and training to be prepared for future positions, while citizens in emerging markets and underdeveloped countries will reap the benefits of large amounts of capital flowing into those countries, which will stimulate growth and development. Critics disagree, noting that the high number of jobs moving abroad as a result of the offshoring of business services jobs to lower-wage countries does not inherently create greater opportunities at home and that the main winners of globalization are the company executives. Proponents claim that job losses are a natural consequence of economic and technological change and that offshoring actually improves the competitiveness of American companies and increases the size of the overall economic pie.[24] Critics point out that growing trade deficits and slow wage growth are damaging economies and that globalization may be moving too fast for some emerging markets, which could result in economic collapse. Moreover, critics argue that when production moves to countries to take advantage of lower labor costs or less regulated environments, it creates a "race to the bottom" in which companies and countries place downward pressure on wages and working conditions.[25]

India is one country at the center of the globalization debate. As noted above, India has been the beneficiary of significant foreign investment, especially in services such as software and information technology (IT). Limited clean water, power, paved roadways, and modern bridges, however, are making it increasingly difficult for companies to expand. There have even been instances of substantial losses for companies using India as an offshore base, such as occurred when several automakers, including Ford, Hyundai, Renault-Nissan, and Daimler, experienced the destruction of inventory and a week-long production stoppage due to flooding in southern India.[26] India's public debt has declined to about 65 percent of GDP over the last ten years, increasing macroeconomic stability and lowering its vulnerability to external risks. Expanding by over 7 percent in 2015, India has eclipsed China as the fastest-growing large economy.[27] It is possible that India will follow in China's footsteps and continue rapid growth in incomes and wealth; however, it is also possible that the challenges India faces are greater than the country's capacity to respond to them. See In the International Spotlight at the end of this chapter for additional insights on India.

This example illustrates just one of the ways in which globalization has raised particular concerns over environmental and social impacts. According to antiglobalization activists, if corporations are free to locate anywhere in the world, the world's poorest countries will relax or eliminate environmental standards and social services in order to attract first-world investment and the jobs and wealth that come with it. Proponents of globalization contend that even within the developing world, it is protectionist policies, not trade and investment liberalization, that result in environmental and social damage. They believe globalization will force higher-polluting countries such as China and Russia into an integrated global community that takes responsible measures to protect the environment. However, given the significant changes required in many developing nations to support globalization, such as better infrastructure, greater educational opportunities, and other improvements, most supporters concede that there may be some short-term disruptions. Over the long term, globalization supporters believe industrialization will

Outsourcing and Offshoring

The concepts of outsourcing and offshoring are not new, but these practices are growing at an extreme rate. *Offshoring* refers to the process by which companies undertake some activities at offshore locations instead of in their countries of origin. *Outsourcing* is the subcontracting or contracting out of activities to external organizations that had previously been performed within the firm and is a wholly different phenomenon. Often the two combine to create "offshore outsourcing." Offshoring began with manufacturing operations. Globalization jump-started the extension of offshore outsourcing of services, including call centers, R&D, information services, and even legal work. American Express, GE, Sony, and Netflix all use attorneys from Pangea3, a Mumbai-based legal firm, to review documents and draft contracts. These companies benefit from the lower costs and higher efficiency that companies like Pangea3 can provide compared to domestic legal firms.[28] This is a risky venture as legal practices are not the same across countries, and the

documents may be too sensitive to rely on assembly-line lawyers. It also raises the question as to whether or not there are limitations to offshore outsourcing. Many companies, including Deutsche Bank, spread offshore outsourcing opportunities across multiple countries such as India and Russia for economic or political reasons. The advantages, concerns, and issues with offshoring span a variety of subjects. Throughout the text we will revisit the idea of offshore outsourcing as it is relevant. Here in Chapter 1 we see how skeptics of globalization wonder if there are benefits to offshore outsourcing, while in Chapter 2 we see how these are related to technology, and, finally, in Chapter 14 we see how offshore practices affect human resource management and the global distribution of work.

Sources: Engardio, Pete; Shameen, Assif, "Let's Offshore the Lawyers," *BusinessWeek*, September 18, 2006, p. 42; Hallett, Tony; McCue, Andy, "Why Deutsche Bank Spreads Its Outsourcing," *BusinessWeek*, March 15, 2007.

create wealth that will enable new industries to employ more modern, environmentally friendly technology. We discuss the social and environmental aspects of globalization in more detail in Chapter 3.

These contending perspectives are unlikely to be resolved anytime soon. Instead, a vigorous debate among countries, MNCs, and civil society will likely continue and affect the context in which firms do business internationally. Business firms operating around the world must be sensitive to different perspectives on the costs and benefits of globalization and adapt and adjust their strategies and approaches to these differences.

Global and Regional Integration

One important dimension of globalization is the increasing economic integration among countries brought about by the negotiation and implementation of trade and investment agreements. Here we provide a brief overview of some of the major developments in global and regional integration.

Over the past six decades, succeeding rounds of global trade negotiations have resulted in dramatically reduced tariff and nontariff barriers among countries. Table 1–3 shows the history of these negotiation rounds, their primary focus, and the number of countries involved. These efforts reached their crest in 1994 with the conclusion of the Uruguay Round of multilateral trade negotiations under the General Agreement on Tariffs and Trade (GATT) and the creation of the **World Trade Organization (WTO)** to oversee the conduct of trade around the world. The WTO is the global organization of countries that oversees rules and regulations for international trade and investment, including agriculture, intellectual property, services, competition, and subsidies. Recently, however, the momentum of global trade agreements has slowed. In December 1999, trade ministers from around the world met in Seattle to launch a new round of global trade talks. In what later became known as the "Battle in Seattle," protesters disrupted the meeting, and representatives of developing countries who felt their views were being left out of the discussion succeeded in ending the discussions early and postponing a new round of trade talks. Two years later, in November 2001, the members of the WTO met

World Trade Organization (WTO)
The global organization of countries that oversees rules and regulations for international trade and investment.

Table 1–3
Completed Rounds of the Negotiations under the GATT and WTO

Year	Place (name)	Subjects Covered	Countries
1947	Geneva	Tariffs	23
1949	Annecy	Tariffs	13
1951	Torquay	Tariffs	38
1956	Geneva	Tariffs	26
1960–1961	Geneva (Dillon Round)	Tariffs	26
1964–1967	Geneva (Kennedy Round)	Tariffs and antidumping measures	62
1973–1979	Geneva (Tokyo Round)	Tariffs, nontariff measures, "framework" agreements	102
1986–1994	Geneva (Uruguay Round)	Tariffs, nontariff measures, services, intellectual property, dispute settlement, textiles, agriculture, creation of WTO	123

Source: *Understanding the WTO*, 5th ed. (Geneva: World Trade Organization, 2015), https://www.wto.org/english/thewto_e/whatis_e/tif_e/understanding_e.pdf.

again and successfully launched a new round of negotiations at Doha, Qatar, to be known as the "Development Round," reflecting the recognition by members that trade agreements needed to explicitly consider the needs of and impact on developing countries.[29] However, after a lack of consensus among WTO members regarding agricultural subsidies and the issues of competition and government procurement, progress slowed. At the most recent meeting, held in Geneva in July 2008, disagreements between the U.S., China, and India over access to agricultural imports from developing countries resulted in an impasse after nine days of discussions.[30] Failure to reach agreement resulted in another setback, and although there have been attempts to restart the negotiations, they have remained stalled, especially in light of rising protectionism in the wake of the global economic crisis.[31]

Partly as a result of the slow progress in multilateral trade negotiations, the United States and many other countries have pursued bilateral and regional trade agreements. The United States, Canada, and Mexico make up the **North American Free Trade Agreement (NAFTA)**, which in essence has removed all barriers to trade among these countries and created a huge North American market. A number of economic developments have occurred because of this agreement that are designed to promote commerce in the region. Some of the more important developments include (1) the elimination of tariffs as well as import and export quotas; (2) the opening of government procurement markets to companies in the other two nations; (3) an increase in the opportunity to make investments in each other's country; (4) an increase in the ease of travel between countries; and (5) the removal of restrictions on agricultural products, auto parts, and energy goods. Many of these provisions were implemented gradually. For example, in the case of Mexico, quotas on Mexican products in the textile and apparel sectors were phased out over time, and customs duties on all textile products were eliminated over 10 years. Negotiations between NAFTA members and many Latin American countries, such as Chile, have concluded, and others are ongoing. Moreover, other regional and bilateral trade agreements, including the U.S.–Singapore Free Trade Agreement, concluded in May 2003, and the U.S.–Central American Free Trade Agreement (CAFTA), later renamed CAFTA-DR to reflect the inclusion of the Dominican Republic in the agreement and concluded in May 2004, were negotiated in the same spirit as NAFTA. The U.S. Congress approved the CAFTA-DR in July 2005, and the president signed it into law on

North American Free Trade Agreement (NAFTA)
A free-trade agreement between the United States, Canada, and Mexico that has removed most barriers to trade and investment.

August 2, 2005. The export zone created will be the United States' second largest free-trade zone in Latin America after Mexico. The United States is implementing the CAFTA-DR on a rolling basis as countries make sufficient progress to complete their commitments under the agreement. The agreement first entered into force between the United States and El Salvador on March 1, 2006; followed by Honduras and Nicaragua on April 1, 2006; Guatemala on July 1, 2006; and the Dominican Republic on March 1, 2007. Implementation by Costa Rica was delayed by concerns over the impact of the opening of Costa Rica's energy and telecommunications monopoly, and a subsequent election and referendum; however, the agreement finally entered into force for Costa Rica on January 1, 2009.[32]

Agreements like NAFTA and CAFTA not only reduce barriers to trade but also require additional domestic legal and business reforms in developing nations to protect property rights. Most of these agreements now include supplemental commitments on labor and the environment to encourage countries to upgrade their working conditions and environmental protections, although some critics believe the agreements do not go far enough in ensuring worker rights and environmental standards. Partly due to the stalled progress with the WTO and FTAA, the United States has pursued bilateral trade agreements with a range of countries, including Australia, Bahrain, Chile, Colombia, Israel, Jordan, Malaysia, Morocco, Oman, Panama, Peru, and Singapore.[33]

Economic activity in Latin America continues to be volatile. Despite the continuing political and economic setbacks these countries periodically experience, economic and export growth continue in Brazil, Chile, and Mexico. In addition, while outside MNCs continually target this geographic area, there also is a great deal of cross-border investment between Latin American countries. Regional trade agreements are helping in this cross-border process, including NAFTA, which ties the Mexican economy more closely to the United States. The CAFTA agreement, signed August 5, 2006, between the United States and Central American countries, presents new opportunities for bolstering trade, investment, services, and working conditions in the region. Within South America there are Mercosur, a common market created by Argentina, Brazil, Paraguay, Uruguay, and Venezuela, and the Andean Common Market, a subregional free-trade compact that is designed to promote economic and social integration and cooperation between Bolivia, Colombia, Ecuador, and Peru.

European Union
A political and economic community consisting of 28 member states.

The **European Union** (EU) has made significant progress over the past decade in becoming a unified market. In 2003 it consisted of 15 nations: Austria, Belgium, Denmark, Finland, France, Germany (see In the International Spotlight at the end of Chapter 13), Great Britain, Greece, the Netherlands, Ireland, Italy, Luxembourg, Portugal, Spain, and Sweden. In May 2004, 10 additional countries joined the EU: Cyprus, the Czech Republic, Estonia, Hungary, Latvia, Lithuania, Malta, Poland, Slovakia, and Slovenia. In January 2007, Romania and Bulgaria acceded to the EU, and in July 2013, Croatia became the 28th and newest member of the EU. Not only have most trade barriers between the members been removed, but a subset of European countries have adopted a unified currency called the euro. As a result, it is now possible for customers to compare prices between most countries and for business firms to lower their costs by conducting business in one uniform currency. With access to the entire pan-European market, large MNCs can now achieve the operational scale and scope necessary to reduce costs and increase efficiencies. Even though long-standing cultural differences remain, and the EU has recently experienced some substantial challenges, the EU is more integrated as a single market than NAFTA, CAFTA, or the allied Asian countries. With many additional countries poised to join the EU, including Albania, Serbia, and Turkey, the resulting pan-European market will be one that no major MNC can afford to ignore (see Figure 1–1). Moreover, the Transatlantic Trade and Investment Partnership (T-TIP) is a proposed trade agreement between the European Union and the United States that could further bolster trade and multilateral economic growth in Europe and North America.[34]

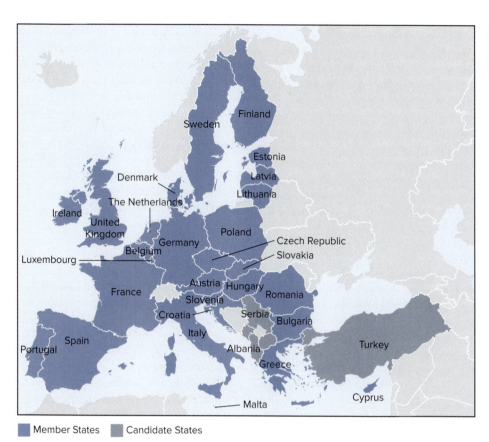

Figure 1–1

European Member States and Candidates, 2016

■ Member States   ■ Candidate States

Source: Original graphic by Ben Littell under supervision of Professor Jonathan Doh.

Although Japan has experienced economic problems since the early 1990s, it continues to be one of the primary economic forces in the Pacific Rim (see In the International Spotlight at the end of Chapter 11). Japanese MNCs want to take advantage of the huge, underdeveloped Asian markets. At the same time, China continues to be a major economic force, with many predictions that it will surpass the United States as the largest economy in the world, in terms of nominal GDP, by 2026.[35] Although all the economies in Asia are now feeling the impact of the economic uncertainty of the post-9/11 era and the Asian economic crisis of the late 1990s, Hong Kong, Taiwan, South Korea, and Singapore have been doing relatively well, and the Southeast Asia countries of Malaysia, Thailand, Indonesia, and even Vietnam are bouncing back to become major export-driven economies. The Association of Southeast Asian Nations (ASEAN), made up of Indonesia, Malaysia, the Philippines, Singapore, Brunei, Thailand, and, in recent years, Cambodia, Myanmar, and Vietnam, is advancing trade and economic integration and now poses challenges to China as a region of relatively low-cost production and export. In addition, under the **Trans-Pacific Partnership** (TPP), Asian-facing countries have concluded negotiations for an ambitious, next-generation, Asia-Pacific trade agreement. The TPP group represents roughly two-fifths of the global economy, consisting of Australia, Brunei, Canada, Chile, Japan, Malaysia, Mexico, New Zealand, Peru, Singapore, the United States, and Vietnam. On October 4, 2015, representatives of the 12 Pacific Rim countries agreed to the 30-chapter deal, with full ratification by each country's legislative bodies expected to take up to two years to complete.[36]

Central and Eastern Europe, Russia (see In the International Spotlight at the end of Chapter 14), and the other republics of the former Soviet Union currently are still trying to make stable transitions to market economies. Although the Czech Republic, Slovenia, Poland, and Hungary have accelerated this process through their accession to

Trans-Pacific Partnership (TPP) or Trans-Pacific Partnership Agreement (TPPA)
A trade agreement among 12 Pacific Rim countries, including Australia, Brunei, Canada, Chile, Japan, Malaysia, Mexico, New Zealand, Peru, Singapore, the United States, and Vietnam.

the EU, others (the Balkan countries, Russia, and the other republics of the former Soviet Union) still have a long way to go. However, all remain a target for MNCs looking for expansion opportunities. For example, after the fall of the Berlin Wall in 1989, Coca-Cola quickly began to sever its relations with most of the state-run bottling companies in the former communist-bloc countries. The soft drink giant began investing heavily to import its own manufacturing, distribution, and marketing techniques. To date, Coca-Cola has pumped billions into Central and Eastern Europe—and this investment is beginning to pay off. Its business in Central and Eastern Europe has been expanding at twice the rate of its other foreign operations.

These are specific, geographic examples of emerging internationalism. Equally important to this new climate of globalization, however, are broader trends that reflect the emergence of developing countries as major players in global economic power and influence.

Changing Global Demographics

The collective world population is aging. In 2016, for the first time since the end of the second World War, the global working-age population will decline. By 2050, the *Wall Street Journal* projects that the working age population will contract by nearly 5 percent worldwide. These demographic changes will have significant effects on the global economy.[37]

Multiple factors are contributing to this increase in the median global population age. Due to improvements in the technology and health care sectors, people are now living longer lives in both developed and developing countries. Global life expectancy, which has increased from 48 years in 1950 to 70 years in 2012, will continue to steadily increase over the next several decades. As more people are living longer, they are spending more time in retirement. People are also having fewer children. In the last 65 years, the global fertility rate has been cut in half—from 5 children per woman in 1950 to 2.5 children per woman in 2015.[38]

Though these demographic changes are projected to occur globally, the most dramatic impact will be seen in the developed nations. Western Europe, which has seen stagnant economic and population growth for the last decade, will face some of the sharpest constrictions of the workforce population. In Germany and Italy, the working-age population will shrink by over 20 percent by 2050. Developed Asian nations, with some of the longest life expectancies, will not be able to repopulate quickly enough to replace the retiring, aging population. In Japan, the number of nonworkers will be nearly equal to that of workers by 2050. Both Japan and South Korea will face a loss of over 25 percent of their working class population.[39]

Even some developing countries will face large challenges. Due to years of a one-child policy, and rapidly rising incomes, which are almost always accompanied by lower birth rates, China faces an unbalanced population pyramid. It is estimated that China will see a 20 percent decline in its working-class population by 2050, as middle-aged workers begin to retire and are replaced by fewer workers. With a lower GDP per capita than Germany, Japan, and other developed nations, Chinese workers will face additional pressure to support the nonworking population.[40]

The increase in the size of the elderly population affects more than just the proportion of workers to nonworkers. The amount of spending on health care–related services will continue to increase rapidly, while the demand for goods such as cars and computers will decline. Whereas younger populations spend income on housing and other capitally financed purchases, elderly populations spend money on health care services.[41]

Although the full impact of these demographic changes will not be known for several years, strategies such as easing the immigration process for workers from developing to developed nations, incentivizing citizens in developed nations to have more children, and encouraging workers to delay retirement could help to offset the problems associated with an aging global population.[42]

The Shifting Balance of Economic Power in the Global Economy

Economic integration and the rapid growth of emerging markets are creating a shifting international economic landscape. Specifically, the developing and emerging countries of the world are now predicted to occupy increasingly dominant roles in the global economic system. Various economists have studied the potential growth of these rapidly expanding economies.

In 2001 the Goldman Sachs global economics team released its initial report on the economic growth projected to occur in the emerging markets of Brazil, Russia, India, and China—which it collectively coined as the "BRIC" nations. Follow-up reports were released in 2004 and 2011. In these reports, Goldman Sachs predicted that the BRIC economies' share of world growth could rise from 20 percent in 2003 to more than 40 percent in 2025, and that the BRIC's total weight in the world economy would rise from approximately 10 percent in 2004 to more than 20 percent in 2025. After the 2009 global recession, Goldman Sachs argued that the BRIC economies were growing at such a fast pace that they may constitute four of the top five most dominant economies by the year 2050, with China surpassing the United States in output by 2027. Additionally, the report estimated that the economies of the four BRIC nations will surpass the collective economies of the G7 nations by 2032.[43,44]

In the years since Goldman Sachs' original reports on the future potential of the BRIC nations, global economic conditions have led to some setbacks for the economies of Brazil, Russia, and China, leading some to reconsider the rate at which the BRIC economies will continue to grow. Low prices for oil and other commodities contributed to the deep 2015 and 2016 recessions in Russia and Brazil, and China's growth has slowed substantially. Unlike its fellow BRIC partners, however, India continues to post strong figures, and the country has actually surpassed China in annual GDP growth rate in recent years.

In 2015, after a few years of losses and weak forecasts for Brazil, Russia, and China, Goldman Sachs dissolved its BRIC fund, folding the remaining assets into its larger emerging markets fund.[45] Whether or not Goldman Sachs' long-term predictions hold true is yet to be seen, but Brazil, Russia, China, and India will continue to assume a broader role in the global economy. It is notable that since 2009 the leaders of the BRIC nations have met for an annual summit, and, in 2010, the leaders of the founding members agreed to admit South Africa to the group, making it the BRICS.

As the BRICS's economies mature and growth slows, some analysts, including Goldman Sachs, are beginning to turn their attention to a new group of emerging markets. In March 2006, PricewaterhouseCoopers (PwC) coined the term E7 to describe seven major emerging economies (Brazil, China, India, Indonesia, Mexico, Russia, and Turkey) that are expected to expand significantly in the coming decades.[46] Unlike the G7 economies, which are primarily located in North America and Europe, the E7 economies are located throughout Latin America and Asia (see Figure 1–2 and Figure 1–3). In 2015, PwC predicted that the GDP of the E7, when measured in terms of MER (market exchange rates), would surpass that of the G7 by around 2030. Furthermore, the GDP of the E7 would expand at an annual rate of 3.8 percent through 2050, while the G7 would only expand by 2.1 percent annually. Per PwC's predictions, by 2050, the GDP of the E7 is predicted to be 50 percent higher than that of the G7.[47]

The N-11 (N stands for "next") are another grouping of economies that may constitute the next wave of emerging markets growth. These countries, which include Bangladesh, Egypt, Indonesia, Iran, Mexico, Nigeria, Pakistan, Philippines, South Korea, Turkey, and Vietnam, represent a diverse global set, with relative strengths (and weaknesses) in terms of their future potential. The MIST countries (Mexico, Indonesia, South

Figure 1–2

G7 (Group of Seven) Economies

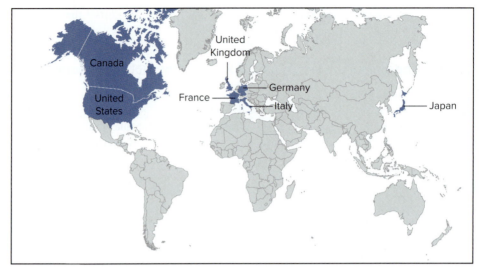

Source: Original graphic by Ben Littell under supervision of Professor Jonathan Doh.

Figure 1–3

E7 (Emerging Seven) Economies

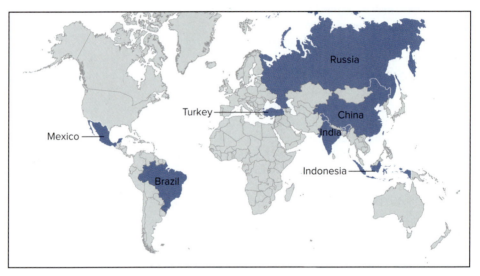

Source: Original graphic by Ben Littell under supervision of Professor Jonathan Doh.

Korea, and Turkey), a subset of the N-11, are sometimes grouped as a particularly attractive subset of the N-11. Goldman views the MIST countries as the most promising and advanced of the N-11, all of which have young, growing populations and other positive good conditions for economic growth. Other groupings of fast-growing developing countries include the CEVITS (Colombia, Egypt, Vietnam, Indonesia, Turkey, and South Africa) and EAGLES (which stands for emerging and growth-leading economies), which includes the original BRIC and MIST countries plus Egypt and Taiwan.[48] Table 1–8 compares the G-7 (advanced countries), BRIC, and N-11 by population, GDP, and GDP per capita in 2000, 2010, and 2020.

Using data from the World Bank, PricewaterhouseCoopers has made estimates about the future growth of emerging versus developed economies, the result of which appear in summary form in Tables 1–4 and 1–5. Table 1–4 shows the world's largest economies in 2014 and 2050 (projected) using (current) market exchange rates. By this calculation, China would surge past the United States and Japan by 2050, and India would move from tenth to third. Viewing the data on a purchasing power parity (PPP) basis, a method that adjusts GDP to account for different prices in countries, a more dramatic picture is presented. Using this method, both China and India would surpass the United States as the largest world economic power by 2050. In both the Goldman Sachs and

Table 1–4
The World's Largest Economies 2014 and 2050 (Projected)
Measured by GDP at Market Exchange Rates
(in billions of dollars)

	2014		2050	
	GDP	**Rank**	**GDP**	**Rank**
United States	17,416	1	41,384	2
China	10,355	2	53,553	1
Japan	4,770	3	7,914	6
Germany	3,820	4	6,338	10
France	2,902	5	5,207	12
United Kingdom	2,848	6	5,744	11
Brazil	2,244	7	8,534	5
Italy	2,129	8	3,617	16
Russia	2,057	9	6,610	8
India	2,048	10	27,937	3
Canada	1,794	11	3,583	17
Australia	1,483	12	2,903	19
South Korea	1,449	13	4,142	15
Spain	1,400	14	3,099	18

Source: The World in 2050: Will the Shift in Global Economic Power Continue?
PricewaterhouseCoopers LLP, 2015.

Table 1–5
The World's Largest Economies 2014 and 2050 (Projected)
Measured by GDP at Purchasing Power Parity
(in millions of dollars)

	2014		2050	
	GDP	**Rank**	**GDP**	**Rank**
China	17,632	1	61,079	1
United States	17,416	2	41,384	3
India	7,277	3	42,205	2
Japan	4,788	4	7,914	7
Germany	3,621	5	6,338	10
Russia	3,559	6	7,575	8
Brazil	3,073	7	9,164	5
France	2,587	8	5,207	13
Indonesia	2,554	9	12,210	4
United Kingdom	2,435	10	5,744	11
Mexico	2,143	11	8,014	6
Italy	2,066	12	3,617	18
South Korea	1,790	13	4,142	17
Saudi Arabia	1,652	14	5,488	12

Source: The World in 2050: Will the Shift in Global Economic Power Continue?
PricewaterhouseCoopers LLP, 2015.

Table 1–6
Cities Expected to Contribute Most to Global Growth 2015–2030
(GDP contribution in billions)

City	Country	GDP Contribution
New York City	United States	874
Shanghai	China	734
Tianjin	China	625
Beijing	China	594
Los Angeles	United States	522
Guangzhou	China	510
Shenzhen	China	508
London	United Kingdom	476
Chongqing	China	432
Suzhou	China	394

Source: "Global Cities 2013," *Oxford Economics,* 2015.

Table 1–7
Changing Global Demographics: Developing Countries on the Rise (ranked by size)

	1950	2017	2050
1	China	China	India
2	Soviet Union	India	China
3	India	United States	Nigeria
4	United States	Indonesia	United States
5	Japan	Brazil	Indonesia
6	Indonesia	Pakistan	Pakistan
7	Germany	Nigeria	Brazil
8	Brazil	Bangladesh	Bangladesh
9	United Kingdom	Russia	Congo
10	Italy	Mexico	Ethiopia
11	France	Japan	Mexico
12	Bangladesh	Ethiopia	Egypt

Source: United Nations: Department of Economic and Social Affairs, *World Population Prospects: the 2015 Revision.* https://esa.un.org/unpd/wpp/

PricewaterhouseCoopers scenarios, global growth over the next decade, and the next 35 years, is heavily supported by Asia, as seen in Table 1–6. In addition, China and India will remain the most populous countries in the world in 2050, although India will surpass China as the most populous (Table 1–7).

Most African countries have not, to date, fully benefited from globalization. However, increases in the price of commodities, such as oil and gas, agricultural products, and mineral and mining products, between 2000 and 2015 have helped boost incomes and wealth in the African continent. Moreover, rapid population growth in many African countries, similar to growth in India and China in earlier periods, may suggest that African countries could constitute the next wave of dynamic emerging markets.

Although the emerging nations have experienced unprecedented GDP growth since the global recession, it is important to note that the growth rates of the developing world are beginning to show signs of a slowdown. The BRIC economies, once thought to be

Table 1–8
Population, GDP, and GDP per Capita of G-7, BRIC, and N-11 Countries, 2000, 2010, and 2020 (projected)

Country	2000 Population (millions)	2000 GDP (billions)	2000 GDP (per cap.)	2010 Population (millions)	2010 GDP (billions)	2010 GDP (per cap.)	2020 (projected) Population (millions)	2020 (projected) GDP (billions)	2020 (projected) GDP (per cap.)
G7									
Canada	31	$ 739	$24,129	34	$ 1,614	$47,531	37	$ 1,958	$52,316
France	59	1,372	23,318	63	2,652	42,249	66	2,940	44,752
Germany	82	1,956	23,774	82	3,423	41,876	82	4,005	48,666
Italy	57	1,146	20,125	59	2,131	35,996	62	2,144	34,599
Japan	127	4,731	37,302	128	5,499	42,943	124	4,747	38,174
United Kingdom	59	1,549	26,301	62	2,407	38,665	67	3,852	57,385
United States	282	10,285	36,433	310	14,964	48,309	332	22,294	67,064
Total/Average	**697**	**$21,778**	**31,245**	**738**	**$32,690**	**44,295**	**770**	**$41,940**	**54,468**
BRICs									
Brazil	173	$ 657	$ 3,789	195	$2,209	$11,301	212	$ 2,054	$ 9,687
China	1,267	1,205	951	1,341	6,340	4,504	1,411	17,100	12,117
India	1,029	477	463	1,195	1,708	1,430	1,380	3,444	2,495
Russia	146	260	1,775	143	1,524	10,671	146	1,792	12,247
Total/Average	**2,615**	**$ 2,599**	**$ 994**	**2,874**	**$11,781**	**$ 4,099**	**3,149**	**$24,390**	**$ 7,745**
Next-11									
Bangladesh	132	$ 55	$ 412	151	$122	$ 808	168	$ 310	$ 1,847
Egypt	64	100	1,562	79	219	2,779	96	—	—
Indonesia	206	179	870	245	755	3,178	273	1,194	4,380
Iran	64	358	5,604	74	464	6,241	83	555	6,692
South Korea	47	562	11,947	49	1,094	22,151	52	1,899	36,750
Mexico	101	684	6,776	114	1,051	9,197	128	1,496	11,668
Nigeria	119	61	515	156	374	2,396	205	595	2,907
Pakistan	138	74	538	172	178	1,034	208	—	—
Philippines	77	81	1,055	93	200	2,155	112	507	4,530
South Korea	47	562	11,947	49	1,094	22,151	52	1,899	36,750
Turkey	64	267	4,149	73	732	10,002	82	906	11,088
Vietnam	78	31	402	87	113	1,297	96	287	2,978
Total/Average	**1,090**	**$ 2,452**	**$ 2,250**	**1,293**	**$ 5,302**	**$ 4,101**	**1,199**	**$ 7,749**	**$ 6,463**

Source: IMF, "World Economic Outlook Database," October 2015, https://www.imf.org/external/pubs/ft/weo/2015/02/weodata/index.aspx.

the backbone of the emerging market growth, have experienced particularly deep setbacks. In 2015, the Brazilian economy dipped into recession, experiencing an economic contraction of roughly 3 percent, double-digit inflation, and a rapidly rising unemployment rate. Russia, which averaged 6.6 percent annual GDP growth between 2002 and 2008, slowed to only 1.5 percent average annual growth between 2011 and 2014.[49] And in China, GDP grew just 6.8 percent in 2015—significantly less than its 14.5 percent growth in 2007.[50] The slowdown extends beyond the BRIC nations; in 2015, emerging markets outside of China and India contributed only 13 percent to global GDP growth. This represents the lowest proportion of GDP growth contributed by emerging markets since 2009.[51] While emerging markets still hold the most potential for growth in the coming years, the rapid rate of expansion that was experienced over the last decade may prove difficult to match.[52]

In the years since the global recession of 2009, in which merchandise exports fell 23 percent to $12.15 trillion and commercial services exports declined 13 percent to $3.31 trillion, global trade and investment have continued to grow at a healthy rate, outpacing domestic growth in most countries. According to the World Trade Organization, in 2014 merchandise exports reached a record high $18.5 trillion, and commercial services exports have rebounded to $4.9 trillion.[53] **Foreign direct investment (FDI)**—the term used to indicate the amount invested in property, plant, and equipment in another country—also has been growing at a slow but steady rate in the years since the global recession of 2009. Despite dropping almost 50 percent in 2009 to $896 billion, global FDI rebounded to $1.5 trillion by 2013. By 2017, FDI is estimated to reach $1.7 trillion, surpassing the all-time high set a decade earlier in 2007. Interestingly, according to data from UNCTAD, in 2014 Hong Kong received more FDI than the United States, and China received twice as much as Canada, showing the shifting balance of economic influence among developed and developing countries.[54] Table 1–9 shows trade flows among major world regions in both absolute and percentage terms. Tables 1–10 and 1–11 show FDI inflows and outflows by leading developed and emerging economies.

> **foreign direct investment (FDI)**
> Investment in property, plant, or equipment in another country.

As nations become more affluent, they begin looking for countries with economic growth potential where they can invest. Over the last two decades, for example, Japanese MNCs have invested not only in their Asian neighbors but also in the United States and the EU. European MNCs, meanwhile, have made large financial commitments in Japan and, more recently, in China and India because they see Asia as having continued growth potential. American multinationals have followed a similar approach in regard to both Europe and Asia.

The following quiz illustrates how transnational today's MNCs have become. This trend is not restricted to firms in North America, Europe, or Asia. An emerging global community is becoming increasingly interdependent economically. Take the quiz and see how well you do by checking the answers given at the end of the chapter. However, although there may be a totally integrated global market in the near future, at present, regionalization, as represented by North America, Europe, Asia, and the less developed countries, is most descriptive of the world economy.

1. Where is the parent company of Braun household appliances (electric shavers, coffee makers, etc.) located?

   a. Italy   *b.* Germany   *c.* the U.S.   *d.* Japan

2. The BIC pen company is

   a. Japanese   *b.* British   *c.* U.S.-based   *d.* French

3. The company that owns Jaguar is based in

   a. Germany   *b.* the U.S.   *c.* the U.K.   *d.* India

4. French's Mustard is produced by a company based in

   a. the U.K.   *b.* the U.S.   *c.* France   *d.* Taiwan

5. The firm that owns Green Giant vegetables is

   a. U.S.-based   *b.* Canadian   *c.* British   *d.* Italian

Table 1–9
World Merchandise Trade by Region and Selected Country, 2015
(in US$ billions and percentages)

	Exports					Imports				
	Values	**Annual Percentage Change**				**Values**	**Annual Percentage Change**			
	2015	**2005–15**	**2013**	**2014**	**2015**	**2015**	**2005–15**	**2013**	**2014**	**2015**
World	16,272	6	2	0	−13	16,613	5	2	1	−13
North America	2,294	5	2	3	−8	3,132	4	0	3	−5
United States	1,505	6	2	3	−7	2,308	4	0	4	−4
Canada	408	2	1	4	−14	419	4	0	0	−10
Mexico	381	7	2	5	−4	405	7	3	5	−2
South and Central America	532	5	−2	−6	−22	609	9	3	−3	−16
Brazil	191	6	0	−7	−15	179	12	7	−5	−25
Argentina	57	5	−5	−10	−17	60	10	10	−12	−8
Europe	5,956	4	5	0	−12	5,900	4	2	1	−13
European Union (28)	5,381	4	5	1	−12	5,309	3	1	2	−13
Germany	1,329	4	3	3	−11	1,050	4	2	2	−13
France	506	2	2	0	−13	572	2	1	−1	−15
Netherlands	567	4	2	0	−16	506	4	0	0	−14
United Kingdom	460	3	14	−7	−9	626	3	−5	5	−9
Italy	459	3	3	2	−13	409	2	−2	−1	−14
Commonwealth of Independent States (CIS)	489	7	−2	−6	−32	339	8	1	−11	−34
Russian Federation	340	6	−1	−5	−32	194	8	2	−10	−37
Africa										
South Africa	82	6	−3	−4	−11	86	6	−1	−3	−14
Algeria	38	2	−9	−4	−40	52	11	9	6	−12
Egypt	21	6	−5	−7	−23	61	12	−9	1	−9
Middle East										
Saudi Arabia	202	4	−3	−9	−41	172	12	8	3	−1
Iran	63	5	−21	8	−29	42	2	−14	4	−17
Asia	5,967	8	3	3	−8	5,448	8	2	0	−14
China	2,275	12	8	6	−3	1,682	11	7	0	−14
Japan	625	2	−11	−3	−9	648	4	−6	−2	−20
India	267	12	6	2	−17	392	13	−5	−1	−15

Source: Adapted from WTO Press Release, April, 2015. Modest trade recovery to continue in 2015 and 2016 following three years of weak expansion. https://www.wto.org/english/news_e/pres15_e/pr739_e.htm.

6. The owners of Godiva chocolate are
    a. U.S.-based   *b.* Swiss   *c.* Dutch   *d.* Turkish
7. The company that produces Vaseline is
    a. French   *b.* Anglo-Dutch   *c.* German   *d.* U.S.-based
8. The company that bought General Electric Appliances is headquartered in
    a. France   *b.* China   *c.* Japan   *d.* Germany
9. The company that owns Holiday Inn is headquartered in
    a. Saudi Arabia   *b.* France   *c.* the U.S.   *d.* Britain
10. Tropicana orange juice is owned by a company that is headquartered in
    a. Mexico   *b.* Canada   *c.* the U.S.   *d.* Japan

Table 1–10
Foreign Direct Investment Inflows, by Region
(in US$ billions)

	2015	2014	2013
Developed economies	$962.5	$522.0	$680.3
Developing economies	764.7	698.5	662.4
Africa	54.1	58.3	52.2
East and Southeast Asia	447.9	383.2	350.3
South Asia	50.5	41.4	35.6
West Asia	42.4	43.3	45.5
Latin America and the Caribbean	167.6	170.3	176.0
Transition economies	35.0	56.4	84.5

Source: UNCTAD, *World Investment Report 2016* (June 21, 2016), Annex Table 1, http://unctad.org/en/Pages/DIAE/World%20Investment%20Report/Annex-Tables.aspx.

Table 1–11
Foreign Direct Investment Outflows, by Region
(in US$ billions)

	2015	2014	2013
Developed economies	$1,474.2	$800.7	$825.9
Developing economies	377.9	445.6	408.9
Africa	11.3	15.2	15.5
East and Southeast Asia	292.8	365.1	312.0
South Asia	7.8	12.1	2.2
West Asia	31.3	20.4	44.7
Latin America and the Caribbean	33.0	31.4	32.3
Transition economies	31.1	72.2	75.8

Source: UNCTAD, *World Investment Report 2016* (June 21, 2016), Annex Table 2, http://unctad.org/en/Pages/DIAE/World%20Investment%20Report/Annex-Tables.aspx.

■ Global Economic Systems

The evolution of global economies has resulted in three main systems: market economies, command economies, and mixed economies. Recognizing opportunities in global expansion includes understanding the differences in these systems, as they affect issues such as consumer choice and managerial behavior.

Market Economy

A *market economy* exists when private enterprise reserves the right to own property and monitor the production and distribution of goods and services while the state simply supports competition and efficient practices. Management is particularly effective here since private ownership provides local evaluation and understanding, opposed to a nationally standardized archetype. This model contains the least restriction as the allocation of resources is roughly determined by the law of demand. Individuals within the community disclose wants, needs, and desires to which businesses may appropriately respond. A general balance between supply and demand sustains prices, while an imbalance creates a price fluctuation. In other words, if demand for a good or service exceeds supply, the price will inevitably rise, while an excess supply over consumer demand will result in a price decrease.

Since the interaction of the community and firms guides the system, organizations must be as versatile as the individual consumer. Competition is fervently encouraged to promote innovation, economic growth, high quality, and efficiency. The focus on how to best serve the customer is necessary for optimal growth as it ensures a greater penetration of niche markets.[55] The government may prohibit such things as monopolies or restrictive business practices in order to maintain the integrity of the economy. Monopolies are a danger to this system because they tend to stifle economic growth and consumer choice with their power to determine supply. Factors such as efficiency of production and quality and pricing of goods can be chosen arbitrarily by monopolies, leaving consumers without a choice and at the mercy of big business.

Command Economy

A *command economy* is comparable to a monopoly in the sense that the organization, in this case the government, has explicit control over the price and supply of a good or service. The particular goods and services offered are not necessarily in response to consumers' stated needs but are determined by the theoretical advancement of society. Businesses in this model are owned by the state to ensure that investments and other business practices are done in the best interest of the nation despite the often contradictory outcomes. Management within this model ignores demographic information. Government subsidies provide firms with enough security so they cannot go out of business, which simply encourages a lack of efficiency or incentive to monitor costs. Devoid of private ownership, a command economy creates an environment where little motivation exists to improve customer service or introduce innovative ideas.[56]

History confirms the inefficiency and economic stagnation of this system with the dramatic decline of communism in the 1980s. Communist countries believe that the goals of the so-called people take precedence over individualism. While the communist model once dominated countries such as Ethiopia, Bulgaria, Hungary, Poland, and the former U.S.S.R., among others, it survives only in North Korea, Cuba (see In the International Spotlight at the end of Chapter 3), Laos, Vietnam, and China today, in various degrees or forms. A desire to effectively compete in the global economy has resulted in the attempt to move away from the communist model, especially in China, which will be considered in greater depth later in the chapter.

Mixed Economy

A *mixed economy* is a combination of a market and a command economy. While some sectors of this system reflect private ownership and the freedom and flexibility of the law of demand, other sectors are subject to government planning. The balance allows competition to thrive while the government can extend assistance to individuals or companies. Regulations concerning minimum wage standards, social security, environmental protection, and the advancement of civil rights may raise the standard of living and ensure that those who are elderly, are sick, or have limited skills are taken care of. Ownership of organizations seen as critical to the nation may be transferred to the state to subsidize costs and allow the firms to flourish.[57]

Below we discuss general developments in key world regions reflective of these economic systems and the impact of these developments on international management.

■ Economic Performance and Issues of Major Regions

From a vantage point of development, performance, and growth, the world's economies can be evaluated as established economies, emerging economies, and developing economies (some of which may soon become emerging).

Established Economies

North America   As noted earlier, North America constitutes one of the four largest trading blocs in the world. The combined purchasing power of the United States, Canada, and Mexico is more than $19 trillion. Even though there will be more and more integration both globally and regionally as time goes on, effective international management still requires knowledge of individual countries.

The free-market-based economy of this region allows considerable freedom in decision-making processes of private firms. This allows for greater flexibility and low barriers for other countries to establish business. Despite factors such as the Iraq War beginning in 2003, Hurricane Katrina in 2005, high oil prices from 2006 to 2008, the global recession in 2009, and Superstorm Sandy in 2012, the U.S. economy continues to grow. U.S. MNCs have holdings throughout the world, and foreign firms are welcomed as investors in the U.S. market. U.S. firms maintain particularly dominant global positions in technology-intensive industries, including computing (hardware and services), telecommunications, media, and biotechnology. At the same time, foreign MNCs are finding the United States to be a lucrative market for expansion. Many foreign automobile producers, such as BMW, Honda, Subaru, Nissan, and Toyota, have established a major manufacturing presence in the United States. Given the near collapse of the "domestic" automotive industries, North American automotive production will come increasingly from these foreign "transplants."

Canada is the United States' largest trading partner, a position it has held for many years. The United States also has considerable foreign direct investment in Canada. This helps explain why most of the largest foreign-owned companies in Canada are totally or heavily U.S.-owned. The legal and business environments in Canada are similar to those in the United States, and the similarity helps promote trade between the two countries. Geography, language, and culture also help, as does NAFTA, which will assist Canadian firms in becoming more competitive worldwide. They will have to be able to go head to head with their U.S. and Mexican competitors as trade barriers are removed, which should result in greater efficiency and market prowess on the part of the Canadian firms, which must compete successfully or go out of business. In recent years, Canadian firms have begun investing heavily in the United States while gaining international investment from both the United States and elsewhere. Canadian firms also do business in many other countries, including Mexico, Great Britain, Germany, and Japan, where they find ready markets for Canada's vast natural resources, including lumber, natural gas, crude petroleum, and agricultural products.

By the early 1990s Mexico had recovered from its economic problems of the previous decade and had become the strongest economy in Latin America. In 1994, Mexico became part of NAFTA, and it appeared to be on the verge of becoming the major economic power in Latin America. Yet, an assassination that year and related economic crisis underscored that Mexico was still a developing country with considerable economic volatility. Mexico now has free-trade agreements with 46 countries, more than any other nation, including agreements with Panama, the Unifying Free Trade Agreement with Central America, the EU, the European Free Trade Area, and the Trans-Pacific Partnership. More than 90 percent of Mexico's trade occurs under free trade agreements.[58] In 2000 the 71-year hold of the Institutional Revolutionary Party on the presidency of the country came to an end, and many investors believe that the administration of Vicente Fox and his successor, Felipe Calderon, have been especially pro-business. Calderon battled Mexico's narcotics gangs, which, unfortunately, have been responsible for an ongoing epidemic of violence and casualties, including those of innocent civilians. In 2012, the Institutional Revolutionary Party returned to power with the election of Enrique Peña Nieto as president, who, despite uncertainty from some, has continued to advance pro-business initiatives, such as expanding the Mexican auto industry, opening the oil industry to the private sector, and forcing greater competition in telecommunications.[59,60]

Because of NAFTA, Mexican businesses are finding themselves able to take advantage of the U.S. market by producing goods for that market that were previously purchased by the U.S. from Asia. Mexican firms are now able to produce products at highly competitive prices thanks to lower-cost labor and proximity to the American market. Location has helped hold down transportation costs and allows for fast delivery. This development has been facilitated by the **maquiladora** system, under which materials and equipment can be imported on a duty- and tariff-free basis for assembly or manufacturing and re-export mostly in Mexican border towns. Mexican firms, taking advantage of a new arrangement that the government has negotiated with the EU, can also now export goods into the European community without having to pay a tariff. The country's trade with both the EU and Asia is on the rise, which is important to Mexico as it wants to reduce its overreliance on the U.S. market (see In the International Spotlight at the end of Chapter 9).

> **maquiladora**
> A factory, the majority of which are located in Mexican border towns, that imports materials and equipment on a duty- and tariff-free basis for assembly or manufacturing and re-export.

The EU The ultimate objective of the EU is to eliminate all trade barriers among member countries (like between the states in the United States). This economic community eventually will have common custom duties as well as unified industrial and commercial policies regarding countries outside the union. Another goal that has finally largely become a reality is a single currency and a regional central bank. With the addition of Croatia in 2013, 28 countries now comprise the EU, with 17 having adopted the euro. Another 9 countries, having joined the EU in either 2004, 2007, or 2013, are legally bound to adopt the euro upon meeting the monetary convergence criteria.[61]

Such developments will allow companies based in EU nations that are able to manufacture high-quality, low-cost goods to ship them anywhere within the EU without paying duties or being subjected to quotas. This helps explain why many North American and Pacific Rim firms have established operations in Europe; however, all these outside firms are finding their success tempered by the necessity to address local cultural differences.

The challenge for the future of the EU is to absorb its eastern neighbors, the former communist-bloc countries. This could result in a giant, single European market. In fact, a unified Europe could become the largest economic market in terms of purchasing power in the world. Between 2004 and 2007, Poland, the Czech Republic, Hungary, Bulgaria, and Romania all joined the EU, improving economic growth, inflation, and employment rates throughout. Such a development is not lost on Asian and U.S. firms, which are working to gain a stronger foothold in Eastern European countries as well as the existing EU. In recent years, foreign governments have been very active in helping to stimulate and develop the market economies of Central and Eastern Europe to enhance their economic growth as well as world peace.

For the last decade, the EU has faced major challenges. Several European governments, including Greece (see In the International Spotlight at the end of Chapter 2), Portugal, Spain, and Ireland, have found themselves with dangerously large deficits that resulted from both structural conditions (stagnant population growth, overly generous pension systems, early retirements) and shorter-term economic pressures (the 2009 global recession). These conditions have placed pressure on the euro, the currency adopted by most EU countries, and have forced substantial rescue packages led by Germany and France. Though the financial situation in Ireland, Portugal, and Spain has significantly improved, the situation in Greece remains challenging.

Having accepted multiple bailout packages from the IMF, the European Commission, and the European Central Bank between 2010 and 2015, Greece has been forced to accept severe austerity measures, including higher taxes, the freezing of government pensions and wages, and cuts to public spending. Though the European community believes that forcing these restrictions on Greece is necessary to assure financial stability and repayment of bailout funds, many in Greece have argued that these austerity measures have made recovery nearly impossible. In July 2015, with Greece facing a repayment of 1.6 billion euro that it would not be able to meet without additional financial assistance, negotiations between Greek officials and its European creditors deadlocked. In a surprising move, the Greek government pushed the decision of whether or not to accept the latest bailout package and accompanying financial restrictions to its citizens via referendum, which the Greek people voted overwhelming to reject. Banks closed across the country and withdrawals were limited to 60 euros per day. Despite the referendum vote, the Greek government ultimately accepted the terms of the bailout deal in exchange for financial assistance, preventing bankruptcy and a potential Greek exit from the EU.[62,63,64,65]

Maintaining a unified EU in the coming decades may be challenging. In the face of growing skepticism about the advantages of integration with Continental Europe, the United Kingdom, part of the EU but not the Euro-zone, held a referendum in June 2016 regarding whether to "remain" in or "leave" the European Union. In a close but decisive vote, the citizens of the United Kingdom became the first to vote to dissolve their membership in the bloc. This vote, though not legally binding, paves the way for invoking Article 50, which establishes the three-year withdrawal procedure for countries wishing to exit. In the morning following the referendum vote, "remain" supporter Prime Minister David Cameron announced his plans to step aside, leaving the task of coordinating the EU exit, or "Brexit," up to the next prime minister.

Japan During the 1970s and 1980s, Japan's economic success had been without precedent. The country had a huge positive trade balance, the yen was strong, and the Japanese became recognized as the world leaders in manufacturing and consumer goods.

Analysts ascribe Japan's early success to a number of factors. Some areas that have received a lot of attention are the Japanese cultural values supporting a strong work ethic and group/team effort, consensus decision making, the motivational effects of guaranteed lifetime employment, and the overall commitment that Japanese workers have to their organizations. However, at least some of these assumptions about the Japanese workforce have turned out to be more myth than reality, and some of the former strengths have become weaknesses in the new economy. For example, consensus decision making turns out to be too time-consuming in the new speed-based economy. Also, there has been a steady decline in Japan's overseas investments since the 1990s due to a slowing Japanese economy, poor management decisions, and competition from emerging economies, such as China.

Some of the early success of the Japanese economy can be attributed to the **Ministry of International Trade and Industry (MITI)**. This is a governmental agency that identifies and ranks national commercial pursuits and guides the distribution of national resources to meet these goals. In recent years, MITI has given primary attention to the so-called ABCD industries: automation, biotechnology, computers, and data processing.

Another major reason for Japanese success may be the use of **keiretsus**. This Japanese term stands for the large, vertically integrated corporations whose holdings supply much of the assistance needed in providing goods and services to end users. Being able to draw from the resources of the other parts of the keiretsu, a Japanese MNC often can get things done more quickly and profitably than its international competitors.

Despite setbacks, Japan remains a formidable international competitor and is well poised in all three major economic regions: the Pacific Rim, North America, and Europe.

Emerging and Developing Economies

In contrast to the fully developed countries of North America, Europe, and Asia are the developing and emerging countries. While there is no precise definition, developing economies typically face relatively low GDP per capita and a workforce that is either unskilled or semiskilled. In many cases, there also is considerable government intervention in economic affairs. Emerging markets can be viewed as developing economies that exhibit sustained economic reform and growth.

Ministry of International Trade and Industry (MITI)
A Japanese government agency that identifies and ranks national commercial pursuits and guides the distribution of national resources to meet these goals.

keiretsu
In Japan, an organizational arrangement in which a large, often vertically integrated group of companies cooperate and work closely with each other to provide goods and services to end users; members may be bound together by cross-ownership, long-term business dealings, interlocking directorates, and social ties.

One objective of multicultural research is to learn more about the customs, cultures, and work habits of people in other countries. After all, a business can hardly expect to capture an overseas market without knowledge of the types of goods and services the people there want to buy. Equally important is the need to know the management styles that will be effective in running a foreign operation. Sometimes this information can change quite rapidly. For example, as Russia continues to move from a central to a market economy, management is constantly changing as the country attempts to adjust to increased exposure in the global environment. Russia entered into a strategic partnership with the United States in 2002. However, while U.S. perspectives of "partnerships" are flexible, they are generally seen as inherently having some hierarchical structure. Russia, on the other hand, sees "partnerships" as entailing equality, especially in the decision-making process. This may be a part of the reason Russia formed a strategic partnership with China in 2005, since both countries emerged from a communist regime and can understand similar struggles. Regardless, as Russia moves to privatize its organizations, the new partnership may pose a threat to the Americas and the West if efforts to understand each other and work together are abandoned.

It is evident that the United States and Russia differ on many horizons. Russian management is still based on authoritarian styles, where the managerial role is to pass orders down the chain of command, and there is

little sense of responsibility, open communication, or voice in the decision-making process. Furthermore, while 64 percent of U.S. employees see retirement as an opportunity for a new chapter in life, only 15 percent of Russian employees feel that way, and another 23 percent see retirement as "the beginning of the end." Despite such differences, there are points of similarity that a U.S. firm can use as leverage when considering opening a business in Russia. About 46 percent of employees in both the United States and Russia would prefer a work schedule that fluctuates between work and leisure, mirroring a pattern of recurring sabbaticals. Also, Russia currently has a post–Cold War mentality, much like the United States experienced after the Great Depression of the 1930s. Looking back at history and incorporating the evolutionary knowledge can assist in understanding emerging economies.

These examples show the importance of studying international management and learning via systematic analysis of culture and history and firsthand information how managers in other countries really do behave toward their employees and their work. Such analysis is critical in a firm's ensuring a strong foothold in effective international management.

Source: Garry Kasparov, "Putin's Gangster State," *The Wall Street Journal*, March 30, 2007, p. A15; The Economist Intelligence Unit, *Country Report: Russia* (Kent, U.K.: EIU, 2007), p. 7; "Trust the Locals," *The Economist* 382, January 25, 2007, pp. 55–56.

Central and Eastern Europe In 1991, the Soviet Union ceased to exist. Each of the individual republics that made up the U.S.S.R. in turn declared its independence and now is attempting to shift from a centrally planned to a market-based economy. The Russian Republic has the largest population, territory, and influence, but others, such as Ukraine, also are industrialized and potentially important in the global economy. Of most importance to the study of international management are the Russian economic reforms, the dismantling of Russian price controls (allowing supply and demand to determine prices), and privatization (converting the old communist-style public enterprises to private ownership).

Russia's economy continues to emerge as poverty declines and the middle class expands. Direct investment in Russia, along with its membership in the International Monetary Fund (IMF), helped to raise GDP and decrease inflation, offsetting the hyperinflation created from the initial attempt at transitioning to a market-based economy in the early 1990s. Abundant oil and high global energy prices greatly boosted Russia's economy in the early 2000s, though recent decreases in demand have pushed Russia into a recession. In addition, the Group of Seven (G7, including the United States, Germany, France, England, Canada, Japan, and Italy) formally expanded to include Russia in 1997, becoming the Group of Eight (G8). However, Russia was suspended from the group in 2014 after a series of political differences between the original G7 and Russia, culminating in the annexation of Crimea. In addition, multilateral sanctions were imposed. These actions, when combined with falling oil and gas prices, have resulted in a dramatic slowdown in Russia's economy and a fall in the value of the ruble. As such, the Russian economy likely will have a number of years of economic instability and many recurrent political problems.

One pervasive set of challenges in Russia is persistent crime, corruption, and lack of public security. As such, many foreign investors feel that the risk is still too high (see The World of International Management at the beginning of Chapter 10). Russia is such a large market, however, and has so much potential for the future that many MNCs feel they must get involved, especially with a promising rise in GDP. There also has been a movement toward teaching Western-style business courses, as well as MBA programs, in all the Central European countries, creating a greater preparation for trends in globalization.

In Hungary, state-owned hotels have been privatized, and Western firms, attracted by the low cost of highly skilled, professional labor, have been entering into joint ventures with local companies. MNCs also have been making direct investments, as in the case of General Electric's purchase of Tungsram, the giant Hungarian electric company. Another example is Britain's Telfos Holdings, which paid $19 million for 51 percent of Ganz, a Hungarian locomotive and rolling stock manufacturer. Still others include Suzuki's investment of $110 million in a partnership arrangement to produce cars with local manufacturer Autokonzern, Ford Motor's construction of a new $80 million car component plant, and Italy's Ilwa's $25 million purchase of the Salgotarjau Iron Works.

Poland had a head start on the other former communist-bloc countries. General political elections were held in June 1989 and the first noncommunist government was established well before the fall of the Berlin Wall. In 1990, the Communist Polish United Workers Party dissolved and Lech Walesa was elected president. Earlier than its neighbors, Poland instituted radical economic reforms (characterized as "shock therapy"). Although the relatively swift transition to a market economy has been very difficult for the Polish people, with very high inflation initially, continuing unemployment, and the decline of public services, Poland's economy has done relatively well. In fact, Poland's economy was the only economy in the EU to continue to grow during the global recession of 2008–2009. In 2015, Poland's GDP grew by around 4 percent. However, political instability and risk, large external debts, a deteriorating infrastructure, and only modest education levels have led to continuing economic problems (see In the International Spotlight at the end of Chapter 5).

Although Russia, the Czech Republic, Hungary, and Poland receive the most media coverage and are among the largest of the former communist countries, others also are struggling to right their economic ships. A small but particularly interesting example is Albania. Ruled ruthlessly by the Stalinist-style dictator Enver Hoxha for over four decades following World War II, Albania was the last, but most devastated, Eastern European country to abandon communism and institute radical economic reforms. At the beginning of the 1990s, Albania started from zero. Industrial output initially fell over 60 percent and inflation reached 40 percent monthly. Today, Albania still struggles but is slowly making progress.

The key for Albania and the other Eastern European countries is to maintain the social order, establish the rule of law, rebuild the collapsed infrastructure, and get factories and other value-added, job-producing firms up and running. Foreign investment must be forthcoming for these countries to join the global economy. A key challenge for Albania and the other "have-not" Eastern European countries will be to make themselves less risky and more attractive for international business.

China   After years of steady, strong growth, China's GDP has been slowing considerably. In 2015, GDP expanded at only 7 percent, its slowest in 25 years.[66] China faces other formidable challenges, including a massive savings glut in the corporate sector, the globalization of manufacturing networks, vast developmental needs, and the requirement for 15–20 million new jobs annually to avoid joblessness and social unrest (see In the International Spotlight at the end of Chapter 7).

China also remains a major risk for investors. The one country, two systems (communism and capitalism) balance is a delicate one to maintain, and foreign businesses are often caught in the middle. Most MNCs find it very difficult to do business in and with

China. Concerns about undervaluation of China's currency, the renminbi (also know as the yuan), and continued policies that favor domestic companies over foreign ones make China a complicated and high-risk venture.[67,68] Even so, MNCs know that China, with its 1.4 billion people, will be a major world market and that they must have a presence there.

Trade relations between China and developed countries and regions, such as the United States and the EU, remain tense. Many in the United States and around the globe had long argued that the value of the Chinese currency was kept artificially low, giving China an unfair advantage in selling its exports. That opinion, however, may be changing. A slowing Chinese economy, coupled with over a decade of steady gains relative to the dollar, resulted in both the IMF and the Peterson Institute stating in 2015 that the yuan was no longer undervalued.[69] In addition, China's policy toward foreign investors continues to be fluid and sometimes unpredictable. Both Walmart and Yum Brands found themselves accused of improper business practices and each had to close stores and issue public apologies. Walmart was forced to pay nearly US$10 million in fines over the three-year period from 2012 through 2014 due to poor-quality food, confusing pricing, and mislabeled meat products.[70] In response, Walmart invested nearly US$50 million through the end of 2015 to improve food safety and testing within China.[71] Similarly, Yum Brands suffered a 29 percent drop in same-store sales in China in April of 2013 after concerns about the safety of some chicken and the spread of Avian flu caused customers to stay away from the outlets.[72]

Other Emerging Markets of Asia   In addition to Japan and China, there are a number of other important economies in the region, including South Korea, Hong Kong, Singapore, and Taiwan. Together, the countries of the ASEAN bloc are also fueling growth and development in the region.

In South Korea, the major conglomerates, called **chaebols**, include such internationally known firms as Samsung, Daewoo, Hyundai, and the LG Group. Many key managers in these huge firms have attended universities in the West, where in addition to their academic programs they learned Western culture, customs, and language. Now they are able to use this information to help formulate competitive international strategies for their firms. This will be very helpful for South Korea, which has shifted to privatizing a wide range of industries and withdrawing some of the restrictions on overall foreign ownership. Unlike most developed economies, South Korea was able to avoid falling into economic recession in 2009. In the years since, South Korea has maintained steady progress, with a solid economy with moderate growth, moderate inflation, low unemployment, an export surplus, and fairly equal distribution of income.

chaebols
Very large, family-held Korean conglomerates that have considerable political and economic power.

Bordering southeast China and now part of the People's Republic of China (PRC), Hong Kong has been the headquarters for some of the most successful multinational operations in Asia. Although it can rely heavily on southeast China for manufacturing, there is still uncertainty about the future and the role that the Chinese government intends to play in local governance.

Singapore is a major success story. Its solid foundation leaves only the question of how to continue expanding in the face of increasing international competition. To date, however, Singapore has emerged as an urban planner's ideal model and the leader and financial center of Southeast Asia.

Taiwan has progressed from a labor-intensive economy to one that is dominated by more technologically sophisticated industries, including banking, electricity generation, petroleum refining, and computers. Although its economy has also been hit by the downturn in Asia, it continues to steadily grow.

Besides South Korea, Singapore, and Taiwan, other countries of Southeast Asia are also becoming dynamic platforms for growth and development. Thailand, Malaysia, Indonesia (see In the International Spotlight at the end of Chapter 12), and now Vietnam have developed economically with a relatively large population base and inexpensive labor despite the lack of considerable natural resources. These countries have been known to have social stability, but in the aftermath of the recent economic crisis, there has been considerable turmoil in this part of the world. This instability first occurred in Indonesia, the fourth most populous country in the world, and more recently in Thailand. In late 2013, Thailand's Prime Minister Yingluck Shinawatra's government proposed sweeping pardons for various past offenses committed by former and current politicians. Although the legislature overwhelmingly rejected those proposed pardons, protests and political unrest, led by the People's Democratic Reform Committee, still unraveled on the streets of Bangkok.[73] In December, Prime Minister Yingluck Shinawatra attempted to contain the protests by dissolving the House of Representatives, declaring a state of emergency, and calling for a new election in February 2014.[74] The continued protests led to disruptions of the February election, leading the Constitutional Court to nullify the election results.[75] In May 2014, a military coup d'etat, led by General Prayut Chan-o-cha, removed Prime Minister Yingluck Shinawatra from power.[76] Since then, Thailand has been ruled by the newly formed National Council for Peace and Order under military dictatorship. Despite the political turmoil that has plagued Thailand and other countries in the region, these export-driven Southeast Asian countries remain attractive to outside investors.

India With a population of about 1.3 billion and growing, India has traditionally had more than its share of political and economic problems. The recent trend of locating software and other higher-value-added services has helped to bolster a large middle- and upper-class market for goods and services and a GDP that is quickly reaching the level of China. India may soon be viewed as a fully developed country if it can withstand the intense growth period.

For a number of reasons, India is attractive to multinationals, especially U.S. and British firms. Many Indian people speak English, are very well educated, and are known for advanced information technology expertise. Also, the Indian government is providing funds for economic development. For example, India is expanding its telecommunication systems and increasing the number of phone lines fivefold, a market that AT&T is vigorously pursuing. Many frustrations remain in doing business in India (see In the International Spotlight at the end of this chapter), but there is little question that the country will receive increased attention in the years ahead.

Developing Economies on the Verge

Around the world there are many economies that can be considered developing (what might formally have been termed "less developed" or in some cases "least developed") that are worthy of attention and understanding. Some of these economies are on the verge of emerging as impressive contributors to global growth and development.

South America Over the years, countries in South America have had difficult economic problems. They have accumulated heavy foreign debt obligations and experienced severe inflation. Although most have tried to implement economic reforms reducing their debt, periodic economic instability and the emergence of populist leaders have had an impact on the attractiveness of countries in this region.

Through the 1990s and 2000s, Brazil had been attracting considerable foreign investment, with foreign companies drawn to opportunities created by Brazil's privatization of power, telecommunications, and other infrastructure sectors. (See the International Management in Action box "Brazilian Economic Reform and Recent Challenges.") Power companies such as AES and General Electric have constructed more than $20 billion worth of electricity plants throughout the country. At the same time, many other well-known companies have set up operations in Brazil, including Yum! Brands, Apple, Gap, McDonald's, and Walmart. Until recently, Brazil has benefited from one of the most stable governments throughout Latin America, which has helped secure the country's place today as the undisputed economic leader of South America.

More recently, Brazil has faced alternating periods of economic progress and setbacks. After a period of robust growth and declining poverty rates in the period 2008–2014,

Brazil slipped into recession in 2015 and 2016. Frustration of economic stagnation and a widespread public corruption scandal resulted in the impeachment of President Dilma Rousseff in May of 2016.[77] Given Brazil's large and relatively well-educated population, ample natural resources, existing industrial base, and strategic geographic position, longer-term prospects are still potentially positive. With an economic output comparable to that of France, the Brazilian economy outweighs that of any other South American country and has become a worldwide presence (see In the International Spotlight at the end of Chapter 10).

Chile's market-based economic growth has fluctuated between 3 and 6 percent since the early 2000s, one of the best and most stable performances in Latin America. Chile attracts a lot of foreign direct investment, mainly dealing with gas, water, electricity, and mining. It continues to participate in globalization by engaging in further trade agreements, including those with Mercosur, China, India, the EU, South Korea, and Mexico.

Argentina has one of the strongest economies overall with abundant natural resources, a highly literate population, an export-oriented agricultural sector, and a diversified industrial base; however, it has suffered the recurring economic problems of inflation, external debt, capital flight, and budget deficits. Although Argentina rebounded from the global recession with over 8 percent GDP growth in 2010 and 2011, economic growth has since slowed significantly. In 2015, inflation soared to over 25 percent. An election in 2015, however, ousted the Peronist government that had ruled the country since 2013. Mauricio Macri was elected with a mandate to reverse the government-driven economic policies of his predecessors, Cristina de Kirchner and her husband, Néstor Kirchner.[78]

Despite the ups and downs, a major development in South America is the growth of intercountry trade, spurred on by the progress toward free-market policies. For example, beginning in 1995, 90 percent of trade among Mercosur members (Brazil, Argentina, Paraguay, and Uruguay) was duty-free. At the same time, South American countries are increasingly looking to do business with the United States. In fact, a survey of businesspeople from Argentina, Brazil, Chile, Colombia, and Venezuela found that the U.S. market, on average, was more important for them than any other. Some of these countries, however, also are looking outside the Americas for growth opportunities. For over two decades, Mercosur has been in discussion with the EU to create free trade between the two blocs, and Chile and Peru have joined the Asia-Pacific Economic Cooperation group and were participants in the TPP negotiations described above. These developments help illustrate the economic dynamism of South America and, especially in light of Asia's recent economic problems, explain why so many multinationals are interested in doing business with this part of the world.

Middle East and Central Asia   Israel, the Arab countries, Iran, Turkey, and the Central Asian countries of the former Soviet Union are a special group of emerging countries. Because of their oil, however, some of these countries are considered to be economically rich. Recently, this region has been in the world news because of the political instability and civil war in Syria, the rise of the Islamic State in Iraq and Syria, and the decade-long wars in Iraq and Afghanistan following the September 11, 2011, terrorist attacks in the United States. Despite the political challenges, these countries continue to try to balance geopolitical/religious forces with economic viability and activity in the international business arena. Students of international management should have a working knowledge of these countries' customs, culture, and management practices since most industrial nations rely, at least to some degree, on imported oil and since many people around the world work for international, and specifically Arab, employers.

The Arab and Central Asian countries rely almost exclusively on oil production. The price of oil greatly fluctuates, and the Organization of Petroleum Exporting Countries (OPEC) has trouble holding together its cartel. After years of relatively high prices, oil prices dipped to a 12-year low in 2016, causing financial shockwaves throughout the

Brazilian Economic Reform and Recent Challenges   http://en.wikipedia.org; http://www.wto.org/

Over the past two decades, Brazil's economic reform and progress have been nothing short of spectacular. Beginning with a comprehensive privatization program in the early and mid-1990s under which dozens of state-owned enterprises were sold to commercial interests, Brazil has transformed itself from a relatively closed and frequently unstable economy to one of the global leading "BRIC" countries and the anchor of South American economic development. Brazil's reforms, which have included macroeconomic stabilization, liberalization of import and export restrictions, and improved fiscal and monetary management, reflect a definitive break from past inward-looking policies that characterized much of Latin America in the 1960s and 1970s. A critical milestone was the introduction of the Plano Real ("Real Plan"), instituted in the spring of 1994, which sought to break inflationary expectations by pegging the real to the U.S. dollar. Inflation was brought down to single-digit annual figures, but not fast enough to avoid substantial real exchange rate appreciation during the transition phase of the Plano Real. This appreciation meant that Brazilian goods were now more expensive relative to goods from other countries, which contributed to large current account deficits. However, no shortage of foreign currency ensued because of the financial community's renewed interest in Brazilian markets as inflation rates stabilized and memories of the debt crisis of the 1980s faded.

The Real Plan successfully eliminated inflation, after many failed attempts to control it. Almost 25 million people turned into consumers. The maintenance of large current account deficits via capital account surpluses became problematic as investors became more risk averse to emerging market exposure as a consequence of the Asian financial crisis in 1997 and the Russian bond default in August 1998. After crafting a fiscal adjustment program and pledging progress on structural reform, Brazil received a $41.5 billion IMF-led international support program in November 1998. In January 1999, the Brazilian Central Bank announced that the real would no longer be pegged to the U.S. dollar. This devaluation helped moderate the downturn in economic growth in 1999 that investors had expressed concerns about over the summer of 1998. Brazil's debt to GDP ratio of 48 percent for 1999 beat the IMF target and helped reassure investors that Brazil will maintain tight fiscal and monetary policy even with a floating currency.

The economy grew 4.4 percent in 2000, but problems in Argentina in 2001, and growing concerns that the presidential candidate considered most likely to win, leftist Luis Inácio Lula da Silva, would default on the debt, triggered a confidence crisis that caused the economy to decelerate. Poverty was down to near 16 percent.

In 2002, Luis Inácio Lula da Silva won the presidential elections, and he was reelected in 2006. During his government, the economy began to grow more rapidly. In 2004 Brazil saw promising growth of 5.7 percent in GDP; following in 2005 with 3.2 percent growth; in 2006, 4.0 percent; in 2007, 6.1 percent; and in 2008, 5.1 percent growth. Although the financial crisis caused some slowdown in Brazil's economy, it has weathered the period much better than nearly every other economy in the Western Hemisphere. From 2009 to 2011, Brazil was the world's fastest-growing car market. By 2011, the size of the Brazilian economy had surpassed that of the United Kingdom.

The years since the financial crisis have been more challenging for the Brazilian economy. Oil producer OXG entered bankruptcy in late 2013—the largest corporate bankruptcy in South American history. Political corruption, including the exchange of millions in bribery and money laundering between Brazilian politicians and state-owned oil producer Petrobras, lowered consumer confidence. Petrobras lost nearly 60 percent of its value between the last quarter of 2014 and early 2015, and the Bovespa, Brazil's stock index, slid sharply downward. Between 2011 and 2015, the real depreciated nearly 50 percent in relation to the U.S. dollar. By 2015, the economy had slipped into recession, and in 2016, the president was impeached due in part to alleged connections to the Petrobras scandal.

Despite the current struggles, there continues to be promise for Brazil's future. Brazil remains the second-biggest destination for foreign direct investment into developing countries after China, and many Brazilian companies continue to expand in the international arena. Embraer (ERJ), the global leader in small and medium-sized airplanes, is now the world's third-largest manufacturer of passenger jets after Boeing and Airbus. Odebrecht, the Brazilian business conglomerate in the fields of engineering, construction, chemicals, and petrochemicals, is responsible for building a number of large infrastructure projects around the world, including roads, bridges, mass transit systems, more than 30 airports, and sports stadiums such as Florida International University's FIU stadium. Brazil remains the world's largest exporter of several agricultural products including beef, chicken, coffee, orange juice, and sugar, and the country's international trade and investment relationships continue to diversify considerably to include manufacturing and services.

Source: Garry Kasparov, "Putin's Gangster State," The Wall Street Journal, March 30, 2007, p. A15; The Economist Intelligence Unit, Country Report: Russia (Kent, U.K.: EIU, 2007), p. 7; "Trust the Locals," *The Economist* 382, January 25, 2007, pp. 55–56.

region.[79] Saudi Arabia, the largest oil producer in the Arab world, was forced to reduce fuel, water, and power subsidies it provides to its citizens after experiencing a U.S.$98 billion budget deficit in 2015 (see In the International Spotlight at the end of Chapter 8).[80] Arab countries have invested billions of dollars in U.S. property and businesses. Many people around the world, including those in the West, work for Arab employers. For example, the bankrupt United Press International was purchased by the Middle East Broadcasting Centre, a London-based MNC owned by the Saudis.

The "Arab Spring," described in the next chapter, has had a profound impact on the political and economic environment of many countries in this region.

Africa Even though they have considerable natural resources, many African nations remain very poor and undeveloped, and international trade is only beginning to serve as a major source of income. One major problem of doing business in the African continent is the overwhelming diversity of approximately one-billion people, divided into 3,000 tribes, that speak 1,000 languages and dialects. Also, political instability is pervasive, and this instability generates substantial risks for foreign investors.

In recent years, Africa, especially sub-Saharan Africa, has had a number of severe problems. In addition to tragic tribal wars, there has been the spread of terrible diseases such as AIDS, malaria, and Ebola. These problems have resulted in serious economic setbacks. According to the World Bank, the 2014–2015 Ebola outbreak cost the economies of Guinea, Liberia, and Sierra Leone an estimated US$1.6 billion of potential economic growth.[81] Although the WTO was able to agree to relax intellectual property rights (IPR) in 2002–2003 to allow for greater and less costly access by African countries to antiviral AIDS medications, similar IPR disputes resulted in a delay of Ebola medicine to the region in 2014.[82] While globalization has opened up new markets for developed countries, developing nations in Africa lack the institutions, infrastructure, and economic capacity to take full advantage of globalization. Other big problems include poverty, malnutrition, illiteracy, corruption, social breakdown, vanishing resources, overcrowded cities, drought, and homeless refugees. There is still hope in the future for Africa despite this bleak situation because the potential of African countries remains virtually untapped. Not only are there considerable natural resources, but the diversity itself also can be used to advantage. For example, many African people are familiar with the European cultures and languages of the former colonial powers (e.g., English, French, Dutch, and Portuguese), and this can serve them well in international business as they strive for continued growth. Uncertain times are ahead, but a growing number of MNCs are attempting to make headway in this vast continent. Also, the spirit of these emerging countries has not been broken. There are continuing efforts to stimulate economic growth. Examples of what can be done include Togo, which has sold off many of its state-owned operations and leased a steel-rolling mill to a U.S. investor, and Guinea, which has sold off some of its state-owned enterprises and cut its civil service force by 30 percent. A special case is South Africa, where apartheid, the former white government's policies of racial segregation and oppression, has been dismantled and the healing process is progressing (see In the International Spotlight at the end of Chapter 4). Long-jailed former black president Nelson Mandela was recognized as a world leader. These significant developments have led to an increasing number of the world's MNCs returning to South Africa; however, there continue to be both social and economic problems that, despite Mandela's and his successors' best efforts, signal uncertain times for the years ahead. One major initiative is the country's Broad-Based Black Economic Empowerment (B-BBEE) program, designed to reintegrate the disenfranchised majority into business and economic life.

Africa's economic growth and dynamism have accelerated in recent years. Real GDP rose by an average of 5.3 percent a year from 2000 through 2015, more than twice its pace in the 1980s and 1990s.[83] Telecommunications, banking, and retailing are all flourishing, while Nigeria and Angola saw their economies accelerate due in part to higher global fuel prices (see In the International Spotlight at the end of Chapter 6).[84] It is important to emphasize, however, that sub-Saharan Africa's recent growth, which has been dependent on foreign direct investment and the high level of global demand for commodities, is particularly sensitive to changes in the global economy. In 2015, sub-Saharan Africa's growth stalled to a 20-year low in the wake of low oil prices and China's economic slowdown (see Table 1–12).[85] Although global pullback from the region, such as China's slowdown, may mean less foreign direct investment in the near-term, McKinsey, the global consultancy, has found that the rate of return on foreign investment in Africa is actually higher than for any other region, offering positive prospects for this historically struggling region.[86]

Table 1–12
Overview of the World Economic Outlook; Projections
(percentage change, unless otherwise noted)

| | Year over Year | | | | Q4 over Q4 | | |
| | | | Projections | | Estimates Projections | | |
	2013	2014	2015	2016	2014	2015	2016
World Output	3.3	3.4	3.1	3.6	3.3	3.0	3.6
Advanced Economies	1.1	1.8	2.0	2.2	1.8	2.0	2.3
United States	1.5	2.4	2.6	2.8	2.5	2.5	2.8
Euro Area	−0.3	0.9	1.5	1.6	0.9	1.5	1.7
Germany	0.4	1.6	1.5	1.6	1.5	1.6	1.6
France	0.7	0.2	1.2	1.5	0.1	1.5	1.5
Italy	−1.7	−0.4	0.8	1.3	−0.4	1.2	1.5
Spain	−1.2	1.4	3.1	2.5	2.0	3.2	2.2
Japan	1.6	−0.1	0.6	1.0	−0.8	1.3	1.3
United Kingdom	1.7	3.0	2.5	2.2	3.4	2.2	2.2
Canada	2.0	2.4	1.0	1.7	2.5	0.5	2.0
Other Advanced Economies	2.2	2.8	2.3	2.7	2.6	2.5	2.6
Emerging and Developing Economies	5.0	4.6	4.0	4.5	4.7	4.0	4.8
Commonwealth of Independent States	2.2	1.0	−2.7	0.5	−0.6	−3.3	0.3
Russia	1.3	0.6	−3.8	−0.6	0.3	−4.6	0.0
Excluding Russia	4.2	1.9	−0.1	2.8	...	...	...
Emerging and Developing Asia	7.0	6.8	6.5	6.4	6.8	6.4	6.4
China	7.7	7.3	6.8	6.3	7.1	6.7	6.3
India	6.9	7.3	7.3	7.5	7.6	7.3	7.5
ASEAN–5	5.1	4.6	4.6	4.9	4.8	4.4	5.2
Emerging and Developing Europe	2.9	2.8	3.0	3.0	2.6	3.2	4.2
Latin America and the Caribbean	2.9	1.3	−0.3	0.8	1.1	−1.5	1.7
Brazil	2.7	0.1	−3.0	−1.0	−0.2	−4.4	1.3
Mexico	1.4	2.1	2.3	2.8	2.6	2.3	2.9
Middle East and North Africa (MENA)	2.3	2.7	2.5	3.9	...	...	...
Sub-Saharan Africa	5.2	5.0	3.8	4.3	...	...	...
South Africa	2.2	1.5	1.4	1.3	1.3	0.7	1.7
Memorandum European Union	0.2	1.5	1.9	1.9	1.5	1.8	2.1
World Growth Based on Market Exchange Rates	2.4	2.7	2.5	3.0	2.5	2.4	3.0
World Trade Volume (goods and services)	5.9	2.8	3.8	5.5	...	...	...
Imports							
Advanced Economies	2.0	3.4	4.0	4.2	...	...	...
Emerging and Developing Economies	5.2	3.6	1.3	4.4	...	...	...
Exports							
Advanced Economies	2.9	3.4	3.1	3.4	...	...	...
Emerging and Developing Economies	4.4	2.9	3.9	4.8	...	...	...

Source: IMF World Economic Outlook, October 2015.

Table 1–13
World's Most Competitive Nations, 2015

Country	Rank
USA	1
China–Hong Kong	2
Singapore	3
Switzerland	4
Canada	5
Luxembourg	6
Norway	7
Denmark	8
Sweden	9
Germany	10

Source: World Competitive Scoreboard, 2015. http://www.imd.org/

Table 1–12 shows economic growth rates and projections for major world regions and countries from 2013 to 2016. Of note is the fact that a number of emerging regions and countries are growing faster than developed countries; notably, China, India, and other Asian economies. Table 1–13 ranks the top 10 countries globally on their "competitiveness" as reported by the World Economic Forum. For 2015, China–Hong Kong and Singapore were ranked second and third, respectively. Table 1–14 ranks emerging markets according to several key indicators.

The World of International Management—Revisited

In the World of International Management at the start of the chapter, you read about how social media is changing how we connect, shaping business strategy and operations, and even affecting diplomacy. Social media and social networks are revolutionizing the nature of international management by allowing producers and consumers to interact directly and bringing populations of the world closer together. Having read this chapter, you should now be more cognizant of the impacts of globalization and many international linkages among countries, firms, and societies on international management. Although controversial, globalization appears unstoppable. The creation of free-trade agreements worldwide has helped to trigger economic gains in many developing nations. The consolidation and expansion of the EU will continue to open up borders and make it easier and more cost-effective for exporters from less developed countries to do business there. In Asia, formerly closed economies such as India and China have opened up, and other emerging Asian countries such as Indonesia, Malaysia, the Philippines, and Thailand are becoming important emerging economies in their own right. Continued efforts to privatize, deregulate, and liberalize many industries will increase consumer choice and lower prices as competition increases. The rapid growth of social media networks around the world is but one reflection of the interconnected nature of global economies and individuals. In some ways, social media are transcending traditional barriers and impediments to global integration; however, differences in economic systems and approaches persist, making international management an ongoing challenge.

In light of these developments, answer the following questions: (1) What are some of the pros and cons of globalization and free trade? (2) How might the rise of social media result in closer connections (and fewer conflicts) among nations? (3) Which regions of the world are most likely to benefit from globalization and integration in the years to come, and which may experience dislocations or setbacks?

Table 1–14
Market Potential Indicators Ranking for Emerging Markets, 2016

Country	Market Size	Market Growth Rate	Market Intensity	Market Consumption Capacity	Commercial Infra-Structure	Economic Freedom	Market Receptivity	Country Risk	Overall Score
China	100	95	1	92	62	22	7	78	100
Hong Kong	1	58	100	43	100	100	100	100	57
Singapore	1	76	76	43	84	70	88	93	50
India	37	78	32	66	28	45	7	67	48
Qatar	1	100	94	54	53	45	27	83	40
South Korea	9	61	48	81	52	63	20	85	38
Brazil	17	59	48	47	40	49	5	56	29
Poland	3	53	53	67	51	66	14	77	29
Israel	2	63	55	58	46	65	21	68	29
Estonia	1	52	37	64	58	74	25	77	28
Turkey	6	71	63	61	40	48	10	50	28
Malaysia	3	68	41	54	47	52	23	77	28
Indonesia	11	69	32	58	30	46	8	61	26
Russia	18	51	42	58	49	24	8	39	26
Mexico	9	54	58	41	27	53	24	67	26
Peru	2	81	45	45	23	57	9	72	24
Vietnam	4	83	39	51	32	24	25	50	24
Latvia	1	43	54	61	50	62	19	61	23
Chile	2	53	58	39	38	75	16	68	23
Philippines	4	65	58	46	27	49	10	72	23
Argentina	4	58	74	60	38	38	6	17	20
Thailand	4	61	30	47	38	37	20	56	20
Egypt	4	56	78	57	27	30	6	23	18
South Africa	5	46	43	1	47	55	10	56	11

Source: globalEDGE: A Market Potential Index for Emerging Markets 2016. http://globaledge.msu.edu/

SUMMARY OF KEY POINTS

1. Globalization—the process of increased integration among countries—continues at an accelerated pace. More and more companies—including those from developing countries—are going global, creating opportunities and challenges for the global economy and international management. Globalization has become controversial in some quarters due to perceptions that the distributions of its benefits are uneven and due to questions raised by offshoring. There have emerged sharp critics of globalization among academics, NGOs, and the developing world, yet the pace of globalization and integration continues unabated.

2. Economic integration is most pronounced in the triad of North America, Europe, and the Pacific Rim. The North American Free Trade Agreement (NAFTA) is turning the region into one giant market. In South America, there is an increasing amount of intercountry trade, sparked by Mercosur. Additionally, trade agreements such as the Central American Free Trade Agreement (CAFTA) are linking countries of the Western Hemisphere together. In Europe, the expansion of the original countries of the European Union (EU) is creating a larger and more diverse union, with dramatic transformation of Central and Eastern European countries such as the Czech Republic, Poland, and Hungary. The Trans-Pacific Partnership (TPP), if implemented, could link together 12 or more major Asian and Asian-facing economies, and the Transatlantic Trade and Investment Partnership (T-TIP), a proposed trade agreement between the European Union and the United States, could further promote trade and multilateral economic growth in Europe and North America. Africa and the Middle East continue to face complex problems but still hold economic promise for the future. Emerging markets in all regions present both opportunities and challenges for international managers.

3. Different growth rates and shifting demographics are dramatically altering the distribution of economic power around the world. Notably, China's rapid growth will make it the largest economic power in the world by midcentury, if not before. India will be the most populous country in the world, and other emerging markets will also become important players. International trade and investment have been increasing dramatically over the years. Major multinational corporations (MNCs) have holdings throughout the world, from North America to Europe to the Pacific Rim to Africa. Some of these holdings are a result of direct investment; others are partnership arrangements with local firms. Small firms also are finding that they must seek out international markets to survive in the future. MNCs from emerging markets are growing rapidly and expanding their global reach. The internationalization of nearly all business has arrived.

4. Different economic systems characterize different countries and regions. These systems, which include market, command, and mixed economies, are represented in different nations and have changed as economic conditions have evolved.

KEY TERMS

chaebols, 29

European Union, 12

foreign direct investment (FDI), 20

globalization, 7

international management, 5

keiretsu, 26

management, 5

maquiladora, 25

Ministry of International Trade and Industry (MITI), 26

MNC, 5

North American Free Trade Agreement (NAFTA), 11

offshoring, 7

outsourcing, 7

Trans-Pacific Partnership, 13

World Trade Organization (WTO), 10

REVIEW AND DISCUSSION QUESTIONS

1. How has globalization affected different world regions? What are some of the benefits and costs of globalization for different sectors of society (companies, workers, communities)?

2. How has NAFTA affected the economies of North America and how has the EU affected Europe? What importance do these economic pacts have for international managers in North America, Europe, and Asia?

3. Why are Russia and Eastern Europe of interest to international managers? Identify and describe some reasons for such interest and also risks associated with doing business in these regions.

4. Many MNCs have secured a foothold in Asia, and many more are looking to develop business relations there. Why does this region of the world hold such interest for international management? Identify and describe some reasons for such interest.

5. Why would MNCs be interested in South America, India, the Middle East and Central Asia, and Africa, the less developed and emerging countries of the world? Would MNCs be better off focusing their efforts on more industrialized regions? Explain.

6. MNCs from emerging markets (India, China, Brazil) are beginning to challenge the dominance of developed country MNCs. What are some advantages that firms from emerging markets bring to their global business? How might MNCs from North America, Europe, and Japan respond to these challenges?

ANSWERS TO THE IN-CHAPTER QUIZ

1. **c.** U.S.-based Procter & Gamble acquired the Braun company in 2005.

2. **d.** BIC SA is a French company.

3. **d.** Tata Motors, a division of the Indian conglomerate the Tata Group, purchased Jaguar, Land Rover, and related brands from Ford in 2008.

4. **a.** United Kingdom–based Reckitt Benckiser acquired French's parent company, Durkee Famous Foods, in 1986.

5. **a.** General Mills, of the United States, acquired the Green Giant product line (together with the Pillsbury company) in 2001 from Britain's Diageo PLC.

6. **d.** Godiva chocolate is owned by Yildiz Holding, a Turkish conglomerate.

7. **b.** Vaseline is manufactured by the Anglo-Dutch MNC Unilever PLC.

8. **d.** Haier Group, the largest appliance manufacturer in the world and headquartered in China, acquired GE Appliances in 2016.

9. **d.** Holiday Inn is owned by Britain's InterContinental Hotels Group PLC.

10. **c.** Tropicana orange juice was purchased by U.S.-based PepsiCo.

INTERNET EXERCISE: GLOBAL COMPETITION IN FAST FOOD

One of the best-known franchise operations in the world is McDonald's, and in recent years, the company has been working to expand its international presence. But emerging market fast-food companies have succeeded in slowing McDonald's global expansion by catering to local and regional tastes. Philippines-based Jollibee is one such success story. Jollibee has 780 outlets in the Philippines and more than 90 around the world, including in the United States. Visit the McDonald's and Jollibee websites, and find out what each has planned in terms of its global expansion. Compare their presence in Asia to each other and to Yum! Brands' KFC and Pizza Hut presence in Asia.

Then, based on this assignment and the chapter material, answer these last three questions: (1) Which of these companies seems best positioned in Southeast Asia? (2) What advantages might a "local" brand like Jollibee have over the global companies? What advantages do the global MNCs have? (3) What is your prediction in terms of future growth potential?

ENDNOTES

1. Brad Stone and Sarah Frier, "Evan Spiegel Reveals Plan to Turn Snapchat into a Real Business," *Bloomberg*, May 26, 2015, http://www.bloomberg.com/news/features/2015-05-26/evan-spiegel-reveals-plan-to-turn-snapchat-into-a-real-business.

2. Ibid.

3. Lars Backstrom, "Anatomy of Facebook," *Facebook.com*, November 21, 2011, http://www.facebook.com/notes/facebook-data-team/anatomy-of-facebook/10150388519243859.

4. Evan LePage, "A Long List of Instagram Statistics and Facts (That Prove Its Importance)," Hootsuite, September 17, 2015, http://blog.hootsuite.com/instagram-statistics-for-business/.

5. Stone and Frier, "Evan Spiegel Reveals Plan to Turn Snapchat into a Real Business."

6. 3V Advertising, Snapchat, https://www.snapchat.com/ads (last visited January 10, 2016).

7. Lara O'Reilly, "If You're Traveling Home for the Holidays, GE Wants You to Use This Snapchat Filter," *Business Insider*, November 24, 2015, http://www.businessinsider.com/ge-launches-snapchat-geofilter-targeting-airports-and-train-stations-2015-11.

8. Erik Qualman, *Socialnomics: How Social Media Transforms the Way We Live and Do Business* (Hoboken, NJ: Wiley, 2009), front flap, pp. 95, 110.

9. Ibid.

10. The UN on Social Media, United Nations, http://www.un.org/en/sections/about-website/un-social-media/.

11. Rose Yu, "China Car Sales Growth Slows Further," *The Wall Street Journal Online*, January 12, 2015, http://www.wsj.com/articles/china-car-sales-growth-slows-further-1452587244.

12. Rajesh Mahapatra, "Cisco to Set Up Center in India," *Associated Press* online, December 6, 2006.

13. Joan Lublin, "India Could Provide Unique Opportunities for Expat Managers," *The Wall Street Journal*, May 8, 2007, p. B1.

14. "Get a First Look at Our New Innovation Center in Singapore," *P&G News Blog*, April 1, 2014, http://news.pg.com/blog/company-strategy/SGIC.

15. Unilever, "Our R&D Locations," https://www.unilever.com/about/innovation/our-r-and-d-locations/ (last visited July 11, 2016).

16. Laurie Burkitt, "GE Bases X-ray Unit in China," *The Wall Street Journal Online*, July 26, 2012, http://online.wsj.com/article/SB100014240531119047723045764678733321597208.html.

17. "American Powerhouse Builds Global Profile," *The Wall Street Journal Online*, November 4, 2012, http://online.wsj.com/article/SB100014240529702047129045780921823017966600.html.

18. Jochelle Mendonca, "Accenture Shoots Past TCS in Headcount; Says 95,000 People Will Join in 2015," *Economic Times*, June 26, 2015, http://articles.economictimes.indiatimes.com/2015-06-26/news/63862376_1_tata-consultancy-services-headcount-strong-growth.

19. "Q1 Fiscal 2016," Accenture, November 30, 2015, https://newsroom.accenture.com/fact-sheet/.

20. "Accenture Earnings: Strong Dollar Impacts Revenue and New Signings Growth," *Forbes*, December 18, 2015, http://www.forbes.com/sites/greatspeculations/2015/12/18/accenture-earnings-strong-dollar-impacts-revenue-and-new-signings-growth/2/#6052f0296ef4.

21. Thomas Friedman, *The World Is Flat: A Brief History of the Twenty-first Century* (New York: Farrar, Straus and Giroux, 2005).

22. "Anti-forum Protests Turn Violent," Associated Press, February 2, 2009.

23. Michael Yaziji and Jonathan P. Doh, *NGOs and Corporations: Conflict and Collaboration* (Cambridge: Cambridge University Press, 2009).

24. For discussions of the benefits of globalization, see Jagdish Bhagwati, *In Defense of Globalization* (New York: Oxford University Press, 2004), and Edward Graham, *Fighting the Wrong Enemy: Antiglobal Activists and Multinational Enterprises* (Washington, DC: Institute for International Economics, 2000).

25. For discussion of some of the emerging concerns surrounding globalization, see Peter Singer, *One World: The Ethics of Globalization* (New Haven: Yale University Press, 2002); George Soros, *George Soros on Globalization* (New York: Public Affairs Books, 2002); Joseph Stiglitz, *Globalization and Its Discontents* (New York: Norton, 2002).

26. G. Balachandar, "Vehicle Makers Sans Ford Resume Production at Chennai Factories," *The Hindu*, December 7, 2015, http://www.thehindu.com/business/Industry/tamil-nadu-floods-vehicle-makers-sans-ford-resume-production-at-chennai-factories/article7958524.ece.

27. Tim Worstall, "India Now Fastest Growing Large Economy at 7.4% Third Quarter GDP Growth," *Forbes*, November 30, 2015, http://www.forbes.com/sites/timworstall/2015/11/30/india-now-fastest-growing-large-economy-at-7-4-third-quarter-gdp-growth/#2715e4857a0b3e2ca881acba.

28. "Offshoring Your Lawyer," *The Economist*, December 16, 2010, http://www.economist.com/node/17733545.

29. Paul Blustein, "EU Offers to End Farm Subsidies," *Washington Post*, May 11, 2004, p. E1.

30. Alan Beattie and Frances Williams, "Doha Trade Talks Collapse," *Financial Times*, July 29, 2008.

31. "Developing Nations Call for WTO Deal to Help Poor," *Reuters.com*, November 29, 2009.

32. CIA, "Costa Rica," *The World Factbook* (2009), https://www.cia.gov/library/publications/the-world-factbook/geos/cs.html.

33. Office of the U.S. Trade Representative, "Trade Agreements," https://ustr.gov/trade-agreements.

34. Office of the U.S. Trade Representative, "Transatlantic Trade and Investment Partnership (T-TIP)," https://ustr.gov/ttip.

35. Elena Holodny, "China's GDP Is Expected to Surpass the US' in 11 Years," *Business Insider*, June 24, 2015, http://www.businessinsider.com/chinas-gdp-is-expected-to-surpass-the-us-in-11-years-2015-6.

36. Office of the U.S. Trade Representative, "Summary of the Trans-Pacific Partnership Agreement," https://ustr.gov/about-us/policy-offices/press-office/press-releases/2015/october/summary-trans-pacific-partnership.

37. Greg Ip, "Population Implosion: How Demographics Rule the Global Economy," WSJ 2050 Demographic Destiny, *The Wall Street Journal Online*, November 22, 2015, http://www.wsj.com/articles/how-demographics-rule-the-global-economy-1448203724.

38. Ibid.

39. Ibid.

40. Ibid.

41. Ibid.

42. Ibid.

43. Goldman Sachs, "Global Economics Paper No. 99: Dreaming with the BRICs: The Path to 2050," October 1, 2003.

44. Goldman Sachs, "Global Economics Paper No. 208: The BRICs 10 Years On: Halfway Through the Great Transformation," December 7, 2011.

45. Mark Fahey and Nicholas Wells, "Emerging Markets Funds, by the Numbers," *CNBC*, November 9, 2015, http://www.cnbc.com/2015/11/09/emerging-markets-funds-by-the-numbers.html.

46. John Hawksworth, "The World in 2050: How Big Will the Major Emerging Market Economies Get and How Can the OECD Compete?," Pricewater-houseCoopers, March 2006.

47. "The World in 2050: Will the Shift in Global Economic Power Continue?" PricewaterhouseCoopers, February 2015.

48. Eric Martin, "Move Over, BRICs. Here Come the MISTs." *BusinessWeek*, August 9, 2012, www.bloomberg.com/news/articles/2012-08-09/move-over-brics-dot-here-come-the-mists.

49. Data Team, "Brazilian Waxing and Waning," *The Economist Online*, December 1, 2015, http://www.economist.com/blogs/graphicdetail/2016/04/economic-backgrounder.

50. IMF, "World Economic Outlook Database," October 2015, https://www.imf.org/external/pubs/ft/weo/2015/02/weodata/index.aspx.

51. "World GDP," *The Economist*, June 13, 2015, http://www.economist.com/news/economic-and-financial-indicators/21654018-world-gdp.

52. Kenneth Rapoza, "This Year's World Growth Slowest Since 2008 Crisis, Forecasts 'The Economist,'" *Forbes Online,* August 22, 2013, www.forbes.com/sites/kenrapoza/2013/08/22/this-years-world-growth-slowest-since-2008-crisis-forecasts-the-economist/#7e77de4138de.

53. WTO, International Trade Statistics (Switzerland, WTO, 2015).

54. UNCTAD, World Investment Report 2015 (Switzerland, United Nations, 2015).

55. R. Glenn Hubbard and Anthony Patrick O'Brien, *Essentials of Economics* (Upper Saddle River, NJ: Pearson Prentice Hall, 2007).

56. Ibid.

57. Ibid.

58. CIA, "Mexico," *The World Factbook* (2015), https://www.cia.gov/library/publications/the-world-factbook/geos/mx.html.

59. Colleen Anne, "Mexico Takes Bids on 25 Offshore Oil Fields Taking One Step Closer to Privatization & Reviving the Energy Sector," *LatinOne.com*, December 16, 2015, http://www.latinone.com/articles/29157/20151216/mexico-takes-bids-25-offshore-oil-fields-taking-one-step.htm.

60. Dave Graham, "Mexico Telecoms Regulator Backs AT&T and Telefonica Spectrum Deal," *Reuters*, December 17, 2015, http://www.reuters.com/article/us-mexico-at-t-idUSKBN0U106B20151218.

61. CIA, "European Union," *The World Factbook* (2015), https://www.cia.gov/library/publications/the-world-factbook/geos/ee.html.

62. Ben Knight, "Greece Bailout Deal: Angela Merkel Expects IMF Involvement," *The Guardian*, August 16, 2015, www.theguardian.com/business/2015/aug/16/greece-bailout-deal-angela-merkel-expects-imf-involvement.

63. Virginia Harrison, "Greek Banks Closed Until Thursday," *CNN Money*, July 14, 2015, http://money.cnn.com/2015/07/13/news/greece-deal-banks-closed/.

64. Abhinav Ramnarayan, "Greece's July 20 Repayment to ECB Moves into Focus," *Reuters*, June 30, 2015, www.reuters.com/article/greece-eurobonds-idUSL8N0ZG1QR20150630.

65. "How Greece's Referendum Works," *The Economist*, July 4, 2015, www.economist.com/blogs/economist-explains/2015/07/economist-explains-2.

66. Xiaoyi Shao and Sue-Lin Wong, "China State Planner Sees 2015 GDP Growth around 7 Percent, Okays More Big Projects," *Reuters*, January 12, 2016, http://www.reuters.com/article/us-china-economy-planning-idUSKCN0UQ0BH20160112.

67. John Boudreau and Brandon Bailey, "Doing Business in China Getting Tougher for U.S. Companies," *Mercury News*, March 27, 2010, www.mercurynews.com/2010/03/26/doing-business-in-china-getting-tougher-for-u-s-companies/.

68. Edward Wong and Mark Landler, "China Rejects U.S. Complaints on Its Currency," *New York Times Online,* February 4, 2010, www.nytimes.com/2010/02/05/world/asia/05diplo.html.

69. Wei Gu, "Is Yuan Undervalued or Overvalued?," *The Wall Street Journal Online*, August 11, 2015, www.wsj.com/articles/yuan-devaluation-enters-debate-on-whether-currency-is-undervalued-1439307298.

70. Laurie Burkitt and Shelly Banjo, "Wal-Mart Cries Foul on China Fines," *The Wall Street Journal Online*, April 13, 2014, www.wsj.com/news/articles/SB10001424052702304157204579473272856969150?cb=logged0.31542067981929367.

71. Laurie Burkitt, "Wal-Mart to Triple Spending on Food-Safety in China," *The Wall Street Journal Online*, June 17, 2014, www.wsj.com/articles/wal-mart-to-triple-spending-on-food-safety-in-china-1402991720.

72. Bloomberg News, "Yum's 29% Sales Collapse in China Goes Beyond Avian Flu," *Bloomberg.com*, May 12, 2013, www.bloomberg.com/news/articles/2013-05-12/yum-s-29-sales-collapse-in-china-goes-beyond-avian-flu.

73. Thomas Fuller, "Antigovernment protesters try to Shut Down Bangkok," New York Times, January 12, 2014, http://www.nytimes.com/2014/01/13/world/asia/protests-thailand.html?_r=0.

74. "Thai Prime Minister Dissolves Parliament," *Al Jazeera*, December 9, 2013, www.aljazeera.com/news/asia-pacific/2013/12/thai-pm-says-she-will-dissolve-parliament-201312913831169537.html.

75. "Thai Court Rules General Election Invalid," *BBC.com*, March 21, 2014, http://www.bbc.com/news/world-asia-26677772.

76. Walden Bello, "Military Coup Follows Judicial Coup in Thailand," *Inquirer.net*, May 24, 2014, http://opinion.inquirer.net/74896/military-coup-follows-judicial-coup-in-thailand.

77. Simon Romero, Vinod Sreeharsha, and Bryant Rousseau, "Brazil Impeachment: The Process for Removing the President," *New York Times*, May 12, 2016, www.nytimes.com/interactive/2016/world/americas/brazil-dilma-rousseff-impeachment.html?_r=0.

78. The Editorial Board, "Argentina's Transformative Election," *New York Times*, November 26, 2015, www.nytimes.com/2015/11/27/opinion/argentinas-transformative-election.html.

79. Mark Shenk, "$30 Oil Just Got Closer as WTI Slides to 12-Year Low on China," *Bloomberg Business Online*, January 6, 2016, www.bloomberg.com/news/articles/2016-01-06/oil-trades-near-34-as-record-cushing-stockpiles-exacerbate-glut.

80. Rick Gladstone, "Saudi Arabia, Squeezed by Low Oil Prices, Cuts Spending to Shrink Deficit," *New York Times Online*, December 28, 2015, www.nytimes.com/2015/12/29/world/middleeast/squeezed-by-low-oil-prices-saudi-arabia-cuts-spending-to-shrink-deficit.html?_r=0.

81. The World Bank, "Ebola: Most African Countries Avoid Major Economic Loss but Impact on Guinea, Liberia, Sierra Leone Remains Crippling," January 20, 2015, www.worldbank.org/en/news/press-release/2015/01/20/ebola-most-african-countries-avoid-major-economic-loss-but-impact-on-guinea-liberia-sierra-leone-remains-crippling.

82. Karen Pauls, "Could Ebola Vaccine Delay Be Due to an Intellectual Property Spat?," *CBC News*, October 3, 2014, www.cbc.ca/news/canada/manitoba/could-ebola-vaccine-delay-be-due-to-an-intellectual-property-spat-1.2786214.

83. The World Bank, "Sub-Saharan Africa: Regional Forecast," *Global Economic Prospects*, https://www.worldbank.org/content/dam/Worldbank/GEP/GEP2015b/Global-Economic-Prospects-June-2015-Sub-Saharan-Africa-analysis.pdf (last visited January 9, 2016).

84. Matina Stevis, "IMF Revises Down Sub-Saharan Africa 2015 Growth," *The Wall Street Journal Online*, October 27, 2015, www.wsj.com/articles/imf-revises-sub-saharan-africa-2015-growth-down-1445936591.

85. Ibid.

86. Acha Leke, Susan Lund, Charles Roxburgh, and Arend van Wamelen, "What's Driving Africa's Growth," *McKinsey Quarterly,* June 2010, www.mckinsey.com/global-themes/middle-east-and-africa/whats-driving-africas-growth.

87. CIA, "India," *The World Factbook* (2016), https://www.cia.gov/library/publications/the-world-factbook/geos/in.html.

88. Ibid.

89. World Bank, "India," *World Development Indicators* (2016), http://data.worldbank.org/country/india#cp_wdi.

90. Ankit Panda, "India's 7.4% GDP Growth Rate Keeps It Ahead of the Emerging Economy Pack," *The Diplomat*, December 2, 2015, http://thediplomat.com/2015/12/indias-7-4-gdp-growth-rate-keeps-it-ahead-of-the-emerging-economy-pack/.

91. Ritika Katyal, "India Census Exposes Extent of Poverty," *CNN*, August 2, 2015, www.cnn.com/2015/08/02/asia/india-poor-census-secc/.

92. "A Brief History of the Kashmir Conflict," *The Telegraph*, September 24, 2001, www.telegraph.co.uk/news/1399992/A-brief-history-of-the-Kashmir-conflict.html.

93. Donald Kirk, "Modi, India's New Prime Minister, Dreams of Economic Reform, Reconciliation with Pakistan," *Forbes*, May 26, 2014, www.forbes.com/sites/donaldkirk/2014/05/26/modi-indias-new-prime-minister-dreams-of-lifting-indias-masses-from-poverty/#5fa99962750c.

94. Ibid.

95. Shashank Bengali, "Wal-Mart, Thwarted by India's Retail Restrictions, Goes Big: Wholesale," *Los Angeles Times*, July 23, 2015.

96. Geeta Anand and Hari Kumar, "Hoping Jobs for India Will Follow, Modi Clears Investors' Path," *New York Times*, June 21, 2016, p. A1.

97. Bengali, "Wal-Mart, Thwarted by India's Retail Restrictions, Goes Big: Wholesale."

India

India is located in southern Asia, with the Bay of Bengal to the country's east and the Arabian Sea to its west. Positioned alongside the important trade corridor of the Indian Ocean, India is approximately one-third the size of the United States in area. Its major natural resources consist of coal (fourth-largest reserves in the world), iron ore, manganese, mica, bauxite, rare earth elements, titanium ore, chromite, natural gas, diamonds, petroleum, limestone, and arable land. The majority of the country's land use (60 percent) is allocated to agriculture. India is a largely rural country that suffers from a significant lack of infrastructure in both metropolitan and rural areas.[87]

India boasts a population of 1.295 billion. The country is approximately 80 percent Hindu and 14 percent Muslim. The population is also relatively young: approximately 85 percent of its population is 54 years old or younger. The population growth rate is a steady 1.22 percent. Hindi is the dominant language, but Indians, depending on their ethnicity and geographic location, speak other languages as well, including Bengali, Telugu, Marathi, Tamil, Urdu, Gujarati, Kannada, Malayalam, Oriya, Punjabi, Assamese, and Maithili. These various languages form the basis on how the states within the country are divided. While Hindi is the dominant language, English is the language primarily used among the educated class and in commercial and political communication. The vast majority of the population is either directly or indirectly dependent on agriculture.[88]

India's GDP in 2014 was US$2.049 trillion.[89] GDP growth in India has been higher and more consistent compared to many of the other larger emerging markets, with recent annual growth rates holding steady at around 7 percent.[90]

India faces numerous socioeconomic and security challenges, including a very high rate of poverty and strained relations with neighboring Pakistan. India's 2014–2015 census indicates that less than 10 percent of the 300 million households surveyed had a salaried job; only 5 percent had earned enough to pay taxes. More than 35 percent of adults are classified as illiterate.[91] India's tense relations with Pakistan date back to the moment each gained independence from the British empire. Split along religious lines, India was intended to remain a largely Hindu state while Pakistan was intended to be a predominantly Muslim one. Fighting between the two neighbors started almost immediately. Kashmir, where the leader of the state was Hindu but the majority of the population

was Muslim, has served as a focal point for disagreements between the nations. The multiple wars over this area are known collectively as the "Kashmir Conflict."[92]

Because India was under British rule, India adopted the "common law" legal system, with certain codes intertwined based on particular religions. As a democratic republic, India's political system is also similar to that of the British system. The country has operated with this form of government since its independence in 1947. The executive branch consists of the president, vice president, prime minister, and a cabinet of appointees; the legislative branch is fashioned as a bicameral Parliamentary system; and the judicial branch is modeled off of the English court system.

In May 2014, India elected Prime Minister Narendra Modi. Support for Prime Minister Modi was based on promises that he would mend the country's relationship with its Asian neighbors, including China and, most importantly, Pakistan. He also promised to create a business-friendly environment in the country.[93] Specifically, Prime Minister Modi promised to invest heavily in infrastructure, including adding high-speed trains, building more schools, and cleaning the badly polluted waterways. These investments were designed to dramatically increase India's manufacturing exports.[94]

Early in his term, Prime Minister Modi was criticized for failing to deliver on his promises. However, India's 7.5 percent annual GDP growth rate has positioned it as the fastest-growing major world economy. Time will tell if India will be able to maintain this growth rate and whether or not the Prime Minister's efforts to open India to foreign business will succeed. Currently, India ranks 130 out of 185 nations in the World Bank's "Ease of Doing Business" Survey, which is up four spots from the previous year.

You Be the International Business Consultant:

Walmart is one of the largest retailers in the world. Despite its size, the company has faced numerous challenges when entering and operating in foreign markets. India has posed an especially difficult situation. Even though the country has opened its economy to the world market over the past 30–40 years, India maintains strict limitations over foreign ownership in its retail sector. For example, foreign companies are prohibited from opening supermarkets and can only own a maximum of 51 percent in local chains. Other retailers, such as Starbucks, have paired up with Indian companies; Starbucks has a 50-50 joint venture with Tata, one of India's largest conglomerates. Walmart also had plans for future joint ventures in India. In 2007, it announced a partnership with Bharti Enterprises, but the relationship fell apart in the face of continued limitations on what the joint venture would be permitted to do. Allegations of corruption also soured the deal. The Indian government has frequently committed to opening the retail sector to foreign investment, only to bow to pressures from local competitors, resulting in delayed or watered-down proposals.[95] Recently, however, the Indian government has once again announced new policies that would appear to open foreign investment in retail.[96]

As a way to remain in the market, Walmart has shifted its attention to serving as a wholesale supplier to India's small mom-and-pop stores, known as kiranas. This is permitted because India does not maintain restrictions on foreign investment in wholesale. The kiranas purportedly sell more than 95 percent of the country's basic foodstuffs, creating a large opportunity for a wholesaler like Walmart. It is unclear, however, as to exactly what retail role Walmart will be able to play long term and whether sales to the kiranas can provide enough revenue to make remaining in India worthwhile.[97]

Questions

1. In light of this situation, what would your recommendation be to Walmart?
2. Should it stick with the wholesale focus, or should it pursue another joint venture with an Indian partner?
3. Alternatively, should it maintain a "wait and see" approach in hopes that the Indian government will finally reform its restrictions on foreign investment?

Source: John F. Burns, "India Now Winning U.S. Investment," *New York Times,* February 6, 1995, pp. C1, C5; Rahual Jacob, "India Gets Moving," *Fortune,* September 5, 1994, pp. 101–102; Jon E. Hilsenrath, "Honda Venture Takes the Bumps in India," *The Wall Street Journal,* August 2, 2000, p. A18; Manjeet Kripalani and Pete Engardio, "India: A Shocking Election Upset Means India Must Spend Heavily on Social Needs," *BusinessWeek,* May 31, 2004; Steve Hamm, "The Trouble with India," *BusinessWeek,* March 19, 2007, pp. 48–58; "The World's Headache," *The Economist,* December 6, 2008, p. 58; Gaurav Choudhury, "How Slow GDP Growth Affects You," *Hindustan Times,* December 4, 2012, http://www.hindustantimes.com/.

Chapter 2

THE POLITICAL, LEGAL, AND TECHNOLOGICAL ENVIRONMENT

The broader political, legal, and technological environment faced by international managers is changing rapidly. Changes in this environment are more common and rapid, presenting challenges for managers seeking to respond and adapt to this environment. Although there are many dimensions of the external environment relevant to international management, economic considerations covered in the last chapter are among the most important, along with cultural issues covered in Part Two. However, the political, legal, regulatory, and technological dimensions also bear on the international manager in highly significant ways. The objective of this chapter is to examine how the political, legal, regulatory, and technological environments have changed in recent years, and how these changes pose challenges and opportunities for international managers. In Chapter 10, we return to some of these themes, especially as they relate to political risk and managing the political environment. In this chapter, we outline some of the major trends in the political, legal, and technological environment that will shape the world in which international managers will compete. The specific objectives of this chapter are

1. **INTRODUCE** the basic political systems that characterize regions and countries around the world and offer brief examples of each and their implications for international management.

2. **PRESENT** an overview of the legal and regulatory environment in which MNCs operate worldwide, and highlight differences in approach to legal and regulatory issues in different jurisdictions.

3. **REVIEW** key technological developments, including the growth of e-commerce, and discuss their impact on MNCs now and in the future.

The World of *International Management*

Social Media and Political Change

The struggle for government reform has traditionally been a long, painful process. In the past, uprisings in the Middle East were often violently and horrifically repressed by corrupt dictators. Governments censored and controlled news organizations, hiding the atrocities of war from the view of the global community. For example, the true scale of the 1982 Hama massacre, where at least 10,000 Syrian revolutionaries were killed by government forces, is still unclear. Over the last few years, however, the transparency of war and the resulting pace of change appear to be rapidly increasing.

The ongoing conflict in Syria, which arose in the wake of the "Arab Spring" that spread across Egypt, Tunisia, and Libya in the early 2010s, has been particularly impacted by the use of social media. Journalism, communication, and transparency from within Syria have all been redefined by the use of social media by ordinary citizens. Unlike past conflicts, the Syrian civil war and resulting refugee crisis are unraveling in real time to a global audience in photos and videos through YouTube, Facebook, and Twitter.

Social Media as an Organizing Tool

While previous uprisings lacked widespread communication tools, those engaged in the Syrian conflict are equipped with smartphones and social media. Syrian government loyalists, Syrian revolutionaries, and the terrorist organization Islamic State of Iraq and Syria (ISIS) have all utilized social media to quickly and efficiently organize their supporters. In the early years of the conflict, the pro-revolution Facebook group "The Syrian Revolution 2011" swelled to nearly half a million members, while the group supporting Syrian President Bashar al-Assad had nearly 3 million. ISIS has released propaganda videos on all forms of social media, and the terror group has maintained multiple Twitter accounts in an attempt to recruit internationally.

Evidence suggests that revolutionaries in particular have mobilized successfully through social media. Inspired by videos uploaded to YouTube showing the Syrian government harshly cracking down on nonviolent protesters, nearly 100,000 Syrians organized via Facebook and staged a protest in Hama in June 2011. The strength in numbers afforded by social media has made the Syrian protests incredibly difficult to dissolve; the mass scale of protests organized through social networking sites far outnumbers the military and government forces sent to suppress them. Tips on how to protect oneself from tear gas and police batons are shared through Facebook groups, and Twitter has served as a communication lifeline when government authorities have attempted to disperse the crowds.[1,2]

Social media has provided such a powerful tool to revolutionaries that the Syrian government has attempted to completely disrupt Internet service on several occasions since 2011, most notably during massive protests demanding the removal of President Bashar al-Assad. Widespread outages spread through nearly all of Syria, including Damascus, essentially shutting off all communication with the outside world.[3] Cyber attacks have also been perpetrated by supporters of the Syrian government in an attempt to censor photos and videos coming from the protesters; malware programs that steal Facebook and YouTube logins have been dispatched on a massive scale.[4] Smartphones have morphed into a symbol of the revolutionary forces, with Syrian government soldiers and ISIS border guards often demanding to inspect cell phones of anyone passing through their posts.[5]

Those fleeing the conflict have also utilized social media to plan safe escape from Syria. Refugees who successfully migrated to Europe assist those still making the journey through online activity. A Facebook group dedicated to sharing knowledge and advice with fellow refugees has over 100,000 members. Topics range from necessary supplies and route information to messages of encouragement. Smugglers, often necessary for safe passage, are recommended and discussed, and even weather conditions are relayed to those making the journey by sea.[6,7] Refugees in past conflicts often separated from their family and friends with the unfortunate yet realistic possibility that they would never reunite. During the Syrian conflict, refugees have been able to send messages to their loved ones and update them on their safety throughout their journey.[8] WhatsApp, the instant messaging application, is popular among refugees not only for familial communication but also for its ability to connect with transportation, smugglers, and even Greek coast guard officials in the event of an emergency.

Social Media as a Journalistic Tool

In the early stages of the war, the Syrian government banned international news media from covering the revolution. As a result, social media became the primary source of photos, videos, and news stories from inside the conflict. The Syrian civil war represented one of the first major conflicts in which citizens could instantly record video from the front lines and, using smartphones, transmit that footage to the Internet in real time. News organizations, unable to gather information from any other source, used the uploaded social media to build their reports.[9]

Syrians from all sides of the conflict created and shared this content on various social networking sites, attempting to build international support for their cause.[10] The sheer amount of content uploaded is staggering; over a million videos from within the revolution were uploaded to YouTube, often taken by cellular phone. Another website, OnSyria, was used by protestors to upload nearly 200,000 videos.

More importantly, smartphones and social networks ensured that any human rights violations from either revolutionaries or the government would be broadcast online, likely eroding any international support that the inflicting party had. In August 2013, one of the most defining moments in the early years of the war occurred when hundreds of civilians were killed in a sarin gas chemical attack in Ghouta, allegedly perpetrated by the Syrian government. Almost instantly, witnesses and first responders uploaded photos and video of the aftermath to social networking sites including YouTube, Reddit, and Twitter. These images marked a critical turning point in the global public opinion and international involvement in the war. The U.S. government had taken a hands-off approach prior to the attacks; however, once these human rights violations were broadcast across social media, the U.S. had no choice but to take a formal stand against the Syrian government.[11]

Social Media as a Support-Building Tool

Unlike written news releases, pictures and videos have the ability to convey information in emotional ways that transcend language. During the Syrian civil war, social media, used as a visual medium, led the global community to unite behind the plight of the Syrian refugees in an unprecedented way. Throughout early 2015, images and videos of overloaded rafts, filled with desperately fleeing Syrians, dominated social media. The emotion and suffering of the refugees were conveyed through these images to a worldwide audience in real time. Though thousands of images, stories, and videos were shared over various social networks during the crisis, the September 2015 photo of a deceased toddler, Aylan Al-Kurdi, who had drowned during his family's attempted escape on a raft across the Mediterranean, provoked global outcry and underscores the power of social media as a support-building tool. As a direct result of this image, financial and emotional support among the global community grew almost instantly.

World leaders, including French President François Hollande, British Prime Minister David Cameron, and Irish Prime Minister Enda Kenny, publically expressed support and shock after seeing the picture of the toddler. Spreading across social networks almost instantly, the hashtag "#kiyiyavuraninsanlik," meaning "Humanity Washed Ashore," was shared more than 200,000 times within 24 hours. In the United States, the United Kingdom, and Canada, the hashtag "#RefugeesWelcome" swelled to 1.5 million shares.[12] Within four days, 78 percent of the British public had seen the photo of Al-Kurdi, and 92 percent had at least heard about it. The photo was directly linked to increased support: Those who had seen the photo were nearly twice as likely to say that the United Kingdom should take in more refugees.[13] Support in the form of financial donations also surged. Migrant Offshore Aid Station, an NGO focused on search and rescue efforts, reported a 1,400 percent increase in donations in the 24 hours immediately after the pictures went viral. Donations to organizations including Oxfam and Care Canada doubled in one week what had been raised all year.[14]

The role of social media as an organizing tool, a journalistic tool, and a support-building tool, all in the context of political change, underscores the interesting interactions of technological progress and political conflict and change. Social media has enabled revolutionaries, governments, journalists, and even terrorists to organize quickly, communicate globally, and build support for their cause, resulting in serious ramifications for international management. It is important for international managers to think through these complex political, legal, and technological issues that arise in a world that embraces rapid change so that they are prepared for potential challenges. MNCs must collaboratively work with new governments as laws, policies, and regulations are introduced and altered. Managing the political and legal environment will continue to be an important challenge for international managers, as will the rapid changes in the technological environment of global business.

■ Political Environment

Both domestic and international political environments have a major impact on MNCs. As government policies change, MNCs must adjust their strategies and practices to accommodate the new perspectives and actual requirements. Moreover, in a growing number of regions and countries, governments appear to be less stable; therefore, these areas carry more risk than they have in the past. The assessment of political risk and strategies to cope with it will be given specific attention in Chapter 10, but in this chapter we focus on general political systems with selected areas used as illustrations relevant to today's international managers.

The political system or system of government in a country greatly influences how its people manage and conduct business. We discussed in Chapter 1 how the government regulates business practices via economic systems. Here we review the general systems currently in place throughout the world. Political systems vary greatly between nation-states across the world. The issue with understanding how to conduct international management extends beyond general knowledge of the governmental practices to the specifics of the legal and regulatory frameworks in place. Underlying the actions of a government is the ideology informing the beliefs, values, behavior, and culture of the nation and its political system. We discussed ideologies and the philosophies underpinning them above. Effective management occurs when these different ideologies and philosophies are recognized and understood.

A political system can be evaluated along two dimensions. The first dimension focuses on the rights of citizens under governments ranging from fully democratic to totalitarian. The other dimension measures whether the focus of the political system is on individuals or the broader collective. The first dimension is the ideology of the system, while the second measures the degree of individualism or collectivism. No pure form of government exists in any category, so we can assume that there are many gradations along the two extremes. The observed correlation suggests that democratic societies emphasize individualism, while totalitarian societies lean toward collectivism.[15]

Ideologies

Individualism Adopters of **individualism** adhere to the philosophy that people should be free to pursue economic and political endeavors without constraint. This means that government interest should not solely influence individual behavior. In a business context, this is synonymous with capitalism and is connected to a free-market society, as discussed in Chapter 1, which encourages diversity and competition, compounded with private ownership, to stimulate productivity. It has been argued that private property is more successful, progressive, and productive than communal property due to increased incentives for maintenance and focus on care for individually owned property. The idea is that working in a group requires less energy per person to achieve the same goal, but an individual will work as hard as he or she has to in order to survive in a competitive environment. Simply following the status quo will stunt progress, while competing will increase creativity and progress. Modern managers may witness this when dealing with those who adopt an individualist philosophy and then must work in a team situation. Research has shown that team performance is negatively influenced by those who consider themselves individualistic; however, competition stimulates motivation and encourages increased efforts to achieve goals.[16]

> **individualism**
> The political philosophy that people should be free to pursue economic and political endeavors without constraint (Chapter 2); the tendency of people to look after themselves and their immediate family only (Chapter 4).

The groundwork for this ideology was founded long ago. Philosophers such as David Hume (1711–1776), Adam Smith (1723–1790), and even Aristotle (384–322 BC) contributed to these principles. While philosophers created the foundation for this belief system long ago, it can be witnessed playing out through modern practice. Eastern Europe, the former Soviet Union, areas of Latin America, Great Britain, and Sweden all have moved toward the idea that the betterment of society is related to the level of freedom individuals have in pursuing economic goals, along with general individual freedoms and self-expression without governmental constraint. The well-known movement in Britain toward privatization was led by Prime Minister Margaret Thatcher during her 11 years in office (1979–1990), when she successfully transferred ownership of many companies from the state to individuals and reduced the government-owned portion of gross national product from 10 to 3.9 percent. She was truly a pioneer in the movement toward a capitalistic society, which has since spread across Europe.

International managers must remain alert as to how political changes may impact their business, as a continuous struggle for a foothold in government power often affects leaders in office. For example, Britain's economy improved under the leadership of Tony Blair; however, his support of the Iraq War severely weakened his position. Conservative David Cameron, first elected prime minister in 2010, sought to integrate traditional conservative principles without ignoring social development policies, something the Labour Party has traditionally focused on. More recently, however, increased concerns about immigration and the role of the EU in managing affairs in member states prompted the United Kingdom to vote to leave the EU, a process that has been termed "Brexit." Government policy, in its attempt to control the economic environment, waxes and wanes, something the international manager must be keenly sensitive to.

Europe has added complexity to the political environment with the unification of the EU, which celebrated its 60th "birthday" in 2017. Notwithstanding the increasing integration of the EU, MNCs still need to be responsive to the political environment of individual countries, some due to the persistence of cultural differences, which will be discussed in Chapter 5. Yet, there are also significant interdependencies. For example, the recent economic crises in Greece, Spain, Portugal, and Ireland have prompted Germany and France to mobilize public and private financial support, even though the two largest economies in the euro zone have residual distrust from earlier eras of conflict and disagreement.[17] Europe is no longer a group of fragmented countries; it is a giant and expanding interwoven region in which international managers must be aware of what is happening politically, not only in the immediate area of operations but also throughout the continent. The EU consists of countries that adhere to individualistic orientations as well as those that follow collectivist ideals.

collectivism
The political philosophy that views the needs or goals of society as a whole as more important than individual desires (Chapter 2); the tendency of people to belong to groups or collectives and to look after each other in exchange for loyalty (Chapter 4).

Collectivism   Collectivism views the needs and goals of society at large as more important than individual desires.[18] The reason there is no one rigid form of collectivism is because societal goals and the decision of how to keep people focused on them differ greatly among national cultures. The Greek philosopher Plato (427–347 BC) believed that individual rights should be sacrificed and property should be commonly owned. While on the surface one may assume that this would lead to a classless society, Plato believed that classes should still exist and that the best suited should rule over the people. Many forms of collectivism do not adhere to that idea.

Collectivism emerged in Germany and Italy as "national socialism," or fascism. Fascism is an authoritarian political ideology (generally tied to a mass movement) that considers individual and other societal interests inferior to the needs of the state and seeks to forge a type of national unity, usually based on ethnic, religious, cultural, or racial attributes. Various scholars attribute different characteristics to fascism, but the following elements are usually seen as its integral parts: nationalism, authoritarianism, militarism, corporatism, collectivism, totalitarianism, anticommunism, and opposition to economic and political liberalism.

We will explore individualism and collectivism again in Chapter 4 in the context of national cultural characteristics.

socialism
A moderate form of collectivism in which there is government ownership of institutions, and profit is not the ultimate goal.

Socialism   Socialism directly refers to a society in which there is government ownership of institutions but profit is not the ultimate goal. In addition to historically communist states such as China, North Korea, and Cuba, socialism has been practiced to varying degrees in recent years in a more moderate form—"democratic socialism"—by Great Britain's Labour Party, Germany's Social Democrats, as well as in France, Spain, and Greece.[19]

Modern socialism draws on the philosophies of Karl Marx (1818–1883), Friedrich Engels (1820–1895), and Vladimir Ilyich Lenin (1870–1924). Marx believed that governments should own businesses because in a capitalistic society only a few would benefit, and it would probably be at the expense of others in the form of not paying wages due to laborers. He advocated a classless society where everything was essentially communal. Socialism is a broad political movement and forms of it are unstable. In modern times, it branched off into two extremes: communism and social democracy.

Communism is an extreme form of socialism that was realized through violent revolution and was committed to the idea of a worldwide communist state. During the 1970s, most of the world's population lived in communist states. The communist party encompassed the former Soviet Union, China, and nations in Eastern Europe, Southeast Asia, Africa, and Latin America. Cuba, Nicaragua, Cambodia, Laos, and Vietnam headed a notorious list. Today much of the communist collective has disintegrated. China still exhibits communism in the form of limiting individual political freedom. China has begun to move away from communism in the economic and business realms because it has discovered the failure of communism as an economic system due to the tendency of common goals to stunt economic progress and individual creativity.

Some transition countries, such as Russia, are postcommunist but still retain aspects of an authoritarian government. Russia presents one of the most extreme examples of how the political environment affects international management. Poorly managed approaches to the economic and political transition resulted in neglect, corruption, and confusing changes in economic policy.[20] Devoid of funds and experiencing regular gas pipeline leaks, toxic drinking water, pitted roads, and electricity shutoffs, Russia did not present attractive investment opportunities as it moved away from communism. Yet more companies are taking the risk of investing in Russia because of increasing ease of entry, the new attempt at dividing and privatizing the Unified Energy System, and the movement by the Kremlin to begin government funding for the good of society including education, housing, and health care.[21] Actions by the Russian government over the past few years, however, continue to call into question the transparency and reliability of the Russian government. BP, Exxon Mobil, and Ikea have each encountered de facto expropriation, corruption, and state-directed industrialization (see The World of International Management at the beginning of Chapter 10).

One of the biggest problems in Russia and in other transition economies is corruption, which we will discuss in greater depth in Chapter 3. The 2014 Corruption Perception Index from Transparency International ranked Russia 136th out of 174 countries, falling behind Egypt and Colombia.[22] Brazil, China, and India, part of the BRIC emerging markets block, consistently score higher than Russia. In the 2015 Heritage Foundation's Index of Economic Freedom, Russia's overall rating in the measurement of economic openness, regulatory efficiency, the rule of law, and competitiveness remained at 52.1 this year, ranking it only 2.1 points away from being a repressive economic business environment.[23] As more MNCs invest in Russia, these unethical practices will face increasing scrutiny if political forces can be contained. To date, some multinationals feel that the risk is too great, especially with corruption continuing to spread throughout the country. Despite the Kremlin's support of citizens, Russia is in danger of becoming a unified corrupt system. Still most view Russia as they do China: Both are markets that are too large and potentially too lucrative to ignore.

Social democracy refers to a socialist movement that achieved its goals through nonviolent revolution. This system was pervasive in such Western nations as Australia, France, Germany, Great Britain, Norway, Spain, and Sweden, as well as in India and Brazil. While social democracy was a great influence on these nations at one time or another, in practice it was not as viable as anticipated. Businesses that were nationalized were quite inefficient due to the guarantee of funding and the monopolistic structure. Citizens suffered a hike in both taxes and prices, which was contrary to the public interest and the good of the people. The 1970s and 1980s witnessed a response to this unfair structure with the success of Britain's Conservative Party and Germany's Christian Democratic Party, both of which adopted free-market ideals. Margaret Thatcher, as mentioned previously, was a great leader in this movement toward privatization. Although many businesses have been privatized, Britain still has a central government that adheres to the ideal of social democracy. With Britain facing severe budget shortfalls, Prime Minister David Cameron, first elected in 2010, proposed a comprehensive restructuring of public services that could further alter the country's longstanding commitment to a broad social support program. Under his administration, austerity measures, including cuts to military and social program spending, were implemented. The Conservatives and David Cameron were reelected in a landslide in 2015, however, the Brexit vote was seen as a repudiation to Cameron and he later resigned.[24]

It is important to note here the difference between the nationalization of businesses and nationalism. The nationalization of businesses is the transference of ownership of a business from individuals or groups of individuals to the government. This may be done for several reasons: The ideologies of the country encourage the government to extract more money from the firm, the government believes the firm is hiding money, the government has a large investment in the company, or the government wants to secure wages and employment status because jobs would otherwise be lost. Nationalism, on the other hand, is an ideal in and of itself whereby an individual is completely loyal to his or her nation. People who are a part of this mindset gather under a common flag for such reasons as language or culture. The confusing thing for the international businessperson is that it can be associated with both individualism and collectivism. Nationalism exists in the United States, where there is a national anthem and all citizens gather under a common flag, even though individualism is practiced in the midst of a myriad of cultures and extensive diversity. Nationalism also exists in China, exemplified in the movement against Japan in the mid-1930s and the communist victory in 1949 when communist leader Mao Tse-tung gathered communists and peasants to fight for a common goal. This ultimately led to the People's Republic of China. In the case of modern China, nationalism presupposes collectivism.

Political Systems

There are two basic anchors to political systems, each of which represents an "ideal type" that may not exist in pure form.

democracy
A political system in which the government is controlled by the citizens either directly or through elections.

Democracy   **Democracy**, with its European roots and strong presence in Northern and Western Europe, refers to the system in which the government is controlled by the citizens either directly or through elections. Essentially, every citizen should be involved in decision-making processes. The representative government ensures individual freedom since anyone who is eligible may have a voice in the choices made.

A democratic society cannot exist without at least a two-party system. Once elected, the representative is held accountable to the electorate for his or her actions, and this ultimately limits governmental power. Individual freedoms, such as freedom of expression and assembly, are secured. Further protections of citizens include impartial public service, such as a police force and court systems that also serve the government and, in turn, the electorate, though they are not directly affiliated with any political party. Finally, while representatives may be reelected, the number of terms is often limited, and the elected representative may be voted out during the next election if he or she does not sufficiently adhere to the goals of the majority ruling. As mentioned above, a social democracy combines a socialist ideology with a democratic political system, a situation that has characterized many modern European states as well as some in Latin America and other regions.

totalitarianism
A political system in which there is only one representative party, which exhibits control over every facet of political and human life.

Totalitarianism   **Totalitarianism** refers to a political system in which there is only one representative party, which exhibits control over every facet of political and human life. Power is often maintained by suppression of opposition, which can be violent. Media censorship, political repression, and denial of rights and civil liberties are dominant ideals. If there is opposition to government, the response is imprisonment or even worse tactics, often torture. This may be used as a form of rehabilitation or simply a warning to others who may question the government.

Because only one party within each entity exists, there are many forms of totalitarian government. The most common is communist totalitarianism. Most dictatorships under the communist party disintegrated by 1989, but as noted above, aspects and degrees of this form of government are still found in Cuba, North Korea, Laos, Vietnam, and China. The evolution of modern global business has substantially altered the political systems in Vietnam, Laos, and China, each of which has moved toward a more market-based and pluralistic environment. However, each still exhibits some oppression of citizens through denial of civil liberties. The political environment in China is very complex because of the government's desire to balance national, immediate needs with the challenge of a free-market economy and globalization. Since joining the WTO in 2001, China has made trade liberalization a top priority. However, MNCs still face a host of major obstacles when doing business with and in China. For example, government regulations severely hamper multinational activity and favor domestic companies, which results in questionable treatment such as longer document processing times for foreign firms.[25] This makes it increasingly difficult for MNCs to gain the proper legal footing. The biggest problem may well be that the government does not know what it wants from multinational investors, and this is what accounts for the mixed signals and changes in direction that it continually sends. All this obviously increases the importance of knowledgeable international managers.

China may be moving further away from its communist tendencies as it begins supporting a more open, democratic society, at least in the economic sphere. China continues to monitor what it considers antigovernment actions and practices, but there is a discernible shift toward greater tolerance of individual freedoms.[26] For now, China continues to challenge the capabilities of current international business theory as it transitions through a unique system favoring high governmental control yet striving to unleash a more dynamic market economy.[27]

Though the most common, the totalitarian form of government exhibited in China is not the only one. Other forms of totalitarianism exhibit other forms of oppression as well. Parties or governments that govern an entity based on religious principles will ultimately oppress religious and political expression of its citizens. Examples are Iran and Saudi Arabia, where the laws and government are based on Islamic principles. Conducting business in the Middle East is, in many ways, similar to operating a business in the Western world. The Arab countries have been a generally positive place to do business, as many of these nations are seeking modern technology and most have the financial ability to pay for quality services. Worldwide fallout from the war on terrorism; the rise of ISIS; the Afghanistan, Iraq, and Syrian wars; and the ongoing Israel–Arab conflicts, however, have raised tensions in the Middle East considerably, making the business environment there risky and potentially dangerous.

The 2011 Arab Spring uprisings have affected business dealings in the authoritarian and/or totalitarian countries across northern Africa and the Middle East. Reasons for the political unrest varied, but most commonly included factors were oppressive government rule, economic decline, high unemployment, and human rights violations. Protesters successfully overthrew four government regimes and forced reforms in almost a dozen others. The political and economic fallout from the Arab Spring, including the Syrian civil war discussed in the opening section of this chapter, has left the business environment with much continued uncertainty. Production and GDP were negatively affected almost overnight, and fuel prices spiked globally. Supply chain routes were disrupted for months, increasing the shipping and logistical costs of goods passing through the region. In Egypt, a military coup overthrew democratically elected Egyptian President Morsi in 2013, and a military general was elected president in a suspect election in 2014. In Libya, the fall of Gaddafi has resulted in a power vacuum, inviting increased acts of terrorism. Unemployment in Egypt and Tunisia has not recovered since the uprisings, and inflation remains around 10 percent.[28] According to a late 2011 study by Grant Thornton, 26 percent of businesses in North America, and 22 percent of businesses globally, reported negative effects from the uprisings.[29] A map of the countries that were impacted by the Arab Spring can be seen in Figure 2–1. Though many countries in the region have

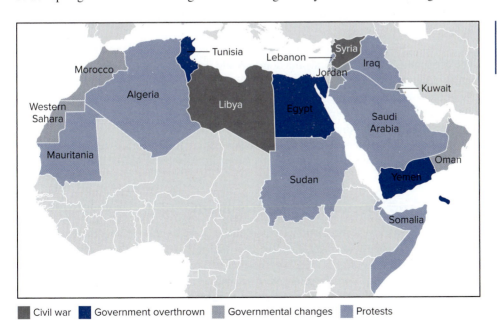

Figure 2–1

Summary of Arab Spring Uprisings

■ Civil war ■ Government overthrown ■ Governmental changes ■ Protests

Source: Original graphic by Ben Littell under supervision of Professor Jonathan Doh.

The Economic Impacts of Global Terrorism

A New Challenge for the International Business Community

As discussed in the opening section of this chapter, social media has made global communication easier, which unfortunately includes the orchestration of terrorist attacks. Global terrorism is a relatively new challenge; no longer are terrorist attacks small, one-person events isolated to a particular region or country. Over the last decade, attacks in Madrid, London, and Paris have involved a high degree of complexity and organization. Organizations like ISIS are recruiting worldwide through social networking sites, working to organize attacks far from their home base in Syria. Living in an interconnected world, it would be naïve to believe that the threat of terrorism does not affect the international business community.

Evidence shows that the tourism industry appears to be especially impacted by the threat of terrorism, at least in the short term. According to the Paris Convention and Visitors Bureau, the November 2015 terrorist attacks in Paris, which killed 130 civilians, resulted in a sudden, yet temporary, decline in tourism activity. Restaurants, shops, and related businesses lost revenue, and hotels reported that the number of visitors declined sharply in the weeks following the attacks. Forty percent of hotel bookings in Brussels were cancelled the weekend following the Paris attacks, when suspected terrorist apartments were raided in Belgium. In places like France, where seven percent of economic activity and nearly two million jobs are dependent on tourism, even a slight decrease in visitors has a high economic impact. There is some evidence that terrorism negatively impacts other sectors of the economy as well. According to a report issued by financial services firm Markit, manufacturing and service providers grew at a slower rate in November 2015 than expected. Service providers specifically stated that the terrorist attacks in Paris contributed to negative performance and a decrease in consumer confidence. Some estimates suggest that the November attacks could ultimately cost the French economy tens of billions of euros.

Despite these setbacks, the long-term economic impact from terrorist attacks does not appear to be substantial. Past terrorist attack locations, such as New York City, quickly rebounded from short-term economic setbacks. Stock market volatility following previous terror attacks has always stabilized fairly quickly, indicating a continued confidence from investors despite living in a world with this new type of uncertainty. The global economy faces a variety of challenges in the 21st century—climate change, political tensions, and demographic shifts, to name a few. Global terrorism, like these other challenges, will likely continue to cause some disruption to the international business community, but it will not stop economic progress.

Sources: Walker, Andrew, "Paris Attacks: Assessing the economic impact," *BBC,* December 2, 2015. http://www.bbc.com/news/business-34965000; "Market Flash France PMI," *Markit Economics,* November 23, 2015. https://www.markiteconomics.com/; Newton-Small, Jay, "The Cost of the Paris Attacks," *Time,* November 23, 2015. http://time.com/4123827/paris-attacks-tourism/.

somewhat stabilized, the fallout from the revolutions will continue to impact international business.

One final form of totalitarianism, sometimes referred to as "right-wing," allows for some economic (but not political) freedoms. While it directly opposes socialist and communist ideas, this form may gain power and support from the military, often in the form of a military leader imposing a government "for the good of the people." This results in military officers filling most government positions. Such military regimes ruled in Germany and Italy from the 1930s to the 1940s and persisted in Latin America and Asia until the 1980s, when the latter moved toward democratic forms. Recent examples include Myanmar, where the military ruled as a dictatorship from 1962 to 2011.

■ Legal and Regulatory Environment

One reason why today's international environment is so confusing and challenging for MNCs is that they face so many different laws and regulations in their global business operations. These factors affect the way businesses are developed and managed within host nations, so special consideration must be paid to the subtle differences in the legal codes from one country to another. Adhering to disparate legal frameworks sometimes prevents large MNCs from capitalizing on manufacturing economies of scale and scope within these regions. In addition, the sheer complexity and magnitude of bureaucracies require special attention. This, in turn, results in slower time to market and greater costs. MNCs must take time to carefully evaluate the legal framework in each market in which they do business before launching products or services in those markets.

There are four foundations on which laws are based around the world. Briefly summarized, these are

1. **Islamic law**. This is law derived from interpretation of the Qur'an and the teachings of the Prophet Muhammad. It is found in most Islamic countries in the Middle East and Central Asia.

2. **Socialist law**. This law comes from the Marxist socialist system and continues to influence regulations in former communist countries, especially those from the former Soviet Union, as well as present-day China, Vietnam, North Korea, and Cuba. Since socialist law requires most property to be owned by the state or state-owned enterprises, MNCs have traditionally shied away from these countries.

3. **Common law**. This comes from English law, and it is the foundation of the legal system in the United States, Canada, England, Australia, New Zealand, and other nations.

4. **Civil or code law**. This law is derived from Roman law and is found in the non-Islamic and nonsocialist countries such as France, some countries in Latin America, and even Louisiana in the United States.

With these broad notions serving as points of departure, the following sections discuss basic principles and examples of the international legal environment facing MNCs today.

Basic Principles of International Law

When compared with domestic law, international law is less coherent because its sources embody not only the laws of individual countries concerned with any dispute but also treaties (universal, multilateral, or bilateral) and conventions (such as the Geneva Convention on Human Rights or the Vienna Convention of Diplomatic Security). In addition, international law contains unwritten understandings that arise from repeated interactions among nations. Conforming to all the different rules and regulations can create a major problem for MNCs. Fortunately, much of what they need to know can be subsumed under several broad and related principles that govern the conduct of international law.

Sovereignty and Sovereign Immunity The **principle of sovereignty** holds that governments have the right to rule themselves as they see fit. In turn, this implies that one country's court system cannot be used to rectify injustices or impose penalties in another country unless that country agrees. So while U.S. laws require equality in the workplace for all employees, U.S. citizens who take a job in Japan cannot sue their Japanese employer under the provisions of U.S. law for failure to provide equal opportunity for them.

International Jurisdiction International law provides for three types of jurisdictional principles. The first is the **nationality principle**, which holds that every country has jurisdiction (authority or power) over its citizens no matter where they are located. Therefore, a U.S. manager who violates the American Foreign Corrupt Practices Act while traveling abroad can be found guilty in the United States. The second is the **territoriality principle**, which holds that every nation has the right of jurisdiction within its legal territory. Therefore, a German firm that sells a defective product in England can be sued under English law even though the company is headquartered outside England. The third is the **protective principle**, which holds that every country has jurisdiction over behavior that adversely affects its national security, even if that conduct occurred outside the country. Therefore, a French firm that sells secret U.S. government blueprints for a satellite system can be subjected to U.S. laws.

Islamic law
Law that is derived from interpretation of the Qur'an and the teachings of the Prophet Muhammad and is found in most Islamic countries.

socialist law
Law that comes from the Marxist socialist system and continues to influence regulations in countries formerly associated with the Soviet Union as well as China.

common law
Law that derives from English law and is the foundation of legislation in the United States, Canada, and England, among other nations.

civil or code law
Law that is derived from Roman law and is found in the non-Islamic and nonsocialist countries.

principle of sovereignty
An international principle of law that holds that governments have the right to rule themselves as they see fit.

nationality principle
A jurisdictional principle of international law that holds that every country has jurisdiction over its citizens no matter where they are located.

territoriality principle
A jurisdictional principle of international law that holds that every nation has the right of jurisdiction within its legal territory.

protective principle
A jurisdictional principle of international law that holds that every country has jurisdiction over behavior that adversely affects its national security, even if the conduct occurred outside that country.

doctrine of comity
A jurisdictional principle of international law that holds that there must be mutual respect for the laws, institutions, and governments of other countries in the matter of jurisdiction over their own citizens.

act of state doctrine
A jurisdictional principle of international law that holds that all acts of other governments are considered to be valid by U.S. courts, even if such acts are illegal or inappropriate under U.S. law.

Doctrine of Comity   The **doctrine of comity** holds that there must be mutual respect for the laws, institutions, and governments of other countries in the matter of jurisdiction over their own citizens. Although this doctrine is not part of international law, it is part of international custom and tradition.

Act of State Doctrine   Under the **act of state doctrine**, all acts of other governments are considered to be valid by U.S. courts, even if such acts are inappropriate in the United States. As a result, for example, foreign governments have the right to set limits on the repatriation of MNC profits and to forbid companies from sending more than this amount out of the host country back to the United States.

Treatment and Rights of Aliens   Countries have the legal right to refuse admission of foreign citizens and to impose special restrictions on their conduct, their right of travel, where they can stay, and what business they may conduct. Nations also can deport aliens. For example, the United States has the right to limit the travel of foreign scientists coming into the United States to attend a scientific convention and can insist they remain within five miles of their hotel. After the horrific events of 9/11, the U.S. government began greater enforcement of laws related to illegal aliens. As a consequence, closer scrutiny of visitors and temporary workers, including expatriate workers from India and elsewhere who have migrated to the United States for high-tech positions, may result in worker shortages.[30]

Forum for Hearing and Settling Disputes   This is a principle of U.S. justice as it applies to international law. At their discretion, U.S. courts can dismiss cases brought before them by foreigners; however, they are bound to examine issues including where the plaintiffs are located, where the evidence must be gathered, and where the property to be used in restitution is located. One of the best examples of this principle is the Union Carbide pesticide plant disaster in Bhopal, India. Over 2,000 people were killed and thousands left permanently injured when a toxic gas enveloped 40 square kilometers around the plant. The New York Court of Appeals sent the case back to India for resolution.

Examples of Legal and Regulatory Issues

The principles described above help form the international legal and regulatory framework within which MNCs must operate. In the following, we examine some examples of specific laws and situations that can have a direct impact on international business.

Financial Services Regulation   The global financial crisis of 2008–2010 underscored the integrated nature of financial markets around the world and the reality that regulatory failure in one jurisdiction can have severe and immediate impacts on others.[31] The global contagion that enveloped the world was exacerbated, in part, by the availability of global derivatives trading and clearing and the relatively lightly regulated private equity and hedge fund industries. The crisis and its broad economic effects have prompted regulators around the world to consider tightening aspects of financial services regulation, especially those related to the risks associated with the derivatives activities of banks and their involvement in trading for their own account. In the United States, financial reform legislation was approved in July of 2010, although the degree to which that legislation would prevent another crisis remained hotly debated.[32] The nearby Closer Look box provides a comparison of proposed and implemented financial reform approaches across the globe.

Foreign Corrupt Practices Act   During the special prosecutor's investigation of the Watergate scandal in the early 1970s, a number of questionable payments made by U.S. corporations to public officials abroad were uncovered. These bribes became the focal point of investigations by the U.S. Internal Revenue Service, Securities and Exchange Commission (SEC), and Justice Department. This concern over bribes in the international arena eventually culminated in the 1977 passage of the **Foreign Corrupt Practices Act (FCPA)**, which makes it illegal to influence foreign officials through personal payment or political contributions. The objectives of the FCPA were to stop U.S. MNCs from initiating or perpetuating corruption in foreign governments and to upgrade the image of both the United States and its businesses abroad.

Critics of the FCPA feared the loss of sales to foreign competitors, especially in those countries where bribery is an accepted way of doing business. Nevertheless, the U.S. government pushed ahead and attempted to enforce the act. Some of the countries that were named in early bribery cases under the law included Algeria, Kuwait, Saudi Arabia, and Turkey. The U.S. State Department tried to convince the SEC and Justice Department not to reveal countries or foreign officials who were involved in its investigations for fear of creating internal political problems for U.S. allies. Although this political sensitivity was justified for the most part, several interesting developments occurred: (1) MNCs found that they could live within the guidelines set down by the FCPA and (2) many foreign governments actually applauded these investigations under the FCPA because it helped them crack down on corruption in their own country.

One analysis reported that since passage of the FCPA, U.S. exports to "bribe prone" countries actually increased.[33] Investigations reveal that once bribes were removed as a key competitive tool, more MNCs were willing to do business in that country. This proved to be true even in the Middle East, where many U.S. MNCs always assumed that bribes were required to ensure contracts. Evidence shows that this is no longer true in most cases; and in cases where it is true, those companies that engage in bribery face a strengthened FCPA that now allows the courts to both fine and imprison guilty parties. In addition, stepped-up enforcement appears to be having a real impact. A report from the law firm Jones Day found that FCPA actions are increasingly targeting individual executives, not just corporations; that penalties imposed under the FCPA have skyrocketed; and that violations have spurred a number of collateral civil actions.[34]

Bureaucratization Very restrictive foreign bureaucracies are one of the biggest problems facing MNCs. This is particularly true when bureaucratic government controls are inefficient and left uncorrected. A good example is Japan, whose political parties feel more beholden to their local interests than to those in the rest of the country. As a result, it is extremely difficult to reorganize the Japanese bureaucracy and streamline the ways things are done because so many politicians are more interested in the well-being of their own districts than in the long-term well-being of the nation as a whole. In turn, parochial actions create problems for MNCs trying to do business there. The administration of Prime Minister Junichiro Koizumi of Japan tried to reduce some of this bureaucracy, although the fact that Japan has had seven different prime ministers from 2006 to 2015 has not helped these efforts. Certainly the long-running recessionary economy of the country is inspiring reforms in the nation's antiquated banking system, opening up the Japanese market to more competition.[35]

Japanese businesses are also becoming more aware of the fact that they are dependent on the world market for many goods and services and that when bureaucratic red tape drives up the costs of these purchases, local consumers pay the price. These businesses are also beginning to realize that government bureaucracy can create a false sense of security and leave them unprepared to face the harsh competitive realities of the international marketplace.

In many developing and emerging markets, bureaucratic red tape impedes business growth and innovation. The World Bank conducts an annual survey to determine the ease of doing business in a variety of countries around the world. The survey includes individual items related to starting a business, dealing with construction permits, employing workers, registering property, getting credit, protecting investors, paying taxes, trading across borders, enforcing contracts, and closing a business. A composite ranking, as

Foreign Corrupt Practices Act (FCPA)
An act that makes it illegal to influence foreign officials through personal payment or political contributions; became U.S. law in 1977 because of concerns over bribes in the international business arena.

Comparing Recent Global Financial Reforms

Preventing More Tax-Funded Bailouts

The G20 wants to end the belief among banks that they are "too big to fail" by requiring resolution mechanisms and "living wills" for speedy windups that don't destabilize markets. As a legislative body for a unified country, the United States' Senate was able to set up an "orderly liquidation" process fairly quickly through Title II of the Dodd-Frank Act. Japan's Diet passed similar reforms by amending its existing Deposit Insurance Act in 2013.

The EU, as a collection of 28 states with no common insolvency laws, faces a much harder task of thrashing out a pan-EU mechanism even though cross-border banks dominate the sector. To ensure that resolution funds can quickly be collected and paid even when banks cross international borders, the European Commission established a centralized banking union in 2012. This banking union essentially transfers the legislating of banking policies from individual nations to the EU as a whole. Two major initiatives have resulted from this shift: the Single Supervisory Mechanism (SSM) and the Single Resolution Mechanism (SRM). The SSM, which became operational in 2014, supervises the financial health of banking institutions across Europe. The SRM, which came into force on January 1, 2016, provides restructuring assistance to failing EU banks. The SRM is funded through contributions made by other banking institutions, thereby protecting taxpayers.

Winners/Losers: Banks face an extra levy on top of higher capital and liquidity requirements. Taxpayers should be better shielded. Messy patchwork for global banks, which will come under pressure to "subsidiarize" operations in different countries.

Over-the-Counter Derivatives

The G20 agreed that derivatives should be standardized where possible so they can be centrally cleared and traded on an exchange by the end of 2012; three-quarters of the G20 members were able to meet this deadline. Some countries have taken reforms a step further. The U.S. Senate adopted legislation (Dodd-Frank Act) requiring banks to spin off their swaps desk to isolate risks from depositors, and, in 2014, Canada expanded the ability of banking regulators to set restrictions over banks that trade standard derivatives.

However, some disagreement has risen between the EU and the U.S. within the international derivatives market. Between 2014 and 2016, regulators in Europe and the United States were unable to agree on whether each other's clearinghouse rules were equivalent. Without an agreement, European traders would have faced higher capital requirements, likely resulting in less transnational trading. In 2016, the EU and the United States finally reached a deal on the oversight of clearinghouses, paving the way for a more unified global market.

Winners/Losers: Cross-border trading within the United States and the EU will continue uninterrupted.

Corporations face costlier hedging as there will be heavier capital charges on uncleared trades, but differences in exemption scope could be exploited.

Bonuses

The G20 has introduced principles to curb excessive pay and bonuses, such as requiring a big chunk of a bonus to be deferred over several years with a clawback mechanism. The United States and the EU are applying these principles and taking their own actions, such as a one-off tax in Britain.

Winners/Losers: Harder to justify big bonuses in the future.

Credit Ratings Agencies

The G20 agreed that ratings agencies should be required to register, report to supervisors, and show how they manage internal conflicts of interest. In 2014 the EU adopted even stricter laws, increasing the disclosure requirements regarding fees charged by credit rating agencies. Also in 2014, the Securities and Exchange Commission in the United States adopted stricter requirements for credit rating agencies, aimed at preventing conflicts of interest and increasing standards and transparency.

Winners/Losers: Ratings agencies will have to justify what they do much more in the future. The "Big Three"—Fitch, S&P, and Moody's—may face more competition in the EU. The sector faces more efforts to dilute their role in determining bank capital requirements.

Hedge Funds/Private Equity

The United States and the EU are working in parallel to introduce a G20 pledge to require hedge fund managers to register and report a range of data on their positions. U.S. law is in line with G20 but exempts private equity and venture capital. The EU wants to go much further by including private equity and requiring third-country funds and managers to abide by strict requirements if they want to solicit European investors, a step the United States says is discriminatory. Managers of alternative funds in the EU would also have curbs on remuneration, an element absent from U.S. reform.

Winners/Losers: U.S. hedge fund managers may find it harder to do business in the EU. European investors may end up with less choice. Regulators will have better data on funds. EU managers may decamp to Switzerland, though also for tax reasons.

Banks Trading

The U.S. Senate has adopted the "Volcker Rule," which would ban risky trading unrelated to customers' needs at deposit-insured banks. The Volcker Rule's associated regulations were fully implemented in the United States in 2014. Similar regulation in Europe has been slower to take shape. Many key EU states are against the rule as they want to preserve their universal banking model, though, in 2015, the European Commission sent a proposal to the European Parliament for consideration.

Winners/Losers: Some trading could switch to the EU from the United States inside global banks.

Systemic Risk

The G20 wants mechanisms in place to spot and tackle systemwide risks better, a core lesson from the crisis. The U.S. Senate bill sets up a council of regulators that includes the Federal Reserve, but the U.S. House wants a bigger role for the Fed. The EU has approved a reform that will make the European Central Bank the hub of a pan-EU systemic risk board.

Winners/Losers: ECB is a big winner with an enhanced role that many see as a platform for a more pervasive role in the future. Banks will have yet another pair of eyes staring down at them.

Bank Capital Requirements

The push to beef up bank capital and liquidity requirements is being led by the global Basel Committee of central bankers and supervisors, which is toughening up its global accord as requested by the G20. It took at the end of 2012. The U.S. bill directs regulators to increase capital requirements on large financial firms as they grow in size or engage in riskier activities. In 2015, the Federal Reserve further increased the capital requirements for the eight largest banks.

The EU has approved new rules to beef up capital on trading books and allow supervisors to slap extra capital requirements if remuneration is encouraging excessively risky behavior. Additional rules were implemented to strengthen corporate governance and increase transparency.

Winners/Losers: Bank return on equity is set to be squeezed. Regulators will have many more tools to control the sector. Higher costs are likely to be passed on to consumer investors. There could be timing issues as the EU has been more willing than the United States in the past to adopt Basel rules.

Fixing Securitization

The U.S. Senate bill forces securitizers to keep a baseline 5 percent of credit risk on securitized assets. The EU has already approved a law to this effect.

Winners/Losers: Banks say privately the 5 percent level is low enough not to make much difference and that the key problem is restoring investor confidence into the tarnished sector.

Sources: Tracy, Ryan; McGrane, Victoria; Baer, Justin, "Fed Lifts Capital Requirements for Banks," *The Wall Street Journal,* July 20, 2015; "SEC Adopts Credit Rating Agency Reform Rules," US Securities and Exchange Commission, August 27, 2014; Brush, Silla; Verlaine, Julia-Ambra, "EU, U.S. Reach Deal on Clearing Rules for Derivatives Market," *BloombergBusiness,* February 10, 2016; Mayeda, Andrew, "Canada to Increase Regulation of Over-the-Counter Derivatives," *BloombergBusiness,* February 11, 2014; "Factbox: Comparing EU and U.S. Financial Reform," *Reuters,* May 19, 2010. Additional research by authors.

shown in Table 2–1, ranks the overall ease of doing business in these countries. Although developed countries generally rank better (higher), there are some developing countries (Georgia, Malaysia) that do well, and some developed economies (Greece) that do poorly.

In Table 2–1 economies are ranked on their ease of doing business, from 1 to 189, with first place being the best. A high ranking on the ease-of-doing-business index means the regulatory environment is conducive to the operation of business. This index averages the country's percentile rankings on 10 topics, made up of a variety of indicators, giving equal weight to each topic. The rankings are benchmarked to June 2015.

Privatization

Another example of the changing international regulatory environment is the current move toward privatization by an increasing number of countries. The German government, for example, has sped up privatization and deregulation of its telecommunications market. This has opened a host of opportunities for MNCs looking to create joint ventures with local German firms. Additionally, the French government has put some of its businesses on the sale block. Meanwhile, in China the government is slowly moving forward with plans to partially privatize many of its state-owned enterprises. In late 2015, the Chinese government announced reforms allowing private investment in state-owned enterprises. These reforms are likely aimed at increasing the profitability of the

Table 2-1
Ease-of-Doing-Business Ranking among Select Countries (2015)

Economy	Ease of Doing Business (Overall) Rank	Starting a Business	Dealing with Construction Permits	Getting Electricity	Registering Property	Getting Credit	Protecting Investors	Paying Taxes	Trading across Borders	Trading Enforcing Contracts	Resolving Insolvency
Singapore	1	10	1	6	17	19	1	5	41	1	27
United Kingdom	6	17	23	15	45	19	4	15	38	33	13
United States	7	49	33	44	34	2	35	53	34	21	5
Sweden	8	16	19	7	11	70	14	37	17	24	19
Finland	10	33	27	16	20	42	66	17	32	30	1
Taiwan	11	22	6	2	18	59	25	39	65	16	21
Australia	13	11	4	39	47	5	66	42	89	4	14
Germany	15	107	13	3	62	28	49	72	35	12	3
Ireland	17	25	43	30	39	28	8	6	48	93	20
Malaysia	18	14	15	13	38	28	4	31	49	44	45
Georgia	24	6	11	62	3	7	20	40	78	13	101
France	27	32	40	20	85	79	29	87	1	14	24
United Arab Emirates	31	60	2	4	10	97	49	1	101	18	91
Japan	34	81	68	14	48	79	36	121	52	51	2
Kazakhstan	41	21	92	71	19	70	25	18	122	9	47
Russian Federation	51	41	119	29	8	42	66	47	170	5	51
Greece	60	54	60	47	144	79	47	66	27	132	54
Bahrain	65	140	9	77	25	109	111	8	85	101	85
Saudi Arabia	82	130	17	24	31	79	99	3	150	86	189
Kenya	108	151	149	127	115	28	115	101	131	102	144
Indonesia	109	173	107	46	131	70	88	148	105	170	77
Brazil	116	174	169	22	130	97	29	178	145	45	62
Argentina	121	157	173	85	116	79	49	170	143	38	95
Cambodia	127	180	181	145	121	15	111	95	98	174	82
India	130	155	183	70	138	42	49	152	127	184	116
Pakistan	138	122	61	157	137	133	25	171	169	151	94
Ethiopia	146	176	73	129	141	167	166	113	166	84	114
Gambia, the	151	169	117	153	124	162	163	177	104	110	111
Zimbabwe	155	182	184	161	114	79	81	145	100	166	152
Bolivia	157	178	150	101	143	126	144	189	124	136	92
Niger	160	134	178	169	126	133	166	156	158	154	121
Iraq	161	154	147	106	117	181	115	59	178	122	189
Bangladesh	174	117	118	189	185	133	88	86	172	188	155
Central African Republic	185	189	155	186	167	133	150	185	144	177	149
Venezuela, RB	186	186	125	171	129	109	178	188	186	141	165

Source: The World Bank, "Table 1.1: Rankings on the Ease of Doing Business," Doing Business 2015, p. 6, www.doingbusiness.org/rankings.

Bitcoin and other Decentralized Currencies in the Digital Age

Alternative, extra-governmental currencies have sparked the interest of many due to the global nature of online transactions. In the past, these virtual currencies were centrally controlled and often quickly shut down by governmental regulations. Virtual currencies in the early 2000s, such as "E-gold" and "Liberty Reserve," were prone to criminal activity and illegal transactions. These virtual currencies acted more as businesses than as peer-to-peer transaction devices, and the currencies provided little flexibility in real, everyday use.

In 2008, a paper published online by Satoshi Nakamoto, titled "Bitcoin: A Peer-to-Peer Electronic Cash System," outlined a new concept for digital currency, in which open peer-to-peer transactions replace the need for centralized currency oversight and regulation. Little is known about "Satoshi Nakamoto," with many now believing that the name is a pseudonym for a group of individuals. In 2009, Nakamoto released the first peer-to-peer Bitcoin software and issued the first round of currency. Unlike its predecessors, Bitcoin is easy to use when purchasing real, tangible goods. In recent years, Bitcoin has quickly grown into the most widely used digital currency.

Like traditional paper currency, Bitcoin depends on faith of the users for the system to work. Rather than relying on a central bank, Bitcoin relies on a decentralized ledger system to maintain the overall value within the market. On a basic level, every registered user maintains a copy of the ledger, which displays the individual balance of Bitcoin for every other user. Transactions in Bitcoin are, in essence, just the debiting and crediting of those balances. The open, public sharing of the value of the transactions occurring in Bitcoin is essential, as this allows for the role of the central banking institution to be completely replaced, thereby "decentralizing" the currency. As of February 2016, the market capitalization of Bitcoin was about US$6 billion. More than 1,000 retailers, both online and in brick-and-mortar locations, now accept Bitcoin.

Bitcoin and other decentralized digital currencies could provide an alternative method of storing value in times of currency uncertainty. In 2015, when Greece's inability to meet its debt repayment schedule led to restrictions on bank withdrawals and growing uncertainty for the future of the European Union, Bitcoin saw a surge in activity across Europe. In July, the number of Greeks registering to buy and sell Bitcoin increased tenfold, and trades increased by 79 percent. Bitcoin markets in Germany, Poland, and China saw large increases in activity from Greek computers.

Governments appear to be cautiously open to the use of Bitcoin within their borders. Almost every country allows the use of Bitcoin for private transactions. The United States and EU have issued only modest warnings regarding the use of digital currencies, and few legal regulations exist. In 2015, the United States officially recognized Bitcoin as a commodity.

Bitcoin's growth has not been completely smooth. A series of rapid increases and decreases in the value of a Bitcoin, from US$0.08 in 2010 to over US$1,200 in 2013, has led to many economists, including former U.S. Federal Reserve Chairman Alan Greenspan, to declare the currency a bubble. Though the currency has stabilized to a value of between US$200 and US$400 in recent years, rapid price swings are still commonplace. Illegal activity, including drug trafficking and money laundering, does occur through Bitcoin marketplaces, though the open ledger concept behind the currency makes these activities easier to trace. As a digital currency, malware and computer viruses have also led to some limited instances of theft. Bitcoin's encryption, however, is still regarded as strong.

Bitcoin appears to be reaching a tipping point. While some economists insist that Bitcoin will ultimately sink to a value of zero, others predict that the currency will rise to a value of over US$40,000. Perhaps the ultimate success or failure of Bitcoin as a digital currency lies not in its own design, but in the uncertainties that led to its initial rise in popularity. If consumers continue to cast doubt over government-issued, centralized currencies, Bitcoin could continue to grow in popularity for years to come.

approximately 115 large state-owned conglomerates. The returns for these businesses, ranging from telecommunications to energy, have been far lower than those from related private enterprises. Despite these small reforms, some still express doubt that the Communist Party will allow a true market-based economy to take hold. The state still controls 80,000 small-scale businesses across the country, plans to maintain a high level of control over the nationalized conglomerates, and continues to exert a level of control over the stock market.[36,37]

Poland, transitioning from a state-planned economy to a free-market economy, underwent extensive privatization of its state-owned enterprises in the early 2000s. The mass privatization of industries, including insurance and coal mining, boosted the Warsaw Stock Exchange into the top ten European markets by value.[38] Turkey had issued various privatization tenders in the energy and electricity sectors; Nigeria finalized the privatization of three of the Power Holding Company of Nigeria successor companies in 2012;

and Pakistan had privatized 167 state-owned enterprises since its inception, yielding US$9 billion in proceeds to the government.[39] As described in the International Management in Action box "Brazilian Economic Reform" in Chapter 1, many developing countries are privatizing their state-owned companies to provide greater competition and access to service.

Regulation of Trade and Investment

The regulation of international trade and investment is another area in which individual countries use their legal and regulatory policies to affect the international management environment. The rapid increase in trade and investment has raised concerns among countries that others are not engaging in fair trade, based on the fundamental principles of international trade as specified in the WTO and other trade and investment agreements. Specifically, international trade rules require countries to provide "national treatment," which means that they will not discriminate against others in their trade relations. Unfortunately, many countries engage in government support (subsidies) and other types of practices that distort trade. For example, many developing countries require that foreign MNCs take on local partners in order to do business. Others mandate that MNCs employ a certain percentage of local workers or produce a specific amount in their country. These practices are not limited to developing countries. Japan, the United States, and many European countries use product standards, "buy local" regulations, and other policies to protect domestic industries and restrict trade.

In addition, most trade agreements require that countries extend most-favored-nation status such that trade benefits accorded one country (such as tariff reductions under the WTO) are accorded all other countries that are parties to that agreement. The emergence of regional trade arrangements has called into question this commitment because, by definition, agreements among a few countries (NAFTA, EU) give preference to those specific members over those who are not part of these trading "blocs." As discussed in Chapter 1, many countries engage in antidumping actions intended to offset the practice of trading partners "dumping" products at below cost or home market price, as well as countervailing duty actions intended to offset foreign government subsidization. In each case, there is evidence that many countries abuse these laws to protect domestic industries, something the WTO has been more vigilant in monitoring in recent years.

■ Technological Environment and Global Shifts in Production

Technological advancements not only connect the world at incredible speed but also aid in the increased quality of products, information gathering, and R&D. Manufacturing, information processing, and transportation are just a few examples of where technology improves organizational and personal business. The need for instant communication increases exponentially as global markets expand. MNCs need to keep their businesses connected; this is becoming increasingly easier as technology contributes to "flattening the world." Thomas Friedman, in his book *The World Is Flat*, writes that such events as the introduction of the Internet or the World Wide Web, along with mobile technologies, open sourcing, and work flow software distribution, not only enable businesses and individuals to access vast amounts of information at their fingertips in real time but are also resulting in the world flattening into a more level playing field.[40]

Trends in Technology, Communication, and Innovation

The innovation of the microprocessor could be considered the foundation of much of the technological and computing advancements seen today.[41] The creation of a digital framework allowed high-power computer performance at low cost. This then gave birth to such breakthroughs as the development of enhanced telecommunication systems, which will be explored in greater depth later in the chapter. Now, computers, telephones, televisions, and wireless forms of communication have merged to create multimedia products and allow users anywhere in the world to communicate with one another. The Internet allows one to obtain information from literally billions of sources.

Global connections do not necessarily level the playing field, however. Throughout the early 2000s, the challenge of integrating telecom standards became an issue for MNCs in China. Qualcomm Corporation had wanted to sell China narrowband CDMA (code division multiple access) technology; however, Qualcomm was initially unsuccessful in convincing the government that it could build enough products locally. Instead, China's network, the world's largest mobile network, used primarily the GSM technology that is popular in Europe.[42] Following the reorganization of China's telecommunication industry in 2009, however, CDMA gained a foothold in China. In 2015 alone, China Telecom was expected to sell an estimated 100 million CDMA handsets.[43]

Furthermore, concepts like the open-source model allow for free and legal sharing of software and code, which may be utilized by underdeveloped countries in an attempt to gain competitive advantage while minimizing costs. India exemplifies this practice as it continues to increase its adoption of the Linux operating system (OS) in place of the global standard Microsoft Windows. The state of Kerala shifted the software of its 2,600 high schools to the Linux system, enabling each user to configure it to his or her needs, with the goal of creating a new generation of adept programmers. Microsoft, through its DreamSpark program, has been providing students access to its latest developer and designer tools at no charge. The program aims to unlock students' creative potential and set them on the path to academic and career success and, since its inception, has provided nearly 50 million free downloads. Originally launched in the United States and United Kingdom, the DreamSpark program is now available to students in over 165 countries.[44] More broadly, a number of for-profit and nonprofit firms have been aggressively working to bring low-cost computers into the hands of the hundreds of millions of children in the developing world who have not benefited from the information and computing revolution.

Next Thing Company, a start-up based in California, has developed an extremely low-cost computer with the goal of providing word processing and Internet access to people in low-income areas. Called C.H.I.P., the computers retail for US$9. The computers are roughly the size of a postcard, allowing for cheap and easy shipment to any part of the world. Despite the low price, C.H.I.P. computers have about as much functionality as a smartphone; every unit has Wi-Fi capability, a 4-gigabyte hard drive, and 512 megabytes of RAM. Accessories can be connected through USB ports, and most televisions can serve as the computer's screen, saving additional costs by negating the need for more expensive monitors. Because of the low cost and small size, the computers are suited to be adapted, or "hacked," to best fit the needs of the user. Next Thing Company plans to actively partner with schools and nonprofits to ensure that the computers ultimately meet the needs of the end users in the developing world. The first 30,000 units were shipped in January 2016.[45]

There also exists a great potential for disruptions as the world relies more and more on digital communication and imaging. The world is connected by a vast network of fiber-optic cables that we do not see because they are buried either underground or underwater. Roughly the width of a garden hose, 200 sets of these cables carry 99 percent of all transoceanic communication, leading to a great deal of system vulnerability.[46] In 2015, a series of accidental disruptions to one cable led to weeks of slower Internet and communication problems throughout Vietnam. The fact that so many were reliant on a mere 4-inch-thick cable shows the potential risks associated with greater global connectivity.[47]

We have reviewed general influences of technology here, but what are some of the specific dimensions of technology and what other ways does technology affect international management? Here, we explore some of the dimensions of the technological environment currently facing international management, with a closer look at biotechnology, e-business, telecommunications, and the connection between technology, outsourcing, and offshoring.

In addition to the trends discussed above, other specific ways in which technology will affect international management in the next decade include

1. Rapid advances in biotechnology that are built on the precise manipulation of organisms, which will revolutionize the fields of agriculture, medicine, and industry.

2. The emergence of nanotechnology, in which nanomachines will possess the ability to remake the whole physical universe.

3. Satellites that will play a role in learning. For example, communication firms will place tiny satellites into low orbit, making it possible for millions of people, even in remote or sparsely populated regions such as Siberia, the Chinese desert, and the African interior, to send and receive voice, data, and digitized images through handheld telephones.

4. Automatic translation telephones, which will allow people to communicate naturally in their own language with anyone in the world who has access to a telephone.

5. Artificial intelligence and embedded learning technology, which will allow thinking that formerly was felt to be only the domain of humans to occur in machines.

6. Silicon chips containing up to 100 million transistors, allowing computing power that now rests only in the hands of supercomputer users to be available on every desktop.

7. Supercomputers that are capable of 1 trillion calculations per second, which will allow advances such as simulations of the human body for testing new drugs and computers that respond easily to spoken commands.[48]

The development and subsequent use of these technologies have greatly benefited the most developed countries in which they were first deployed. However, the most positive effects should be seen in developing countries where inefficiencies in labor and production impede growth. Although all these technological innovations will affect international management, specific technologies will have especially pronounced effects in transforming economies and business practices. The following discussion highlights some specific dimensions of the technological environment currently facing international management.

Biotechnology

The digital age has given rise to such innovations as computers, cellular phones, and wireless technology. Advancements within this realm allow for more efficient communication and productivity to the point where the digital world has extended its effect from information systems to biology. Biotechnology is the integration of science and technology, but more specifically it is the creation of agricultural or medical products through industrial use and manipulation of living organisms. At first glance, it appears that the fusion of these two disciplines could breed a modern bionic man immune to disease, especially with movements toward technologically advanced prosthetics, cell regeneration through stem cell research, or laboratory-engineered drugs to help prevent or cure diseases such as HIV or cancer.

Pharmaceutical competition is also prevalent on the global scale with China's raw material reserve and the emergence of biotech companies such as Genentech and Merck, after its acquisition of Swiss biotech company Serono. India is emerging as a major player, with its largest, mostly generic, pharmaceutical company Ranbaxy's ability to produce effective and affordable drugs (for further discussion on drug affordability internationally and the ethics of drug pricing, see In-Depth Integrative Case 1.2 at the end of Part One).[49] While pharmaceutical companies mainly manufacture drugs through a process similar to that of organic chemistry, biotech companies attempt to discover genetic abnormalities or medicinal solutions through exploring organisms at the molecular level or by formulating compounds from inorganic materials that mirror organic substances. DNA manipulation in the laboratory extends beyond human research. As mentioned above, another aspect of biotech research is geared toward agriculture. In the United States and Brazil, ethanol production is expected to increase for the foreseeable future, with corn and sugarcane serving as feedstock. Automobile gasoline in Brazil is now mandated to consist of nearly 25 percent ethanol, and blended gasoline was initially encouraged in the United States through tax subsidies.[50] However, some have raised concerns regarding increased food prices caused by using sugarcane and corn as a fuel alternatives. For this and many other reasons, global companies like Monsanto are collaborating with others such as BASF AG to work toward creating genetically modified seeds such as drought-tolerant corn and herbicide-tolerant soybeans.[51] (See the supplemental online simulation related to the U.S.-EU dispute over trade in genetically modified organisms.) Advancements in this industry include nutritionally advanced crops that may help alleviate world hunger.[52]

Aside from crops, the meat industry can also benefit from this process. The outbreak of mad cow disease in Great Britain sparked concern when evidence of the disease spread throughout Western Europe; however, the collaborative work of researchers in the United States and Japan may have engineered a solution to the problem by eliminating the gene that is the predecessor to making the animal susceptible to this ailment.[53] Furthermore, animal cloning, which simply makes a copy of preexisting DNA, could boost food production by producing more meat or dairy-producing animals. The first evidence of a successful animal clone was Dolly, born in Scotland in 1996. Complications arose, and Dolly aged at an accelerated rate, indicating that while she provided hope, there still existed many flaws in the process. While the EU has banned the cloning of livestock, the United States allows cloned animal products to be incorporated in the food supply.[54] Other countries actively cloning animals include Australia, China, Japan, New Zealand, and South Korea. The world is certainly changing, and the trend toward technological integration is far from over. Whether one desires laser surgery to correct eyesight, a vaccine for emerging viruses, or more nutritious food, there is a biotechnology firm competing to be the first to achieve these goals. Hunger and poor health care are worldwide issues, and advancement in global biotechnology is working to raise the standards.

E-Business

As the Internet becomes increasingly widespread, it is having a dramatic effect on international commerce. Table 2–2 shows Internet penetration rates for major world regions,

Table 2–2
World Internet Usage and Population Statistics

World Regions	Population (2015 Est.)	Internet Users 2000	Internet Users 2015	Penetration (% Population)	Growth 2000–2015	Users % of Total
Africa	1,158,355,663	4,514,400	327,145,889	28.2%	7,146.7%	9.8%
Asia	4,032,466,882	114,304,000	1,611,048,215	40.0	1,309.4	48.1
Europe	821,555,904	105,096,093	604,147,280	73.5	474.9	18.1
Middle East	236,137,235	3,284,800	123,172,132	52.2	3,649.8	3.7
North America	357,178,284	108,096,800	313,867,363	87.9	190.4	9.4
Latin America/ Caribbean	617,049,712	18,068,919	339,251,363	55.5	1,777.5	10.1
Oceania/Australia	37,158,563	7,620,480	27,200,530	73.2	256.9	0.8
WORLD TOTAL	7,259,902,243	360,985,492	3,345,832,772	46.1	826.9	100.0

Source: "Usage and Population Statistice," *Internet World Stats*, www.internetworldstats.com/stats.htm. Estimated Internet users are 3,345,832,772 for November 15, 2015.

illustrating the dramatic increase from 2000 to 2015 and the accompanying growth rates, with Africa exhibiting the highest rate at more than 7,000 percent.

Tens of millions of people around the world have now purchased books from Amazon.com, and the company has now expanded its operations around the world (see The World of International Management at the beginning of Chapter 11). So have a host of other electronic retailers (e-tailers), which are discovering that their home-grown retailing expertise can be easily transferred and adapted for the international market.[55] Dell Computer has been offering B2C (electronic business-to-consumer) goods and services in Europe for a number of years, and the automakers are now beginning to move in this direction. Tesla sells most of its cars directly to customers through the Internet, and Toyota is testing a similar model.[56] Other firms are looking to use e-business to improve their current operations. For example, Deutsche Bank has overhauled its entire retail network with the goal of winning affluent customers across the continent.[57] Yet the most popular form of e-business is for business-to-business (B2B) dealings, such as placing orders and interacting with suppliers worldwide. Business-to-consumer (B2C) transactions will not be as large, but this is an area where many MNCs are trying to improve their operations.

The area of e-business that will most affect global customers is e-retailing and financial services. For example, customers can now use their keyboard to pay by credit card, although security remains a problem. However, the day is fast approaching when electronic cash (e-cash) will become common. This scenario already occurs in a number of forms. A good example is prepaid smart cards, which are being used mostly for telephone calls and public transportation. An individual can purchase one of these cards and use it in lieu of cash. This idea is blending with the Internet, allowing individuals to buy and sell merchandise and transfer funds electronically. The result will be global digital cash, which will take advantage of existing worldwide markets that allow buying and selling on a 24-hour basis.

Some companies, such as Capital One 360, the U.S.'s largest direct bank, are completely "disintermediating" banking by eliminating the branches and other "bricks-and-mortar" facilities altogether. Through Capital One 360, all banking transactions occur online, with higher interest rates often offered to those who agree to "paperless" statements and communication. To align with its Internet-savvy clientele, Capital One 360 has developed a comprehensive social media "Savers Community," including Twitter, Facebook, Pinterest, and its YouTube "Challenge Your Savings" video series. And so far, not one of the 275-plus bank failures in the U.S., since the financial crisis began in 2008, has been online banks.[58] HSBC and other global banks are learning from Capital One 360's success and growing their Internet banking globally(see In-Depth Integrative Case 4.1 after Part Four).

Telecommunications

One of the most important dimensions of the technological environment facing international management today is telecommunications. To begin with, global access to affordable cell phone services is resulting in a form of technological leapfrogging, in which regions of the world are moving from a situation where phones were completely unavailable to one where cell phones are available everywhere, including rural areas, due to the quick and relatively inexpensive installation of cellular infrastructure. This is especially true in sub-Saharan Africa. According to a 2015 Pew Research study, the number of land-line phone users is nearly zero percent in the countries of Ghana, Kenya, Nigeria, Senegal, South Africa, Tanzania, and Uganda, while cellular phone access in those same countries averages over 80 percent.[59] In addition, technology has merged two previously discrete methods of communication: the telephone and the Internet. Internet access through cellular phones has, in many ways, replaced access via computers. By 2016, nearly half of all e-mails were opened on mobile phones. Social networking sites have seen an even larger shift to mobile; over 900 million people were checking Facebook daily via their smartphones, and 90 percent of all video views on Twitter were occurring on mobile devices.[60] Wireless technology is proving to be a boon for less developed countries, such as in South America, Africa, and Eastern Europe where customers once waited years to get a telephone installed.

One reason for this rapid increase in telecommunications services is many countries believe that without an efficient communications system, their economic growth may stall. Additionally, governments are accepting the belief that the only way to attract foreign investment and know-how in telecommunications is to cede control to private industry. As a result, while most telecommunications operations in the Asia-Pacific region were state-run a few decades ago, a growing number are now in private hands. Singapore Telecommunications, Pakistan Telecom, Thailand's Telecom Asia, Korea Telecom, and Globe Telecom in the Philippines all have been privatized, and MNCs have helped in this process by providing investment funds. Today, First Pacific holds a 25 percent stake in the Philippine Long Distance Telephone Company, and the Japanese government has privatized nearly two-thirds of Nippon Telegraph & Telephone (NTT). At the same time, Australia's Telestra is moving into the Philippines; Thailand is loosening regulations on foreign investment in telecom; and Korea Telecom has operations in Brunei, Mongolia, and Uzbekistan.

Many governments are reluctant to allow so much private and foreign ownership of such a vital industry; however, they also are aware that foreign investors will go elsewhere if the deal is not satisfactory. The Hong Kong office of Salomon Brothers, a U.S. investment bank, estimates that to meet the expanding demand for telecommunication service in Asia, companies will need to considerably increase the investment, most of which will have to come from overseas. MNCs are unwilling to put up this much money unless they are assured of operating control and a sufficiently high return on their investment.

Developing countries are eager to attract telecommunication firms and offer liberal terms. This liberalization has resulted in rapid increases in wireless penetration, with more than 1.2 billion wireless devices in circulation in China and about a billion in India. Between 2000 and 2012, the total number of mobile subscribers in developing countries grew dramatically—from 250 million to nearly 4.5 billion.[61] According to the International Telecommunications Union, nearly 80 percent of people in developing nations have mobile phones.[62] Growth was rapid in all regions, but fastest in sub-Saharan Africa. It is estimated that mobile phone penetration in Africa stands at over 60 percent, and, in Nigeria alone, there are nearly 150 million mobile phones. This represents a nearly one-to-one ratio of people to mobile devices.[63] In Africa, mobile users are increasingly relying on their devices for commerce and payment. Transactions are conducted via text message, and users aren't even required to hold a bank account.[64] Apple and Samsung, two of the largest mobile phone producers globally, have been aggressively penetrating emerging markets with smartphone technology (see The World of International Management at the beginning of Chapter 5). Since 2012, China has held the largest share of smartphone sales worldwide.[65] Although the counterfeiting of smartphones remains an issue in many emerging markets, there are signs that some effort is being taken to protect authentic products; in 2015, police in Beijing busted a large-scale counterfeiting operation that included hundreds of employees and six production lines. According to the *Wall Street Journal,* this particular counterfeiter manufactured over 40,000 fake iPhones in 2015 alone.[66]

Technological Advancements, Outsourcing, and Offshoring

As MNCs use advanced technology to help them communicate, produce, and deliver their goods and services internationally, they face a new challenge: how technology will affect the nature and number of their employees. Some informed observers note that technology already has eliminated much and in the future will eliminate even more of the work being done by middle management and white-collar staff. Mounting cost pressures resulting from increased globalization of competition and profit expectations exerted by investors have placed pressure on MNCs to outsource or offshore production to take advantage of lower labor and other costs.[67] In the past century, machines replaced millions of manual laborers, but those who worked with their minds were able to thrive and survive. During the past three decades in particular, employees in blue-collar, smokestack industries such as steel and autos have been downsized by technology, and the result has been a permanent restructuring of the number of employees needed to run factories efficiently. In the 1990s, a similar trend unfolded in the white-collar service industries (insurance, banks, and even government). Most recently, this trend has affected high-tech companies in the late 1990s and early 2000s, when after the dot-com bubble burst, hundreds of thousands of jobs were lost, and again in 2008–2010, when many jobs were lost in finance and related industries as a result of the financial crisis and global recession. Furthermore, the job recovery in the wake of the financial crisis has been largely dependent on lower-wage jobs. According to the National Employment Law Project, 78 percent of jobs lost during the global recession were in finance, manufacturing, and construction, but only 57 percent of the jobs created from 2009 to 2015 were in those fields.[68]

Some experts predict that in the future, technology has the potential to displace employees in all industries, from those doing low-skilled jobs to those holding positions traditionally associated with knowledge work. For example, voice recognition is helping to replace telephone operators; the demand for postal workers has been reduced substantially by address-reading devices; and cash-dispensing machines can do 10 times more transactions in a day than bank tellers, so tellers can be reduced in number or even eliminated entirely in the future. Also, expert (sometimes called "smart") systems can eliminate human thinking completely. For example, American Express has an expert system that performs the credit analysis formerly done by college-graduate financial analysts. In the medical field, expert systems can diagnose some illnesses as well as doctors can, and robots capable of performing certain operations are starting to be used.

Emerging information technology also makes work more portable. As a result, MNCs have been able to move certain production activities overseas to capitalize on cheap labor resources. This is especially true for work that can be easily contracted with overseas locations. For example, low-paid workers in India and Asian countries now are being given subcontracted work such as labor-intensive software development and code-writing jobs. A restructuring of the nature of work and of employment is a result of such information technology; Table 2–3 identifies some winners and losers in the workforce in recent years.

The new technological environment has both positives and negatives for MNCs and societies as a whole. On the positive side, the cost of doing business worldwide should decline thanks to the opportunities that technology offers in substituting lower-cost machines for higher-priced labor. Over time, productivity should go up, and prices should go down. On the negative side, many employees will find either their jobs eliminated or their wages and salaries reduced because they have been replaced by machines and their skills are no longer in high demand. This job loss from technology can be especially devastating in developing countries. However, it doesn't have to be this way. A case in point is South Africa's showcase for automotive productivity as represented by the Delta Motor Corporation's Opel Corsa plant in Port Elizabeth. To provide as many jobs as possible, this world-class operation automated only 23 percent, compared to more than 85 percent auto assembly in Europe and North America.[69] Even some manufacturing processes in developed countries have traded robots for humans; in 2014, Toyota replaced automated manufacturing machines with manual jobs in an effort to increase quality.[70] Some industries can also add jobs. For example, the positive has outweighed the negative in the computer and information technology industry, despite its ups and downs. Specifically, employment in the U.S. computer software industry has increased over the last decade. In less developed countries such as India, a high-tech boom in recent years has created jobs and opportunities for a growing number of people.[71] Even though developed countries such as Japan and the United States are most affected by technological displacement of workers, both nations still lead the world in creating new jobs and shifting their traditional industrial structure toward a high-tech, knowledge-based economy.

Table 2–3
Winners and Losers in Selected Occupations: Percentage Change Forecasts for 2014–2024

The 10 occupations with the largest projected employment growth 2014–2024

Occupation	Employment in millions		Difference	Percent change
	2014	2024		
Personal care aides	1768.4	2226.5	458.1	25.9%
Registered nurses	2751.0	3190.3	439.3	16.0
Home health aides	931.5	1261.9	348.4	38.1
Combined food preparation and serving workers, including fast food	3159.7	3503.2	343.5	10.9
Retail salespersons	4624.9	4939.1	314.2	6.8
Nursing assistants	1492.1	1754.1	262.0	17.6
Customer service representatives	2581.8	2834.8	252.9	9.8
Cooks, restaurant	1109.7	1268.7	158.9	14.3
General and operations managers	2124.1	2275.2	151.1	7.1
Construction laborers	1159.1	1306.5	147.4	12.7

The 10 occupations with the largest projected employment declines, 2014–2024

Occupation	Employment in millions		Difference	Percent change
	2014	2024		
Bookkeeping, accounting, and auditing clerks	1760.3	1611.5	−148.7	−8.4%
Cooks, fast food	524.4	444.0	−80.4	−15.3
Postal service mail carriers	297.4	219.4	−78.1	−26.2
Executive secretaries and executive administrative assistants	776.6	732.0	−44.6	−5.7
Farmworkers and laborers, crop, nursery, and greenhouse	470.2	427.3	−42.9	−9.1
Sewing machine operators	153.9	112.2	−41.7	−27.1
Tellers	520.5	480.5	−40.0	−7.7
Postal service mail sorters, processors, and processing machine operators	117.6	78.0	−39.7	−33.7
Cutting, punching, and press machine setters, operators, and tenders, metal and plastic	192.2	152.7	−39.5	−20.6
Switchboard operators, including answering service	112.4	75.4	−37.0	−32.9

Source: Bureau of Labor Statistics, "Tables 4 & 6," *Employment Projections.* December 15, 2015. http://www.bls.gov/emp/tables.htm.

The precise impact that the advanced technological environment will have on international management over the next decade is difficult to forecast. One thing is certain, however; there is no turning back the technological clock. MNCs and nations alike must evaluate the impact of these changes carefully and realize that their economic performance is closely tied to keeping up with, or ahead of, rapidly advancing technology.

The World of International Management—Revisited

Political, legal, and technological environments can alter the landscape for global companies. The chapter opening The World of International Management described how social media can be used a tool for political change—both positive and negative. It has allowed political groups to organize, journalists to communicate and report on political developments, and citizens to mobilize and build support for political movements. This situation underscores the increasing uncertainty in the global business environment and the rapidity and extent of political and legal change. It also highlights how technology is contributing to accelerating change and how traditional legal systems have difficulty keeping pace with these changes. International managers need to be aware of how differing political, legal, and technological environments are affecting their business and how globalization, security concerns, and other developments influence these environments. Changes in political, legal, and environmental conditions also open up new business opportunities but close some old ones.

In light of the information you have learned from reading this chapter, you should have a good understanding of these environments and some of the ways in which they will affect companies doing business abroad. Drawing on this knowledge, answer the following questions: (1) How will changes in the political and legal environment in the Middle East and North Africa, including the potential economic impacts of terrorism, affect U.S. MNCs conducting business there? (2) How might evolving political interests and legal systems affect future investment in the region? (3) How does technology result in greater integration and dependencies among economies, political systems, and financial markets, but also greater fragility?

SUMMARY OF KEY POINTS

1. The global political environment can be understood via an appreciation of ideologies and political systems. Ideologies, including individualism and collectivism, reflect underlying tendencies in society. Political systems, including democracy and totalitarianism, incorporate ideologies into political structures. There are fewer and fewer purely collectivist or socialist societies, although totalitarianism still exists in several countries and regions. Many countries are experiencing transitions from more socialist to democratic systems, reflecting related trends discussed in Chapter 1 toward more market-oriented economic systems.

2. The current legal and regulatory environment is both complex and confusing. There are many different laws and regulations to which MNCs doing business internationally must conform, and each nation is unique. Also, MNCs must abide by the laws of their own country. For example, U.S. MNCs must obey the rules set down by the Foreign Corrupt Practices Act. Privatization and regulation of trade also affect the legal and regulatory environment in specific countries.

3. The technological environment is changing quickly and is having a major impact on international business. This will continue in the future with, for example, digitization, higher-speed telecommunication, and advancements in biotechnology as they offer developing countries new opportunities to leapfrog into the 21st century. New markets are being created for high-tech MNCs that are eager to provide telecommunications service. Technological developments also impact both the nature and the structure of employment, shifting the industrial structure toward a more high-tech, knowledge-based economy. MNCs that understand and take advantage of this high-tech environment should prosper, but they also must keep up, or go ahead, to survive.

KEY TERMS

act of state doctrine, *54*

civil or code law, *53*

collectivism, *48*

common law, *53*

democracy, *50*

doctrine of comity, *54*

Foreign Corrupt Practices Act (FCPA), *55*

individualism, *47*

Islamic law, *53*

nationality principle, *53*

principle of sovereignty, *53*

protective principle, *53*

socialism, *48*

socialist law, *53*

territoriality principle, *53*

totalitarianism, *50*

REVIEW AND DISCUSSION QUESTIONS

1. In what ways do different ideologies and political systems influence the environment in which MNCs operate? Would these challenges be less for those operating in the EU than for those in Russia or China? Why or why not?

2. How do the following legal principles impact MNC operations: the principle of sovereignty, the nationality principle, the territoriality principle, the protective principle, and principle of comity?

3. How will advances in technology and telecommunications affect developing countries? Give some specific examples.

4. Why are developing countries interested in privatizing their state-owned industries? What opportunities does privatization have for MNCs?

INTERNET EXERCISE: HITACHI GOES WORLDWIDE

Hitachi products are well known in the United States, as well as in Europe and Asia. However, in an effort to maintain its international momentum, the Japanese MNC is continuing to push forward into new markets, especially emerging markets, while also developing new products. Visit the MNC at its website www.hitachi.com and examine some of the latest developments that are taking place. Begin by reviewing the firm's current activities in Asia, specifically Hong Kong and Singapore. Then look at how it is doing business in North America. Finally, read about its European operations. Then answer these three questions: (1) What kinds of products and systems does the firm offer? What are its primary areas of emphasis? (2) In what types of environments does it operate? Is Hitachi primarily interested in developed markets, or is it also pushing into newly emerging markets? (3) Based on what it has been doing over the last two to three years, what do you think Hitachi's future strategy will be in competing in the environment of international business?

ENDNOTES

1. "Syrian Protests Grow Despite Attacks, Internet Cut," *USA Today*, June 3, 2011, http://usatoday30. usatoday.com/news/world/2011-06-03-syria-unrest_n. htm.

2. Nicholas Blanford, "On Facebook and Twitter, Spreading Revolution in Syria," *The Christian Sience Monitor*, April 8, 2011, www.csmonitor.com/ World/Middle-East/2011/0408/On-Facebook-and-Twitter-spreading-revolution-in-Syria.

3. Rosemary D'Amour, "Syria Utilites 'Kill Switch' as Internet Freedom Debate Heats Up," *Broadband-Breakfast*, June 17, 2011, http://broadbandbreakfast. com/2011/06/syria-utilizes-kill-switch-as-internet-freedom-debate-heats-up/.

4. Eva Galperin, "Fake YouTube Site Targets Syrian Activists with Malware," *Electronic Frontier Foundation*, March 12, 2012, www.eff.org/ deeplinks/2012/03/fake-youtube-site-targets-syrian-activists-malware.

5. Matthew Brunwasser, "A 21st Century Migrant's Essentials: Food, Shelter, Smartphone," *New York Times*, August 25, 2015, http://mobile.nytimes. com/2015/08/26/world/europe/a-21st-century-migrants-checklist-water-shelter-smartphone.html?_ r=3&referer=http://jilltxt.net/?p=4332.

6. Andrew Byme and Erika Solomon, "Refugees Seek Help from Social Media," *Financial Times*, September 11, 2015, www.ft.com/intl/cms/s/ 0/09625b90-56fc-11e5-a28b-50226830d644. html#axzz3xjqWWaD1.

7. Brunwasser, "A 21st Century Migrant's Essentials: Food, Shelter, Smartphone."

8. Ibid.

9. Zeina Karam, "Syria's Civil War Plays Out on Social Media," *Huffington Post*, October 19, 2013, www.huffingtonpost.com/huff-wires/20131019/ ml--syria-youtube-war/?utm_hp_ref=world&ir=world.

10. Ibid.

11. Jennifer Moire, "5 Ways Social Media Spread Word of Syrian Chemical Attack," *Adweek Social Times*, August 27, 2013, www.adweek.com/socialtimes/5-ways-social-media-spread-word-of-syrian-chemical-attack/135905.

12. Mukul Devichand, "Alan Kurdi's Aunt: My Dead Nephew's Picture Saved Thousands of Lives," *BBC News*, January 2, 2016, www.bbc.com/news/blogs-trending-35116022.

13. "BBC Newsnight Refugee Poll," *ComRes*, September 2015, www.comres.co.uk/polls/bbc-newsnight-refugee-poll/.

14. Rachelle Younglai and Jacqueline Nelson, "Until Now, Syria a Hard Sell for Donations," *UNHCR*, September 6, 2015, www.unhcr.org/cgi-bin/texis/vtx/refdaily?pass=52fc6fbd5&id=55ed341e5.

15. Michael Gundlach, "Understanding the Relationship Between Individualism-Collectivism and Team Performance Through an Integration of Social Identity Theory and the Social Relations Model," *Human Relations* 59, no. 12 (2006), pp. 1603–1632.

16. Donald Ball, Michael Geringer, Michael Minor, and Jeanne McNett, *International Business: The Challenge of Global Competition* (New York: McGraw-Hill, 2009).

17. Alessandra Galloni, Charles Forelle, and Stephen Fidler, "France, Germany Weigh Rescue Plan for Greece," *The Wall Street Journal Online*, February 11, 2010.

18. Henry W. Spiegel and Ann Hubbard, *The Growth of Economic Thought* (Durham, NC: Duke University Press, 1991).

19. Ball et al., *International Business: The Challenge of Global Competition*.

20. Daniel J. McCarthy, Sheila M. Puffer, and Alexander I. Naumov, "Russia's Retreat to Statization and the Implications for Business," *Journal of World Business* 35, no. 3 (2000), p. 258.

21. Jason Bush, "Russia's New Deal," *BusinessWeek Online*, March 29, 2007, www.bloomberg.com/news/articles/2007-03-29/russias-new-dealbusinessweek-business-news-stock-market-and-financial-advice.

22. Transparency International, *Corruption Perceptions Index* 2014.

23. Heritage Foundation, *Index of Economic Freedom* 2015.

24. Kim Hjelmgaard, "Cameron Gets a Go-Ahead for His British Austerity Programs," *USA Today*, May 8, 2015, www.usatoday.com/story/news/world/2015/05/08/british-election-analysis-conservatives-cameron/26968731/.

25. Keith Bradsher, "As China Stirs Economy, Some See Protectionism," *New York Times,* June 24, 2009, p. B1.

26. "When Opium Can Be Benign," *The Economist*, February 1, 2007, pp. 25–27.

27. John Child and David K. Tse, "China's Transition and Its Implications for International Business," *Journal of International Business Studies*, First Quarter 2001, pp. 5–21.

28. Andre Tartar and Salma El Wardany, "The Grim Economic Legacy of the Arab Spring Poster Children," *Bloomberg Businessweek*, October 27, 2015, www.bloomberg.com/news/articles/2015-10-28/the-grim-economic-legacy-of-the-arab-spring-poster-children.

29. "Business Counts the Cost of the Arab Spring," *Grant Thornton*, June 21, 2011.

30. Paul Nadler, "Making a Mystery out of How to Comply with Patriot Act," *American Banker*, May 19, 2004, p. 5.

31. "International: Financial Crisis Goes Global," *New York Times*, September 19, 2008.

32. David M. Herszenhorn, "Financial Overhaul Wins Final Approval in House," *New York Times*, June 30, 2010, p. A1.

33. John Graham, "Foreign Corrupt Practices Act: A Manager's Guide," *California Management Review*, Summer 1987, p. 9.

34. R. Christopher Cook and Stephanie Connor, "The Foreign Corruption Practices Act: 2010 and Beyond," *Jonesday.com*, January 2010.

35. Katsunori Nagayasu, "How Japan Restored Its Financial System," *The Wall Street Journal Online*, August 6, 2009.

36. Scott Cendrowski, "Why China's SOE Reform Would Always Disappoint," *Fortune*, September 15, 2015, http://fortune.com/2015/09/15/why-chinas-soe-reform-would-always-disappoint/.

37. Gabriel Wildau, "China Cautiously Embraces Privatisation of State-Owned Enterprises," *The Financial Times*, September 25, 2015, www.ft.com/intl/cms/s/0/69253d76-633c-11e5-97e9-7f0bf5e7177b.html#axzz3y5XO5C6p.

38. Marcin Sobczyk, "Warsaw Rows Back from Large-Scale Asset Sales," *The Wall Street Journal Online*, July 4, 2014, www.wsj.com/articles/polish-government-rows-back-from-large-scale-asset-sales-1404469210.

39. Privatization Alert, Fdi.net, May 2010.

40. Thomas Friedman, *The World Is Flat (Updated and Expanded): A Brief History of the Twenty-first Century* (New York: Farrar, Straus and Giroux, 2006).

41. Charles W. L. Hill, *International Business* (New York: McGraw-Hill/Irwin, 2011).

42. Rebecca Buckman, "China Keeps Telecom Firms Waiting on 3G," *The Wall Street Journal*, May 13, 2004, p. B4.

43. "China Telecom Announces 2015 Plan in 4G Business," *CRI English*, December 24, 2014, http://english.cri.cn/12394/2014/12/24/1261s858097.htm.

44. Lee Stott, "What Does DreamSpark Offer for UK Education?" *Microsoft.com*, April 2, 2014, https://www.microsoft.com/en-gb/developers/articles/week01apr14/what-does-dreamspark-offer-for-uk-education/.

45. Andrew Rosenblum, "For Oakland Startup, a $9 Computer About More Than Getting Rich," *Mercury News*, February 9, 2016, www.mercurynews.com/news/ci_29491760/west-oakland-startup-9-computer-about-more-than?source=infinite-up.

46. Greg Miller, "Undersea Internet Cables Are Surprisingly Vulnerable," *Wired.com*, October 29, 2015, www.wired.com/2015/10/undersea-cable-maps/.

47. "Vietnam Suffers Second Internet Cable Cut in Less Than 4 Months," *Tuoi Tre News*, April 23, 2015, http://tuoitrenews.vn/society/27677/vietnam-suffers-second-internet-cable-cut-in-less-than-4-months.

48. "Supercomputers: The Race Is On," *BusinessWeek*, June 7, 2004, p. 76.

49. Nicholas Zamiska and Eric Bellman, "Ranbaxy Unveils Its Ambition to Be a Generics Powerhouse," *The Wall Street Journal*, January 10, 2007, p. A11.

50. Congressional Budget Office, "Using Biofuel Tax Credits to Achieve Energy and Environmental Policy Goals," July 14, 2010, https://www.cbo.gov/publication/21444?index=11477.

51. Christopher Leonard, "Monsanto, BASF Join Forces," *BusinessWeek Online*, March 21, 2007, www.businessweek.com.

52. Doris De Guzman, "Monsanto Sows More Seeds," *ICIS Chemical Business Americas* 270, no. 2 (2007), p. 26.

53. "World's First BSE-Immune Cow," *Asia Pacific Biotech News* 8, no. 12 (2004), p. 682.

54. Gretchen Vogel, "E.U. Parliament Votes to Ban Cloning of Farm Animals," *Science Magazine*, September 8, 2015, www.sciencemag.org/news/2015/09/eu-parliament-votes-ban-cloning-farm-animals.

55. David Mildenberg, "SDN Sees Growth in High Speed Links," *The Business Journal*, May 14, 2004, p. 1.

56. James Ayre, "Toyota Following Tesla's Lead, Trying Out Direct Online Sales," *Clean Technica*, August 29, 2015, http://cleantechnica.com/2015/08/29/toyota-following-teslas-lead-trying-direct-online-sales/.

57. "Deutsche Bank Govvie Honcho: Business as Usual Now," *Bondweek*, June 22, 2003, p. 1.

58. FDIC, "Failed Bank List," https://www.fdic.gov/bank/individual/failed/banklist.html (last visited February 11, 2016).

59. "Cell Phones in Africa: Communication Lifeline," *Pew Research Center*, April 15, 2015, www.pewglobal.org/2015/04/15/cell-phones-in-africa-communication-lifeline/.

60. Govind Bansal, "Trends in Multimedia Consumption on Mobile," *Business World*, January 21, 2016, http://businessworld.in/article/Trends-In-Multimedia-Consumption-On-Mobile/21-01-2016-90515/.

61. David Yanofsky and Christopher Mims, "Since 2000, the Number of Mobile Phones in the Developing World Has Increased 1700%," *Quartz*, October 2, 2012, http://qz.com/9101/mobile-phones-developing-world/.

62. Chandra Steele, "How the Mobile Phone Is Evolving in Developing Countries," *PC Mag*, May 11, 2012, www.pcmag.com/slideshow/story/297822/how-the-mobile-phone-is-evolving-in-developing-countries.

63. Morgan Winsor, "Nigeria's Telephone Penetration Expands in First Half of 2015 Amid Mobile Phone Boom," *International Business Times*, September 29, 2015, www.ibtimes.com/nigerias-telephone-penetration-expands-first-half-2015-amid-mobile-phone-boom-2118947.

64. Heidi Vogt, "Making Change: Mobile Pay in Africa," *The Wall Street Journal Online*, January 2, 2015, www.wsj.com/articles/making-change-mobile-pay-in-africa-1420156199.

65. mobiThinking, "Global Mobile Statistics 2014 Part A: Mobile Subscribers; Handset Market Share; Mobile Operators," *mobiForge*, May 16, 2014, https://mobiforge.com/research-analysis/global-mobile-statistics-2014-part-a-mobile-subscribers-handset-market-share-mobile-operators.

66. Yang Jie, "Chinese Firm Made Fake iPhones Worth $19.4 Million, Police Say," *The Wall Street Journal Online*, July 27, 2015, http://blogs.wsj.com/chinarealtime/2015/07/27/chinese-firm-made-fake-iphones-worth-19-4-million-police-say/.

67. Jonathan P. Doh, Kraiwinee Bunyaratavej, and Eugene E. Hahn, "Separable but Not Equal: The Location Determinants of Discrete Offshoring Activities," *Journal of International Business Studies* 40, no. 6 (2009), pp. 926–943.

68. Cole Strangler, "Unemployment Report: Six Years after the Great Recession, Are the Good Jobs Ever Coming Back?" *International Business Times*, March 6, 2015, www.ibtimes.com/unemployment-report-six-years-after-great-recession-are-good-jobs-ever-coming-back-1838178.

69. Jan Syfert, "Up There with the Best," *Productivity SA*, November–December 1998, p. 49.

70. Craig Trudell, "Humans Replacing Robots Herald Toyota's Vision of Future," *BloombergBusiness*, April 7, 2014, www.bloomberg.com/news/articles/2014-04-06/humans-replacing-robots-herald-toyota-s-vision-of-future.

71. Ashok Bhattacharjee, "India's Outsourcing Tigers Seek Cover, Markets, in Europe's East," *The Wall Street Journal,* December 18, 2003, p. A16.

72. CIA, "Greece," *The World Factbook* (2016), https://www.cia.gov/library/publications/the-world-factbook/geos/gr.html.

73. Ibid.

74. World Bank, "Greece," *World Development Indicators* (2016), http://data.worldbank.org/indicator/NY.GDP.MKTP.KD.ZG/countries/GR?display=graph.

75. CIA, "Greece."

76. Liz Alderman, James Kanter, Jim Yardley, and Jack Ewing, "Greece's Debt Crisis Explained," *New York Times*, November 9, 2015, www.nytimes.com/interactive/2015/business/international/greece-debt-crisis-euro.html?_r=0.

77. Ibid.

Greece

Greece is located in southern Europe, positioned geographically between the Aegean and Mediterranean Seas, Albania, and Turkey. The country's land mass is slightly smaller than that of Alabama. Major natural resources include lignite, petroleum, iron ore, bauxite, lead, zinc, nickel, magnesite, marble, salt, and hydro-power potential.[72]

Greece has a population of 10.78 million people, with Athens, the capital, home to 3 million people. Population growth has stabilized at zero in recent years. Greece is a fairly homogeneous country, with close to 95 percent of the population with Greek ethnicity. Nearly all in the country practice the Greek Orthodox religion. With a median age of 44 years, Greece has an older population than most countries in the world. Approximately 34 percent of the population is 55 years or older. In recent years, the country has struggled economically, leading to the third highest unemployment rate in the world.[73]

Greece's GDP is estimated at US$238 billion. After years of negative growth, and declines of 9.1 percent in 2011 and 7.3 percent in 2012, the country's GDP finally grew in 2014 by 0.7 percent. GDP per capita in Greece is estimated at $26,000. Greece has a capitalist economy, but the public sector accounts for approximately 40 percent of GDP.[74]

Greece was significantly impacted by the financial crisis of 2008. Greece's poor financial management of the country's budget and its failure to report massive deficits in a timely fashion to its borrowers amplified the impact of the crisis, causing the economy to spiral downward. As a consequence, Greece was no longer able to borrow in global markets. Ultimately, Greece was required to take a US$316 billion bailout from the European Union. In return for the bailout, the Greek government was required to implement dramatic spending cuts and tax increases to reduce its budget deficits. In total, aid from the European Union has amounted to approximately 3 percent of the country's GDP.[75]

The country has started to show some limited signs of progress and has recently agreed to further economic reforms in return for liquidity from its lenders. Greece is not out of the woods, however. The bailout money has largely gone to the country's lenders and has not yet been able to support the restructuring of the economy.[76]

You Be the International Management Consultant

In 2015, Greece received its third bailout in five years. Relations between Greece and its creditors remain strained and contentious. On several occasions, Greece has threatened to default on its loans and has even contemplated exiting the European Union. The 2015 bailout allowed creditors to demand harsh austerity programs and require deep economic and structural reforms. These measures included raising the retirement age, cutting pensions, liberalizing the energy market, opening up protected professions, enlarging a property tax that Greeks already despise, and moving ahead with a program to sell state-owned enterprises and other assets.[77]

Questions

1. If you are a consultant for a business looking to expand in Europe, is Greece even an option?
2. Do the facts that its population is comprised largely of government workers, that the citizens were largely in favor of defaulting on its national debt, and that the country nearly left the European Union constitute a deal breaker?
3. If the government does, in fact, implement the agreed-upon austerity measures, would that be a sign that the country is on the right track?
4. What other concerns would you have about entering the Greek market?

Chapter 3

ETHICS, SOCIAL RESPONSIBILITY, AND SUSTAINABILITY

OBJECTIVES OF THE CHAPTER

Recent concerns about ethics, social responsibility, and sustainability transcend national borders. In this era of globalization, MNCs must be concerned with how they carry out their business and their social role in foreign countries. This chapter examines business ethics and social responsibility in the international arena, and it looks at some of the critical social issues that will be confronting MNCs in the years ahead. The discussion includes ethical decision making in various countries, regulation of foreign investment, the growing trends toward environmental sustainability, and current responses to social responsibility by today's multinationals. The specific objectives of this chapter are

1. **EXAMINE** ethics in international management and some of the major ethical issues and problems confronting MNCs.

2. **DISCUSS** some of the pressures on and actions being taken by selected industrialized countries and companies to be more socially and environmentally responsive to world problems.

3. **EXPLAIN** some of the initiatives to bring greater accountability to corporate conduct and limit the impact of corruption around the world.

The World of *International Management*

Sustaining Sustainable Companies

With a more environmentally aware public, becoming a "sustainable" business has become an important part of the business model for many MNCs. Three of these companies—Patagonia, Nestlé, and Tesla—have in different ways transformed their corporate strategy to emphasize "doing good" socially and environmentally while "doing well" economically.

Sustainability in the Supply Chain—Patagonia

Founded by Yvon Chouinard in 1972, Patagonia is a private, outdoor-clothing company. Patagonia's transition to a sustainability-focused company started in 1988 after several employees in one of their Boston retail stores suddenly fell ill. After a thorough investigation, it was discovered that formaldehyde, emitted from Patagonia's cotton-based merchandise, was cycling into the air. In response, Patagonia committed in 1994 to use only formaldehyde-free, 100 percent organic cotton in the manufacture of its clothing; within just 18 months, they achieved that goal.[1] Since then, Patagonia has examined and modified its entire supply chain from both a corporate social responsibility and environmental viewpoint. Its revised mission statement reflects that ideal: "Build the best product, cause no unnecessary harm, and use business to inspire and implement solutions to the environmental crisis."[2]

Internally, recycled products constitute a large percentage of the material used in Patagonia's products. Recycled polyester and nylon, made of postconsumer soda bottles and waste fabric, are used in the production of fleece and linings.[3] This reuse cuts down on oil usage and CO_2 emissions. All of Patagonia's wool products are now chlorine-free, preventing the contamination of wastewater in the developing countries where the products are manufactured. Furthermore, Patagonia's finished products are fully recyclable, and the company has encouraged its customers to properly dispose of their products. Any Patagonia product can be dropped off at a retail store for guaranteed recycling.[4]

Social sustainability, with an emphasis on employee welfare, has also become a key tenet of Patagonia's strategy. Beginning in 1990, Patagonia instituted a policy of visiting every factory that manufactured its goods to evaluate and score working conditions.[5] Patagonia refuses to do business with any factory that does not allow full access or breaks local labor laws. Additionally, third-party audits of factories were established to provide nonbiased assessments of the factories. Every factory along its supply chain is listed on its website. In 1999, Patagonia became one of the founding members of the Fair Labor Association.[6] Since 1985, Patagonia has donated one percent of its sales to environmental nonprofits.[7] In 2002, Chouinard expanded on his vision for corporate sustainability by cofounding "One Percent for the Planet," an international nonprofit dedicated to philanthropy for environmental organizations. The program encourages companies to follow Patagonia's lead and donate one percent of sales to worthwhile, environmentally focused causes. As of 2015, over 1,200 companies across 48 countries have joined the organization. Over 3,300 different nonprofits have received funding from the over US$100 million donated by the member companies.[8]

The decision to invest in sustainable products has not been without repercussions. Chlorine-free wool has been more costly to manufacture, cutting down on profits. Following the shift to 10 percent organic cotton, Patagonia's profits dropped.[9] Furthermore, the high priority that Patagonia puts on only using factories that follow its strict standards means higher labor costs than the competition. However, Patagonia has gained a competitive advantage by doing good. The company has developed a loyal customer base that is willing to pay a premium for the sustainability that Patagonia provides.

Sustainability in Operations and Products—Nestlé

Founded over 150 years ago, Nestlé S.A., a Swiss MNC, is best known for its chocolate and other snack products. With sales of over US$1.1 billion in 2015, the company employs over 339,000 people across 447 factories. Nestlé maintains operations in 197 countries and boasts over 2,000 brands. For Nestlé, sustainability means improving its environmental impact along the entire value chain.[10]

Nestlé's sustainable efforts are centered on six core categories: resource efficiency, packaging, products, climate change, natural capital, and information. In each category,

Nestlé sets environmental objectives, resulting in trackable and measurable progress. From 2005 to 2015, Nestlé cut overall energy consumption by a quarter and greenhouse gas emissions by 40 percent. The use of industrial refrigerants has been cut by 92 percent, and Nestlé's chest freezers now consume 50 percent less energy. In 2015, Nestlé was able to achieve zero waste in 15 percent of its global factories. By 2017, Nestlé plans to eliminate 100,000 tons of packaging material.[11]

Environmental efforts extend down Nestlé's supply chain, from raw material sourcing to final distribution. Environmental standards are set for all farmers conducting business with Nestlé, and Nestlé supports those farmers through training and informational support. Whenever possible, local farmers are utilized to decrease the environmental impacts from shipping raw materials long distances. During the manufacturing process, the Nestlé Environmental Management System tracks energy performance and improves efficiency and quality. Areas for improvement are identified, leading to new manufacturing processes that lead to less waste. Final distribution, though handled by third parties, is subject to Nestlé's environmental performance standards. Mileage and fuel consumption are tracked, distribution networks are altered to decrease congestion and noise, and greenhouse gas emissions are monitored.[12]

Continual environmental-friendly innovation is a priority for Nestlé. Nestlé developed an eco-design tool, called the Eco-dEX, to assist with sustainability in its research and development efforts. Since 2013, over 5,000 products have been tested and assessed using this tool. All new products now undergo an environmental assessment.[13] As with Patagonia, customers seem eager to purchase products that are sustainable, giving Nestlé a competitive advantage over the competition. Nestlé reached number 18 on *Fortune* magazine's 2014 "Best Global Green Brands" list.[14]

Sustainability as a Competitive Advantage—Tesla Motors

Tesla Motors, an independent Silicon Valley–based auto manufacturer, focuses on creating and mass-producing reliable electric automobiles. Using technology descended from 19th-century physicist Nikola Tesla, Tesla Motors has developed the longest-range electric car battery on the market. Visionary billionaire Elon Musk, who is also behind SpaceX, cofounded the company in 2003.[15]

Unlike previously developed electric cars, which were clunky and unattractive, Tesla aimed to design automobiles that were attractive and high-quality. Tesla's first vehicle, the Roadster, was designed to be a high-performance sports car. Released in 2008, the Roadster can accelerate from zero to 60 in less than four seconds, reaching top speeds of over 125 miles per hour.[16] The Model S, released in 2012, was designed to be a luxury sedan for the masses. Starting at US$57,400, the Model S was introduced for less than half of the cost of the Roadster. The car won multiple awards upon its release, including Motor Trend's "Car of the Year" award for 2013, and sold over 100,000 units within its first four years.[17] In late 2015, Tesla introduced a full-size SUV, named the Model X, as the latest addition to its fleet and in early 2016, the company started taking pre-orders for its forthcoming US$35,000 Model 3. More than a quarter of a million people pre-ordered the car within the first 72 hours, shattering expectations.[18]

Inspiring sustainability across the entire automobile industry is a secondary goal for the company. To achieve that goal, Tesla has collaborated with several other researchers and car manufacturers to produce greener automobiles. Panasonic joined Tesla's US$5 billion "Gigafactory" battery production project in 2014, and from 2009 to 2015, Tesla partnered with Mercedes to provide powertrain components for its electric models.[19,20,21] In its partnerships with Smart and Toyota, Tesla produced batteries and chargers.[22,23]

As an innovator, Tesla has faced some major obstacles. Tesla's first automobile, the Roadster, faced two high-profile recalls, one of which dealt with the potential loss of control of the car.[24,25] In a highly publicized February 2013 article, a *New York Times* reporter took the Model S on an infamous test drive along the East Coast. Not only did the car fall short of the estimated 200-mile range per charge, but the battery actually ran completely out of power and the car ended up having to be towed.[26] Musk estimated that the negative *New York Times* review resulted in several hundred vehicle cancellations and cost Tesla US$100 million in valuation.[27] Financially, Tesla has invested hundreds of millions of dollars into its operations. Since its founding in 2003, Tesla has only earned a quarterly profit once; Tesla posted a US$300 million loss in 2014.[28]

Tesla, despite its setbacks, still maintains a competitive advantage from its dedicated investor and customer bases. Customers seem willing to deal with minor issues and recalls for the sake of the overall sustainability goal of the company. By targeting high-income customers with the Roadster, Tesla was able to spend the funds necessary to develop and fine-tune its technology. Investors have also been willing to bet on the idea of Tesla Motors. The IPO on June 29, 2010, raised US$226 million for the company, and in the years since, Tesla's share price has increased nearly tenfold.[29,30]

Our opening discussion of Patagonia, Nestlé, and Tesla demonstrates how corporations are shifting their focus from traditional market-responsive strategies to broader approaches that incorporate both business and social or environmental goals. Patagonia has radically transformed its business to focus on what it expects to be increasing demand for "green" products as well as those that contribute to improved working conditions in developing countries. Focusing on six core categories for creating and tracking sustainable goals allowed Nestlé to achieve measurable progress in emissions reductions. Tesla Motors's Model S is focused on developing and deploying a reasonably priced all-electric car to the masses. By combining their commitment to social and environmental sustainability, aligned with their business and commercial objectives, these three companies appear to be setting an example for a new approach to integrating social and business goals among global corporations, tapping into consumers' desire for products and services that are consistent with their values. This "triple bottom line" approach, which simultaneously considers social, environmental, and economic sustainability ("people, planet, profits") could make a real and lasting impact on the world's human and environmental conditions by harnessing business and managerial skills and techniques.

More broadly, recent scandals have called attention to the perceived lack of ethical values and corporate governance standards in business. In addition, assisting impoverished countries by helping them gain a new level of independence is both responsible and potentially profitable. Indeed, corporate social responsibility is becoming more than just good moral behavior. It can assist in avoiding future economic and environmental setbacks and may be the key to keeping companies afloat.

■ Ethics and Social Responsibility

The ethical behavior of business and the broader social responsibilities of corporations have become major issues in the United States and all countries around the world. Ethical scandals and questionable business practices have received considerable media attention, aroused the public's concern about ethics in international business, and brought attention to the social impact of business operations.

Ethics and Social Responsibility in International Management

Unbiased ethical decision-making processes are imperative to modern international business practices. It is difficult to determine a universal ethical standard when the views and norms in one country can vary substantially from those in others. **Ethics,** the study of morality and standards of conduct, is often the victim of subjectivity as it yields to the will of cultural relativism, or the belief that the ethical standard of a country is based on the culture that created it and that moral concepts lack universal application.[31]

> **ethics**
> The study of morality and standards of conduct.

The adage "When in Rome, do as the Romans do" is derived from the idea of cultural relativism and suggests that businesses and their managers should behave in accordance with the ethical standards of the country they are active in, regardless of MNC headquarters location. It is necessary, to some extent, to rely on local teams to execute under local rule; however, this can be taken to extremes. While a business whose only objective is to make a profit may opt to take advantage of these differences in norms and standards in order to legally gain leverage over the competition, it may find that negative consumer opinion about unethical business practices, not to mention potential legal action, could affect the bottom line. Dilemmas that arise from conflicts between ethical standards of a country and business ethics, or the moral code guiding business behavior, are most evident in employment and business practices; recognition of human rights, including women in the workplace; and corruption. The newer area of **corporate social responsibility (CSR)** is closely related to ethics. However, we discuss CSR issues separately. Ethics is the study of or the learning process involved in understanding morality, while CSR involves taking action. Furthermore, the area of ethics has a lawful component and implies right and wrong in a legal sense, while CSR is based more on voluntary actions. Business ethics and CSR therefore may be viewed as two complementary dimensions of a company's overall social profile and position.

> **corporate social responsibility (CSR)**
> The actions of a firm to benefit society beyond the requirements of the law and the direct interests of the firm.

Ethics Theories and Philosophy

There are a range of ethical theories and approaches around the world, many emanating from religious and cultural traditions. We focus on the cultural factors in Part Two of the book. Here we review three tenets from Western philosophy and briefly describe Eastern philosophy, which can be used to evaluate and inform international management decisions. The International Management in Action feature explores how these perspectives might be used to inform the ethics of a specific international business decision.

Kantian philosophical traditions argue that individuals (and organizations) have responsibilities based on a core set of moral principles that go beyond those of narrow self-interest. In fact, a Kantian moral analysis rejects consequences (either conceivable or likely) as morally irrelevant when evaluating the choice of an agent: "The moral worth of an action does not lie in the effect expected from it, nor in any principle of action which requires to borrow its motive from this expected effect."[32] Rather, a Kantian approach asks us to consider our choices as implying a general rule, or maxim, that must be evaluated for its consistency as a universal law. For Kant, what is distinctive about rational behavior is not that it is self-interested or even purpose driven, though all actions do include some purpose as part of their explanation. Instead, rational beings, in addition to having purposes and being able to reason practically in their pursuit, are also capable of evaluating their choices through the lens of a universal law, what Kant calls the moral law, or the "categorical imperative."[33] From this perspective, we ought always to act under a maxim that we can will consistently as a universal law for all rational beings similarly situated.

Aristotelian virtue ethics focus on core, individual behaviors and actions and how they express and form individual character. They also consider social and institutional arrangements and practices in terms of their contribution to the formation of good character in individuals. A good, or virtuous, individual does what is right for the right reasons and derives satisfaction from such actions because his or her character is rightly formed. For Aristotle, moral success and failure largely come down to a matter of right desire, or appetite: "In matters of action, the principles of initiating motives are the ends at which our actions are aimed. But as soon as people become corrupted by pleasure or pain, the goal no longer appears as a motivating principle: he no longer sees that he should choose and act in every case for the sake of and because of this end. For vice tends to destroy the principle or initiating motive of action."[34] It is important to have an understanding of what is truly good and practical wisdom to enable one to form an effective plan of action toward realizing what is good; however, absent a fixed and habitual desire for the good, there is little incentive for good actions. There is also an important social component to virtue theory insofar as one's formation is a social process. The exemplars and practices one finds in one's cultural context guide one's moral development. Virtue theory relies heavily on existing practices to provide an account of what is good and what character traits contribute to pursuing and realizing the good in concrete ways.

Utilitarianism—a form of consequentialism—favors the greatest good for the greatest number of people under a given set of constraints.[35] A given act is morally correct if it maximizes utility, that is, if the ratio of benefit to harm (calculated by taking everyone affected by the act into consideration) is greater than the ratio resulting from an alternative act. This theory was given its most famous modern expression in the works of Jeremy Bentham (1988) and John Stuart Mill (1957), two English utilitarians writing in the 18th and 19th centuries, both of whom emphasized the greatest happiness principle as their moral standard.[36,37] Utilitarianism is an attractive perspective for business decision making, especially in Western countries, because its logic is similar to an economic calculation of utility or cost-benefit, something many Western managers are accustomed to doing.

Eastern philosophy—which broadly can include various philosophies of Asia, including Indian philosophy, Chinese philosophy, Iranian philosophy, Japanese philosophy, and Korean philosophy—tends to view the individual as part of, rather than separate from, nature. Many Western philosophers generally assume as a given that the individual is something distinct from the entire universe, and many Western philosophers attempt to describe and categorize the universe from a detached, objective viewpoint. Eastern perspectives, on the other hand, typically hold that people are an intrinsic and inseparable part of the universe and that attempts to discuss the universe from an objective viewpoint, as though the individual speaking were something separate and detached from the whole, are inherently absurd.

In international management, executives may rely upon one or more of these perspectives when confronted with decisions that involve ethics or morality. While they may not invoke the specific philosophical tradition by name, they likely are drawing from these fundamental moral and ethical beliefs when advancing a specific agenda or decision. The International Management in Action box regarding an offshoring decision shows how a given action could be informed by each of these perspectives.

The Ethics of an Offshoring Decision

The financial services industry has been especially active in offshoring. Western investment banks including Citigroup, Deutsche Bank, Goldman Sachs, Credit Suisse, and UBS have established back-office functions in India. JP Morgan was the first to offshore staff to the country in 2001 and has more than 8,000 staff in Mumbai, nearly 5 percent of its 170,000 employees worldwide. In October 2007, Credit Suisse announced the expansion of its center of excellence in Pune, India, with 300 new jobs, bringing staff numbers to 1,000 by December. Deutsche Bank has 3,500 staff in Bangalore and Mumbai. UBS began outsourcing work to third-party information technology vendors in 2003 and has 1,220 employees in Hyderabad and Mumbai. Goldman Sachs started offshoring to India three years ago and has about 2,500 employees there. On October 17, 2007, JP Morgan announced plans to build a back-office workforce of 5,000 in the Philippines over the next two years. Its traditional offshoring center of Mumbai in India has become overcrowded by investment banks that have set up similar operations. The bank will develop credit card and treasury services in the Philippines. A source close to the bank said the move was to diversify its back-office locations and because JP Morgan has strong links with a human resources network in the country. Mark Kobayashi-Hillary, an outsourcing specialist, said: "Because India's finance center is almost wholly based in Mumbai, the resources are finite and there is a supply and demand problem. It's no surprise people are looking elsewhere. But banks are not just after keeping costs down; these moves are also strategic." He said he was surprised that banks had not opened more offices in the Philippines,

considering its strong links with the U.S., cheap rent, and wealth of resources. "In Manila there is a high density of people who have worked in the financial sector with the skills that investment banks look for. We should see more banks setting up shop there soon."

Ethical philosophy and reasoning could be used to inform offshoring decisions such as these. A *Kantian* approach to offshoring would require us to consider a set of principles in accord with which offshoring choices were made such that decisions were measured against these core tenets, such as a corporate code of conduct. A *virtue theory* perspective would suggest that the decision should consider the impact on communities and a goal of humans flourishing more generally; such an analysis could include economic as well as social impacts. A *utilitarian* perspective would urge that benefits and costs be measured; e.g., who is losing jobs, who is gaining, and do the gains (measured in either jobs, income, utility, or quality of life) outweigh the losses. An *Eastern* philosophical approach would suggest a broader, more integrative and longer-term view, considering impacts not just on humans but also on the broader natural environment in which they operate.

Taken together, an understanding of these ethical perspectives could help managers to decide how to make their own ethical decisions in the international business environment.

Source: Jonathan Doh and Bret Wilmot, "The Ethics of Offshoring," Working Paper, Villanova University, 2010; David Smith, "Offshoring: Political Myths and Economic Reality," *World Economy,* March 2006, pp. 249–256.

■ Human Rights

Human rights issues present challenges for MNCs as there is currently no universally adopted standard of what constitutes acceptable behavior. It is difficult to list all rights inherent to humanity because there is considerable subjectivity involved, and cultural differences exist among societies. Some basic rights include life, freedom from slavery or torture, freedom of opinion and expression, and a general ambiance of nondiscriminatory practices.[38] One violation of human rights that resonated with MNCs and made them question whether to move operations into China was the violent June 1989 crackdown on student protesters in Beijing's Tiananmen Square. Despite this horrific event, most MNCs continued their involvement in China, although friction still exists between countries with high and low human rights standards. Even South Africa is beginning to experience the healing process of transitioning to higher human rights standards after the 1994 dismantling of apartheid, the former white government's policy of racial segregation. Unfortunately, human rights violations are still rampant worldwide. For several decades, for example, Russia has experienced widespread human trafficking, but this practice has accelerated in recent years.[39] Here, we take a closer look at women in the workplace.

Women's rights and gender equity can be considered a subset of human rights. While the number of women in the workforce has increased substantially worldwide, most are still experiencing the effects of a "glass ceiling," meaning that it is difficult, if not impossible, to reach the upper management positions. Japan is a good example because both harassment and a glass ceiling have existed in the workplace. Sexual harassment also remains a major social issue in Japan. Many women college graduates in Japan are still offered only secretarial or low-level jobs. Japanese management still believes that women will quit and get married within a few years of employment, leading to a two-track recruiting process: one for men and one for women.[40,41] Japan ranked 101st in the "gender gap index" study by the World Economic Forum, an international nonprofit organization that measured the economic opportunities and political empowerment of women by nation in 2015. Iceland ranked no. 1, and the U.S. was no. 28. Japanese women make up only 8 percent of senior executives and managers, a tiny share compared with 21 percent in the U.S., 38 percent in China, and 26 percent in France, according to Grant Thornton's 2015 Women in Business report. Two-thirds of Japanese businesses still have no female members on their senior leadership teams.[42]

Equal employment opportunities may be more troubled in Japan than other countries, but the glass ceiling is pervasive throughout the world. Today, women earn less than men for the same job in the United States, although progress has been made in this regard. France, Germany, and Great Britain have seen an increase in the number of women not only in the workforce but also in management positions. Unfortunately, women in management tend to represent only the lower level and do not seem to have the resources to move up in the company. This is partially due to social factors and perceived levels of opportunity or lack thereof. The United States, France, Germany, and Great Britain all have equal opportunity initiatives, whether they are guaranteed by law or are represented by growing social groups. Despite the existence of equal opportunity in French and German law, the National Organization for Women in the United States, and British legislation, there is no guarantee that initiatives will be implemented. It is a difficult journey as women attempt to make their mark in the workplace, but soon it may be possible for them to break through the glass ceiling.

Labor, Employment, and Business Practices

Labor policies vary widely among countries around the world. Issues of freedom to work, freedom to organize and engage in collective action, and policies regarding notification and compensation for layoffs are treated differently in different countries. Political, economic, and cultural differences make it difficult to agree on a universal foundation of employment practices. It does not make much sense to standardize compensation packages within an MNC that spans both developed and underdeveloped nations. Elements such as working conditions, expected consecutive work hours, and labor regulations also create challenges in deciding which employment practice is the most appropriate. For example, the low cost of labor entices businesses to look to China; however, workers in China are not well paid, and to meet the demand for output, they often are forced to work 12-hour days, seven days a week. In some cases, children are used for this work. Child labor initially invokes negative associations and is considered an unethical employment practice. The reality is that of the 168 million children age 5–17 working globally in 2016, most are engaged in work to help support their families.[43] In certain countries it is necessary for children to work due to low wages. UNICEF and the World Bank recognize that in some instances, family survival depends on all members working, and that intervention is necessary only when the child's developmental welfare is compromised. There has been some progress in the reduction of child labor. It continues to decline, especially among girls, but only modestly, with the International Labour Organization reporting a 25 percent reduction between 2000 and 2015.[44] There has also been considerable progress in the ratification of ILO standards concerning child labor. Convention 182 (on the worst forms of child labor) has been ratified by 180 countries, with only India and a few Pacific island nations yet to endorse. Convention 138 (on minimum age), however, has found less acceptance and remains yet to be ratified by nearly two dozen countries, including the United States, India, and Australia. Roughly one-quarter of the children in the world live in countries that have not ratified Convention 138.[45]

In early 2010, the issue of relatively low wages paid by Chinese subcontractors made the headlines after a number of suicides by workers at factories run by Foxconn, one of the largest contractors for electronics firms such as Apple, and a strike by workers at a Honda plant. A year later, in May 2011, an explosion at a Foxconn iPad factory killed two employees. In a survey of Foxconn employees, over 43 percent of workers stated that they have seen or been part of a workplace accident.[46] As a result of these controversies, Foxconn, which employs more than 800,000 workers in China making products for companies such as Dell, Hewlett-Packard, and Apple, agreed to raise its base wage by more than 30 percent. Earlier, Honda had raised wages at some of its factories by 24 percent.[47] Additional pressure from Apple in 2012 further improved employee safety and reduced working hours at Foxconn. By July 2013, weekly work hours were limited to just 49 per employee; this reduced overtime hours from 80 per month to just 36. Apple also partnered with the Fair Labor Association to independently audit the safety of the Foxconn plants.[48] Some analysts believe these higher wages, combined with the longstanding shortage and high turnover of factory workers in China, will eventually result in the lowest wage manufacturing moving to other countries, such as Vietnam, while higher value-added production will remain in China.

Ensuring that all contractors along the global supply chain are compliant with company standards is an ongoing issue and one that is not without challenges. This issue came to a head once again when a Bangladesh factory that produced products for Walmart caught fire in November 2012, killing 112 workers. Walmart immediately responded by severing all ties with suppliers who use subcontractors without Walmart's knowledge and began requiring all overseas factories to pass audits before they could be used to produce Walmart products.[49] Yet, a subsequent collapse of a garment factory in Bangladesh in April of 2013 that killed more than 1,000 and a fire not two weeks later, also in Bangladesh, killing eight, underscored the challenges companies face in trying to develop and implement policies for production that is largely outsourced. After a number of NGOs pressed companies to take responsibility for the conditions that allowed for these tragedies, several global apparel firms, including Swedish-based retailer H&M; Inditex, owner of the Zara chain; the Dutch retailer C&A; and British companies Primark and Tesco, agreed to a plan to help pay for fire safety and building improvements in Bangladesh. The Bangladesh government announced that it would improve its labor laws, raise wages, and ease restrictions on forming trade unions.[50] Walmart and Gap chose not to sign on to the European-led agreement out of concerns that they could be subject to litigation. Instead, they initiated a separate agreement with U.S. retail trade groups and a bipartisan think tank. These challenges, and the reforms they bring, should contribute to improved workers' conditions and help prevent similar tragedies.

Environmental Protection and Development

Conservation of natural resources is another area of ethics and social responsibility in which countries around the world differ widely in their values and approach. Many poor, developing countries are more concerned with improving the basic quality of life for their citizens than worrying about endangered species or the quality of air or water. There are several hypotheses regarding the relationship between economic development, as measured by per capita income, and the quality of the natural environment. The most widely accepted thesis is represented in the Environmental Kuznets Curve (EKC), which hypothesizes that the relationship between per capita income and the use of natural resources and/or the emission of wastes has an inverted U-shape. (See Figure 3–1.) According to this specification, at relatively low levels of income, the use of natural resources and/or the emission of wastes increase with income. Beyond some turning point, the use of the natural resources and/or the emission of wastes decline with income. Reasons for this inverted U-shaped relationship are hypothesized to include income-driven changes in (1) the composition of production and/or consumption, (2) the preference for environmental quality, (3) institutions that are needed to internalize externalities, and/or (4) increasing returns to scale associated with pollution abatement. The term

Figure 3–1

The Environmental Kuznets Curve

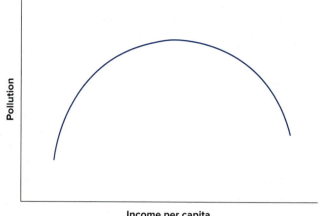

"EKC" is based on its similarity to the time-series pattern of income inequality described by Simon Kuznets in 1955. A 1992 World Bank Development Report made the notion of an EKC popular by suggesting that environmental degradation can be slowed by policies that protect the environment and promote economic development. Subsequent statistical analysis, however, showed that while the relationship might hold in a few cases, it could not be generalized across a wide range of resources and pollutants.[51]

Despite difficulty in achieving international consensus on environmental reform, recent progress holds promise. For two weeks in December 2015, representatives from over 185 countries converged in the suburbs of Paris at the 21st annual United Nations Climate Change Conference. Throughout the conference, representatives debated and drafted a wide-ranging greenhouse gas agreement that aims to drastically reduce global emissions beginning in 2020. On December 12, 2015, the text of the "Paris Agreement" was adopted by all 196 parties at the convention. A summary of some of the agreement's 27 articles is included in Table 3-1.

Table 3–1
Highlights of the Paris Agreement on Climate Policy

Article 2

• Outlines the objectives of the agreement, which includes limiting the increase in the average temperature globally to under 2 degrees Celsius and aiming for just a 1.5 degrees Celsius increase. Also states goals of developing lower greenhouse gas emissions technology and structuring financing to nations so that adaption to the impacts of climate change and lower greenhouse gas emissions technology is implemented.

Article 4

• Affirms that the global peaking of greenhouse gas emissions should be reached as soon as possible to ensure that goals can be reached. The long-term goal is to achieve net zero global emissions by 2070. Each individual country is tasked with determining its own contributions, with developed countries tasked with taking the lead. Smaller, less developed nations are to be assisted by developed nations.

Article 7

• Requires countries to submit reports indicating their strategies for adapting to the effects of climate change.

Article 8

• Provides a method for smaller, more vulnerable countries to mitigate potential financial losses due to climate change.

Article 9

• Requires more developed countries to provide financing to developing countries to meet emissions goals and adapt to the effects of climate change.

Article 13

• Requires all countries to be transparent with their progress towards emissions reduction goals.

Article 14

• Requires that every five years, countries are to update, evaluate, and set new targets based on their progress.

Source: Summarized from the Paris Agreement, https://unfccc.int/.

For the Paris Agreement to officially take effect, ratification of the deal must now take place by at least 55 countries representing at least 55 percent of global emissions. As the two largest emitters of greenhouse gas, China and the United States are critical in reaching the 55 percent emission threshold. The signing of the agreement officially commenced on April 22, 2016, in New York City. If fully ratified, the Paris Agreement will be the largest international agreement on environmental reform since the Kyoto Protocol of 1997.

Despite improvements in environmental protection and ethical business practices, many companies continue to violate laws and/or jeopardize safety and environmental concerns in their operations. This is particularly true in emerging and developing countries, where environmental laws may be reasonably strong but are not as vigorously enforced as in higher income countries. As one example, in April 2016, China's government announced it would investigate a report that nearly 500 students became sick with various ailments, including cancer, at a school built near a recently closed chemical plant in Changzhou.[52] As citizens become more demanding that governments and businesses take action to address environmental pollution, and the media report on these controversies, officials are likely to feel pressure to respond.

■ Globalization and Ethical Obligations of MNCs

All this prompts the question, how much responsibility do MNCs have in changing these practices? Should they adopt the regulations in the country of origin or yield to those in the country of operation? One remedy could be to instill a business code of ethics that extends to all countries, or to create contracts for situations that may arise. The nearby International Management in Action box regarding Volkswagen underscores how, despite a strong code of conduct, VW found itself the subject of numerous ethical problems, which resulted in lawsuits and severely tarnished its reputation.

"Doing the right thing" is not always as simple as it appears. Some years back, Levi Strauss experienced this issue with its suppliers from Bangladesh. Children under the age of 14 were working at two locations, which did not violate the law in Bangladesh but did go against the policy of Levi Strauss. Ultimately, Levi Strauss decided to continue paying the wages of the children and secured a position for them once they reached the age of 14, after their return from schooling.[53] While the level of involvement is hard to standardize, having a basic set of business ethics and appropriately applying it to the culture in which one is managing is a step in the right direction. Managers need to be cautious not to blur the lines of culture in these situations. The Prince of Wales was once quoted as saying, "Business can only succeed in a sustainable environment. Illiterate, poorly trained, poorly housed, resentful communities, deprived of a sense of belonging or of roots, provide a poor workforce and an uncertain market."[54] Businesses face much difficulty in attempting to balance organizational and cultural roots with the advancement of globalization.

One recent phenomenon in response to globalization has been not just to offshore low-cost labor-intensive practices, as described in Chapter 1, but to transfer a large percentage of current employees of all types to foreign locations. The inexpensive labor available through offshore outsourcing in India has aided many institutions, but also has put a strain on some industries, particularly home-based technology services. More than a third of the global IT workforce is now located in India. It is estimated that IBM now bases more than 30 percent of its employees in India and Accenture, a company specializing in management consulting, technology services, and outsourcing, now has more than double the number of employees in India than it has in the United States. With labor costs in India at less than half of those in the United States, companies like Accenture gain a competitive advantage by offering similar low-cost services, but with consulting expertise that is not yet matched by Indian cohorts.[55]

Volkswagen's Challenges with Ethical Business Practices

In the fiercely competitive global automotive industry, the Volkswagen Group (VW) has pursued an ongoing global strategy that emphasizes both centralization and regional adaptation and leverages the range of capabilities from its various brands and their production. VW operates manufacturing facilities in nearly 30 countries, including two joint ventures in China, and sells its cars in over 150 countries. After two decades of sales leadership in Europe, VW reached a significant milestone in its 78-year history when, for the first half of 2015, it surpassed Toyota to become the top automobile producer by sales worldwide. However, celebrations would be short-lived.

In late 2015, VW found itself in a major ethical crisis after numerous independent investigations confirmed that VW's engine software was intentionally bugged to alter a car's performance when the vehicle was undergoing emissions testing. The VW-manufactured diesel engines were programmed to function in such a way that good gas mileage could be achieved during road tests (when emissions were not being tested) and acceptable nitrogen oxide readings were emitted during lab tests (when gas mileage was not being tested). In reality, however, the amount of nitrogen oxide emitted during regular road driving was nearly 40 times greater than what was emitted during testing, far exceeding permissible emissions levels regulated in the United States and Europe. In September 2015, the U.S. Environmental Protection Agency (EPA) formally issued a Notice of Violation to VW. The software modification was installed on nearly 11 million vehicles across the globe, affecting all VW diesel engines manufactured between 2009 and 2015. It has been speculated that over 30 management-level employees participated in or had knowledge of the intentional attempt to cheat on these emissions tests.

Within hours of the issuance of the EPA Notice of Violation, the scandal was receiving worldwide news coverage. Perhaps learning from the experience of other companies entangled in ethical scandals over the last several years, VW was quick to assume full responsibility. A number of key figureheads, including global CEO Martin Winterkorn and American President Michael Horn, resigned. Maintaining transparency, including open testimony before the U.S. Congress, was a key element of VW's approach to rebuilding public trust. "We've totally screwed up," stated former American VW President Horn.

The financial fallout from the scandal has been devastating to VW. After starting the year as the top global automaker, VW slumped in the final few months of 2015, and annual sales declined for the first time in 13 years. The company's stock price dropped by a third over the last several months of 2015. In the third quarter of 2015, VW posted its first quarterly loss in 15 years. VW has set aside over $7 billion to cover costs incurred due to the recall and repair of the vehicles. However, as of mid 2016, Volkswagen still did not have an economical approach to lowering emissions in the affected cars.

In November 2015, the company offered vouchers worth $1,000 to all U.S. affected customers, and in April 2016, Volkswagen gave U.S. customers the option to return their vehicle for a full refund. No compensation package, however, has been extended to those customers outside of the U.S. Fines and associated lawsuits are likely to cost VW even more in the coming years. The EPA has the ability to fine VW $37,500 per car sold in the United States—or about $18 billion. Over 500 lawsuits have already been filed in the United States against VW, with additional pressure due to a pending $46 billion suit filed by the U.S. Department of Justice.

In its 15-page code of conduct, published in the years prior to the emissions scandal, VW emphasizes its commitment to its strong reputation. The trust that the public placed in the VW brand aided in its growth from a small German automaker to a global giant. Now, that reputation appears to be in jeopardy. Will VW be able to recover?

Sources: Volkswagen website, www.vw.com/; Russell Hotten, "Volkswagen: The Scandal Explained," *BBC*, December 10, 2015, www.bbc.com/news/business-34324772.

The transfer of the labor force overseas creates an interesting dynamic in the scope of ethics and corporate responsibility. While most international managers concern themselves with understanding the social culture in which the corporation is enveloped and how that can mesh with the corporate culture, this recent wave involves the extension of an established corporate culture into a new social environment. The difference here is that the individuals being moved offshore are part of a corporate citizenship, meaning that they will identify with the corporation and not necessarily the outside environment; the opposite occurs when the firm moves to another country and seeks to employ local citizens. Accenture proves that it is possible to succeed with such an effort, but as more and more companies follow suit, other questions and concerns may arise. How will the two cultures work together? Will employees adhere to the work schedule of the home or the host country? Will the host country be open or reluctant to an influx of new citizens?

The latter may not be a current concern due to the infrequency of offshoring, but MNCs may face a time when they have to consider more than just survival of the company. One must also bear in mind the effects these choices will have on both cultures.

Reconciling Ethical Differences across Cultures

As noted in the introduction to this section, ethical dilemmas arise from conflicts between ethical standards of a country and business ethics, or the moral code guiding business behavior. Most MNCs seek to adhere to a code of ethical conduct while doing business around the world, yet must make some adjustments to respond to local norms and values. Navigating this natural tension can be challenging. One approach advocated by two prominent business ethicists suggests that there exist implied social contracts that generally govern behavior around the world, some of which are universal or near universal. These "hyper" norms include fundamental principles like respect for human life or abstention from cheating, lying, and violence. Local community norms are respected within the context of such hyper norms when they deviate from one society to another.

This approach, called "Integrative Social Contracts Theory" (ISCT), attempts to navigate a moral position that does not force decision makers to engage exclusively in relativism versus absolutism. It allows substantial latitude for nations and economic communities to develop their unique concepts of fairness but draws the line at flagrant neglect of core human values. It is designed to provide international managers with a framework when confronted with a substantial gap between the apparent moral and ethical values in the country in which the MNC is headquartered and the many countries in which it does business. Although ISCT has been criticized for its inability to provide precise guidance for managers under specific conditions, it nonetheless offers one approach to helping reconcile a fundamental contradiction in international business ethics.[56]

Corporate Social Responsibility and Sustainability

In addition to expectations that they adhere to specific ethical codes and principles, corporations are under increasing pressure to contribute to the societies and communities in which they operate and to adopt more socially responsible business practices throughout their entire range of operations. Corporate social responsibility (CSR) can be defined as the actions of a firm to benefit society beyond the requirements of the law and the direct interests of the firm.[57] It is difficult to provide a list of obligations since the social, economic, and environmental expectations of each company will be based on the desires of the stakeholders. Pressure for greater attention to CSR has emanated from a range of stakeholders, including civil society (the broad societal interests in a given region or country) and from **nongovernmental organizations (NGOs)**. These groups have urged MNCs to be more responsive to the range of social needs in developing countries, including concerns about working conditions in factories or service centers and the environmental impacts of their activities.[58] The increased CSR efforts by businesses appear to be effective in increasing public opinion; more than 50 percent of global respondents to a recent Edelman survey expressed trust in business and government in 2016, reaching a record high (see Figure 3–2).[59]

nongovernmental organizations (NGOs) Private, not-for-profit organizations that seek to serve society's interests by focusing on social, political, and economic issues such as poverty, social justice, education, health, and the environment.

Many MNCs such as Intel, HSBC, Lenovo, TOMS, and others take their CSR commitment seriously (see Brief Integrative Case 1.2 at the end of Part One). These firms have integrated their response to CSR pressures into their core business strategies and operating principles around the world (see the section "Response to Social and Organizational Obligations".

Civil Society, NGOs, MNCs, and Ethical Balance   The emergence of organized civil society and NGOs has dramatically altered the business environment globally and the role of MNCs within it. Although social movements have been part of the political and economic landscape for centuries, the emergence of NGO activism in the United States

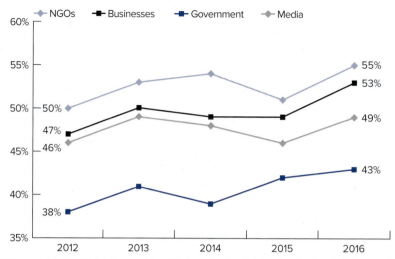

Figure 3–2

Public Trust Reaches Record Highs in 2016

Source: Original graphic by Ben Littell under supervision of Professor Jonathan Doh based on data from *2016 Edelman Trust Barometer*, www.edelman.com/insights/intellectual-property/2016-edelman-trust-barometer/.

during the modern era can be traced to mid-1984, when a range of NGOs, including church and community groups, human rights organizations, and other antiapartheid activists, built strong networks and pressed U.S. cities and states to divest their public pension funds of companies doing business in South Africa. This effort, combined with domestic unrest, international governmental pressures, and capital flight, posed a direct, sustained, and ultimately successful challenge to the white minority rule, resulting in the collapse of apartheid.

Since then, NGOs generally have grown in number, power, and influence. Large global NGOs such as Save the Children, Oxfam, CARE, Amnesty International, World Wildlife Fund, and Conservation International are active in all parts of the world. Their force has been felt in a range of major public policy debates, and NGO activism has been responsible for major changes in corporate behavior and governance. Some observers now regard NGOs as a counterweight to business and global capitalism. NGO criticisms have been especially sharp in relation to the activities of MNCs, such as Nike, Levi's, Chiquita, and others whose sourcing practices in developing countries have been alleged to exploit low-wage workers, take advantage of lax environmental and workplace standards, and otherwise contribute to social and economic problems. Three recent examples illustrate the complex and increasingly important impact of NGOs on MNCs.

In November 2015, on the opening day of the United Nations climate summit in Paris, Morgan Stanley and Wells Fargo announced that they would no longer provide financing to coal-mining companies in both the developed and developing world. Morgan Stanley also stated that it, as a financier, has a responsibility to guide the global community towards a low-carbon economy. This announcement came after several months of aggressive pressure and lobbying by environmental protection groups, including the Rainforest Action Network (RAN). An online petition initiated by RAN drew thousands of signatures.[60] After heavy lobbying from NGOs, in August 2003, the U.S. pharmaceutical industry dropped its opposition to relaxation of intellectual property provisions under the WTO to make generic, low-cost antiviral drugs available to developing countries facing epidemics or other health emergencies.[61] In November 2009, after nearly two years of student campaigning in coordination with the apparel workers, a Honduran workers' union concluded an agreement with Russell Athletics, the apparel manufacturer owned by Fruit of the Loom, that puts all of the workers back to work, provides compensation for lost wages, recognizes the union and agrees to collective bargaining, and provides access for the union to all other Russell apparel plants in Honduras for union organizing drives in which the company will remain neutral. According to a November 18,

2009, press release of United Students Against Sweatshops, this has been an "unprecedented victory for labor rights."[62]

Many NGOs recognize that MNCs can have positive impacts on the countries in which they do business, often adhering to higher standards of social and environmental responsibility than local firms. In fact, MNCs may be in a position to transfer "best practices" in social or environmental actions from their home to host countries' markets. In some instances, MNCs and NGOs collaborate on social and environmental projects and in so doing contribute both to the well-being of communities and to the reputation of the MNC. The emergence of NGOs that seek to promote ethical and socially responsible business practices is beginning to generate substantial changes in corporate management, strategy, and governance.

Response to Social and Organizational Obligations MNCs are increasingly engaged in a range of responses to growing pressures to contribute positively to the social and environmental progress of the communities in which they do business. One response is the agreements and codes of conduct in which MNCs commit to maintain certain standards in their domestic and global operations. These agreements, which include the U.N. Global Compact (see Table 3–2), the Global Reporting Initiative, the social accountability "SA8000" standards, and the ISO 14000 environmental quality standards, provide some assurances that when MNCs do business around the world, they will maintain a minimum level of social and environmental standards in the workplaces and communities in which they operate.[63,64] These codes help offset the real or perceived concern that companies move jobs to avoid higher labor or environmental standards in their home markets. They may also contribute to the raising of standards in the developing world by "exporting" higher standards to local firms in those countries.

Another interesting trend among businesses and NGOs is the movement toward increasing the availability of "fairly traded" products. Beginning with coffee and moving to chocolate, fruits, and other agricultural products, **fair trade** is an organized social movement and market-based approach that aims to help producers in developing countries obtain better trading conditions and promote sustainability. See the A Closer Look box for a discussion of fair trade systems and products.

fair trade
An organized social movement and market-based approach that aims to help producers in developing countries obtain better trading conditions and promote sustainability.

Table 3–2
Principles of the Global Compact

Human Rights

Principle 1: Support and respect the protection of international human rights within their sphere of influence.

Principle 2: Make sure their own corporations are not complicit in human rights abuses.

Labor

Principle 3: Freedom of association and the effective recognition of the right to collective bargaining.

Principle 4: The elimination of all forms of forced and compulsory labor.

Principle 5: The effective abolition of child labor.

Principle 6: The elimination of discrimination with respect to employment and occupation.

Environment

Principle 7: Support a precautionary approach to environmental challenges.

Principle 8: Undertake initiatives to promote greater environmental responsibility.

Principle 9: Encourage the development and diffusion of environmentally friendly technologies.

Anticorruption

Principle 10: Business should work against all forms of corruption, including extortion and bribery.

Source: From *The Ten Principles of the UN Global Compact,* by The United Nations, © 2016 United Nations. Reprinted with the permission of the United Nations.

Fair Trade in the U.S.: Fair trade USA

Fair Trade helps farming families across Latin America, Africa, and Asia to improve the quality of life in their communities. Fair Trade certification empowers farmers and farm workers to lift themselves out of poverty by investing in their farms and communities, protecting the environment, and developing the business skills necessary to compete in the global marketplace. Fair Trade is much more than a fair price. Fair Trade principles include

- **Fair price:** Democratically organized farmer groups receive a guaranteed minimum floor price and an additional premium for certified organic products. Farmer organizations are also eligible for preharvest credit.

- **Fair labor conditions:** Workers on Fair Trade farms enjoy freedom of association, safe working conditions, and living wages. Forced child labor is strictly prohibited.

- **Direct trade:** With Fair Trade, importers purchase from Fair Trade producer groups as directly as possible, eliminating unnecessary middlemen and empowering farmers to develop the business capacity necessary to compete in the global marketplace.

- **Democratic and transparent organizations:** Fair Trade farmers and farm workers decide democratically how to invest Fair Trade revenues.

- **Community development:** Fair Trade farmers and farm workers invest Fair Trade premiums in social and business development projects like scholarship programs, quality improvement training, and organic certification.

- **Environmental sustainability:** Harmful agrochemicals and GMOs are strictly prohibited in favor of environmentally sustainable farming methods that protect farmers' health and preserve valuable ecosystems for future generations.

Fair Trade USA, a nonprofit organization, is the only independent, third-party certifier of Fair Trade products in the U.S. and one of 20 members of Fairtrade Labeling Organizations International (FLO). Fair Trade USA's rigorous audit system, which tracks products from farm to finished product, verifies industry compliance with Fair Trade criteria. Fair Trade USA allows U.S. companies to display the Fair Trade Certified label on products that meet strict Fair Trade standards. Fair Trade certification is currently available in the U.S. for coffee, tea and herbs, cocoa and chocolate, fresh fruit, sugar, rice, and vanilla.

---

sustainability
Development that meets humanity's needs without harming future generations.

Sustainability In the boardroom, the term **sustainability** may first be associated with financial investments or the hope of steadily increasing profits, but for a growing number of companies, this term means the same to them as it does to an environmental conservationist. Partially this is due to corporations recognizing that dwindling resources will eventually halt productivity, but the World Economic Forum in Davos, Switzerland, has also played a part in bringing awareness to this timely subject. In a report published in 2012, the World Economic Forum discussed the challenges created by the speed of business growth. With half as many people living in poverty as just 30 years ago, the consumer class is growing rapidly in emerging markets. The report focused on how sustainable consumption of energy and resources can be used to ease the problems brought about from this need for rapid business scaling.[65]

While the United States has the Environmental Protection Agency to provide information about and enforce environmental laws,[66] the United Nations also has a division dedicated to the education, promotion, facilitation, and advocacy of sustainable practices and environmentally sound concerns called the United Nations Environment Programme (UNEP).[67] The degree to which global awareness and concern are rising extends beyond laws and regulations, as corporations are now taking strides to be leaders in this "green" movement.

Walmart, one of the most well-known and pervasive global retailers, has begun to recognize the numerous benefits of the adage, "Think globally, act locally." Walmart has set three broad corporate goals in regards to sustainability: to use 100 percent renewable energy, to achieve zero-waste, and to sell products that are sustainable for the environment and people.[68] Working with environmentalists, it discovered that many changes in production and supply chain practices could reduce waste and pollution and therefore reduce costs. By cutting back on packaging, Walmart saves an estimated $2.4 million a year, 3,800 trees, and 1 million barrels of oil. Over 80,000 suppliers compete to put their products on Walmart shelves, which means that this company has a strong influence on how manufacturers do business.[69,70] To encourage sustainability from these suppliers, Walmart created a "Sustainability Hub" website to share standards and encourage innovation.[71] And Walmart's efforts are truly global. In line with the three corporate goals, the company is buying solar and wind power in Mexico, sourcing local food in China and India, and analyzing the life-cycle impact of consumer products in Brazil. Alleviating hunger has become a goal of Walmart's charitable efforts, and so with CARE it is backing education, job-training, and entrepreneurial programs for women in Peru, Bangladesh, and India. Walmart is attempting to change global standards as it offers higher prices to coffee growers in Brazil and increases pressures on the factory owners in China to reduce energy and fuel costs.[72] Although Walmart has faced some setbacks in its global CSR efforts, it continues to respond to pressures for social responsibility and sustainability (see In-Depth Integrated Case 2.2 at the end of Part Two).

GE has pursued an aggressive initiative to integrate environmental sustainability with its business goals through the "ecomagination" program. Management styles again are changing as agendas are refocused on not only seeing the present but also looking to the future of human needs and the environment. Ecomagination is a GE strategic initiative to use innovation to improve energy efficiency across the globe. By meeting the demand for "green" products and services, GE is generating value for shareholders as well as promoting environmental sustainability. At a GE Hitachi Nuclear Energy power plant in North Carolina, a new wastewater system "has reduced water usage by 25 million gallons annually, avoiding nearly 80 tons per year of CO_2 emissions and realizing annual savings of $160,000 in water and energy costs." GE's ecomagination ZeeWeed® membrane bioreactor (MBR) technology transforms up to 65,000 gallons per day of wastewater into treated water that can be used in the facility's cooling towers. GE Jenbacher engines capture gas from various fuel sources, even garbage, to create power. Jenbacher engines are at the core of a Mexican landfill gas-to-energy project, which President Felipe Calderón called "a model renewable energy project" for Latin America. This project's power supports "Monterrey's light-rail system during the day and city street lights at night."

In addition, GE's Flight Management System (FMS) for Boeing 737 planes has enabled airlines to lower fuel costs and reduce emissions. According to a GE Ecomagination Annual Report, "The FMS enables pilots to determine, while maintaining a highly efficient cruise altitude, the exact point where the throttle can be reduced to flight idle while allowing the aircraft to arrive precisely at the required runway approach point without the need for throttle increases."[73] SAS Scandinavian Airlines estimates that FMS will save the airline $10 million annually. According to CEO Jeffrey R. Immelt and vice president of Ecomagination Steven M. Fludder, "Ecomagination is playing a role in boosting economic recovery, supporting the jobs of the future, improving the environmental impact of our customers' (and our own) operations, furthering energy independence, and fostering innovation and growth in profitable environmental solutions."[74]

Corporate Governance

The recent global, ethical, and governance scandals have placed corporations under intense scrutiny regarding their oversight and accountability. Adelphia, Arthur Andersen, Enron, Olympus, HSBC, Tyco, and Barclays are just a few of the dozens of companies that have been found to engage in inappropriate and often illegal activities related to governance. In addition, a number of financial services firms, including Credit Suisse, Deutsche Bank, Lehman Brothers, Citigroup, and many others, have been found to have engaged in inappropriate trading or other activities. Corporate governance is increasingly high on the agenda for directors, investors, and governments alike in the wake of financial collapses and corporate scandals in recent years. The collapses and scandals have not been limited to a single country, or even a single continent, but have been a global phenomenon.

corporate governance
The system by which business corporations are directed and controlled.

Corporate governance can be defined as the system by which business corporations are directed and controlled.[75] The corporate governance structure specifies the distribution of rights and responsibilities among different participants in the corporation—such as the board, managers, shareholders, and other stakeholders—and spells out the rules and procedures for making decisions on corporate affairs. By doing this, it also provides the structure through which the company objectives are set and the means of attaining those objectives and monitoring performance.

Governance rules and regulations differ among countries and regions around the world. For example, the UK and U.S. systems have been termed "outsider" systems because of dispersed ownership of corporate equity among a large number of outside investors. Historically, although institutional investor ownership was predominant, institutions generally did not hold large shares in any given company; hence, they had limited direct control.[76] In contrast, in an insider system, such as that in many continental European countries, ownership tends to be much more concentrated, with shares often being owned by holding companies, families, or banks. In addition, differences in legal systems, as described in Chapter 2, also affect shareholders' and other stakeholders' rights and, in turn, the responsiveness and accountability of corporate managers to these constituencies. Notwithstanding recent scandals, in general, North American and European systems are considered comparatively responsive to shareholders and other stakeholders. In regions with less well-developed legal and institutional protections and poor property rights, such as some countries in Asia, Latin America, and Africa, forms of "crony capitalism" may emerge in which weak corporate governance and government interference can lead to poor performance, risky financing patterns, and macroeconomic crises.

Corporate governance will undoubtedly remain high on the agenda of governments, investors, NGOs, and corporations in the coming years, as pressure for accountability and responsiveness continues to increase.

Corruption

As noted in Chapter 2, government corruption is a pervasive element in the international business environment. Recently publicized scandals in Brazil, China, Costa Rica, Egypt, Pakistan, Russia, South Africa, and elsewhere underscore the extent of corruption globally, especially in the developing world. However, a number of initiatives have been taken by governments and companies to begin to stem the tide of corruption.[77,78]

The Foreign Corrupt Practices Act (FCPA) makes it illegal for U.S. companies and their managers to attempt to influence foreign officials through personal payments or political contributions. Prior to passage of the FCPA, some American multinationals had engaged in this practice, but realizing that their stockholders were unlikely to approve of these tactics, the firms typically disguised the payments as entertainment expenses, consulting fees, and so on. Not only does the FCPA prohibit these activities, but the U.S. Internal Revenue Service also continually audits the books of MNCs. Those firms that take deductions for such illegal activities are subject to high financial penalties, and individuals who are involved can even end up going to prison. Strict enforcement of the FCPA has been applauded by many people, but some critics wonder if such a strong stance has hurt the competitive ability of American MNCs. On the positive side, many U.S. multinationals have now increased the amount of business in countries where they used to pay bribes. Additionally, many institutional investors in the United States have made it clear that they will not buy stock in companies that engage in unethical practices and will sell their holdings in such firms. Given that these institutions have hundreds of billions of dollars invested, senior-level management must be responsive to their needs.

Looking at the effect of the FCPA on U.S. multinationals, it appears that the law has had far more of a positive effect than a negative one. Given the growth of American MNCs in recent years, it seems fair to conclude that bribes are not a basic part of business in many countries, for when multinationals stopped this activity, they were still able to sell in that particular market. On the other hand, this does not mean that bribery and corruption are a thing of the past.

Indeed bribery continues to be a problem for MNCs around the world. In fact, recent scandals at ALSTOM, BAE, Daimler, Halliburton, Siemens, Walmart, and many other multinationals underscore the reality that executives continue to participate in bribery and corruption. Although Siemens paid a record fine, U.S. authorities are still concerned about enforcement of corruption laws in other countries.[79] Figure 3–3 gives the latest corruption index of countries around the world. Notice that the United States ranks 16th in this independent analysis. These rankings fluctuate somewhat from year to year. Factors that appear to contribute to these fluctuations include changes in government or political party in power, economic crises, and crackdowns in individual countries.

In complying with the provisions of the FCPA, U.S. firms must be aware of changes in the law that make FCPA violators subject to Federal Sentencing Guidelines. The origin of this law and the guidelines that followed can be traced to two Lockheed Corporation executives who were found guilty of paying a $1 million bribe to a member of the Egyptian parliament in order to secure the sale of aircraft to the Egyptian military. One of the executives was sentenced to probation and fined $20,000 and the other, who initially fled prosecution, was fined $125,000 and sentenced to 18 months in prison.[80]

Another development that promises to give teeth to "antibribing" legislation is the recent formal agreement by a host of industrialized nations to outlaw the practice of bribing foreign government officials. The treaty, which initially included 29 nations that belong to the Organization for Economic Cooperation and Development (OECD), marked a victory for the United States, which outlawed foreign bribery two decades previously but had not been able to persuade other countries to follow its lead. As a result, American firms had long complained that they lost billions of dollars in contracts each year to rivals that bribed their way to success.[81]

This treaty does not outlaw most payments to political party leaders. In fact, the treaty provisions are much narrower than U.S. negotiators wanted, and there undoubtedly will be ongoing pressure from the American government to expand the scope and coverage of the agreement. For the moment, however, it is a step in the direction of a more ethical and level playing field in global business. Additionally, in summing up the impact and value of the treaty, one observer noted: "For their part, business executives say the treaty . . . reflects growing support for antibribery initiatives among corporations in Europe and Japan that have openly opposed the idea. Some of Europe's leading industrial corporations, including a few that have been embroiled in recent allegations of bribery, have spoken out in favor of tougher measures and on the increasingly corrosive effect of corruption."[82]

In addition to the 34 members of the OECD, a number of developing countries, including Argentina, Brazil, Bulgaria, and South Africa, have signed on to the OECD agreement. Latin American countries have established the Organization of American States (OAS) Inter-American Convention Against Corruption, which entered into force in March 1997, and more than 25 Western Hemisphere countries are signatories to the convention, including Argentina, Brazil, Chile, Mexico, and the United States. As a way to prevent the shifting of corrupt practices to suppliers and intermediaries, the Transparent Agents Against Contracting Entities (TRACE) standard was developed after a review of the practices of 34 companies. It applies to business intermediaries, including sales agents, consultants, suppliers, resellers, subcontractors, franchisees, and joint-venture partners, so that final producers, distributors, and customers can be confident that no party within a supply chain has participated in corruption.

Both governments and companies have made important steps in their efforts to stem the spread of corruption, but much more needs to be done in order to reduce the impact of corruption on companies and the broader societies in which they operate.[83]

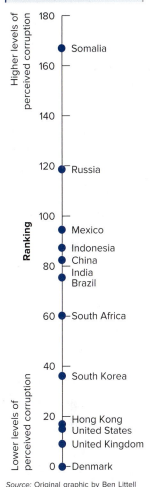

Figure 3–3

Transparency International Corruption Perceptions Index Ratings, Selected Countries, 2016

Source: Original graphic by Ben Littell under supervision of Jonathan Doh based on data from *Transparency International Corruption Perceptions Index Ratings 2016.*

International Assistance

In addition to government- and corporate-sponsored ethics and social responsibility practices, governments and corporations are increasingly collaborating to provide assistance to communities around the world through global partnerships. This assistance is particularly important for those parts of the world that have not fully benefited from globalization and economic integration. Using a cost-benefit analysis of where investments would have the greatest impact, a recent study identified the top priorities around the world for development assistance. The results of this analysis are presented in Table 3–3. Fighting malnutrition, controlling malaria, and immunizing children are shown to be the best investments. Governments, international institutions, and corporations are involved in several ongoing efforts to address some of these problems.

At a United Nations summit in September 2015, world leaders placed development at the heart of the global agenda by adopting the Sustainable Development Goals (see Table 3–4). The seventeen Sustainable Development Goals constitute an ambitious agenda to significantly improve the human condition by 2030. The goals set clear targets for reducing poverty, hunger, disease, and inequalities, while protecting the environment and climate. For each goal, targets and indicators have been defined and are used to track the progress in meeting the goals.[84]

A more specific initiative is the Global Fund to Fight AIDS, Tuberculosis and Malaria, which was established in 2001. Through the end of 2015, the Global Fund had committed over US$33 billion in grants to over 151 countries.[85]

Through these and other efforts, MNCs, governments, and international organizations are providing a range of resources to communities around the world to assist them as they respond to the challenges of globalization and development. International managers will increasingly be called upon to support and contribute to these initiatives.

Table 3–3
Copenhagen Consensus Investment Priorities

Ranking	Investment
1	Bundled micronutrient interventions to fight hunger and improve education
2	Expanding the subsidy for malaria combination treatment
3	Expanded childhood immunization coverage
4	Deworming of schoolchildren, to improve educational and health outcomes
5	Expanding tuberculosis treatment
6	R&D to increase yield enhancements, to decrease hunger, fight biodiversity destruction, and lessen the effects of climate change
7	Investing in effective early warning systems to protect populations against natural disaster
8	Strengthening surgical capacity
9	Hepatitis B immunization
10	Using low-cost drugs in the case of acute heart attacks in poorer nations (these are already available in developed countries)
11	Salt reduction campaign to reduce chronic disease
12	Geo-engineering R&D into the feasibility of solar radiation management
13	Conditional cash transfers for school attendance
14	Accelerated HIV vaccine R&D
15	Extended field trial of information campaigns on the benefits from schooling
16	Borehole and public hand pump intervention

Source: Copenhagen Consensus 2012.

Table 3–4
The U.N. Sustainable Development Goals

Goal 1: Poverty—End poverty in all its forms everywhere.

Goal 2: Food—End hunger, achieve food security and improved nutrition, and promote sustainable agriculture.

Goal 3: Health—Ensure healthy lives and promote well-being for all at all ages.

Goal 4: Education—Ensure inclusive and equitable quality education and promote lifelong learning opportunities for all.

Goal 5: Women—Achieve gender equality and empower all women and girls.

Goal 6: Water—Ensure availability and sustainable management of water and sanitation for all.

Goal 7: Energy—Ensure access to affordable, reliable, sustainable, and modern energy for all.

Goal 8: Economy—Promote sustained, inclusive, and sustainable economic growth; full and productive employment; and decent work for all.

Goal 9: Infrastructure—Build resilient infrastructure, promote inclusive and sustainable industrialization, and foster innovation.

Goal 10: Inequality—Reduce inequality within and among countries.

Goal 11: Habitation—Make cities and human settlements inclusive, safe, resilient, and sustainable.

Goal 12: Consumption—Ensure sustainable consumption and production patterns.

Goal 13: Climate—Take urgent action to combat climate change and its impacts.

Goal 14: Marine ecosystems—Conserve and sustainably use the oceans, seas, and marine resources for sustainable development.

Goal 15: Ecosystems—Protect, restore, and promote sustainable use of terrestrial ecosystems; sustainably manage forests; combat desertification; halt and reverse land degradation; and halt biodiversity loss.

Goal 16: Institutions—Promote peaceful and inclusive societies for sustainable development; provide access to justice for all; and build effective, accountable, and inclusive institutions at all levels.

Goal 17: Sustainability—Strengthen the means of implementation and revitalize the global partnership for sustainable development

Source: www.un.org/sustainabledevelopment/sustainable-development-goals/.

The World of International Management—Revisited

The World of International Management feature that opened this chapter outlines how three companies have sought to incorporate social responsibility and sustainability into their business strategy and operations. In each case, the companies have responded to changes in the external environment and sought to capitalize on increasing interest in and support of sustainability in business. This interest has spread around the globe such that both developed and developing countries and their companies are increasingly committed to a sustainable future.

In this chapter we focused on ethics and social responsibility in global business activities, including the role of governments, MNCs, and NGOs in advancing greater ethical and socially responsible behavior. MNCs' new focus on environmental sustainability and "doing well by doing good" is an important dimension of this broad trend.

Global ethical and governance scandals have rocked the financial markets and implicated dozens of individual companies. New corporate ethics guidelines passed in the United States have forced many MNCs to take a look at their own internal ethical practices and make changes accordingly. Lawmakers in Europe and Asia have also made adjustments in rules over corporate financial disclosure. The continuing trend toward globalization and free trade appears to be encouraging development of a set of global ethical, social responsibility, and anticorruption standards. This may actually help firms cut compliance costs as they realize that economies have common global frameworks.

Having read the chapter, answer the following questions: (1) Do governments and companies in developed countries have an ethical responsibility to contribute to economic growth and social development in developing countries? (2) Are governments, companies, or NGOs best equipped to provide this assistance? How might collaboration among these sectors provide a comprehensive approach? (3) Do corporations have a responsibility to use their "best" ethics and social responsibility practices when they do business in other countries, even if those countries' practices are different? (4) How can companies leverage their ethical reputation and social and environmental responsibility to improve business performance?

SUMMARY OF KEY POINTS

1. Ethics is the study of morality and standards of conduct. It is important in the study of international management because ethical behavior often varies from one country to another. Ethics manifests itself in the ways societies and companies address issues such as employment conditions, human rights, and corruption. A danger in international management is the ethical relativism trap—"When in Rome, do as the Romans do."

2. During the years ahead, multinationals likely will become more concerned about being socially responsible. NGOs are forcing the issue. Countries are passing laws to regulate ethical practices and governance rules for MNCs. MNCs are being more proactive (often because they realize it makes good business sense) in making social contributions in the regions in which they operate and in developing codes of conduct to govern ethics and social responsibility. One area in which companies have been especially active is in pursuing strategies that blend environmental sustainability and business objectives.

3. MNCs—in conjunction with governments and NGOs—are also contributing to international development assistance and working to ensure that corporate governance practices are sound and effective.

KEY TERMS

corporate governance, *90*

corporate social responsibility (CSR), *77*

ethics, *77*

fair trade, *87*

nongovernmental organizations (NGOs), *85*

sustainability, *88*

REVIEW AND DISCUSSION QUESTIONS

1. How might different ethical philosophies influence how managers make decisions when it comes to offshoring of jobs?

2. What lessons can U.S. multinationals learn from the bribery and corruption scandals in recent years, such as those affecting contractors doing business in Iraq (Halliburton), as well as large MNCs such as Siemens, HP, and others? Discuss two.

3. In recent years, rules have tightened such that those who work for the U.S. government in trade negotiations are now restricted from working for lobbyists for foreign firms. Is this a good idea? Why or why not?

4. What are some strategies for overcoming the impact of counterfeiting? Which strategies work best for discretionary (for instance, movies) versus nondiscretionary (pharmaceutical) goods?

5. Why are MNCs getting involved in corporate social responsibility and sustainable business practice? Are they displaying a sense of social responsibility, or is this merely a matter of good business, or both? Defend your answer.

ENDNOTES

1. "Becoming a Responsible Company," *Patagonia. com*, www.patagonia.com/responsible-company.html.

2. "Patagonia Mission Statement: Our Reason for Being," *Patagonia.com.* www.patagonia.com/company-info.html.

3. "Becoming a Responsible Company."

4. Ibid.

5. "Corporate Responsibility: Promoting Fair Labor Practices and Safe Working Conditions throughout Patagonia's Supply Chain," *Patagonia.com,* www.patagonia.com/corporate-responsibility.html.

6. Ibid.

7. "Becoming a Responsible Company."

8. "About us," *1% for the Planet*, http://onepercentfortheplanet.org/about/.

9. "Supply Chain: The Footprint Chronicles: 20 Years of Organic Cotton," *Patagonia.com*, www.patagonia.com/20-years-of-organic-cotton.html.

10. "About Us," *Nestlé*, www.nestle.com/aboutus (last visited January 30, 2016).

11. "Environmental Sustainability," *Nestlé*, www.nestle.com/csv/environmental-sustainability (last visited January 30, 2016).

12. Ibid.

13. Ibid.

14. Brian Dumaine, "Is Apple 'Greener' Than Starbucks?" *Fortune*, June 24, 2014, http://fortune.com/2014/06/24/50-best-global-green-brands-2014/.

15. "About Tesla," *Tesla Motors*, www.teslamotors.com/about.

16. "Features and Specs," *Tesla Motors,* http://maben.homeip.net/static/auto../tesla/Tesla%20roadster%20specifications%201.pdf.

17. "Model S: Features and Specs," *Tesla Motors*, www.teslamotors.com/models/features#/performance.

18. Joe Romm, "Tesla's Model 3 Is Already Shattering Expectations," *Climate Progress*, April 6, 2016, http://thinkprogress.org/climate/2016/04/06/3766982/next-apple-tesla-model-3-presales/.

19. "Panasonic, Tesla Agree to Partnership for US Car Battery Plant," *Nikkei Asian Review*, July 29, 2014, http://asia.nikkei.com/Business/Deals/Panasonic-Tesla-agree-to-partnership-for-US-car-battery-plant.

20. "Mercedes Electric Car by Tesla Test Drive–Video Tesla Mercedes A Class," *The Daily Green*, September 3, 2010.

21. Steve Hanley, "Mercedes Is Saying Goodbye to Tesla," *GAS2*, August 21, 2015, http://gas2.org/2015/08/21/mercedes-is-saying-goodbye-to-tesla/.

22. Chuck Squatriglia, "Tesla Motors Joins Daimler on a Smart EV | Autopia," *Wired.com*, January 13, 2009, www.wired.com/autopia/2009/01/tesla-motors-jo/.

23. Tori Tellem, "2012 Toyota RAV4-EV: Take Two," *The New York Times*, November 17, 2011.

24. Tesla Motors, "Tesla Initiates Voluntary Recall after Single Customer Incident," press release, October 1, 2010, www.teslamotors.com/about/press/releases/tesla-initiates-voluntary-recall-after-single-customer-incident.

25. Suzanne Ashe, "Tesla Motors Recalls Electric Roadster," *CNET*, May 28, 2009, http://reviews.cnet.com/8301-13746_7-10251758-48.html.

26. John M. Broder, "Stalled Out on Tesla's Electric Highway," *The New York Times*, February 8, 2013, www.nytimes.com/2013/02/10/automobiles/stalled-on-the-ev-highway.html.

27. Paul Chesser, "Tesla CEO Elon Musk Fights Perceptions as Stock Drops," *NLPC.org*, February 26, 2013, http://nlpc.org/stories/2013/02/25/tesla-ceo-elon-musk-fights-perceptions-stock-drops.

28. John Lippert, "Will Tesla Ever Make Money?" *Bloomberg Markets*, March 4, 2015, www.bloomberg.com/news/articles/2015-03-04/as-tesla-gears-up-for-suv-investors-ask-where-the-profits-are.

29. Ibid.

30. Kristen Scholer and Lee Spears, "Tesla Posts Second-Biggest Rally for 2010 U.S. IPO," *Bloomberg Businessweek*, June 29, 2010.

31. Thomas Donaldson, *The Ethics of International Business* (New York: Oxford University Press, 1989).

32. I. Kant, *Fundamental Principles of the Metaphysics of Morals*, trans. Thomas K. Abbott (New York: Macmillan, 1949 [1785]), p. 18.

33. Ibid.

34. Aristotle, *Nicomachean Ethics*, trans. Martin Ostwald New York: Macmillan, 1962, p. 153.

35. W. Frankena, *Ethics*, 2nd ed. (Engelwood Cliffs, NJ: Prentice Hall, 1973).

36. J. Bentham, *The Principles of Morals and Legislation* (Amherst, NY: Prometheus Books, 1988 [1789]),

37. J. S. Mill, *Utilitarianism* (Indianapolis: Bobbs-Merrill, 1957 [1861]).

38. R. J. Vincent, *Human Rights and International Relations* (New York: Cambridge University Press, 1986).

39. Vladimir Kovalev, "EU Presses Russia on Human Trafficking,"*BusinessWeek,* February 23, 2007, www.bloomberg.com/news/articles/2007-02-23/eu-presses-russia-on-human-traffickingbusinessweek-business-news-stock-market-and-financial-advice.

40. Andrew Pollack, "In Japan, It's See No Evil; Have No Harassment," *The New York Times*, May 7, 1996, p. C5.

41. Howard W. French, "Diploma at Hand, Japanese Women Find Glass Ceiling Reinforced with Iron," *The New York Times*, January 1, 2001, p. A4.

42. Grant Thornton, "Women in Business: The Path to Leadership," *Grant Thornton International Business Report 2015*, www.grantthornton.global/globalassets/1.-member-firms/global/insights/ibr-charts/ibr2015_wib_report_final.pdf.

43. "Child Labour," *International Labour Organization* (2015), http://www.ilo.org/global/topics/child-labour/lang--en/index.htm.

44. Ibid.

45. "C138—Minimum Age Convention, 1973 (No. 138): Countries That Have Not Ratified This Convention," *International Labour Organization* (2015), www.ilo.org/dyn/normlex/en/f?p=NORMLEXPUB:11310:0::NO:11310:P11310_INSTRUMENT_ID:312283:NO.

46. Mikey Campbell, "Foxconn Promises to Fix a Multitude of Violations Found by FLA Audit," *Apple Insider*, March 29, 2012, http://appleinsider.com/articles/12/03/29/foxconn_promises_to_fix_violations_found_by_fla_audit.html.

47. David Barboza, "After Spate of Suicides, Technology Firm in China Raises Workers' Salaries," *The New York Times*, June 3, 2010, p. B3.

48. Campbell, "Foxconn Promises to Fix a Multitude of Violations Found by FLA Audit."

49. Shelly Banjo, "Wal-Mart Toughens Supplier Policies," *The Wall Street Journal*, January 21, 2013. http://online.wsj.com/article/SB10001424127887323301104578256183164905720.html.

50. Steven Greenhouse and Jim Yardley, "Global Retailers Join Safety Plan for Bangladesh," *The New York Times*, May 14, 2013, p. A1.

51. David Stern, "The Rise and Fall of the Environmental Kuznets Curve," *World Development* 32, no. 8 (2004), pp. 1419–1439.

52. Gerry Shih, "School in China Near Closed Plants Has 500 Sick Kids," *U.S. News and World Report*, April 18, 2016, www.usnews.com/news/articles/2016-04-18/changzhou-china-school-has-500-sick-kids-due-to-toxins-report-says.

53. Ron Duska and Nicholas M. Rongione, *Ethics and Corporate Responsibility: Theory, Cases and Dilemmas* (New York: Thomas Custom Publishing, 2003).

54. Paul M. Minus, *The Ethics of Business in a Global Economy* (Boston: Kluwer Academic Publishers, 1993).

55. Shilpa Phadnis and Sujit John, "Top Global IT Firms Have More Staff in India Than Home Nations," *The Times of India*, November 6, 2013, http://timesofindia.indiatimes.com/tech/jobs/Top-global-IT-firms-have-more-staff-in-India-than-home-nations/articleshow/25280494.cms.

56. Thomas Donaldson and Thomas W. Dunfee, *Ties That Bind: A Social Contracts Approach to Business Ethics* (Cambridge, MA: Harvard Business Press, 1999).

57. Abagail McWilliams and Donald Siegel, "Corporate Social Responsibility: A Theory of the Firm Perspective," *Academy of Management Review* 26, no. 1 (2001), pp. 117–127.

58. "Non-governmental Organizations and Business: Living with the Enemy," *The Economist*, August 9, 2002, pp. 49–50.

59. "2016 Edelman Trust Barometer: Annual Global Study," *Edelman* (2016), www.edelman.com/insights/intellectual-property/2016-edelman-trust-barometer/.

60. Blair FitzGibbon, "Morgan Stanley and Wells Fargo Cut Coal Financing, Join Growing Movement by Banks in U.S. and Europe," *RAN* press release, November 30, 2015, www.ran.org/morgan_stanley_and_wells_fargo_cut_coal_financing.

61. "WTO to Allow Access to Cheap Drug Treatments," *Los Angeles Times*, August 31, 2003, p. A4.

62. "USAS Press Release on Jerzees de Honduras Victory," *USAS*, November 18, 2009, http://usas.org/2009/11/18/usas-press-release-on-jerzees-de-honduras-victory/.

63. Jonathan P. Doh and Terrence R. Guay, "Globalization and Corporate Social Responsibility: How Nongovernmental Organizations Influence Labor and Environmental Codes of Conduct," *Management International Review* 44, no. 3 (2004), pp. 7–30.

64. Petra Christmann and Glen Taylor, "Globalization and the Environment: Strategies for International Voluntary Environmental Initiatives," *Academy of Management Executive* 16, no. 30 (2002), pp. 121–135.

65. *More with Less: Scaling Sustainable Consumption and Resource Efficiency* (Geneva: World Economic Forum, 2012).

66. For more information, visit www.epa.gov.

67. For more information regarding the role of the UNEP, visit www.unep.org.

68. "Sustainability," *Walmart*, http://corporate.walmart.com/global-responsibility/sustainability/.

69. Marc Gunther, "The Green Machine," *Fortune*, August 7, 2006, pp. 42–57.

70. Marc Gunther, "Wal-Mart: Still the Green Giant," May 19, 2010, www.marcgunther.com/2010/05/19/walmart-still-the-green-giant/.

71. "SustainabilityHUB," *Walmart*, www.walmartsustainabilityhub.com/.

72. Gunther, "The Green Machine."

73. GE Ecomagination, *2008 Ecomagination Annual Report*, p. 29, www.ge.com/about-us/ecomagination.

74. Ibid., p. 3.

75. Organization for Economic Cooperation and Development, *Corporate Governance: A Survey of OECD Countries* (Paris: OECD, 2003).

76. Stijn Claessens and Joseph P. H. Fan, "Corporate Governance in Asia: A Survey," *International Review of Finance* 3, no. 2 (2002), pp. 71–103.

77. Bob Davis, "The Economy: U.S. Nears Pact on Corruption Treaty," *The Wall Street Journal*, August 13, 2003, p. A2.

78. See also Jonathan P. Doh, Peter Rodriguez, Klaus Uhlenbruck, Jamie Collins, and Lorraine Eden, "Coping with Corruption in Foreign Markets," *Academy of Management Executive* 17, no. 3 (2003), pp. 114–127.

79. Ken Stier, "Too Big to Be Nailed," *Fortune*, April 19, 2001, http://archive.fortune.com/2010/04/19/news/companies/hewlett_packard_bribery.fortune/index.htm.

80. Tipton F. McCubbins, "Somebody Kicked the Sleeping Dog—New Bite in the Foreign Corrupt Practices Act," *Business Horizons*, January–February 2001, p. 27.

81. Greg Steinmetz, "U.S. Firms Are among Least Likely to Pay Bribes Abroad, Survey Finds," *The Wall Street Journal*, August 25, 1997, p. 5.

82. Edmund L. Andrews, "29 Nations Agree to Outlaw Bribing Foreign Officials," *The New York Times*, November 21, 1997, p. C2.

83. "Special Report: The Short Arm of the Law—Bribery and Business," *The Economist*, March 2, 2002, p. 85.

84. "Sustainable Development Goals," *United Nations*, www.un.org/sustainabledevelopment/sustainable-development-goals/.

85. "Financials," *The Global Fund*, www.theglobalfund.org/en/financials/ (last visited February 14, 2016).

86. CIA, "Cuba," *The World Factbook* (2016), https://www.cia.gov/library/publications/the-world-factbook/geos/cu.html.

87. Ibid.

88. Ibid.

89. Ibid.

90. Heritage Foundation, "Cuba," *Index of Economic Freedom* (2016), http://www.heritage.org/index/country/cuba.

91. Miguel Heft, "Why Airbnb Thinks Cuba Can Become a Case Study," *Forbes*, September 6, 2015, www.forbes.com/sites/miguelhelft/2015/09/06/inside-airbnbs-cuba/#42de19b7c3ec.

Cuba

Cuba is an island nation located between the Atlantic Ocean and the Caribbean Sea. The country is positioned just 150 kilometers from Key West, Florida. Cuba is slightly smaller in area than Pennsylvania. The country has few natural resources, but it does possess some deposits of cobalt, nickel, iron ore, chromium, copper, salt, timber, silica, petroleum, and arable land.[86]

Cuba's population is estimated at 11 million people. Havana, the capital, is home to over 2 million Cubans. The country's population is currently decreasing, at 0.15 percent per year, and the country boasts a higher-than-average median age of 40.4 years old. More than 70 percent of the population is older than 25.[87]

Cuba's GDP stands at US$77.15 billion, although this number is disputed due to Cuba's economic isolation from many other countries. For 50 years, foreign exchange of currency has been highly limited. Additionally, the country has two currencies in circulation, one for local Cubans and one for tourists and traders. After a significant recession and steady economic decline from 2006 until 2009, Cuba's GDP growth stabilized at about 1 percent annually. In 2015, GDP grew at about 1.3 percent. The country's GDP per capita is estimated at around US$10,000, but some believe this number is highly inflated.[88]

Cuba is a communist state. The president is indirectly elected by the legislative body, the National Assembly, for a five-year term. There are no term limits and, since 1976, there have only been two presidents: Fidel Castro, who stepped aside in 2008, and his brother Raul Castro.

The economy remains sluggish due to the effects of the long-time communist regime and poor economic policies and management. Cuba's public sector, which controls nearly all public services and private businesses in the country, employs well over 75 percent of the employed population.[89] The country suffers from corruption that occurs within its state-owned businesses, its military, and the political elite class. In the past, Cuba has been able to gain the majority of its foreign investment from countries like Venezuela, but due to dramatic drops in oil prices, Cuba may now be looking towards the United States and other Western investors. In 2014, President Barack Obama and President Raul Castro announced that the two countries would seek to normalize their relationship. As a consequence, each country reopened its embassy in the other and travel restrictions have been eased. In 2016, Presidents Obama and Castro held a series of in-person meetings over several days on the island. Telecom giants Verizon and Sprint have been able to establish roaming agreements with the state-owned telecommunications company in Cuba for U.S. citizens, and U.S. citizens can now use debit cards in Cuba.[90]

You Be the International Management Consultant

As the tension in the relations between the United States and Cuba have begun to thaw, trade and business opportunities may open up, making Cuba a potentially attractive investment for U.S. companies. One company that has already taken advantage of this new market is "Airbnb," the private house and room rental website, which opened in the Cuban marketplace in April 2015. As the Cuban government begins allowing more and more private enterprise in the country, room rentals are quickly becoming one of the most successful ways for Cubans to earn foreign currency. Airbnb's hope is that, as relations continue to normalize, it can provide reliable rentals in this previously unvisited country. As it will take time for a full restoration of Cuban-U.S relations, Airbnb does not see the island nation as a major source of profit any time in the near future. But with over 200,000 American visitors expected in 2017, and with that number projected to grow by 30 percent in the coming years, Airbnb believes that its early investment in Cuba will pay off.[91]

Questions

Although Cuba is allowing more private enterprise into the country, it is still very much under communist rule, and the government still has a deplorable record when dealing with human rights.

1. Would you advise a company to become an early investor in Cuba?
2. Do you think Airbnb's investment in Cuba will eventually see success and become a reliable profit stream?
3. Do you think Cuba will ultimately become an attractive long-term tourist destination for Americans?

Brief Integrative Case 1.1

Advertising or Free Speech? The Case of Nike and Human Rights

Nike Inc., the global leader in the production and marketing of sports and athletic merchandise including shoes, clothing, and equipment, has enjoyed unparalleled worldwide growth for many years. Consumers around the world recognize Nike's brand name and logo. As a supplier to and sponsor of professional sports figures and organizations, and as a large advertiser to the general public, Nike is widely known. Nike was a pioneer in offshore manufacturing, establishing company-owned assembly plants and engaging third-party contractors in developing countries.

In 1996, *Life* magazine published a landmark article about the labor conditions of Nike's overseas subcontractors, entitled "On the Playgrounds of America, Every Kid's Goal Is to Score: In Pakistan, Where Children Stitch Soccer Balls for Six Cents an Hour, Their Goal Is to Survive." Accompanying the article was a photo of a 12-year-old Pakistani boy stitching a Nike-embossed soccer ball. The photo caption noted that the job took a whole day, and the child was paid US$0.60 for his effort. Up until this time, the general public was neither aware of the wide use of foreign labor nor familiar with the working arrangements and treatment of laborers in developing countries. Almost instantly, Nike became a poster child for the questionable unethical use of offshore workers in poorer regions of the world. This label continued to plague the corporation as many global human interest and labor rights organizations have monitored and often condemned Nike for its labor practices around the world.

In the years following, Nike executives were frequent targets at public events, especially at universities where students pressed administrators and athletic directors to ban products that had been made under "sweatshop" conditions. Indeed, at the University of Oregon, a major gift from Phil Knight, Nike's CEO, was held up in part because of student criticism and activism against Nike on campus.[1]

Nike took immediate action to repair its damaged brand. In 2001, the company established a Corporate Responsibility and Sustainability Committee to ensure that labor practices were ethical across its supply chain. By 2003, the company employed 86 compliance officers (up from just three in 1996) to monitor its plant operations and working conditions and ensure compliance with its published corporate code of conduct. In 2005, Nike became the first among its peers to release a complete listing of all of the overseas factories that it contracts for labor. That same year, Nike released the pay scales of the factory workers and addressed actions it was taking to further improve conditions. Even so, the stigma of past practices—whether perceived or real—remained emblazoned on its image and brand name. Nike found itself constantly defending its activities, striving to shake this reputation and perception.

In 2002, Marc Kasky sued Nike, alleging that the company knowingly made false and misleading statements in its denial of direct participation in abusive labor conditions abroad. Through corporate news releases, full-page ads in major newspapers, and letters to editors, Nike defended its conduct and sought to show that allegations of misconduct were unwarranted. The action by the plaintiff, a local citizen, was predicated on a California state law prohibiting unlawful business practices. He alleged that Nike's public statements were motivated by marketing and public relations and were simply false. According to the allegation, Nike's statements misled the public and thus violated the California statute. Nike countered by claiming its statements fell under and within the protection of the First Amendment, which protects free speech. The state court concluded that a firm's public statements about its operations have the effect of persuading consumers to buy its products and therefore are, in effect, advertising. Therefore, the suit could be adjudicated on the basis of whether Nike's pronouncements were false and misleading. The court stated that promoting a company's reputation was equivalent to sales solicitation, a practice clearly within the purview of state law. The majority of justices summarized their decision by declaring, "because messages in question were directed by a commercial speaker to a commercial audience, and because they made representations of fact about the speaker's own business operations for the purpose of promoting sales of its products, we conclude that these messages are commercial speech for purposes of applying state laws barring false and misleading commercial messages" (*Kasky v. Nike Inc.*, 2002). The conclusion reached by the court was that statements by a business enterprise to promote its reputation must, like advertising, be factual representations and that companies have a clear duty to speak truthfully about such issues.[2]

In January 2003, the U.S. Supreme Court agreed to hear Nike's appeal of the decision in *Kasky v. Nike Inc.* from the California Supreme Court. In particular, the U.S. Supreme Court agreed to rule on whether Nike's previous statements about the working conditions at its subcontracted, overseas plants were in fact "commercial speech" and, separately, whether a private individual (such as Kasky) has the right to sue on those grounds. Numerous amici briefs were filed on both sides. Supporters of Kasky included California, as well as 17 other states; Ralph Nader's Public Citizen Organization; California's AFL/CIO; and California's attorney general. Nike's friends of the court included the American Civil Liberties Union, the Business Roundtable, the U.S. Chamber of Commerce, other MNCs including Exxon/Mobil and Microsoft, and the Bush administration (particularly on the grounds that it does not support private individuals acting as public censors).[3]

Despite the novelty of this First Amendment debate and the potentially wide-reaching effects for big business (particularly MNCs), the U.S. Supreme Court dismissed the case (6 to 3) in June 2003 as "improvidently granted" due to procedural issues surrounding the case. In their dissenting opinion, Justices Stephen G. Breyer and Sandra Day O'Connor suggested that Nike would likely win the appeal at the U.S. Supreme Court level. In both the concurring and dissenting opinions, Nike's statements were described as a mix of "commercial" and "noncommercial" speech.[4] This suggested to Nike, as well as other MNCs, that if the Court were to have ruled on the substantive issue, Nike would have prevailed.

Although this case has set no nationwide precedent for corporate advertising about business practices or corporate social responsibility (CSR) in general, given the sensitivity of the issue, Nike has allowed its actions to speak louder than words in recent years. As part of its international CSR profile, Nike has assisted relief efforts (donating $1 million to tsunami relief in 2004) and advocated fair wages and employment practices in its outsourced operations. Nike claims that it has not abandoned production in certain countries in favor of lower-wage labor in others and that its factory wages abroad are actually in accordance with local regulations, once one accounts for purchasing power and cost-of-living differences.[5] The Nike Foundation, a nonprofit organization supported by Nike, is also an active supporter of the Millennium Development Goals, particularly those directed at improving the lives of adolescent girls in developing countries (specifically Bangladesh, Brazil, China, Ethiopia, and Zambia) through better health, education, and economic opportunities.[6] Environmental impact is also a key component of Nike's CSR profile. The company has focused on preserving water in the areas where its products are manufactured, incorporating new technology that minimizes the amount of water needed for dyeing processes. Nike has pledged to eliminate all hazardous chemicals from its supply chain by 2020.

As part of its domestic CSR profile, Nike is primarily concerned with keeping youth active, presumably for health, safety, educational, and psychological/esteem reasons. Nike has worked with Head Start (2005) and Special Olympics Oregon (2007), as well as created its own community program, NikeGO, to advocate physical activity among youth. Partnering with then First Lady Michelle Obama, Nike worked to implement the "Let's Move" campaign (2013) into schools across the U.S. Nike also sponsors Project Play (2014), which aims to reshape the direction of youth sports by encouraging children to stay involved and feel included. Furthermore, Nike is committed to domestic efforts such as Hurricane Katrina relief and education, the latter through grants made by the Nike School Innovation Fund in support of the Primary Years Literacy Initiative.[7]

Despite Nike's impressive CSR profile, if the California State Supreme Court decision is sustained and sets a global precedent, Nike's promotion or "advertisement" of its global CSR initiatives could still be subjected to legal challenge. This could create a minefield for multinational firms. It would effectively elevate statements on human rights treatment by companies to the level of corporate marketing and advertising. Under these conditions, it might be difficult for MNCs to defend themselves against allegations of human rights abuses. In fact, action such as the issuance and dissemination of a written company code of conduct could fall into the category of advertising declarations. Although *Kasky v. Nike* was never fully resolved in court, the issues that it raised remain to be addressed by global companies.

Also to be seen is what effect a court decision would have on Nike's financial success. Despite the publicity of the case, at both the state and Supreme Court levels, and the lingering criticism about its labor practices overseas, Nike has maintained strong and growing sales and profits. The company has expanded its operations into different types of clothing and sports equipment and has continued to choose successful athletes to advertise its gear. Nike has shown no signs of slowing down, suggesting that its name and logo have not been substantially tarnished in the global market.

Questions for Review

1. What ethical issues faced by MNCs in their treatment of foreign workers could bring allegations of misconduct in their operations?

2. Would the use of third-party independent contractors insulate MNCs from being attacked? Would that practice offer MNCs a good defensive shield against charges of abuse of "their employees"?

3. Do you think that statements by companies that describe good social and moral conduct in the treatment of their workers are part of the image those companies create and therefore are part of their advertising message? Do consumers judge companies and base their buying decision on their perceptions of corporate behavior and values? Is the historic "made in" question (e.g., "Made in the USA") now being replaced by a "made by" inquiry (e.g., "Made by Company X" or "Made for Company X by Company Y")?

4. Given the principles noted in the case, how can companies comment on their positive actions to promote human rights so that consumers will think well of them? Would you propose that a company (a) do nothing, (b) construct a corporate code of ethics, or (c) align itself with some of the universal covenants or compacts prepared by international agencies?

5. What does Nike's continued financial success, in spite of the lawsuit, suggest about consumers' reactions to negative publicity? Have American media and NGOs exaggerated the impact of a firm's labor practices and corporate social responsibility on its sales? How should managers of an MNC respond to such negative publicity?

Source: This case was prepared by Lawrence Beer, W. P. Carey School of Business, Arizona State University as the basis for class discussion. It is not intended to illustrate either effective or ineffective managerial capability or administrative responsibility.

ENDNOTES

1. "Nike CEO Retracts University Donation over Human Rights," *SocialFunds.com*, May 3, 2000, www.socialfunds.com/news/print. cgi?sfArticleId=237.

2. Marc Kasky v. Nike Inc., No. 994446, 02 C.D.O.S. 3790 (Cal., San Francisco Superior Ct. 2002), http://law.justia.com/cases/california/supreme-court/4th/27/939.html (accessed November, 15, 2016).

3. Linda Greenhouse, "Free Speech for Companies on Justices' Agenda," *New York Times*, April 20, 2003, p. A17.

4. Linda Greenhouse, "Nike Free Speech Case Is Unexpectedly Returned to California," *New York Times*, June 27, 2003, p. A16.

5. "Nike and child labour – how it went from laggard to leader," www.mallenbaker.net/csr/CSRfiles/nike. html (accessed November 16, 2016).

6. Nike Inc., "Nike Foundation Secures Footing in Helping to Reach Millennium Development Goals," press release, www.nikebiz.com (accessed September 15, 2005).

7. Nike Inc., "Nike Announces $200,000 Grant to Hillsboro Schools," press release, www.nikebiz. com (accessed March 6, 2007).

TOMS Puts Its Right Foot Forward

Nearing 30 years old and tired from working long hours on his fourth start-up, serial entrepreneur Blake Mycoskie took a much-needed extended vacation to Argentina in 2006.[1] While there, Mycoskie fully immersed himself in the local culture, learning to dance the tango, enjoying fine Argentine wine, and engaging in sports such as polo.[2] Mycoskie also took note of the diverse Argentine fashion culture. One trend in particular that caught Mycoskie's eye was the soft canvas footwear called the "alpargata," worn by nearly all Argentines.[3] During his stay, Mycoskie purchased and began wearing his own alpargatas. He quickly realized how functional and comfortable the shoes were, leading him to wonder: Would consumers in the United States also be interested in such a product?

Blake Mycoskie: Serial Entrepreneur

Blake Mycoskie, born in Arlington, Texas, is the founder and "Chief Shoe Giver" for TOMS Shoes. A world traveler and former realty show contestant, Mycoskie has spent his entire career involved in start-ups.[4] Much of Mycoskie's business knowledge was self-taught through reading biographies of successful businesspeople. Though originally enrolled at Southern Methodist University (SMU), Mycoskie dropped out after just two years when he lost his tennis scholarship due to an injury.[5] This newly found freedom gave Mycoskie the chance to put his entrepreneurial spirit into action.

His first start-up business, EZ Laundry, was a small laundry service located at SMU. The university, with no campus dry cleaning service, provided steady demand.[6] By 1999, EZ Laundry had expanded to three more universities, and Mycoskie sold the company to his partner.[7] Following this experience, Mycoskie moved to Nashville and founded his next venture, Mycoskie Media. As an outdoor billboard company, Mycoskie Media focused on marketing country music. The company turned a steady profit, and Mycoskie sold it in just nine months.[8]

With two successful businesses behind him, Mycoskie and his sister, Paige, applied to be on the reality show *Survivor* in 2001. Although they did not make the cut for Survivor, they were ultimately cast in the travel-based reality series, *The Amazing Race*. Through this experience, Mycoskie was able to venture to Africa, Asia, and South America. Ultimately finishing the race as second runner-ups, the brother/sister team missed out on the million U.S. dollar prize by just a few minutes. However, and perhaps more importantly, the adventure exposed Mycoskie to

Argentina for the first time.[9] Later that year, Mycoskie moved to Los Angeles, where he co-founded his third start-up, cable network Reality Central. For this new venture, Mycoskie joined forces with Larry Namer, a founder of E! Entertainment Television.[10] The network debuted in 2003, with a planned format of airing both new, original programming as well as reruns of past successful realty shows. The venture was able to raise large amounts of funding from backers and proved successful until 2005, when competitor channel Fox Reality began to dominate ratings.[11] A short time later, Mycoskie (holding true to his entrepreneurial spirit) partnered with the founders of Trafficschool.com to create his fourth business, Drivers Ed Direct, which functioned as an online-based drivers education service.[12] To increase brand awareness, Mycoskie created a viral marketing company, the Closer Marketing Group, to better promote his driver education business.[13]

The TOMS Experiment

On the heels of these successes, Mycoskie took his pivotal trip to Argentina in 2006. As his adventure was nearing its conclusion, Mycoskie happened to stumble upon an aid worker conducting a volunteer shoe drive. She was working to provide impoverished children with new shoes, explaining to Mycoskie that, even in more-developed countries like Argentina, children in poverty often lacked shoes.[14] Without shoes, simple daily tasks can be quite difficult and children are also especially vulnerable to disease and illness when lacking proper footwear. According to the volunteer, inconsistent donations limited the success of events like shoe drives.

Over the next few days, Mycoskie's eyes were opened to the realities of poverty across Argentina. He traveled with the volunteer to several local villages, observing poverty among children first hand. The experience left an strong impression on Mycoskie, stimulating him to consider getting involved in addressing poverty.[15] Mycoskie strategized how to address the problem. Although he considered forming a charity to fund shoe donations for the children, the uncertainty posed by often inconsistent and uneven donations led Mycoskie to consider more business-oriented solutions. Having a constant flow of shoes available for donation was deemed as a critical element to the success of the effort. Mycoskie therefore settled on creating a for-profit business in which the sale of each pair of shoes would fund the donation of a pair of shoes for impoverished children. Mycoskie, reflecting on his

Figure 1   **A Brief Timeline of TOMS**

February 2006	Blake Mycoskie founds TOMS & begins development of his first shoe line.
May 2006	Sales begin. Following a string of positive press, shoe sales skyrocket.
October 2006	The company reaches 10,000 shoes sold, and the first "shoe drop" occurs in Argentina.
April 2007	The first "A Day Without Shoes" social media campaign is launched, increasing donations and brand awareness.
August 2011	TOMS launches its eyewear brand, maintaining the same "One for One" concept.
December 2011	TOMS reaches the milestone of over 2 million shoes donated.
June 2013	TOMS reaches the milestone of over 10 million shoes donated.
March 2014	TOMS Roasting Company begins business, expanding TOMS's product line into consumable products.
February 2015	TOMS Bag Collection is launched, focusing on donations to aid mothers in childbirth.
June 2016	TOMS reaches the milestone of over 60 million shoes donated.

Argentine adventure, based the shoe design on the "alpargata" shoes, which he believed held potential for success in the U.S. market. "Shoes for a Better Tomorrow," which Mycoskie originally named the company, was based on shoe sales today leading to donated shoes tomorrow. The name was eventually shortened to "Tomorrow's Shoes," which again was shortened to TOMS (see Figure 1).[16]

Products That Solve Problems

TOMS is built around the concept of expanding community outreach efforts through reliable business practices. As often discussed, TOMS was founded with the "One for One" company philosophy: every pair of shoes purchased would fund the donation of a pair of shoes to a child in need. First focusing on developing and selling the simple Argentine alpargata shoe, the company has since diversified its product line greatly. Current shoe selection includes winter boots, wet-weather shoes, sports shoes, and even locally produced shoes. Through this program, local locations manufacture their own traditional shoe, spurring job creation in developing areas. Each type of shoe that is donated is tailored to the specific geographic region to which it is sent.[17]

In 2011, the company expanded to incorporate eyeglasses. With every pair of sunglasses purchased, TOMS funds the donation of a pair of prescription glasses to a person in need.[18] Furthermore, the purchase of sunglasses funds more intensive eye-related procedures, including sight-saving surgery and medical treatments. Educational programs regarding proper eye care have also been sponsored through TOMS's donations. Through this venture, TOMS partners with 14 different organizations in 13 different countries to help diverse communities.[19]

TOMS continues to expand its product line and the scope of its social outreach programs. TOMS formed its first consumable product offering, a coffee business called TOMS Roasting Company, in 2014. With each bag of coffee purchased, TOMS provides 140 liters of water to a community in need. This equates to a week's supply of fresh, safe water to an individual person.[20] To date, TOMS has provided over 250,000 weeks of safe water to locations around the globe.[21] In 2015, TOMS expanded into the handbag industry, with the charitable link of ensuring safe childbirth for expecting mothers in developing locations. A leading cause of childbirth complications for both the mother and the infant is infections; with a portion of the profits from the sale of its bags, TOMS is financially supporting partners in its network by delivering materials and training that is needed, decreasing the chance of an infection for delivering mothers by up to 80 percent.[22]

As TOMS carries on its "One for One" philosophy, it continues to expand its product line. It is effectively generating more revenue and at the same time helping more people in need. TOMS is also spreading its philosophy and gaining more partners to help it with the same cause.

The Unconventional Leader

Mycoskie takes a somewhat unconventional approach to managing the everyday operations at TOMS. While many entrepreneurs spend long days at the office, Mycoskie takes his duties on the road with him, acting as a traveling brand representative. This allows him to personally convey the TOMS philosophy to potential customers. Back at the office, a carefully selected management team handles the day-to-day operations.[23] Even when he is in the office, Mycoskie takes an unorthodox approach to managing his staff. Informal meetings are often held out on his sailboat.

Mycoskie's personal life is equally unconventional. Prior to his recent marriage and the birth of his child, Mycoskie resided in his sailboat, docked in Marina del Ray, California. He would arise around 8:30 a.m., consume a Cliff Bar for breakfast, and spend several hours writing before finally heading into the office. Mycoskie is also a long-time user of a personal diary, allowing him to track his thoughts as they occur.[24] In fact, his journaling has filled over 50 books, containing his thoughts on all aspects of his life. He usually revisits these notes months later. In a world where instant communication is often demanded by employers, Mycoskie is notorious for leaving his e-mail inbox untouched for several days at a time. He also has been known to frequently bypass e-mail completely, utilizing handwritten letters instead. On many days, however, Mycoskie is up early to head to the airport and function as the company's traveling spokesperson.[25] Mycoskie spends much of his time speaking at different events and universities to promote personal social responsibility, the TOMS ideology, and other messages that he believes create positive impact in the world. For two or three months in the year, Mycoskie also takes time off to go travel as it continues to inspire him through seeing the world and meeting new people.[26]

In the years since visiting Argentina and building the TOMS brand, Mycoskie has largely focused on the corporate responsibility and charitable side of the business. Several times a year, Mycoskie leads teams of volunteers and employees on "shoe drops." "Shoe drop" is the term that is used to describe when a TOMS team, composed of roughly 10 to 15 staff and volunteers, heads out into the field to hand out shoes to those in need.[27] This opportunity is considered an honor; an employee must earn the ability to participate by staying with the company for several years. TOMS now donates shoes in over 40 countries, preventing more diseases and providing the means for many children to live better lives.[28]

Social Responsibility, Sustainability, and Business Strategy

Early on, one of the most common criticisms of TOMS's philanthropic programs was that it was not creating new jobs within local populations.[29] Using this feedback constructively, Mycoskie expanded the "One for One" philosophy and focused his company's next efforts on creating job opportunities for those in the developing nations where donations were being directed.

In 2013, TOMS committed to producing one-third of its shoes within the regions where they are actually distributed. This effort has proven successful; over 700 jobs have been created in the regions where shoes are donated. Furthermore, employment opportunities have been kept at an equal ratio for male and female workers, promoting gender equality in developing locations.[30] Today, TOMS maintains factories in all six countries in which it donates shoes: Argentina, China, Ethiopia, Haiti, India, and Kenya. Another example of TOMS's recent push towards social responsibility can be seen through TOMS Roasting Company. The coffee-producing subsidiary now engages in sourcing practices that provide farmers with a fair wage and ensure that clean water is accessible to people in the regions in which it sources its coffee beans. Interestingly, TOMS's internally conducted studies indicate that its overseas production initiatives are not negatively affecting domestic shoe manufacturers.[31]

Helping like-minded start-ups has evolved into another priority for TOMS. Specifically, TOMS seeks to assist new socially oriented enterprises in developing locations. Major end-goals of these efforts are the creation of additional jobs in poverty-stricken areas and the reinvestment of revenue into the improvement of the lives of locals.[32] To help facilitate these efforts, TOMS has created a platform called TOMS Marketplace to highlight specific social enterprises and to assist them in their efforts to improve communities.

Another program that Mycoskie started is funded directly by sales of his award winning book, *Start Something That Matters*.[33] Mycoskie donates 100 percent of the profits from the book to the Start Something That Matters Foundation, which has helped create over 20 socially responsible start-ups including Charlize Theron's African Outreach Project, Charity: Water, Movember, and Ben Affleck's Eastern Congo Initiative.[34]

Charity: Water is a nonprofit organization focused on solving the water shortage problems common to areas all over the world. Charity: Water takes donations from individuals that are then reinvested into organizations experienced in building sustainable, community-owned water projects.[35] Charity: Water now maintains operations in 24 different countries, funding almost 20,000 projects and providing over 6 million people with safe water.[36]

Movember, another nonprofit organization, is committed to the happiness and health of men. The organization has raised over US$650 million and funded over 1,000 projects. Efforts are primarily focused on combating testicular and prostate cancers, the first and second most common cancers in males, as well as poor mental health and physical inactivity. An interesting symbol of this organization is their pride in having moustaches.[37]

Global Impact and Influence

Through TOMS's ideology of "One for One," the original organization and its offshoots have had a significant impact on the lives of those in need. TOMS partners with several different organizations in its Giving Partners program. These partners, numbering more than 100, provide expertise and input, working closely with TOMS in its shoes, sight, water, safe birth, and bullying-prevention efforts.

The statistics highlight how effective many of the company's efforts have been. An estimated 2 million children have been protected from hookworm with the TOMS shoes provided, and, following shoe distribution, there has been a 42 percent increase in maternal health-care program participation and a 1,000-student increase in enrollment.[38] The awareness program One Day Without Shoes has reached millions, showing the difficulties that people without shoes experience while also donating a pair of shoes for every social media photo shared that shows someone without shoes.[39]

The statistics from TOMS's other product initiatives are just as encouraging. TOMS's sunglasses purchases have funded hospitals and doctors with the help of 14 different partners. An estimated 325,000 people with curable eye ailments have had their sight restored as a result of TOMS's efforts, and another 175,000 have received needed eye surgeries.[40] Funds raised through TOMS Roasting Co. have supported partners like Water for People and Aguayuda with the development and maintenance of safe water systems in local communities.[41] From bag sales, TOMS and three of its partners have helped 40 million women in four countries during childbirth, decreasing the likelihood of infection or death.[42]

Socially responsible companies have gained traction in the global society as people work to raise awareness and promote a higher standard of life; TOMS, leveraging this trend, is now valued at US$625 million.[43] Building on the one-for-one model pioneered by TOMS, other companies have pursued similar approaches, such as Blanket America, which gives a blanket for every blanket purchased, and Smile Squared, which donates a toothbrush for every one bought. It appears as if some consumers find the direct connection between buying and giving to be appealing, and companies such as TOMS—and the charities they support—are thriving as a result.[44,45]

Questions for Review

1. How might combining commercial objectives and social goals improve the impact of corporate social responsibility efforts? How might the two conflict?

2. What aspects of the "One for One" philosophy appeal to consumers? How might it appeal to consumers who may not otherwise be motivated to support corporate social responsibility?

3. Could a company like TOMS have come about absent the role of Blake Mycoskie? What is the role of the individual in entrepreneurial ventures such as TOMS?

Source: This case was prepared by Otto Eberle of Villanova University under the supervision of Professor Jonathan Doh as the basis for class discussion. Additional research assistance was provided by Ben Littell. It is not intended to illustrate either effective or ineffective managerial capability or administrative responsibility.

ENDNOTES

1. Blake Mycoskie, "How I Did It: The TOMS Story," *Entrepreneur*, September 20, 2011, https://www.entrepreneur.com/article/220350.

2. Ibid.

3. Ibid.

4. Kelsey Hubbard, "Sole Man Blake Mycoskie," *The Wall Street Journal*, January 7, 2012, www.wsj.com/articles/SB1000142405297020463220457713103103171906.

5. Jessica Shambora, "How TOMS Shoes Founder Blake Mycoskie Got Started," *CNN*, March 16, 2010, http://archive.fortune.com/2010/03/16/smallbusiness/toms_shoes_blake_mycoskie.fortune/index.htm.

6. Karen Bates, "'Soul Mates': Shoe Entrepreneur Finds Love in Giving," *NPR*, March 7, 2014, www.npr.org/2010/11/23/131550142/-soul-mates-shoe-entrepreneur-finds-love-in-giving.

7. Shambora, "How TOMS Shoes Founder Blake Mycoskie Got Started."

8. Imran Amed and Vikram Alexei Kansara, "Founder Stories: Blake Mycoskie of Toms on Social Entrepreneurship and Finding His 'Business Soulmate,'" *Business of Fashion*, July 29, 2013, https://www.businessoffashion.com/articles/founder-stories/founder-stories-blake-mycoskie-of-toms-on-social-entrepreneurship-and-finding-his-business-soulmate.

9. Gillian Telling, "Saving Soles," *Hemispheres*, April 1, 2009, http://old.hemimag.us/2009/04/01/blake-mycoskie-saves-the-world-step-by-step/.

10. J. J. Colao, "The Trials of Entrepreneurship: TOMS Founder Blake Mycoskie on Starting Up Again . . . and Again," *Forbes*, March 3, 2014, www.forbes.com/sites/jjcolao/2014/03/03/the-trials-of-

entrepreneurship-toms-founder-blake-mycoskie-on-starting-up-again-and-again/#76895a42669d.

11. "Get to the Top with Mycoskie's 5 tips," *CNN World Business*, September 26, 2008, www.cnn.com/2008/BUSINESS/09/26/mycoskie.tips/index.html?iref=nextin.

12. Colao, "The Trials of Entrepreneurship."

13. "Blake Mycoskie, Contributor Profile," *Huffington Post*, 2014, www.huffingtonpost.com/author/blake-mycoskie.

14. Blake Mycoskie, "Blake Mycoskie Conceived the Idea for TOMS Shoes While Sitting on a Farm, Pondering Life, in Argentina," *Business Insider*, September 21, 2011, www.businessinsider.com/blake-mycoskie-argentina-toms-shoes-2011-09.

15. Ibid.

16. Mycoskie, "How I Did It."

17. "Improving Lives," http://www.toms.com/improving-lives.

18. Booth Moore, "Toms Founder Blake Mycoskie Is Known for Pairing Fashion and Causes," *Los Angeles Times*, June 11, 2011, http://articles.latimes.com/2011/jun/11/image/la-ig-toms-20110611.

19. "What We Give: Giving Sight," *TOMS*, www.toms.com/what-we-give-sight.

20. Stephanie Strom, "Turning Coffee into Water to Expand Business Model," *New York Times*, March 11, 2014, www.nytimes.com/2014/03/12/business/turning-coffee-into-water-to-expand-a-one-for-one-business-model.html.

21. Jefferson Graham, "SXSW | Toms Expands to Coffee," *USA Today*, March 12, 2014, www.usatoday.com/story/tech/2014/03/12/sxsw--toms-expands-to-coffee/6284525/.

22. "Every Newborn: An Action Plan to End Preventable Deaths," *World Health Organization*, June 2014, www.who.int/maternal_child_adolescent/topics/newborn/enap_consultation/en/.

23. Tamara Schweitzer, "The Way I Work: Blake Mycoskie of Toms Shoes," *Inc.com*, June 1, 2010, www.inc.com/magazine/20100601/the-way-i-work-blake-mycoskie-of-toms-shoes.html.

24. Ibid.

25. Ibid.

26. Ibid.

27. Ibid.

28. Michael Murray, "Person of the Week: TOMS Shoes Founder Blake Mycoskie," *ABC News*, April 8, 2011, abcnews.go.com/International/PersonOfWeek/person-week-toms-shoes-founder-blake-mycoskie/story?id=13331473.

29. Cheryl Davenport, "The Broken 'Buy-One, Give-One' Model: 3 Ways to Save Toms Shoes," *factscoexist.com*, April 10, 2012, www.fastcoexist.com/1679628/the-broken-buy-one-give-one-model-three-ways-to-save-toms-shoes.

30. Kevin Short, "Toms CEO Blake Mycoskie Offers Surprising Answer to His Critics," *Huffington Post*, November 14, 2013, www.huffingtonpost.com/2013/11/14/toms-ceo-critics_n_4274637.html.

31. "TOMS: One for One," *TOMS*, www.toms.com/#expanding-local-production.

32. "Beyond One for One: Social Enterprise," *TOMS*, www.toms.com/beyond-one-for-one.

33. "Hardcover Business Books," *New York Times*, October 2011, www.nytimes.com/books/best-sellers/2011/10/09/hardcover-business-books/.

34. Sandi L. Gordon, "Change the World—Start Something That Matters," *Ezine*, January 3, 2013, http://ezinearticles.com/?Change-the-World—Start-Something-That-Matters&id=7447820.

35. Gregory Ferenstein, "Trickle-Forward Economics: Scott Harrison's Water-Based Experiment in Viral Philanthropy," *Fast Company*, October 24, 2011, https://www.fastcompany.com/1790136/trickle-forward-economics-scott-harrisons-water-based-experiment-viral-philanthropy.

36. *Charity: Water* home page, www.charitywater.org/.

37. *Movember Foundation* home page, https://us.movember.com/?home.

38. "What We Give: Giving Shoes," *TOMS*, www.toms.com/what-we-give-shoes.

39. Julee Wilson, "TOMS Shoes Annual 'One Day Without Shoes,' Plus Barefoot Celebs," *Huffington Post*, April 10, 2012, www.huffingtonpost.com/2012/04/10/toms-one-day-without-shoes_n_1414470.html.

40. "What We Give: Giving Sight," *TOMS*, http://www.toms.com/what-we-give-sight

41. "What We Give: Giving Water," *TOMS*, www.toms.com/what-we-give-water.

42. "What We Give: Safe Births," *TOMS*, www.toms.com/what-we-give-safe-births.

43. Marcela Isaza and Leanne Italie, "Blake Mycoskie on 10 Years of Toms," *Business of Fashion*, May 6, 2016, https://www.businessoffashion.com/articles/news-analysis/blake-mycoskie-on-10-years-of-toms.

44. Adam L. Penenberg, "Blanket America's Charitable Capitalism Is Going Viral," *Fast Company*, November 12, 2009, https://www.fastcompany.com/1449664/blanket-americas-charitable-capitalism-going-viral.

45. Michelle Juergen, "Smile Squared Donates Toothbrushes to Children in Need," *Entrepreneur*, November 7, 2012, https://www.entrepreneur.com/article/224444.

Student Advocacy and "Sweatshop" Labor: The Case of Russell Athletic

Introduction

In November 2009, after nearly two years of student campaigning in coordination with the apparel workers, the Honduran workers' union concluded an agreement with Russell Athletic, a major supplier of clothing and sportswear to college campuses around the country. The agreement included a commitment by Russell to put all of the workers back to work, to provide compensation for lost wages, to recognize the union and agree to collective bargaining, and to allow access for the union to all other Russell apparel plants in Honduras for union organizing drives in which the company will remain neutral. According to a November 18, 2009, press release of United Students Against Sweatshops (USAS), this has been an "unprecedented victory for labor rights."[1]

Outsourcing of production facilities and labor to developing countries has been one of the important business strategies of large U.S. corporations. While in the United States, a typical corporation is subject to various regulations and laws such as minimum wage law, labor laws, safety and sanitation requirements, and trade union organizing provisions, in some developing countries these laws are soft and rudimentary, allowing a large corporation to derive significant cost benefits from outsourcing. Moreover, many developing countries like Bangladesh, China, Honduras, India, Pakistan, and Vietnam encourage the outsourcing of work from the developed world to factories within their borders as a source of employment for their citizens, who otherwise would suffer from lack of jobs in their country.

However, in spite of the obvious positive fact of creating new jobs in the hosting country, large multinational corporations very often have been criticized for violating the rights of the workers, creating unbearable working conditions, and increasing workloads while cutting compensation. They have been attacked for creating a so-called sweatshop environment for their employees. A few of the recent targets of the criticism have been Walmart,[2] Disney,[3] JCPenney, Target, Sears,[4] ToysRUs,[5] Nike,[6] Reebok,[7] adidas,[8] Gap,[9] IBM, Dell, HP,[10] Apple, and Microsoft,[11] etc.

This case addresses advocacy by students and other stakeholders toward one of these companies and documents the evolution and outcome of the dispute.

What Is a Sweatshop?

By common agreement, a sweatshop is a workplace that provides low or subsistence wages under harsh working conditions, such as long hours, unhealthy conditions, and/or an oppressive environment. Some observers see these work environments as essentially acceptable if the laborers freely contract to work in such conditions. For others, to call a workplace a sweatshop implies that the working conditions are illegitimate and immoral. The U.S. Government Accountability Office (the name since July 7, 2004) would hone this definition for U.S. workplaces to include those environments where an employer violates more than one federal or state labor, industrial homework, occupational safety and health, workers' compensation, or industry registration laws. The AFL-CIO Union of Needletrades, Industrial and Textile Employees would expand on that to include workplaces with systematic violations of global fundamental workers' rights. The Interfaith Center on Corporate Responsibility (ICCR) defines sweatshops much more broadly than either of these; even where a factory is clean, well organized, and harassment free, the ICCR considers it a sweatshop if its workers are not paid a sustainable living wage. The purpose of reviewing these varied definitions is to acknowledge that, by definition, sweatshops are oppressive, unethical, and patently unfair to workers.[12]

History of Sweatshops

Sweatshop labor systems were most often associated with garment and cigar manufacturing of the period 1880–1920. Sweated labor can also be seen in laundry work, green grocers, and most recently in the "day laborers," often legal or illegal immigrants, who landscape suburban lawns.[13] Now, sweatshops are often found in the clothing industry because it is easy to separate higher- and lower-skilled jobs and contract out the lower-skilled ones. Clothing companies can do their own designing, marketing, and cutting and contract out sewing and finishing work. New contractors can start up easily; all they need are a few sewing machines in a rented apartment or factory loft located in a neighborhood where workers can be recruited.[14] Sweatshops make the most fashion-oriented clothing—women's and girls'—because production has to be flexible, change quickly, and be done in small batches. In less style-sensitive sectors—men's and boys' wear, hosiery, and knit products—there is less change and longer production runs, and clothing can be made competitively in large factories using advanced technology.[15]

Since their earliest days, sweatshops have relied on immigrant labor, usually women, who were desperate for work under any pay and conditions. Sweatshops in New York City, for example, opened in Chinatown, the mostly Jewish Lower East Side, and Hispanic neighborhoods in the boroughs. Sweatshops in Seattle are near neighborhoods of Asian immigrants. The evolution of sweatshops in London and Paris—two early and major centers of the garment industry—followed the pattern in New York City. First, garment manufacturing was localized in a few districts: the Sentier of Paris and the Hackney, Haringey, Islington, Tower Hamlets, and Westminster boroughs of London. Second, the sweatshops employed mostly immigrants, at first men but then primarily women, who had few job alternatives.[16]

In developing countries, clothing sweatshops tend to be widely dispersed geographically rather than concentrated in a few districts of major cities, and they often operate alongside sweatshops, some of which are very large, that produce toys, shoes (primarily athletic shoes), carpets, and athletic equipment (particularly baseballs and soccer balls), among other goods. Sweatshops of all types tend to have child labor, forced unpaid overtime, and widespread violations of workers' freedom of association (i.e., the right to unionize). The underlying cause of sweatshops in developing nations—whether in China, Southeast Asia, the Caribbean, or India and Bangladesh—is intense cost-cutting done by contractors who compete among themselves for orders from larger contractors, major manufacturers, and retailers.[17] Sweatshops became visible through the public exposure given to them by reformers in the late 19th and early 20th centuries in both England and the United States. In 1889–1890, an investigation by the House of Lords Select Committee on the Sweating System brought attention in Britain. In the United States, the first public investigations came as a result of efforts to curb tobacco homework, which led to the outlawing of the production of cigars in living quarters in New York State in 1884.[18]

The spread of sweatshops was reversed in the United States in the years following a horrific fire in 1911 that destroyed the Triangle Shirtwaist Company, a women's blouse manufacturer near Washington Square in New York City. The company employed 500 workers in notoriously poor conditions. One hundred forty-six workers perished in the fire; many jumped out windows to their deaths because the building's emergency exits were locked. The Triangle fire made the public acutely aware of conditions in the clothing industry and led to pressure for closer regulation. The number of sweatshops gradually declined as unions organized and negotiated improved wages and conditions and as government regulations were stiffened (particularly under the 1938 Fair Labor Standards Act, which imposed a minimum wage and required overtime pay for work of more than 40 hours per week).[19] Unionization and government regulation never completely eliminated clothing sweatshops, and many continued on the edges of the industry; small

sweatshops were difficult to locate and could easily close and move to avoid union organizers and government inspectors. In the 1960s, sweatshops began to reappear in large numbers among the growing labor force of immigrants, and by the 1980s sweatshops were again "business as usual." In the 1990s, atrocious conditions at a sweatshop once again shocked the public.[20] A 1994 U.S. Department of Labor spot check of garment operations in California found that 93 percent had health and safety violations, 73 percent of the garment makers had improper payroll records, 68 percent did not pay appropriate overtime wages, and 51 percent paid less than the minimum wage.[21]

Sweatshop Dilemma

The fight against sweatshops is never a simple matter; there are mixed motives and unexpected outcomes. For example, unions object to sweatshops because they are genuinely concerned about the welfare of sweated labor, but they also want to protect their own members' jobs from low-wage competition even if this means ending the jobs of the working poor in other countries.[22] Also, sweatshops can be evaluated from moral and economic perspectives. Morally, it is easy to declare sweatshops unacceptable because they exploit and endanger workers. But from an economic perspective, many now argue that, without sweatshops, developing countries might not be able to compete with industrialized countries and achieve export growth. Working in a sweatshop may be the only alternative to subsistence farming, casual labor, prostitution, and unemployment. At least most sweatshops in other countries, it is argued, pay their workers above the poverty level and provide jobs for women who are otherwise shut out of manufacturing. And American consumers have greater purchasing power and a higher standard of living because of the availability of inexpensive imports.[23]

NGOs' Anti-Sweatshop Initiatives

International nongovernmental organizations (NGOs) have attempted to step into the sweatshop conflict to suggest voluntary standards to which possible signatory countries or organizations could commit. For instance, the International Labour Office has promulgated its Tripartite Declaration of Principles Concerning Multinational Enterprises and Social Policy, which offers guidelines for employment, training, conditions of work and life, and industrial relations. The "Tripartite" nature refers to the critical cooperation necessary from governments, employers' and workers' organizations, and the multinational enterprises involved.[24]

On December 10, 1948, the General Assembly of the United Nations adopted its Universal Declaration of Human Rights, calling on all member countries to publicize the text of the Declaration and to cause it to be disseminated, displayed, and read. The Declaration recognizes that all humans have an inherent dignity and specific equal and inalienable rights. These rights are based on the foundation of freedom, justice, and peace. The UN stated that the rights should be guaranteed without distinction of any kind, such as race, color, sex, language, religion, political or other opinion, national or social origin, property, birth, or other status. Furthermore, no distinction shall be made on the basis of the political, jurisdictional, or international status of the country or territory to which a person belongs. The foundational rights also include the right to life, liberty, and security of person and protection from slavery or servitude, torture, or cruel, inhuman, or degrading treatment or punishment.[25] Articles 23, 24, and 25 discuss issues with immediate implications for sweatshops. By extrapolation, they provide recognition of the fundamental human right to nondiscrimination, personal autonomy or liberty, equal pay, reasonable working hours and the ability to attain an appropriate standard of living, and other humane working conditions. All these rights were reinforced by the United Nations in its 1966 International Covenant on Economic, Social, and Cultural Rights.[26]

These are but two examples of standards promulgated by the international labor community, though the enforcement of these and other norms is spotty. In the apparel industry in particular, the process of internal and external monitoring has matured such that it has become the norm at least to self-monitor, if not to allow external third-party monitors to assess compliance of a supplier factory with the code of conduct of a multinational corporation or with that of NGOs. Though a number of factors affected this evolution, one such factor involved pressure by American universities on their apparel suppliers, which resulted in two multistakeholder efforts—the Fair Labor Association, primarily comprising and funded by the multinational retailers, and the Worker Rights Consortium, originally perceived as university driven. Through a cooperative effort of these two organizations, large retailers such as Nike and Adidas not only have allowed external monitoring, but Nike has now published a complete list of each of its suppliers.[27]

The Case of Russell Athletic

While some argue that sweatshop scandals cause little or no impact on the corporate giants because people care more for the ability to buy cheap and affordable products rather than for working conditions of those who make these products,[28] the recent scandal around the Russell Athletic brand has proved that it may no longer be as easy for a corporation to avoid the social responsibility for its outsourcing activities as it has been for a long time. November 2009 became a tipping point in the many years of struggle between the student anti-sweatshop movement and the corporate world. An unprecedented victory was won by the United Students Against Sweatshops (USAS) coalition against Russell Athletic, a corporate giant owned by Fruit of the Loom, a Berkshire-Hathaway portfolio

company. USAS pressure tactics persuaded one of the nation's leading sportswear companies, Russell Athletic, to agree to rehire 1,200 workers in Honduras who lost their jobs when Russell closed their factory soon after the workers had unionized.[29]

Russell Corporation, founded by Benjamin Russell in 1902, is a manufacturer of athletic shoes, apparel, and sports equipment. Russell products are marketed under many brands, including Russell Athletic, Spalding, Brooks, Jerzees, Dudley Sports, and others. This company with more than 100 years of history has been a leading supplier of team uniforms at the high school, college, and professional level. Russell Athletic™ active wear and college-licensed products are broadly distributed and marketed through department stores, sports specialty stores, retail chains, and college bookstores.[30] After an acquisition in August 2006, Russell's brands joined Fruit of the Loom in the Berkshire-Hathaway family of products.

Russell/Fruit of the Loom is the largest private employer in Honduras. Unlike other major apparel brands, Russell/Fruit of the Loom owns all eight of its factories in Honduras rather than subcontracting to outside manufacturers.[31] The incident related to Russell Athletic's business in Honduras that led to a major scandal in 2009 was the company's decision to fire 145 workers in 2007 for supporting a union. This ignited the anti-sweatshop campaign against the company. Russell later admitted its wrongdoing and was forced to reverse its decision. However, the company continued violating worker rights in 2008 by constantly harassing the union activists and making threats to close the Jerzees de Honduras factory. It finally closed the factory on January 30, 2009, after months of battling with a factory union.[32]

NGOs' Anti-Sweatshop Pressure

The Worker Rights Consortium (WRC) has conducted a thorough investigation of Russell's activities, and ultimately released a 36-page report on November 7, 2008, documenting the facts of worker rights violations by Russell in its factory Jerzees de Honduras, including the instances of death threats received by the union leaders.[33] The union's vice president, Norma Mejia, publicly confessed at a Berkshire-Hathaway shareholders' meeting in May 2009 that she had received death threats for helping lead the union.[34] The Worker Rights Consortium continued monitoring the flow of the Russell Athletic scandal and issued new reports and updates on this matter throughout 2009, including its recommendation for Russell's management on how to mediate the situation and resolve the conflict.

As stated in its mission statement, the Worker Rights Consortium is an independent labor rights monitoring organization, whose purpose is to combat sweatshops and protect the rights of workers who sew apparel and make other products sold in the United States. The WRC conducts independent, in-depth investigations, issues public reports on factories producing for major U.S. brands, and aids workers at these factories in their efforts to end labor abuses and defend their workplace rights. The WRC is supported by over 175 college and university affiliates and is primarily focused on the labor practices of factories that make apparel and other goods bearing university logos.[35]

Worker Rights Consortium assessed that Russell's decision to close the plant represented one of the most serious challenges yet faced to the enforcement of university codes of conduct. If allowed to stand, the closure would not only unlawfully deprive workers of their livelihoods, it would also send an unmistakable message to workers in Honduras and elsewhere in Central America that there is no practical point in standing up for their rights under domestic or international law and university codes of conduct and that any effort to do so will result in the loss of one's job. This would have a substantial chilling effect on the exercise of worker rights throughout the region.[36]

The results of the WRC investigation of Russell Athletic unfair labor practices in Honduras spurred the nationwide student campaign led by United Students Against Sweatshops (USAS), who persuaded the administrations of Boston College, Columbia, Harvard, NYU, Stanford, Michigan, North Carolina, and 89 other colleges and universities to sever or suspend their licensing agreements with Russell. The agreements—some yielding more than $1 million in sales—allowed Russell to put university logos on T-shirts, sweatshirts, and fleeces.[37]

As written in its mission statement, USAS is a grassroots organization run entirely by youth and students. USAS strives to develop youth leadership and run strategic student-labor solidarity campaigns with the goal of building sustainable power for working people. It defines "sweatshop" broadly and considers all struggles against the daily abuses of the global economic system to be a struggle against sweatshops. The core of its vision is a world in which society and human relationships are organized cooperatively, not competitively. USAS struggles toward a world in which all people live in freedom from oppression, in which people are valued as whole human beings rather than exploited in a quest for productivity and profits.[38]

The role of USAS in advocating for the rights of the Honduran workers in the Russell Athletic scandal is hard to overestimate. One can only envy the enthusiasm and effort contributed by students fighting the problem that did not seem to have any direct relationship to their own lives. They did not just passively sit on campus, but went out to the public with creative tactical actions such as picketing the NBA finals in Orlando and Los Angeles to protest the league's licensing agreement with Russell, distributing fliers inside Sports Authority sporting goods stores, and sending Twitter messages to customers of Dick's Sporting Goods urging them to boycott Russell

products. The students even sent activists to knock on Warren Buffett's door in Omaha because his company, Berkshire-Hathaway, owns Fruit of the Loom, Russell's parent company.[39]

United Students Against Sweatshops involved students from more than 100 campuses where it did not have chapters in the anti-Russell campaign. It also contacted students at Western Kentucky University in Bowling Green, where Fruit of the Loom has its headquarters.[40] The USAS activists even reached Congress, trying to gain more support and inflict more political and public pressure on Russell Athletic. On May 13, 2009, 65 congressmen signed the letter addressed to Russell CEO John Holland expressing their grave concern over the labor violations.

In addition, the Fair Labor Association (FLA), a nonprofit organization dedicated to ending sweatshop conditions in factories worldwide, issued a statement on June 25, 2009, putting Russell Athletic on probation for noncompliance with FLA standards.[41] The Fair Labor Association, one of the powerful authorities that oversees the labor practices in the industry, represents a powerful coalition of industry and nonprofit sectors. The FLA brings together colleges and universities, civil society organizations, and socially responsible companies in a unique multistakeholder initiative to end sweatshop labor and improve working conditions in factories worldwide. The FLA holds its participants, those involved in the manufacturing and marketing processes, accountable to the FLA Workplace Code of Conduct.[42] The 19-member Board of Directors, the FLA's policy-making body, comprises equal representation from each of its three constituent groups: companies, colleges and universities, and civil society organizations.[43]

Victory for USAS and WRC

As mentioned at the start of this case, on November 2009, after nearly two years of student campaigning in coordination with the apparel workers, the Honduran workers' union concluded an agreement with Russell that put all of the workers back to work, provided compensation for lost wages, recognized the union and agreed to collective bargaining, and provided access for the union to all other Russell apparel plants in Honduras for union-organizing drives in which the company will remain neutral. According to the November 18, 2009, press release of USAS, this has been an "unprecedented victory for labor rights."[44] Rod Palmquist, USAS International Campaign Coordinator and University of Washington alumnus, noted that there were no precedents for a factory apparently being shut down to dislodge a union and "later reopened after a worker-activist campaign."[45]

This was not an overnight victory for the student movement and the coalition of NGOs such as USAS, WCR, and FLA. It took over 10 years of building a movement that persuaded scores of universities to adopt detailed codes of conduct for the factories used by licensees like Russell.[46] It is another important lesson for the corporate world in the era of globalization, which can no longer expect to conduct business activities in isolation from the rest of the world. The global corporations such as Russell Athletic, Nike, Gap, Walmart, and others will have to assess the impact of their business decisions on all the variety of stakeholders and take higher social responsibility for what they do in any part of the world.

More recently, a fire at a Bangalore textile factory in late 2012, and two horrific accidents at garment factories in Bangladesh in 2013, have placed renewed pressure on U.S. and European clothing brands to take greater responsibility for the working conditions of the factories from which they source products. On April 24, 2013, more than 1,000 workers were killed when an eight-story building collapsed while thousands of people were working inside. Less then two weeks later, eight people were killed in a fire at a factory in Dhaka that was producing clothes for Western retailers. After a number of investor, religious, labor, and human rights groups voiced concerns about the lack of oversight and accountability by the major companies, several of the world's largest apparel firms agreed to a plan to help pay for fire safety and building improvements. Companies agreeing to the plan included the Swedish-based retailer H&M; Inditex, owner of the Zara chain; the Dutch retailer C&A; and British companies Primark and Tesco. At the same time, the Bangladesh government announced that it would improve its labor laws and raise wages, and ease restrictions on forming trade unions. U.S. retailers Walmart and Gap did not commit to the agreement, expressing concerns about legal liability in U.S. courts. Instead, with the help of a U.S.-based think tank, they announced they would pursue a separate accord to improve factory conditions in Bangladesh.[47]

Despite these promises by various companies and governmental organizations, and a commitment of over a quarter of a billion dollars, much work remains to be done. According to December 2015 report by NYU Stern Center for Business and Human Rights, only eight out of over 3,000 factories in Bangladesh had cleared violations in the years since the garment fires and building collapse.[48]

Questions for Review

1. Assume that you are an executive of a large U.S. multinational corporation planning to open new manufacturing plants in China and India to save on labor costs. What factors should you consider when making your decision? Is labor outsourcing to developing countries a legitimate business strategy that can be handled without risk of running into a sweatshop scandal?

2. Do you think that sweatshops can be completely eliminated throughout the world in the near future? Provide an argument as to why you think this can or cannot be achieved.

3. Would you agree that in order to eliminate sweatshop conflicts, large corporations such as Russell Athletic should retain the same high labor standards and regulations that they have in the home country (for example, in the U.S.) when they conduct business in developing countries? How hard or easy can this be to implement?

4. Do you think that the public and NGOs like USAS should care about labor practices in other countries? Isn't this a responsibility of the government of each particular country to regulate the labor practices within the borders of its country? Who do you think provides a better mechanism of regulating and improving the labor practices: NGOs or country governments?

5. Would you agree that Russell Athletic made the right decision by conceding to USAS and union demands? Isn't a less expensive way to handle this sort of situation simply to ignore the scandal? Please state your pros and cons regarding Russell's decision to compromise with the workers' union and NGOs as opposed to ignoring this scandal.

Source: This case was prepared by Professor Jonathan Doh and Tetyana Azarova of Villanova University as the basis for class discussion. Additional research assistance was provided by Ben Littell. It is not intended to illustrate either effective or ineffective managerial capability or administrative responsibility.

ENDNOTES

1. USAS Press Release on "Jerzees de Honduras Victory," *USAS*, November 18, 2009, usas. org/2009/11/18/usas-press-release-on-jerzees-de-honduras-victory/.

2. David Barboza, "In Chinese Factories, Lost Fingers and Low Pay," *New York Times*, January 5, 2008, www.nytimes.com/2008/01/05/business/worldbusiness/05sweatshop.html.

3. Ibid.

4. "Tearing Down a Sweatshop," *Duke University News*, June 15, 2001, https://today.duke.edu/2001/06/peterle615.html.

5. Dexter Roberts and Aaron Bernstein, "Inside a Chinese Sweatshop: A Life of Fines and Beating," *BusinessWeek*, October 2, 2000, www.bloomberg.

com/news/articles/2000-10-01/inside-a-chinese-sweatshop-a-life-of-fines-and-beating.

6. Tim Connor, "Still Waiting for Nike to Do It," *Global Exchange*, May 2001, www.globalexchange. org/campaigns/sweatshops/nike/stillwaiting.html.

7. Ann Harrison and Jason Scorse, "Multinationals and Anti-Sweatshop Activism,"*American Economic Review* 100, no. 1 (March 2010), https://www. aeaweb.org/articles?id=10.1257/aer.100.1.247.

8. Ibid.

9. Ibid.

10. "Working in a Chinese Sweatshop for HP, Micro-soft, Dell and IBM," *France 24,* December 2, 2009, observers.france24.com/en/20090212-working-hp-microsoft-china-serving-prison-sentence-sweatshop-dell-ibm-china.

11. Jonathan Adams and Kathleen E. McLaughlin, "Special Report: Silicon Sweatshops," *Globalpost,* November 17, 2009, sacom.hk/special-report-silicon-sweatshops/.

12. Laura P. Hartman, *Encyclopedia of Business Ethics and Society*, vol. 4, ed. Robert W. Kolb (Thousand Oaks, CA: Sage Publications, 2008), pp. 2034–2041.

13. Richard A. Greenwald, *Dictionary of American History*, 3rd ed., vol. 8, ed. Stanley I. Kutler (New York: Charles Scribner's Sons, 2003), pp. 34–35.

14. Gary Chaison, *Encyclopedia of Clothing and Fashion*, vol. 3, ed. Valerie Steele (Detroit: Charles Scribner's Sons, 2005), pp. 247–250.

15. Ibid.

16. Ibid.

17. Ibid.

18. Greenwald, *Dictionary of American History*, pp. 34–35.

19. Chaison, *Encyclopedia of Clothing and Fashion*, pp. 247–250.

20. Ibid.

21. Hartman, *Encyclopedia of Business Ethics and Society*, pp. 2034–2041.

22. Chaison, *Encyclopedia of Clothing and Fashion*, pp. 247–250.

23. Ibid.

24. Hartman, *Encyclopedia of Business Ethics and Society*, pp. 2034–2041.

25. Ibid.

26. Ibid.

27. Ibid.

28. Laura Fitch, "Do Sweatshop Scandals Really Damage Brands?" *Brandchannel*, November 20, 2009, www.brandchannel.com/home/post/2009/ 11/20/Do-Sweatshop-Scandals-Really-Damage-Brands.aspx#continue.

29. Steven Greenhouse, "Labor Fight Ends in Win for Students," *New York Times*, November 17, 2009, www.nytimes.com/2009/11/18/ business/18labor.html.

30. Russell Athletic home page, www.fotlinc.com/pages/ russell-athletic-classic-athletic-apparel-and-uniforms. html#.WCNTKPorKUk.

31. "USAS Press Release on Jerzees de Honduras Victory."

32. "Russell Corporation's Rights Violations in Hondu-ras," *Worker Rights Consortium, News and Projects*, http://workersrights.org/RussellRightsViolations.asp.

33. Ibid.

34. Greenhouse, "Labor Fight Ends in Win for Students."

35. "Mission," *Worker Rights Consortium*, http:// workersrights.org/about/.

36. "Russell Corporation's Rights Violations in Honduras."

37. Greenhouse, "Labor Fight Ends in Win for Students."

38. USAS, "Mission and Vision," http://usas.org/about/ mission-vision-organizing/.

39. Greenhouse, "Labor Fight Ends in Win for Students."

40. Ibid.

41. FLA Board Resolution on Special Review for Russell Corporation, adopted June 25, 2009, *Fair Labor Association*, www.fairlabor.org/sites/default/ files/documents/reports/board_resolution_06.28.09.pdf.

42. "FLA Workplace Code of Conduct," *Fair Labor Association*, www.fairlabor.org/our-work/labor-standards.

43. "Board of Directors," *Fair Labor Association*, www. fairlabor.org/about-us/board-directors.

44. USAS Press Release on "Jerzees de Honduras Victory."

45. Ibid.

46. Greenhouse, "Labor Fight Ends in Win for Students."

47. Steven Greenhouse and Jim Yardley, "Global Retailers Join Safety Plan for Bangladesh." *New York Times*, May 14, 2013, p. A1.

48. Gillian B. White, "Are Factories in Bangladesh Any Safer Now?," *The Atlantic Magazine,* December 17, 2015, www.theatlantic.com/business/archive/2015/12/ bangladesh-factory-workers/421005/.

The Ethics of Global Drug Pricing

In September 2015, Turing Pharmaceuticals, headed by former hedge fund manager Martin Shrkeli, increased the price of a 62-year-old drug used for treating life-threatening parasitic infections in HIV and cancer patients by over 5,000 percent—from US$13.50 to US$750 per tablet.[1] Also in 2015, Valeant Pharmaceuticals raised the price of a standard-use diabetes pill from US$896 to US$10,020, pills used for Wilson's Disease from US$1,395 and US$888 to US$21,267 and US$26,139 respectively, and a heart rate medication from $4,489 to $36,811.[2] In the same year, Rodelis Therapeutics increased the price of a drug used to treat multidrug-resistant tuberculosis from around US$500 to US$10,800 per 30 pills.[3] These highlight just a few examples of numerous recent extreme price increases that have fueled the debate regarding the cost of prescription medication in the United States, prompting comparisons to drug prices in other industrialized countries. Moreover, a related debate has simmered regarding access to life-saving medicine in developing countries, the relatively low investments by major global pharma companies in developing new medicines for diseases such as tuberculosis and malaria, and the prices major pharmaceutical companies charge for HIV/AIDS medications.

Pharmaceuticals and Pricing—A Complicated Calculation

The issue of drug pricing is incredibly complex and, as more prescription medications are becoming available to the growing global population, that complexity is increasing. Debates regarding prescription medication pricing involve such hot-button issues as the appropriate levels of corporate profits, the responsibility of the corporations who own the medication (profit for shareholders versus providing a need for suffering patients), and insurance coverage, to name a few. The ethical debate over drug pricing is not confined to just the United States, but extends to developed and developing companies alike.

The pricing of pharmaceuticals is influenced by a myriad of stakeholders who represent a wide range of competing interests. These include the patients taking the drugs, the doctors prescribing the drugs, the insurance companies paying for the drugs, the pharmaceutical manufacturers that either produce or acquire the rights and supply the drug, and the governmental forces that often act as a bulk purchaser and regulator, policing the entire process. Tensions among these diverse stakeholders are aggravated by continued growth in prescription-drug

spending. In 2014, drug prices grew by 12.2 percent from the previous year, and prices for some medications, including effective treatments for hepatitis-C, cancer, and multiple sclerosis, grew by as much as $50,000.[4]

Patients need reliable drugs that can be used to treat their conditions; however, the costs to patients vary widely based on the health-care system of the countries in which they live, whether they are subject to public or private insurance (or no insurance at all), and various other factors. In the United States, insurance options vary widely, with some patients paying out of pocket, others opting for coverage under their employer-paid or commercial insurance, and some utilizing a form of government-paid insurance, like Medicare. The type of provider and type of plan ultimately determine the cost that the patient must pay out of pocket for any prescription medications. Some plans require co-pays, premiums, or deductibles to cover the costs of prescriptions and some pay a certain percentage of prescription costs, leaving the balance to the patient. In many countries featuring single-payer models, health plans determine which drugs are available and how they are to be allocated to patients. In a similar vein, insurance plans in the United States maintain a "booklet" or listing of what prescription medications are covered under a given plan. This booklet can change from year-to-year, meaning that one year a given insurance company will cover costs for a certain medication and, due to factors like huge price increases, the medication may not be covered the following year.

In the United States, prescribing doctors are an important stakeholder in this issue. Until recently, their responsibility and incentives were not always well established. In the past, it was common practice for pharmaceutical companies to offer doctors fees for research and clinical assessments. Because these fees created at least the appearance of a conflict of interest, legislation and regulation began to require greater disclosure and reporting. Now, all compensation, including nonmonetary items such as food and entertainment, that pharmaceutical companies provide to doctors in exchange for research and promotional activities must be reported.[5]

Putting that role aside, doctors are generally expected to treat patients with whatever means result in the highest efficacy levels. Higher prescription drug prices inevitably interact with that responsibility. Recent trends seem to indicate that these tensions will only grow; the number of Americans using prescription medication has increased nearly 10 percent since 1999, to 60 percent of Americans, and the number of patients who take five or more medications has doubled to 15 percent.[6] As drug prices continue to soar, doctors are placed in the difficult situation of prescribing their patients medication that may not be affordable or performing alternative methods with lower efficacy.

In defending relatively high prices of drugs, pharmaceutical companies routinely cite the high failure rate of new drugs during the FDA approval process and the steep costs of research and development. Indeed, some estimates put the price of developing a new drug at nearly $3 billion when including the cost of failures and drugs that never reach the marketplace.[7] Opponents of this argument cite the fact that, in cases where a new drug is successful, it enjoys approximately two decades of protection from any competition under strict patent laws. Additionally, some companies, especially in the "orphan" drug industry, which will be discussed later, receive grants for research and development. Finally, in extreme cases of companies like Valeant and Turing, critics point to the fact that those companies do not appear to invest much if any financial resources into developing new drugs. Valeant, for example, invests less than 3 percent of revenue into research and development activities.[8]

The Wall Street Journal conducted an exhaustive investigation into the pricing of drugs at Pfizer, which involved interviewing management regarding pricing for its new breast cancer medication Ibrance. The results revealed that Pfizer's multistep pricing process is not based on a single algorithm but is derived—and adjusted—based on a range of external inputs and internal benchmarks. According to the report, research and development costs had minimal influence on the ultimate price per dose set by the company. Rather, factors including demand in the marketplace, competition, the opinions of medical professionals, and potential pressure from insurers heavily influenced the resulting pricing strategy.[9] Pfizer explained that it seeks to reduce this complex analysis into a three-point approach: patients receive maximum access to the drug; payers, such as insurers, will accept the price; and Pfizer receives strong financial returns. In this case, Pfizer spent three years of market research to determine pricing for what was a revolutionary medication to treat advanced breast cancer. The final step of the process was a meeting of Pfizer economists to determine the financial impact to the company, the health insurers, and the patients. Finally, the commercial team decided to set the price at $9,850 per month. This price was approved by Pfizer and, just as the medication was set to go to market, a competitor raised the price of its comparable medication by 9.9 percent, putting the monthly cost of that medication at US$687 more than Pfizer's, on the basis of "reflecting an evolving health-care and competitive environment."[10] According to *The Wall Street Journal*, Pfizer was left thinking, "was $9,850 too low?"[11]

In the most egregious cases of price increases, companies like Valeant and Turing buy the rights to specialty medications that have been on the market for years and for which there are few direct substitutes. These companies then raise the prices of the drugs exponentially. Decades-old specialty medications often do not have generic alternatives due to traditionally low sales volumes. Therefore, patients who require these medications and have been using them as standard care are left without any real cost-effective alternative when prices skyrocket.

Pharmaceutical companies also argue that they provide subsidies—sometimes significant ones—for patients who are not able to pay the full cost. These programs include providing medication free of charge to patients in both developed and developing countries, as well as offering a type of financial aid to help other patients obtain the medication at a discount. Pharma companies' programs to provide access to medicines for patients in developing countries are discussed below.

When taken together, the many considerations associated with drug costs and pricing conspire to create a confusing web of social, economic, and political challenges, some of which are detailed below.

Drug Pricing in the United States and around the World

Although the United States is facing rapidly increasing prescription medication prices, this is not the case in much of the world. In the United States, a mostly market-based system provides economic and other incentives for companies that develop new drugs or improve existing ones. The drug companies in market-based systems, benefiting from patent-protected exclusivity, ultimately recoup their large research and development investments with higher market-based prices for their breakthrough products. In other parts of the world, where public health care and prescription drug purchasing systems are commonplace, different factors prevail.

The Wall Street Journal conducted a study comparing prescription drug prices in the market-based United States, using the data available through Medicare Part B, to the prices found in three countries with public health care systems: Norway, England, and Canada's Ontario province. This investigation used both public and nonpublic data.[12] Table 1 summarizes the results of that study. Among the findings was that, in the case of the top 40 selling drugs, prices in the United States were 93 percent higher than in Norway. Similarly, England and Ontario also showed significantly cheaper prices than those found in the U.S. Research seems to conclude that, in general, branded prescription drugs are more expensive in the market-based U.S. system than in other developed countries.[13]

The patent protection and exclusivity prevalent in the market-based U.S. system are not the only reason for steep

Table 1 **Drug Price Comparison**

Drug	Dose Size	Medicare (U.S.)	Norway	England	Ontario	Drug Used for
Lucentis	0.5 mg	US $1,936	US $ 894	US $1,159	US $1,254	Macular degeneration
Eylea	2 mg	1,930	919	1,274	1,129	Macular degeneration
Rituxan/MabThera	500 mg	3,679	1,527	1,364	1,820	Rheumatoid arthritis
Neulasta	6 mg	3,620	1,018	1,072	n/a	White blood cell deficiency
Ayastin	100 mg	685	399	379	398	Cancer
Prolia	60 mg	893	260	286	285	Osteoporosis
Alimta	100 mg	604	313	250	342	Lung cancer
Velcade	3.5 mg	1,610	1,332	1,191	n/a	Cancer
Herceptin	100 mg	858	483	424	493	Breast cancer
Eligard	7.5 mg	217	137	n/a	247	Prostate cancer

Source: Jeanne Whalen, "Why the U.S. Pays More Than Other Countries for Drugs," *The Wall Street Journal*, December 1, 2015.

drug prices; structural differences in the health-care system, the lobbying and political power of pharmaceutical companies, and the fear of rationing all contribute to the increased prices in the market.[14] Conversely, the state-run health systems in other developed countries, like Norway, exert strong negotiating leverage with drug companies. In these countries, nearly all drug purchasing is completed by government agencies, shifting the power from pure market demand to a single government purchaser. In these systems, it is common for government health-care agencies to set firm caps on pricing, require strong evidence that breakthrough drugs truly provide higher value than existing medications, and refuse to pay for higher-priced drugs that offer only minimal improvements over cheaper alternatives.[15] By contrast, the U.S. marketplace is more disjointed. Individuals, employers, large and small insurance companies, and even state and federal government agencies foot the bill for medications, resulting in decreased bargaining power. Furthermore, Medicare, which pays for more medications than any other company or agency in the country, is legally prevented from negotiating pricing.[16]

Drug manufacturers and developers are quick to note the huge financial disincentives posed by European public health-care systems. Lower returns coupled with strong governmental control arguably result in decreased research investment and less patient access to life-saving drugs. Without the large profits achieved through the U.S. pricing model, new drug development would sharply decline.[17] Per Pharmaceutical Research and Manufacturers of America (PhRMA) executive vice president Lori Reilly, "The U.S. has a competitive biopharmaceutical marketplace that works to control costs while encouraging the development of new treatments and cures."[18]

Below is a brief summary of drug pricing approaches in key European countries.

Norway, Canada, and the United Kingdom

Norway created the Norwegian Medicines Agency (NMA) to determine the appropriateness of specific drugs for treatment. The agency evaluates patient information to determine the cost-effectiveness of new drugs. Pharmaceutical companies submit a price for reimbursement, which must be below the maximum price set by the agency, and the pharmaceutical companies must file detailed documents outlining the additional benefits and value that the new drug provides that existing drugs do not. QALY, or quality-adjusted life year, is a metric that is often used to measure the value of the drug.[19] Interestingly, Medicare in the U.S. is prohibited from incorporating such an approach. Many drug companies ultimately discount their drugs to ensure that they are accepted by NMA for inclusion in the health-care system, though companies are able to resubmit rejected drugs if they can improve the value proposition.[20]

England's health-care cost agency, the National Institute for Health and Care Excellence (NICE), is one of Europe's strictest regulators. Providing a high value is critical to any specific drug's acceptance by NICE; the agency evaluates the cost versus effectiveness of drugs, ultimately determining whether the medication provides enough benefit to warrant coverage. If NICE determines that the value offered by the new drug is too low compared to the price, drug makers have the opportunity to try for acceptance again with a revised price point.[21] The level of spending by the National Health Service (NHS) on individual drugs is also capped, and the pharmaceutical industry must reimburse the NHS for any additional spending over that cap. Nearly every drug covered by both Medicare Part B and the English health-care system was more expensive in the U.S.[22]

Though the Canadian health-care system does not include a centralized government agency responsible for all drug payments and negotiations, the country has been able to maintain lower drug costs due to government regulation.[23] First, maximum drug prices, based on the effectiveness and overall value of the pharmaceutical product as well as the cost of the drug in the U.S. and Europe, are set by Canada's Patented Medicine Prices Review Board. After the price ceiling is set on a particular drug, the pharmaceutical company producing the product is prohibited from increasing the price above the comparable U.S. or

European price. Additionally, the annual rate of price increase is capped at Canada's rate of inflation.[24] Because Canada has a nationalized system with heavy subsidies for low- and fixed-income citizens, the Canadian government also must determine whether or not any specific drug will be available to seniors and those on government assistance. The Canadian Agency for Drugs and Technologies in Health ultimately makes this decision. These regulations appear to effectively reduce costs, especially when compared to the U.S. For example, of 30 pharmaceutical drugs covered by both Ontario's Ministry of Health and Long-Term Care and the U.S.'s Medicare Part B, only 7 percent of the drugs were more expensive in Canada.[25]

Obviously, the significant difference in health-care systems and prescription medication practices makes it extremely difficult to debate whether the U.S. approach or the Norway-England-Canada approach is better. Of more practical relevance, it would be extremely difficult for the U.S. to adopt the approach used in these three countries. Indeed, the U.S. has (so far) rejected a universal, government-paid health-care system.[26] The arguments for and against that type of system are well-documented and will not be addressed here, but it is worth mentioning that there are valid reasons for opposing it. One is that adopting a universal system could result in the government being unwilling to pay for certain medications, something that is quite controversial in the U.S., where freedom and choice are highly valued.[27] This reality complicates the process for encouraging development of specialty and orphan drugs that by definition treat a very small portion of the population. In these cases, there is usually a lack of effective alternatives or generic medications and it is only with strong economic incentives that pharmaceutical companies are willing to take the risk of development new products. As such, a public health-care system does not provide a solution to high drug prices in cases where there are little to no alternative treatments.[28]

Germany, Spain, and Italy

Another approach to drug pricing, which has features of both a private, market-based system, like that of the United States, and a public system, like that of Norway, can be found in Germany, Spain, and Italy. A *New York Times* analysis described how these countries approach the pricing challenge.

In Germany, Spain, and Italy, pharmaceutical drugs are categorized into groupings with other similar drugs.[29] Insurers, whether public or private, then set a single specific price that they will pay for any drug that is grouped within a specific category. This price is referred to as the "reference price." If any individual drug within a category is priced higher than the set reference price for that category, the consumer must pay the excess cost if he or she wants the more expensive drug.[30] This approach results in

significant consumer pressure on the drug manufacturer. When a low reference price is set, consumers become more willing to switch the specific drug that they are taking to avoid any additional, uncovered cost. Drug companies, with the desire to keep consumers, respond by lowering their price to as close to the reference price as possible.[31] Germany, Italy, and Spain vary slightly in how reference prices are actually set. In Germany and Spain, averages are used to calculate the proper reference price, while in Italy, the lowest price in each drug category effectively acts as the reference price.

Price controls, whether through government agencies or insurers, are often blamed for slowing drug research and development. While this may be rooted in some truth, the reference price strategy can still result in financial incentive for innovation. When a new, breakthrough drug is developed, reference pricing allows for that drug to be placed into a category by itself, eliminating the price competition seen in categories of drugs established with multiple competitors. The new drug is still able to reap the financial benefits of being a first-to-market innovator, likely for many years.[32] Additionally, the reference pricing strategy can encourage innovations within long-established drug categories. When an existing drug within a crowed, competitive drug category is improved and its cost to manufacture is reduced, the drug manufacturer can likewise lower its price point in an attempt to steal market share. This results in savings to the end consumer.

As stated already, it is difficult to argue against a system that has prices a fraction of those in the U.S., but it is worth mentioning that this system is still difficult to implement in cases where there are no comparable drugs. Furthermore, companies could shave margins on drugs that have comparable alternatives but attempt to make up those margins in areas where they provide novel medications. Finally, as seen with Pfizer's pricing example, pharmaceutical companies routinely look to competitors for guidance on pricing. Implementing a reference-pricing system could incentivize companies to set higher prices knowing that the government will be imposing a bottom price or average price and encourage a type of price-fixing.

Specialty and "Orphan" Drugs

Specialty drugs—which are generally understood to be drugs that are structurally complex and often require special handling or delivery mechanisms—are typically priced much higher than traditional drugs. While some of these drugs have been groundbreaking in the treatment of cancer, rheumatoid arthritis, multiple sclerosis, and other chronic conditions, the cost of treating a patient with specialty drugs can exceed tens of thousands of dollars a year. Over the past decade, the industry has seen significant increases to the pricing of specialty drugs. Figure 1 shows the growth in these costs.

Figure 1   **Growth in Average Annual Cost of Specialty Drug Regime**

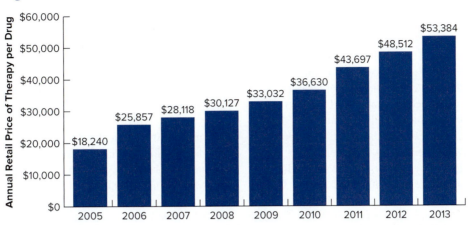

Source: Anna Gorman, "California Voters Will Have Their Say on Drug Prices," *Kaiser Health News.* January 29, 2015, http://khn.org/news/california-voters-will-have-their-say-on-drug-prices/.

Depending on the effectiveness, demand, and disease being treated, some specialty drugs cost upwards of three-quarters of a million U.S. dollars annually. In fact, within the last few years, a third of all spending on prescription drugs in the U.S. has been dedicated to specialty drugs. This has resulted in a surge in the development of new specialty drugs; since 2010, the U.S. Food and Drug Administration (FDA) has been approving more specialty drugs than traditional drugs. For example, in 2014, specialty drugs accounted for 54 percent of all FDA approvals.[33]

Another classification of drugs—called "orphan drugs"—are pharmaceutical products aimed at rare diseases or disorders. In the market-based U.S. system, orphan drugs can be financially lucrative for drug developers, especially since the passage of the Orphan Drug Act of 1983. Since the passage of the law, over 400 new orphan drugs have received FDA approval, resulting in treatments for nearly 400 rare diseases. In the U.S., orphan drugs often cost 20 times that of drugs used to treat traditional disease. Additionally, the market for orphan drugs continues to grow. More than 30 million U.S. citizens, representing almost 10 percent of the entire population, are estimated to be inflicted with a rare disease. While demand for traditional prescription drugs is only expected to increase 4 percent annually in Japan, the U.S., and Europe through 2020, total sales for orphan drugs will increase by 11 percent year-over-year. By 2020, nearly a fifth of all nongeneric drugs sold globally will be orphan drugs.[34]

As discussed previously, the U.S. spending on prescription medication is substantially higher than in most other countries. One argument justifying these high prices is that the high prices for medications in the U.S. and some other developed countries make it possible for the same companies to offer medications needed in developing countries at a significant discount.

Access to Medicine and Pricing in Developing Countries

Prescription drugs are the primary method of medical treatment in most developing countries and largely dominate total health-care spending in these economies. As a result, drug affordability in emerging countries is critical to ensuring medical treatment for those who are in need. Despite aid from the international community, developing countries still lack access to life-saving medications. Less than 20 percent of all drug importing, and only 6 percent of all drug exporting, occurs in emerging nations. Furthermore, a full third of people in these countries are without consistent access to prescription drugs.[35]

One grouping of major global initiatives that are helping to make medication more available to the developing countries is the Neglected Tropical Disease (NTD) programs. NTDs are defined as common, easily transmitted diseases that are most often found in the approximately 150 developing nations located in tropical regions. The economic impact of these diseases is estimated to be in the US$ billions annually, directly and indirectly affecting more than a fifth of the world's population. Often, factors such as unsanitary water and livestock contribute to the spread of NTDs.[36] Specific programs, such as the one established by the Centers for Disease Control and Prevention (CDC), aim to combat NTDs directly. This includes attempting to completely eliminate diseases through Mass Drug Administration (MDA) programs, as well as working together with pharmaceutical companies and local NGOs. With a lack of formal doctors and nurses in many of these areas, localized community leaders and volunteers, such as teachers, function as drug administrators. These volunteers have the training required to effectively and properly provide drugs to the community members. Pharmaceutical companies provide support through large drug donations.[37,38] The U.S. Agency for

International Development (USAID) is a key partner with organizations like the CDC and the World Health Organization (WHO). In addition, USAID, CDC, and WHO also collaborate with other organizations, including foundations such as the Bill and Melinda Gates Foundation, as well as individual pharmaceutical companies that donate medications that can combat these diseases.

In the United States, concern about NTDs and the lack of incentives for pharmaceutical companies to develop drugs for those diseases caught the attention of three academics from Duke University. In their 2006 paper, researchers David Ridley, Henry Grabowski, and Jeffery Moe proposed a voucher system based on the Orphan Drug program to reward companies for investing in the development of drugs targeted at treating NTDs.[39] Under this system, the incentive provided to pharmaceutical companies developing NTD treatments would be the expedited FDA review of a subsequent drug of the company's choice, potentially generating millions of dollars of added revenue due to the fact that the chosen drug would gain market access earlier than would otherwise be the case. The researchers also suggested providing some flexibility in redeeming this reward, including allowing the benefit to be sold to another company. In the U.S., the voucher system idea quickly transformed from concept into law; U.S. Senator Sam Brownback adapted and included the program in the Food and Drug Administration Amendments Act (FDAAA) of 2007.[40]

In addition to the above initiatives, pharmaceutical companies are increasingly evaluated and assessed based on their ability and willingness to make drugs available to poor countries. The Access to Medicine Foundation, an independent nongovernmental organization, publishes the "Access to Medicine Index," which ranks pharmaceutical companies by their access-related policies and practices. The index is based on an analysis of 95 indicators, in relation to 106 countries and 47 diseases.[41] Each company is ranked separately according to its commitment to its performance in seven categories: (1) General Access to Medicine Management; (2) Public Policy and Marketing Influence; (3) Research and Development; (4) Pricing, Manufacturing, and Distribution; (5) Patents and Licensing; (6) Capability Advancement; and (7) Donations and Philanthropy. Figure 2 shows the overall ranking for the top 20 pharmaceutical companies globally.

In addition, individual companies have taken it upon themselves to provide free or low-cost access to their own production and distribution channels or with partners. For example, the pharmaceutical giant Merck developed a drug—Mectizan—to fight onchocerciasis, also known as river blindness, in 1987 and established the Mectizan Donation Program (MDP) to oversee the initiative.[42] Onchocerciasis is found primarily in Latin America and Africa. It is transmitted through the bites of black flies and can cause disfiguring dermatitis, eye lesions,

and, over time, blindness. MDP approves more than 140 million treatments for onchocerciasis annually.[43] Another company, Novartis, developed a highly effective malaria treatment called Coartem that was made available in a lemon-flavored disbursable format, making it easier for children to take. It has become one of the largest access-to-medicine programs in the health-care industry, measured by the number of patients reached annually.[44] Since 2001, working with a range of international organizations such as the World Health Organization and the Gates Foundation, Novartis has provided more than 600 million treatments for adults and children, to more than 60 malaria-endemic countries, contributing to a dramatic reduction of the malaria burden in Africa.[45] It is estimated that 3.3 million lives have been saved as a result.[46] Interestingly, Novartis chose to sell the drug on a cost-recovery (not-for-profit) basis rather than give away the drug, perhaps because it believes this approach will make the program more sustainable over the long term. Novartis was the first recipient of an NTD priority review voucher described above.

The Future of Drug Pricing around the World

The question of how to price pharmaceutical drugs is difficult and ethically complex. As an industry directly related to the health and welfare of humankind, political and ideological decisions regarding health-care provision and delivery can be deeply personal for many. In addition, income disparities both within countries and across the developing world are on the rise, and these differences pose difficult questions about fairness, equity, and moral obligations.

It seems clear that drug pricing will remain a contentious and debated issue. From the perspective of globalization, it is interesting to consider whether or not price differentials for drugs will persist, or, as is the case in many other areas, prices will converge due to growing wealth in developing and emerging markets, regulatory coordination across jurisdictions, increasing market pressures, or some combination of these factors.

Questions for Review

1. What is the proper balance for pharmaceutical companies between delivering the fiduciary obligation of earning a profit for owners and providing life-saving or life-extending drugs to customers? How much profit is too much profit and who determines the amount? How does that balance get achieved?

2. Should the United States consider other methods for controlling drug pricing, such as those used in some European countries? Are there other ways the United States might use market forces or incentives from government programs to control drug prices? Given that one of the most prevalent and persuasive

Figure 2   **The Access to Medicine Index 2014—Overall Ranking**

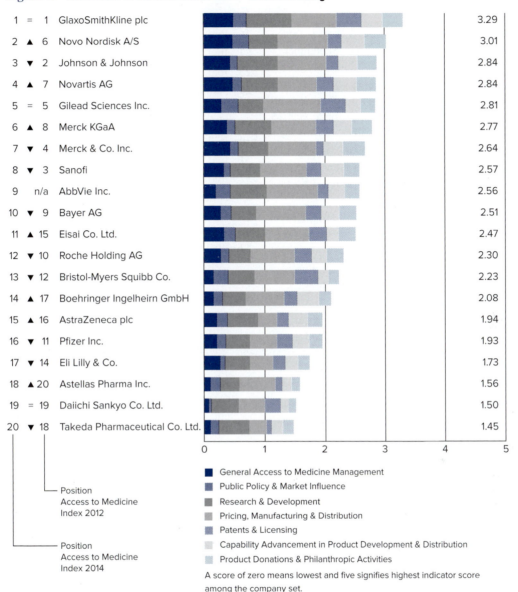

1 = 1	GlaxoSmithKline plc	3.29
2 ▲ 6	Novo Nordisk A/S	3.01
3 ▼ 2	Johnson & Johnson	2.84
4 ▲ 7	Novartis AG	2.84
5 = 5	Gilead Sciences Inc.	2.81
6 ▲ 8	Merck KGaA	2.77
7 ▼ 4	Merck & Co. Inc.	2.64
8 ▼ 3	Sanofi	2.57
9 n/a	AbbVie Inc.	2.56
10 ▼ 9	Bayer AG	2.51
11 ▲ 15	Eisai Co. Ltd.	2.47
12 ▼ 10	Roche Holding AG	2.30
13 ▼ 12	Bristol-Myers Squibb Co.	2.23
14 ▲ 17	Boehringer Ingelheirn GmbH	2.08
15 ▲ 16	AstraZeneca plc	1.94
16 ▼ 11	Pfizer Inc.	1.93
17 ▼ 14	Eli Lilly & Co.	1.73
18 ▲ 20	Astellas Pharma Inc.	1.56
19 = 19	Daiichi Sankyo Co. Ltd.	1.50
20 ▼ 18	Takeda Pharmaceutical Co. Ltd.	1.45

Position Access to Medicine Index 2012

Position Access to Medicine Index 2014

■ General Access to Medicine Management
■ Public Policy & Market Influence
■ Research & Development
■ Pricing, Manufacturing & Distribution
■ Patents & Licensing
■ Capability Advancement in Product Development & Distribution
■ Product Donations & Philanthropic Activities

A score of zero means lowest and five signifies highest indicator score among the company set.

arguments for relatively high drug prices is the high cost associated with research and development and regulatory compliance, is there a way to combat those costs?

3. What are your views on the role of patents in prescription medication? What is the proper balance of patent protection for costly research and development versus lack of competition?

4. What should be done on the issue of orphan drugs to combat high costs without viable alternatives? Should there be cost restrictions? Should there be patent restrictions?

5. What should be done in cases like Turing and Valeant Pharmaceuticals, where decades-old medications that do not have competitors are purchased and

prices are raised exponentially? If you think restrictions should be imposed, what is the justification for treating that case differently than the case where a drug, with patent protection, comes to market and is priced for hundreds or thousands of dollars?

6. How can the United States and other developed countries stimulate greater research and development of treatments for NTDs and offer those drugs at prices that are affordable?

Source: This case was prepared by Matthew Vassil of Villanova University under the supervision of Professor Jonathan Doh as the basis for class discussion. Additional research assistance was provided by Ben Littell. It is not intended to illustrate either effective or ineffective managerial capability or administrative responsibility.

ENDNOTES

1. Andrew Pollock, "Drug Goes from $13.50 a Tablet to $750, Overnight," *New York Times*, September 21, 2015, p. B1.

2. Andrew Pollock and Sabrina Tavernise, "Valeant's Drug Price Strategy Enriches It, but Infuriates Patients and Lawmakers," *New York Times*, October 5, 2015, p. A1.

3. Carolyn Y. Johnson, "How an Obscure Drug's 4,000% Price Increase Might Finally Spur Action on Soaring Health-Care Costs," *Washington Post*, September 21, 2015.

4. Joseph Walker, "Patients Struggle with High Drug Prices," *The Wall Street Journal,* December 31, 2015.

5. Andrew Pollock, "Drug Prices Soar, Prompting Calls for Justification," *New York Times*, July 23, 2015.

6. Jessica Firger, "Prescription Drugs on the Rise: Estimates Suggest 60 Percent of Americans Take at Least One Medication," *Newsweek*, November 3, 2015.

7. Joseph A. DiMasi and Henry G. Grabowski, "The Cost of Biopharmaceutical R&D: Is Biotech Different?," *Managerial and Decision Economics* 28, no. 4–5 (2011), pp. 469–479.

8. Pollock and Tavernise, "Valeant's Drug Price Strategy Enriches It, but Infuriates Patients and Lawmakers."

9. Jonathan D. Rockoff, "How Pfizer Set the Cost of Its New Drug at $9,850 a Month," *The Wall Street Journal*, December 9, 2015.

10. Ibid.

11. Ibid.

12. Jeanne Whalen, "Why the U.S. Pays More Than Other Countries for Drugs," *The Wall Street Journal*, December 1, 2015.

13. Ibid.

14. Ibid.

15. Ibid.

16. Ibid.

17. Ibid.

18. Ibid.

19. Ibid.

20. Ibid.

21. Ibid.

22. Ibid.

23. Ibid.

24. Ibid.

25. Ibid.

26. Ibid.

27. Ibid.

28. Ibid.

29. Andrew Frakt, "To Reduce the Costs of Drugs, Look to Europe," *New York Times*, October 19, 2015.

30. Ibid.

31. Ibid.

32. Ibid.

33. America's Health Insurance Plans Center for Policy and Research, "Issue Brief: Specialty Drugs—Issues and Challenges," July 2015.

34. EvaluatePharma, *Orphan Drug Report 2014*, October 2014, www.evaluategroup.com/public/Reports/EvaluatePharma-Orphan-Drug-Report-2014.aspx.

35. "Trade, Foreign Policy, Diplomacy, and Health—Access to Medicines," *World Health Organization*, http://www.who.int/trade/en/.

36. "Neglected Tropical Diseases," *World Health Organization*, www.who.int/neglected_diseases/diseases/en/.

37. Neglected Tropical Diseases," Centers for Disease Control and Prevention, November 22, 2013, www.cdc.gov/globalhealth/ntd/global_program.html.

38. Neglected Tropical Diseases Program, *USAID*, https://www.neglecteddiseases.gov/about/what-we-do.

39. Alexander Gaffney and Michael Mezher, "Regulatory Explainer: Everything You Need to Know About FDA's Priority Review Vouchers," July 2, 2015, www.raps.org/Regulatory-Focus/News/2015/07/02/21722/Regulatory-Explainer-Everything-You-Need-to-Know-About-FDA%E2%80%99s-Priority-Review-Vouchers/#sthash.1NDz9gW3.dpuf.

40. Food and Drug Administration Amendments Act of 2007, Pub. L. No. 110-85, 121 Stat. 823.

41. Access to Medicine Foundation, *Access to Medicine Index 2014* (November 2014), www.accesstomedicineindex.org/sites/2015.atmindex.org/files/2014_accesstomedicineindex_fullreport_clickablepdf.pdf.

42. "About," *Mectizan Donation Program*, www.mectizan.org/about (last visited July 12, 2016).

43. Ibid.

44. "The Novartis Malaria Initiative," *Novartis*, www.malaria.novartis.com/images/Brochure-Malaria-Initiative.pdf (last visited July 12, 2016).

45. Ibid.

46. Ibid.

PART TWO

THE ROLE
OF CULTURE

Chapter 4

THE MEANINGS AND DIMENSIONS OF CULTURE

A major challenge of doing business internationally is to respond and adapt effectively to different cultures. Such adaptation requires an understanding of cultural diversity, perceptions, stereotypes, and values. In recent years, a great deal of research has been conducted on cultural dimensions and attitudes, and the findings have proved useful in providing integrative profiles of international cultures. However, a word of caution must be given when discussing these country profiles. It must be remembered that stereotypes and overgeneralizations should be avoided; there are always individual differences and even subcultures within every country.

This chapter examines the meaning of culture as it applies to international management, reviews some of the value differences and similarities of various national groups, studies important dimensions of culture and their impact on behavior, and examines country clusters. The specific objectives of this chapter are

1. **DEFINE** the term *culture*, and discuss some of the comparative ways of differentiating cultures.

2. **DESCRIBE** the concept of cultural values, and relate some of the international differences, similarities, and changes occurring in terms of both work and managerial values.

3. **IDENTIFY** the major dimensions of culture relevant to work settings, and discuss their effects on behavior in an international environment.

4. **DISCUSS** the value of country cluster analysis and relational orientations in developing effective international management practices.

The World of *International Management*

Culture Clashes in Cross-Border Mergers and Acquisitions

In one of the largest cross-border deals ever proposed, Belgian-Brazilian beverage giant ABInBev offered US$104.2 billion to acquire British-owned SABMiller. Both companies have multiple investments and brands in every major beer market in the world. The merger brings ABInBev's brands of Budweiser, Busch, Corona, and Stella Artois together with SABMiller's brands of Miller, Foster, Grolsch, Peroni, Castle, and Carlton, resulting in the largest beverage company on the globe. The combined company will account for 30 percent of beer sales worldwide and 60 percent of sales in the U.S. market. In late 2015, SABMiller's shareholders agreed to the terms of the deal.[1]

Mergers and acquisitions are among the most challenging strategic moves by companies seeking to grow their markets and reap hoped-for efficiencies. Many cross-border mergers and acquisitions have failed or experienced extreme difficulties in the face of cultural differences that manifest in communication, work policies, compensation systems, and other aspects of strategy and operations. These cultural differences can be aggravated by geographic, institutional, and psychological distance. With operations spanning the globe, and leadership teams in both Latin America and Europe, the combined ABInBev and SABMiller company will need to address the interests of its culturally diverse constituencies.

Although both SABMiller and ABInBev have recent, extensive experience with cross-border mergers and acquisitions, neither company has been involved in a deal this large. How can this integrated company fully realize the benefits of combining people, production, and brands from diverse cultures? Will ABInBev be able to achieve its aggressive sales goal of US$100 billion annually by 2020? Looking at some past cross-border mergers, both successful and failed, may provide some insight.

DuPont in Denmark

When DuPont, the U.S.-based giant chemicals company, set out to acquire Danisco, a Danish producer of food ingredients, shareholders in Denmark initially voiced skepticism and disapproval. To better understand the concerns of the Danish investment community, DuPont sent executives to Copenhagen.[2] Gaining an understanding of the cultural and business perspectives of those shareholders through face-to-face, in-person meetings, DuPont executives were able to determine that their original offer was seen as offensively low. In response, DuPont adjusted its offer, resulting in a 92 percent approval rate from Danisco's shareholders. Dupont's CEO claims, "These face-to-face conversations were critical for the actions we took next, and, ultimately, for the successful outcome of the deal."[3]

After the deal was complete, DuPont made culture a strong focus of itsintegration efforts by first hosting a "Welcome Week" with presentations to all employees about the new combined firm, adjusted to local communication styles. After this week-long celebration, designed to encourage excitement and positive thinking, the company gauged successes and failures using regular pulse surveys. These surveys "created a heat map of potential geographic locations where there might be confusion or miscommunication."[4] Anticipating and measuring potential places of difficulty allowed managers to address issues as quickly and transparently as possible, easing the integration process. DuPont's CEO reflected on the successful acquisition of Danisco, saying, "If we didn't execute and integrate well, and if we didn't get synergies quickly, it wouldn't be a victory."[5]

DuPont's careful, level-headed due diligence, strong communication, and appreciation for Danisco's corporate and national cultures ultimately helped the firm evaluate the potential success of a combined business venture and avoided deal-ending cultural conflicts. Forming the right deal and designing an integration process with the goal of maximizing the value of the deal provided the merging companies with the tools necessary to optimize their combined value and avoid the pitfalls of cultural miscommunications.[6]

The Daimler-Chrysler Debacle

Looking at failed cross-border mergers can lend some valuable insight as well. One classic case is that of Daimler-Chrysler, two companies that came together in a US$36 billion acquisition that faced severe challenges from the start. Although it was hailed as a historic "merger of equals," enthusiasm dissolved in the face of cultural and personality clashes.[7] From the onset, German executives were uncomfortable with the lack of protocol and loose structure at Chrysler. Conversely, the American managers felt that their German bosses were too formal and lacked any flexibility.

In its first attempt to resolve these issues, top leaders at the company quickly worked to establish firm-wide processes that would dictate a unified approach to planning, information exchange, communication, and decision making. Executives believed that a unified company culture—part American, part German—would lead to a better working relationship between employees and result in improved fiscal results for the company. After just a few months, however, continued cultural difficulty led executives to conclude that imposing a single culture on its diverse workforce was a short-sighted strategy. Engineers between the two companies continued to disagree over quality and design, and personality conflicts persisted. Americans found Germans to have an "attitude," while Germans found Americans to be "chaotic."[8]

In response to these failures, Daimler-Chrysler took a more drastic approach to altering its operations. Rather than attempting to impose the Daimler culture on Chrysler employees, individual business groups were permitted to adopt whichever culture worked best for them. Essentially, two cultures were allowed to persist at the merged company—those of American Chrysler and of German Daimler. Though this strategy worked well for groups that were located solely in the United States or Germany, business divisions that spanned both countries continued to face challenges. Communication was often misinterpreted, and the approach to staffing was questioned by executives on both sides.[9]

After a decade of struggle, the merger was ultimately reversed. Daimler sold nearly its entire stake in Chrysler to an American private equity group for a fraction of its original investment, and Chrylser entered bankruptcy proceedings just two years later. Roland Klein, former manager of corporate communications at the merged Daimler-Chrysler, remarked that "Maybe we should have had a cultural specialist to counsel us. But we wanted to achieve the integration without outside help."[10]

ABInBev's Past Experiences

In many ways, ABInBev's own history may provide the best example of a previously successful cross-border merger. In 2008, Belgian-Brazilian-based InBev acquired U.S.-based Anheuser Busch, creating the world's largest brewing company. InBev first bid $65 per share for Anheuser Bush, which was initially rejected. The final price agreed to was $70 per share. With operations on every continent, the newly combined company had to quickly adapt to diverse national and organizational culture backgrounds. InBev's organizational culture, heavily influenced by AmBev, was described as "a work atmosphere reminiscent of an athletic locker room . . . a culture that includes ferocious cost cutting and lucrative incentive-based compensation programs."[11] In contrast to this, Anheuser-Busch was known as a family-friendly company founded in St. Louis in the 1800s with strong emphasis on community involvement. Anheuser-Busch "won numerous awards for its philanthropy, diversity, community involvement, and employer of choice. The company was known for luxurious executive offices and lots of perks, with six planes and two helicopters to transport its employees."[12]

It was clear to leadership that these two distinct cultures—one very competitive and low cost, the other inclusive with many expensive corporate reward systems—would create conflicts in regards to communication, informal relationships between employees, employee satisfaction, and mentorship.[13] In response, ABInBev formulated an integration plan that, among other actions, led to the creation of a new board of directors for the combined company, which included the current directors of the InBev board, the Anheuser-Busch president and CEO, as well as one other current or former director of the Anheuser-Busch board. The management team consisted of executives from both companies' current leadership teams.[14] Ultimately, the ABInBev merger was a financial success, with EBITDA rising from 23 percent to 38 percent in the three years following the deal. Despite initial cultural clashes, this merger succeeded due to the recognition and education of these differences and the international management experience of the company's leaders.[15]

Going Forward

Companies from the same cultural clusters inherently understand one another's values, expectations of leadership, and communication styles better than people from different cultural clusters would. With diligent planning and education of their workforce, two firms from different organizational and national cultural backgrounds, such as SABMiller and ABInBev, can still find success through mergers or acquisitions. Although companies from different geographic regions would not have an "inherent understanding," it is possible to replicate it through employee training and strong leadership, as past mergers at DuPont and ABInBev demonstrated. Managers and executives at a newly merged company should educate its employees on the cultural differences of the two joining firms, putting the combined company in a position to leverage the merger as an opportunity to create a new corporate culture that emphasizes elements and values common to both companies' national cultures while preserving, where necessary, attributes of the distinct cultures of each.

Despite diversity among its British, Belgian, Brazilian, and American roots, cultural commonalities and understanding may help to propel the SABMiller and ABInBev merger forward. The companies certainly face challenges ahead, but, as demonstrated by past successes, proper management and careful planning can maximize their chances for long-term success.

Our opening discussion in "The World of International Management" shows how culture can have a great impact on mergers. For some companies, like DuPont and ABInBev, early recognition of differences led to more successful company integration. National cultural characteristics can strengthen, empower, and enrich management effectiveness and success. MNCs that are aware of the potential positives and negatives of different cultural characteristics will be better equipped to manage under both smooth and trying times and environments.

■ The Nature of Culture

The word *culture* comes from the Latin *cultura*, which is related to cult or worship. In its broadest sense, the term refers to the result of human interaction.[16] For the purposes of the study of international management, **culture** is acquired knowledge that people use to interpret experience and generate social behavior.[17] This knowledge forms values, creates attitudes, and influences behavior. Most scholars of culture would agree on the following characteristics of culture:

culture
Acquired knowledge that people use to interpret experience and generate social behavior. This knowledge forms values, creates attitudes, and influences behavior.

1. *Learned.* Culture is not inherited or biologically based; it is acquired by learning and experience.
2. *Shared.* People as members of a group, organization, or society share culture; it is not specific to single individuals.
3. *Transgenerational.* Culture is cumulative, passed down from one generation to the next.
4. *Symbolic.* Culture is based on the human capacity to symbolize or use one thing to represent another.
5. *Patterned.* Culture has structure and is integrated; a change in one part will bring changes in another.
6. *Adaptive.* Culture is based on the human capacity to change or adapt, as opposed to the more genetically driven adaptive process of animals.[18]

Because different cultures exist in the world, an understanding of the impact of culture on behavior is critical to the study of international management.[19] If international managers do not know something about the cultures of the countries they deal with, the results can be quite disastrous. For example, a partner in one of New York's leading private banking firms tells the following story:

> I traveled nine thousand miles to meet a client and arrived with my foot in my mouth. Determined to do things right, I'd memorized the names of the key men I was to see in Singapore. No easy job, inasmuch as the names all came in threes. So, of course, I couldn't resist showing off that I'd done my homework. I began by addressing top man Lo Win Hao with plenty of well-placed Mr. Hao's—sprinkled the rest of my remarks with a Mr. Chee this and a Mr. Woon that. Great show. Until a note was passed to me from one man I'd met before, in New York. Bad news. "Too friendly too soon, Mr. Long," it said. Where diffidence is next to godliness, there I was, calling a room of VIPs, in effect, Mr. Ed and Mr. Charlie. I'd remembered everybody's name—but forgot that in Chinese the surname comes first and the given name last.[20]

■ Cultural Diversity

There are many ways of examining cultural differences and their impact on international management. Culture can affect technology transfer, managerial attitudes, managerial ideology, and even business-government relations. Perhaps most important, culture affects how people think and behave. Table 4–1, for example, compares the most important cultural values of the United States, Japan, and Arab countries. A close look at this table shows a great deal of difference among these three cultures. Culture affects a host of business-related activities, even including the common handshake. Here are some contrasting examples:

Culture	Type of Handshake
United States	Firm
Asian	Gentle (shaking hands is unfamiliar and uncomfortable for some; the exception is the Korean, who usually has a firm handshake)
British	Soft
French	Light and quick (not offered to superiors); repeated on arrival and departure
German	Brusque and firm; repeated on arrival and departure
Latin American	Moderate grasp; repeated frequently
Middle Eastern	Gentle; repeated frequently
South Africa	Light/soft; long and involved

Source: Lillian H. Chaney and Jeanette S. Martin, *Intercultural Business Communication* (Englewood Cliffs, NJ: Prentice Hall, 1995), p. 115.

Table 4–1
Priorities of Cultural Values: United States, Japan, and Arab Countries

United States	Japan	Arab Countries
1. Freedom	1. Belonging	1. Family security
2. Independence	2. Group harmony	2. Family harmony
3. Self-reliance	3. Collectiveness	3. Parental guidance
4. Equality	4. Age/seniority	4. Age
5. Individualism	5. Group consensus	5. Authority
6. Competition	6. Cooperation	6. Compromise
7. Efficiency	7. Quality	7. Devotion
8. Time	8. Patience	8. Patience
9. Directness	9. Indirectness	9. Indirectness
10. Openness	10. Go-between	10. Hospitality

Note: "1" represents the most important cultural value, "10" the least.
Source: Adapted from information found in F. Elashmawi and Philip R. Harris, *Multicultural Management* (Houston: Gulf Publishing, 1993), p. 63.

In overall terms, the cultural impact on international management is reflected by basic beliefs and behaviors. Here are some specific examples where the culture of a society can directly affect management approaches:

- *Centralized vs. decentralized decision making.* In some societies, top managers make all important organizational decisions. In others, these decisions are diffused throughout the enterprise, and middle- and lower-level managers actively participate in, and make, key decisions.
- *Safety vs. risk.* In some societies, organizational decision makers are risk-averse and have great difficulty with conditions of uncertainty. In others, risk taking is encouraged and decision making under uncertainty is common.
- *Individual vs. group rewards.* In some countries, personnel who do outstanding work are given individual rewards in the form of bonuses and commissions. In others, cultural norms require group rewards, and individual rewards are frowned on.
- *Informal vs. formal procedures.* In some societies, much is accomplished through informal means. In others, formal procedures are set forth and followed rigidly.
- *High vs. low organizational loyalty.* In some societies, people identify very strongly with their organization or employer. In others, people identify with their occupational group, such as engineer or mechanic.
- *Cooperation vs. competition.* Some societies encourage cooperation between their people. Others encourage competition between their people.
- *Short-term vs. long-term horizons.* Some cultures focus most heavily on short-term horizons, such as short-range goals of profit and efficiency. Others are more interested in long-range goals, such as market share and technological development.
- *Stability vs. innovation.* The culture of some countries encourages stability and resistance to change. The culture of others puts high value on innovation and change.

These cultural differences influence the way that international management should be conducted.

Another way of depicting cultural diversity is through visually separating its components. Figure 4–1 provides an example by using concentric circles. The outer ring consists of the explicit artifacts and products of the culture. This level is observable and consists of such things as language, food, buildings, and art. The middle ring contains the norms and values of the society. These can be both formal and informal, and they are designed to help people understand how they should behave. The inner circle contains the implicit, basic assumptions that govern behavior. By understanding these assumptions, members of a culture are able to organize themselves in a way that helps them increase the effectiveness of their problem-solving processes and interact well with each other. In explaining the nature of the inner circle, Trompenaars and Hampden-Turner have noted that

> [t]he best way to test if something is a basic assumption is when the [situation] provokes confusion or irritation. You might, for example, observe that some Japanese bow deeper than others. . . . If you ask why they do it the answer might be that they don't know but that the other person does it too (norm) or that they want to show respect for authority (value). A typical Dutch question that might follow is: "Why do you respect authority?" The most likely Japanese reaction would be either puzzlement or a smile (which might be hiding their irritation). When you question basic assumptions you are asking questions that have never been asked before. It might lead others to deeper insights, but it also might provoke annoyance. Try in the USA or the Netherlands to raise the question of why people are equal and you will see what we mean.[21]

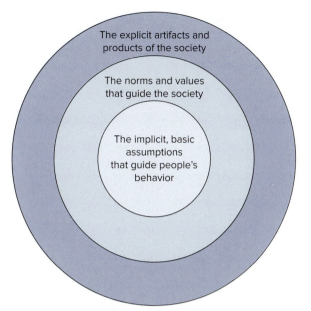

Figure 4–1

A Model of Culture

Source: Adapted from Fons Trompenaars and Charles Hampden-Turner, *Riding the Waves of Culture: Understanding Diversity in Global Business,* 2nd ed. (New York: McGraw-Hill, 1998).

A supplemental way of understanding cultural differences is to compare culture as a normal distribution, as in Figure 4–2, and then to examine it in terms of stereotyping, as in Figure 4–3. Chinese culture and American culture, for example, have quite different norms and values. So the normal distribution curves for the two cultures have only limited overlap. However, when one looks at the tail-ends of the two curves, it is possible to identify stereotypical views held by members of one culture about the other. The stereotypes are often exaggerated and used by members of one culture in describing the other, thus helping reinforce the differences between the two while reducing the likelihood of achieving cooperation and communication. This is one reason why an understanding of national culture is so important in the study of international management.

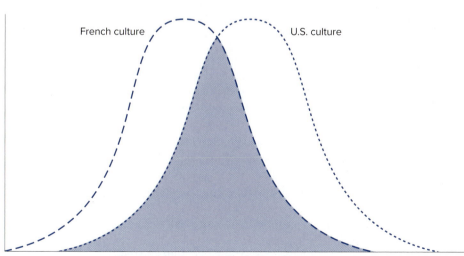

Figure 4–2

Comparing Cultures as Overlapping Normal Distributions

Source: Revised and adapted from various sources, including Fons Trompenaars and Charles Hampden-Turner, *Riding the Waves of Culture: Understanding Diversity in Global Business,* 2nd ed. (New York: McGraw-Hill, 1998), p. 25.

Figure 4–3

Stereotyping from the Cultural Extremes

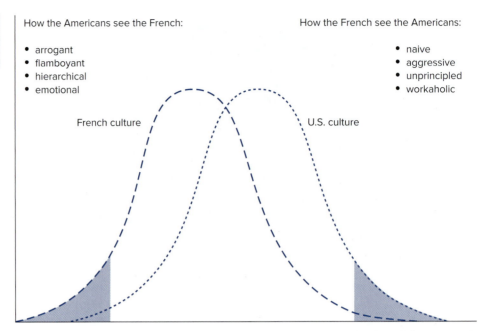

How the Americans see the French:

- arrogant
- flamboyant
- hierarchical
- emotional

French culture

How the French see the Americans:

- naive
- aggressive
- unprincipled
- workaholic

U.S. culture

Source: Revised and adapted from various sources, including Fons Trompenaars and Charles Hampden-Turner, *Riding the Waves of Culture: Understanding Diversity in Global Business,* 2nd ed. (New York: McGraw-Hill, 1998), p. 23.

■ Values in Culture

values

Basic convictions that people have regarding what is right and wrong, good and bad, and important and unimportant.

A major dimension in the study of culture is values. **Values** are basic convictions that people have regarding what is right and wrong, good and bad, and important and unimportant. These values are learned from the culture in which the individual is reared, and they help direct the person's behavior. Differences in cultural values often result in varying management practices.

Values in Transition

Do values change over time? Past research indicates that personal value systems are relatively stable and do not change rapidly.[22] However, changes are taking place in managerial values as a result of both culture and technology. A good example is provided by examining the effects of the U.S. environment on the cultural values of Japanese managers working for Japanese firms in the United States. Researchers, focusing attention on such key organizational values as lifetime employment, formal authority, group orientation, seniority, and paternalism, found that

1. Lifetime employment is widely accepted in Japanese culture, but the stateside Japanese managers did not believe that unconditional tenure in one organization was of major importance. They did believe, however, that job security was important.

2. Formal authority, obedience, and conformance to hierarchic position are very important in Japan, but the stateside managers did not perceive obedience and conformity to be very important and rejected the idea that one should not question a superior. However, they did support the concept of formal authority.

3. Group orientation, cooperation, conformity, and compromise are important organizational values in Japan. The stateside managers supported these values but also believed it was important to be an individual, thus maintaining a balance between a group and a personal orientation.

4. In Japan, organizational personnel often are rewarded based on seniority, not merit. Support for this value was directly influenced by the length of time the Japanese managers had been in the United States. The longer they had been there, the lower their support for this value.

5. Paternalism, often measured by a manager's involvement in both personal and off-the-job problems of subordinates, is very important in Japan. Stateside Japanese managers disagreed, and this resistance was positively associated with the number of years they had been in the United States.[23]

There is increasing evidence that individualism in Japan is on the rise, indicating that Japanese values are changing—and not just among managers outside the country. The country's long economic slump has convinced many Japanese that they cannot rely on the large corporations or the government to ensure their future. They have to do it for themselves. As a result, today a growing number of Japanese are starting to embrace what is being called the "era of personal responsibility." Instead of denouncing individualism as a threat to society, they are proposing it as a necessary solution to many of the country's economic ills. A vice chair of the nation's largest business lobby summed up this thinking at the opening of a recent conference on economic change when he said, "By establishing personal responsibility, we must return dynamism to the economy and revitalize society."[24] This thinking is supported by past research, which reveals that a culture with a strong entrepreneurial orientation is important to global competitiveness, especially in the small business sector of an economy. This current trend may well be helpful to the Japanese economy in helping it meet foreign competition at home.[25]

Other countries, such as China, have more recently undergone a transition of values. As discussed in Chapter 2, China is moving away from a collectivist culture, and it appears as though even China is not sure what cultural values it will adhere to. Confucianism was worshipped for over 2,000 years, but the powerful messages through Confucius's teachings were overshadowed in a world where profit became a priority. Now, Confucianism is slowly gaining popularity once again, emphasizing respect for authority, concern for others, balance, harmony, and overall order. While this may provide sanctuary for some, it poses problems within the government because it will have to prove its worthiness to remain in power. As long as China maintains economic momentum, despite its recent slowdown, hope for a unified culture may be on the horizon.[26]

■ Cultural Dimensions

Understanding the cultural context of a society, and being able to respond and react appropriately to cultural differences, is becoming increasingly important as the global environment becomes more interconnected. Over the past several decades, researchers have attempted to provide a composite picture of culture by examining its subparts, or dimensions.

Hofstede

In 1980, Dutch researcher Geert Hofstede identified four original, and later two additional, dimensions of culture that help explain how and why people from various cultures behave as they do.[27] His initial data were gathered from two questionnaire surveys with over 116,000 respondents from over 70 different countries around the world—making it the largest organizationally based study ever conducted. The individuals in these studies all worked in the local subsidiaries of IBM. As a result, Hofstede's research has been sometimes criticized because of its focus on just one company; however, samples for cross-national comparison need not be representative, as long as they are functionally equivalent. Because they are so similar in respects other than nationality (their employers, their kind of work, and—for matched occupations—their level of education), employees of multinational companies like IBM form attractive sources of information for comparing national traits. The only thing that can account for systematic and consistent differences between national groups within such a homogeneous multinational population is nationality itself—the national environment in which people were brought up before they joined this employer. Comparing IBM subsidiaries therefore shows national culture differences with unusual clarity.[28] Despite being first published nearly 40 years ago, Hofstede's massive study continues to be a focal point for additional research, including the most recent **GLOBE** project, discussed at the end of this chapter.

The original four dimensions that Hofstede examined were (1) power distance, (2) uncertainty avoidance, (3) individualism, and (4) masculinity.[29] Further research by Hofstede led to the recent identification of the fifth and sixth cultural dimensions: (5) time orientation, identified in 1988, and (6) indulgence versus restraint, identified in 2010.[30]

Power Distance   **Power distance** is "the extent to which less powerful members of institutions and organizations accept that power is distributed unequally."[31] Countries in which people blindly obey the orders of their superiors have high power distance. In many societies, lower-level employees tend to follow orders as a matter of procedure. In societies with high power distance, however, strict obedience is found even at the upper levels; examples include Mexico, South Korea, and India. For example, a senior Indian executive with a PhD from a prestigious U.S. university related the following story:

> What is most important for me and my department is not what I do or achieve for the company, but whether the [owner's] favor is bestowed on me. . . . This I have achieved by saying "yes" to everything [the owner] says or does. . . . To contradict him is to look for another job. . . . I left my freedom of thought in Boston.[32]

The effect of this dimension can be measured in a number of ways. For example, organizations in low-power-distance countries generally will be decentralized and have flatter organization structures. These organizations also will have a smaller proportion of supervisory personnel, and the lower strata of the workforce often will consist of highly qualified people. By contrast, organizations in high-power-distance countries will tend to be centralized and have tall organization structures. Organizations in high-power-distance countries will have a large proportion of supervisory personnel, and the people at the lower levels of the structure often will have low job qualifications. This latter structure encourages and promotes inequality between people at different levels.[33]

Uncertainty Avoidance   **Uncertainty avoidance** is "the extent to which people feel threatened by ambiguous situations and have created beliefs and institutions that try to avoid these."[34] Countries populated with people who do not like uncertainty tend to have a high need for security and a strong belief in experts and their knowledge; examples include Germany, Japan, and Spain. Cultures with low uncertainty avoidance have people who are more willing to accept that risks are associated with the unknown and that life must go on in spite of this. Examples include Denmark and Great Britain.

The effect of this dimension can be measured in a number of ways. Countries with high-uncertainty-avoidance cultures have a great deal of structuring of organizational activities, more written rules, less risk taking by managers, lower labor turnover, and less ambitious employees.

Low-uncertainty-avoidance societies have organization settings with less structuring of activities, fewer written rules, more risk taking by managers, higher labor turnover, and more ambitious employees. The organization encourages personnel to use their own initiative and assume responsibility for their actions.

Individualism   We discussed individualism and collectivism in Chapter 2 in reference to political systems. **Individualism** is the tendency of people to look after themselves and their immediate family only.[35] Hofstede measured this cultural difference on a bipolar continuum with individualism at one end and collectivism at the other. **Collectivism** is

---

GLOBE (Global Leadership and Organizational Behavior Effectiveness)
A multicountry study and evaluation of cultural attributes and leadership behaviors among more than 17,000 managers from 951 organizations in 62 countries.

power distance
The extent to which less powerful members of institutions and organizations accept that power is distributed unequally.

uncertainty avoidance
The extent to which people feel threatened by ambiguous situations and have created beliefs and institutions that try to avoid these.

individualism
The political philosophy that people should be free to pursue economic and political endeavors without constraint (Chapter 2); the tendency of people to look after themselves and their immediate family only (Chapter 4).

collectivism
The political philosophy that views the needs or goals of society as a whole as more important than individual desires (Chapter 2); the tendency of people to belong to groups or collectives and to look after each other in exchange for loyalty (Chapter 4).

Table 4–2
Countries and Regions Used in Hofstede's Research

Arabic-speaking countries (Egypt, Iraq, Kuwait, Lebanon, Libya, Saudi Arabia, United Arab Emirates)	Ecuador	Panama
	Estonia	Peru
	Finland	Philippines
	France	Poland
	Germany	Portugal
	Great Britain	Romania
	Greece	Russia
Argentina	Guatemala	Salvador
Australia	Hong Kong (China)	Serbia
Austria		Singapore
Bangladesh	Hungary	Slovakia
Belgium Flemish (Dutch speaking)	India	Slovenia
	Indonesia	South Africa
Belgium Walloon (French speaking)	Iran	Spain
	Ireland	Suriname
Brazil	Israel	Sweden
Bulgaria	Italy	Switzerland French
Canada Quebec	Jamaica	Switzerland German
Canada total	Japan	Taiwan
Chile	Korea (South)	Thailand
China	Luxembourg	Trinidad
Colombia	Malaysia	Turkey
Costa Rica	Malta	United States
Croatia	Mexico	Uruguay
Czech Republic	Morocco	Venezuela
Denmark	Netherlands	Vietnam
East Africa (Ethiopia, Kenya, Tanzania, Zambia)	New Zealand	West Africa (Ghana, Nigeria, Sierra Leone)
	Norway	
	Pakistan	

Source: From G. Hofstede and G. J. Hofstede, *Cultures and Organizations: Software of the Mind*, 2nd ed. (New York: McGraw-Hill, 2005).

the tendency of people to belong to groups or collectives and to look after each other in exchange for loyalty.[36]

Like the effects of the other cultural dimensions, the effects of individualism and collectivism can be measured in a number of different ways.[37] Hofstede found that wealthy countries have higher individualism scores and poorer countries higher collectivism scores (see Table 4–2 for the 74 countries used in Figure 4–4 and subsequent figures). Note that in Figure 4–4, the United States, Canada, Australia, France, and the United Kingdom, among others, have high individualism and high GNP. Conversely, China, Mexico, and a number of South American countries have low individualism (high collectivism) and low GNP. Countries with high individualism also tend to have greater support for the Protestant work ethic, greater individual initiative, and promotions based on market value. Countries with low individualism tend to have less support for the Protestant work ethic, less individual initiative, and promotions based on seniority.

Masculinity **Masculinity** is defined by Hofstede as "a situation in which the dominant values in society are success, money, and things."[38] Hofstede measured this

masculinity
A cultural characteristic in which the dominant values in society are success, money, and things.

Figure 4–4

GDP per Capita in 2015 versus Individualism

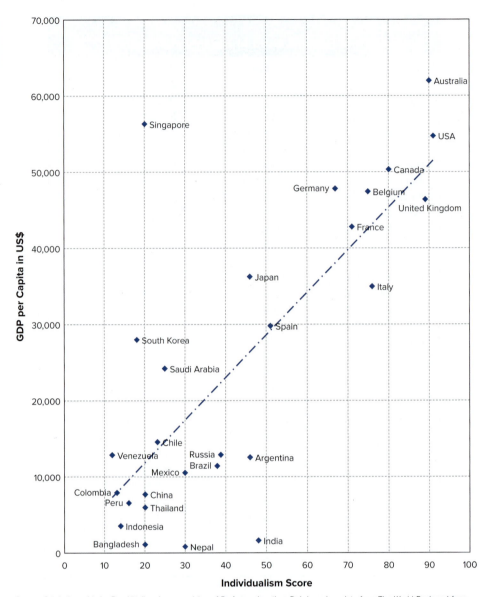

Source: Original graphic by Ben Littell under supervision of Professor Jonathan Doh based on data from The World Bank and from G. Hofstede and G. J. Hofstede, *Cultures and Organizations: Software of the Mind*, 2nd ed. (New York: McGraw-Hill, 2005).

femininity

A cultural characteristic in which the dominant values in society are caring for others and the quality of life.

dimension on a continuum ranging from masculinity to femininity. Contrary to some stereotypes and connotations, **femininity** is the term used by Hofstede to describe "a situation in which the dominant values in society are caring for others and the quality of life."[39]

Countries with a high masculinity index, such as the Germanic countries, place great importance on earnings, recognition, advancement, and challenge. Individuals are encouraged to be independent decision makers, and achievement is defined in terms of recognition and wealth. The workplace is often characterized by high job stress, and many managers believe that their employees dislike work and must be kept under some degree of control. The school system is geared toward encouraging high performance. Young men expect to have careers, and those who do not often view themselves as failures. Historically, fewer women hold higher-level jobs, although this is changing. The school system is geared toward encouraging high performance.

Table 4–3
Ten Differences between Short- and Long-Term-Oriented Societies

Short-Term Orientation	Long-Term Orientation
Most important events in life occurred in the past or take place now	Most important events in life will occur in the future
Personal steadiness and stability: a good person is always the same	A good person adapts to the circumstances
There are universal guidelines about what are good and evil	What are good and evil depend on the circumstances
Traditions are sacrosanct	Traditions are adaptable to changed circumstances
Family life is guided by imperatives	Family life is guided by shared tasks
Supposed to be proud of one's country	Trying to learn from other countries
Service to others is an important goal	Thrift and perseverance are important goals
Social spending and consumption	Large savings quote, funds available for investment
Students attribute success and failure to luck	Students attribute success to effort and failure to lack of effort
Slow or no economic growth of poor countries	Fast economic growth of countries up until a level of prosperity

Source: From G. Hofstede, "Dimensionalizing Cultures: The Hofstede Model in Context," *Online Readings in Psychology and Culture,* Unit 2 (2011), http://scholarworks.gvsu.edu/orpc/vol2/iss1/8/.

Countries with a low masculinity index (Hofstede's femininity dimension), such as Norway, tend to place great importance on cooperation, a friendly atmosphere, and employment security. Individuals are encouraged to be group decision makers, and achievement is defined in terms of layman contacts and the living environment. The workplace tends to be characterized by low stress, and managers give their employees more credit for being responsible and allow them more freedom. Culturally, this group prefers small-scale enterprises, and they place greater importance on conservation of the environment. The school system is designed to teach social adaptation. Some young men and women want careers; others do not. Many women hold higher-level jobs and do not find it necessary to be assertive.

Time Orientation Originally called Confucian Work Dynamism, time orientation is defined by Hofstede as "dealing with society's search for virtue." Long-term-oriented societies tend to focus on the future. They have the ability to adapt their traditions when conditions change, have a tendency to save and invest for the future, and focus on achieving long-term results. Short-term-oriented cultures focus more on the past and present than on the future. These societies have a deep respect for tradition, focus on achieving quick results, and do not tend to save for the future.[40] Hofstede's original time orientation research only included 23 countries, leading to some criticism. However, in 2010, the research was expanded to include 93 countries. Table 4–3 highlights ten differences between long- and short-term-oriented cultures.

Asian cultures primarily exhibit long-term orientation. Countries with a high long-term orientation index include China, Japan, and Indonesia (see Figure 4–5). In these cultures, individuals are persistent, thrifty with their money, and highly adaptable to unexpected circumstances. Relationships tend to be ordered by status, which can affect the way that situations are handled. Additionally, people in long-term-oriented cultures are more likely to believe that there are multiple truths to issues that arise, rather than just one, absolute answer.

Figure 4–5

Countries with Very High Long-Term and Short-Term Orientation Scores

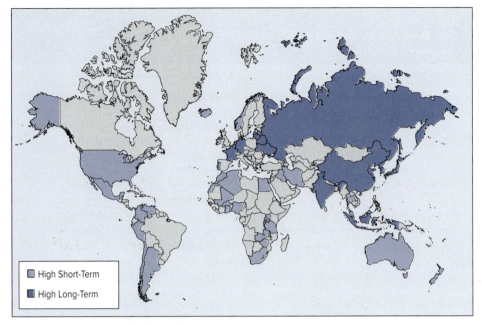

High Short-Term
High Long-Term

Note: Country rankings were completed using Geert Hofstede's Long-Term Orientation (LTO) scores. *High Short-Term* refers to countries with scores less than 35 and *High Long-Term* refers to countries with scores greater than 60.

Source: Original graphic by Ben Littell under supervision of Professor Jonathan Doh based on data from Geert Hofstede, "Dimensionalizing Cultures: The Hofstede Model in Context," *Online Readings in Psychology and Culture*, Unit 2 (2011), http://scholarworks.gvsu.edu/orpc/vol2/iss1/8/.

Spain, the USA, and the UK were identified as having a low long-term orientation index (Hofstede's short-term orientation). Individuals in short-term-oriented societies believe in absolutes (good and evil), value stability and leisure time, and spend money more freely. Traditional approaches are respected, and feedback cycles tend to be short. Gift giving and greetings are shared and reciprocated.[41]

Indulgence versus Restraint   Based on research related to relative happiness around the world, Hofstede's most recent dimension measures the freedom to satisfy one's natural needs and desires within a society. Indulgent societies encourage instant gratification of natural human needs, while restrained cultures regulate and control behavior based on social norms.[42] The research leading to the identification of this sixth dimension included participants from 93 countries. Table 4–4 highlights ten differences between indulgent and restrained cultures.

Countries that show a high indulgence index tend to be located in the Americas and Western Europe, including the USA, Australia, Mexico, and Chile (see Figure 4–6). Freely able to satisfy their basic human desires, individuals in these societies tend to live in the moment. They participate in more sports and activities, express happiness freely, and view themselves as being in control of their own destiny. Freedom of speech is considered vital, and smaller police forces are commonplace. People in indulgent cultures tend to view friendships as important, have less moral discipline, and exhibit a more extroverted, positive personality.

Countries that show a low indulgence index (Hofstede's dimension of high restraint) tend to be located in Asia and Eastern Europe, including Egypt, Russia, India, and China. In these societies, individuals participate in fewer activities and sports, express less happiness, and believe that their own destiny is not in their control. Maintaining order is seen as vital, resulting in larger police forces and less crime. People tend to value work ethic over friendships, exhibit introverted personalities, and follow a stricter moral discipline.[43]

Table 4–4
Ten Differences between Indulgent and Restrained Societies

Indulgent	Restrained
Higher percentage of people declaring themselves very happy	Fewer very happy people
A perception of personal life control	A perception of helplessness: what happens to me is not my own doing
Freedom of speech seen as important	Freedom of speech is not a primary concern
Higher importance of leisure	Lower importance of leisure
More likely to remember positive emotions	Less likely to remember positive emotions
In countries with educated populations, higher birthrates	In countries with educated populations, lower birthrates
More people actively involved in sports	Fewer people actively involved in sports
In countries with enough food, higher percentages of obese people	In countries with enough food, fewer obese people
In wealthy countries, lenient sexual norms	In wealthy countries, stricter sexual norms
Maintaining order in the nation is not given a high priority	Higher number of police officers per 100,000 population

Source: From Geert Hofstede, "Dimensionalizing Cultures: The Hofstede Model in Context," *Online Readings in Psychology and Culture*, Unit 2 (2011), http://scholarworks.gvsu.edu/orpc/vol2/iss1/8/.

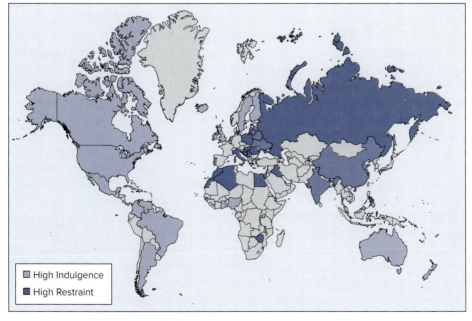

Figure 4–6

Countries with Very High Indulgence and Restraint Scores

■ High Indulgence
■ High Restraint

Note: Country rankings were completed using Geert Hofstede's Indulgence versus Restraint (IVR) scores. *High Indulgence* refers to countries with scores greater than 50 and *High Restraint* refers to countries with scores less than 25.

Source: Original graphic by Ben Littell under supervision of Professor Jonathan Doh based on data from Geert Hofstede, "Dimensionalizing Cultures: The Hofstede Model in Context," *Online Readings in Psychology and Culture*, Unit 2 (2011), http://scholarworks.gvsu.edu/orpc/vol2/iss1/8/.

Integrating the Dimensions A description of the four original and two additional dimensions of culture is useful in helping to explain the differences between various countries, and Hofstede's research has extended beyond this focus and shown how countries can be described in terms of pairs of dimensions. In Hofstede's and later research, pairings and clusters can provide useful summaries for international managers. It is always best to have an in-depth understanding of the multicultural environment, but the general groupings outline common ground that one can use as a starting point. Figure 4–7, which incorporates power distance and individualism, provides an example.

Upon first examination of the cluster distribution, the data may appear confusing. However, they are very useful in depicting what countries appear similar in values and to what extent they differ from other country clusters. The same countries are not always clustered together in subsequent dimension comparisons. This indicates

Figure 4–7

Power Distance versus Individualism

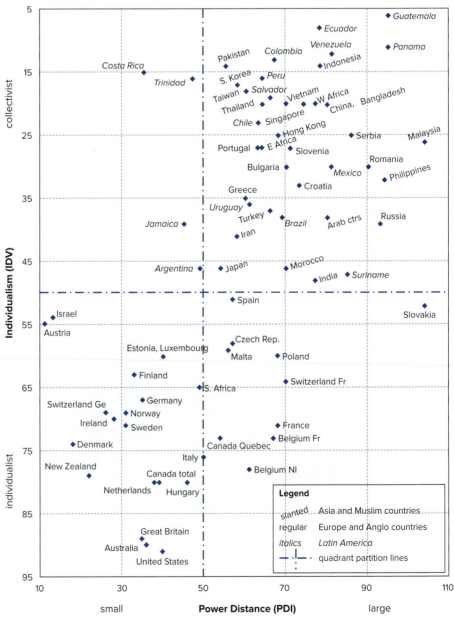

Source: From G. Hofstede and G. J. Hofstede, *Cultures and Organizations: Software of the Mind*, 2nd ed. (New York: McGraw-Hill, 2005).

that while some beliefs overlap between cultures, it is where they diverge that makes groups unique to manage.

In Figure 4–7, the United States, Australia, Canada, Britain, Denmark, and New Zealand are located in the lower-left-hand quadrant. Americans, for example, have very high individualism and relatively low power distance. They prefer to do things for themselves and are not upset when others have more power than they do. The other countries, while they may not be a part of the same cluster, share similar values. Conversely, many of the underdeveloped or newly industrialized countries, such as Colombia, Hong Kong, Portugal, and Singapore, are characterized by large power distance and low individualism. These nations tend to be collectivist in their approach.

Similarly, Figure 4–8 plots the uncertainty-avoidance index against the power-distance index. Once again, there are clusters of countries. Many of the Anglo nations tend to be in the upper-left-hand quadrant, which is characterized by small power distance

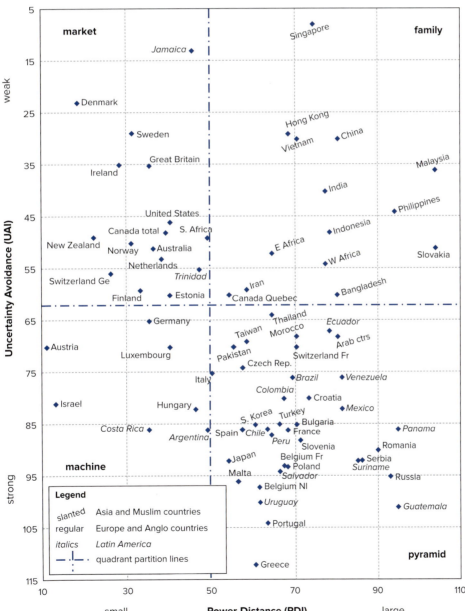

Figure 4–8

Power Distance versus Uncertainty Avoidance

Source: From G. Hofstede and G. J. Hofstede, *Cultures and Organizations: Software of the Mind,* 2nd ed. (New York: McGraw-Hill, 2005).

Chapter 5

MANAGING ACROSS CULTURES

OBJECTIVES OF THE CHAPTER

Traditionally, both scholars and practitioners assumed the universality of management. There was a tendency to take the management concepts and techniques that worked at home into other countries and cultures. It is now clear, from both practice and cross-cultural research, that this universality assumption, at least across cultures, does not hold up. Although there is a tendency in a borderless economy to promote a universalist approach, there is enough evidence from many cross-cultural researchers to conclude that the universalist assumption that may have held for U.S. organizations and employees is not generally true in other cultures.[1]

The overriding purpose of this chapter is to examine how MNCs can and should manage across cultures. This chapter puts into practice Chapter 4's discussion on the meaning and dimensions of culture and serves as a foundation and point of departure for Chapters 8 and 9 on strategic management. The first part of this chapter addresses the traditional tendency to attempt to replicate successful home-country operations overseas without taking into account cultural differences. Next, attention is given to cross-cultural challenges, focusing on how differences can impact multinational management strategies. Finally, the cultures in specific countries and geographic regions are examined. The specific objectives of this chapter are

1. **EXAMINE** the strategic dispositions that characterize responses to different cultures.

2. **DISCUSS** cross-cultural differences and similarities.

3. **REVIEW** cultural differences in select countries and regions, and note some of the important strategic guidelines for doing business in each.

The World of *International Management*

Taking a Bite Out of Apple: Corporate Culture and an Unlikely Chinese Start-Up

Since first introducing the iPhone in 2007, Apple has achieved tremendous success in the smartphone industry. User-friendly innovations, including the first touchscreen display, transformed the smartphone market. Through 2015, Apple has sold over 800 million iPhones, becoming one of the most admired and recognizable brands worldwide.[2] Though Apple has faced competition from traditional rivals Samsung and Motorola for several years, new competition from unexpected companies in developing markets is beginning to disrupt the smartphone market. Xiaomi, a Chinese start-up formed in 2010, is perhaps the largest and most successful of these new smartphone marketplace entrants. Xiaomi released its first phone in 2011; since then, sales have soared. By 2013, Xiaomi had surpassed Apple in terms of sales within China, the world's largest smartphone market. And in 2015, Xiaomi became the fourth largest smartphone producer worldwide.

Though they are competing for the same customers, Apple and Xiaomi could not be more different. Their approaches to innovation, their supply chains, their product lines, and even their ideas about intellectual property rights are diametrically opposed. How have these two incredibly different companies achieved success, and will Xiaomi's corporate culture and accompanying strategy ultimately propel the company to rival Apple in the smartphone battle?

Individual versus the Collective

At Apple, individual achievement is highly regarded. Innovating for the company, as an individual, is expected and required. In fact, according to an urban legend, Steve Jobs allegedly once fired an employee in the elevator for not having an answer to the question, "So what have you done for Apple lately?" Personal excellence is required by every employee, with an overall focus on end results and exceeding corporate goals.[3] Internal competition, and challenging others, is strongly encouraged. Hierarchy exists, but individuals are encouraged to speak up if it means achieving a better, more innovative product. According to a former employee, "There's a mentality that it's okay to shred somebody in the spirit of making the best products."[4]

Collectivism and group achievement, on the other hand, permeate Xiaomi's corporate culture. From initial design to final production, collaboration between employees and the public is more celebrated than individual creativity. Rather than developing innovations in secret, Xiaomi takes an unconventional approach to design by using crowd-sourcing as a key element of its strategy.[5] End users provide input and feedback continuously to Xiaomi, shaping the direction in which Xiaomi takes it products. This feedback results in continual product evolution; rather than release new phones annually, like Apple, Xiaomi actually releases new, incrementally better smartphone models every week.[6]

Supply Chain Management

Apple has been able to maximize profits through its complex, yet carefully doctored, supply chain. To minimize costs, Apple outsources the majority of its production processes. Nearly a thousand factories produce components for Apple across the globe, with over 600 in Southeast Asia alone.[7] As a result of its low manufacturing costs, Apple is able to sell the majority of its products with a 70 percent gross profit margin. Relinquishing its control over the manufacturing process, however, has led to some major negative consequences for Apple. In 2012, Apple was unable to meet customer demand for the iPad Mini due to supply chain issues that resulted in lower-than-expected production numbers.[8] Furthermore, the lack of control over its suppliers' actions has exposed Apple to criticism over human rights violations. Highly publicized worker suicides and alleged underage labor have tarnished Apple's image, even though the abuses occurred at the suppliers' facilities.

Like Apple, Xiaomi works with a variety of suppliers throughout Asia to produce its products. A key advantage for Xiaomi's approach to its supply chain, however, is its unique ability to adjust production to meet demand. To achieve this, Xiaomi maintains a strict policy with its suppliers that demand alone drives the production quantity. This has allowed for great flexibility in its supply. For example, in 2015, Xiaomi was able to set the world record for most smartphones sold in 24 hours when it sold and shipped 2.1 million units. To keep costs along its supply chain low, Xiaomi sells its products for longer periods of time than its competitors, reducing

production expenses over the life of the product. While Apple and other competitors retire their products nearly every year, Xiaomi will continue to manufacture the same phone for nearly two years.[9] This flexibility also lowers inventory carrying costs. Xiaomi owns no warehouses for long-term inventory holding, considering itself more of an Internet-based merchant.[10]

Product Focus

Apple is dedicated to maintaining first-mover advantage. As a result, Apple focuses narrowly on a few key products, with little variation in features and price. The iPhone, for example, is the only phone offered by Apple. When purchasing the latest Apple product, customers know that they are buying the most current technology on the market. By continually being the first to market with new technology, Apple is able to maintain a loyal customer base that is willing to put up with minor defects and flaws in design. This narrow product focus has created a trendy "brand" image for the company. However, by only offering one product line, Apple sacrifices sales to potential customers who are less concerned with the latest technology.

Knowing that it cannot compete for the first-mover customers who want the newest technology fastest, Xiaomi focuses on competing on price. Xiaomi aims to provide the best value in the marketplace to its customers by not sacrificing quality to meet consumer pricing demands; the hardware specifications of Xiaomi phones rival those of Apple and Samsung but remain at a fraction of the cost. Unlike Apple, Xiaomi offers a wide array of products at multiple price points. In fact, Xiaomi plans to introduce regionally specific models for every new market it enters. With dozens of different phone products, for example, customers can sacrifice features and the most current technology for a phone within their budget. Xiaomi is willing to quickly try multiple products, releasing slightly updated models nearly every week.[11]

Intellectual Property

Apple, as a company that differentiates itself through innovation, values its intellectual property as an important asset. This culture starts at the top and permeates through the company: Steve Jobs alone was listed as the inventor on over 300 patents.[12] Having spent millions in research and development for new technology and improved designs, Apple has accused Samsung and others of essentially stealing patent-protected technology. Apple has sued numerous companies to protect its

Table 5–1
Orientation of an MNC under Different Profiles

	Orientation of the Firm			
	Ethnocentric	**Polycentric**	**Regiocentric**	**Geocentric**
Mission	Profitability (viability)	Public acceptance (legitimacy)	Both profitability and public acceptance (viability and legitimacy)	Same as regiocentric
Governance	Top-down	Bottom-up (each subsidiary decides on local objectives)	Mutually negotiated between region and its subsidiaries	Mutually negotiated at all levels of the corporation
Strategy	Global integration	National responsiveness	Regional integration and national responsiveness	Global integration and national responsiveness
Structure	Hierarchical product divisions	Hierarchical area divisions, with autonomous national units	Product and regional organization tied through a matrix	A network of organizations (including some stakeholders and competitor organizations)
Culture	Home country	Host country	Regional	Global
Technology	Mass production	Batch production	Flexible manufacturing	Flexible manufacturing
Marketing	Product development determined primarily by the needs of home country customers	Local product development based on local needs	Standardized within region, but not across regions	Global product, with local variations
Finance	Repatriation of profits to home country	Retention of profits in host country	Redistribution within region	Redistribution globally
Personnel practices	People of home country developed for key positions everywhere in the world	People of local nationality developed for key positions in their own country	Regional people developed for key positions anywhere in the region	Best people everywhere in the world developed for key positions everywhere in the world

Source: From Balaji S. Chakravarthy and Howard V. Perlmutter, "Strategic Planning for a Global Business," *Columbia Journal of World Business*, Summer 1985, pp. 5–6.

tries to integrate a global systems approach to decision making. Table 5–1 provides details of each of these orientations.

If an MNC relies on one of these profiles over an extended time, the approach may become institutionalized and greatly influence strategic planning. By the same token, a predisposition toward any of these profiles can provide problems for a firm if it is out of step with the economic or political environment. For example, a firm with an ethnocentric predisposition may find it difficult to implement a geocentric strategy because it is unaccustomed to using global integration. Commonly, successful MNCs use a mix of these predispositions based on the demands of the current environment described in the chapters in Part One.

Meeting the Challenge

globalization imperative
A belief that one worldwide approach to doing business is the key to both efficiency and effectiveness.

Despite the need for and, in general, the tendency of MNCs to address regional differentiation issues, many MNCs remain committed to a **globalization imperative**, which is a belief that one worldwide approach to doing business is the key to both efficiency and effectiveness. However, despite this predilection to use home strategies, effective MNCs are continuing their efforts to address local needs. A number of factors are moving companies to facilitate the development of unique strategies for different cultures, including

   1. The diversity of worldwide industry standards such as those in broadcasting, where television sets must be manufactured on a country-by-country basis.

2. A continual demand by local customers for differentiated products, as in the case of consumer goods that must meet local tastes.

3. The importance of being an insider, as in the case of customers who prefer to "buy local."

4. The difficulty of managing global organizations, as in the case of some local subsidiaries that want more decentralization and others that want less.

5. The need to allow subsidiaries to use their own abilities and talents and not be restrained by headquarters, as in the case of local units that know how to customize products for their market and generate high returns on investment with limited production output.

Responding to the cultural needs of local operations and customers, MNCs find that regional strategies can be used effectively in capturing and maintaining worldwide market niches. One example is Haier, which is discussed in the opening World of International Management section at the beginning of Chapter 9. Another example is appliance producer Whirlpool, which has manufacturing facilities spread across the United States. Each plant is specialized and produces a small number of products for the entire North American market; in this way, each can focus on tailoring products for the unique demands of the various markets.

The globalization versus national responsiveness challenge is even more acute when marketing cosmetics and other products that vary greatly in consumer use. For example, marketers sell toothpaste as a cosmetic product in Spain and Greece but as a cavity fighter in the Netherlands and United States. Soap manufacturers market their product as a cosmetic item in Spain but as a functional commodity in Germany. Moreover, the way in which the marketing message is delivered also is important. For example:

- Germans want advertising that is factual and rational; they fear being manipulated by "the hidden persuader." The typical German spot features the standard family of two parents, two children, and grandmother.

- The French avoid reasoning or logic. Their advertising is predominantly emotional, dramatic, and symbolic. Spots are viewed as cultural events—art for the sake of money—and are reviewed as if they were literature or films.

- The British value laughter above all else. The typical broad, self-deprecating British commercial amuses by mocking both the advertiser and consumer.[28]

In some cases, however, both the product and the marketing message are similar worldwide. This is particularly true for high-end products, where the lifestyles and expectations of the market niche are similar regardless of the country. Heineken beer, Hennessey brandy, Porsche cars, and the *Financial Times* all appeal to consumer niches that are fairly homogeneous, regardless of geographic locale. The same is true at the lower end of the market for goods that are impulse purchases, novel products, or fast foods, such as Coca-Cola's soft drinks, Levi's jeans, pop music, and ice-cream bars. In most cases, however, it is necessary to modify products as well as the market approach for the regional or local market. One analysis noted that the more marketers understand about the way in which a particular culture tends to view emotion, enjoyment, friendship, humor, rules, status, and other culturally based behaviors, the more control they have over creating marketing messages that will be interpreted in the desired way.

The need to adjust global strategies for regional markets presents three major challenges for most MNCs. First, the MNC must stay abreast of local market conditions and sidestep the temptation to assume that all markets are basically the same. Second, the MNC must know the strengths and weaknesses of its subsidiaries so that it can provide these units with the assistance needed in addressing local demands. Third, the multinational must give the subsidiary more autonomy so that it can respond to changes in local demands. The International Management in Action "Ten Key Factors for MNC Success" provides additional insights into the ways that successful MNCs address these challenges.

Ten Key Factors for MNC Success

Why are some international firms successful while others are not? Some of the main reasons are that successful multinational firms take a worldwide view of operations, support their overseas activities, pay close attention to political winds, and use local nationals whenever possible. These are the overall findings of a report that looked into the development of customized executive education programs. Specifically, there are 10 factors or guidelines that successful global firms seem to employ. Successful global competitors

1. See themselves as multinational enterprises and are led by a management team that is comfortable in the world arena.

2. Develop integrated and innovative strategies that make it difficult and costly for other firms to compete.

3. Aggressively and effectively implement their worldwide strategy and back it with large investments.

4. Understand that innovation no longer is confined to the United States and develop systems for tapping innovation abroad.

5. Operate as if the world were one large market rather than a series of individual, small markets.

6. Have organization structures that are designed to handle their unique problems and challenges and thus provide them the greatest efficiency.

7. Develop a system that keeps them informed about political changes around the world and the implications of these changes on the firm.

8. Have management teams that are international in composition and thus better able to respond to the various demands of their respective markets.

9. Allow their outside directors to play an active role in the operation of the enterprise.

10. Are well managed and tend to follow such important guidelines as sticking close to the customer, having lean organization structures, and encouraging autonomy and entrepreneurial activity among the personnel.

Source: James F. Bolt, "Global Competitors: Some Criteria for Success," *Business Horizons*, January–February 1988, pp. 34–41; Alan S. Rugman and Richard M. Hodgetts, *International Business*, 2nd ed. (London: Pearson, 2000), chapter 1; Sheida Hodge, *Global Smarts: The Art of Communicating and Deal Making Anywhere in the World* (New York: Wiley, 2000).

■ Cross-Cultural Differences and Similarities

As you saw in Chapter 4, cultures can be similar or quite different across countries. The challenge for MNCs is to recognize and effectively manage the similarities and differences. Generally, the way in which MNCs manage their home businesses often should be different from the way they manage their overseas operations.[29] After recognizing the danger for MNCs of drifting toward parochialism and simplification in spite of cultural differences, the discussion in this section shifts to some examples of cultural similarities and differences and how to effectively manage across cultures by a *contingency approach*.

Parochialism and Simplification

parochialism
The tendency to view the world through one's own eyes and perspectives.

Parochialism is the tendency to view the world through one's own eyes and perspectives. This can be a strong temptation for many international managers, who often come from advanced economies and believe that their state-of-the-art knowledge is more than adequate to handle the challenges of doing business in less developed countries. In addition, many of these managers have a parochial point of view fostered by their background.[30] A good example is provided by Randall and Coakley, who studied the impact of culture on successful partnerships in the former Soviet Union. Initially after the breakup of the Soviet Union, the republics called themselves the Commonwealth of Independent States (CIS). Randall and Coakley found that while outside MNC managers typically entered into partnerships with CIS enterprises with a view toward making them efficient and profitable, the CIS managers often brought a different set of priorities to the table.

Commenting on their research, Randall and Coakley noted that the way CIS managers do business is sharply different from that of their American counterparts. CIS managers are still emerging from socially focused cultural norms embedded in their history, past training, and work experiences that emphasize strategic values unlike those that exist in an international market-driven environment. For example, while an excess of unproductive workers may lead American managers to lay off some individuals for the good of the company, CIS managers would focus on the good of the working community and allow the company to accept significant profit losses as a consequence. This led the researchers to conclude:

> As behavioral change continues to lag behind structural change, it becomes imperative to understand that this inconsistency between what economic demands and cultural norms require manifests problems and complexities far beyond mere structural change. In short, the implications of the different perspectives on technology, labor, and production . . . for potential partnerships between U.S. and CIS companies need to be fully grasped by all parties entering into any form of relationship.[31]

Simplification is the process of exhibiting the same orientation toward different cultural groups. For example, the way in which a U.S. manager interacts with a British manager is the same way in which he or she behaves when doing business with an Asian executive. Moreover, this orientation reflects one's basic culture. Table 5–2 provides an example, showing several widely agreed-on, basic cultural orientations and the range of variations for each. Asterisks indicate the dominant U.S. orientation. Quite obviously, U.S. cultural values are not the same as those of managers from other cultures; as a result, a U.S. manager's attempt to simplify things can result in erroneous behavior. Here is an example of a member of the purchasing department of a large European oil company who was negotiating an order with a Korean supplier:

> At the first meeting, the Korean partner offered a silver pen to the European manager. The latter, however, politely refused the present for fear of being bribed (even though he knew about the Korean custom of giving presents). Much to our manager's surprise, the second

simplification
The process of exhibiting the same orientation toward different cultural groups.

Table 5–2
Six Basic Cultural Variations

Orientations	Range of Variations
What is the nature of people?	Good (changeable/unchangeable)
	A mixture of good and evil*
	Evil (changeable/unchangeable)
What is the person's relationship to nature?	Dominant*
	In harmony with nature
	Subjugation
What is the person's relationship to other people?	Lineal (hierarchic)
	Collateral (collectivist)
	Individualist*
What is the modality of human activity?	Doing*
	Being and becoming
	Being
What is the temporal focus of human activity?	Future*
	Present
	Past
What is the conception of space?	Private*
	Mixed
	Public

Note: *Indicates the dominant U.S. orientation.
Source: Adapted from the work of Florence Rockwood Kluckhohn and Fred L. Stodtbeck.

meeting began with the offer of a stereo system. Again the manager refused, his fear of being bribed probably heightened. When he gazed at a piece of Korean china on the third meeting, he finally realized what was going on. His refusal had not been taken to mean "let's get on with business right away," but rather "If you want to get into business with me, you had better come up with something bigger."[32]

Understanding the culture in which they do business can make international managers more effective.[33] Unfortunately, when placed in a culture with which they are unfamiliar, most international managers are not culturally knowledgeable, so they often misinterpret what is happening. This is particularly true when the environment is markedly different from the one from which they come. Consider, for example, the difference between the cultures in Malaysia and the United States. Malaysia has what could be called a high-context culture, which possesses characteristics such as

1. Relationships between people are relatively long lasting, and individuals feel deep personal involvement with each other.
2. Communication often is implicit, and individuals are taught from an early age to interpret these messages accurately.
3. People in authority are personally responsible for the actions of their subordinates, and this places a premium on loyalty to both superiors and subordinates.
4. Agreements tend to be spoken rather than written.
5. Insiders and outsiders are easily distinguishable, and outsiders typically do not gain entrance to the inner group.

These Malaysian cultural characteristics are markedly different from those of low-context cultures such as the United States, which possess the following characteristics:

1. Relationships between individuals are relatively short in duration, and in general, deep personal involvement with others is not valued greatly.
2. Messages are explicit, and individuals are taught from a very early age to say exactly what they mean.
3. Authority is diffused throughout the bureaucratic system, and personal responsibility is hard to pin down.
4. Agreements tend to be in writing rather than spoken.
5. Insiders and outsiders are not readily distinguished, and the latter are encouraged to join the inner circle.[34]

These differences are exacerbated by the fact that Malaysian culture is based on an amalgamation of diverse religions, including Hinduism, Buddhism, and Islam. The belief is pervasive that success and failure are the will of God, which may create issues with American managers attempting to make deals, as Malaysians will focus less on facts and more on intuitive feelings.

At the same time, it is important to realize that while there are cultural differences, there also are similarities. Therefore, in managing across cultures, not everything is totally different. Some approaches that work at home also work well in other cultural settings.

Similarities across Cultures

When internationalization began to take off in the 1970s, many companies quickly admitted that it would not be possible to do business in the same way in every corner of the globe. There was a secret hope, however, that many of the procedures and strategies that worked so well at home could be adopted overseas without modification. This has proved to be a false hope. At the same time, some similarities across cultures have been uncovered by researchers. For example, a co-author of this text (Luthans) and his associates studied through direct observation a sample of managers in the largest textile factory in Russia to determine their activities. Like U.S. managers studied earlier, Russian managers carried out traditional management, communication, human resources, and networking activities. The study also found that, as in the United States, the relative attention given to the networking activity increased the Russian managers' opportunities for promotion, and that communication activity was a significant predictor of effective performance in both Russia and the United States.[35]

Besides the similarities of managerial activities, another study at the same Russian factory tested whether organizational behavior modification (O.B.Mod.) interventions that led to performance improvements in U.S. organizations would do so in Russia.[36,37] As with the applications of O.B.Mod. in the United States, Russian supervisors were trained to administer social rewards (attention and recognition) and positive feedback when they observed workers engaging in behaviors that contributed to the production of quality fabric. In addition, Russian supervisors were taught to give corrective feedback for behaviors that reduced product quality. The researchers found that this O.B.Mod. approach, which had worked so well in the United States, produced positive results in the Russian factory. They concluded that the hypothesis that "the class of interventions associated with organizational behavior modification are likely to be useful in meeting the challenges faced by Russian workers and managers [is] given initial support by the results of this study."[38,39]

In another cross-cultural study, this time using a large Korean sample, Luthans and colleagues analyzed whether demographic and situational factors identified in the U.S.-based literature had the same antecedent influence on the commitment of Korean employees.[40,41] As in the U.S. studies, Korean employees' position in the hierarchy, tenure in their current position, and age all related to organizational commitment. Other similarities with U.S. firms included (1) as organizational size increased, commitment declined; (2) as structure became more employee-focused, commitment increased; and (3) the more positive the perceptions of organizational climate, the greater the employee commitment. The following conclusion was drawn:

> This study provides beginning evidence that popular constructs in the U.S. management and organizational behavior literature should not be automatically dismissed as culture bound. Whereas some organizational behavior concepts and techniques do indeed seem to be culture specific . . . a growing body of literature is demonstrating the ability to cross-culturally validate other concepts and techniques, such as behavior management. . . . This study contributed to this cross-cultural evidence for the antecedents to organizational commitment. The antecedents for Korean employees' organizational commitment were found to be similar to their American counterparts.[42]

Many Differences across Cultures

We have stressed throughout the text how different cultures can be from one another and how important it is for MNCs to understand the points of disparity. Here, we look at some differences from a human resources perspective, a topic that will be covered in depth in Chapter 14. We introduce human resource management (HRM) here as a way to illustrate that the cultural foundations utilized in the selection of employees can further form the culture that international managers will oversee. In other words, understanding the HRM strategies before becoming a manager in the industry can aid in effective performance. The focus here is more from a socially cultural perspective; the organizational perspective will be discussed further in Chapter 14.

Despite similarities between cultures in some studies, far more differences than similarities have been found. MNCs are discovering that they must carefully investigate and understand the culture where they intend to do business and modify their approaches appropriately. Sometimes these cultures are quite different from the United States—as well as from each other! One human resource management example has been offered by Trompenaars, who examined the ways in which personnel in international subsidiaries were appraised by their managers. The head office had established the criteria to be used in these evaluations but left the prioritization of the criteria to the national operating company.

As a result, the outcome of the evaluations could be quite different from country to country because what was regarded as the most important criterion in one subsidiary might be ranked much lower on the evaluation list of another subsidiary. In the case of Shell Oil, for example, Trompenaars found that the firm was using a HAIRL system of appraisal. The five criteria in this acronym stood for (a) helicopter—the capacity to take a broad view from above; (b) analysis—the ability to evaluate situations logically and completely; (c) imagination—the ability to be creative and think outside the box; (d) reality—the ability to use information realistically; and (e) leadership—the ability to effectively galvanize and inspire personnel. When staff in Shell's operating companies in four countries were asked to prioritize these five criteria from top to bottom, the results were as follows:

Netherlands	France	Germany	Britain
Reality	Imagination	Leadership	Helicopter
Analysis	Analysis	Analysis	Imagination
Helicopter	Leadership	Reality	Reality
Leadership	Helicopter	Imagination	Analysis
Imagination	Reality	Helicopter	Leadership

Quite obviously, personnel in different operating companies were being evaluated differently. In fact, no two of the operating companies in the four countries had the same criterion at the top of their lists. Moreover, the criterion at the top of the list for operating companies in the Netherlands—reality—was at the bottom of the list for those in France; and the one at the top of the list in French operating companies—imagination—was at the bottom of the list of the Dutch firms. Similarly, the German operating companies put leadership at the top of the list and helicopter at the bottom, while the British companies did the opposite! In fact, the whole list for the Germans is in the exact reverse order of the British list.[43]

Other HRM differences can be found in areas such as wages, compensation, pay equity, and maternity leave. Here are some representative examples.

1. The concept of an hourly wage plays a minor role in Mexico. Labor law requires that employees receive full pay 365 days a year.

2. In Austria and Brazil, employees with one year of service are automatically given 30 days of paid vacation.

3. Some jurisdictions in Canada have legislated pay equity—known in the United States as comparable worth—between male- and female-intensive jobs.

4. In Japan, compensation levels are determined by using the objective factors of age, length of service, and educational background rather than skill, ability, and performance. Performance does not count until after an employee reaches age 45.

5. In the United Kingdom, employees are allowed up to 40 weeks of maternity leave, and employers must provide a government-mandated amount of pay for 18 of those weeks.

6. In 87 percent of large Swedish companies, the head of human resources is on the board of directors.[44]

These HRM practices certainly are quite different from those in the United States, and U.S. MNCs need to modify their approaches when they go into these countries if they hope to be successful. Compensation plans, in particular, provide an interesting area of contrast across different cultures.

Drawing on the work of Hofstede (see Chapter 4), it is possible to link cultural clusters and compensation strategies. Each cluster requires a different approach to formulating an effective compensation strategy:

1. In Pacific Rim countries, incentive plans should be group-based. In high-masculinity cultures (Japan, Hong Kong, Malaysia, the Philippines, Singapore), high salaries should be paid to senior-level managers.

2. In EU nations such as France, Spain, Italy, and Belgium, compensation strategies should be similar. In the latter two nations, however, significantly higher salaries should be paid to local senior-level managers because of the high masculinity index. In Portugal and Greece, both of which have a low individualism index, profit-sharing plans would be more effective than individual incentive plans, while in Denmark, the Netherlands, and Germany, personal-incentive plans would be highly useful because of the high individualism in these cultures.

3. In Great Britain, Ireland, and the United States, managers value their individualism and are motivated by the opportunity for earnings, recognition, advancement, and challenge. Compensation plans should reflect these needs.[45]

Figure 5–1 shows how specific HRM areas can be analyzed contingently on a country-by-country basis. Take, for example, the information on Japan. When it is contrasted with U.S. approaches, a significant number of differences are found. Recruitment and selection in Japanese firms often are designed to help identify those individuals who will do the best job over the long run. In the United States, people often are hired based on what they can do for the firm in the short run because many of them eventually will quit or be downsized. Similarly, the Japanese use a great deal of cross-training, while the Americans tend to favor specialized training. The Japanese use group performance appraisal and reward people as a group; at least traditionally, Americans use manager-subordinate performance appraisal and reward people as individuals. In Japan, unions are regarded as partners; in the United States, management and unions view each other in a much more adversarial way. Only in the area of job design, where the Japanese use a great deal of participative management and autonomous work teams, are the Americans beginning to employ a similar approach. The same types of differences can be seen in the matrix of Figure 5–1 among Japan, Germany, Mexico, and China.

These differences should not be interpreted to mean that one set of HRM practices is superior to another. In fact, recent research from Japan and Europe shows these firms often have a higher incidence of personnel-related problems than do U.S. companies. Figure 5–1 clearly indicates the importance of MNCs using a contingency approach to HRM across cultures. Not only are there different HRM practices in different cultures, but there also are different practices within the same cultures. For instance, one study involving 249 U.S. affiliates of foreign-based MNCs found that in general, affiliate HRM practices closely follow local practices when dealing with the rank and file but even more closely approximate parent-company practices when dealing with upper-level management.[46] In other words, this study found that a hybrid approach to HRM was being used by these MNCs.

Aside from the different approaches used in different countries, it is becoming clear that common assumptions and conventional wisdom about HRM practices in certain countries no longer are valid. For example, for many years, it has been assumed that Japanese employees do not leave their jobs for work with other firms, that they are loyal to their first employer, and that it would be virtually impossible for MNCs operating in Japan to recruit talent from Japanese firms. Recent evidence, however, reveals that job-hopping among Japanese employees is increasingly common. One report concluded:

> While American workers, both the laid-off and the survivors, grapple with cutbacks, one in three Japanese workers willingly walks away from his job within the first 10 years of his career, according to the Japanese Institute of Labor, a private research organization. And many more are thinking about it. More than half of salaried Japanese workers say they would switch jobs or start their own business if a favorable opportunity arose, according to a survey by the Recruit Research Corporation.[47]

These findings clearly illustrate one important point: Managing across cultures requires careful understanding of the local environment because common assumptions and stereotypes may not be valid. Cultural differences must be addressed, and this is why cross-cultural research will continue to be critical in helping firms learn how to manage across cultures.[48,49]

Figure 5–1 | **A Partially Completed Contingency Matrix for International Human Resource Management**

	Japan	Germany	Mexico	China
Recruitment and selection	• Prepare for long process • Ensure that your firm is "here to stay" • Develop trusting relationship with recruit	• Obtain skilled labor from government-subsidized apprenticeship program	• Use expatriates sparingly • Recruit Mexican nationals at U.S. colleges	• Recent public policy shifts encourage use of sophisticated selection procedures
Training	• Make substantial investment in training • Use general training and cross-training • Training is everyone's responsibility	• Reorganize and utilize apprenticeship programs • Be aware of government regulations on training	• Use bilingual trainers	• Carefully observe existing training programs • Utilize team training
Compensation	• Use recognition and praise as motivators • Avoid pay for performance	• Note high labor costs for manufacturing	• Consider all aspects of labor cost	• Use technical training as reward • Recognize egalitarian values • Use "more work, more pay" with caution
Labor relations	• Treat unions as partners • Allow time for negotiations	• Be prepared for high wages and short workweek • Expect high productivity from unionized workers	• Understand changing Mexican labor law • Prepare for increasing unionization of labor	• Tap large pool of labor cities • Lax labor laws may become more stringent
Job design	• Include participation • Incorporate group goal setting • Use autonomous work teams • Use uniform, formal approaches • Encourage co-worker input • Empower teams to make decision	• Utilize works councils to enhance worker participation	• Approach participation cautiously	• Determine employee's motives before implementing participation

Source: From Fred Luthans, Paul A. Marsnik, and Kyle W. Luthans, "A Contingency Matrix Approach to IHRM," *Human Resource Management Journal* 36, no. 2 (1997), pp. 183–199.

■ Cultural Differences in Selected Countries and Regions

As noted in Part One and in Chapter 4, MNCs are increasingly active in all parts of the world, including the developing and emerging regions because of their recent growth and future potential. Chapter 4 introduced the concept of country clusters, which is the idea that certain regions of the world have similar cultures. For example, the way that Americans do business in the United States is very similar to the way that the British do business in England. Even in this Anglo culture, however, there are pronounced differences, and in other clusters, such as in Asia, these differences become even more pronounced. The next sections focus on cultural highlights and differences in selected countries and regions that provide the necessary understanding and perspective for effective management across cultures.

Using the GLOBE Project to Compare Managerial Differences

Examination of the GLOBE project has resulted in an extensive breakdown of how managers behave and how different cultures can yield managers with similar perspectives in some realms, with quite divergent opinions in other sectors. One example, as illustrated in Figure 5–2, shows how the value scores for managers in China compare to those of managers in the United States and Argentina. The web structure, based on factors such as individualism, consciousness of social and professional status, and risky behaviors, can be used to show both similarities and differences between multiple cultures at once, indicating potential areas of cultural misunderstanding when conducting business. As can be seen through the web structure shown, Chinese managers typically score higher than their Argentine and U.S. counterparts in the area of uncertainty avoidance. This indicates that Chinese managers prefer structured situations, rules, and careful planning, while their counterparts in the U.S. and Argentina are more open to looser restrictions and more unplanned situations. When managers from the U.S. and Argentina are conducting business in a culture with high uncertainty avoidance preferences, like China, it is suggested that they give their employees a clear plan and a structural framework to complete their assigned tasks. Interestingly, all three countries score similarly low in the area of power distance, indicating that managers

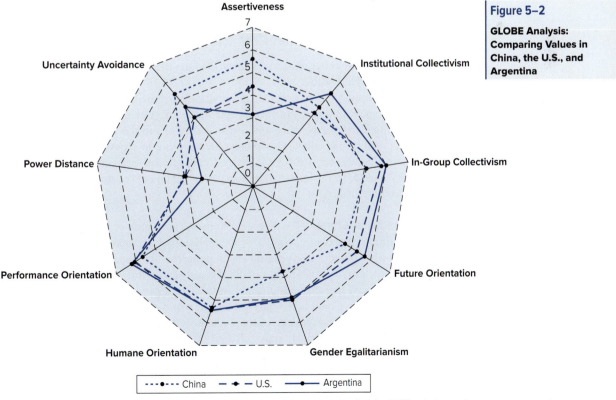

Figure 5–2

GLOBE Analysis: Comparing Values in China, the U.S., and Argentina

Source: Original graphic by Ben Littell under supervision of Professor Jonathan Doh based on data from the GLOBE project research.

in these cultures prefer structures with less hierarchy and more equality—even if, in practice, the opposite is true within their country.[50]

As shown in the figure, Chinese managers tend to value assertiveness significantly more than managers from Argentina, indicating that aggressive or confrontational behavior in a business negotiation, for example, would not be viewed in a negative way by Chinese businesspeople but might well by Argentine businesspeople. A Chinese businessperson may walk away from intense negotiation feeling as though things went well, while an Argentine counterpart across the table might view the same meeting as unproductive and detrimental.[51]

One interesting development is the increasing frequency of managers and executives from one part of the world assuming leadership roles in another. For example, in 2015, Takeda Pharmaceutical Company named Christophe Weber as its new CEO, becoming the first non-Japanese CEO in the company's history. He joins the ranks of the few—but increasing—number of foreign heads of Japanese firms, who now include Brian Prince of Aozora Bank, Eva Chen of Trend Micro, and Carlos Ghoshen of Nissan Motor Co. Foreign CEOs still face cultural difficulties, however. At Nippon Sheet Glass, for example, American Craig Naylor resigned suddenly in 2012 after just two years as CEO. Naylor cited "fundamental disagreements with the board on company strategy" as the key reason for his departure.[52] Chapters 13 and 14 provide an in-depth discussion of leadership and human resource management across cultures, respectively. Because of the increasing importance of developing and emerging regions and countries in the global economy, knowledge of these contexts is more and more important for global managers. In a study by the China Europe International Business School's Leadership Behavioral Laboratory and the Center for Creative Leadership, executives identified critical characteristics in their careers that contributed to their development as managers in emerging markets settings. These included setting an example for junior employees and learning to thrive in unstable environments.[53] In addition, managers emphasized the importance of learning about their business and the emerging markets environment, through formal classes, mentoring, and direct experience.

Managing Culture in Selected Countries and Regions

More specific insight on cultural practices specific to the BRIC countries, Arab countries, and France are presented below.

Before this discussion, however, it is important to provide a word of caution on overgeneralizing about cultures. Businesspeople from all cultures are individuals with unique personalities and styles; there are always exceptions to the general cultural characteristics discussed in the following sections. Stereotyping in cross-cultural dealings is unwarranted. In this chapter, we review general cultural characteristics, but from your own experience, you know the importance of an understanding of the particular individuals or situations you are dealing with.

Managing Culture in China   The People's Republic of China (China, for short) has had a long tradition of isolation. In 1979, Deng Xiaoping opened this country to the world. Although his bloody 1989 put-down of protesters in Tiananmen Square was a definite setback for progress, China is rapidly trying to close the gap between itself and economically advanced nations and to establish itself as a power in the world economy. As noted in Chapter 1, China is actively trading in world markets, is a member of the WTO, and is a major trading partner of the United States. Despite this global presence, many U.S. and European multinationals still find that doing business in China can be a long, grueling process.[54,55] Foreign firms still find it difficult to make a profit in China. One primary reason is that Western-based MNCs do not appreciate the important role and impact of Chinese culture.

Experienced executives report that the primary criterion for doing business in China is technical competence. For example, in the case of MNCs selling machinery,

Chinese businesspeople tend to want to know exactly how the machine works, what its capabilities are, and how repairs and maintenance must be handled. Sellers must be prepared to answer these questions in precise detail. This is why successful multinationals send only seasoned engineers and technical people to China. They know that the questions to be answered will require both knowledge and experience, and young, fresh-out-of-school engineers will not be able to answer them.

A major cultural difference between China and many Western countries is the issue of time. Chinese culture tends to value punctuality, so it is important that those who do business with them arrive on time, as discussed in Chapter 4. During meetings, such as those held when negotiating a contract, Chinese businesspeople may ask many questions and nod their assent at the answers. This nodding usually means that they understand or are being polite; it seldom means that they like what they are hearing and want to enter into a contract. For this reason, when dealing with Chinese businesspeople, one must keep in mind that patience is critically important. Chinese businesspeople will make a decision in their own good time, and it is common for outside businesspeople to make several trips to China before a deal is finally concluded. Moreover, not only are there numerous meetings, but sometimes these are unilaterally cancelled at the last minute and rescheduled. This often tries the patience of outsiders and is inconvenient in terms of rearranging travel plans and other problems.

Another important dimension of Chinese culture is **guanxi**, which means "good connections."[56] In turn, these connections can result in such things as lower costs for doing business.[57] Yet guanxi goes beyond just lower costs. Yi and Ellis surveyed Hong Kong and Chinese managers and found that both groups agreed that guanxi networking offered a number of potential benefits, including increased business, higher sales revenue, more sources of information, greater prospecting opportunities, and the facilitation of future transactions.[58] In practice, guanxi resembles nepotism, where individuals in authority make decisions on the basis of family ties or social connections rather than objective indices.[59] Additionally, outsiders doing business in China must be aware that Chinese people will typically argue that they have the guanxi to get a job done, when in reality they may or may not have the necessary connections.

When conducting business in China, one must realize that the Chinese are a collective society in which people pride themselves on being members of a group. Chinese people are very proud of their collective economic accomplishments and want to share these feelings with outsiders. This is in sharp contrast to the situation in the United States and other Western countries, where individualism is highly prized. For this reason, one must never single out a Chinese employee and praise him or her for a particular quality, such as intelligence or kindness, because doing so may embarrass the individual in the presence of his or her peers. It is equally important to avoid using self-centered conversation, such as excessive use of the word "I," because it appears that the speaker is trying to single him- or herself out for special consideration.

In negotiations, reciprocity is important. If Chinese partners give concessions, they expect some in return. Additionally, it is common to find them slowing down negotiations to take advantage of Westerners' desire to conclude arrangements as quickly as possible. The objective of this tactic is to extract further concessions. Another common strategy used by Chinese businesspeople is to pressure the other party during final arrangements by suggesting that this counterpart has broken the spirit of friendship in which the business relationship originally was established. Again, through this strategy, the Chinese partners are trying to gain additional concessions. Because negotiating can involve a loss of face, it is common to find Chinese businesspeople carrying out the whole process through intermediaries. This allows them to convey their ideas without fear of embarrassment.[60] During negotiations, it is also important not to show excessive emotion of any kind. Anger or frustration, for example, is viewed as antisocial and unseemly. Negotiations should be viewed with a long-term perspective. Those who will do best are the ones who realize they are investing in a long-term relationship.[61]

guanxi
In Chinese, it means "good connections."

While these are the traditional behaviors of Chinese businesspeople, the transitioning economy (see Chapter 1) has also caused a shift in business culture, which has affected working professionals' private lives. Performance, which was once based on effort, is now being evaluated from the angle of results as the country continues to maintain its flourishing profits. While traditional Chinese culture focused on family first, financial and material well-being has become a top priority. This performance orientation has increased stress and contributed to growing incidence of burnout, depression, substance abuse, and other ailments. Some U.S. companies have attempted to curb these psychological ailments by offering counseling; however, this service is not as readily accepted by Chinese culture. Instead of bringing attention to the "counseling" aspect, firms instead promote "workplace harmony" and "personal well-being services."[62] This suggests that while some aspects of Chinese culture are changing, international managers must recognize the foundational culture of the country and try to deal with such issues according to local beliefs.

Managing Culture in Russia   As pointed out in Chapter 1, the Russian economy has experienced severe problems, and the risks of doing business there cannot be overstated. Recent tensions between the governments of Russia and the G7 nations, resulting from Russian intervention in Crimea and Syria, have made business dealings even more complicated. At the same time, however, by following certain guidelines, MNCs can begin to tap the potential opportunities.

When conducting business in Russia, it is important to build personal relationships with partners. Business laws and contracts do not mean as much in Russia as they do in the West. When there are contract disputes, there is little protection for the aggrieved party because of the time and effort needed to legally enforce the agreement. Detailed contracts can be hammered out later on; in the beginning, all that counts is friendship.

Local consultants can be valuable. Because the rules of business have changed so much in recent years, it pays to have a local Russian consultant working with the company. Russian expatriates often are not up to date on what is going on and, quite often, are not trusted by local businesspeople who have stayed in the country. So the consultant should be someone who has been in Russia all the time and understands the local business climate.

Ethical behavior in Europe and the United States is not always the same as in Russia. For example, it is traditional in Russia to give gifts to those with whom one wants to transact business, an approach that may be regarded as bribery in the United States. In recent years, large companies such as IKEA have faced repercussions in their home markets due to bribery allegations from their business conduct in Russia (see Brief Integrative Case 4.1 at the end of Part 4).

When conducting business in Russia, businesspeople should be careful about compromising or settling things too quickly, as this is often seen as a sign of weakness. Because of the history of complexity during the Soviet Union days, Russians today tend to be suspicious of anything that is conceded easily. If agreements are not reached after a while, a preferred tactic on their part is to display patience and then wait it out. However, they will abandon this approach if the other side shows great patience because they will realize that their negotiating tactic is useless.[63]

Conducting business in Russia requires careful consideration of cultural factors, and it often takes a lot longer than initially anticipated. However, the benefits may be worth the wait. And when everything is completed, there is a final cultural tradition that should be observed: Fix and reinforce the final agreements with a nice dinner together and an invitation to the Russians to visit your country and see your facilities.[64]

Managing Culture in India   In recent years, India has begun to attract the attention of large MNCs. Unsaturated consumer markets, coupled with cheap labor and production locations, have helped make India a desirable market for global firms. The government continues to play an important role in this process, although recently many of the bureaucratic restrictions have been lifted as India works to attract foreign investment and raise its economic growth rate.[65,66] In addition, although most Indian businesspeople speak English, many of their values and beliefs are markedly different from those in the West. Thus, understanding Indian culture is critical to successfully doing business in India.

Shaking hands with male business associates is almost always an acceptable practice. U.S. businesspeople in India are considered equals, however, and the universal method of greeting an equal is to press one's palms together in front of the chest and say, "namaste," which means "greetings to you." Therefore, if a handshake appears to be improper, it always is safe to use "namaste."

For Western businesspeople in India, shirt, trousers, tie, and suit are proper attire. In the southern part of India, where the climate is very hot, a light suit is preferable. In the north during the winter, a light sweater and jacket are a good choice. Indian businesspeople, on the other hand, often will wear local dress. In many cases, this includes a dhoti, which is a single piece of white cloth (about five yards long and three feet wide) that is passed around the waist up to half its length and then the other half is drawn between the legs and tucked at the waist. Long shirts are worn on the upper part of the body. In some locales, such as Punjab, Sikhs will wear turbans, and well-to-do Hindus sometimes will wear long coats like the rajahs. This coat, known as a sherwani, is the dress recognized by the government for official and ceremonial wear. Foreign businesspeople are not expected to dress like locals, and in fact, many Indian businesspeople will dress like Europeans. Therefore, it is unnecessary to adopt local dress codes.[67]

Finally, it is important to remember that Indians are very tolerant of outsiders and understand that many are unfamiliar with local customs and procedures. Therefore, there is no need to make a phony attempt to conform to Indian cultural traditions. Making an effort to be polite and courteous is sufficient.[68]

Managing Culture in France   Many in the United States believe that it is more difficult to get along with the French than with other Europeans. This feeling probably reflects the French culture, which is markedly different from that in the United States. In France, one's social class is very important, and these classes include the aristocracy, the upper bourgeoisie, the upper-middle bourgeoisie, the middle, the lower middle, and the lower. Social interactions are affected by class stereotypes, and during their lifetime, most French people do not encounter much change in social status. Additionally, the French are very status conscious, and they like to provide signs of their status, such as knowledge of literature and the arts; a well-designed, tastefully decorated house; and a high level of education.

In the workplace, many French people are not motivated by competition or the desire to emulate fellow workers. They often are accused of not having as intense a work ethic as, for example, Americans or Asians. Many French workers frown on overtime, and statistics show that on average, they have the longest vacations in the world (four to five weeks annually). On the other hand, few would disagree that they work extremely hard in their regularly scheduled time and have a reputation for high productivity. Part of this reputation results from the French tradition of craftsmanship. Part of it also is accounted for by a large percentage of the workforce being employed in small, independent businesses, where there is widespread respect for a job well done. In general, French employees do not derive much motivation from professional accomplishment. Rather, they believe that quality of life is what really matters. As a result, they attach a great deal of importance to leisure time, and many are unwilling to sacrifice the enjoyment of life for dedication to work.

Most French organizations tend to be highly centralized and have rigid structures. As a result, it usually takes longer to carry out decisions. Because this arrangement is quite different from the more decentralized, flattened organizations in the United States, both middle- and lower-level U.S. expatriate managers who work in French subsidiaries often find bureaucratic red tape a source of considerable frustration. There also are marked differences at the upper levels of management. In French companies, top managers have far more authority than their U.S. counterparts, and they are less accountable for their actions. While top-level U.S. executives must continually defend their decisions to the CEO or board of directors, French executives are challenged only if the company has poor performance. As a result, those who have studied French management find that they take a more autocratic approach.[69]

Managing Culture in Brazil   Brazil is considered a Latin American country, but it is important to highlight this nation since some characteristics make it markedly different to manage as compared to other Latin American countries.[70] Brazil was originally colonized by Portugal, and remained affiliated with its parent country until 1865. Even though today Brazil is extremely multicultural, the country still demonstrates many attributes derived from its Portuguese heritage, including its official language. For example, the Brazilian economy was once completely centrally controlled like many other Latin American countries, yet was motivated by such Portuguese influences as flexibility, tolerance, and commercialism.[71] This may be a significant reason behind its successful economic emergence.

Brazilian businesspeople tend to have a relaxed work ethic, often respecting those who inherit wealth and have strong familial roots over those seeking entrepreneurial opportunities. They view time in a very relaxed manner, so punctuality is not a strong suit in this country. Overall, the people are very good-natured and tend to avoid confrontation, yet they seek out risky endeavors.

In Brazil, physical contact is acceptable as a form of communication. Brazilian businesspeople tend to stand very close to others when having a conversation, and will touch the person's back, arm, or elbow as a greeting or sign of respect. Additionally, face-to-face interaction is preferred as a way to communicate, so avoid simply e-mailing or calling. Do not be surprised if business meetings begin anywhere from 10 to 30 minutes after the scheduled time because Brazilian culture tends to not be governed by the clock.

Appearance can be very important to Brazilian culture, as it will reflect both you and your company. When conducting business, men should wear conservative dark suits, shirts, and ties. Women should dress nicely but avoid too conservative or formal attire. Brazilian managers often wonder, for example, if Americans make so much money, why do they dress like they are poor?

Patience is key when managing business in Brazil. Many processes are longer and more drawn out than in other cultures, including negotiations. Expressing frustration or impatience and attempting to speed up procedures may lose the deal. The slow processes and relaxed atmosphere do not imply that it is acceptable to be ill-prepared. Presentations should be informative and expressive, and consistency is important. It is common for Brazilian businesspeople to bring a lot of people to attend negotiations, mostly to observe and learn. Subsequent meetings may include members of higher management, requiring a rehashing of information.[72,73]

Managing Culture in Arab Countries   The intense media attention given to the Iraq War, terrorist actions, and continuing conflicts in the Middle East have perhaps revealed to everyone that Arab cultures are distinctly different from Anglo cultures.[74,75] Europeans and Americans often find it extremely hard to do business in Arab countries, and a number of Arab cultural characteristics can be cited for this difficulty.

One is the Arab view of time. In the United States, it is common to use the cliché, "Time is money." In Arab countries, a favorite expression is *Bukra insha Allah,* which means "Tomorrow if God wills," an expression that explains the fatalistic approach to time common to many Arab cultures. As a result, if Arab businesspeople commit themselves to a date in the future and fail to show up, they may feel no guilt or concern because they believe they have no control over time in the first place.

When conducting business in an Arab country, it is important to understand that culture generally holds that destiny depends more on the will of a supreme being than on the behavior of individuals. A higher power dictates the outcome of important events, so individual action is of little consequence. Also of importance is that, in the culture of many Arab countries, social status is largely determined by family position and connections, not necessarily by accomplishments. This view helps to explain why some Middle Easterners take great satisfaction in appearing to be helpless. This approach is quite different from that in the United States, where the strong tend to be compensated and rewarded. If a person was ill, such as in this example, the individual would be relieved of his responsibility until he or she had regained full health. In the interim, the rest of the group would go on without the sick person, and he or she might lose power.

In Arab countries, initial meetings typically are used to get to know the other party. Business-related discussions may not occur until the third or fourth meeting. Also, in contrast to the common perception among many Western businesspeople who have never been to an Arab country, it is not necessary to bring the other party a gift. If this is done, however, it should be a modest gift. A good example is a novelty or souvenir item from the visitor's home country. Also, Arab businesspeople tend to attach a great deal of importance to status and rank. When meeting with them, one should pay deference to the senior person first. It also is important never to criticize or berate anyone publicly. This causes the individual to lose face, and the same is true for the person who makes these comments. Mutual respect is required at all times.[76]

The World of International Management—Revisited

Management at many companies and in many countries is becoming more and more multicultural, yet individual corporate cultures persist. Apple and Xiaomi are both examples of highly successful companies with radically different approaches to strategy and management. Apple prides itself on groundbreaking innovation, individual achievement, and excellence. At Xiaomi, the emphasis is on extending innovations and applications and on group achievement and collective responsibility, all geared toward companywide success. The two companies even take a very different approach to their supply chains, with Apple outsourcing the entirety of its production and only manufacturing its new phone models for about a year, while Xiaomi produces its new phone models for a longer period of time and maintains contracts with suppliers who can adjust production based on frequent changes in demand. In terms of products, Apple is a first-mover with a universal product focus, while Xiaomi is a "fast follower" with a variety of phones for its different markets. In some ways, these two companies epitomize the cultures from which they emanate, but both are now global players.

Cross-border investments by Chinese, Indian, and other developing-country firms have prompted investing firms, especially in Europe and North America, to more thoughtfully consider cultural issues as they seek to integrate local companies and employees into their global organizations. As we saw in Chapter 4, East Asian, U.S., and Western European cultures differ on many dimensions, which may pose challenges for companies seeking to operate across these geographical/cultural boundaries.

Now that you have read this chapter, you should have a good understanding of the importance and the difficulties of managing across cultures. Using this knowledge as a platform, answer the following questions: (1) Which aspects of Apple's culture have helped it succeed in its global growth and which may have impeded it? (2) Which aspects of Xiaomi's culture have helped it succeed in its global growth and which may have impeded it? (3) How would you characterize Apple and Xiaomi in terms of the four basic strategic predispositions? (4) What might Apple learn from Xiaomi and Xiaomi learn from Apple?

SUMMARY OF KEY POINTS

1. One major problem facing MNCs is that they some-times attempt to manage across cultures in ways similar to those of their home country. MNC dispo-sitions toward managing across cultures can be characterized as (1) ethnocentric, (2) polycentric, (3) regiocentric, and (4) geocentric. These different approaches shape how companies adapt and adjust to cultural pressures around the world.

2. One major challenge when dealing with cross-cultural problems is that of overcoming parochialism and simplification. Parochialism is the tendency to view the world through one's own eyes and per-spectives. Simplification is the process of exhibiting the same orientation toward different cultural groups. Another problem is that of doing things the same way in foreign markets as they are done in domestic markets. Research shows that in some cases, this approach can be effective; however,

effective cross-cultural management more com-monly requires approaches different than those used at home. One area where this is particularly evident is human resource management. Recruitment, selec-tion, training, and compensation often are carried out in different ways in different countries, and what works in the United States may have limited value in other countries and geographic regions.

3. Doing business in various parts of the world requires the recognition and understanding of cul-tural differences. Some of these differences revolve around the importance the society assigns to time, status, control of decision making, personal accom-plishment, and work itself. These types of cultural differences help to explain why effective managers in China or Russia often are quite different from those in France, and why a successful style in the United States will not be ideal in Arab countries.

KEY TERMS

ethnocentric predisposition, *159*

geocentric predisposition, *159*

globalization imperative, *160*

guanxi, *171*

parochialism, *162*

polycentric predisposition, *159*

regiocentric predisposition, *159*

simplification, *163*

REVIEW AND DISCUSSION QUESTIONS

1. Define the four basic predispositions MNCs have toward their international operations.

2. If a locally based manufacturing firm with sales of $350 million decided to enter the EU market by set-ting up operations in France, which orientation would be the most effective: ethnocentric, polycentric, regio-centric, or geocentric? Why? Explain your choice.

3. In what way are parochialism and simplification barriers to effective cross-cultural management? In each case, give an example.

4. Many MNCs would like to do business overseas in the same way that they do business domestically. Do research findings show that any approaches that

work well in the United States also work well in other cultures? If so, identify and describe two.

5. In most cases, local managerial approaches must be modified for doing business overseas. What are three specific examples that support this statement? Be complete in your answer.

6. What are some categories of cultural differences that help make one country or region of the world different from another? In each case, describe the value or norm and explain how it would result in different behavior in two or more countries. If you like, use the countries discussed in this chapter as your point of reference.

INTERNET EXERCISE: HAIER'S APPROACH

Haier is a China-based multinational corporation that sells a wide variety of commercial and household appliances in the international marketplace. These range from washers, dryers, and refrigerators to industrial heating and ventila-tion systems. Visit Haier.com and read about some of the latest developments in which the company is engaged: (1) What type of cultural challenges does Haier face when it attempts to market its products worldwide? Is demand

universal for all these offerings, or is there a "national responsiveness" challenge, as discussed in the chapter, that must be addressed? (2) Investigate the way in which Haier has adapted its products in different countries and regions, especially emerging markets. What are some examples? (3) In managing its far-flung enterprise, what are two cul-tural challenges that the company is likely to face and what will it need to do to respond to these?

ENDNOTES

1. Nancy J. Adler, *International Dimensions of Organizational Behavior*, 5th ed. (Cincinnati, OH: Southwestern, 2007).

2. Evan Niu, "How Many iPhones Has Apple Sold?" *The Motley Fool*, November 14, 2015, www.fool.com/investing/general/2015/11/14/iphones-sold.aspx.

3. Dylan Love, "At Apple, They Really Are After You," *Business Insider*, January 9, 2013, www.businessinsider.com/apple-corporate-culture-2013-1.

4. Adam Lashinsky, "This Is How Apple Keeps the Secrets," *Fortune*, January 18, 2012, http://fortune.com/2012/01/18/the-secrets-apple-keeps/.

5. Parmy Olson, "How China's Xiaomi Does in a Week What Apple Does in a Year: Update Devices," *Forbes*, October 22, 2013, www.forbes.com/sites/parmyolson/2013/10/22/how-chinas-xiaomi-does-in-a-week-what-apple-does-in-a-year-update-devices/2/#15201d7b2c16.

6. Ibid.

7. David M. Barreda, "Who Supplies Apple? (It's Not Just China)," *China File*, February 14, 2013, www.chinafile.com/who-supplies-apple-it-s-not-just-china-interactive-map.

8. Peter Cohan, "Apple Can't Innovate or Manage Supply Chain," *Forbes*, October 26, 2012. http://www.forbes.com/sites/petercohan/2012/10/26/apple-cant-innovate-or-manage-supply-chain/.

9. "Xiaomi & the Supply Chain Behind the World's Highest Valued Startup," *Elementum News*, April 16, 2015, http://news.elementum.com/how-supply-chain-is-building-xiaomis-empire.

10. Ibid.

11. Devindra Hardawar, "What China's Xiaomi Can Teach Apple, Google, and the Western Tech World," *Venture Beat*, September 1, 2013, http://venturebeat.com/2013/09/01/what-xiaomi-can-teach-google-apple-and-the-western-tech-world/.

12. Miguel Helft and Shan Carter, "A Chief Executive's Attention to Detail, Noted in 313 Patents," *The New York Times*, August 25, 2011, www.nytimes.com/2011/08/26/technology/apple-patents-show-steve-jobss-attention-to-design.html?_r=2.

13. Nick Bilton, "Bits: What Apple vs. HTC Could Mean," *The New York Times*, March 2, 2010, http://bits.blogs.nytimes.com/2010/03/02/what-apple-vs-htc-could-mean/.

14. Leo Kelion, "Apple v Samsung Patent Verdict Reconsidered in Court," *BBC*, December 6, 2012, www.bbc.com/news/technology-20615376.

15. Parmy Olson, "Xiaomi May Have a Major Patent Problem," *Forbes*, January 29, 2015, www.forbes.com/sites/parmyolson/2015/01/29/xiaomi-patent-problem/#37415e5322ec.

16. Salvador Rodriguez, "Why Xiaomi Is Not Coming to America Anytime Soon: It Only Has 2 US Patents," *International Business Times*, March 30, 2015, www.ibtimes.com/why-xiaomi-not-coming-america-anytime-soon-it-only-has-2-us-patents-1863838.

17. "Smartphone Vendor Market Share, 2015 Q2," IDC, http://www.idc.com/prodserv/smartphone-market-share.jsp.

18. Carrie Mihalcik, "Xiaomi Made Only $56M Last Year, Filing Shows," *CNet*, December 16, 2014, www.cnet.com/news/upstart-phone-maker-xiaomi-values-growth-over-profit/.

19. Nissan Motor Corporation, "Nissan Reports Net Income of 389 Billion Yen for FY2013," news releases, May 12, 2014, www.nissan-global.com/EN/NEWS/2014/_STORY/140512-01-e.html.

20. Nissan Motor Corporation, "Nissan Reports Net Income of $4.2 Billion (¥457.6 billion) for FY2014," news release, May 13, 2015, http://nissan-news.com/en-US/nissan/usa/releases/nissan-reports-net-income-of-4-2-billion-457-6-billion-for-fy2014.

21. Yuro Kageyama, "Nissan Reports 38 Percent Rise in Profit, Raises Forecasts," *AP*, November 2, 2015, http://bigstory.ap.org/article/80dda8efe70041f4b8aa312b14d67996/nissan-reports-38-percent-rise-profit-raises-forecasts.

22. "New models lift Renault profit despite Russia writedown." *Reuters,* February 12, 2016. http://www.reuters.com/article/us-renault-results-idUSKCN0VL0KP.

23. "World Motor Vehicle Production," *OICA*, February 2016, www.oica.net/category/production-statistics/.

24. "Dacia Exceeded the Threshold of 500,000 Vehicles Sold Worldwide," *Dacia Group*, January 19, 2015, www.daciagroup.com/en/press/press-releases/2015/dacia-exceeded-the-threshold-of-500000-vehicles-sold-worldwide.

25. Luca Ciferri, "How Renault's Low-Cost Dacia Has Become a 'Cash Cow,'" *Automotive News Europe*, January 2, 2013, http://europe.autonews.com/article/20130102/ANE/312259994/how-renaults-low-cost-dacia-has-become-a-cash-cow.

26. Greeshma M, "5 Reasons Why Renault Kwid Will Be a Game Changer," *Economic Times of India*, September 26, 2015, www.ibtimes.co.in/5-reasons-why-renault-kwid-will-be-game-changer-648139.

27. "Renault-Nissan Alliance Celebrates 15th Anniversary as Four Key Business Units Prepare to Converge," *Renault Nissan*, March 27, 2014, www.media.blog.alliance-renault-nissan.com/news/renault-nissan-alliance-celebrates-15th-anniversary-as-four-key-business-units-prepare-to-converge/.

28. Lisa Hoecklin, *Managing Cultural Differences: Strategies for Competitive Advantage* (Workingham, England: Addison-Wesley, 1995), pp. 98–99.

29. Marcy Beitle, Arjun Sethi, Jessica Milesko, and Alyson Potenza, "The Offshore Culture Clash," *AT Kearney Executive Agenda* XI, no. 2 (2008), pp. 32–39.

30. Matt Ackerman, "State St.: New Markets Key to Growth," *American Banker*, May 3, 2004, p. 1.

31. Linda M. Randall and Lori A. Coakley, "Building a Successful Partnership in Russia and Belarus: The Impact of Culture on Strategy," *Business Horizons*, March–April 1998, pp. 15–22.

32. Fons Trompenaars and Charles Hampden-Turner, *Riding the Waves of Culture: Understanding Diversity in Global Business*, 2nd ed. (New York: McGraw-Hill, 1998), p. 202.

33. See, for example, Anisya S. Thomas and Stephen L. Mueller, "A Case for Comparative Entrepreneurship: Assessing the Relevance of Culture," *Journal of International Business Studies*, Second Quarter 2000, pp. 287–301.

34. Adapted from Richard Mead, *International Management* (Cambridge, MA: Blackwell, 1994), pp. 57–59.

35. Fred Luthans, Dianne H. B. Welsh, and Stuart A. Rosenkrantz, "What Do Russian Managers Really Do? An Observational Study with Comparisons to U.S. Managers," *Journal of International Business Studies*, Fourth Quarter 1993, pp. 741–761.

36. Diane H. B. Welsh, Fred Luthans, and Steven M. Sommer, "Organizational Behavior Modification Goes to Russia: Replicating an Experimental Analysis Across Cultures and Tasks," *Journal of Organizational Behavior Management* 13, no. 2 (1993), pp. 15–35.

37. Diane H. B. Welsh, Fred Luthans, and Steven M. Sommer, "Managing Russian Factory Workers: The Impact of U.S.-Based Behavioral and Participative Techniques," *Academy of Management Journal*, February 1993, pp. 58–79.

38. Welsh, Luthans, and Sommer, "Organizational Behavior Modification," p. 31.

39. The summary of positive (17 percent average) performance from O.B.Mod. for U.S. samples can be found in Fred Luthans and Alexander Stajkovic, "Reinforce for Performance," *Academy of Management Executive* 13, no. 2 (1999), pp. 49–57.

40. Steven M. Sommer, Seung-Hyun Bae, and Fred Luthans, "The Structure-Climate Relationship in Korean Organizations," *Asia Pacific Journal of Management* 12, no. 2 (1995), pp. 23–36.

41. Also see Steven Sommer, Seung-Hyun Bae, and Fred Luthans, "Organizational Commitment Across Cultures: The Impact of Antecedents on Korean Employees," *Human Relations* 49, no. 7 (1996), pp. 977–993.

42. Sommers, Bae, and Luthans, "The Structure-Climate Relationship in Korean Organizations."

43. Trompenaars and Hampden-Turner, *Riding the Waves of Culture*, p. 196.

44. Shari Caudron, "Lessons for HR Overseas," *Personnel Journal*, February 1995, p. 92.

45. Richard M. Hodgetts and Fred Luthans, "U.S. Multinationals' Compensation Strategies for Local Management: Cross-Cultural Implications," *Compensation and Benefits Review*, March–April 1993, pp. 42–48.

46. Philip M. Rosenzweig and Nitin Nohria, "Influences on Human Resource Management Practices in Multinational Corporations," *Journal of International Business Studies*, Second Quarter 1994, pp. 229–251.

47. "Disillusioned Workers Cost Japanese Economy up to $180.18 Billion," *The Wall Street Journal*, September 5, 2001, p. B18.

48. Also see Richard W. Wright, "Trends in International Business Research: Twenty-Five Years Later," *Journal of International Business Studies*, Fourth Quarter 1994, pp. 687–701.

49. Also see Schon Beechler and John Zhuang Yang, "The Transfer of Japanese-Style Management to American Subsidiaries: Contingencies, Constraints, and Competencies," *Journal of International Business Studies*, Third Quarter 1994, pp. 467–491.

50. Mansour Javidan, Peter W. Dorfman, et al., "In the Eye of the Beholder: Cross Cultural Lessons in Leadership from Project GLOBE," *Academy of Management Perspectives* 20, no. 1 (2006), pp. 67–90.

51. Ibid.

52. Jacob M. Schlesinger, "Another Foreign CEO Leaves Japan's Executive Ranks," *The Wall Street Journal Online*, April 18, 2012, http://blogs.wsj.com/japanrealtime/2012/04/18/another-foreign-ceo-leaves-japans-executive-ranks/.

53. Jean Lee, "Emerging Need: How Companies in Developing Markets Can Cultivate the Leaders

They Lack," *The Wall Street Journal Online*, May 24, 2010, www.wsj.com/articles/SB10001424052748 7048789045750309011196923746.

54. John Boudreau and Brandon Bailey, "Doing Business in China Getting Tougher for U.S. Companies," *Mercury News*, March 27, 2010.

55. Emily Rauhala, "Q. and A.: Doing Business in China," *The New York Times* online, June 16, 2010, www.nytimes.com/2010/06/17/business/global/17iht-chinqa.html.

56. Eric W. K. Tsang, "Can Guanxi Be a Source of Sustained Competitive Advantage for Doing Business in China?" *Academy of Management Executive* 12, no. 2 (1998), p. 64.

57. Stephen S. Standifird and R. Scott Marshall, "The Transaction Cost Advantage of Guanxi-Based Business Practices," *Journal of World Business* 35, no. 1 (2000), pp. 21–42.

58. Lee Mei Yi and Paul Ellis, "Insider-Outsider Perspective of Guanxi," *Business Horizons*, January–February 2000, p. 28.

59. Rosalie L. Tung, "Managing in Asia: Cross-Cultural Dimensions," in *Managing Across Cultures: Issues and Perspectives*, ed. Pat Joynt and Malcolm Warner (London: International Thomson Business Press, 1996), p. 239.

60. For more on this topic, see Philip R. Harris and Robert T. Moran, *Managing Cultural Differences*, 3rd ed. (Houston: Gulf Publishing, 1991), pp. 410–411.

61. Ming-Jer Chen, *Inside Chinese Business* (Boston: Harvard Business School Press, 2001), p. 153.

62. Michelle Conlin, "Go-Go-Going to Pieces in China," *BusinessWeek*, April 23, 2007, p. 88.

63. For additional insights into how to interact and negotiate effectively with the Russians, see Richard D. Lewis, *When Cultures Collide* (London: Nicholas Brealey, 1999), pp. 314–318.

64. William B. Snavely, Serguel Miassaoedov, and Kevin McNeilly, "Cross-Cultural Peculiarities of the Russian Entrepreneur: Adapting to the New Russians," *Business Horizons*, March–April 1998, pp. 13.

65. "The AU: Challenges for India," *Chicago Tribune*, May 27, 2004, p. 28.

66. Amy Waldman, "In India, Economic Growth and Democracy Do Mix," *The New York Times*, May 26, 2004, p. A13.

67. Adapted from Harris and Moran, *Managing Cultural Differences*, p. 447.

68. Also see Lewis, *When Cultures Collide*, pp. 341–346.

69. Jean-Louis Barsoux and Peter Lawrence, "The Making of a French Manager," *Harvard Business Review*, July–August 1991, pp. 58–67.

70. T. Lenartowicz and James Patrick Johnson, "A Cross-National Assessment of Values of Latin America Managers: Contrasting Hues or Shades of Gray?" *Journal of International Business Studies* 34, no. 3 (May 2003), p. 270.

71. Reed E. Nelson and Suresh Gopalan, "Do Organizational Cultures Replicate National Cultures? Isomorphism, Rejection and Reciprocal Opposition in the Corporate Values of Three Countries," *Organization Studies* 24, no. 7 (September 2003), pp. 1115–1154.

72. Derived from Raul Gouvea, "Brazil: A Strategic Approach," *Thunderbird International Business Review* 46, no. 2 (March–April 2004), pp. 183–184.

73. David Hannon, "Brazil Offers the Best of Both Worlds," *Purchasing*, October 5, 2006, pp. 51–52, https://www.highbeam.com/doc/1G1-152695481.html.

74. Sean Van Zyl, "Global Political Risks: Post 9/11," *Canadian Underwriter* 71, no. 3 (March 2004), p. 16.

75. Marvin Zonis, "Mideast Hopes: Endless Surprises," *Chicago Tribune*, January 18, 2004, p. 1.

76. Adapted from Harris and Moran, *Managing Cultural Differences*, p. 503.

77. CIA, "Poland," *The World Factbook* (2016), https://www.cia.gov/library/publications/the-world-factbook/geos/pl.html.

78. Ibid.

79. "Poland: Selected Indicators," *Organization for Economic Co-operation and Development*, https://data.oecd.org/poland.htm.

80. CIA, "Poland." This is Op. cit of Endnote 77.

81. "Poland: Selected Indicators." This is Op. Cit of Endnote 79.

82. CIA, "Poland." This is Op. cit of Endnote 77.

83. Ibid.

84. Deyana Ivanova, "Tesco Share Price: Grocer's Polish Business at Risk," *Invezz*, February 10, 2016, http://invezz.com/news/equities/22323-Tesco-share-price-Grocers-Polish-business-at-risk-.

Poland

Poland is located in Central Europe and is bordered by Germany, the Czech Republic, Slovakia, Ukraine, Belarus, and Lithuania. The Baltic Sea is located to the northwest. Slightly smaller than New Mexico, the country's terrain is largely flat with mountain ranges along its southern border. Its climate is relatively cool, with moderately severe winters and mild summer temperatures. Poland's natural resources include coal, sulfur, copper, natural gas, silver, lead, salt, amber, and arable land.[77]

Poland's population, estimated at 38,562,000, has remained steady for the last several years. Poland, with a median age of 40 years old, has an older-than-average population. The country is essentially entirely made up of native Poles. Immigrants do not comprise a significant proportion of the population. Poland has no citizenship by birth; instead, citizenship is awarded by descent, which requires both parents to be citizens of Poland. The country is almost exclusively Roman Catholic.[78]

Poland's GDP stands at US$545 billion, or US$24,952 per capita. Unlike most of Europe, Poland has seen years of steady economic gains. In 2015, the economy expanded at 3.5 percent.[79] Poland was one of the only countries in the European Union to avoid a recession during 2008–2009: The government of Prime Minister Donald Tusk steered the Polish economy through the economic downturn by skillfully managing public finances and adopting controversial pension and tax reforms to further shore up public finances. Once a largely agricultural nation, the country's economy has transitioned to one based primarily on industry (41 percent) and services (56 percent).[80] The labor force, with 18.29 million people, ranks 34th in the world in size.[81] Poland's main export partners include Germany, the UK, the Czech Republic, France, Italy, the Netherlands, and Russia. Machinery and transportation equipment, intermediate manufactured goods, miscellaneous manufactured goods, foodstuffs, and live animals are all major exports.[82]

Poland has adopted a republic form of government. It was one of the first ex-communist countries to embrace a capitalistic economy with privatization and economic liberalization. The country's economic success following the fall of the Soviet Union was largely attributed to the government's success at privatizing most of the small and medium state-owned companies and encouraging foreign direct investment. Poland's major difficulties lie in its somewhat deficient infrastructure, its rigid labor codes, a burdensome commercial court system, its extensive government red tape, a lack of energy mix, and its burdensome tax system.[83]

You Be the International Management Consultant

Tesco, a multinational grocery and general merchandise retailer, operates over 6,000 stores around the world and 442 stores in Poland. Tesco has a large online presence and handles online orders for customers in its various markets. The company has enjoyed considerable success across the world but has faced some recent difficulty with its Polish investments.

The Polish government has recently announced a plan to increase revenues to pay for various initiatives, including the proposed imposition on large retailers of a 1.9 percent tax on gross revenue. This tax is targeted at "foreign-dominated industries" like supermarkets and banks. Moody's estimates that this new tax could cost Tesco as much as 3.5 percent of earnings.[84]

Questions

1. If you were a consultant for Tesco, how would you advise Tesco to deal with the new tax?
2. Would this new tax be enough for you to advise the company to end business in Poland?
3. Does the fact that this regulation is specifically targeted at foreign-dominated industries and businesses create concern for future regulations should you choose to continue operations in Poland?

Chapter 6

ORGANIZATIONAL CULTURES AND DIVERSITY

OBJECTIVES OF THE CHAPTER

The previous two chapters focused on national cultures. The overriding objective of this chapter is to examine the interaction of national culture (diversity) and organizational cultures and to discuss ways in which MNCs can manage the often inherent conflicts between national and organizational cultures. Many times, the cultural values and resulting behaviors that are common in a particular country are not the same as those in another. To be successful, MNCs must balance and integrate the national cultures of the countries in which they do business with their own organizational culture. Employee relations, which includes how organizational culture responds to national culture or diversity, deals with internal structures and defines how the company manages. Customer relations, associated with how national culture reacts to organizational cultures, reflects how the local community views the company from a customer service and employee satisfaction perspective.

Although the field of international management has long recognized the impact of national cultures, only recently has attention been given to the importance of managing organizational cultures and diversity. This chapter first examines common organizational cultures that exist in MNCs, and then presents and analyzes ways in which multiculturalism and diversity are being addressed by the best, world-class multinationals. The specific objectives of this chapter are

1. **DEFINE** exactly what is meant by *organizational culture*, and discuss the interaction of national and MNC cultures.

2. **IDENTIFY** the four most common categories of organizational culture that have been found through research, and discuss the characteristics of each.

3. **PROVIDE** an overview of the nature and degree of multiculturalism and diversity in today's MNCs.

4. **DISCUSS** common guidelines and principles that are used in building multicultural effectiveness at the team and the organizational levels.

The World of *International Management*

Managing Culture and Diversity in Global Teams

According to many international consultants and managers, diverse and global teams are one of the most consistent sources of competitive advantage for any organization. Deloitte Touche Tohmatsu, the international accounting and consulting firm, has embraced a global mindset when building its teams. According to the company, "strength from cultural diversity is one of Deloitte's shared values." With more than 200,000 employees spread across offices in 150 countries, the company has implemented a corporate culture that regards diversity as a key competitive advantage.[1]

At Deloitte, as with most multinational organizations, global teams are also virtual teams. According to a study by Kirkman, Rosen, Gibson, and Tesluk, virtual teams are "groups of people who work interdependently with shared purpose across space, time, and organization boundaries using technology to communicate and collaborate."[2] These teams are often cross-cultural and cross-functional. Furthermore, Kirkman and colleagues explain that virtual teams allow "organizations to combine the best expertise regardless of geographic location."[3] To manage a global team, international managers must take into consideration three factors: culture, communication, and trust.

Culture

At Deloitte, leadership is trained to adapt to the cultural differences that their globally located employees exhibit. Leveraging the experiences of one of their global teams, the company conducted a three-month study into how cultural dynamics impact performance and success. The team included employees from Spain, Germany, Australia, the United States, and Japan. Through this study, Deloitte identified four key findings regarding culture and global leadership:[4]

1. "Cultural and/or personality diversity is in the eye of the beholder." Despite prior assumptions that cultural differences would have the largest impact on the team's final deliverable, the team members in the study were split as to whether culture or personality led to a greater

impact. In many instances, the individual personalities of the team members, irrespective of national origin, were shown to be equally as differentiating.

2. "Cultural diversity can positively contribute to people's professional and personal enjoyment of the project, as well as a project's outcome." The team members in the study universally expressed an enhanced experience from working with others of differing cultures. A few factors seemed to lead to this. Genuine curiosity about their fellow team members, learning how to build new types of relationships, and being challenged to think differently were all found to be enjoyable by the employees.

3. "Cultural diversity can indirectly encourage project members to rethink their usual working habits and expectations, behave with fewer assumptions about the 'right' way to address an issue and promote linguistic clarity." Unexpectedly, the lack of a common first language between team members actually enhanced communication. Employees spent more time ensuring that the content of their communication was clearly understood by the team, and team members reported that they actually found themselves transforming into better listeners.

4. "The dominance of cultural diversity amongst team members reduces the bias to interact with people who have common characteristics and create a unique bond." With each employee bringing a different set of perspectives to the table, the playing field among the team members was more level. The employees expressed a sense of synergy, with many stating that they felt better prepared to overcome challenges by having such a diverse set of skills at their disposal. Ironically, the lack of similarities between the employees in the study actually led to greater personal connections to each other, with team members expressing a familial feeling among the group.[5]

Communication

Communicating without face-to-face interaction can have its drawbacks. Being consciously aware of the way that both you and your teammates communicate can increase the chances of success for your team.

To help team members gain a better understanding of each other's communication styles, Deloitte developed "Business Chemistry," a program that identifies the preferred business behaviors of team members to help build better, stronger cross-cultural teams. Through the program, individuals are identified as having one or more of the four types of "chemistries": Pioneer, Driver, Integrator, or Guardian. By sharing their "chemistry" with the team, team members can adapt their style of delivery to better communicate with each other. Deloitte delivers "Business Chemistry" to external clients as well as to its internal teams. To date, more than 90,000 people in 150 countries have used the program.[6]

In her article "Tips for Working in Global Teams," Melanie Doulton provides helpful suggestions for good communication in a global team:

- When starting a project with a new team, hold an initial meeting in which all members introduce themselves and describe the job each one is going to do.

- Hold regular meetings throughout the project to ensure everyone is "on the same page." Follow up conference calls with written minutes to reinforce what was discussed and what individual team members are responsible for.

- Put details of the project in writing, especially for a new team in which everyone speaks in different accents and uses different idioms and colloquialisms.

- Communicate using the most effective technology. For example, decide when e-mail is preferable to a phone call or instant messaging is preferable to a videoconference. In addition, try to understand everyone's communication style. For example, for a high-context culture such as India's, people tend to speak in the passive voice, whereas in North America, people use the active voice.[7]

Moreover, while acknowledging the challenges of communication in virtual teams, Steven R. Rayner also points out that written communication can have an advantage. He states, "The process of writing—where the sender must carefully examine how to communicate his/her message—provides the sender with the opportunity to create a more refined response than an 'off-the-cuff' verbal comment."[8]

Likelihood of Message Getting Interpreted Correctly

LOW				HIGH
			Video	Face-to-Face
Fax/Letter	E-mail	Telephone	Conferencing	Interaction

Source: Adapted from Steven R. Rayner, "The Virtual Team Challenge," Rayner & Associates, Inc., 1997.

Trust

Kirkman and colleagues emphasize that "a specific challenge for virtual teams, compared to face-to-face teams, is the difficulty of building trust between team members who rarely, or never, see each other."[9] Rayner notes that "by some estimates, as much as 30 percent of senior management time is spent in 'chance' encounters (such as unplanned hallway, parking lot, and lunch room conversations). . . . In a virtual team setting, these opportunities for relationship building and idea sharing are far more limited."[10]

How can managers build trust among virtual team members? From their research, Kirkman and colleagues discovered that "building trust requires rapid responses to electronic communications from team members, reliable performance, and consistent follow-through. Accordingly, team leaders should coach virtual team members to avoid long lags in responding, unilateral priority shifts, and failure to follow up on commitments."[11] In addition, Doulton recommends that virtual team members "exchange feedback early" and allow an extra day or two for responses due to time zone differences.[12]

Team building activities also build trust. According to Kirkman and colleagues, as part of the virtual team launch, it is recommended that all members meet face-to-face to "set objectives, clarify roles, build personal relationships, develop team norms, and establish group identity."[13] Picking the right team members can help the teams become more cohesive as well. When Kirkman and colleagues interviewed 75 team leaders and members in virtual teams, people responded that skills in communication, teamwork, thinking outside the box, and taking initiative were more important than technical skills. This finding was surprising, considering most managers select virtual team members based on technical skills. Having people with the right skills is essential to bring together a successful virtual team.[14]

At Deloitte, training employees to trust and harness the benefits of global, diverse teaming starts at the intern level. Through Deloitte's Global Project Challenge, interns cross-collaborate with other Deloitte employees across the world to solve real business problems. Employees learn strategies to cope with both the logistical challenges, such as time zone differences, and cultural challenges that arise when working in a virtual team.

Advantages of Global Virtual Teams

In addition to its challenges of overcoming cultural and communication barriers, global virtual teams have certain advantages over face-to-face teams.

First, Kirkman and colleagues concluded that "working virtually can reduce team process losses associated with stereotyping, personality conflicts, power politics, and cliques commonly experienced by face-to-face teams. Virtual team members may be unaffected by potentially divisive demographic differences when there is minimal face-to-face contact." Managers may even give fairer assessments of team members' work because managers are compelled to rely on objective data rather than being influenced by their perceptual biases.[15]

Second, Rayner observes that "having members span many different time zones can literally keep a project moving around the clock. . . . Work doesn't stop—it merely shifts to a different time zone."[16]

Third, according to Rayner, "The ability for an organization to bring people together from remote geography and form a cohesive team that is capable of quickly solving complex problems and making effective decisions is an enormous competitive advantage."[17]

For an international manager, this competitive advantage makes overcoming challenges of managing global teams worth the effort.

As can be seen from Deloitte's experiences, there are both benefits and challenges inherent in multinational, multicultural teams. These teams, which almost always include a diverse group of members with varying functional, geographic, ethnic, and cultural backgrounds, can be an efficient and effective vehicle for tackling increasingly multidimensional business problems. At the same time, this very diversity brings challenges that are often exacerbated when the teams are primarily "virtual." Research has demonstrated the benefits of diversity and has also offered insight on how best to overcome the inherent challenges of global teams, including those that are "virtual."

In this chapter we will explore the nature and characteristics of organizational culture as it relates to doing business in today's global context. In addition, strategies and guidelines for establishing a strong organizational culture in the presence of diversity are presented.

■ The Nature of Organizational Culture

The chapters in Part One provided the background on the external environment, and the chapters so far in Part Two have been concerned with the external culture. Regardless of whether this environment or cultural context affects the MNC, when individuals join an MNC, not only do they bring their national culture, which greatly affects their learned beliefs, attitudes, values, and behaviors, but they also enter into an organizational culture. Employees of MNCs are expected to "fit in." For example, at PepsiCo, personnel are expected to be cheerful, positive, and enthusiastic and have committed optimism; at Ford, they are expected to show self-confidence, assertiveness, and machismo.[18] Regardless of the external environment or their national culture, managers and employees must understand and follow their organization's culture to be successful. In this section, after first defining organizational culture, we analyze the interaction between national and organizational cultures. An understanding of this interaction has become recognized as vital to effective international management.

Definition and Characteristics

Organizational culture has been defined in several different ways. In its most basic form, organizational culture can be defined as the shared values and beliefs that enable members to understand their roles in and the norms of the organization. A more detailed definition is offered by organizational cultural theorist Edgar Schein, who defines it as a pattern of shared basic assumptions that the group learned as it solved its problems of external adaptation and internal integration, and that has worked well enough to be considered valid and, therefore, to be taught to new members as the correct way to perceive, think, and feel in relation to those problems.[19]

> **organizational culture**
> Shared values and beliefs that enable members to understand their roles and the norms of the organization.

Regardless of how the term is defined, a number of important characteristics are associated with an organization's culture. These have been summarized as

1. Observed behavioral regularities, as typified by common language, terminology, and rituals.
2. Norms, as reflected by things such as the amount of work to be done and the degree of cooperation between management and employees.
3. Dominant values that the organization advocates and expects participants to share, such as high product and service quality, low absenteeism, and high efficiency.
4. A philosophy that is set forth in the MNC's beliefs regarding how employees and customers should be treated.
5. Rules that dictate the dos and don'ts of employee behavior relating to areas such as productivity, customer relations, and intergroup cooperation.
6. Organizational climate, or the overall atmosphere of the enterprise, as reflected by the way that participants interact with each other, conduct themselves with customers, and feel about the way they are treated by higher-level management.[20]

This list is not intended to be all-inclusive, but it does help illustrate the nature of organizational culture.[21] The major problem is that sometimes an MNC's organizational culture in one country's facility differs sharply from organizational cultures in other countries. For example, managers who do well in England may be ineffective in Germany, despite the fact that they work for the same MNC. In addition, the cultures of the English and German subsidiaries may differ sharply from those of the home U.S. location. Effectively dealing with multiculturalism within the various locations of an MNC is a major challenge for international management.

A good example is provided by the British-Swedish MNC AstraZeneca PLC, the seventh-largest pharmaceutical company in the world. With operations in over 100 countries on six continents, AstraZeneca's 13-member senior executive team includes leaders from the United Kingdom, France, Australia, the United States, and the Netherlands.[22] Over 23 percent of the company's employees work in North America, and about 31 percent are employed in Asia.[23] To unite such a diverse set of employees under a common corporate culture, AstraZeneca's Global Steering Group has focused on three universal cultural pillars: "Leadership and Management Capability," "Transparency in Talent Management and Career Progression," and "Work/Life Challenges."[24] Furthermore, the company introduced a new cross-cultural mentorship program, called Insight Exchange. By pairing senior- and junior-level employees from different cultural and professional backgrounds, AstraZeneca hopes to create a more open culture.

In some cases companies have deliberately maintained two different business cultures because they do not want one culture influencing the other. A good example is provided by the Tata Group, the giant conglomerate based in India, which has made multiple transnational acquisitions in recent years. When its automobile subsidiary, Tata Motors, bought control of Daewoo, a Korean automaker, it used a strategy that is not very common when one company controls another. Rather than impose its own culture on the chain, Tata's management took a back seat. To emphasize this approach, Tata Group chairman Ratan Tata publicly stated that "Tata Motors will operate Daewoo as a Korean company, in Korea, managed by Koreans."[25] Tata maintained the Daewoo brand name, appointed a Korean as the new CEO, and operated as a Korean business. The union vice president even remarked that "Though Tata is a foreign company, we were able to confirm that it recognizes and respects Korea in many aspects." In the first four years after the acquisition, revenue doubled, operating profit grew sevenfold, and trust between the employees' union and management improved.[26]

Tata Chemicals took a similar approach when it purchased British soda ash producer Brunner Mond and its Kenyan subsidy Magadi Soda. To maintain the existing company culture at Brunner Mond and Magadi Soda, Tata Chemicals did not change the companies' names or logos, kept all existing senior executives in place, and made it clear that all major decisions would be made jointly between Brunner Mond, Magadi Soda, and Tata Chemicals. To ensure a smooth ownership transition, executives from all three companies jointly created a plan of action for the first 100 days post-acquisition. Since then, Tata Chemicals has leveraged resources from all three companies to build strong relationships with external suppliers, expand global growth opportunities, and coordinate sales and operations.[27]

■ Interaction between National and Organizational Cultures

There is a widely held belief that organizational culture tends to moderate or erase the impact of national culture. The logic of such conventional wisdom is that if a U.S. MNC set up operations in, say, France, it would not be long before the French employees began to "think like Americans." In fact, evidence is accumulating that just the opposite may be true. Hofstede's research found that the national cultural values of employees have a significant impact on their organizational performance, and that the cultural values employees bring to the workplace with them are not easily changed by the organization. So, for example, while some French employees would have a higher power distance than Swedes and some a lower power distance, chances are "that if a company hired locals in Paris, they would, on the whole, be less likely to challenge hierarchical power than would the same number of locals hired in Stockholm."[28]

Andre Laurent's research supports Hofstede's conclusions.[29] He found that cultural differences are actually more pronounced among foreign employees working within the same multinational organization than among personnel working for firms in their native lands. Nancy Adler summarized these research findings as follows:

> When they work for a multinational corporation, it appears that Germans become more German, Americans become more American, Swedes become more Swedish, and so on. Surprised by these results, Laurent replicated the research in two other multinational corporations, each with subsidiaries in the same nine Western European countries and the United States. Similar to the first company, corporate culture did not reduce or eliminate national differences in the second and third corporations. Far from reducing national differences, organization culture maintains and enhances them.[30]

There often are substantial differences between the organizational cultures of different subsidiaries, and, of course, this can cause coordination problems. For example, when Lucent Technologies, Inc., of Murray Hill, New Jersey, merged with Alcatel SA of Paris, France, both parties failed to realize some of the cultural differences between themselves and their new partners. Leadership concerns due to cultural misunderstandings arose from the very beginning of the merger. Frenchman Serge Tchuruk was appointed chair of the combined company, while American Patricia Russo was appointed as CEO. In France, the chair is often seen as the company's leader, while in the United States, the CEO is viewed as the person highest in command. This cultural difference led to confusion as to whether Russo or Tchuruk was actually in charge.[31] Additionally, Patricia Russo did not speak French, despite leading a now-French company, resulting in additional confusion.[32]

When the combined company faced financial crises, the cultural response differed greatly between the American and French executives, leading to further disagreement. In the United States, jobs are often cut when finances are pressured, whereas in France, companies tend to reach out to the government for assistance. As a result, Alcatel-Lucent was unable to cut costs, but also unable to secure government assistance.[33] Local restrictions, overlooked before the merger, further hindered the combined company's success and added to the financial strain; in Bonn, Germany, for example, the company was required to keep both Lucent's and Alcatel's original offices open, despite employing only a combined 75 employees.[34] After just a few years, both top executives were forced to step aside. The merger never did result in profitability for the company; for all seven years that Alcatel-Lucent operated independently before being acquired by Nokia in 2015, the company posted negative cash flows.

In examining and addressing the differences between organizational cultures, Hofstede provided the early database of a set of proprietary cultural-analysis techniques and programs known as DOCSA (Diagnosing Organizational Culture for Strategic Application). This approach identifies the dimensions of organizational culture summarized in Table 6–1.

Table 6–1
Dimensions of Corporate Culture

Motivation	
Activities	**Outputs**
To be consistent and precise. To strive for accuracy and attention to detail. To refine and perfect. Get it right.	To be pioneers. To pursue clear aims and objectives. To innovate and progress. Go for it.
Relationship	
Job	**Person**
To put the demands of the job before the needs of the individual.	To put the needs of the individual before the needs of the job.
Identity	
Corporate	**Professional**
To identify with and uphold the expectations of the employing organizations.	To pursue the aims and ideals of each professional practice.
Communication	
Open	**Closed**
To stimulate and encourage a full and free exchange of information and opinion.	To monitor and control the exchange and accessibility of information and opinion.
Control	
Tight	**Loose**
To comply with clear and definite systems and procedures.	To work flexibly and adaptively according to the needs of the situation.
Conduct	
Conventional	**Pragmatic**
To put the expertise and standards of the employing organization first. To do what we know is right.	To put the demands and expectations of customers first. To do what they ask.

Source: Adapted from a study by the Diagnosing Organizational Culture for Strategic Application (DOCSA) group and reported in Lisa Hoecklin, *Managing Cultural Differences: Strategies for Competitive Advantage* (Workingham, England: Addison-Wesley, 1995), p. 146.

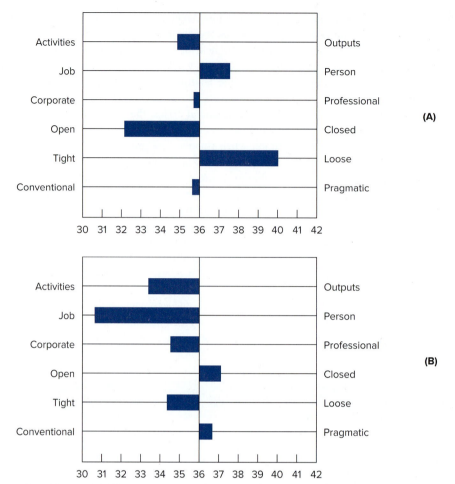

Figure 6–1

Europeans' Perception of the Cultural Dimensions of U.S. Operations (*A*) and European Operations (*B*) of the Same MNC

Source: Adapted from a study by the Diagnosing Organizational Culture for Strategic Application (DOCSA) group and reported in Lisa Hoecklin, *Managing Cultural Differences: Strategies for Competitive Advantage* (Workingham, England: Addison-Wesley, 1995), pp. 147–148.

It was found that when cultural comparisons were made between different subsidiaries of an MNC, different cultures often existed in each one. Such cultural differences within an MNC could reduce the ability of units to work well together. An example is provided in Figure 6–1, which shows the cultural dimensions of a California-based MNC and its European subsidiary as perceived by the Europeans. A close comparison of these perceptions reveals some startling differences.

The Europeans viewed the culture in the U.S. facilities as only slightly activities oriented (see Table 6–1 for a description of these dimensions), but they saw their own European operations as much more heavily activities oriented. The U.S. operation was viewed as moderately people oriented, but their own relationships were viewed as very job oriented. The Americans were seen as having a slight identification with their own organization, while the Europeans had a much stronger identification. The Americans were perceived as being very open in their communications; the Europeans saw themselves as moderately closed. The Americans were viewed as preferring very loose control, while the Europeans felt they preferred somewhat tight control. The Americans were seen as somewhat conventional in their conduct, while the Europeans saw themselves as somewhat pragmatic. If these perceptions are accurate, then it obviously would be necessary for both groups to discuss their cultural differences and carefully coordinate their activities to work well together.

This analysis is relevant to multinational alliances. It shows that even though an alliance may exist, the partners will bring different organizational cultures with them.

Lessem and Neubauer, who have portrayed Europe as offering four distinct ways of dealing with multiculturalism (based on the United Kingdom, French, German, and Italian characteristics), provide an example in Table 6–2, which briefly describes each of these sets of cultural characteristics. A close examination of the differences highlights how difficult it can be to do business with two or more of these groups because each group perceives things differently from the others. Another example is the way in which negotiations occur between groups; here are some contrasts between French and Spanish negotiators:[35]

French	Spanish
Look for a meeting of minds.	Look for a meeting of people.
Intellectual competence is very important.	Social competence is very important.
Persuasion through carefully prepared and skilled rhetoric is employed.	Persuasion through emotional appeal is employed.
Strong emphasis is given to a logical presentation of one's position coupled with well-reasoned, detailed solutions.	Socialization always precedes negotiations, which are characterized by an exchange of grand ideas and general principles.
A contract is viewed as a well-reasoned transaction.	A contract is viewed as a long-lasting relationship.
Trust emerges slowly and is based on the evaluation of perceived status and intellect.	Trust is developed on the basis of frequent and warm interpersonal contact and transaction.

Such comparisons also help explain why it can be difficult for an MNC with a strong organizational culture to break into foreign markets where it is not completely familiar with divergent national cultures. The International Management in Action "Doing Things the Walmart Way" provides an illustration. When dealing with these challenges, MNCs must work hard to understand the nature of the country and institutional practices to both moderate and adapt their operations in a way that accommodates the company and customer base.

Table 6–2
European Management Characteristics

	Characteristic			
Dimension	**Western (United Kingdom)**	**Northern (France)**	**Eastern (Germany)**	**Southern (Italy)**
Corporate	Commercial	Administrative	Industrial	Familial
Management attributes				
Behavior	Experiential	Professional	Developmental	Convivial
Attitude	Sensation	Thought	Intuition	Feeling
Institutional models				
Function	Salesmanship	Control	Production	Personnel
Structure	Transaction	Hierarchy	System	Network
Societal ideas				
Economics	Free market	Dirigiste	Social market	Communal
Philosophy	Pragmatic	Rational	Holistic	Humanistic
Cultural images				
Art	Theatre	Architecture	Music	Dance
Culture	(Anglo-Saxon)	(Gallic)	(Germanic)	(Latin)

Source: Adapted from Ronald Lessen and Fred Neubauer, *European Management Systems* (McGraw-Hill, London, 1994), and reported in Lisa Hoecklin, *Managing Cultural Differences: Strategies for Competitive Advantage* (Workingham, England: Addison-Wesley, 1995), p. 149.

Doing Things the Walmart Way; Germans Say, "Nein, vielen Dank"

Across the globe, Walmart employees engage in the "Walmart cheer" to start their day. It is a way to show inclusivity and express their pride in the company, and can be heard in many different languages. Walmart not only operates in more than two dozen countries but is also a leader in diversity in the workplace. In 2015, Walmart was named a noteworthy company for diversity by *DiversityInc* magazine, and, in 2012, then-CEO Mike Duke was inducted into the CPG/Retail Diversity Hall of Fame. However, despite Walmart's multinational presence and representation, its internal culture proved to be less than satisfactory to the German market.

Walmart has experienced a fair share of negative PR over the years, so it is no surprise that some may have adverse reactions to news of Walmart moving into the neighborhood. Before the unflattering buzz, Walmart sometimes discovers that even the best intentions can fall flat. Walmart entered the German market in 1997 and stressed the idea of friendly service with a smile, where the customers always come first. Even before the employees walked onto the sales room floor, employee dissatisfaction became clear.

The pamphlet that outlined the workplace code of ethics was simply translated from English to German, but the message was not expressed the way Walmart had intended. It warned employees of potential supervisor-employee relationships, implying sexual harassment, and encouraged reports of "improper behavior," which spoke more to legal matters. The Germans interpreted this to mean that there was a ban on any romantic relationships in the workplace and saw the reporting methods as more of a way to rat out co-workers than benefit the company. As we saw in Chapter 3, ethical values in one country may not be the same as in another, and Walmart experienced this firsthand. Another employee relations issue that arose dealt with local practices. Walmart has never been open to unionized employees, so when the German operations began dealing with workers' councils and adhering to co-determination rules, a common practice there, Walmart was less than willing to listen to suggestions as to how to improve employee working conditions. As if this was not enough, Walmart soon experienced problems with customer relations as well.

Doing things the Walmart way included smiling at customers and assisting them by bagging their groceries at the Supercenter locations. This policy presented problems in the German environment. Male employees who were ordered to smile at customers were often seen as flirtatious to male customers, and Germans do not like strangers handling their groceries. These are just a few reasons that customers did not enjoy their shopping experience. This does not mean that everything Walmart attempted was wrong. Products that are popular in Germany were available on the shelves in place of products that would be common in other countries. Enhanced distribution processes guaranteed availability of most requested items, and efficiency was pervasive.

Despite some successes and good intentions and numerous attempts to improve the German stores, the Walmart culture proved to be a poor fit for the German market, and Walmart vacated Germany in 2006. Unfortunately, Walmart learned the hard way that in the retail or service industry, local customs are often more important than a strong, unyielding organizational culture. The challenge to incorporate everyone into the Walmart family certainly fell short of expectations. If the Walmart culture does not become more flexible, or locally relevant, it may be chastised from numerous global markets, and the company could hear, "no, thank you" in even more languages than German as it continues to expand. (See In-Depth Integrative Case 2.2 at the end of Part Two for more detail on Walmart's experiences around the world.)

Source: Mark Landler and Michael Barbaro, "Wal-Mart Finds That Its Formula Doesn't Fit Every Culture," *New York Times,* August 2, 2006, http://www.nytimes.com/2006/08/02/business/worldbusiness/02walmart.html.

■ Organizational Cultures in MNCs

Organizational cultures of MNCs are shaped by a number of factors, including the cultural preferences of the leaders and employees. In the international arena, some MNCs have subsidiaries that, except for the company logo and reporting procedures, would not be easily recognizable as belonging to the same multinational.[36]

Given that many recent international expansions are a result of mergers or acquisition, the integration of these organizational cultures is a critical concern in international management. Numeroff and Abrahams have suggested that there are four steps that are critical in this process:

1. The two groups have to establish the purpose, goal, and focus of their merger.
2. Then they have to develop mechanisms to identify the most important organizational structures and management roles.
3. They have to determine who has authority over the resources needed for getting things done.
4. They have to identify the expectations of all involved parties and facilitate communication between both departments and individuals in the structure.[37]

Companies all over the world are finding out firsthand that there is more to an international merger or acquisition than just sharing resources and capturing greater market share. Differences in workplace cultures sometimes temporarily overshadow the overall goal of long-term success of the newly formed entity. With the proper management framework and execution, successful integration of cultures is not only possible, but also the most preferable paradigm in which to operate. It is the role of the sponsors and managers to keep sight of the necessity to create, maintain, and support the notion of a united front. It is only when this assimilation has occurred that an international merger or acquisition can truly be labeled a success.[38]

In addition, there are three aspects of organizational functioning that seem to be especially important in determining MNC organizational culture: (1) the general relationship between the employees and their organization; (2) the hierarchical system of authority that defines the roles of managers and subordinates; and (3) the general views that employees hold about the MNC's purpose, destiny, goals, and their place in them.[39]

When examining these dimensions of organizational culture, Trompenaars suggested the use of two continua: One distinguishes between equity and hierarchy; the other examines orientation to the person and the task. Along these continua, which are shown in Figure 6–2, he identifies and describes four different types of organizational cultures: family, Eiffel Tower, guided missile, and incubator.[40]

In practice, of course, organizational cultures do not fit neatly into any of these four, but the groupings can be useful in helping examine the bases of how individuals relate to each other, think, learn, change, are motivated, and resolve conflict. The following discussion examines each of these cultural types.

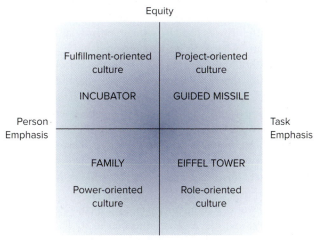

Figure 6–2

Organizational Cultures

Source: Adapted from Fons Trompenaars, *Riding the Waves of Culture: Understanding Diversity in Global Business* (Burr Ridge, IL: Irwin, 1994), p. 154.

Family Culture

family culture
A culture that is characterized by a strong emphasis on hierarchy and orientation to the person.

Family culture is characterized by a strong emphasis on hierarchy and orientation to the person. The result is a family-type environment that is power-oriented and headed by a leader who is regarded as a caring parent and one who knows what is best for the personnel. Trompenaars found that this organizational culture is common in countries such as Turkey, Pakistan, Venezuela, China, Hong Kong, and Singapore.[41]

In this culture, personnel not only respect the individuals who are in charge but look to them for both guidance and approval as well. In turn, management assumes a paternal relationship with personnel, looks after employees, and tries to ensure that they are treated well and have continued employment. Family culture also is characterized by traditions, customs, and associations that bind together the personnel and make it difficult for outsiders to become members. When it works well, family culture can catalyze and multiply the energies of the personnel and appeal to their deepest feelings and aspirations. When it works poorly, members of the organization end up supporting a leader who is ineffective and drains their energies and loyalties.

This type of culture is foreign to most managers in the United States, who believe in valuing people based on their abilities and achievements, not on their age or position in the hierarchy. As a result, many managers in U.S.-based MNCs fail to understand why senior-level managers in overseas subsidiaries might appoint a relative to a high-level, sensitive position even though that individual might not appear to be the best qualified for the job. They fail to realize that family ties are so strong that the appointed relative would never do anything to embarrass or let down the family member who made the appointment. Here is an example:

> A Dutch delegation was shocked and surprised when the Brazilian owner of a large manufacturing company introduced his relatively junior accountant as the key coordinator of a $15 million joint venture. The Dutch were puzzled as to why a recently qualified accountant had been given such weighty responsibilities, including the receipt of their own money. The Brazilians pointed out that the young man was the best possible choice among 1,200 employees since he was the nephew of the owner. Who could be more trustworthy than that? Instead of complaining, the Dutch should consider themselves lucky that he was available.[42]

Eiffel Tower Culture

Eiffel Tower culture
A culture that is characterized by strong emphasis on hierarchy and orientation to the task.

Eiffel Tower culture is characterized by strong emphasis on hierarchy and orientation to the task. Under this organizational culture, jobs are well defined, employees know what they are supposed to do, and everything is coordinated from the top. As a result, this culture—like the Eiffel Tower itself—is steep, narrow at the top, and broad at the base. Unlike family culture, where the leader is revered and considered to be the source of all power, the person holding the top position in the Eiffel Tower culture could be replaced at any time, and this would have no effect on the work that organization members are doing or on the organization's reasons for existence. In this culture, relationships are specific, and status remains with the job. Therefore, if the boss of an Eiffel Tower subsidiary were playing golf with a subordinate, the subordinate would not feel any pressure to let the boss win. In addition, these managers seldom create off-the-job relationships with their people because they believe this could affect their rational judgment. In fact, this culture operates very much like a formal hierarchy—impersonal and efficient.

Each role at each level of the hierarchy is described; rated for its difficulty, complexity, and responsibility; and has a salary attached to it. Then follows a search for a person to fill it. In considering applicants for the role, the personnel department will treat everyone equally and neutrally, match the person's skills and aptitudes with the job requirements, and award the job to the best fit between role and person. The same procedure is followed in evaluations and promotions.[43]

Eiffel Tower culture most commonly is found in northwestern European countries. Examples include Denmark, Germany, and the Netherlands. The way that people in this culture learn and change differs sharply from that in the family culture. Learning involves the accumulation of skills necessary to fit a role, and organizations will use qualifications in deciding how to schedule, deploy, and reshuffle personnel to meet their needs. The organization also will employ such rational procedures as assessment centers, appraisal systems, training and development programs, and job rotation in managing its human resources. All these procedures help ensure that a formal hierarchic or bureaucracy-like approach works well. When changes need to be made, however, the Eiffel Tower culture often is ill-equipped to handle things. Manuals must be rewritten, procedures changed, job descriptions altered, promotions reconsidered, and qualifications reassessed.

Because the Eiffel Tower culture does not rely on values that are similar to those in most U.S. MNCs, U.S. expatriate managers often have difficulty initiating change in this culture. As Trompenaars notes:

> An American manager responsible for initiating change in a German company described to me the difficulties he had in making progress, although the German managers had discussed the new strategy in depth and made significant contributions to its formulation. Through informal channels, he had eventually discovered that his mistake was not having formalized the changes to structure or job descriptions. In the absence of a new organization chart, this Eiffel Tower company was unable to change.[44]

Guided Missile Culture

Guided missile culture is characterized by strong emphasis on equality in the workplace and orientation to the task. This organizational culture is oriented to work, which typically is undertaken by teams or project groups. Unlike the Eiffel Tower culture, where job assignments are fixed and limited, personnel in the guided missile culture do whatever it takes to get the job done. This culture gets its name from high-tech organizations such as the National Aeronautics and Space Administration (NASA), which pioneered the use of project groups working on space probes that resembled guided missiles. In these large project teams, more than a hundred different types of engineers often were responsible for building, say, a lunar landing module. The team member whose contribution would be crucial at any given time in the project typically could not be known in advance. Therefore, all types of engineers had to work in close harmony and cooperate with everyone on the team.

guided missile culture
A culture that is characterized by strong emphasis on equality in the workplace and orientation to the task.

To be successful, the best form of synthesis must be used in the course of working on the project. For example, in a guided missile project, formal hierarchical considerations are given low priority, and individual expertise is of greatest importance. Additionally, all team members are equal (or at least potentially equal) because their relative contributions to the project are not yet known. All teams treat each other with respect because they may need the other for assistance. This egalitarian and task-driven organizational culture fits well with the national cultures of the United States and United Kingdom, which helps explain why high-tech MNCs commonly locate their operations in these countries.

Unlike family and Eiffel Tower cultures, change in guided missile culture comes quickly. Goals are accomplished, and teams are reconfigured and assigned new objectives. People move from group to group, and loyalties to one's profession and project often are greater than loyalties to the organization itself.

Trompenaars found that the motivation of those in guided missile cultures tends to be more intrinsic than just concern for money and benefits. Team members become enthusiastic about, and identify with, the struggle toward attaining their goal. For example, a project team that is designing and building a new computer for the Asian market may be highly motivated to create a machine that is at the leading edge of technology, user-friendly, and likely to sweep the market. Everything else is secondary to this overriding objective. Thus, both intragroup and intergroup conflicts are minimized and petty problems between team members set aside; everyone is so committed to the project's main goal that no one has time for petty disagreements. As Trompenaars notes:

> This culture tends to be individualistic since it allows for a wide variety of differently specialized persons to work with each other on a temporary basis. The scenery of faces keeps changing. Only the pursuit of chosen lines of personal development is constant. The team is a vehicle for the shared enthusiasm of its members, but is itself disposable and will be discarded when the project ends. Members are garrulous, idiosyncratic, and intelligent, but their mutuality is a means, not an end. It is a way of enjoying the journey. They do not need to know each other intimately, and may avoid doing so. Management by objectives is the language spoken, and people are paid for performance.[45]

Incubator Culture

incubator culture
A culture that is characterized by strong emphasis on equality and orientation to the person.

Incubator culture is the fourth major type of organizational culture that Trompenaars identified, and it is characterized by strong emphasis on equality and personal orientation. This culture is based heavily on the existential idea that organizations per se are secondary to the fulfillment of the individuals within them. This culture is based on the premise that the role of organizations is to serve as incubators for the self-expression and self-fulfillment of their members; as a result, this culture often has little formal structure. Participants in an incubator culture are there primarily to perform roles such as confirming, criticizing, developing, finding resources for, or helping complete the development of an innovative product or service. These cultures often are found among start-up firms in Silicon Valley, California, or Silicon Glen, Scotland. These incubator-type organizations typically are entrepreneurial and often founded and made up by a creative team who left larger, Eiffel Tower-type employers. They want to be part of an organization where their creative talents will not be stifled.

Incubator cultures often create environments where participants thrive on an intense, emotional commitment to the nature of the work. For example, the group may be in the process of gene splitting that could lead to radical medical breakthroughs and extend life. Often, personnel in such cultures are overworked, and the enterprise typically is underfunded. As breakthroughs occur and the company gains stability, however, it starts moving down the road toward commercialization and profit. In turn, this engenders the need to hire more people and develop formalized procedures for ensuring the smooth flow of operations. In this process of growth and maturity, the unique characteristics of the incubator culture begin to wane and disappear, and the culture is replaced by one of the other types (family, Eiffel Tower, or guided missile).

As noted, change in the incubator culture often is fast and spontaneous. All participants are working toward the same objective. Because there may not yet be a customer who is using the final output, however, the problem itself often is open to redefinition, and the solution typically is generic, aimed at a universe of applications. Meanwhile, motivation of the personnel remains highly intrinsic and intense, and it is common to find employees working 70 hours a week—and loving it. The participants are more concerned with the unfolding creative process than they are in gathering power or ensuring personal monetary gain. In sharp contrast to the family culture, leadership in this incubator culture is achieved, not gained by position.

The four organizational cultures described by Trompenaars are "pure" types and seldom exist in practice. Rather the types are mixed and, as shown in Table 6–3, overlaid with one of the four major types of culture dominating the corporate scene. Recently, Trompenaars and his associates have created a questionnaire designed to identify national patterns of corporate culture, as shown in Figure 6–3.

Table 6–3
Summary Characteristics of the Four Corporate Cultures

Characteristic	Corporate Culture			
	Family	**Eiffel Tower**	**Guided Missile**	**Incubator**
Relationships between employees	Diffuse relationships to organic whole to which one is bonded.	Specific role in mechanical system of required interaction.	Specific tasks in cybernetic system targeted on shared objectives.	Diffuse, spontaneous relationships growing out of shared creative process.
Attitude toward authority	Status is ascribed to parent figures who are close and powerful.	Status is ascribed to superior roles that are distant yet powerful.	Status is achieved by project group members who contribute to targeted goal.	Status is achieved by individuals exemplifying creativity and growth.
Ways of thinking and learning	Intuitive, holistic, lateral, and error correcting.	Logical, analytical, vertical, and rationally efficient.	Problem centered, professional, practical, and cross-disciplinary.	Process oriented, creative, ad hoc, and inspirational.
Attitudes toward people	Family members.	Human resources.	Specialists and experts.	Co-creators.
Ways of changing	"Father" changes course.	Change rules and procedures.	Shift aim as target moves.	Improvise and attune.
Ways of motivating and rewarding	Intrinsic satisfaction in being loved and respected.	Promotion to greater position, larger role.	Pay or credit for performance and problems solved.	Participation in the process of creating new realities.
	Management by subjectives.	Management by job description.	Management by objectives.	Management by enthusiasm.
Criticism and conflict resolution	Turn other cheek, save other's face, do not lose power game.	Criticism is accusation of irrationalism unless there are procedures to arbitrate conflicts.	Constructive task-related only, then admit error and correct fast.	Improve creative idea, not negate it.

Source: Adapted from Fons Trompenaars and Charles Hampden-Turner, *Riding the Waves of Culture: Understanding Diversity in Global Business*, 2nd ed. (New York: McGraw-Hill, 1998), p. 183.

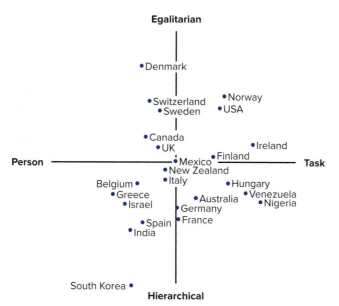

Figure 6–3
National Patterns of Corporate Culture

Source: Adapted from Fons Trompenaars and Charles Hampden-Turner, *Riding the Waves of Culture: Understanding Diversity in Global Business*, 2nd ed. (New York: McGraw-Hill, 1998), p. 184.

Matsushita Goes Global

In recent years, growing numbers of multinationals have begun to expand their operations, realizing that if they do not increase their worldwide presence now, they likely will be left behind in the near future. In turn, this has created a number of different challenges for these MNCs, including making a fit between their home organizational culture and the organizational cultures at local levels in the different countries where the MNC operates. Matsushita provides an excellent example of how to handle this challenge with its macromicro approach. This huge, Japanese MNC has developed a number of guidelines that it uses in setting up and operating its more than 150 industrial units. At the same time, the company complements these macro guidelines with on-site micro techniques that help create the most appropriate organizational culture in the subsidiary.

At the macro level, Matsushita employs six overall guidelines that are followed in all locales: (1) Be a good corporate citizen in every country by, among other things, respecting cultures, customs, and languages. (2) Give overseas operations the best manufacturing technology the company has available. (3) Keep the expatriate head count down, and groom local management to take over. (4) Let operating plants set their own rules, fine-tuning manufacturing processes to match the skills of the workers. (5) Create local research and development to tailor products to markets. (6) Encourage competition between overseas outposts and plants back home. Working within these macro guidelines, Matsushita then allows each local unit to create its own culture. The Malaysian operations are a good example. Matsushita has erected 23 subsidiaries in Malaysia that collectively consist of about 30,000 employees. Less than 1 percent of the employee population, however, is Japanese. From these Malaysian operations, Matsushita has been producing more than 1.3 million televisions and 1.8 million air conditioners annually, and 75 percent of these units are shipped overseas. To produce this output, local plants reflect Malaysia's cultural mosaic of Muslim Malays, ethnic Chinese, and Indians. To accommodate this diversity, Matsushita cafeterias offer Malaysian, Chinese, and Indian food, and to accommodate Muslim religious customs, Matsushita provides special prayer rooms at each plant and allows two prayer sessions per shift.

How well does this Malaysian workforce perform for the Japanese MNC? In the past, the Malaysian plants' slogan was "Let's catch up with Japan." Today, however, these plants frequently outperform their Japanese counterparts in both quality and efficiency. The comparison with Japan no longer is used. Additionally, Matsushita has found that the Malaysian culture is very flexible, and the locals are able to work well with almost any employer.

Today, Matsushita faces a number of important challenges, including remaining profitable in a slow-growth, high-cost Japanese economy. Fortunately, this MNC is doing extremely well overseas, which is buying it time to get its house in order back home. A great amount of this success results from the MNC's ability to nurture and manage overseas organizational cultures (such as in Malaysia) that are both diverse and highly productive.

Source: P. Christopher Earley and Harbir Singh, "International and Intercultural Management Research: What's Next," *Academy of Management Journal,* June 1995, pp. 327–340; Karen Lowry Miller, "Siemens Shapes Up," *BusinessWeek,* May 1, 1995, pp. 52–53; Christine M. Riordan and Robert J. Vandenberg, "A Central Question in Cross-Cultural Research: Do Employees of Different Cultures Interpret Work-Related Measures in an Equivalent Manner?" *Journal of Management* 20, no. 3 (1994), pp. 643–671; Brenton R. Schlender, "Matsushita Shows How to Go Global," *Fortune,* July 11, 1994, pp. 159–166.

■ Managing Multiculturalism and Diversity

As the International Management in Action box on Matsushita indicates, success in the international arena often is greatly determined by an MNC's ability to manage both multiculturalism and diversity.[46] Both domestically and internationally, organizations find themselves leading workforces that have a variety of cultures (and subcultures) and consist of a largely diverse population of women, men, young and old people, blacks, whites, Latins, Asians, Arabs, Indians, and many others.

Phases of Multicultural Development

The effect of multiculturalism and diversity will vary depending on the stage of the firm in its international evolution. Figure 6–4 depicts the characteristics of the major phases in this evolution. For example, Adler has noted that international cultural diversity has minimal impact on domestic organizations, although domestic multiculturalism has a highly significant impact. As firms begin exporting to foreign clients, however, and become what she calls "international corporations" (Phase II in Figure 6–4), they must

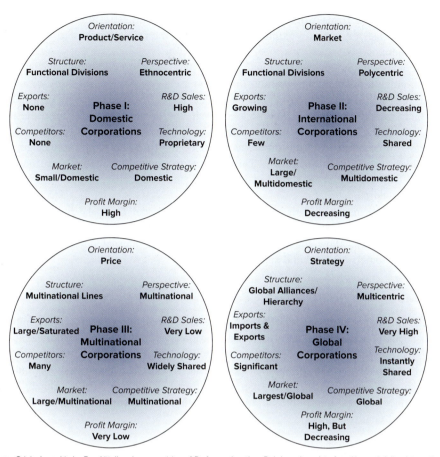

Figure 6–4

International Corporation Evolution

Source: Original graphic by Ben Littell under supervision of Professor Jonathan Doh based on data from Nancy J. Adler, *International Dimensions of Organizational Behavior*, 5th ed. © 2008 South-Western, a part of Cengage Learning, Inc.

adapt their approach and products to those of the local market. For these international firms, the impact of multiculturalism is highly significant. As companies become what she calls "multinational corporations" (Phase III), they often find that price tends to dominate all other considerations and the direct impact of culture may lessen slightly. For those who continue this international evolution and become full-blown "global corporations" (Phase IV), the impact of culture again becomes extremely important.[47]

As shown in Figure 6–5, international cultural diversity traditionally affects neither the domestic firm's organizational culture nor its relationship with its customers

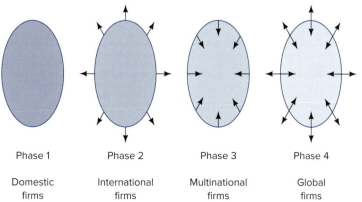

Figure 6–5

Locations of International Cross-Cultural Interaction

Source: From Nancy J. Adler, *International Dimensions of Organizational Behavior*, 5th ed. © 2008 South-Western, a part of Cengage Learning, Inc. Reproduced by permission. www.cengage.com/permissions.

or clients. These firms work domestically, and only domestic multiculturalism has a direct impact on their dynamics as well as on their relationship to the external environment.

Conversely, among international firms, which focus on exporting and producing abroad, cultural diversity has a strong impact on their external relationships with potential buyers and foreign employees. In particular, these firms rely heavily on expatriate managers to help manage operations; as a result, the diversity focus is from the inside out. This is the reverse of what happens in multinational firms, where there is less emphasis on managing cultural differences outside the firm and more on managing cultural diversity within the company. This is because multinational firms hire personnel from all over the world. As shown in Figure 6–5, this results in a diversity focus that is primarily internal.

Global firms need both an internal and an external diversity focus (again see Figure 6–5). To be effective, everyone in the global organization needs to develop cross-cultural skills that allow them to work effectively with internal personnel as well as external customers, clients, and suppliers.

Types of Multiculturalism

For the international management arena, there are several ways of examining multiculturalism and diversity. One is to focus on the domestic multicultural and diverse workforce that operates in the MNC's home country. In addition to domestic multiculturalism, there is the diverse workforce in other geographic locales, and increasingly common are the mix of domestic and overseas personnel found in today's MNCs. The following discussion examines both domestic and group multiculturalism and the potential problems and strengths.

Domestic Multiculturalism It is not necessary for today's organizations to do business in another country to encounter people with diverse cultural backgrounds. Culturally distinct populations can be found within organizations almost everywhere in the world. In Singapore, for example, there are four distinct cultural and linguistic groups: Chinese, Eurasian, Indian, and Malay. In Switzerland, there are four distinct ethnic communities: French, German, Italian, and Romansch. In Belgium, there are two linguistic groups: French and Flemish. In the United States, millions of first-generation immigrants have brought both their languages and their cultures. In Los Angeles, for example, there are more Samoans than on the island of Samoa, more Israelis than in any other city outside Israel, and more first- and second-generation Mexicans than in any other city except Mexico City. In Miami, over one-half the population is Latin, and most residents speak Spanish fluently. More Puerto Ricans live in New York City than in Puerto Rico.

It is even possible to examine domestic multiculturalism within the same ethnic groups. For example, Lee, after conducting research in Singapore among small Chinese family businesses, found that the viewpoints of the older generation differ sharply from those of the younger generation.[48] Older generations tend to stress hierarchies, ethics, group dynamics, and the status quo, while the younger generations focus on worker responsibility, strategy, individual performance, and striving for new horizons. These differences can slow organizational processes as one generation considers the other to be ineffective in its methods. Managers, therefore, need to consider employees on an individual basis and try to compile techniques that convey a common message, ultimately maximizing productivity while satisfying everyone across the ages. In short, there is considerable multicultural diversity domestically in organizations throughout the world, and this trend will continue. For example, the U.S. civilian labor force of the next decade will change dramatically in ethnic composition. In particular, there will be a significantly lower percentage of white males in the workforce and a growing percentage of women, African Americans, Hispanics, and Asians.

Group Multiculturalism There are a number of ways that diverse groups can be categorized. Four of the most common include

1. **Homogeneous groups**, in which members have similar backgrounds and generally perceive, interpret, and evaluate events in similar ways. An example would be a group of male German bankers who are forecasting the economic outlook for a foreign investment.

2. **Token groups**, in which all members but one have the same background. An example would be a group of Japanese retailers and a British attorney who are looking into the benefits and shortcomings of setting up operations in Bermuda.

3. **Bicultural groups**, in which two or more members represent each of two distinct cultures. An example would be a group of four Mexicans and four Canadians who have formed a team to investigate the possibility of investing in Russia.

4. **Multicultural groups**, in which there are individuals from three or more different ethnic backgrounds. An example is a group of three American, three German, three Uruguayan, and three Chinese managers who are looking into mining operations in Chile.

As the diversity of a group increases, the likelihood of all members perceiving things in the same way decreases sharply. Attitudes, perceptions, and communication in general may be a problem. On the other hand, there also are significant advantages associated with the effective use of multicultural, diverse groups. Sometimes, local laws require a certain level of diversity in the workplace. More and more, people are moving to other countries to find the jobs that match their skills. International managers need to be cognizant of the likelihood that they will oversee a group that represents many cultures, not just the pervasive culture associated with that country. The following sections examine the potential problems and the advantages of workplace diversity.

Potential Problems Associated with Diversity

Overall, diversity may cause a lack of cohesion that results in the unit's inability to take concerted action, be productive, and create a work environment that is conducive to both efficiency and effectiveness. These potential problems are rooted in people's attitudes. An example of an attitudinal problem in a diverse group may be the mistrust of others. For example, many U.S. managers who work for Japanese operations in the United States complain that Japanese managers often huddle together and discuss matters in their native language. The U.S. managers wonder aloud why the Japanese do not speak English. What are they talking about that they do not want anyone else to hear? In fact, the Japanese often find it easier to communicate among themselves in their native language, and because no Americans are present, the Japanese managers ask why they should speak English. If there is no reason for anyone else to be privy to our conversation, why should we not opt for our own language? Nevertheless, such practices do tend to promote an atmosphere of mistrust.

Another potential problem may be perceptual. Unfortunately, when culturally diverse groups come together, they often bring preconceived stereotypes with them. In initial meetings, for example, engineers from economically advanced countries often are perceived as more knowledgeable than those from less advanced countries. In turn, this perception can result in status-related problems because some of the group initially are regarded as more competent than others and likely are accorded status on this basis. As the diverse group works together, erroneous perceptions often are corrected, but this takes time. In one diverse group consisting of engineers from a major Japanese firm and a world-class U.S. firm, a Japanese engineer was assigned a technical task because of his stereotyped technical educational background. The group soon realized that this particular

homogeneous group
A group in which members have similar backgrounds and generally perceive, interpret, and evaluate events in similar ways.

token groups
A group in which all members but one have the same background, such as a group of Japanese retailers and a British attorney.

bicultural group
A group in which two or more members represent each of two distinct cultures, such as four Mexicans and four Taiwanese who have formed a team to investigate the possibility of investing in a venture.

multicultural group
A group in which there are individuals from three or more different ethnic backgrounds, such as three American, three German, three Uruguayan, and three Chinese managers who are looking into mining operations in South Africa.

Japanese engineer was not capable of doing this job because for the last four years, he had been responsible for coordinating routine quality and no longer was on the technological cutting edge. His engineering degree from the University of Tokyo had resulted in the other members perceiving him as technically competent and able to carry out the task; this perception proved to be incorrect.

A related problem is inaccurate biases. For example, it is well known that Japanese companies depend on groups to make decisions. Entrepreneurial behavior, individualism, and originality are typically downplayed.[49] However, in a growing number of Japanese firms, this stereotype is proving to be incorrect.[50] Here is an example.

> Mr. Uchida, a 28-year-old executive in a small software company, dyes his hair brown, keeps a sleeping bag by his desk for late nights in the office and occasionally takes the day off to go windsurfing. "Sometimes I listen to soft music to soothe my feelings, and sometimes I listen to hard music to build my energy," said Mr. Uchida, who manages the technology development division of the Rimnet Corporation, an Internet access provider. "It's important that we always keep in touch with our sensibilities when we want to generate ideas." The creative whiz kid, a business personality often prized by corporate America, has come to Japan Inc. Unlikely as it might seem in a country renowned for its deference to authority and its devotion to group solidarity, freethinkers like Mr. Uchida are popping up all over the workplace. Nonconformity is suddenly in.[51]

Still another potential problem with diverse groups is miscommunication or inaccurate communication, which can occur for a number of reasons. Misunderstandings can be caused by a speaker using words that are not clear to other members. For example, in a diverse group in which one of the authors was working, a British manager told her U.S. colleagues, "I will fax you this report in a fortnight." When the author asked the Americans when they would be getting the report, most of them believed it would be arriving in four days. They did not know that the common British word fortnight (14 nights) means two weeks.

Another contribution to miscommunication may be the way in which situations are interpreted. Many Japanese nod their heads when others talk, but this does not mean that they agree with what is being said. They are merely being polite and attentive. In many societies, it is impolite to say no, and if the listener believes that the other person wants a positive answer, the listener will say yes even though this is incorrect. As a result, many U.S. managers find out that promises made by individuals from other cultures cannot be taken at face value—and in many instances, the other individual assumes that the American realizes this!

Diversity also may lead to communication problems because of different perceptions of time. For example, many Japanese will not agree to a course of action on the spot. They will not act until they have discussed the matter with their own people because they do not feel empowered to act alone. Many Latin managers refuse to be held to a strict timetable because they do not have the same time urgency that U.S. managers do. Here is another example, as described by a European manager:

> In attempting to plan a new project, a three-person team composed of managers from Britain, France, and Switzerland failed to reach agreement. To the others, the British representative appeared unable to accept any systematic approach; he wanted to discuss all potential problems before making a decision. The French and Swiss representatives agreed to examine everything before making a decision, but then disagreed on the sequence and scheduling of operations. The Swiss, being more pessimistic in their planning, allocated more time for each suboperation than did the French. As a result, although everybody agreed on its validity, we never started the project. If the project had been discussed by three Frenchmen, three Swiss, or three Britons, a decision, good or bad, would have been made. The project would not have been stalled for lack of agreement.[52]

Advantages of Diversity

While there are some potential problems to overcome when using culturally diverse groups in today's MNCs, there are also very many benefits to be gained.[53] In particular, there is growing evidence that culturally diverse groups can enhance creativity, lead to better decisions, and result in more effective and productive performance.[54]

One main benefit of diversity is the generation of more and better ideas. Because group members come from a variety of cultures, they often are able to create a greater number of unique (and thus creative) solutions and recommendations. For example, a U.S. MNC recently was preparing to launch a new software package aimed at the mass consumer market. The company hoped to capitalize on the upcoming Christmas season with a strong advertising campaign in each of its international markets. A meeting of the sales managers from these markets in Spain, the Middle East, and Japan helped the company revise and better target its marketing effort. The Spanish manager suggested that the company focus its campaign around the coming of the Magi (January 6) and not Christmas (December 25) because in Latin cultures, gifts typically are exchanged on the date that the Magi brought their gifts. The Middle Eastern manager pointed out that most of his customers were not Christians, so a Christmas campaign would not have much meaning in his area. Instead, he suggested the company focus its sales campaign around the value of the software and how it could be useful to customers and not worry about getting the product shipped by early December at all. The Japanese manager concurred with his Middle Eastern colleague but further suggested that some of the colors being proposed for the sales brochure be changed to better fit with Japanese culture. Thanks to these diverse ideas, the sales campaign proved to be one of the most effective in the company's history.

A second major benefit is that culturally diverse groups can prevent **groupthink**, which is caused by social conformity and pressures on individual members of a group to conform and reach consensus. When groupthink occurs, group participants come to believe that their ideas and actions are correct and that those who disagree with them are either uninformed or deliberately trying to sabotage their efforts. Multicultural diverse groups often are able to avoid this problem because the members do not think similarly or feel pressure to conform. As a result, they typically question each other, offer opinions and suggestions that are contrary to those held by others, and must be persuaded to change their minds. Therefore, unanimity is achieved only through a careful process of deliberation. Unlike homogeneous groups, where everyone can be "of one mind," diverse groups may be slower to reach a general consensus, but the decision may be more effective and free of "groupthink."

Diversity in the workplace enhances more than just the internal operations—it enhances relationships to customers as well. It is commonly held that anyone will have insight into and connect better with others of the same nationality or cultural background, resulting in more quickly building trust and understanding of one another's preferences. Therefore, if the customer base is composed of many cultures, it may benefit the company to have representatives from corresponding nationalities. The U.S. multinational cosmetic firm Avon adopted this philosophy over a decade ago. When Avon observed an increase in the number of Korean shoppers at one of its U.S. locations, it quickly employed Korean sales staff.[55] The external environment, even in the MNC home country, can encompass many cultures that managers should bear in mind. Expanding diversity in the workplace to better serve the customer means that even local managers have an international exposure, further emphasizing the importance of learning about the multicultural surroundings.

groupthink
Social conformity and pressures on individual members of a group to conform and reach consensus.

Building Multicultural Team Effectiveness

Multiculturally diverse teams have a great deal of potential, depending on how they are managed. As shown in Figure 6–6, Dr. Carol Kovach, who conducted research on the importance of leadership in managing cross-cultural groups, reports that if cross-cultural groups are led properly, they can indeed be highly effective; unfortunately, she also found that if they are not managed properly, they can be highly ineffective. In other words, diverse groups are more powerful than single-culture groups. They can hurt the organization, but

Figure 6–6

Group Effectiveness and Culture

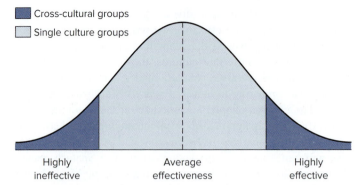

Source: From Nancy J. Adler. *International Dimensions of Organizational Behavior*, 5th ed. © 2008 South-Western, a part of Cengage Learning, Inc. Reproduced by permission. www.cengage.com/permissions.

if managed effectively, they can be the best.[56] The following sections provide the conditions and guidelines for managing diverse groups in today's organizations effectively.

Understanding the Conditions for Effectiveness   Multicultural teams are most effective when they face tasks requiring innovativeness. They are far less effective when they are assigned to routine tasks.[57] To achieve the greatest effectiveness from diverse teams, the focus of attention must be determined by the stage of team development (e.g., entry, working, and action stages). In the entry stage, the focus should be on building trust and developing team cohesion, as we saw in The World of International Management at the opening of the chapter. This can be difficult for diverse teams, whose members are accustomed to working in different ways. For example, Americans, Germans, and Swiss typically spend little time getting to know each other; they find out the nature of the task and set about pursuing it on their own without first building trust and cohesion. This contrasts sharply with individuals from Latin America, Southern Europe, and the Middle East, where team members spend a great deal of initial time getting to know each other. This contrast between task-oriented and relationship-oriented members of a diverse team may slow progress due to communication and strategic barriers. To counteract this problem, it is common in the entry stage of development to find experienced multicultural managers focusing attention on the team members' equivalent professional qualifications and status. Once this professional similarity and respect are established, the group can begin forming a collective unit. In the work stage of development, attention may be directed more toward describing and analyzing the problem or task that has been assigned. This stage often is fairly easy for managers of multicultural teams because they can draw on the diversity of the members in generating ideas. As noted earlier, diverse groups tend to be most effective when dealing with situations that require innovative approaches.

In the action stage, the focus shifts to decision making and implementation. This can be a difficult phase because it often requires consensus building among the members. In achieving this objective, experienced managers work to help the diverse group recognize and facilitate the creation of ideas with which everyone can agree. In doing so, it is common to find strong emphasis on problem-solving techniques such as the nominal group technique (NGT), where the group members individually make contributions before group interaction takes place and consensus is reached.

Using the Proper Guidelines   Some specific guidelines have proved to be helpful as a quick reference for managers when setting out to manage a culturally diverse team. Here are some of the most useful ideas:

1. Team members must be selected for their task-related abilities and not solely based on ethnicity. If the task is routine, homogeneous membership often is preferable; if the task is innovative, multicultural membership typically is best.

2. Team members must recognize and be prepared to deal with their differences. The goal is to facilitate a better understanding of cross-cultural differences and generate a higher level of performance and rapport. In doing so, members need to become aware of their own stereotypes, as well as those of the others, and use this information to better understand the real differences that exist between them. This can then serve as a basis for determining how each individual member can contribute to the overall effectiveness of the team.

3. Because members of diverse teams tend to have more difficulty agreeing on their purpose and task than members of homogeneous groups, the team leader must help the group to identify and define its overall goal. This goal is most useful when it requires members to cooperate and develop mutual respect in carrying out their tasks.

4. Members must have equal power so that everyone can participate in the process; cultural dominance always is counterproductive. As a result, managers of culturally diverse teams distribute power according to each person's ability to contribute to the task, not according to ethnicity.

5. It is important that all members have mutual respect for each other. This is often accomplished by managers choosing members of equal ability, making prior accomplishments and task-related skills known to the group, and minimizing early judgments based on ethnic stereotypes.

6. Because teams often have difficulty determining what is a good or a bad idea or decision, managers must give teams positive feedback on their process and output. This feedback helps the members see themselves as a team, and it teaches them to value and celebrate their diversity, recognize contributions made by the individual members, and trust the collective judgment of the group.

The World of International Management—Revisited

Our discussion in The World of International Management at the outset of the chapter introduced the challenges and the benefits of diverse, multicultural teams. These teams have become commonplace in organizations around the world as work becomes more flexible and less geographically bound. In addition, companies are looking to such teams to solve intractable problems and bring creativity and fresh thinking to their organizations. Using what you have learned from this chapter, answer the following: (1) What steps should organizations take to get the most out of their global virtual teams? (2) What types of organizational culture (family, Eiffel Tower, guided missile, incubator) would be best for leveraging global teams? (3) What advantages and problems associated with diversity have been experienced by global teams? How might they be overcome? (4) What features of multicultural teams are most critical for successful global team collaboration?

SUMMARY OF KEY POINTS

1. Organizational culture is a pattern of basic assumptions developed by a group as it learns to cope with its problems of external adaptation and internal integration and taught to new members as the correct way to perceive, think, and feel in relation to these problems. Some important characteristics of organizational culture include observed behavioral regularities, norms, dominant values, philosophy, rules, and organizational climate.

2. Organizational cultures are shaped by a number of factors. These include the general relationship between employees and their organization; the hierarchic system of authority that defines the roles of managers and subordinates; and the general views

that employees hold about the organization's purpose, destiny, and goals and their place in the organization. When examining these differences, Trompenaars suggested the use of two continua: equity-hierarchy and person-task orientation, resulting in four basic types of organizational cultures: family, Eiffel Tower, guided missile, and incubator.

3. Family culture is characterized by strong emphasis on hierarchic authority and orientation to the person. Eiffel Tower culture is characterized by strong emphasis on hierarchy and orientation to the task. Guided missile culture is characterized by strong emphasis on equality in the workplace and orientation to the task. Incubator culture is characterized by strong emphasis on equality and orientation to the person.

4. Success in the international arena often is heavily determined by a company's ability to manage multiculturalism and diversity. Firms progress through four phases in their international evolution: (1) domestic corporation, (2) international corporation, (3) multinational corporation, and (4) global corporation.

5. There are a number of ways to examine multiculturalism and diversity. One is by looking at the domestic multicultural and diverse workforce that operates in the MNC's home country. Another is by examining the variety of diverse groups that exist in MNCs, including homogeneous groups, token groups, bicultural groups, and multicultural groups. Several potential problems as well as advantages are associated with multicultural, diverse teams. Diverse teams are not only helpful to internal operations but can enhance sales to customers as well, as shown at Avon.

6. A number of guidelines have proved to be particularly effective in managing culturally diverse groups. These include careful selection of the members, identification of the group's goals, establishment of equal power and mutual respect among the participants, and delivering of positive feedback on performance.

KEY TERMS

bicultural group, *199*

Eiffel Tower culture, *192*

family culture, *192*

groupthink, *201*

guided missile culture, *193*

homogeneous group, *199*

incubator culture, *194*

multicultural group, *199*

organizational culture, *185*

token group, *199*

REVIEW AND DISCUSSION QUESTIONS

1. Some researchers have found that when Germans work for a U.S. MNC, they become even more German, and when Americans work for a German MNC, they become even more American. Why would this knowledge be important to these MNCs?

2. When comparing the negotiating styles and strategies of French versus Spanish negotiators, a number of sharp contrasts are evident. What are three of these, and what could MNCs do to improve their position when negotiating with either group?

3. In which of the four types of organizational cultures—family, Eiffel Tower, guided missile, incubator—would most people in the United States feel comfortable? In which would most Japanese feel comfortable? Based on your answers, what conclusions could you draw regarding the importance of

understanding organizational culture for international management?

4. Most MNCs need not enter foreign markets to face the challenge of dealing with multiculturalism. Do you agree or disagree with this statement? Explain your answer.

5. What are some potential problems that must be overcome when using multicultural, diverse teams in today's organizations? What are some recognized advantages? Identify and discuss two of each.

6. A number of guidelines can be valuable in helping MNCs to make diverse teams more effective. What are five of these? How do these relate to the guidelines established by Matsushita, as discussed in the International Management in Action box?

INTERNET EXERCISE: LENOVO'S INTERNATIONAL FOCUS

Based in China, Lenovo is one of the largest computer brands in the world. Several years ago, Lenovo purchased IBM's PC business and now sells more computers to retail customers and businesses than any other company in the world. From its base in China, it is moving aggressively into global markets, especially emerging countries like India.

Visit Lenovo's website at lenovo.com and review some of the latest developments. In particular, pay close attention to its product line and international expansion. Using the country/language tab in the bottom right of the screen, choose three different countries where the firm is doing business: one from the Americas, one from Europe, and one from Southeast Asia or India. (The sites are all presented in the local language, so you might want to make India or Hong Kong your choice because this site is in English.) Compare and contrast the product offerings and ways in which HP goes about marketing itself over the web in these locations. What do you see as some of the major differences? Second, using Figure 6–2 and Table 6–3 as your guide, in what way are differences in organizational cultures internationally likely to present significant challenges to Lenovo's efforts to create a smooth-running international enterprise? Look at the web page showing Lenovo's leadership team. What do you notice? What would you see as two of the critical issues with which management will have to deal? Third, what are two steps that you think Lenovo will have to take in order to build multicultural team effectiveness? What are two guidelines that can help it do this?

ENDNOTES

1. "A Shared Value Around the World," *Deloitte,* www2.deloitte.com/bh/en/pages/about-deloitte/articles/shared-value.html.

2. Bradley L. Kirkman, Benson Rosen, Cristina Gibson, and Paul E. Tesluk, "Five Challenges to Virtual Team Success: Lessons from Sabre, Inc.," *Academy of Management Executive* 16, no. 3 (August 2002), pp. 67–79, retrieved from EBSCOhost: http://turbo.kean.edu/~jmcgill/sabre.htm.

3. Ibid.

4. Juliet Bourke, "Working in Multicultural Teams: A Case Study," *Deloitte,* www2.deloitte.com/au/en/pages/human-capital/articles/working-multicultural-teams.html.

5. Ibid.

6. Deloitte, "Deloitte Celebrates Five-Year Anniversary of Business Chemistry," press release, April 6, 2015, www2.deloitte.com/us/en/pages/about-deloitte/articles/press-releases/deloitte-business-chemistry-relationships-teamwork.html.

7. Melanie Doulton, "Tips for Working in Global Teams," *The Institute* (IEEE), January 5, 2007.

8. Steven R. Rayner, "The Virtual Team Challenge," Rayner & Associates, Inc., 1997.

9. Kirkman, Rosen, Gibson, and Tesluk, "Five Challenges to Virtual Team Success."

10. Rayner, "The Virtual Team Challenge."

11. Kirkman, Rosen, Gibson, and Tesluk, "Five Challenges to Virtual Team Success."

12. Doulton, "Tips for Working in Global Teams."

13. Kirkman, Rosen, Gibson, and Tesluk, "Five Challenges to Virtual Team Success."

14. Ibid.

15. Ibid.

16. Rayner, "The Virtual Team Challenge."

17. Ibid.

18. Lisa Hoecklin, *Managing Cultural Differences: Strategies for Competitive Advantage* (Workingham, England: Addison-Wesley, 1995), p. 146.

19. Edgar H. Schein, *Organizational Culture and Leadership,* 2nd ed. (San Francisco: Jossey-Bass, 1997), p. 12.

20. Fred Luthans, *Organizational Behavior,* 10th ed. (New York: McGraw-Hill/Irwin, 2005), pp. 110–111.

21. In addition, see W. Mathew Jeuchter, Caroline Fisher, and Randall J. Alford, "Five Conditions for High-Performance Cultures," *Training and Development Journal*, May 1998, pp. 63–67.

22. "Our Leadership Team," *AstraZeneca,* https://www.astrazeneca.com/our-company/leadership.html#!.

23. AstraZeneca, *What Science Can Do: AstraZeneca Annual Report and Form 20-F Information 2014* (March 23, 2015), https://www.astrazeneca.com/content/dam/az/our-company/Documents/2014-Annual-report.pdf.

24. AstraZeneca, *Health: AstraZeneca Annual Report and Form 20-F Information 2011* (2012), https://www.astrazeneca.com/content/dam/az/our-company/investor-relations/presentations-and-webcast/Annual-Reports/2011-Annual-report.pdf.

25. Prashant Kale, Harbir Singh, and Anand Raman, "Don't Integrate Your Acquisitions, Partner with Them," *Harvard Business Review*, December 2009, https://webcache.googleusercontent.com/searc h?q=cache:lajyv0FdxQQJ:https://hbr.org/2009/12/ dont-integrate-your-acquisitions-partner-with-them+&cd=1&hl=en&ct=clnk&gl=us.

26. Oh Hwa-seok, "Tata Daewoo: An Indian Success Story in Korea," *Asia-Pacific Business & Technology Report*, January 1, 2010, www.biztechreport.com/ story/378-tata-daewoo-indian-success-story-korea.

27. Kale, Singh, and Raman, "Don't Integrate Your Acquisitions, Partner with Them."

28. Hoecklin, *Managing Cultural Differences*, p. 145.

29. Andre Laurent, "The Cultural Diversity of Western Conceptions of Management," *International Studies of Management and Organization*, Spring–Summer 1983, pp. 75–96.

30. Nancy J. Adler, *International Dimensions of Organizational Behavior*, 2nd ed. (Boston: PWS-Kent Publishing, 1991), pp. 58–59.

31. William Holstein, "Lucent-Alcatel: Why Cross-Cultural Mergers Are So Tough," *CBS Money Watch*, November 6, 2007, www.cbsnews.com/news/lucent-alcatel-why-cross-cultural-mergers-are-so-tough/.

32. David Jolly, "Culture Clash Hits Home at Alcatel-Lucent," *New York Times*, July 29, 2008, www.nytimes.com/2008/07/29/business/ worldbusiness/29iht-alcatel.4.14867263.html?_r=0.

33. Holstein, "Lucent-Alcatel: Why Cross-Cultural Mergers Are So Tough."

34. Jolly, "Culture Clash Hits Home at Alcatel-Lucent."

35. Hoecklin, *Managing Cultural Differences*, p. 151.

36. Robert Hughes, "Weekend Journal: Futures and Options: Global Culture," *The Wall Street Journal*, October 10, 2003, p. W2.

37. Rita A. Numeroff and Michael N. Abrams, "Integrating Corporate Culture from International M&As," *HR Focus*, June 1998, p. 12.

38. Ibid.

39. See Maddy Janssens, Jeanne M. Brett, and Frank J. Smith, "Confirmatory Cross-Cultural Research: Testing the Viability of a Corporation-Wide Safety Policy," *Academy of Management Journal*, June 1995, pp. 364–382.

40. Fons Trompenaars, *Riding the Waves of Culture: Understanding Diversity in Global Business* (Burr Ridge, IL: Irwin, 1994), p. 154.

41. Ibid.

42. Ibid., p. 156.

43. Ibid., p. 164.

44. Ibid., p. 167.

45. Ibid., p. 172.

46. For more, see Rose Mary Wentling and Nilda Palma-Rivas, "Current Status of Diversity Initiatives in Selected Multinational Corporations," *Human Resource Development Quarterly*, Spring 2000, pp. 35–60.

47. Adler, *International Dimensions of Organizational Behavior*, p. 121.

48. Jean Lee, "Culture and Management: A Study of Small Chinese Family Business in Singapore," *Journal of Small Business Management*, July 1996, p. 65.

49. Noboru Yoshimura and Philip Anderson, *Inside the Kaisha: Demystifying Japanese Business Behavior* (Boston: Harvard Business School Press, 1997).

50. Edmund L. Andrews, "Meet the Maverick of Japan, Inc." *New York Times*, October 12, 1995, pp. C1, C4.

51. Sheryl WuDunn, "Incubators of Creativity," *New York Times*, October 9, 1997, pp. C1, C21.

52. Adler, *International Dimensions of Organizational Behavior*, p. 132.

53. Adele Thomas and Mike Bendixen, "The Management Implications of Ethnicity in South Africa," *Journal of International Business Studies*, Third Quarter 2000, pp. 507–519.

54. John M. Ivencevich and Jacqueline A. Gilbert, "Diversity Management: Time for a New Approach," *Public Personnel Management*, Spring 2000, pp. 75–92.

55. "Over the Rainbow," *Economist Online*, November 20, 1997, http://www.economist.com/node/106483.

56. See, for example, Betty Jane Punnett and Jason Clemens, "Cross-National Diversity: Implications for International Expansion Decisions," *Journal of World Business* 34, no. 2 (1999), pp. 128–138.

57. Adler, *International Dimensions of Organizational Behavior*, p. 137.

58. CIA, "Nigeria," *The World Factbook* (2016), https:// www.cia.gov/library/publications/the-world-factbook/ geos/ni.html.

59. Ibid.

60. CIA. 2016. "The World Factbook," https://www.cia. gov/library/publications/the-world-factbook/geos/ ni.html.

61. Ibid.

62. Jim Stenman and Peter Guest, "The Man Who Wants to Make Hollywood Move to Nigeria," *CNN. com*, October 25, 2015, www.cnn.com/2015/10/23/ africa/nollywood-hits-london-mpkaru-abudu/.

63. Ibid.

Nigeria

Located in western Africa, Nigeria is situated between the countries of Benin and Cameroon on the Gulf of Guinea. The Niger River, perhaps the most important river in western Africa, flows into the country through Niger and empties into the Gulf of Guinea. The total land mass of Nigeria is six times the size of Georgia and slightly larger than twice the size of California. Natural resources include natural gas, petroleum, tin, iron ore, coal, limestone, niobium, lead, zinc, and arable land. The climate is tropical in most of the country, although the northern portion of the country is quite arid.[58]

With over 181,562,000 people and a growth rate of 2.5 percent, Nigeria is Africa's most populous nation and one of the fastest growing. The official spoken language is English, due to Nigeria's history as a part of the British Empire. The country is incredibly diverse, with more than 250 ethnic groups. Religiously, Nigeria is split evenly between Muslims and Christians. This spiritual division has led to significant unrest and civil wars from the time of its independence until recent history.[59]

The country's population is younger than most. The largest segment of the population (43 percent) is 0–14 years old, and the second largest segment is 25–54 years old (30 percent). Wealth inequality is especially pronounced in Nigeria, leaving a large gap between the "haves" and "have nots." With a GDP per capita in 2014 of US$3,001, 60 percent of the country's population lives below the poverty line. Nigeria's total 2014 GDP stood at US$568.5 billion and has been experiencing a strong decade of growth. In 2014, the economy expanded by 6.3 percent.[60]

The British Empire controlled a majority of Africa and, specifically, Nigeria from the early 19th century until the end of World War II. Nigeria gained its independence in 1960, but its politics consisted of military regimes and numerous coups. Military rule continued until the adoption of a new constitution in 1999, which transitioned the country's government into a civilian one. Since this transition, the political environment has been relatively stable, consisting of legitimate and regular elections. The country is, however, still feeling the effects of the four decades of corruption and mismanagement.[61]

You Be the International Management Consultant

The Nigerian owner of the Filmhouse Cinemas franchise, Kene Mpkaru, has announced a significant expansion of his company's presence in the country. Although the movie industry in Nigeria currently consists of viewers watching movies in their homes, Mpkaru believes there is growth potential for in-theater watching. Mpkaru has some expertise in the movie theater business; prior to owning his Nigerian franchise, he worked for a European franchise and oversaw substantial expansion. Currently, Filmhouse has nine movie theaters in Nigeria, and the company plans to open 16 additional locations. The greatest challenge to doing business in the country is the relatively low purchasing power of the consumers, with more than 60 percent of the population living below the poverty line. Prior to Filmhouse, Nigeria's main movie theater option was a high-end theater that included a full dining experience, costing approximately US$40 per ticket.[62]

Nigeria has built a film industry of its own in recent years. The country's movies, generally shot with very small budgets, are often released direct to DVD. This industry, referred to as "Nollywood," accounts for approximately 1.5 percent of the nation's GDP, or US$7 billion. For Filmhouse, this domestic industry could serve as an attractive expansion vehicle.[63]

Questions

1. If you were a consultant for Filmhouse, how would you advise Kene Mpkaru regarding his next moves in Nigeria?
2. What specific aspects of the country would be positive for the company? What factors are negatives?
3. How would you deal with the wealth gap in the country?
4. Would you advise Filmhouse to concentrate on Nollywood productions or would you try to attract Hollywood movies?

Chapter 7

CROSS-CULTURAL COMMUNICATION AND NEGOTIATION

OBJECTIVES OF THE CHAPTER

Communication takes on special importance in international management because of the difficulties in conveying meanings between parties from different cultures. The problems of misinterpretation and error are compounded in the international context. Chapter 7 examines how the communication process in general works, and it looks at the downward and upward communication flows that commonly are used in international communication. Then the chapter examines the major barriers to effective international communication and reviews ways of dealing with these communication problems. Finally, one important dimension of international communication, international negotiation, is examined, with particular attention to how negotiation approaches and strategies must be adapted to different cultural environments. The specific objectives of this chapter are

1. **DEFINE** the term *communication*, examine some examples of verbal communication styles, and explain the importance of message interpretation.

2. **ANALYZE** the common downward and upward communication flows used in international communication.

3. **EXAMINE** the language, perception, and culture of communication and nonverbal barriers to effective international communications.

4. **PRESENT** the steps that can be taken to overcome international communication problems.

5. **DEVELOP** approaches to international negotiations that respond to differences in culture.

6. **REVIEW** different negotiating and bargaining behaviors that may improve negotiations and outcomes.

The World of *International Management*

Netflix's Negotiations: China and Russia

The year 2015 was a break-through year for Netflix. Just eight years after first entering the digital video-streaming industry, the company had evolved into the world's largest provider of Internet-based content. In 2015 alone, Netflix launched service in 130 new countries, tripling the number of international markets it served.[1] By the start of 2016, the company, which originally started as a mail-order DVD rental service in 1997, had established video-streaming operations in nearly every country in the world. Of its 82 million subscribers, over 40 percent were outside of the U.S.[2]

Critical to this rapid expansion was Netflix's entry strategy. As a digital service provider, without physical goods or merchandise being imported and exported into the countries in which it operates, Netflix has been able to skip the lengthy, typically required governmental negotiations that most other companies must endure when expanding into foreign markets. For the most part, Netflix's strategy appears to have worked; the company has been able to operate across North and South America, Africa, and Europe without any governmental challenge. However, in two major markets, Netflix is facing an increasing number of setbacks due to negotiation and communication difficulties: in China, the company has found entry to require a long negotiation process, while in Russia, setbacks implemented by government officials appear to have resulted from Netflix's lack of communication and negotiation prior to entry.

The Long Road Ahead in China

Of the four nations without access to Netflix, China stands out. While Crimea, North Korea, and Syria all suffer from political turmoil or sanctions that prevent Netflix's entry, China seems like an ideal market for video-streaming services. With one billion consumers—many of whom are ascending into the middle class—the country has the potential to be Netflix's largest subscription base. Why, then, hasn't the company commenced operations in the world's most populous country?

Unlike in other markets, Netflix must have specific governmental approval to operate in China. Negotiations in China have notoriously taken long periods of time to complete; Apple spent years negotiating with Chinese officials to receive permission to sell its iPhone within the country.[3] Additionally, Chinese regulators exert heavy control over content. All shows, including original programming produced by Netflix, would undergo censoring prior to inclusion on the Chinese Netflix platform.[4]

Domestic streaming services, though lacking the infrastructure and content selection that Netflix boasts, add an additional layer of complexity to negotiations. Most of the domestic streaming services are free to the public and funded by the government, giving the Chinese government a stake in Netflix's competitors. Netflix may be required to partner with one of these local providers to gain a media license, resulting in a loss of some control over its operations.[5]

To ensure success in China, Netflix will first have to manage the negotiation process with government officials. Any misunderstanding will likely result in further setbacks for Netflix. According to *Harvard Business Review*, there are multiple cultural differences when negotiating in China of which companies like Netflix should be aware, a few of which include

- Formality in business dealings is critical in China, whereas informality is commonplace in the U.S. Failure to address Chinese business partners by their rank or importance could be seen as insulting, ultimately leading to a deterioration of negotiations.
- The presence of a high-level company official, like the CEO, at the bargaining table is culturally seen as increasing the level of seriousness and can significantly improve the outcome of the negotiations for the company.
- Chinese negotiators tend to require a longer period of relationship-building than their U.S. counterparts. It is not uncommon for several months of vetting to be required before discussions become more serious and detailed. Rushing a deal may be perceived as culturally rude.[6]

Netflix appears prepared for a long period of continued negotiations in China. Early in 2016, Netflix CEO Reed Hastings stated that the company has "a very long term look" regarding China. "It could be a many years discussion or it could happen faster than that."[7]

Russian Troubles Mounting?

In January 2016, Netflix successfully launched in Russia to much fanfare and consumer excitement. In the hours after the initial announcement, expatriates and Russians alike took their excitement to social media. Despite the successful launch, Netflix has since been saddled with numerous government-initiated setbacks.

Culturally, Netflix may have misjudged the regulatory and governmental environment in Russia. The Russian government funds and controls much of the country's media services, and Netflix's lack of open communication and disclosure regarding its expansion plans may have resulted in a backlash against the company. Shortly have Netflix's launch, the Russian government insisted that Netflix must approach and initiate discussions with government officials if it wishes to continue operating in the country. Russian deputy communications manager Alexei Volin warned that "Before entering the market, Netflix should have had consultations with Russian representatives, including the regulatory agencies."[8]

In February 2016, one month after Netflix's arrival in Russia, the government increased its demands, directly stating that Netflix must receive broadcasting licenses to operate within the country or face suspension.[9] Legislation was also introduced that would create a value-added tax on digital sales, increasing the cost of doing business for Netflix within Russia.[10]

By March 2016, the Russian government had begun developing new regulations for foreign video-streaming services, like Netflix. Under the new rules, Netflix would be required to partner with a local Russian media provider. Additionally, 80 percent of Netflix's content would have to be available in the Russian language, and 30 percent would have to be produced in Russia.[11]

Netflix may have been able to avoid these setbacks if it had fully understood the cultural differences between the governments in Russia and the U.S. Though its entry strategy worked in more democratic nations, Netflix's lack of communication with the regulatory agencies in Russia resulted in swift restrictions and increased taxes. Whether or not Netflix decides to continue its operations in Russia remains to be seen. Decreasing interest from Russian consumers, coupled with additional headache from regulators, may ultimately result in a withdrawal from Russia altogether.[12]

The opening World of International Management illustrates how cultural differences between a U.S. multinational company, like Netflix, and foreign governments can result in long or troublesome negotiations, and how the misjudgment of culture can result in difficulties for a company attempting to expand into new markets. Netflix's lack of understanding in regards to the operation of the Russian government resulted in setbacks after launching service in the country, and Netflix's ongoing negotiations with China will likely take many years to complete. Though fast expansion, like Netflix was able to achieve, can result in profits and high success, the cultural differences in communication and negotiations can lead to financial setbacks.

In this chapter, we explore communication and negotiation styles across cultures, emphasizing the importance of understanding different approaches to the development of effective international communication and negotiation strategies.

■ The Overall Communication Process

communication
The process of transferring meanings from sender to receiver.

Communication is the process of transferring meanings from sender to receiver. On the surface, this appears to be a fairly straightforward process. On analysis, however, there are a great many problems in the international arena that can result in the failure to transfer meanings correctly.

In addition, as suggested in the opening World of International Management, the means and modes of communication have changed dramatically in recent decades. For example, the advent of the telephone, then Internet, and most recently personal communication devices ("smartphones") has influenced how, when, and why people communicate. These trends have both benefits and disadvantages. On the plus side, we have many more opportunities to communicate rapidly, without delays or filters, and often can incorporate rich content, such as photos, videos, and links to other information, in our exchanges. On the other hand, some are concerned that these devices are rendering our communication less meaningful and personal. In a recent book, Nicholas Carr argues that when we go online, "we enter an environment that promotes cursory reading, hurried and distracted thinking, and superficial learning." Mr. Carr calls the web "a technology of forgetfulness." Web pages draw us into a myriad of embedded links while we are assaulted by other messages via e-mail, RSS, and Twitter and Facebook accounts. He suggests that greater access to knowledge is not the same as greater knowledge and that an ever-increasing plethora of facts and data is not the same as wisdom.[13]

Despite these concerns, communication—verbal and otherwise—remains an important dimension of international management. In this chapter, we survey different communication styles, how communication is processed and interpreted, and how culture and language influence communication (and miscommunication).

Verbal Communication Styles

context
Information that surrounds a communication and helps convey the message.

One way of examining the ways in which individuals convey information is by looking at their communication styles. In particular, as has been noted by Hall, context plays a key role in explaining many communication differences.[14] **Context** is information that surrounds a communication and helps convey the message. In high-context societies, such as Japan and many Arab countries, messages are often highly coded and implicit. As a result, the receiver's job is to interpret what the message means by correctly filtering through what is being said and the way in which the message is being conveyed. This approach is in sharp contrast to low-context societies such as the United States and Canada, where the message is explicit and the speaker says precisely what he or she means. These contextual factors must be considered when marketing messages are being developed in disparate societies. For example, promotions in Japan should be subtle and convey a sense of community (high context). Similar segments in the United States, a low-context environment, should be responsive to expectations for more explicit messages. Figure 7–1 provides an international comparison of high-context and low-context societies. In addition, Table 7–1 presents some of the major characteristics of communication styles.

Researche   ve
power-distance,   ective
Ghana. In contr
alistic, low-cont

Affective and I

that requires the
sender is preser
nonverbal and re
is being said. Th
the part that is
focuses on the s
wants the other

The affect
dle East, Latin
individualistic, l

Table 7–2
select countries.
great difficulty
versa: The verba

Interpretation

The effectivenes
how closely the
If this meaning
the U.S. firm tha   nted
firm put an indi   l inc
pay based on the
was a total flop
rewarded as a gr
provide suggestic
this idea becaus
ductivity. It is al
rewarding group

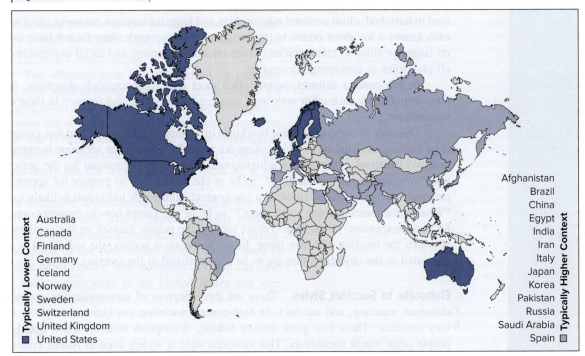

Figure 7–1 **High-/Low-Context Communication: An International Comparison**

Typically Lower Context: Australia, Canada, Finland, Germany, Iceland, Norway, Sweden, Switzerland, United Kingdom, United States

Typically Higher Context: Afghanistan, Brazil, China, Egypt, India, Iran, Italy, Japan, Korea, Pakistan, Russia, Saudi Arabia, Spain

Source: Original graphic by Ben Littell under supervision of Professor Jonathan Doh based on data from Terence Brake, Danielle Medina Walker, and Thomas D. Walker, *Doing Business Internationally: The Guide to Cross-Cultural Success* (Burr Ridge, IL: Irwin, 1994), and Sarah Griffith, "Intercultural Business Communication: High Context vs. Low Context Communication," *HubPages,* 2011, http://hubpages.com/business/Intercultural-Business-Communication-High-Context-vs-Low-Context-Communication.

Table 7–2
Verbal Styles

Country

Australia
Canada
Denmark
Egypt
England
Japan
Korea
Saudi Arabia
Sweden
United States

Source: Anne Marie F   and
1st ed. (Upper Saddle

Table 7–1
Major Characteristics of Verbal Styles

Verbal Style	Major Variation	Interaction Focus and Content	Cultures in Which Characteristic Is Found
Indirect vs. direct	Indirect	Implicit messages	Collective, high context
	Direct	Explicit messages	Individualistic, low context
Succinct vs. elaborate	Elaborate	High quantity of talk	Moderate uncertainty avoidance, high context
	Exacting	Moderate amount of talk	Low uncertainty avoidance, low context
	Succinct	Low amount of talk	High uncertainty avoidance, high context
Contextual vs. personal	Contextual	Focus on the speaker and role relationships	High power distance, collective, high context
	Personal	Focus on the speaker and personal relationships	Low power distance, individualistic, low context
Affective vs. Instrumental	Affective	Process-oriented and receiver-focused language	Collective, high context
	Instrumental	Goal-oriented and sender-focused language	Individualistic, low context

Kinesics   **Kinesics** is the study of communication through body movement and facial expression. Primary areas of concern include eye contact, posture, and gestures. For example, when one communicates verbally with someone in the United States, it is good manners to look the other person in the eye. This area of communicating through the use of eye contact and gaze is known as **oculesics**. In some areas of the world, oculesics is an important consideration because of what people should not do, such as stare at others or maintain continuous eye contact, because it is considered impolite to do these things.

Another area of kinesics is posture, which can also cause problems. For example, when Americans are engaged in prolonged negotiations or meetings, it is not uncommon for them to relax and put their feet up on a chair or desk, but this is insulting behavior in the Middle East. Here is an example from a classroom situation:

> In the midst of a discussion of a poem in the sophomore class of the English Department, the professor, who was British, took up the argument, started to explain the subtleties of the poem, and was carried away by the situation. He leaned back in his chair, put his feet up on the desk, and went on with the explanation. The class was furious. Before the end of the day, a demonstration by the University's full student body had taken place. Petitions were submitted to the deans of the various facilities. The next day, the situation even made the newspaper headlines. The consequences of the act, that was innocently done, might seem ridiculous, funny, baffling, incomprehensible, or even incredible to a stranger. Yet, to the native, the students' behavior was logical and in context. The students and their supporters were outraged because of the implications of the breach of the native behavioral pattern. In the Middle East, it is extremely insulting to have to sit facing two soles of the shoes of somebody.[48]

Gestures are also widely used and take many different forms. For example, Canadians shake hands, Japanese bow, and Middle Easterners of the same sex kiss on the cheek. Communicating through the use of bodily contact is known as **haptics**, and it is a widely used form of nonverbal communication.

Sometimes gestures present problems for expatriate managers because these behaviors have different meanings depending on the country. For example, in the United States, putting the thumb and index finger together to form an "O" is the sign for "okay." In Japan, this is the sign for money; in southern France, the gesture means "zero" or "worthless"; and in Brazil, it is regarded as a vulgar or obscene sign. In France and Belgium, snapping the fingers of both hands is considered vulgar; in Brazil, this gesture is used to indicate that something has been done for a long time. In Britain, the "V for victory" sign is given with the palm facing out; if the palm is facing in, this roughly means "shove it"; in non-British countries, the gesture means two of something and often is used when placing an order at a restaurant.[49] Gibson, Hodgetts, and Blackwell found that many foreign students attending school in the United States have trouble communicating because they are unable to interpret some of the most common nonverbal gestures.[50] A survey group of 44 Jamaican, Venezuelan, Colombian, Peruvian, Thai, Indian, and Japanese students at two major universities were given pictures of 20 universal cultural gestures, and each was asked to describe the nonverbal gestures illustrated. In 56 percent of the choices, the respondents either gave an interpretation that was markedly different from that of Americans or reported that the nonverbal gesture had no meaning in their culture. These findings help to reinforce the need to teach expatriates about local nonverbal communication.

Proxemics   **Proxemics** is the study of the way that people use physical space to convey messages. For example, in the United States, there are four "distances" people use in communicating on a face-to-face basis (see Figure 7–2). **Intimate distance** is used for very confidential communications. **Personal distance** is used for talking with family and close friends. **Social distance** is used to handle most business transactions. **Public distance** is used when calling across the room or giving a talk to a group.

One major problem for Americans communicating with people from the Middle East or South America is that the intimate or personal distance zones are violated.

---

kinesics
The study of communication through body movement and facial expression.

oculesics
The area of communication that deals with conveying messages through the use of eye contact and gaze.

haptics
Communicating through the use of bodily contact.

proxemics
The study of the way people use physical space to convey messages.

intimate distance
Distance between people that is used for very confidential communications.

personal distance
In communicating, the physical distance used for talking with family and close friends.

social distance
In communicating, the distance used to handle most business transactions.

public distance
In communicating, the distance used when calling across the room or giving a talk to a group.

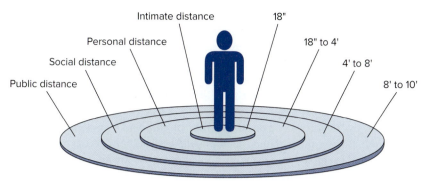

Intimate distance — 18"
Personal distance — 18" to 4'
Social distance — 4' to 8'
Public distance — 8' to 10'

Source: Adapted from Richard M. Hodgetts and Donald F. Kuratko, *Management*, 2nd ed. (San Diego, CA: Harcourt Brace Jovanovich, 1991), p. 384.

Figure 7–2

Personal Space Categories for Those in the United States

Americans often tend to be moving away in interpersonal communication with their Middle Eastern or Latin counterparts, while the latter are trying to physically close the gap. The American cannot understand why the other is standing so close; the latter cannot understand why the American is being so reserved and standing so far away. The result is a breakdown in communication.

Office layout is another good example of proxemics. In the United States, the more important the manager, the larger the office, and often a secretary screens visitors and keeps away those whom the manager does not wish to see. In Japan, most managers do not have large offices, and even if they do, they spend a great deal of time out of the office and with the employees. Thus, the Japanese have no trouble communicating directly with their superiors. A Japanese manager staying in his office would be viewed as a sign of distrust or anger toward the group.

Another way that office proxemics can affect communication is that in many European companies, no wall separates the space allocated to the senior-level manager from that of the subordinates. Everyone works in the same large room. These working conditions often are disconcerting to Americans, who tend to prefer more privacy.

Chronemics   **Chronemics** refers to the way in which time is used in a culture. When examined in terms of extremes, there are two types of time schedules: *monochronic* and *polychronic*. A **monochronic time schedule** is one in which things are done in a linear fashion. A manager will address Issue A first and then move on to Issue B. In individualistic cultures such as the United States, Great Britain, Canada, and Australia, as well as many of the cultures in Northern Europe, managers adhere to monochronic time schedules. In these societies, time schedules are very important, and time is viewed as something that can be controlled and should be used wisely.

This is in sharp contrast to **polychronic time schedules**, which are characterized by people tending to do several things at the same time and placing higher value on personal involvement than on getting things done on time. In these cultures, schedules are subordinated to personal relationships. Regions of the world where polychronic time schedules are common include Latin America and the Middle East.

When doing business in countries that adhere to monochronic time schedules, it is important to be on time for meetings. Additionally, these meetings typically end at the appointed time so that participants can be on time for their next meeting. When doing business in countries that adhere to polychronic time schedules, it is common to find business meetings starting late and finishing late.

Chromatics   **Chromatics** is the use of color to communicate messages. Every society uses chromatics, but in different ways. Colors that mean one thing in the United States may mean something entirely different in Asia. For example, in the United States it is common to wear black when one is in mourning, while in some locations in India people wear white when they are in mourning. In Hong Kong red is used to signify

chronemics
The way in which time is used in a culture.

monochronic time schedule
A time schedule in which things are done in a linear fashion.

polychronic time schedule
A time schedule in which people tend to do several things at the same time and place higher value on personal involvement than on getting things done on time.

chromatics
The use of color to communicate messages.

happiness or luck and traditional bridal dresses are red; in the United States it is common for the bride to wear white. In many Asian countries shampoos are dark in color because users want the soap to be the same color as their hair and believe that if it were a light color, it would remove color from their hair. In the United States shampoos tend to be light in color because people see this as a sign of cleanliness and hygiene. In Chile a gift of yellow roses conveys the message "I don't like you," but in the United States it says quite the opposite.

Knowing the importance and the specifics of chromatics in a culture can be very helpful because, among other things, such knowledge can help you avoid embarrassing situations. A good example is the American manager in Peru who, upon finishing a one-week visit to the Lima subsidiary, decided to thank the assistant who was assigned to him. He sent her a dozen red roses. The lady understood the faux pas, but the American manager was somewhat embarrassed when his Peruvian counterpart smilingly told him, "It was really nice of you to buy her a present. However, red roses indicate a romantic interest!"

■ Achieving Communication Effectiveness

A number of steps can be taken to improve communication effectiveness in the international arena. These include improving feedback systems, providing language and cultural training, and increasing flexibility and cooperation.

Improve Feedback Systems

One of the most important ways of improving communication effectiveness in the international context is to open up feedback systems. Feedback is particularly important between parent companies and their affiliates. There are two basic types of feedback systems: personal (e.g., face-to-face meetings, telephone conversations, and personalized e-mail) and impersonal (e.g., reports, budgets, and plans). Both systems help affiliates keep their home office aware of progress and, in turn, help the home office monitor and control affiliate performance as well as set goals and standards.

At present, there seem to be varying degrees of feedback between the home offices of MNCs and their affiliates. For example, one study evaluated the communication feedback between subsidiaries and home offices of 63 MNCs headquartered in Europe, Japan, and North America.[51] A marked difference was found between the way that U.S. companies communicated with their subsidiaries and the way that European and Japanese firms did. Over one-half of the U.S. subsidiaries responded that they received monthly feedback from their parent companies, in contrast to less than 10 percent for the subsidiaries of European and Japanese firms. In addition, the Americans were much more inclined to hold regular management meetings on a regional or worldwide basis. Seventy-five percent of the U.S. companies had annual meetings for their affiliate top managers, compared with less than 50 percent for the Europeans and Japanese. These findings may help explain why many international subsidiaries and affiliates are not operating as efficiently as they should. The units may not have sufficient contact with the home office. They do not seem to be getting continuous assistance and feedback that are critical to effective communication.

Provide Language Training

Besides improving feedback systems, another way to make communication more effective in the international arena is through language training. Many host-country managers cannot communicate well with their counterparts at headquarters. Because English has become the international language of business, those who are not native speakers of English should learn the language well enough so that face-to-face and telephone conversations and e-mail are possible. If the language of the home office is not English, this other language also should be learned. As a U.S. manager working for a Japanese MNC recently told one of the authors, "The official international language of this company is English. However, whenever the home-office people show up, they tend to cluster together with their countrymen and speak Japanese. That's why I'm trying to learn Japanese. Let's face it. They say all you need to know is English, but if you want to really know what's going on, you have to talk their language."

Written communication also is extremely important in achieving effectiveness. As noted earlier, when reports, letters, and e-mail messages are translated from one language to another, preventing a loss of meaning is virtually impossible. Moreover, if the communications are not written properly, they may not be given the attention they deserve. The reader will allow poor grammar and syntax to influence his or her interpretation and subsequent actions. Moreover, if readers cannot communicate in the language of those who will be receiving their comments or questions about the report, their messages also must be translated and likely will further lose meaning. Therefore, the process can continue on and on, each party failing to achieve full communication with the other. Hildebrandt has described the problems in this two-way process when an employee in a foreign subsidiary writes a report and then sends it to his or her boss for forwarding to the home office:

> The general manager or vice president cannot be asked to be an editor. Yet they often send statements along, knowingly, which are poorly written, grammatically imperfect, or generally unclear. The time pressures do not permit otherwise. Predictably, questions are issued from the States to the subsidiary and the complicated bilingual process now goes in reverse, ultimately reaching the original . . . staff member, who receives the English questions retranslated.[52]

Language training would help to alleviate such complicated communication problems.

Provide Cultural Training

It is very difficult to communicate effectively with someone from another culture unless at least one party has some understanding of the other's culture.[53] Otherwise, communication likely will break down. This is particularly important for multinational companies that have operations throughout the world.[54] Although there always are important differences between countries, and even between subcultures of the same country, firms that operate in South America find that the cultures of these countries have certain commonalities. These common factors also apply to Spain and Portugal. Therefore, a basic understanding of Latin cultures can prove to be useful throughout a large region of the world. The same is true of Anglo cultures, where norms and values tend to be somewhat similar from one country to another. When a multinational has operations in South America, Europe, and Asia, however, multicultural training becomes necessary. The International Management in Action box "Communicating in Europe" provides some specific examples of cultural differences.

As Chapter 4 pointed out, it is erroneous to generalize about an "international" culture because the various nations and regions of the globe are so different. Training must be conducted on a regional or country-specific basis. Failure to do so can result in continuous communication breakdown.[55] Many corporations are investing in programs to help train their executives in international communication. Such training has become more common since it began in the 1970s as many Americans returned from the Peace Corps with increased awareness of cultural differences. And this training is not limited to those who travel themselves but is increasingly important for employees who frequently interact with individuals from other cultures in their workplace or in their communication.

"Whether a multinational or a start-up business out of a garage, everybody is global these days," said Dean Foster, president of Dean Foster Associates, an intercultural consultancy in New York. "In today's economy, there is no room for failure. Companies have

Communicating in Europe

In Europe, many countries are within easy commuting distance of their neighbors, so an expatriate who does business in France on Monday may be in Germany on Tuesday, Great Britain on Wednesday, Italy on Thursday, and Spain on Friday. Each country has its own etiquette regarding how to greet others and conduct oneself during social and business meetings. The following sections examine some of the things that expatriate managers need to know to communicate effectively.

France

When one is meeting with businesspeople in France, promptness is expected, although tardiness of 5 to 10 minutes is not considered a major gaffe. The French prefer to shake hands when introduced, and it is correct to address them by title plus last name. When the meeting is over, a handshake again is proper manners.

French executives try to keep their personal and professional lives separate. As a result, most business entertaining is done at restaurants or clubs. When gifts are given to business associates, they should appeal to intellectual or aesthetic pursuits as opposed to being something that one's company produces for sale on the world market. In conversational discussions, topics such as politics and money should be avoided. Also, humor should be used carefully during business meetings.

Germany

German executives like to be greeted by their title, and one should never refer to someone on a first-name basis unless invited to do so. When introducing yourself, do not use a title, just state your last name. Business appointments should be made well in advance, and punctuality is important. Like the French, the Germans usually do not entertain clients at home, so an invitation to a German manager's home is a special privilege and always should be followed with a thank-you note. Additionally, as is the case in France, one should avoid using humor during business meetings. They are very serious when it comes to business, so be as prepared as possible and keep light-hearted banter to the German hosts' discretion.

Great Britain

In Britain, it is common to shake hands on the first meeting, and to be polite one should use last names and appropriate titles when addressing the host, until invited to use their first name. Punctuality again is important to the British, so be prepared to be on time and get down to business fairly quickly. The British are quite warm, though, and an invitation to a British home is more likely than in most other areas of Europe. You should always bring a gift if invited to the host's house; flowers, chocolates, or books are acceptable.

During business meetings, suits and ties are common dress; however, striped ties should be avoided if they appear to be a copy of those worn by alumni of British universities and schools or by members of military or social clubs. Additionally, during social gatherings it is a good idea not to discuss politics, religion, or gossip about the monarchy unless the British person brings the topic up first.

Italy

In traditional companies, executives are referred to by title plus last name. It is common to shake hands when being introduced, and if the individual is a university graduate, the professional title *dottore* should be used.

Business appointments should be made well in advance, and if you expect to be late, call the host and explain the situation. In most cases, business is done at the office, and when someone is invited to a restaurant, this invitation is usually done to socialize and not to continue business discussions. If an expatriate is invited to an Italian home, it is common to bring a gift for the host, such as a bottle of wine or a box of chocolates. Flowers are also acceptable, but be sure to send an uneven number and avoid chrysanthemums, a symbol of death, and red roses, a sign of deep passion. Be sure to offer high-quality gifts with the wrapping done well, as the Italians are very generous when it comes to gifts. It is not a common practice to exchange them during business, but it is recommended that you are prepared. During the dinner conversation, there are a wide variety of acceptable topics, including business, family matters, and soccer.

Spain

It is common to use first names when introducing or talking to people in Spain, and close friends typically greet each other with an embrace. Appointments should be made in advance, but punctuality is not essential.

If one is invited to the home of a Spanish executive, flowers or chocolates for the host are acceptable gifts. If the invitation includes dinner, any business discussions should be delayed until after coffee is served. During the social gathering, some topics that should be avoided include religion, family, and work. Additionally, humor rarely is used during formal occasions.

Source: Rosalie J. Tung, "How to Negotiate with the Japanese," *California Management Review*, Summer 1984, pp. 62–77; Carla Rapoport, "You Can Make Money in Japan," *Fortune*, February 12, 1990, pp. 85–92; Margaret A. Neale and Max H. Bazerman, "Negotiating Rationally," *Academy of Management Executive*, August 1992, pp. 42–51; Martin J. Gannon, *Understanding Global Cultures*, 2nd ed. (Thousand Oaks, CA: Sage, 2001), pp. 35–56; Sheida Hodge, *Global Smarts* (New York: Wiley, 2000), chapter 14; Richard D. Lewis, *When Cultures Collide* (London: Nicholas Brealey, 1999), pp. 400–415.

to understand the culture they are working in from Day 1." Mr. Foster recounted how an American businessman recently gave four antique clocks wrapped in white paper to a prospective client in China. What the man did not realize, he said, was that the words in Mandarin for clock and the number four are similar to the word for death, and white is a funeral color in many Asian countries. "The symbolism was so powerful," Mr. Foster said, that the man lost the deal.[56] Chapter 14 will give considerable attention to cultural training as part of selection for overseas assignments and human resource development.

Increase Flexibility and Cooperation

Effective international communications require increased flexibility and cooperation by all parties.[57] To improve understanding and cooperation, each party must be prepared to give a little.[58] Take the case of International Computers Ltd., a mainframe computer firm that does a great deal of business in Japan. This firm urges its people to strive for successful collaboration in their international partnerships and ventures. At the heart of this process is effective communication. As Kenichi Ohmae put it:

> We must recognize and accept the inescapable subtleties and difficulties of intercompany relationships. This is the essential starting point. Then we must focus not on contractual or equity-related issues but on the quality of the people at the interface between organizations. Finally, we must understand that success requires frequent, rapport-building meetings by at least three organizational levels: top management, staff, and line management at the working level.[59]

■ Managing Cross-Cultural Negotiations

Closely related to communications but deserving special attention is managing negotiations.[60,61] **Negotiation** is the process of bargaining with one or more parties to arrive at a solution that is acceptable to all. It has been estimated that managers can spend 50 percent or more of their time on negotiation processes.[62] Therefore, it is a learnable skill that is imperative not only for the international manager but for the domestic manager as well because more and more domestic businesses are operating in multicultural environments (see Chapter 6). Negotiation often follows assessing political environments and is a natural approach to conflict management. Often, the MNC must negotiate with the host country to secure the best possible arrangements. The MNC and the host country will discuss the investment the MNC is prepared to make in return for certain guarantees or concessions. The initial range of topics typically includes critical areas such as hiring practices, direct financial investment, taxes, and ownership control. Negotiation also is used in creating joint ventures with local firms and in getting the operation off the ground. After the firm is operating, additional areas of negotiation include expansion of facilities, use of more local managers, additional imports or exports of materials and finished goods, and recapture of profits.

On a more macro level of international trade are the negotiations conducted between countries. The current balance-of-trade problem between the United States and China is one example. The massive debt problems of less developed countries and the opening of trade with Eastern European and newly emerging economies are other current examples.

Types of Negotiation

People enter into negotiations for a multitude of reasons, but the nature of the goal determines what kind of negotiation will take place. There are two types of negotiations that we will discuss here: distributive and integrative negotiations. **Distributive negotiations** occur when two parties with opposing goals compete over a set value.[63] Consider a person who passes a street vendor and sees an item he likes but considers the price, or set value, a bit steep. The goal of the buyer is to procure the item at the lowest price, getting more

negotiation
Bargaining with one or more parties for the purpose of arriving at a solution acceptable to all.

distributive negotiations
Bargaining that occurs when two parties with opposing goals compete over a set value.

value for his money, while the goal of the seller is to collect as much as possible to maximize profits. Both are trying to get the best deal, but what translates into a gain by one side is usually experienced as a loss by the other, otherwise known as a win-lose situation. The relationship is focused on the individual and based on a short-term interaction. More often than not, the people involved are not friends, or at least their personal relationship is put aside in the matter. Information also plays an important role because you do not want to expose too much and be vulnerable to counterattack.

Research has shown that first offers in a negotiation can be good predictors of outcomes, which is why it is important to have a strong initial offer.[64] This does not imply that overly greedy or aggressive behavior is acceptable; this could be off-putting to the other negotiator, causing her or him to walk away. In addition to limiting the amount of information you disclose, it can be advantageous to know a little about the other side.

Integrative negotiation involves cooperation between the two groups to integrate interests, create value, and invest in the agreement. Both groups work toward maximizing benefits for both sides and distributing those benefits. This method is sometimes called the win-win scenario, which does not mean that everyone receives exactly what they wish for, but instead that the compromise allows both sides to keep what is most important and still gain on the deal. The relationship in this instance tends to be more long term since both sides take time to really get to know the other side and what motivates them. The focus is on the group, reaching for a best-case outcome where everyone benefits. This is the most useful tactic when dealing with business negotiation, so from this point on, we assume the integrative approach. Table 7–8 provides a summary of the two types of negotiation.

integrative negotiation
Bargaining that involves cooperation between two groups to integrate interests, create value, and invest in the agreement.

The Negotiation Process

Several basic steps can be used to manage the negotiation process. Regardless of the issues or personalities of the parties involved, this process typically begins with planning.

Planning Planning starts with the negotiators identifying the objectives they would like to attain. Then they explore the possible options for reaching these objectives. Research shows that the greater the number of options, the greater the chances for successful negotiations. While this appears to be an obvious statement, research also reveals that many negotiators do not alter their strategy when negotiating across cultures.[65,66] Next, consideration is given to areas of common ground between the parties. Other major areas include (1) the setting of limits on single-point objectives, such as deciding to pay no more than $10 million for the factory and $3 million for the land; (2) dividing issues into short- and long-term considerations and deciding how to handle each; and (3) determining the sequence in which to discuss the various issues.

Interpersonal Relationship Building The second phase of the negotiation process involves getting to know the people on the other side. This "feeling out" period is

Table 7–8 Negotiation Types and Characteristics		
Characteristic	**Distributive Negotiations**	**Integrative Negotiations**
Objective	Claim maximum value	Create and claim value
Motivation	Individual-selfish benefit	Group-cooperative benefit
Interests	Divergent	Overlapping
Relationship	Short term	Long term
Outcome	Win-lose	Win-win

Source: Adapted from *Harvard Business Essentials: Negotiation* (Boston: Harvard Business School Press, 2003), pp. 2–6.

characterized by the desire to identify those who are reasonable and those who are not. In contrast to negotiators in many other countries, those in the United States often give little attention to this phase; they want to get down to business immediately, which often is an ineffective approach. Adler notes:

> Effective negotiators view luncheon, dinner, reception, ceremony, and tour invitations as times for interpersonal relationship building and therefore as key to the negotiating process. When American negotiators, often frustrated by the seemingly endless formalities, ceremonies, and "small talk," ask how long they must wait before beginning to "do business," the answer is simple: wait until your counterparts bring up business (and they will). Realize that the work of conducting a successful negotiation has already begun, even if business has yet to be mentioned.[67]

Exchanging Task-Related Information   In this part of the negotiation process, each group sets forth its position on the critical issues. These positions often will change later in the negotiations. At this point, the participants are trying to find out what the other party wants to attain and what it is willing to give up.

Persuasion   This step of negotiations is considered by many to be the most important. No side wants to give away more than it has to, but each knows that without giving some concessions, it is unlikely to reach a final agreement. The success of the persuasion step often depends on (1) how well the parties understand each other's position, (2) the ability of each to identify areas of similarity and difference, (3) the ability to create new options, and (4) the willingness to work toward a solution that allows all parties to walk away feeling they have achieved their objectives.

Agreement   The final phase of negotiations is the granting of concessions and hammering out a final agreement. Sometimes, this phase is carried out piecemeal, and concessions and agreements are made on issues one at a time. This is the way negotiators from the United States like to operate. As each issue is resolved, it is removed from the bargaining table and interest is focused on the next. Asians and Russians, on the other hand, tend to negotiate a final agreement on everything, and few concessions are given until the end.

Once again, as in all areas of communication, to negotiate effectively in the international arena, it is necessary to understand how cultural differences between the parties affect the process.

Cultural Differences Affecting Negotiations

In international negotiations, participants tend to orient their approach and interests around their home culture and their group's needs and aspirations. This is natural. Yet, to negotiate effectively, it is important to have a sound understanding of the other side's culture and position to better empathize and understand what they are about.[68] The cultural aspects managers should consider include communication patterns, time orientation, and social behaviors.[69] A number of useful steps can help in this process of understanding. One negotiation expert recommends the following:

1. Do not identify the counterpart's home culture too quickly. Common cues (e.g., name, physical appearance, language, accent, location) may be unreliable. The counterpart probably belongs to more than one culture.
2. Beware of the Western bias toward "doing." In Arab, Asian, and Latin groups, ways of being (e.g., comportment, smell), feeling, thinking, and talking can shape relationships more powerfully than doing.
3. Try to counteract the tendency to formulate simple, consistent, stable images.
4. Do not assume that all aspects of the culture are equally significant. In Japan, consulting all relevant parties to a decision is more important than presenting a gift.

5. Recognize that norms for interactions involving outsiders may differ from those for interactions between compatriots.

6. Do not overestimate your familiarity with your counterpart's culture. An American studying Japanese wrote New Year's wishes to Japanese contacts in basic Japanese characters but omitted one character. As a result, the message became "Dead man, congratulations."[70]

Other useful examples have been offered by Trompenaars and Hampden-Turner, who note that a society's culture often plays a major role in determining the effectiveness of a negotiating approach. This is particularly true when the negotiating groups come from decidedly different cultures such as an ascription society and an achievement society. As noted in Chapter 4, in an ascription society, status is attributed based on birth, kinship, gender, age, and personal connections. In an achievement society, status is determined by accomplishments. As a result, each side's cultural perceptions can affect the outcome of the negotiation. Here is an example:

> Sending whiz-kids to deal with people 10–20 years their senior often insults the ascriptive culture. The reaction may be: "Do these people think that they have reached our own level of experience in half the time? That a 30-year-old American is good enough to negotiate with a 50-year-old Greek or Italian?" Achievement cultures must understand that some ascriptive cultures, the Japanese especially, spend much on training and in-house education to ensure that older people actually are wiser for the years they have spent in the corporation and for the sheer number of subordinates briefing them. It insults an ascriptive culture to do anything which prevents the self-fulfilling nature of its beliefs. Older people are held to be important so that they will be nourished and sustained by others' respect. A stranger is expected to facilitate this scheme, not challenge it.[71]

U.S. negotiators have a style that often differs from that of negotiators in many other countries. Americans believe it is important to be factual and objective. In addition, they often make early concessions to show the other party that they are flexible and reasonable. Moreover, U.S. negotiators typically have authority to bind their party to an agreement, so if the right deal is struck, the matter can be resolved quickly. This is why deadlines are so important to Americans. They have come to do business, and they want to get things resolved immediately.

A comparative example would be the Arabs, who in contrast to Americans, with their logical approach, tend to use an emotional appeal in their negotiation style. They analyze things subjectively and treat deadlines as only general guidelines for wrapping up negotiations. They tend to open negotiations with an extreme initial position. However, the Arabs believe strongly in making concessions, do so throughout the bargaining process, and almost always reciprocate an opponent's concessions. They also seek to build a long-term relationship with their bargaining partners. For these reasons, Americans typically find it easier to negotiate with Arabs than with representatives from many other regions of the world.

Another interesting comparative example is provided by the Chinese. In initial negotiation meetings, it is common for Chinese negotiators to seek agreement on the general focus of the meetings. The hammering out of specific details is postponed for later get-togethers. By achieving agreement on the general framework within which the negotiations will be conducted, the Chinese seek to limit and focus the discussions. Many Westerners misunderstand what is happening during these initial meetings and believe the dialogue consists mostly of rhetoric and general conversation. They are wrong and quite often are surprised later on when the Chinese negotiators use the agreement on the framework and principles as a basis for getting agreement on goals—and then insist that all discussions on concrete arrangements be in accord with these agreed-upon goals. Simply put, what is viewed as general conversation by many Western negotiators is regarded by the Chinese as a formulation of the rules of the game that must be adhered to throughout the negotiations. So in negotiating with the Chinese, it is important to come prepared to ensure that one's own agenda, framework, and principles are accepted by both parties.

Table 7–9
Negotiation Styles from a Cross-Cultural Perspective

Element	United States	Japanese	Arabians	Mexicans
Group composition	Marketing oriented	Function oriented	Committee of specialists	Friendship oriented
Number involved	2–3	4–7	4–6	2–3
Space orientation	Confrontational; competitive	Display harmonious relationship	Status	Close, friendly
Establishing rapport	Short period; direct to task	Longer period; until harmony	Long period; until trusted	Longer period; discuss family
Exchange of information	Documented; step by step; multimedia	Extensive; concentrate on receiving side	Less emphasis on technology, more on relationship	Less emphasis on technology, more on relationship
Persuasion tools	Time pressure; loss of saving/making money	Maintain relationship references; intergroup connections	Go-between; hospitality	Emphasis on family and on social concerns; goodwill measured in generations
Use of language	Open, direct, sense of urgency	Indirect, appreciative, cooperative	Flattery, emotional, religious	Respectful, gracious
First offer	Fair ±5 to 10%	±10 to 20%	±20 to 50%	Fair
Second offer	Add to package; sweeten the deal	−5%	−10%	Add an incentive
Final offer package	Total package	Makes no further concessions	−25%	Total
Decision-making process	Top management team	Collective	Team makes recommendation	Senior manager and secretary
Decision maker	Top management team	Middle line with team consensus	Senior manager	Senior manager
Risk taking	Calculated personal responsibility	Low group responsibility	Religion based	Personally responsible

Source: Lillian H. Chaney and Jeanette S. Martin, *International Business Communication*, 3rd Edition © 2004. Electronically reproduced by permission of Pearson Education, Inc., Upper Saddle River, New Jersey.

Before beginning any negotiations, negotiators should review the negotiating style of the other parties. (Table 7–9 provides some insights regarding negotiation styles of the United States, Japanese, Arabians, and Mexicans.) This review should help to answer certain questions: What can we expect the other side to say and do? How are they likely to respond to certain offers? When should the most important matters be introduced? How quickly should concessions be made, and what type of reciprocity should be expected? These types of questions help effectively prepare the negotiators. In addition, the team will work on formulating negotiation tactics. The International Management in Action "Negotiating with the Japanese" demonstrates such tactics, and the following discussion gets into some of the specifics.

Sometimes, simply being familiar with the culture is still falling short of being aptly informed. We discussed in Chapter 2 how the political and legal environment of a country can have an influence over an MNC's decision to open operations, and those external factors are good to bear in mind when coming to an agreement. Both parties may believe that the goals have been made clear, and on the surface a settlement may deliver positive results. However, the subsequent actions taken by either company could prove to exhibit even more barriers. Take Pirelli, an Italian tire maker that acquired Continental Gummiwerke, its German competitor. Pirelli purchased the majority holdings of Continental's stock, a transaction that would translate into Pirelli having control of the company if it occurred in the United States. When Pirelli attempted to make key managerial decisions for its Continental unit, it discovered that in Germany, the corporate governance in place allows German companies to block such actions, regardless of the shareholder position. Furthermore, the labor force has quite a bit of leverage with its

Negotiating with the Japanese

Some people believe that the most effective way of getting the Japanese to open up their markets to the United States is to use a form of strong-arm tactics, such as putting the country on a list of those to be targeted for retaliatory action. Others believe that this approach will not be effective because the interests of the United States and Japan are intertwined and we would be hurting ourselves as much as them. Regardless of which group is right, one thing is certain: U.S. MNCs must learn how to negotiate more effectively with the Japanese. What can they do? Researchers have found that besides patience and a little table pounding, a number of important steps warrant consideration.

First, business firms need to prepare for their negotiations by learning more about Japanese culture and the "right" ways to conduct discussions. Those companies with experience in these matters report that the two best ways of doing this are to read books on Japanese business practices and social customs and to hire experts to train the negotiators. Other steps that are helpful include putting the team through simulated negotiations and hiring Japanese to assist in the negotiations.

Second, U.S. MNCs must learn patience and sincerity. Negotiations are a two-way street that require the mutual cooperation and efforts of both parties. The U.S. negotiators must understand that many times, Japanese negotiators do not have full authority to make on-the-spot decisions. Authority must be given by someone at the home office, and this failure to act quickly should not be interpreted as a lack of sincerity on the part of the Japanese negotiators.

Third, the MNC must have a unique good or service. So many things are offered for sale in Japan that unless the company has something that is truly different, persuading the other party to buy it is difficult.

Fourth, technical expertise often is viewed as a very important contribution, and this often helps to win concessions with the Japanese. The Japanese know that the Americans, for example, still dominate the world when it comes to certain types of technology and that Japan is unable to compete effectively in these areas. When such technical expertise is evident, it is very influential in persuading the Japanese to do business with the company.

These four criteria are critical to effective negotiations with the Japanese. MNCs that use them report more successful experiences than those that do not.

ability to elect members of the supervisory board, which in turn chooses the management board.[72] Pirelli essentially lost on an investment; that is, unless Continental can be profitable under its current management. If Pirelli had known that this was going to happen, it probably would have reconsidered. One solution could be for Pirelli's management to begin some positive rapport with the labor force to try to sway viewpoints internally. The better option, though, would be for international managers to be as informed as possible and avoid trouble before it occurs.

Negotiation Tactics

A number of specific tactics are used in international negotiation. The following discussion examines some of the most common.

Location   Where should negotiations take place? If the matter is very important, most businesses will choose a neutral site. For example, U.S. firms negotiating with companies from the Far East will meet in Hawaii, and South American companies negotiating with European firms will meet halfway, in New York City. A number of benefits derive from using a neutral site. One is that each party has limited access to its home office for receiving a great deal of negotiating information and advice and thus gaining an advantage on the other. A second is that the cost of staying at the site often is quite high, so both sides have an incentive to conclude their negotiations as quickly as possible. (Of course, if one side enjoys the facilities and would like to stay as long as possible, the negotiations could drag on.) A third is that most negotiators do not like to return home with nothing to show for their efforts, so they are motivated to reach some type of agreement.

Time Limits   Time limits are an important negotiation tactic when one party is under a time constraint. This is particularly true when this party has agreed to meet at the home site of the other party. For example, U.S. negotiators who go to London to discuss a joint venture with a British firm often will have a scheduled return flight. Once their hosts find out how long these individuals intend to stay, the British can plan their strategy accordingly. The "real" negotiations are unlikely to begin until close to the time that the Americans must leave. The British know that their guests will be anxious to strike some type of deal before returning home, so the Americans are at a disadvantage.

Time limits can be used tactically even if the negotiators meet at a neutral site. For example, most Americans like to be home with their families for Thanksgiving, Christmas, and the New Year holiday. Negotiations held right before these dates put Americans at a disadvantage because the other party knows when the Americans would like to leave.

Buyer-Seller Relations   How should buyers and sellers act? As noted earlier, Americans believe in being objective and trading favors. When the negotiations are over, Americans walk away with what they have received from the other party, and they expect the other party to do the same. This is not the way negotiators in many other countries think, however.

The Japanese, for example, believe that the buyers should get most of what they want. On the other hand, they also believe that the seller should be taken care of through reciprocal favors. The buyer must ensure that the seller has not been "picked clean." For example, when many Japanese firms first started doing business with large U.S. firms, they were unaware of U.S. negotiating tactics. As a result, the Japanese thought the Americans were taking advantage of them, whereas the Americans believed they were driving a good, hard bargain.

The Brazilians are quite different from both the Americans and Japanese. Researchers have found that Brazilians do better when they are more deceptive and self-interested and their opponents more open and honest than they are.[73,74] Brazilians also tend to make fewer promises and commitments than their opponents, and they are much more prone to say no. However, Brazilians are more likely to make initial concessions. Overall, Brazilians are more like Americans than Japanese in that they try to maximize their advantage, but they are unlike Americans in that they do not feel obligated to be open and forthright in their approach. Whether they are buyer or seller, they want to come out on top.

Negotiating for Mutual Benefit

When managers enter a negotiation with the intent to win and are not open to flexible compromises, it can result in a stalemate. Ongoing discussion with little progress can increase tensions between the two groups and create an impasse where groups become more frustrated and aggressive, and no agreement can be reached.[75] Ultimately, too much focus on the plan with little concern for the viewpoint of the other group can lead to missed opportunities. It is important to keep objectives in mind and at the forefront, but it should not be a substitute for constructive discussions. Fisher and Ury, authors of the book *Getting to Yes*, present five general principles to help avoid such disasters: (1) separate the people from the problem, (2) focus on interests rather than positions, (3) generate a variety of options before settling on an agreement (as mentioned earlier in this section), (4) insist that the agreement be based on objective criteria, and (5) stand your ground.[76]

Separating the People from the Problem   Often, when managers spend so much time getting to know the issue, many become personally involved. Therefore, responses to a particular position can be interpreted as a personal affront. In order to preserve the personal relationship and gain a clear perspective on the issue, it is important to distinguish the problem from the individual.

When dealing with people, one barrier to complete understanding is the negotiating parties' perspectives. Negotiators should try to put themselves in the other's shoes. Avoid blame, and keep the atmosphere positive by attempting to alter proposals to better translate the objectives. The more inclusive the process, the more willing everyone will be to find a solution that is mutually beneficial.

Emotional factors arise as well. Negotiators often experience some level of an emotional reaction during the process, but it is not seen by the other side. Recognize your own emotions and be open to hearing and accepting emotional concerns of the other party. Do not respond in a defensive manner or give in to intense impulses. Ignoring the intangible tension is not recommended; try to alleviate the situation through sympathetic gestures such as apologies.

As mentioned earlier, good communication is imperative to reaching an agreement. Talk to each other, instead of just rehashing grandiose aspects of the proposal. Listen to responses and avoid passively sitting there while formulating a response. When appropriate, summarize the key points by vocalizing your interpretation to the other side to ensure correct evaluation of intentions.

Overall, don't wait for issues to arise and react to them. Instead, go into discussion with these guidelines already in play.

Focusing on Interests over Positions   The position one side takes can be expressed through a simple outline, but still does not provide the most useful information. Focusing on interests gives one insight into the motivation behind why a particular position was chosen. Digging deeper into the situation by both recognizing your own interests and becoming more familiar with others' interests will put all active partners in a better position to defend their proposal. Simply stating, "This model works, and it is the best option," may not have much leverage. Discussing your motivation, such as, "I believe our collaboration will enhance customer satisfaction, which is why I took on this project," will help others see the why, not just the what.

Hearing the incentive behind the project will make both sides more sympathetic, and may keep things consistent. Be sure to consider the other side, but maintain focus on your own concerns.

Generating Options   Managers may feel pressured to come to an agreement quickly for many reasons, especially if they hail from a country that puts a value on time. If negotiations are with a group that does not consider time constraints, there may be temptation to have only a few choices to narrow the focus and expedite decisions. It turns out, though, that it is better for everyone to have a large number of options in case some proposals prove to be unsatisfactory.

How do groups go about forming these proposals? First, they can meet to brainstorm and formulate creative solutions through a sort of invention process. This includes shifting thought focus among stating the problem, analyzing the issue, pondering general approaches, and strategizing the actions. After creating the proposals, the groups can begin evaluating the options and discuss improvements where necessary. Try to avoid the win-lose approach by accentuating the points of parity. When groups do not see eye to eye, find options that can work with both viewpoints by "look[ing] for items that are of low cost to you and high benefit to them, and vice versa."[77] By offering proposals that the other side will agree to, you can pinpoint the decision makers and tailor future suggestions toward them. Be sure to support the validity of your proposal, but not to the point of being overbearing.

Using Objective Criteria   In cases where there are no common interests, avoid tension by looking for objective options. Legitimate, practical criteria could be formed by using reliable third-party data, such as legal precedent. If both parties would accept being bound to certain terms, then chances are the suggestions were derived from objective criteria. The key is to emphasize the communal nature of the process. Inquire about why the other group chose its particular ideas. It will help you both see the other side and give you a springboard from which you can argue your views, which can be very persuasive. Overall, effective negotiations will result from international managers being flexible but not folding to external pressures.

These are just general guidelines to abide by to try and reach a mutual agreement. The approaches will be more effective if the group adhering to the outline was the one with more power. Fisher and Ury also looked at what managers should do if the other party has the power.

Standing Ground   Every discussion will have some imbalance of power, but there is something negotiators can do to defend themselves. It may be tempting to create a "bottom line," or lowest possible set of options that one will accept, but it does not necessarily accomplish the objective. When negotiators make a definitive decision before engaging in discussion, they may soon find out that the terms never even surface. That is not to say that their bottom line is below even the lowest offer, but instead that without working with the other negotiators, they cannot accurately predict the proposals that will be devised. So what should the "weaker" opponent do?

The reason two parties are involved in a negotiation is because they both want a situation that will leave them better off than before. Therefore, no matter how long negotiations drag on, neither side should agree to terms that will leave it worse off than its best alternative to a negotiated agreement, or BATNA. Clearly defining and understanding the BATNA will make it easier to know when it is time to leave a negotiation and empower that side. An even better scenario would be if the negotiator learns of the other side's BATNA. As Fisher and Ury say: "Developing your BATNA thus not only enables you to determine what is a minimally acceptable agreement, it will probably raise that minimum."[78]

Even the most prepared manager can walk into a battle zone. At times, negotiators will encounter rigid, irritable, caustic, and selfish opponents. A positional approach to bargaining can cause tension, but the other side can opt for a principled angle. This entails a calm demeanor and a focus on the issues. Instead of counterattacking, redirect the conversation to the problem and do not take any outbursts as personal attacks. Inquire about their reasoning and try to take any negative statements as constructive. If no common ground is reached, a neutral third party can come in to assess the desires of each side and compose an initial proposal. Each group has the right to suggest alternative approaches, but the third-party person has the last word in what the true "final draft" is. If the parties decide it is still unacceptable, then it is time to walk away from negotiations.

Fisher and Ury compiled a comprehensive guide as to how to approach negotiations. While no guideline has a 100 percent effective rate, their method helps gain a position where both sides win.

Bargaining Behaviors

Closely related to the discussion of negotiation tactics are the different types of bargaining behaviors, including both verbal and nonverbal behaviors. Verbal behaviors are an important part of the negotiating process because they can improve the final outcome. Research shows that the profits of the negotiators increase when they make high initial offers, ask a lot of questions, and do not make many verbal commitments until the end of the negotiating process. In short, verbal behaviors are critical to the success of negotiations.

Use of Extreme Behaviors   Some negotiators begin by making extreme offers or requests. The Chinese and Arabs are examples. Some negotiators, however, begin with an initial position that is close to the one they are seeking. The Americans and Swedes are examples here.

Is one approach any more effective than the other? Research shows that extreme positions tend to produce better results. Some of the reasons relate to the fact that an extreme bargaining position (1) shows the other party that the bargainer will not be exploited, (2) extends the negotiation and gives the bargainer a better opportunity to gain information on the opponent, (3) allows more room for concessions, (4) modifies the opponent's beliefs about the bargainer's preferences, (5) shows the opponent that the bargainer is willing to play the game according to the usual norms, and (6) lets the bargainer gain more than would probably be possible if a less extreme initial position had been taken.

Although the use of extreme position bargaining is considered to be "un-American," many U.S. firms have used it successfully against foreign competitors. When Peter Ueberroth managed the Olympic Games in the United States in 1984, he turned a profit of well over $100 million—and that was without the participation of Soviet-bloc countries, which would have further increased the market potential of the games. In most other Olympiads, sponsoring countries have lost hundreds of millions of dollars. How did Ueberroth do it? One way was by using extreme position bargaining. For example, the Olympic Committee felt that the Japanese should pay $10 million for the right to televise the games in the country, so when the Japanese offered $6 million for the rights, the Olympic Committee countered with $90 million. Eventually, the two sides agreed on $18.5 million. Through the effective use of extreme position bargaining, Ueberroth got the Japanese to pay over three times their original offer, an amount well in excess of the committee's budget.

Promises, Threats, and Other Behaviors   Another approach to bargaining is the use of promises, threats, rewards, self-disclosures, and other behaviors that are designed to influence the other party. These behaviors often are greatly influenced by the culture. Graham conducted research using Japanese, U.S., and Brazilian businesspeople and found that they employed a variety of different behaviors during a buyer-seller negotiation simulation.[79] Table 7–10 presents the results.

Table 7–10
Cross-Cultural Differences in Verbal Behavior of Japanese, U.S., and Brazilian Negotiators

Behavior and Definition	Number of Times Tactic Was Used in a Half-Hour Bargaining Session		
	Japanese	United States	Brazilian
Promise. A statement in which the source indicated an intention to provide the target with a reinforcing consequence that the source anticipates the target will evaluate as pleasant, positive, or rewarding.	7	8	3
Threat. Same as promise, except that the reinforcing consequences are thought to be noxious, unpleasant, or punishing.	4	4	2
Recommendation. A statement in which the source predicts that a pleasant environmental consequence will occur to the target. Its occurrence is not under the source's control.	7	4	5
Warning. Same as recommendation except that the consequences are thought to be unpleasant.	2	1	1
Reward. A statement by the source that is thought to create pleasant consequences for the target.	1	2	2
Punishment. Same as reward, except that the consequences are thought to be unpleasant.	1	3	3
Positive normative appeal. A statement in which the source indicates that the target's past, present, or future behavior was or will be in conformity with social norms.	1	1	0
Negative normative appeal. Same as positive normative appeal, except that the target's behavior is in violation of social norms.	3	1	1
Commitment. A statement by the source to the effect that its future bids will not go below or above a certain level.	15	13	8
Self-disclosure. A statement in which the source reveals information about itself.	34	36	39
Question. A statement in which the source asks the target to reveal information about itself.	20	20	22
Command. A statement in which the source suggests that the target perform a certain behavior.	8	6	14
First offer. The profit level associated with each participant's first offer.	61.5	57.3	75.2
Initial concession. The differences in profit between the first and second offer.	6.5	7.1	9.4
Number of no's. Number of times the word "no" was used by bargainers per half-hour.	5.7	9.0	83.4

Source: Adapted from John L. Graham, "The Influence of Culture on the Process of Business Negotiations in an Exploratory Study," *Journal of International Business Studies*, Spring 1983, p. 88. Reprinted by permission from Macmillan Publishers Ltd., *Journal of International Business Studies*, March 1, 1985. Published by Palgrave Macmillan.

The table shows that Americans and Japanese make greater use of promises than do Brazilians. The Japanese also rely heavily on recommendations and commitment. The Brazilians use a discussion of rewards, commands, and self-disclosure more than Americans and Japanese. The Brazilians also say no a great deal more and make first offers that have higher-level profits than those of the others. Americans tend to operate between these two groups, although they do make less use of commands than either of their opponents and make first offers that have lower profit levels than their opponents'.

Nonverbal Behaviors   Nonverbal behaviors also are very common during negotiations. These behaviors refer to what people do rather than what they say. Nonverbal behaviors sometimes are called the "silent language." Typical examples include silent periods, facial gazing, touching, and conversational overlaps. As seen in Figure 7–3, the Japanese tend to use silent periods much more often than either Americans or Brazilians during negotiations. In fact, in this study, the Brazilians did not use them at all. The Brazilians did, however, make frequent use of other nonverbal behaviors. They employed facial gazing almost four times more often than the Japanese and almost twice as often as the Americans. In addition, although the Americans and Japanese did not touch their opponents, the Brazilians made wide use of this nonverbal tactic. They also relied heavily on conversational overlaps, employing them more than twice as often as the Japanese and almost three times as often as Americans.

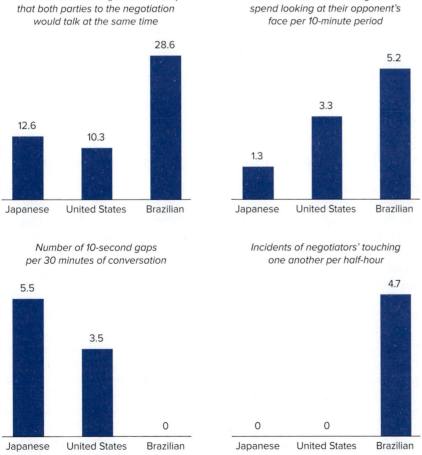

The number of times (per 10 minutes) that both parties to the negotiation would talk at the same time

Japanese 12.6   United States 10.3   Brazilian 28.6

The number of minutes negotiators spend looking at their opponent's face per 10-minute period

Japanese 1.3   United States 3.3   Brazilian 5.2

Number of 10-second gaps per 30 minutes of conversation

Japanese 5.5   United States 3.5   Brazilian 0

Incidents of negotiators' touching one another per half-hour

Japanese 0   United States 0   Brazilian 4.7

Figure 7–3

Cross-Cultural Differences in Nonverbal Behavior of Japanese, U.S., and Brazilian Negotiators

Source: Original graphic by Ben Littell under supervision of Professor Jonathan Doh based on data from John L. Graham, "The Influence of Culture on the Process of Business Negotiations in an Exploratory Study," *Journal of International Business Studies*, Spring 1983, p. 88. Reprinted by permission from Macmillan Publishers Ltd., *Journal of International Business Studies*, March 1, 1985. Published by Palgrave Macmillan.

Table 7–11 Culture-Specific Characteristics Needed by International Managers for Effective Negotiations	
U.S. managers	• Preparation and planning skill Ability to think under pressure Judgment and intelligence Verbal expressiveness Product knowledge Ability to perceive and exploit power Integrity
Japanese managers	• Dedication to job Ability to perceive and exploit power Ability to win respect and confidence Integrity Listening skill Broad perspective Verbal expressiveness
Chinese managers (Taiwan)	• Persistence and determination Ability to win respect and confidence Preparation and planning skill Product knowledge Interesting Judgment and intelligence
Brazilian managers	• Preparation and planning skill Ability to think under pressure Judgment and intelligence Verbal expressiveness Product knowledge Ability to perceive and exploit power Competitiveness

Source: Adapted from Nancy J. Adler, *International Dimensions of Organizational Behavior,* 2nd ed. (Boston: PWS-Kent Publishing, 1991), p. 187; and from material provided by Professor John Graham, School of Business Administration, University of Southern California, 1983.

Quite obviously, the Brazilians rely very heavily on nonverbal behaviors in their negotiating.

The important thing to remember is that in international negotiations, people use a wide variety of tactics, and the other side must be prepared to counter or find a way of dealing with them. The response will depend on the situation. Managers from different cultures will employ different tactics. Table 7–11 suggests some characteristics needed in effective negotiators, as exemplified by various cultures. To the extent that international managers have these characteristics, their success as negotiators should increase.

The World of International Management—Revisited

The chapter's opening World of International Management explored some of the international communication and negotiation challenges that Netflix has faced when expanding into Russia and attempting to enter China. Despite an entry strategy that proved successful in markets in Europe and the Americas, Netflix encountered a longer and more complex negotiation process in China than expected. And in Russia, Netflix's lack of communication and its failure to recognize the necessary involvement of government officials in its expansion plans resulted in a political backlash. As this chapter revealed, understanding the communication styles of different cultures is a critical variable in entering foreign markets, managing relationships among employees and customers, managers and subordinates, and in all business relationships.

A key to success in today's global economy is being able to communicate effectively within and across national boundaries and to engage in effective negotiations across cultures. Considering the communication challenges faced by offshoring firms, along with what you have read in this chapter, answer the following questions: (1) How is communication in India similar to that of Europe and North America? How is it different? (2) What kind of managerial relationships could you assume exist between an American financial services firm and its employees in India? (3) What kind of negotiations could help engage Indian employees and overcome some of the cultural problems encountered? How might culture play a role in the approach the Indian employees take in their negotiation with the financial firm?

SUMMARY OF KEY POINTS

1. Communication is the transfer of meaning from sender to receiver. The key to the effectiveness of communication is how accurately the receiver interprets the intended meaning.

2. Communicating in the international business context involves both downward and upward flows. Downward flows convey information from superior to subordinate; these flows vary considerably from country to country. For example, the downward system of organizational communication is much more prevalent in France than in Japan. Upward communication conveys information from subordinate to superior. In the United States and Japan, the upward system is more common than in South America or some European countries.

3. The international arena is characterized by a number of communication barriers. Some of the most important are intrinsic to language, perception, culture, and nonverbal communication. Language, particularly in written communications, often loses considerable meaning during interpretation. Perception and culture can result in people's seeing and interpreting things differently, and as a result, communication can break down. Nonverbal communication such as body language, facial expressions, and use of physical space, time, and even color often varies from country to country and, if improper, often results in communication problems.

4. A number of steps can be taken to improve communication effectiveness. Some of the most important include improving feedback, providing language and cultural training, and encouraging flexibility and cooperation. These steps can be particularly helpful in overcoming communication barriers in the international context and can lead to more effective international management.

5. Negotiation is the process of bargaining with one or more parties to arrive at a solution that is acceptable to all. There are two basic types of negotiation: distributive negotiation involves bargaining over opposing goals while integrative negotiation involves cooperation aimed at integrating interests. The negotiation process involves five basic steps: planning, interpersonal relationship building, exchanging task-related information, persuasion, and agreement. The way in which the process is carried out often will vary because of cultural differences, and it is important to understand them.

6. There are a wide variety of tactics used in international negotiating. These include location, time limits, buyer-seller relations, verbal behaviors, and nonverbal behaviors.

7. Negotiating for mutual benefit is enhanced by separating the people from the problem, focusing on interests rather than positions, generating a variety of options, insisting that the agreement be based on objective criteria, and standing one's ground.

KEY TERMS

chromatics, *225*

chronemics, *225*

communication, *210*

context, *210*

distributive negotiations, *229*

downward communication, *214*

haptics, *224*

integrative negotiation, *230*

intimate distance, *224*

kinesics, *224*

monochronic time schedule, *225*

negotiation, *229*

nonverbal communication, *223*

oculesics, *224*

perception, *219*

personal distance, *224*

polychronic time schedule, *225*

proxemics, *224*

public distance, *224*

social distance, *224*

upward communication, *215*

REVIEW AND DISCUSSION QUESTIONS

1. How does explicit communication differ from implicit communication? Which is one culture that makes wide use of explicit communication? Implicit communication? Describe how one would go about conveying the following message in each of the two cultures you identified: "You are trying very hard, but you are still making too many mistakes."

2. One of the major reasons that foreign expatriates have difficulty doing business in the United States is that they do not understand American slang. A business executive recently gave the authors the following three examples of statements that had no direct meaning for her because she was unfamiliar with slang: "He was laughing like hell." "Don't

worry; it's a piece of cake." "Let's throw these ideas up against the wall and see if any of them stick." Why did the foreign expat have trouble understanding these statements, and what could be said instead?

3. Yamamoto Iron & Steel is considering setting up a minimill outside Atlanta, Georgia. At present, the company is planning to send a group of executives to the area to talk with local and state officials regarding this plant. In what way might misperception be a barrier to effective communication between the representatives for both sides? Identify and discuss two examples.

4. Diaz Brothers is a winery in Barcelona. The company would like to expand operations to the United States and begin distributing its products in the Chicago area. If things work out well, the company then will expand to both coasts. In its business dealings in the Midwest, how might culture prove to be a communication barrier for the company's representatives from Barcelona? Identify and discuss two examples.

5. Why is nonverbal communication a barrier to effective communication? Would this barrier be greater for Yamamoto Iron & Steel (question 3) or Diaz Brothers (question 4)? Defend your answer.

6. For U.S. companies going abroad for the first time, which form of nonverbal communication barrier would be the greatest, kinesics or proxemics? Why? Defend your answer.

7. If a company new to the international arena was negotiating an agreement with a potential partner in an overseas country, what basic steps should it be prepared to implement? Identify and describe them.

8. Which elements of the negotiation process should be done with only your group? Which events should take place with all sides present? Why?

9. An American manager is trying to close a deal with a Brazilian manager but has not heard back from him for quite some time. The American is getting very nervous that if he waits too long, he is going to miss out on any backup options lost while waiting for the Brazilian. What should the American do? How can the American tell it is time to drop the deal? Give some signs that suggest negotiations will go no further.

10. Wilsten Inc. has been approached by a Japanese firm that wants exclusive production and selling rights for one of Wilsten's new high-tech products. What does Wilsten need to know about Japanese bargaining behaviors to strike the best possible deal with this company? Identify and describe five.

INTERNET EXERCISE: WORKING EFFECTIVELY AT TOYOTA

For 11 straight years, the Toyota Camry has been the best-selling car in the United States, and the firm's share of the American automobile market was solid. However, the company is not resting on its laurels. Toyota has expanded worldwide and is now doing business in scores of countries. Visit the firm's website and find out what it has been up to lately. The address is www.toyota.com. Then take a tour of the company's products and services including cars, air services, and sports vehicles. Next, go to the jobs section site and see what types of career opportunities there are at Toyota. Finally, find out what Toyota is doing in your particular locale. Then, drawing upon this information and the material you read in the chapter, answer these three questions: (1) What type of communication and negotiation challenges do you think you would face if you worked for Toyota and were in constant communication with home-office personnel in Japan? (2) What type of communication training do you think the firm would need to provide to you to ensure that you were effective in dealing with senior-level Japanese managers in the hierarchy? (3) Using Table 7–1 as your guide, what conclusions can you draw regarding communicating with the Japanese managers, and what guidelines would you offer to a non-Japanese employee who just entered the firm and is looking for advice and guidance regarding how to communicate and negotiate more effectively?

ENDNOTES

1. Adam Levine-Weinberg, "Netflix, Inc. Completes Its Global Expansion (with 1 Big Asterisk)," *The Motley Fool*, January 10, 2016, www.fool.com/investing/general/2016/01/10/netflix-inc-completes-its-global-expansion-with-on.aspx.

2. Julia Greenberg, "Netflix Expects to Add Fewer US Users, So It's Looking Abroad," *Wired*, April 18, 2016, www.wired.com/2016/04/netflix-expects-add-fewer-us-users-looking-abroad/.

3. Julia Greenberg, "Netflix Is in 'No Hurry' to Go to China," *Wired*, January 19, 2016, www.wired.com/2016/01/netflix-is-in-no-hurry-to-go-to-china/.

4. Julia Greenberg, "Netflix May Never Break into China," *Wired*, January 12, 2016, www.wired.com/2016/01/netflix-may-never-break-into-china/.

5. Ibid.

6. John L. Graham and N. Mark Lam, "The Chinese Negotiation," *Harvard Business Review*, October 1, 2013.

7. Greenberg, "Netflix Is in 'No Hurry' to Go to China."

8. Vladimir Kozlov, "Netflix May Have to Suspend Operations in Russia, Says Government Minister," *Hollywood Reporter*, February 10, 2016, www.hollywoodreporter.com/news/netflix-may-have-suspend-operations-864130.

9. Ibid.

10. Vladimir Kozlov, "Netflix Faces More Restrictions in Russia," *Hollywood Reporter,* March 2, 2016, www.hollywoodreporter.com/news/netflix-faces-more-restrictions-russia-872455.

11. Ibid.

12. Nathan McAlone, "Netflix Seems to Be Tanking in Russia, but India and Other International Markets Are Going Strong," *Business Insider*, April 5, 2016, www.businessinsider.com/how-netflix-is-doing-internationally-2016-4.

13. Nicholas Carr, *The Shallows* (New York: Norton, 2010).

14. E. T. Hall and E. Hall, "How Cultures Collide," in *Culture, Communication, and Conflict: Readings in Intercultural Relations*, ed. G. R. Weaver (Needham Heights, MA: Ginn Press, 1994).

15. Noboru Yoshimura and Philip Anderson, *Inside the Kaisha: Demystifying Japanese Business Behavior* (Boston: Harvard Business School Press, 1997), p. 59.

16. William C. Byham and George Dixon, "Through Japanese Eyes," *Training and Development Journal*, March 1993, pp. 33–36.

17. Linda S. Dillon, "West Meets East," *Training and Development Journal*, March 1993, pp. 39–43.

18. Fons Trompenaars and Charles Hampden-Turner, *Riding the Waves of Culture: Understanding Diversity in Global Business*, 2nd ed. (New York: McGraw-Hill, 1998), p. 204.

19. Nancy J. Adler (with Allison Gunderson), *International Dimensions of Organizational Behavior*, 5th ed. (Mason, OH: South-Western, 2008), p. 80.

20. Toddi Gutner, "Delivering Unpopular News—When You Haven't Bought In," *The Wall Street Journal*, June 14, 2010, www.wsj.com/articles/SB10001424052748703303904575293212841558170.

21. Giorgio Inzerilli, "The Legitimacy of Managerial Authority: A Comparative Study," *National Academy of Management Proceedings* (Detroit, 1980), pp. 58–62.

22. Ibid., p. 62.

23. Richard Tanner Pascale and Anthony G. Athos, *The Art of Japanese Management* (New York: Warner Books, 1981), pp. 82–83.

24. Justin Fox, "The Triumph of English," *Fortune*, September 18, 2000, pp. 209–212.

25. See "Double or Quits," *The Economist*, February 25, 1995, pp. 84–85.

26. Brock Stout, "Interviewing in Japan," *HR Magazine*, June 1998, p. 73.

27. Ibid., p. 75.

28. H. W. Hildebrandt, "Communication Barriers between German Subsidiaries and Parent American Companies," *Michigan Business Review*, July 1973, p. 9.

29. John R. Schermerhorn Jr., "Language Effects in Cross-Cultural Management Research: An Empirical Study and a Word of Caution," *National Academy of Management Proceedings* (New Orleans, 1987), p. 103.

30. Heather Berry, Mauro F. Guillén, and Nan Zhou, "An Institutional Approach to Cross-national Distance," *Journal of International Business Studies* 41 (2010), pp. 1460–1480. doi: 10.1057/jibs.2010.28.

31. Brenda R. Sims and Stephen Guice, "Differences between Business Letters from Native and Non-Native Speakers of English," *Journal of Business Communication*, Winter 1991, p. 37.

32. James Calvert Scott and Diana J. Green, "British Perspectives on Organizing Bad-News Letters: Organizational Patterns Used by Major U.K. Companies," *The Bulletin*, March 1992, p. 17.

33. Ibid., pp. 18–19.

34. Mi Young Park, W. Tracy Dillon, and Kenneth L. Mitchell, "Korean Business Letters: Strategies for Effective Complaints in Cross-Cultural Communication," *Journal of Business Communication*, July 1998, pp. 328–345.

35. As an example, see Jeremiah Sullivan, "What Are the Functions of Corporate Home Pages?" *Journal of World Business* 34, no. 2 (1999), pp. 193–211.

36. Joseph Kahn, "Fraying U.S.-Sino Ties Threaten Business," *The Wall Street Journal*, July 7, 1995, p. A6.

37. Nathaniel C. Nash, "China Gives Big Van Deal to Mercedes," *New York Times*, July 13, 1995, pp. C1, C5.

38. Seth Faison, "China Times a Business Deal to Make a Point to America," *New York Times*, July 16, 1995, pp. 1, 6.

39. David A. Ricks, *Big Business Blunders: Mistakes in Multinational Marketing* (Homewood, IL: Dow Jones/Irwin, 1983), p. 39.

40. Ibid., p. 55.

41. John Kass, "Some Bright Ideas Get Lost in Translation," *Chicago Tribune* online, April 20, 2007, http://articles.chicagotribune.com/2007-04-20/news/0704190692_1_gst-blunders-hungarian.

42. Edwin Miller, Bhal Bhatt, Raymond Hill, and Julian Cattaneo, "Leadership Attitudes of American and German Expatriate Managers in Europe and Latin America," *National Academy of Management Proceedings* (Detroit, 1980), pp. 53–57.

43. Abdul Rahim A. Al-Meer, "Attitudes Towards Women as Managers: A Comparison of Asians, Saudis and Westerners," *Arab Journal of the Social Sciences*, April 1988, pp. 139–149.

44. Sheryl WuDunn, "In Japan, Still Getting Tea and No Sympathy," *New York Times*, August 27, 1995, p. E3.

45. Fathi S. Yousef, "Cross-Cultural Communication: Aspects of the Contrastive Social Values between North Americans and Middle Easterners," *Human Organization*, Winter 1974, p. 385.

46. Peter McKiernan and Chris Carter, "The Millennium Nexus: Strategic Management at the Crossroads," *European Management Review* 1, no. 1 (Spring 2004), p. 3.

47. R. Bruce Money, "Word-of-Mouth Referral Sources for Buyers of International Corporate Financial Services," *Journal of World Business* 35, no. 3 (2000), pp. 314–329.

48. Yousef, "Cross-Cultural Communication," p. 383.

49. See Roger E. Axtell, ed., *Do's and Taboos around the World* (New York: Wiley, 1990), chapter 2.

50. Jane Whitney Gibson, Richard M. Hodgetts, and Charles W. Blackwell, "Cultural Variations in Nonverbal Communication," *55th Annual Business Communication Proceedings*, San Antonio, November 8–10, 1990, pp. 211–229.

51. William K. Brandt and James M. Hulbert, "Patterns of Communications in the Multinational Corporation: An Empirical Study," *Journal of International Business Studies*, Spring 1976, pp. 57–64.

52. Hildebrandt, "Communication Barriers," p. 9.

53. See, for example, George Ming-Hong Lai, "Knowing Who You Are Doing Business with in Japan: A Managerial View of Keiretsu and Keiretsu Business Groups," *Journal of World Business* 34, no. 4 (1999), pp. 423–449.

54. Nicholas Athanassiou and Douglas Nigh, "Internationalization, Tacit Knowledge and the Top Management Teams of MNCs," *Journal of International Business Studies*, Third Quarter 2000, pp. 471–487.

55. Also see Linda Beamer, "Bridging Business Cultures," *China Business Review*, May–June 1998, pp. 54–58.

56. Tanya Mohn, "Going Global, Stateside," *New York Times*, March 9, 2010, p. B9.

57. Michael D. Lord and Annette L. Ranft, "Organizational Learning about New International Markets: Exploring the Internal Transfer of Local Market Knowledge," *Journal of International Business Studies*, Fourth Quarter 2000, pp. 573–589.

58. Jennifer W. Spencer, "Knowledge Flows in the Global Innovation System: Do U.S. Firms Share More Scientific Knowledge Than Their Japanese Rivals?" *Journal of International Business Studies*, Third Quarter 2000, pp. 521–530.

59. Kenichi Ohmae, "The Global Logic of Strategic Alliances," *Harvard Business Review*, March–April 1989, p. 154.

60. See Hildy Teegen and Jonathan P. Doh, "U.S./Mexican Alliance Negotiations: Cultural Impacts on Trust, Authority and Performance," *Thunderbird International Business Review* 44, no. 6 (2002), pp. 749–775.

61. See also Elise Campbell and Jeffrey J. Reuer, "International Alliance Negotiations: Legal Issues for General Managers," *Business Horizons*, January–February 2001, pp. 19–26.

62. Nina Reynolds, Antonis Simintiras, and Efi Vlachou, "International Business Negotiations: Present Knowledge and Direction for Future Research," *International Marketing Review* 20, no. 3 (2003), p. 236.

63. *Harvard Business Essentials: Negotiation* (Boston: Harvard Business School Press, 2003), p. 2.

64. Ibid., p. 4.

65. David K. Tse, June Francis, and Ian Walls, "Cultural Differences in Conducting Intra- and Inter-Cultural Negotiations: A Sino-Canadian Comparison," *Journal of International Business Studies*, Third Quarter 1994, pp. 537–555.

66. Teegen and Doh, "U.S./Mexican Alliance Negotiations," pp. 749–775.

67. Adler and Gundersen, *International Dimensions of Organizational Behavior*, p. 241.

68. Daniel Druckman, "Group Attachments in Negotiation and Collective Action," *International Negotiation* 11 (2006), pp. 229–252.

69. Jeanne M. Brett, Debra L. Shapiro, and Anne L. Lytle, "Breaking the Bonds of Reciprocity in

Negotiations," *Academy of Management Journal*, August 1998, pp. 410–424.

70. Stephen E. Weiss, "Negotiating with 'Romans'—Part 2," *Sloan Management Review*, Spring 1994, p. 89.

71. Trompenaars and Hampden-Turner, *Riding the Waves of Culture*, p. 112.

72. James K. Sebenius, "The Hidden Challenge of Cross-Border Negotiations," *Harvard Business Review*, March 2002, pp. 4–12.

73. John L. Graham, "Brazilian, Japanese, and American Business Negotiations," *Journal of International Business Studies*, Spring–Summer 1983, pp. 47–61.

74. John L. Graham, "The Influence of Culture on the Process of Business Negotiations in an Exploratory Study," *Journal of International Business Studies*, Spring 1983, pp. 81–96.

75. William Zartman, "Negotiating Internal, Ethnic and Identity Conflicts in a Globalized World," *International Negotiation* 11 (2006), pp. 253–272.

76. Roger Fisher and William Ury, *Getting to Yes: Negotiating Agreement Without Giving In* (New York: Penguin Books, 1983), p. 11.

77. Ibid., p. 79.

78. Ibid., p. 111.

79. Graham, "The Influence of Culture on the Process of Business Negotiations in an Exploratory Study," pp. 84, 88.

80. CIA, "China," *The World Factbook* (2016), https://www.cia.gov/library/publications/the-world-factbook/geos/ch.html.

81. Ibid.

82. Neil Gough, "China G.D.P. Growth at Slowest Pace Since 2009, Data Shows," *New York Times*, January 18, 2016, www.nytimes.com/2016/01/19/business/international/china-gdp-economy.html?_r=0.

83. Hao Li, "Doing Business in China: Cultural Differences to Watch for," *International Business Times*, February 16, 2012, www.ibtimes.com/doing-business-china-cultural-differences-watch-411996.

84. Jason Kirby, "Why China Is So Worried about Labour Unrest," *Maclean's*, June 10, 2015, www.macleans.ca/economy/economicanalysis/why-china-is-so-worried-about-labour-unrest/.

85. Shaun Rein, "What Coca-Cola Did Wrong, and Right, in China," *Forbes.com*, March 24, 2009, www.forbes.com/2009/03/24/coca-cola-china-leadership-citizenship-huiyuan.html.

86. Ibid.

In the International Spotlight

China

Located in the eastern portion of Asia, China's main waterways are the East China Sea, Korean Bay, Yellow Sea, and South China Sea. China shares a border with many important economies in East, South, and Central Asia, including India, North Korea, Pakistan, Russia, and Vietnam. The country has an extremely diverse climate, ranging from subarctic in the north to tropical in the south. Natural resources are extensive and include coal, iron ore, petroleum, natural gas, mercury, tin, tungsten, antimony, manganese, molybdenum, vanadium, magnetite, aluminum, lead, zinc, rare earth elements, uranium, hydropower potential (world's largest), and arable land.[80]

The current population is estimated at 1.37 billion people, making China, for now, the most populous country in the world. With 56 separate ethnic groups recognized within the country, China is much more diverse than many assume. The citizens in China speak one of three main languages: Mandarin, which is the official language; Cantonese; and Shanghainese. Religion is divided among Buddhism, Christianity, and a smaller segment of "folk religions." China is a fairly average-aged nation. The largest age group is made up of those between the ages of 25 and 54 years old, which is estimated at around 50 percent of the population. The median age is 36.8 years old. Once a largely agricultural country, urban centers of China now account for slightly more than half the population.[81]

China's GDP for 2014 was US$10.36 trillion. However, having experienced annual GDP growth rates of between 7 and 14 percent for more than 15 years, China's economic expansion of 6.8 percent in 2015 was perceived by economists as dangerously slow. China, like many countries, faces issues stemming from pollution. Air pollution (greenhouse gases) and acid rain are common. Today, the country is the world's largest single emitter of carbon dioxide from the burning of fossil fuels.[82]

China ranks 84th out of 185 nations in the World Bank's survey of "Ease of Doing Business." Foreign companies can find it difficult to compete on an equal playing field with domestic competitors, often based on either real or perceived favoritism from the government. Associated with this issue is a perceived lack of transparency from the government and relatively poor intellectual property rights enforcement. Culturally, Western companies often find it difficult to manage Chinese employees due to stark differences between the two countries. U.S. managers tend

to be more accustomed to flexibility, while Chinese employees tend to be more comfortable in structured and hierarchical work environments.[83]

China operates under a communist political system. While the country continues to address criticisms regarding corruption, censorship, and a lack of transparency, political unrest remains evident. In 2014, the number of reported labor strikes reached 1,300. Chinese officials have attempted to control labor protests by banning independent labor unions, requiring any organization that wishes to unionize to register with the government. In addition, relations between the U.S. and China have sometimes been strained, fueled by allegations that the Chinese government has orchestrated security hacks of U.S. private firms and government agencies.[84]

In addition to the environmental pollution challenges mentioned above, China has been facing several geopolitical challenges. First, the government is seeking to take a more prominent role in global security and economic issues. Second, China has faced challenges in controlling its real estate and stock market. After a dramatic increase in real estate values in the 2010–2015 period and a turbulent stock market in 2016, Chinese officials are attempting to address concerns about excessive liquidity and lack of market transparency. Some foreign investors have become somewhat leery, adopting a "wait and see" attitude for the time being.

You Be the International Management Consultant

In 2009, the Chinese government rejected a proposed acquisition of Huiyuan Juice by Coca Cola. As part of the deal, worth US$2.3 billion, Coke would have invested a further US$2 billion in its Chinese operations in addition to the purchase price of Huiyan. The Chinese government nonetheless scotched the deal, due to concerns of potential monopolization of the fruit juice and beverage industry by the combined company. The rejection of the deal caused other foreign investors to wonder if the Chinese government was sending a signal that it intended to scrutinize foreign investment projects more closely in the future.[85]

Retail sales in China continue to grow at double-digit rates despite the global financial crisis and the overall slowdown of China's economy. Indeed, when it comes to certain durable and nondurable goods, some economists believe China should no longer be considered an emerging market. The country is now the largest market for cars globally and, despite its own recent setbacks, Yum! Brands generates about a third of its revenue from its KFC and Pizza Hut sales within China. The country remains an especially attractive host for foreign direct investment, given its large market and continued growth.[86]

Questions

1. If you are working as a consultant for Coca Cola, how does the dismissal of the deal by the Chinese government affect your continued investment in the country?

2. What more could private business, like Coca Cola, do to convince the government that new enterprise can bring positive economic development to the country?

3. Is the prospect of China's sheer volume of potential customers too good to pass up? Or do the actions of the government and the country's recent stock market woes indicate a signal that investment should be reconsidered?

Source: "China's Economy: After the Stimulus," *China Business Review,* July 2010, pp. 30–33; Tran Van Hoa, "Impact of the WTO Membership, Regional Economic Integration, and Structural Change on China's Trade and Growth," *Review of Development Economics,* August 2010, pp. 577–591; James Miles, "After the Olympics," *Economist,* December 21, 2008, p. 58; "The Next China," *Economist,* July 31, 2010, pp. 48–50; "China Revises Up 2010 GDP Expansion," *People's Daily Online,* September 8, 2011, english.peopledaily.com.cn/.

Coca-Cola in India

Coca-Cola is a brand name known throughout the entire world. With stagnant soft drink sales in markets like Europe and North America, Coca-Cola has aggressively looked to new, expanding markets to continue to grow its brand. India, with 1.2 billion consumers, has been a primary target for Coca-Cola; through acquisitions and clever marketing, the company now covers 60 percent of India's $1 billion soft drink market.

Coca-Cola's expansion in India has not been without minor setbacks, however. In 2006–2007, Coca-Cola faced some difficult challenges in the region of Kerala, India, after it was accused of using water that contained pesticides in its bottling plants. An environmental group, the Center for Science and Environment (CSE), found 57 bottles of Coke and Pepsi products from 12 Indian states that contained unsafe levels of pesticides.[1] The Kerala minister of health, R. Ashok, imposed a ban on the manufacture and sale of Coca-Cola products in the region. Coca-Cola then arranged to have its drinks tested in a British lab, and the report found that the amount of pesticides found in Pepsi and Coca-Cola drinks was harmless to the body.[2] Coca-Cola then ran numerous ads to regain consumers' confidence in its products and brand. However, these efforts did not satisfy the environmental groups or the minister of health.

India's Changing Marketplace

During the 1960s and 1970s, India's economy faced many challenges, growing only an average of 3–3.5 percent per year. Numerous obstacles hindered foreign companies from investing in India, and many restrictions on economic activity caused huge difficulties for Indian firms and a lack of interest among foreign investors. For many years the government had problems implementing reform and overcoming bureaucratic and political divisions. Business activity has traditionally been undervalued in India; leisure is typically given more value than work. Stemming from India's colonial legacy, Indians are highly suspicious of foreign investors. Indeed, there have been a few well-publicized disputes between the Indian government and foreign investors.[3]

More recently, however, many Western companies are finding an easier time doing business in India.[4] In 1991, political conditions had changed, many restrictions were eased, and economic reforms came into force. With more than 1 billion consumers, India has become an increasingly attractive market.[5] From 2003–2006, foreign investment doubled to $6 billion. Imported goods have become a status symbol for the burgeoning middle class.[6]

Coca-Cola has been targeting India for potential growth, as Indians consume an average of 12 eight-ounce beverages per year. In comparison, Brazil consumers drink roughly 240 beverages per year on average. Despite the relatively low amount of beverages consumed by India on average, India has been one of Coke's best emerging market plays. In 2014, India surpassed Germany as Coca-Cola's sixth largest market. During the January to March period of 2014, sales volumes in India increased 6 percent. This growth is on par with Coca-Cola's other emerging market operations in China (12 percent growth over the same period) and Brazil (4 percent growth over the same period).[7] As part of its investment plan, Coca-Cola plans to expand capacity at all 13 of its bottling plants, which should help expand the company's distribution throughout the country. Coca-Cola is aiming to double both revenue and volume in India by the year 2020.[8]

In 2014 FDI in India stood at $33.9 billion.[9] In 2015, India overtook the United States and China as the top destination for FDI, according to a report by the *Financial Times*.[10] A 2015 survey of Japanese manufacturers conducted by the Japan Bank for International Cooperation ranked India as the most promising country for overseas business operations.[11]

India's GDP grew at the impressive average annual rate of 8.5 percent during the six years spanning 2003–2008. Even the global financial crisis, which began in September 2008, only cut the rate of growth by 2–3 percentage points, and the economy has continued to grow at the annual rate of 6–7 percent in the years since the crisis.[12,13] But the country needs more investment in manufacturing if it hopes to improve the lives of the 350 million people living in poverty.[14]

Coca-Cola and Other Soft Drink Investment in India

Coca-Cola had experienced previous confrontations with the Indian government. In 1977, Coke had pulled out of India when the government demanded its secret formula.[15]

Circumstances have dramatically improved over the years for soft drink providers of India. Coke and Pepsi have invested nearly $2 billion in India over the years. They employ about 12,500 people directly and support

200,000 indirectly through their purchases of sugar, packaging material, and shipping services. Coke is India's number-one consumer of mango pulp for its local soft drink offerings.[16] Coca-Cola in India is also the largest domestic buyer of sugar and green coffee beans.[17] From 1994 to 2003, Coca-Cola sales in India more than doubled.

In 2008–2009 Coca-Cola announced its plans to invest more than $250 million in India over the next three years. The money would be used for everything from expanding bottling capacity to buying delivery trucks and refrigerators for small retailers. The new money meant around a 20 percent increase in the total Coca-Cola has invested in India.[18] Coca-Cola's sales in India climbed 31 percent in the three months ended March 31, 2009, compared to a year earlier. That's the highest volume growth of any of Coke's markets.[19]

Furthermore, Coca-Cola announced plans in 2012 to invest upwards of US$5 billion in India by 2020. This investment marks a 150 percent increase over the announced plans from 2011 to invest up to US$2 billion in India over the next five years. Putting this investment in perspective, Coca-Cola has invested a total of just over US$2 billion in its India operations over the past 20 years. Despite the large investment in India, Coca-Cola will see serious competition from Pepsi in this market. Together Coke and Pepsi make up 97 percent of the market for carbonated soft drinks in India, where soda sales overall are estimated to be US$1.05 billion. Coke accounted for 60 percent of all sales while Pepsi received 37 percent of the market share.[20]

Royal Crown Cola (RC Cola) is the world's third largest brand of soft drinks. The brand was purchased in 2001 by Cott Beverages and entered the Indian market in 2003. For production in India, the company hired three licensing and franchising bottlers. In order to ensure that it was not associated with the pesticide accusations against Pepsi and Coke, RC Cola immediately had its groundwater tested by the testing institute SGS India Pvt Ltd.[21]

The Charges against Coke

The pesticide issue began in 2002 in Plachimada, India. Villagers thought that water levels had sunk and the drinking water was contaminated by Coke's plant. They launched a vigil at the plant, and two years later, Coke's license was canceled. Coca-Cola's most recent pesticide issue began at a bottling plant in Mehdiganj. The plant was accused of exploiting the groundwater and polluting it with toxic metals.[22] Karnataka R. Ashok, the health minister of Kerala, India, banned the sale of all Coca-Cola and PepsiCo products, claiming that the drinks contained unsafe levels of pesticides.

The alleged contamination of the water launched a debate on everything from pesticide-polluted water to the Indian middle-class's addiction to unhealthy, processed foods. "It's wonderful," said Sunita Narin, director of CSE.

"Pepsi and Coke are doing our work for us. Now the whole nation knows that there is a pesticide problem."[23]

Coca-Cola fought back against the accusations. "No Indian soft drink makers have been tested for similar violations even though pesticides could be in their products such as milk and bottled teas. If pesticides are in the groundwater, why isn't anyone else being tested? We are continuously being challenged because of who we are," said Atul Singh, CEO of Coca-Cola India.[24]

Some believe that Coca-Cola was targeted to bring the subject of pesticides in consumer products to light. "If you target multinational corporations, you get more publicity," adds Arvind Kumar, a researcher at the watchdog group Toxic Links. "Pesticides are in everything in India."[25]

India's Response to the Allegations

After CSE's discovery of the unsafe levels of pesticides,[26] some suggested the high levels of pesticides came from sugar, which is 10 percent of the soft drink content. However, laboratories found the sugar samples to be pesticide free.[27]

Kerala is run by a communist government and a chief minister who still claims to have a revolutionary objection to the evils of capitalism.[28] Defenders of Coca-Cola claim that this is a large reason for the pesticide findings in Coca-Cola products. After the ban was placed on all Coca-Cola and PepsiCo products in the region of Kerala, Coca-Cola took its case to the state court to defend its products and name. The court said that the state government had no jurisdiction to impose a ban on the manufacture and sale of products.[29] Kerala then lifted the statewide ban on Coke products.[30]

In March 2010, after several years of tense battles, the Indian unit of Coca-Cola Company was asked to pay $47 million in compensation for causing environmental damage at its bottling plant in the southern Indian state of Kerala. A state government panel said Coca-Cola's subsidiary, Hindustan Coca-Cola Beverages Pvt Ltd (HCBPL), was responsible for depleting groundwater and dumping toxic waste around its Palakkad plant between 1999 and 2004. Protests by farmers, complaining about the alleged pollution, forced Coca-Cola to close down the plant in 2005. Coca-Cola responded that HCBPL was not responsible for pollution in Palakkad, but the final decision on the compensation will be taken by the state government.[31]

Pepsi's Experience in India

PepsiCo has had an equally noticeable presence in India, and it is not surprising that the company has weathered the same storms as its rival Coca-Cola. In addition to claims of excessive water use, a CSE pesticide study, performed in August 2006, accused Pepsi of having 30 times the "unofficial" pesticide limit in its beverages (Coke was claimed to be 27 times the limit in this study).[32] These findings, coupled with the original 2003 CSE study that first tarnished the cola companies' image, have prompted numerous consumers to stop their cola consumption. Some have even taken to the streets, burning pictures of Pepsi bottles in protest.

Indra Nooyi, CEO of PepsiCo Inc. and a native of India, is all too familiar with the issues of water contamination and water shortages. Yet, in light of the recent claims made against Pepsi, she has expressed frustration with the exaggerated CSE findings (local tea and coffee have thousands of times the alleged pesticide level found in Pepsi products) and the disproportionate reaction to Pepsi's water-use practices (pointing out that soft drinks and bottled water account for less than 0.04 percent of industrial water usage in India).[33]

In order to reaffirm the safety and popularity of its products, Pepsi has taken on a celebrity-studded ad campaign across India, as well as continued its legacy of corporate social responsibility (CSR). Some of Pepsi's CSR efforts have involved digging village wells, "harvesting" rainwater, and teaching better techniques for growing rice and tomatoes.[34] Pepsi has also initiated efforts to reduce water waste at its Indian facilities.

Although Pepsi sales are back on the rise, Nooyi realizes that she should have acted sooner to counteract CSE's claims about Pepsi products. From here on out, the company must be more attentive to its water-use practices; but Nooyi also notes, "We have to invest, too, in educating communities in how to farm better, collect water, and then work with industry to retrofit plants and recycle."[35]

Coke's Social Responsibility Commitments

Coca-Cola has recently employed The Energy and Resources Institute (TERI) to assess its operations in India. The investigations have been conducted because of claims that Coca-Cola has engaged in unethical production practices in India. These alleged practices include causing

severe water shortages, locating water-extracting plants in "drought prone" areas, further limiting water access by contaminating the surrounding land and groundwater, and irresponsibly disposing of toxic waste. Colleges and universities throughout the United States, U.K., and Canada have joined in holding the company accountable for its overseas business practices by banning Coca-Cola products on their campuses until more positive results are reported. However, critics have argued that TERI's assessment would undoubtedly be biased because the organization has been largely funded by the Coca-Cola Company.[36]

Coca-Cola stands behind the safety of its products. "Multinational corporations provide an easy target," says Amulya Ganguli, a political analyst in New Delhi. "These corporations are believed to be greedy, devoted solely to profit, and uncaring about the health of the consumers." There is also a deeply rooted distrust of big business, and particularly foreign big business, in India.[37] This is a reminder that there will continue to be obstacles, as there were in the past, to foreign investments in India.

In order to reaffirm their presence in India, Coke and Pepsi have run separate ads insisting that their drinks are safe. Coke's ad said, "Is there anything safer for you to drink?" and invited Indians to visit its plants to see how the beverage is made.[38] Nevertheless, in July 2006, Coke reported a 12 percent decline in sales.[39]

Coca-Cola has undertaken various initiatives to improve the drinking water conditions around the world. It has formally pledged support for the United Nations Global Compact and co-founded the Global Water Challenge, which improves water access and sanitation in countries in critical need. It is improving energy efficiency through the use of hydrofluorocarbon-free insulation for 98 percent of new refrigerator sales and marketing equipment. Specifically, in India, Coke has stated, "More than one-third of the total water that is used in operations is renewed and returned to groundwater systems."[40] Among its first water renewal projects was installation of 270 rainwater

Table 1   **A Timeline of Coca-Cola in Kerala, India**

1977	Coca-Cola pulls out of India when the government demands its secret formula.
1991	Restrictions are eased in India for easier international business development.
1999	A report is published by the All-Indian Coordinated Research Program stating that 20% of all Indian food commodities exceed the maximum pesticide residue level and 43% of milk exceeds the maximum residue levels of DDT.
2002	Villagers in Plachimada, India, make the accusation that Coke's bottling plant is contaminating their drinking water.
2003	The Center for Science and Environment produces a study that finds unsafe levels of pesticides in Coca-Cola products in India.
January 2004	Parliament in India forms a Joint Parliamentary Committee to investigate the charges by the CSE.
March 2004	A Coca-Cola bottling facility is shut down in Plachimada, India.
2004	Indian government announces new regulations for carbonated soft drinks based on European Union standards.
2005	Coca-Cola co-founds the Global Water Challenge, develops the Global Community-Watershed Partnership, and establishes the Ethics and Compliance Committee.
August 2006	The CSE produces another report finding 57 Coke and Pepsi products from 12 Indian states that contain unsafe pesticide levels.
September 2006	India's high court overturns the ban on the sale of Coke products in Kerala.
March 2010	Indian unit of Coca-Cola Co. asked by state government to pay $47 million compensation for causing environmental damage at its bottling plant in Kerala.

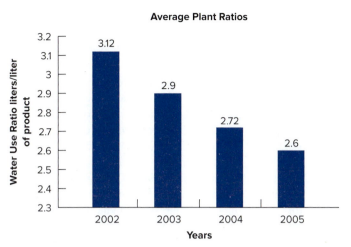

Average Plant Ratios

Source: The Coca-Cola Company, *2005 Environmental Report,* www.thecocacolacompany.com/citizenship/environmental_report2005.pdf.

Figure 1

Coca-Cola's Water Use: Historical Average Plant Ratios

catching devices.[41] Later, Coca-Cola expanded the number of rainwater harvesting projects by partnering with the Central Ground Water Authority (CGWA), State Ground Water Boards, schools, colleges, NGOs, and local communities to combat water scarcity. According to Coca-Cola India's 2007–2008 Environment Report, the company was actively engaged in 400 rainwater harvesting projects running across 17 states. These efforts were contributing to the company's eventual target of being a "net zero" user of groundwater, a goal that it achieved in 2009.[42]

Having inspected its own water-use habits, Coca-Cola has vowed to reduce the amount of water it uses in its bottling operations. As of 2014, Coca-Cola had reduced the amount of water needed to make one liter of Coke to 2.03 liters (compared with 2.70 liters a decade before).[43]

At the June 2007 annual meeting of the World Wildlife Fund (WWF) in Beijing, Coca-Cola announced its multi-year partnership with the organization "to conserve and protect freshwater resources," and in 2013, the partnership was expanded to include new goals. E. Neville Isdell, chair and CEO of the Coca-Cola Company, said, "Our goal is to replace every drop of water we use in our beverages and their production. For us that means reducing the amount of water used to produce our beverages, recycling water used for manufacturing processes so it can be returned safely to the environment, and replenishing water in communities and nature through locally relevant projects." Coca-Cola hopes to spread these practices to other members of its supply chain, particularly the sugar cane industry. The Coca-Cola–WWF partnership is also focused on climate protection and protection of seven of the world's "most critical freshwater basins," including the Yangtze in China. Although Coca-Cola's corporate social responsibility efforts have included other projects with the WWF in the past, it hopes that this official partnership will help achieve larger-scale results.[44]

As a part of its 2013 goals, Coca-Cola and the WWF committed to achieve 100 percent replenishment of all water used, 75 percent recycling rate in developing markets, 30 percent plant-based packaging by 2020, and 25 percent improvement to water efficiency by 2020.[45] Figures 1 and 2 highlight Coca-Cola's rapidly declining water use on a per-plant and systemwide basis that occurred between 2002 and 2005.

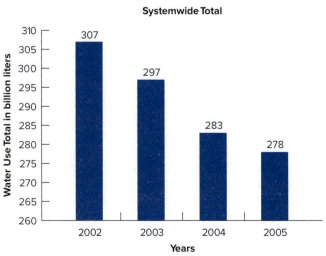

Systemwide Total

Figure 2

Coca-Cola's Water Use: Systemwide Total

Source: The Coca-Cola Company, *2005 Environmental Report,* www.thecocacolacompany.com/citizenship/environmental_report2005.pdf.

Coca-Cola has also established EthicsLine, which is a global web and telephone information and reporting service that allows anyone to report confidential information to a third party. Service is toll free—24 hours a day—and translators are available. Coca-Cola is currently focusing on improving standards through the global water challenge and enhancing global packaging to make it more environmentally friendly. It is also working on promoting nutrition and physical education by launching programs throughout the world. For example, in January 2009, Coca-Cola India announced a partnership with the Bharat Integrated Social Welfare Agency (BISWA) to build awareness regarding micro-nutrient malnutrition (or "hidden hunger") in the "bottom of the socio-economic pyramid" population in India. The two partners will work together to establish a successful income-generation model for communities through self-help groups in Sambalpur in Odisha and also provide them with affordable alternatives to alleviate "hidden hunger." The first product developed by Coca-Cola India to address the issue of "hidden hunger" is Vitingo, a tasty, affordable, and refreshing orange-flavored beverage fortified with micronutrients.

During the past decade, the Coca-Cola Company has invested more than US$1 billion in India, making it one of India's top international investors. By 2020, the company will have invested over US$5 billion. Almost all the goods and services required to produce and market Coca-Cola are made in India. The Coca-Cola Company directly employs approximately 5,500 local people in India; and indirectly, its business in India creates employment for more than 150,000 people.[46] Hindustan Coca-Cola Beverages Pvt Ltd operates 22 bottling plants, some of which are located in economically underdeveloped areas of the country. The Coca-Cola system also includes 23 franchise-operated plants and has one facility that manufactures concentrates or beverage bases.[47]

Lessons Learned

Yet Coca-Cola was caught off guard by its experience in India. Coke did not fully appreciate how quickly local politicians would attack Coke in light of the test results, nor did it respond quickly enough to the anxieties of its consumers. The company failed to realize how fast news travels in modern India. India represents only about 1 percent of Coca-Cola's global volume, but it is central to the company's long-term growth strategy. The company needed to take action fast.[48]

In what Coke thought to be a respectful and immediate time frame, it formed committees in India and the United States. The committees worked on rebuttals and had their own labs commission the tests, and then they commented in detail. Coke also directed reporters to Internet blogs full of entries that were pro-Coke. Critics say that Coke focused too much on the charges instead of winning back the support of its customers. "Here people interpret silence as guilt," said Mr. Seth, Coke's Indian public relations expert.

Ms. Bjorhus, the Coke communications director, said she could now see how the environmental group had picked Coca-Cola as a way of attracting attention to the broader problem of pesticide contamination in Indian food products. Coca-Cola stands behind its products as being pesticide free. It is now up to the Indian consumer to decide the success of Coca-Cola in future years.

Nevertheless, Coca-Cola has been optimistic about its future in India. While India was still among the countries with the lowest per capita consumption of Coke, in 2014 it was the second-fastest-growing region in terms of Coca-Cola unit case volume growth. Coca-Cola recorded a 2 percent growth in sales in 2014 and most of it came from India, Russia, Brazil, and China, even as the company faced hard economic times elsewhere in the world.[49]

The Global Water Challenge

A decade ago in 2007, one out of every five people globally lacked access to clean drinking water.[50] In August 2006, an international conference was held in Stockholm, Sweden, to discuss global water issues. A UN study reported that many large water corporations have decreased their investments in developing countries because of high political and financial risks. Even nations that have had abundant water supplies are experiencing significant reductions. These reductions are believed to be caused by two factors: the decline in rainfall and increased evaporation of water due to global warming and the loss of wetlands. Water is something that affects every person each and every day. The executive director of the Stockholm Water Institute, Anders Berntell, noted that water affects the areas of agriculture, energy, transportation, forestry, trade, financing, and social and political security. The Food and Agriculture Organization points out, "Agriculture is the world's largest water consumer. Any water crisis will therefore also create a food crisis."

There have been attempts to improve the water conditions around the world. The United Nations recently released the World Water Development Report. This report was compiled by 24 UN agencies and claimed that, in actuality, only 12 percent of the funds targeted for water and sanitation improvement reached those most in need. The United Nations stated that more than 1.1 billion people still lack access to improved water resources. Nearly two-thirds of the 1.1 billion live in Asia.[51] In China, nearly a quarter of the population is unable to access clean drinking water. Over half of China's major waterways are also polluted. The Institute of Public and Environmental Affairs reported that 34 foreign-owned or joint-venture companies, including Pepsi, have caused water pollution problems in China. Ma Jun, the institute's founder, said, "We're not talking about very high standards. These companies are known for their commitment to the environment."[52]

According to the 2016 UN World Water Development Report, the world's population will grow by 33 percent by 2050, resulting in over 2 billion more people living in water-stressed areas. An estimated one-third of the global population does not have access to safe drinking water or adequate sanitation. By 2050, the population living in urban environments will double.[53]

With businesses expanding globally, water is a crucial resource, and water issues will increasingly affect all industries. With water conditions improving at a slower rate than business development, businesses will have to take on the responsibility of not only finding an adequate supply of the diminishing resource but also making sure the water is safe for all to consume. This responsibility is going to be an additional cost to companies, but a necessary one that will prevent loss of sales in the future. Coca-Cola's specific situation in India is a reminder for all global corporations.

Questions for Review

1. What aspects of U.S. culture and of Indian culture may have been causes of Coke's difficulties in India?

2. How might Coca-Cola have responded differently when this situation first occurred, especially in terms of responding to negative perceptions among Indians of Coke and other MNCs?

3. If Coca-Cola wants to obtain more of India's soft drink market, what changes does it need to make?

4. How might companies like Coca-Cola and PepsiCo demonstrate their commitment to working with different countries and respecting the cultural and natural environments of those societies?

Source: This case was prepared by Jaclyn Johns of Villanova University under the supervision of Professor Jonathan Doh as the basis for class discussion. Additional research assistance was provided by Courtney Asher, Tetyana Azarova, and Ben Littell. It is not intended to illustrate either effective or ineffective managerial capability or administrative responsibility.

ENDNOTES

1. Peter Wonacott and Chad Terhune, "Politics & Economics: Path to India's Market Dotted with Potholes; Savvy Cola Giants Stumble over Local Agendas; KFC Climbs Back from Abyss," *The Wall Street Journal*, September 12, 2006, p. A6.

2. "CSE Report on Pesticide Residue Inconclusive," *Businessline*, August 27, 2006, p. 1.

3. Rajesh Kumar and Verner Worm, "Institutional Dynamics and the Negotiation Process: Comparing India and China," *International Journal of Conflict Management* 15, no. 3 (2004), p. 304.

4. Wonacott and Terhune, "Politics & Economics."

5. Archna Shukla, "Message Will Always Be More Important Than Medium," *Business Today*, August 27, 2006, p. 102.

6. Mark Sappenfield, "India's Cola Revolt Taps into Old Distrust: Behind Contradictory Reports of Pesticides in Coke and Pepsi Is an Underlying Wariness of Foreign Companies," *The Christian Science Monitor*, September 1, 2006, p. 6.

7. Siddharth Cavale, "Coca-Cola Sales Beat Estimates as China Volumes Soar," *Reuters*, April 15, 2014, www.reuters.com/article/us-cocacola-results-idUSBREA3E0R220140415.

8. Nikhil Gulati and Runman Ahmed, "India Has 1.2 Billion People but Not Enough Drink Coke," *The Wall Street Journal Online*, July 13, 2012, http:// www.wsj.com/articles/SB1000142405270230487030 4577490092413939410.

9. "Foreign Direct Investment, Net Inflows (BoP, current US$)," *World Bank*, http://data.worldbank.org/indicator/BX.KLT.DINV.CD.WD.

10. Courtney Fingar, "India Grabs Investment League Pole Position," *Financial Times*, September 29, 2915, www.ft.com/intl/cms/s/3/fdd0e3c2-65fc-11e5-97d0-1456a776a4f5.html#axzz45LofBnIo.

11. "Survey Shows India as the Favorite Investment Target," *Nikkei Asian Review*, December 9, 2015, http://asia.nikkei.com/Business/Trends/Survey-shows-India-as-the-favorite-investment-target.

12. Arvind Panagariya, "Building a Modern India," *Business Standard India 2010*.

13. "GDP Growth (annual %)," *World Bank*, http://data.worldbank.org/indicator/NY.GDP.MKTP.KD.ZG.

14. Brian Bremner, Nandini Lakshman, and Diane Brady, "India: Behind the Scare over Pesticides in Pepsi and Coke," *BusinessWeek*, September 4, 2006, p. 43.

15. Sappenfield, "India's Cola Revolt Taps into Old Distrust."

16. Bremner, Lakshman, and Brady, "India: Behind the Scare over Pesticides in Pepsi and Coke."

17. Coca-Cola India, "Environment Report 2007–2008." Accessed 2008.

18. Eric Bellman, "Coke Sees Strong Demand across India, Plans Investment," *The Wall Street Journal*, June 30, 2009, http://online.wsj.com/article/SB124055692273452331.html?mod= googlenews_wsj.

19. Ibid.

20. Gulati and Ahmed, "India Has 1.2 Billion People but Not Enough Drink Coke."

21. Ratna Bhushan, "RC Cola Comes to India," *Businessline*, October 7, 2003, p. 1.

22. "India: Reports of Contaminated Soda Dry up Coke, Pepsi Sales," *Global Information Network*, September 7, 2006, p. 1.

23. Aryn Baker, "India's Storm in a Cola Cup," *Time International*, August 21, 2006, p. 8.

24. Bremner, Lakshman, and Brady, "India: Behind the Scare over Pesticides in Pepsi and Coke."

25. Sappenfield, "India's Cola Revolt Taps into Old Distrust."

26. Wonacott and Terhune, "Politics & Economics."

27. "India: Reports of Contaminated Soda Dry up Coke, Pepsi Sales."

28. Sappenfield, "India's Cola Revolt Taps into Old Distrust."

29. "Coca-Cola Co.: India's Kerala State Cancels Ban on Coke, Pepsi Drinks," *The Wall Street Journal*, September 25, 2006, p. A11.

30. Ibid.

31. "Coca-Cola India Unit Asked to Pay $47 Million Damages," *Reuters*, March 23, 2010, www.reuters.com/article/idUSSGE62M0AV20100323.

32. Diane Brady, "Pepsi: Repairing a Poisoned Reputation in India," *BusinessWeek*, June 11, 2007.

33. Ibid.

34. Ibid.

35. Ibid.

36. Amit Srivastava, "Coca-Cola Funded Group Investigates Coca-Cola in India," *India Resource Center*, April 16, 2007, www.indiaresource.org/campaigns/coke/2007/coketeri.html.

37. Sappenfield, "India's Cola Revolt Taps into Old Distrust."

38. Amelia Gentleman, "For 2 Giants of Soft Drinks, a Crisis in Crucial Market," *New York Times*, August 23, 2006, p. C3.

39. Wonacott and Terhune, "Politics & Economics."

40. "CSR Initiatives: Strengthening Communities through Water Conservation," *CSR News*, October 2007, http://newsletters.cii.in/newsletters/csr/october07/spot_lite.html.

41. Ibid.

42. Coca-Cola India, "Environment Report 2007–2008."

43. "Improving Our Water Efficiency," *Coca-Cola Company*, www.coca-colacompany.com/stories/setting-a-new-goal-for-water-efficiency/.

44. Coca-Cola Company, "The Coca-Cola Company Pledges to Replace the Water It Uses in Its Beverages and Their Production," press release, June 5, 2007, http://www.worldwildlife.org/press-releases/the-coca-cola-company-pledges-to-replace-the-water-it-uses-in-its-beverages-and-their-production.

45. Jay Moye, "Beyond Water: Coca-Cola Expands Partnership with WWF, Announces Ambitious Environmental Goals," *Coca-Cola Company*, July 9, 2013, www.coca-colacompany.com/stories/beyond-water-coca-cola-expands-partnership-with-wwf-announces-ambitious-environmental-goals/.

46. Coca-Cola India, "Environment Report 2007–2008."

47. Ibid.

48. Gentleman, "For 2 Giants of Soft Drinks, a Crisis in Crucial Market."

49. Cavale, "Coca-Cola Sales Beat Estimates as China Volumes Soar."

50. Kenneth E. Behring, "Water Research; Researchers Are Raising Awareness of the Global Drinking Water Crisis," *Health & Medicine Week*, October 16, 2006, p. 1339.

51. Thalif Deen, "Development: Water, Water Everywhere Is Thing of the Past," *Global Information Network*, August 22, 2006, p. 1.

52. Loretta Chao and Shai Oster, "China Study Says Foreigners Violate Clean-Water Rules," *The Wall Street Journal*, October 30, 2006, p. B7.

53. United Nations, *World Water Development Report 2016: Water and Jobs* (March 22, 2016), http://unesdoc.unesco.org/images/0024/002439/243938e.pdf.

Brief Integrative Case 2.2

Danone's Wrangle with Wahaha

In 1996, Danone Group and Wahaha Group combined forces in a joint venture (JV) to form the largest beverage company in China. A longstanding trademark dispute between the JV members, embedded within a broader clash of national and organizational cultures, came to a head. Valuable lessons can be learned from this dispute for investors considering joint ventures in China.

The Wahaha Joint Venture was established in 1996 by Hangzhou Wahaha Food Group Co. Ltd., Danone Group, and Bai Fu Qin Ltd. In 1997, Danone bought the interests of Bai Fu Qin and gained legal control of the JV with 51 percent of the shares. While members of the JV are entitled to use the JV's Wahaha trademark, in 2000, the Wahaha Group developed companies outside of the JV that sold products similar to those of the JV and used the JV's trademark. The Danone Group objected and sought to purchase those non-JV companies.[1]

In April 2007, Danone offered RMB4 billion to acquire 51 percent of the shares of Wahaha's five non-JV companies. Wahaha Group rejected the offer. Subsequently, Danone filed more than 30 lawsuits against Wahaha for violating the contract and illegally using the JV's Wahaha trademark in countries such as France, Italy, the U.S., and China.[2]

Danone's Background

Danone traces its routes to Europe in the early 20th century. In 1919, Isaac Carasso opened a small yogurt stand in Spain. He named it "Danone," meaning "Little Daniel," after his son. Carasso was aware of new methods of milk fermentation conducted at the Pasteur Institute in Paris. He decided to merge these new techniques with traditional practices for making yogurt. The first industrial manufacturer of yogurt was started.[3]

Following his success in Europe, Carasso immigrated to the U.S. to expand his market. He changed the Danone name to Dannon Milk products, Inc., and founded the first American yogurt company in 1942 in New York. Distribution began on a small scale. When Dannon introduced the "fruit on the bottom" line in 1947, sales soared. The following year, he sold his company's interest and returned to Spain to manage his family's original business.[4]

By 1950, Dannon had expanded to other U.S. states in the Northeast. It also broadened the line by introducing low-fat yogurt that targeted the health-conscious consumer. Sales continued to rise. Dannon expanded across the country throughout the 1960s and 1970s. In 1979,

Dannon became the first company to sell perishable dairy products coast to coast in the U.S.[5]

In 1967, Danone merged with leading French fresh cheese producer Gervais to become Gervais Danone. In 1973, Gervais Danone merged with Boussois-Souchon-Neuvesel (BSN), a company that had also acquired the Alsacian brewer Kronenbourg and Evian mineral water.[6] In 1987, Gervais Danone acquired European biscuit manufacturer Général Biscuit, owners of the LU brand, and in 1989, it bought out the European biscuit operations of Nabisco.

In 1994, BSN changed its name to Groupe Danone, adopting the name of the Group's best-known international brand. Under its current CEO, Franck Riboud, the company has pursued its focus on the three product groups: dairy, beverages, and cereals.[7] Today, Danone's mission is to produce healthy, nutritious, and affordable food and beverage products for as many people as possible.

Danone's Global Growth

Danone, with 160 plants and nearly 100,000 employees, has a presence in all five continents and over 120 countries. In 2015, Danone recorded €21.1 billion in sales, a nearly 30 percent increase from its €15.2 billion in sales in 2008. Danone enjoys leading positions in healthy food:[8]

- No. 1 worldwide in fresh dairy products
- No. 2 worldwide in bottled water
- No. 2 worldwide in baby nutrition
- No. 1 in Europe in medical nutrition

Its portfolio of brands and products includes Activia, a probiotic dairy product line; Danette, a brand of cream desserts; Nutricia, an infant product line; Danonino, a brand of yogurts; and Evian, a brand of bottled water.[9]

Listed on Euronext Paris, Danone is also ranked among the main indexes of social responsibility: Dow Jones Sustainability Index Stoxx and World, ASPI Eurozone (Advanced Sustainable Performance Indices), and Ethibel Sustainability index. Danone has ranked number 51 in top 100 international brands according to Interbrand 2015 Best Global Brand valuation, with the brand value of $8.6 billion.[10]

In 2014, Danone recorded an organic growth rate of 4.7 percent despite a weak European economy, further strengthening its global standing. The group's performance is the result of a balanced strategy that builds on international expansion, a growing commitment to inno-vation, and strengthening health-oriented brands. Danone invests heavily in research and development—€276 mil-lion in 2015. One hundred percent of projects currently in the pipeline focus on health and nutrition.[11]

As of 2014, Danone is the world's second largest pro-ducer of bottled water. Danone owns the world's top-selling brand of packaged water, Aqua, which recorded sales of 11 billion liters in 2014. With Evian and Volvic, Danone also owns two of the five worldwide brands of bottled water.[12] Its revenue from water products amounted to €4.2 billion in 2014: China, France, Indonesia, and Mexico accounted for the most sales. Growth is strongest in China, Indonesia, and Argentina, with emerging mar-kets accounting for 70 percent of all of Danone's bottled water sales.[13]

In the mid-1990s, Danone did 80 percent of its busi-ness in Western Europe. Until 1996, the company was present in about a dozen markets including pasta, confec-tionery, biscuits, ready-to-serve meals, and beer. The company realized that it is difficult to achieve simultane-ous growth in all these markets. Therefore, they decided to concentrate on the few markets that showed the most growth potential and were consistent with Danone's focus on health. Starting in 1997, the Group decided to focus on three business lines worldwide (Fresh Dairy Products, Beverages, as well as Biscuits and Cereal Products), and the rest of the business lines were divested. This freed the company's financial and human resources and allowed for quick expansion into new markets in Asia, Africa, Eastern Europe, and Latin America. In less than 10 years, the contribution of emerging markets to sales rose from zero to 40 percent while that of Western Europe went below 50 percent.[14] By 2014, emerging markets accounted for 60 percent of all growth, with over 60 percent of all employees working outside of Europe.[15]

In 2007, the same year that it attempted to acquire 51 percent of the shares of Wahaha's five non-JV com-panies, Danone marked the end of a 10-year refocusing strategy period during which the Group's activities were refocused in the area of health. That year, the Group sold nearly all of its Biscuits and Cereal Products busi-ness to the Kraft Foods group, while adding Baby Nutrition and Medical Nutrition to its portfolio by acquiring Numico.

Danone is now centered on 4 business lines:

1. Fresh Dairy Products, representing approximately 53 percent of consolidated sales for 2014.

2. Waters, representing approximately 20 percent of consolidated sales for 2014.

3. Baby Nutrition, representing approximately 21 per-cent of consolidated sales for 2014.

4. Medical Nutrition, representing approximately 7 per-cent of consolidated sales for 2014.

Danone Strategy in China

Danone entered the Chinese market in the late 1980s. Since then, it has invested heavily in China, building fac-tories and expanding production. Today, Danone has 70 factories in China, including Danone Biscuits, Robust, Wahaha, and Health. Ten percent of Danone's workforce is located in China. Danone sells primarily yogurt, bis-cuits, and beverages in the Chinese market.[16] By 2014, Danone's Asia-Pacific division employed 28,000 people in the Asia-Pacific area, which was almost 30 percent of Danone's total employees.

In the early 2000s, Danone's Wahaha was China's larg-est beverage company. In 2008, 57 percent of Danone's Asian sales were in China. Two billion liters of Wahaha were sold in 2004, making it the market leader in China with a 30 percent market share.[17] In Asia, in 2007, Danone Group was the market leader with a 20 percent share of a 34-billion-liter market. In comparison, rivals Coca-Cola and Nestlé had a 7 percent and 2 percent share, respec-tively. Evian, its global brand, was sold alongside of local brands such as China's Wahaha.

In the past 20 years, Danone has purchased shares of many of the top beverage companies in China: 51 percent of the shares of the companies owned by Wahaha Group, 98 percent of Robust Group, 50 percent of Shanghai Mal-ing Aquarius Co., Ltd., 54.2 percent of Shenzhen Yili Mineral Water Company, 22.18 percent of China Huiyuan Group, 50 percent of Mengniu, and 20.01 percent of Bright dairy. These companies, leaders in their industry, all own trademarks that are well-known in China.[18]

However, while expanding into the Chinese market, Danone faced challenges due to lack of market knowl-edge. In 2000, Danone purchased Robust, the then-second-largest company in the Chinese beverage industry. Sales of Robust had reached RMB2 billion in 1999. After the purchase, Danone dismissed the original management and managed Robust directly. Because its new management was not familiar with the Chinese beverage market, Robust struggled. Its tea and milk products almost disappeared from the market. During 2005–2006, the company lost RMB 150 million.[19]

Wahaha Company

The Wahaha company was established in 1987 by a retired teacher, Mr. Zong Qinghou. In 1989, the enterprise opened its first plant, Wahaha Nutritional Food Factory, to pro-duce "Wahaha Oral Liquid for Children," a nutritional drink for kids. The name Wahaha was meant to evoke a laughing child, combining the character for baby (wa) with the sound of laughter.[20] After its launch, Wahaha won a rapid public acceptance. By 1991, the company's sales revenue grew beyond 100 million renminbi (¥).[21]

In 1991, with the support of the Hangzhou local district government, Wahaha Nutritional Food Factory merged with Hangzhou Canning Food Factory, a state-owned enterprise, to form the Hangzhou Wahaha Group Corporation. After mergers with three more companies, Wahaha became the biggest corporation of its district.[22]

Since 1997, Wahaha has set up many new subsidiaries. It was aided by state and local government because its continuous expansion helped create new jobs and its increased profits led to more tax revenues.

In 1996, the Hangzhou Wahaha Group Corporation began a joint venture with Danone Group and formed five new subsidiaries, which attracted a $45 million foreign investment and then added another $26.2 million investment. With the investment funds, Wahaha brought world-class advanced production lines from Germany, America, Italy, Japan, and Canada into its sites. The terms of the Danone-Wahaha joint venture allowed Wahaha to retain all managerial and operating rights as well as the brand name Wahaha. In the next eight years, the company established 40 subsidiaries in China, and in 1998 launched its own brand, "Future Cola," to compete against Coke and Pepsi.[23]

In 2000, the company produced 2.24 million tons of beverages with sales revenue of $5.4 billion. The production accounted for 15 percent of the Chinese output of beverages. The group became the biggest company in the beverage industry of China with total assets of $4.4 billion.[24]

Back in 2007, it produced 6.89 million tons of beverage with a sales revenue of $25.8 billion. Today, Hangzhou Wahaha Group Co., Ltd., is still a leading beverage producer in China with over 60,000 employees and 150 subsidiaries, though sales have dropped since 2013 due to the shrinking carbonated beverage market. The company product category contains more than 100 varieties, such as milk drinks, drinking water, carbonated drinks, tea drinks, canned food, and health care products.[25]

According to a report on the "Top 10 Beverage Companies" released by the China Beverage Industry Association, Wahaha contributed 55.57 percent to the Association Top 10's overall production, 65.84 percent to its revenue, and 73.16 percent to its profit tax. According to Zong Qinghou, the president of Wahaha: "As China becomes the world's largest food and beverage market, we'll be a major player in the global market." Wahaha implements a strategy of "local production and local distribution" and has built an excellent production-distribution network. Its Wahaha R&D center and Analysis Center provide guarantees for high product quality.[26]

Danone-Wahaha Joint Venture Conflict

The Wahaha joint venture (JV) was formed in 1996 with three participants: Hangzhou Wahaha Food Group (Wahaha Group); Danone Group, a French corporation (Danone); and Bai Fu Qin, a Hong Kong corporation (Baifu). Danone and Baifu did not invest directly in the JV. Instead, Danone and Baifu formed Jin Jia Investment, a Singapore corporation (Jinjia). Upon the formation of the JV, Wahaha Group owned 49 percent of the shares of the JV and Jinjia owned 51 percent of the shares of the JV. This structure led to immediate misunderstandings between the participants. From Wahaha Group's point of view—with the division of ownership at 49 percent Wahaha Group, 25.5 percent Danone, and 25.5 percent Baifu—it was the majority shareholder in the JV. Figure 1 shows the initial structure of the JV. Since Wahaha Group felt it controlled the JV, it was relatively unconcerned when it transferred its trademark to the JV.[27]

In 1998, Danone bought out the interest of Baifu in Jinjia, becoming 100 percent owner of Jinjia and effectively the 51 percent owner of the JV. This gave it legal control over the JV because of its right to elect the board of directors. For the first time, the Wahaha Group and Zong realized two things: (1) They had given complete

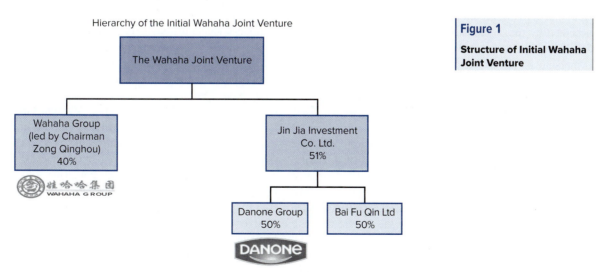

Hierarchy of the Initial Wahaha Joint Venture

Figure 1

Structure of Initial Wahaha Joint Venture

Source: Steven M. Dickinson, "Danone v. Wahaha," *China Economic Review*, September 1, 2007, http://www.chinaeconomicreview.com/node/24126.

control over their trademark to the JV and (2) a foreign company was now in control of the JV. From a legal standpoint, this result was implied by the structure of the JV from the very beginning. However, it is clear from public statements that the Wahaha Group did not understand the implications when they entered into the venture. The Danone "takeover" in 1998 therefore produced significant resentment on the part of Wahaha Group. Rightly or not, Wahaha felt that Danone misled them from the very beginning.[28]

When the JV was formed, Wahaha Group was a state-owned enterprise owned by the Hangzhou city government. After formation of the JV, it was converted into a private corporation, effectively controlled by Zong. This set the stage for Wahaha Group's decision to take back control of the trademark it felt had been unfairly transferred to Danone. Zong and his employees now viewed the transferred trademark as their personal property.[29]

When the JV was formed, Wahaha Group obtained an appraisal of its trademark valuing it at RMB100 million (US$13.2 million). The trademark was its sole contribution to the JV, while Jinjia contributed RMB500 million (US$66.1 million) in cash. Wahaha Group also agreed not to use the trademark for any independent business activity or allow it to be used by any other entity. However, the trademark transfer was rejected by China's Trademark Office. It took the position that, as the well-known mark of a state-owned enterprise, the trademark belonged to the state and Wahaha Group did not have the right to transfer it to a private company.[30]

Rather than terminate the JV, the shareholders (now Danone and Wahaha Group) decided to work around the approval issue by entering into an exclusive license agreement for the trademark in 1999. Because the license agreement was intended to be the functional equivalent of a sale of the trademark, they were concerned the Trademark Office would refuse to register the license. Therefore, they only registered an abbreviated license. This was accepted by the Trademark Office, which never saw the full license. As a result, Wahaha Group never transferred ownership of the Wahaha trademark to the JV, just the exclusive license. Thus, Wahaha Group never complied with its basic obligation for capitalization of the JV. It does not appear that any of the JV documents were revised to deal with this changed situation.[31]

Although Danone was the majority shareholder and maintained a majority interest on the board of directors, day-to-day management of the JV was delegated entirely to Zong. He filled management positions with his family members and employees of the Wahaha Group. Under Zong's management, the JV became the largest Chinese bottled water and beverage company.[32]

Beginning in 2000, the Wahaha Group created a series of companies that sold the same products as the JV and used the Wahaha trademark. The non-JV companies appear to have been owned in part by Wahaha Group and in part by an offshore British Virgin Islands company controlled by Zong's daughter and wife. Neither Danone nor Wahaha Group receives any benefits from the profits of these non-JV companies. According to press reports in China, products from the non-JV companies and the JV were sold by the same sales staff working for the same sales company, all ultimately managed by Zong.[33]

In 2005, Danone realized the situation and insisted it be given a 51 percent ownership interest in the non-JV companies. Wahaha Group and Zong, who by this time was one of the richest men in China, refused.[34]

Details of the Dispute

In April 2006, Wahaha was informed by its 10-year JV partner Danone that it had breached the contract by establishing nonjoint ventures that had infringed upon the interests of Danone. Danone proposed to purchase 51 percent of the shares of Wahaha's nonjoint ventures.[35] The move was opposed by Wahaha. In May 2007, Danone formally initiated a proceeding, claiming that Wahaha's establishment of nonjoint ventures as well as the illegal use of the "Wahaha" trademark had seriously violated the noncompete clause. The two parties carried on 10 lawsuits in and out of China, and all the ruled cases between Wahaha and Danone have ended in Wahaha's favor.[36]

On February 3, 2009, a California court in the United States dismissed Danone's accusation against the wife and daughter of Zong Qinghou and ruled that the dispute between Danone and Wahaha should be settled in China. In addition, Danone's lawsuits against Wahaha were rejected by courts in Italy and France; and a series of lawsuits brought by Danone in China against Zong Qinghou and Wahaha's nonjoint ventures all ended in failure.[37]

The rationality of the existence of the nonjoint ventures, the ownership of the "Wahaha" trademark, and the noncompete clause issue were the key points of the Danone-Wahaha dispute.[38] In 1996, Wahaha offered a list of 10 subsidiaries to Danone, which, after evaluation, selected four. Jinja Investments Pte Ltd. (a Singapore-based joint venture between Danone Asia Pte Ltd. and Hong Kong Peregrine Investment, of which Danone is the controlling shareholder); Hangzhou Wahaha Group Co., Ltd.; and Zhejiang Wahaha Industrial Holdings Ltd. jointly invested to form five joint venture enterprises, with shareholdings of 51 percent, 39 percent, and 10 percent, respectively. In 1998, Hong Kong Peregrine sold its stake in Jinja Investments to Danone, which makes Danone the sole shareholder of Jinja Investments, giving it the control of over 51 percent of the joint ventures. Wahaha and Danone cooperated on the basis of joint venture enterprises, rather than the complete acquisition of Wahaha by Danone. As a result, Wahaha was always independent, and its nonjoint ventures have existed and developed since

1996. Relevant transactions of Wahaha's nonjoint ventures and joint ventures were disclosed fully and frankly by the auditing reports of PricewaterhouseCoopers, an accounting firm appointed by Danone. Meanwhile, during the 11-year cooperation, Danone assigned a finance director to locate in the headquarters of Wahaha Group to audit the latter's financial information.[39]

Danone and Wahaha had signed in succession three relevant agreements concerning the ownership of the "Wahaha" brand name. In 1997, the two parties signed a trademark transfer agreement, with an intention to transfer the "Wahaha" trademark to the joint ventures. The move, however, was not approved by the State Trademark Office.[40] For this reason, the two parties signed in 1999 the trademark licensing contract. According to law, the same subject cannot be synchronously transferred and licensed for use to others by the same host. Therefore, the signing and fulfillment of the trademark licensing contract showed that the two parties had agreed to the invalidation of the transfer agreement. The "Wahaha" brand should belong to the Wahaha Group, while the joint ventures only have the right of use.[41]

In October 2005, the two parties signed the No. 1 amendment agreement to the trademark licensing contract, in which it confirmed Party A (Hangzhou Wahaha Group Co., Ltd.) as owner of the trademark. In addition, the second provision of the amendment agreement clearly stated that the several Wahaha subsidiaries listed in the fifth annex of the licensing contract as well as other Wahaha subsidiaries (referred to as "licensed Wahaha enterprises") established by Party A or its affiliates following the signing of the licensing contract also have the right granted by one party to use the trademark. The "licensed Wahaha enterprises" involved in the amendment agreement refer to the nonjoint ventures.[42] According to related files, Wahaha maintains the ownership of the "Wahaha" trademark, while its nonjoint ventures have the right to use the trademark.[43] The Wahaha brand is among the most famous in China. It ranked No. 16 among domestic brands and is worth US$2.2 billion, according to a recent report by Shanghai research firm Hurun Report. Wahaha doesn't publicly disclose financial figures.[44]

Ventures and Acquisitions

Several years ago, as Wahaha sought to expand its market, Wahaha suggested adding online new production lines by increasing investment, while Danone requested Wahaha outsource to product processing suppliers for its joint ventures. Wahaha saw the shortcomings in using product processing suppliers, so it set up nonjoint ventures to meet production needs. Wahaha believed that the existence and operation of the nonjoint ventures did not adversely affect the interest of Danone.[45]

During the 11 years that followed 1996, Danone invested less than RMB1.4 billion in Wahaha's joint ventures but received a profit of RMB3.554 billion as of 2007. On the other hand, Danone acquired several strong competitors of Wahaha including Robust, Huiyuan, and Shanghai Maling Aquariust. Wahaha saw Robust as its biggest rival. Wahaha was disappointed that Danone failed to hold up its end of the bargain of "jointly exploring markets in and out of China" listed in the JV contract.[46]

Through the influence of the Chinese and French governments, Danone and Wahaha reached a peaceful settlement in late 2007. However, Danone's proposal to sell its shares in the joint ventures to Wahaha for RMB50 billion (finally reduced to approximately RMB20 billion) was rejected by Wahaha.[47]

After the negotiations were suspended, the two parties again turned to legal action. All the ruled cases, both in China and abroad, have ruled against Danone.[48]

Conflict Resolution

In late September 2009, France's Groupe Danone SA agreed to accept a cash settlement to relinquish claims to the name Wahaha. In a joint statement issued September 30, 2009, Danone announced a settlement with China's Hangzhou Wahaha Group Co. by saying its 51 percent share in joint ventures that make soft drinks and related products will be sold to the businesses' Chinese partners. "The completion of this settlement will put an end to all legal proceedings related to the disputes between the two parties," the statement said.[49]

The feud over control of the Wahaha empire offered a glimpse into the breakup of a major Asian–foreign joint venture. Danone's strategy to publicly confront its partner and Wahaha's strategy to respond with its own accusations marked a break with prevailing business practice in China, where problems have usually been settled with face-saving, private negotiations.[50]

Analysts said the case served to reinforce how difficult it is to operate a partnership in China. "That's a key lesson: To build a [brand] business in China you need to build from the ground up," said Jonathan Chajet, China managing director for consultancy Interbrand.[51] Foreign firms such as Procter & Gamble, Starbucks, and General Motors have operated wholly or in part through joint ventures in China. But executives involved say the expectations of foreign and local parties can conflict in a JV; for instance, when an international company is striving for efficiencies and profits that match its global goals while the local partner—sometimes an arm of the Chinese government— strives to maximize employment or improve technology. At other times, partners have stolen corporate secrets or cheated and otherwise sabotaged a venture, while legal avenues have had little effect on disputes over operations.[52]

Danone, which reported the Wahaha business generated about 10 percent of its global revenue in 2006 but has since adjusted how it accounted for Wahaha, said it expects no impact on its income statement from the settlement. In China, it will be left with a much smaller footprint and is essentially starting over.[53] Danone's CEO Franck Riboud stated: "Danone has a long-standing commitment to China, where it has been present since 1987, and we are keen to accelerate the success of our Chinese activities." China is Danone's fourth-largest market after France, Spain, and the U.S., contributing about €1bn, or 8 percent, of Danone's revenues.[54]

Lessons Learned[55]

What can potential foreign investors learn from this dispute? Although JVs in China can be quite difficult, with proper planning and management, they can be successful. In the case of the Wahaha–Danone JV, many basic rules of JV operations in China were violated, virtually guaranteeing the JV's destruction. According to Steve Dickinson, lawyer at Harris Moure PLC, the primary rules violated are as follows:[56]

1. Don't use technical legal techniques to assert or gain control in a JV.

2. Do not expect that a 51 percent ownership interest in a JV will necessarily provide effective control.

3. Do not proceed with a JV formed on a weak or uncertain legal basis.

4. The foreign party must actively supervise or participate in the day-to-day management of the JV.

Questions for Review

1. When and how did Danone expand into the Chinese market? What problems did Danone Group encounter while operating in China?

2. How was the Danone and Wahaha JV formed? What was its structure? Why did Danone decide to form a joint venture rather than establish a 100 percent-owned subsidiary?

3. What was the problem of the Danone-Wahaha joint venture that triggered the conflict between the companies? What were the differences in Danone's and Wahaha's understanding of their own respective roles and responsibilities in this venture? What aspects of national and organizational culture affected this perspective?

4. Was Danone successful in proving its claims in court? How was the conflict between the two companies resolved? What were the key lessons for Danone about doing business in China?

5. Did Danone follow the advice regarding JVs in China mentioned in the list just above? Which aspects did it follow and which did it not?

Source: This case was prepared by Tetyana Azarova of Villanova University under the supervision of Professor Jonathan Doh as the basis for class discussion. Additional research assistance was provided by Kelley Bergsma and Ben Littell. It is not intended to illustrate either effective or ineffective managerial capability or administrative responsibility.

ENDNOTES

1. Patti Waldmeir and Sundeep Tucker, "Danone to Quit Joint Venture with Wahaha French Group to Focus on Expanding Own Units in China," *Financial Times*, September 30, 2009, https://www.ft.com/content/849e7eda-ad87-11de-bb8a-00144feabdc0.

2. Wahaha Group, "Danone Encounters Continuous Frustration in China and a Murky Future Due to Unsuccessful Litigations," press release, *PR Newswire*, September 9, 2008, www.prnewswire.co.uk/news-releases/danone-encounters-continuous-frustration-in-china-and-a-murky-future-due-to-unsuccessful-litigations-152564955.html.

3. "Our Heritage," *Danone*, www.danone.com/en/for-all/our-mission-in-action/our-heritage/.

4. Ibid.

5. Ibid.

6. Bill Bruce, "Danone Celebrates Its 90th Birthday," April 14, 2009, www.foodbev.com/news/danone-celebrates-its-90th-birthday/.

7. Ibid.

8. Danone, 2014 Annual Report, February 20, 2015.

9. Danone, www.danone.com/en.

10. "Rankings," *Interbrand*, http://interbrand.com/best-brands/best-global-brands/2015/ranking/.

11. "Research at Danone," *Danone*, www.danone.com/en/for-all/research-innovation/our-research-at-a-glance/.

12. "Waters," *Danone*, www.danone.com/en/brands/business/beverages.html.

13. Ibid.

14. Danone 2008 Annual Report: *Economic and Social Report*.

15. Danone 2014 Annual Report: *Economic and Social Report*.

16. Shangguan Zhoudong, "Danone's Quick Expansion in China," *China Daily*, June 15, 2007, www.chinadaily.com.cn/bizchina/2007–06/15/content_895462.htm.

17. T. C. Melewar, E. Badal, and J. Small, "Danone Branding Strategy in China," *Brand Management* 13, no. 6 (July 2006), pp. 407–417.

18. "Danone Encounters Continuous Frustration in China."

19. Ibid.

20. Vivian Wai-yin Kwok, "A Pyrrhic Victory for Danone in China," *Forbes*, August 6, 2007, www.forbes.com/2007/06/08/wahaha-danone-zong-markets-equity-cx_vk_0608markets2.html.

21. Wahaha, http://en.wahaha.com.cn/aboutus/index.htm.

22. Ibid.

23. Ibid.

24. Ibid.

25. Ibid.

26. Ibid.

27. Steven M. Dickinson, "Danone v. Wahaha," *China Economic Review*, September 1, 2007, www.chinaeconomicreview.com/node/24126.

28. Dickinson, "Views You Can Use."

29. Dickinson, "Danone v. Wahaha."

30. Ibid.

31. Ibid.

32. Ibid.

33. Ibid.

34. Ibid.

35. Baoxiu Ye, "Wahaha Reviews 21:0 Whitewash Against Danone," *PR Newswire*, April 13, 2009, http://www.journalist-association.eu/archive/news.php?newsid=19477.

36. Ibid.

37. Ibid.

38. Ibid.

39. Ibid.

40. Ibid.

41. Ibid.

42. Ibid.

43. Ibid.

44. Ibid.

45. Ibid.

46. Ibid.

47. Ibid.

48. Ibid.

49. J. T. Areddy, "Danone Pulls Out of Disputed China Venture," *The Wall Street Journal*, October 1, 2009, http://online.wsj.com/article/SB125428911997751859.html.

50. Ibid.

51. Ibid.

52. Ibid.

53. Ibid.

54. Waldmeir and Tucker, "Danone to Quit Joint Venture with Wahaha."

55. Dickinson, "Danone v. Wahaha."

56. Ibid.

Euro Disneyland

On January 18, 1993, Euro Disneyland chair Robert Fitzpatrick announced he would leave that post on April 12 to begin his own consulting company. Quitting his position exactly one year after the grand opening of Euro Disneyland, Fitzpatrick with his resignation removed U.S. management from the helm of the French theme park and resort.

Fitzpatrick's position was taken by a Frenchman, Philippe Bourguignon, who had been Euro Disneyland's senior vice president for real estate. Bourguignon, 45 years old, faced a net loss of FFr 188 million for Euro Disneyland's fiscal year, which ended September 1992. Also, between April and September 1992, only 29 percent of the park's total visitors were French. Expectations were that closer to half of all visitors would be French.

It was hoped that the promotion of Philippe Bourguignon would have a public relations benefit for Euro Disneyland—a project that had been a publicist's nightmare from the beginning. One of the low points was at a news conference prior to the park's opening when protesters pelted Michael Eisner, CEO of the Walt Disney Company, with rotten eggs. Within the first year of operation, Disney had to compromise its "squeaky clean" image and lift the alcohol ban at the park. Wine is now served at all major restaurants.

Euro Disneyland, 49 percent owned by Walt Disney Company, Burbank, California, originally forecasted 11 million visitors in the first year of operation. In January 1993 it appeared attendance would be closer to 10 million. In response, management temporarily slashed prices at the park for local residents to FFr 150 ($27.27) from FFr 225 ($40.91) for adults and to FFr 100 from FFr 150 for children in order to lure more French during the slow, wet winter months. The company also reduced prices at its restaurants and hotels, which registered occupancy rates of just 37 percent.

Bourguignon also faced other problems, such as the second phase of development at Euro Disneyland, which was expected to start in September 1993. It was unclear how the company planned to finance its FFr 8–10 billion cost. The company had steadily drained its cash reserves (FFr 1.9 billion in May 1993) while piling up debt (FFr 21 billion in May 1993). Euro Disneyland admitted that it and the Walt Disney Company were "exploring potential sources of financing for Euro Disneyland." The company was also talking to banks about restructuring its debts.

Despite the frustrations, Eisner was tirelessly upbeat about the project. "Instant hits are things that go away quickly, and things that grow slowly and are part of the culture are what we look for," he said. "What we created in France is the biggest private investment in a foreign country by an American company ever. And it's gonna pay off."

In the Beginning

Disney's story is the classic American rags-to-riches story, which started in a small Kansas City advertising office where Mickey was a real mouse prowling the unknown Walt Disney floor. Originally, Mickey was named Mortimer, until a dissenting Mrs. Disney stepped in. How close Mickey was to Walt Disney is evidenced by the fact that when filming, Disney himself dubbed the mouse's voice. Only in later films did Mickey get a different voice. Disney made many sacrifices to promote his hero-mascot, including selling his first car, a beloved Moon Cabriolet, and humiliating himself in front of Louis B. Mayer. "Get that mouse off the screen!" was the movie mogul's reported response to the cartoon character. Then, in 1955, Disney had the brainstorm of sending his movie characters out into the "real" world to mix with their fans, and he battled skeptics to build the very first Disneyland in Anaheim, California.

When Disney died in 1966, the company went into virtual suspended animation. Its last big hit of that era was 1969's *The Love Bug*, about a Volkswagen named Herbie. Today, Disney executives trace the problem to a tyrannical CEO named E. Cardon Walker, who ruled the company from 1976 to 1983, and to his successor, Ronald W. Miller. Walker was quick to ridicule underlings in public and impervious to any point of view but his own. He made decisions according to what he thought Walt would have done. Executives clinched arguments by quoting Walt like the Scriptures or Marx, and the company eventually supplied a little book of the founder's sayings. Making the wholesome family movies Walt would have wanted formed a key article of Walker's creed. For example, a poster advertising the unremarkable *Condorman* featured actress Barbara Carrera in a slit skirt. Walker had the slit painted over. With this as the context, studio producers ground out a thin stream of tired, formulaic movies that fewer and fewer customers would pay to see. In mid-1983, a similar low-horsepower approach to television production led to CBS's cancellation of the hour-long program *The Wonderful World of Disney*, leaving the company without a regular network show for the first time in 29 years. Like a reclusive hermit, the company lost touch with the contemporary world.

Ron Miller's brief reign was by contrast a model of decentralization and delegation. Many attributed Miller's ascent to his marrying the boss's daughter rather than to any special gift. To shore Miller up, the board installed Raymond L. Watson, former head of the Irvine Co., as part-time chair. He quickly became full time.

Miller sensed the studio needed rejuvenation, and he managed to produce the hit film *Splash*, featuring an apparently (but not actually) bare-breasted mermaid, under the newly devised Touchstone label. However, the reluctance of freelance Hollywood talent to accommodate Disney's narrow range and stingy compensation often kept his sound instincts from bearing fruit. "Card [Cardon Walker] would listen but not hear," said a former executive. "Ron [Ron Miller] would listen but not act."

Too many box office bombs contributed to a steady erosion of profit. Profits of $135 million on revenues of $915 million in 1980 dwindled to $93 million on revenues of $1.3 billion in 1983. More alarmingly, revenues from the company's theme parks, about three-quarters of the company's total revenues, were showing signs of leveling off. Disney's stock slid from $84.375 a share to $48.75 between April 1983 and February 1984.

Through these years, Roy Disney Jr. simmered while he watched the downfall of the national institution that his uncle, Walt, and his father, Roy Disney Sr., had built. He had long argued that the company's constituent parts all worked together to enhance each other. If movie and television production weren't revitalized, not only would that source of revenue disappear, but the company and its activities would also grow dim in the public eye. At the same time, the stream of new ideas and characters that kept people pouring into the parks and buying toys, books, and records would dry up. Now his dire predictions were coming true. His own personal shareholding had already dropped from $96 million to $54 million. Walker's treatment of Ron Miller as the shining heir apparent and Roy Disney as the idiot nephew helped drive Roy to quit as Disney vice president in 1977 and to set up Shamrock Holdings, a broadcasting and investment company.

In 1984, Roy teamed up with Stanley Gold, a tough-talking lawyer and a brilliant strategist. Gold saw that the falling stock price was bound to flush out a raider and afford Roy Disney a chance to restore the company's fortunes. They asked Frank Wells, vice chair of Warner Bros., if he would take a top job in the company in the event they offered it. Wells, a lawyer and a Rhodes scholar, said yes. With that, Roy knew that what he would hear in Disney's boardroom would limit his freedom to trade in its stock, so he quit the board on March 9, 1984.

"I knew that would hang a 'For Sale' sign over the company," said Gold.

By resigning, Roy pushed over the first of a train of dominoes that ultimately led to the result he most desired. The company was raided, almost dismantled, greenmailed, raided again, and sued left and right. But it miraculously emerged with a skilled new top management with big plans for a bright future. Roy Disney proposed Michael Eisner as the CEO, but the board came close to rejecting Eisner in favor of an older, more buttoned-down candidate. Gold stepped in and made an impassioned speech to the directors. "You see guys like Eisner as a little crazy . . . but every studio in this country has been run by crazies. What do you think Walt Disney was? The guy was off the goddamned wall. This is a creative institution. It needs to be run by crazies again."

Meanwhile Eisner and Wells staged an all-out lobbying campaign, calling on every board member except two, who were abroad, to explain their views about the company's future. "What was most important," said Eisner, "was that they saw I did not come in a tutu, and that I was a serious person, and I understood a P&L, and I knew the investment analysts, and I read *Fortune*."

In September 1984, Michael Eisner was appointed CEO and Frank Wells became president. Jeffrey Katzenberg, the 33-year-old, maniacal production chief, followed Fisher from Paramount Pictures. He took over Disney's movie and television studios. "The key," said Eisner, "is to start off with a great idea."

Disneyland in Anaheim, California

For a long time, Walt Disney had been concerned about the lack of family-type entertainment available for his two daughters. The amusement parks he saw around him were mostly filthy traveling carnivals. They were often unsafe and allowed unruly conduct on the premises. Disney envisioned a place where people from all over the world would be able to go for clean and safe fun. His dream came true on July 17, 1955, when the gates first opened at Disneyland in Anaheim, California.

Disneyland strives to generate the perfect fantasy. But magic does not simply happen. The place is a marvel of modern technology. Literally dozens of computers, huge banks of tape machines, film projectors, and electronic controls lie behind the walls, beneath the floors, and above the ceilings of dozens of rides and attractions. The philosophy is that "Disneyland is the world's biggest stage, and the audience is right here on the stage," said Dick Hollinger, chief industrial engineer at Disneyland. "It takes a tremendous amount of work to keep the stage clean and working properly."

Cleanliness is a primary concern. Before the park opens at 8 a.m., the cleaning crew will have mopped, hosed, and dried every sidewalk, street, floor, and counter.

More than 350 of the park's 7,400 employees come on duty at 1 a.m. to begin the daily cleanup routine. The thousands of feet that walk through the park each day and chewing gum do not mix; gum has always presented major cleanup problems. The park's janitors found long ago that fire hoses with 90 pounds of water pressure would not do the job. Now they use steam machines, razor scrapers, and mops towed by Cushman scooters to literally scour the streets and sidewalks daily.

It takes one person working a full eight-hour shift to polish the brass on the Fantasyland merry-go-round. The scrupulously manicured plantings throughout the park are treated with growth-retarding hormones to keep the trees and bushes from spreading beyond their assigned spaces and destroying the carefully maintained five-eighths scale modeling that is utilized in the park. The maintenance supervisor of the Matterhorn bobsled ride personally walks every foot of track and inspects every link of tow chain every night, thus trusting his or her own eyes more than the $2 million in safety equipment that is built into the ride.

Eisner himself pays obsessive attention to detail. Walking through Disneyland one Sunday afternoon, he peered at the plastic leaves on the Swiss Family Robinson tree house, noting that they periodically wear out and need to be replaced leaf by leaf at a cost of $500,000. As his family strolled through the park, he and his eldest son Breck stooped to pick up the rare piece of litter that the cleanup crew had somehow missed. This old-fashioned dedication has paid off. Since opening day in 1955, Disneyland has been a consistent moneymaker.

Disney World in Orlando, Florida

By the time Eisner arrived, Disney World in Orlando was already on its way to becoming what it is today—the most popular vacation destination in the United States. But the company had neglected a rich niche in its business: hotels. Disney's three existing hotels, probably the most profitable in the United States, registered unheard-of occupancy rates of 92 percent to 96 percent versus 66 percent for the industry. Eisner promptly embarked on an ambitious $1 billion hotel expansion plan. Two major hotels, Disney's Grand Floridian Beach Resort and Disney's Caribbean Beach Resort, were opened during 1987–89. Disney's Yacht Club and Beach Resort along with the Dolphin and Swan Hotels, owned and operated by Tishman Realty & Construction, Metropolitan Life Insurance, and Aoki Corporation, opened during 1989–90. Adding 3,400 hotel rooms and 250,000 square feet of convention space made it the largest convention center east of the Mississippi.

In October 1982, Disney made a new addition to the theme park—the Experimental Prototype Community of Tomorrow, or EPCOT Center. E. Cardon Walker, then president of the company, announced that EPCOT would be a "permanent showcase, industrial park, and experimental housing center." This new park consists of two large complexes: Future World, a series of pavilions designed to show the technological advances of the next 25 years, and World Showcase, a collection of foreign "villages."

Tokyo Disneyland

It was Tokyo's nastiest winter day in four years. Arctic winds and 8 inches of snow lashed the city. Roads were clogged and trains slowed down. But the bad weather didn't keep 13,200 hardy souls from Tokyo Disneyland. Mikki Mausu, better known outside Japan as Mickey Mouse, had taken the country by storm.

Located on a fringe of reclaimed shoreline in Urayasu City on the outskirts of Tokyo, the park opened to the public on April 15, 1983. In less than one year, over 10 million people had passed through its gates, an attendance figure that has been bettered every single year. On August 13, 1983, 93,000 people helped set a one-day attendance record that easily eclipsed the old records established at the two parent U.S. parks. Four years later, records again toppled as the turnstiles clicked. The total this time: 111,500. By 1988, approximately 50 million people, or nearly half of Japan's population, had visited Tokyo Disneyland since its opening. The steady cash flow pushed revenues for fiscal year 1989 to $768 million, up 17 percent from 1988.

The 204-acre Tokyo Disneyland is owned and operated by Oriental Land under license from the Walt Disney Co. The 45-year contract gives Disney 10 percent of admissions and 5 percent of food and merchandise sales, plus licensing fees. Disney opted to take no equity in the project and put no money down for construction. "I never had the slightest doubt about the success of Disneyland in Japan," said Masatomo Takahashi, president of Oriental Land Company. Oriental Land was so confident of the success of Disney in Japan that it financed the park entirely with debt, borrowing ¥180 billion ($1.5 billion at February 1988 exchange rates). Takahashi added, "The debt means nothing to me," and with good reason. According to Fusahao Awata, who co-authored a book on Tokyo Disneyland: "The Japanese yearn for [American culture]."

Soon after Tokyo Disneyland opened in April 1983, five Shinto priests held a solemn dedication ceremony near Cinderella's castle. It is the only overtly Japanese ritual seen so far in this sprawling theme park. What visitors see is pure Americana. All signs are in English, with only small katakana (a phonetic Japanese alphabet) translations. Most of the food is American style, and the attractions are cloned from Disney's U.S. parks. Disney also held firm on two fundamentals that strike the Japanese as strange—no alcohol is allowed and no food may be brought in from outside the park.

However, in Disney's enthusiasm to make Tokyo a brick-by-brick copy of Anaheim's Magic Kingdom, there were a few glitches. On opening day, the Tokyo park discovered that almost 100 public telephones were placed too high for Japanese guests to reach them comfortably. And many

Exhibit 1   How the Theme Parks Grew

1955	Disneyland
1966	Walt Disney's death
1971	Walt Disney World in Orlando
1982	Epcot Center
1983	Tokyo Disneyland
1992	Euro Disneyland

Source: Stephen Koepp, "Do You Believe in Magic?" *Time,* April 25, 1988, pp. 66–73.

Exhibit 2   Investor's Snapshot: The Walt Disney Company (December 1989)

Sales (latest four quarters)	$4.6 billion
Change from year earlier	Up 33.6%
Net profit	$703.3 million
Change	Up 34.7%
Return on common stockholders' equity	23.4%
Five-year average	20.3%
Stock price average (last 12 months)	$60.50–$136.25
Recent share price	$122.75
Price/Earnings Multiple	27
Total return to investor (12 months to 11/3/89)	90.6%

Source: Fortune, December 4, 1989.

hungry customers found countertops above their reach at the park's snack stands.

"Everything we imported that worked in the United States works here," said Ronald D. Pogue, managing director of Walt Disney Attractions Japan Ltd. "American things like McDonald's hamburgers and Kentucky Fried Chicken are popular here with young people. We also wanted visitors from Japan and Southeast Asia to feel they were getting the real thing," said Toshiharu Akiba, a staff member of the Oriental Land publicity department.

Still, local sensibilities dictated a few changes. A Japanese restaurant was added to please older patrons. The Nautilus submarine is missing. More areas are covered to protect against rain and snow. Lines for attractions had to be redesigned so that people walking through the park did not cross in front of patrons waiting to ride an attraction. "It's very discourteous in Japan to have people cross in front of somebody else," explained James B. Cora, managing director of operations for the Tokyo project. The biggest differences between Japan and America have come in slogans and ad copy. Although English is often used, it's "Japanized" English—the sort that would have native speakers shaking their heads while the Japanese nod happily in recognition. "Let's Spring" was the motto for one of their highly successful ad campaigns.

Pogue, visiting frequently from his base in California, supervised seven resident American Disney managers who work side by side with Japanese counterparts from Oriental Land Co. to keep the park in tune with the Disney doctrine. American it may be, but Tokyo Disneyland appeals to such deep-seated Japanese passions as cleanliness, order, outstanding service, and technological wizardry. Japanese executives are impressed by Disney's detailed training manuals, which teach employees how to make visitors feel like VIPs. Most worth emulating, say the Japanese, is Disney's ability to make even the lowliest job seem glamorous. "They have changed the image of dirty work," said Hakuhodo Institute's Sekizawa.

Disney Company did encounter a few unique cultural problems when developing Tokyo Disneyland:

> *The problem:* how to dispose of some 250 tons of trash that would be generated weekly by Tokyo Disneyland visitors?
> *The standard Disney solution:* trash compactors.
> *The Japanese proposal:* pigs to eat the trash and be slaughtered and sold at a profit.

James B. Cora and his team of some 150 operations experts did a little calculating and pointed out that it would take 100,000 pigs to do the job. And then there would be the smell . . .

The Japanese relented.

The Japanese were also uneasy about a rustic-looking Westernland, Tokyo's version of Frontierland. "The Japanese like everything fresh and new when they put it in," said Cora. "They kept painting the wood and we kept saying, 'No, it's got to look old.'" Finally the Disney crew took the Japanese to Anaheim to give them a firsthand look at the Old West.

Tokyo Disneyland opened just as the yen escalated in value against the dollar, and the income level of the Japanese registered a phenomenal improvement. During this era of affluence, Tokyo Disneyland triggered an interest in leisure. Its great success spurred the construction of "leisurelands" throughout the country. This created an increase in the Japanese people's orientation toward leisure. But demographics are the real key to Tokyo Disneyland's success. Thirty million Japanese live within 30 miles of the park. There are three times more than the number of people in the same proximity to Anaheim's Disneyland. With the park proven such an unqualified hit, and nearing capacity, Oriental Land and Disney mapped out plans for a version of the Disney-MGM studio tour next door. This time, Disney talked about taking a 50 percent stake in the project.

Building Euro Disneyland

On March 24, 1987, Michael Eisner and Jacques Chirac, the French prime minister, signed a contract for the building of a Disney theme park at Marne-la-Vallee. Talks between Disney and the French government had dragged on for more than a year. At the signing, Robert Fitzpatrick, fluent in French, married to the former Sylvie Blondet, and the recipient of two awards from the French government, was introduced as the president of Euro Disneyland. He was expected to be a key player in wooing

Exhibit 3   **Chronology of the Euro Disneyland Deal**

1984–85	Disney negotiates with Spain and France to create a European theme park. Chooses France as the site.
1987	Disney signs letter of intent with the French government.
1988	Selects lead commercial bank lenders for the senior portion of the project. Forms the Société en Nom Collectif (SNC). Begins planning for the equity offering of 51% of Euro Disneyland as required in the letter of intent.
1989	European press and stock analysts visit Walt Disney World in Orlando. Begin extensive news and television campaign. Stock starts trading at 20–25 percent premium from the issue price.

Source: Geraldine E. Willigan, "The Value-Adding CFO: An Interview with Disney's Gary Wilson," *Harvard Business Review*, January–February 1990, pp. 85–93.

Disney World in Florida as part of an 'American experience,'" said Patrick P. Roper, marketing director of Alton Towers, a successful British theme park near Manchester. He doubted they would seek the suburbs of Paris as eagerly as America and predicted attendance would trail Disney projections. Exhibit 3 summarizes the history and major milestones of Euro Disneyland.

The Layout of Euro Disneyland

Euro Disneyland is determinedly American in its theme. There was an alcohol ban in the park despite the attitude among the French that wine with a meal is a God-given right. Designers presented a plan for a Main Street USA based on scenes of America in the 1920s because research indicated that Europeans loved the Prohibition era. Eisner decreed that images of gangsters and speakeasies were too negative. Though made more ornate and Victorian than Walt Disney's idealized Midwestern small town, Main Street remained Main Street. Steamships leave from Main Street through the Grand Canyon Diorama en route to Frontierland.

The familiar Disney Tomorrowland, with its dated images of the space age, was jettisoned entirely. It was replaced by a gleaming brass and wood complex called Discoverland, which was based on themes of Jules Verne and Leonardo da Vinci. Eisner ordered $8 or $10 million in extras to the "Visionarium" exhibit, a 360-degree movie about French culture that was required by the French in their original contract. French and English are the official languages at the park, and multilingual guides are available to help Dutch, German, Spanish, and Italian visitors.

With the American Wild West being so frequently captured on film, Europeans have their own idea of what life was like back then. Frontierland reinforces those images. A runaway mine train takes guests through the canyons and mines of Gold Rush country. There is a paddle-wheel steamboat reminiscent of Mark Twain, Indian explorer canoes, and a phantom manor from the Gold Rush days.

In Fantasyland, designers strived to avoid competing with the nearby European reality of actual medieval towns, cathedrals, and chateaux. While Disneyland's castle is based on Germany's Neuschwanstein and Disney World's is based on a Loire Valley chateau, Euro Disney's *Le Château de la Belle au Bois Dormant*, as the French insisted Sleeping Beauty be called, is more cartoonlike with stained glass windows built by English craftspeople and depicting Disney characters. Fanciful trees grow inside as well as a beanstalk.

The park is criss-crossed with covered walkways. Eisner personally ordered the installation of 35 fireplaces in hotels and restaurants. "People walk around Disney World in Florida with humidity and temperatures in the 90s and they walk into an air-conditioned ride and say, 'This is the greatest,'" said Eisner. "When it's raining and miserable, I hope they will walk into one of these lobbies with the fireplace going and say the same thing."

Children all over Europe were primed to consume. Even one of the intellectuals who contributed to *Le Figaro*'s Disney-bashing broadsheet was forced to admit with resignation that his 10-year-old son "swears by Michael Jackson." At Euro Disneyland, under the name "Captain EO," Disney just so happened to have a Michael Jackson attraction awaiting him.

Food Service and Accommodations at Euro Disneyland

Disney expected to serve 15,000 to 17,000 meals per hour, excluding snacks. Menus and service systems were developed so that they varied in both style and price. There is a 400-seat buffeteria, 6 table service restaurants, 12 counter service units, 10 snack bars, 1 Discovery food court seating 850, 9 popcorn wagons, 15 ice-cream carts, 14 specialty food carts, and 2 employee cafeterias. Restaurants were, in fact, to be a showcase for American foods. The only exception to this is Fantasyland, which recreates European fables. Here, food service will reflect the fable's country of origin: Pinocchio's facility having German food; Cinderella's, French; Bella Notte's, Italian; and so on.

Of course recipes were adapted for European tastes. Because many Europeans don't care much for very spicy food, Tex-Mex recipes were toned down. A special coffee blend had to be developed that would have universal appeal. Hot dog carts would reflect the regionalism of American tastes. There would be a ball park hot dog (mild, steamed, a mixture of beef and pork), a New York hot dog (all beef, and spicy), and a Chicago hot dog (Vienna-style, similar to bratwurst).

Euro Disneyland has six theme hotels, which would offer nearly 5,200 rooms on opening day; a campground (444 rental trailers and 181 camping sites); and single-family homes on the periphery of the 27-hole golf course. Exhibit 4 provides an overview of the size, and main features of Euro Disneyland. Exhibit 5 compares daily pass and accommodation prices of Euro Disneyland with Disney World Orlando.

Exhibit 4 **The Euro Disneyland Resort**

5,000 acres in size

30 attractions

12,000 employees

6 hotels (with 5,184 rooms)

10 theme restaurants

414 cabins

181 camping sites

Source: Roger Cohen, "Threat of Strikes in Euro Disney Debut," *New York Times*, April 10, 1992, p. 20.

Disney's Strict Appearance Code

Antoine Guervil stood at his post in front of the 1,000-room Cheyenne Hotel at Euro Disneyland, practicing his "Howdy!" When Guervil, a political refugee from Haiti, said the word, it sounded more like "Audi." Native French speakers have trouble with the aspirated "h" sound in words like "hay" and "Hank" and "howdy." Guervil had been given the job of wearing a cowboy costume and booming a happy, welcoming howdy to guests as they entered the Cheyenne, styled after a Western movie set.

"Audi," said Guervil, the strain of linguistic effort showing on his face. This was clearly a struggle. Unless things got better, it was not hard to imagine objections from Renault, the French car company that was one of the corporate sponsors of the park. Picture the rage of a French auto executive arriving with his or her family at the Renault-sponsored Euro Disneyland, only to hear the doorman of a Disney hotel advertising a German car.

Such were the problems Disney faced while hiring some 12,000 people to maintain and populate its Euro Disneyland theme park. A handbook of detailed rules on acceptable clothing, hairstyles, and jewelry, among other things, embroiled the company in a legal and cultural dispute. Critics asked how the brash Americans could be so insensitive to French culture, individualism, and privacy. Disney officials insisted that a ruling that barred them from imposing a squeaky-clean employment standard could threaten the image and long-term success of the park.

"For us, the appearance code has a real effect from a product identification standpoint," said Thor Degelmann, vice president for human resources for Euro Disneyland. "Without it we wouldn't be presenting the Disney product that people would be expecting."

The rules, spelled out in a video presentation and detailed in a guide handbook, went beyond height and weight standards. They required men's hair to be cut above the collar and ears with no beards or mustaches. Any tattoos must be covered. Women must keep their hair in one "natural color" with no frosting or streaking, and they may make only limited use of makeup like mascara. False eyelashes, eyeliners, and eye pencil were completely off limits. Fingernails can't pass the end of the fingers. As for jewelry, women can wear only one earring in each ear, with the earring's diameter no more than three-quarters of an inch. Neither men nor women can wear more than one ring on each hand. Further, women were required to wear appropriate undergarments and only transparent panty hose, not black or anything with fancy designs. Though a daily bath was not specified in the rules, the applicant's video depicted a shower scene and informed applicants that they were expected to show up for work "fresh and clean each day." Similar rules are in force at Disney's three other theme parks in the United States and Japan.

In the United States, some labor unions representing Disney employees have occasionally protested the company's strict appearance code, but with little success. French labor unions began protesting when Disneyland opened its "casting center" and invited applicants to "play the role of [their lives]" and to take a "unique opportunity to marry work and magic." The CGT handed out leaflets in front of the center to warn applicants of the appearance code, which they believed represented "an attack on individual liberty." A more mainstream union, the Confédération Française Démocratique du Travail (CFDT), appealed to the Labor Ministry to halt Disney's violation of "human dignity." French law prohibits employers from restricting individual and collective liberties unless the restrictions can be justified by the nature of the task to be accomplished and are proportional to that end.

Degelmann, however, said that the company was "well aware of the cultural differences" between the United States and France and as a result had "toned down" the wording in the original American version of the guidebook. He pointed out that many companies, particularly airlines, maintained appearance codes just as strict. "We happened to put ours in writing," he added. In any case, he said that he knew of no one who had refused to take the job because of the rules and that no more than 5 percent of the people showing up for interviews had decided not to proceed after watching the video, which also detailed transportation and salary.

Fitzpatrick also defended the dress code, although he conceded that Disney might have been a little naive in presenting things so directly. He added, "Only in France is there still a communist party. There is not even one in Russia any more. The ironic thing is that I could fill the park with CGT requests for tickets."

Another big challenge lay in getting the mostly French "cast members," as Disney calls its employees, to break their ancient cultural aversions to smiling and being consistently polite to park guests. The individualistic French had to be molded into the squeaky-clean Disney image. Rival theme parks in the area, loosely modeled on the Disney system, had already encountered trouble keeping smiles on the faces of the staff, who sometimes took on the demeanor of subway ticket clerks.

The delicate matter of hiring French citizens as opposed to other nationals was examined in the more than two-year-long preagreement negotiations between the French govern-

Other Asian Ventures

The Walt Disney Company has also looked into building other theme parks and resorts in Asia. Based on its successful operation of two theme parks in the United States (at Anaheim and Orlando), Disney believes that it can have more than one park per region. Another strategically located park in Asia, officials agreed, would not compete with Tokyo Disneyland, Hong Kong Disneyland, or Shanghai Disneyland, but rather bring in a new set of customers.

One such strategic location is the state of Johor in Malaysia. Malaysian officials wanted to develop Johor in order to rival its neighbor, Singapore, as a tourist attraction. (Two large casinos were built in Singapore in 2006.) However, Disney claimed to have no existing plans or discussions for building a park in Malaysia. Alannah Goss, a spokeswoman for Disney's Asian operations based in Hong Kong, said, "We are constantly evaluating strategic markets in the world to grow our park and resort business and the Disney brand. We continue to evaluate markets but at this time, we have no plans to announce regarding a park in Malaysia."[34]

Singapore, in its effort to expand its tourism industry, had also expressed interest in being host to the next Disneyland theme park. Although rumors of a Singapore Disneyland were quickly dismissed, some reports suggested there were exploratory discussions of locations at either Marina East or Seletar. Residents of Singapore expressed concern that the park would not be competitive, even against the smaller-scale Hong Kong Disneyland. Their primary fears included limited attractions (based on size and local regulations), hot weather, and high ticket prices.

Disney's Future in Asia

Although Disney is wise to enter the Asian market with its new theme parks, it still faces many obstacles. One is finding the right location. Lee Hoon, professor of tourism management at Yanyang University in Seoul, noted, "Often, more important than content is whether a venue is located in a metropolis, whether it's easily accessible by public transportation." Often tied to issues of location is the additional threat of competition, both from local attractions and from those of other international corporations. It seems that Asian travelers are loyal to their local attractions, evidenced by the success of South Korea's Everland theme park and Hong Kong's own Ocean Park (which brought in more visitors than Hong Kong Disneyland in 2006).[35] The stiff competition of the theme park industry in Asia will center on not only which park can create a surge of interest in its first year but also which can build a loyal base of repeat customers.

Despite its already large size, the Asian theme park industry is still developing. Disney officials will need to be innovative and strategic in order to maintain sales. Existing theme parks in the region have proven that a carefully crafted strategy can lead to increased sales; after a 20 percent drop in attendance in the early 2000s, Universal Studios in Japan was able to rebound to record growth in 2015 by introducing new innovative attractions, including a Harry Potter-themed area within the park and a multiple-month-long Anime event.[36]

In spite of underperformance of some theme parks, Asia is still viewed by many as the most attractive region for the entertainment industry. Attendance may be stagnating in some parts of the world, but a growing middle class with disposable incomes to match is making the Asia-Pacific region a prime target for investors and theme park owners. "China will lead the way," said Kelven Tan, Southeast Asia's representative for the International Association of Amusement Parks and Attractions, an industry group. "The critical mass really came about with the resurgence of China. You need a good source of people; you also need labor and you need cheap land."[37]

That's what the people behind the Universal Studios in Singapore are betting. Developers aim to tap the wallets of Singapore's 4.6 million residents and 9.7 million tourists a year and its proximity to populous areas of Indonesia and southern Malaysia. Opening in spring of 2010, it became the island nation's first bona fide amusement park. Outside this and other foreign brands like Legoland, which opened parks in Johor, Malaysia, in 2012 and in Dubai, UAE, in 2016, home-grown companies like Genting in Malaysia and OTC Enterprise Corp. in China are aggressively looking to take advantage of the burgeoning market in their backyards.[38]

Overall spending on entertainment and media in Asia Pacific is set to increase to over US$700 billion by 2019, doubling the amount spent just ten years earlier, according to a 2015 report by McKinsey. By 2019, Asia Pacific will account for over 40 percent of global spending on entertainment and media.[39] "It's an up-and-coming market, and growing quite fast," said Christian Aaen, Hong Kong–based regional director for AECOM Economics, a consulting firm that specializes in the entertainment and leisure industries. MGM Studios and Paramount, too, are scouting around Asia for future projects.

In light of these optimistic projections, it is reasonable to assume that Disney may consider expansion to other Asian countries such as Malaysia, South Korea, or Singapore, where Disney appeared to have seriously considered a park. Given that the Hong Kong and Shanghai park future expansions are on track, Disney now has the experience and motivation to further penetrate the Asian region. In this regard, Disney has opened English language learning centers across China.[40] This could constitute a broader push by Disney to establish a strong Asian presence across its businesses and brands, a move that would undoubtedly involve the theme park operations as a central component.

Questions for Review

1. What cultural challenges are posed by Disney's expansion into Asia? How are these different from those in Europe?

2. How do cultural variables influence the location choice of theme parks around the world?

3. Why was Disney's Shanghai theme park so controversial? What are the risks and benefits of this project? What do you think is the likelihood that it will "cannibalize" the Hong Kong park?

4. What location would you recommend for Disney's next theme park in Asia? Why?

Source: This case was prepared by Courtney Asher under the supervision of Professor Jonathan Doh of Villanova University as the basis for class discussion. Additional research assistance was provided by Benjamin Littell. It is not intended to illustrate either effective or ineffective managerial capability or administrative responsibility.

ENDNOTES

1. Raymond H. Lopez, "Disney in Asia, Again?" March 2002, http://appserv.pace.edu/emplibrary/FINAL.Asiacasestudy.doc.

2. Ibid.

3. Thomas Crampton, "Disney's New Hong Kong Park to Be 'Culturally Sensitive': Mickey Mouse Learns Chinese," *International Herald Tribune*, January 13, 2003, www.iht.com/articles/2003/01/13/disney_ed3__0.php.

4. Michael Schuman, "Disney's Hong Kong Headache," *Time*, May 8, 2006, www.time.com/time/magazine/article/0,9171,501060515-1191881,00.html.

5. Kim Soyoung and George Chen, "Hollywood Chases Asia Theme Park Rainbow," *Reuters BusinessNews*, May 23, 2007, www.reuters.com/article/businesspro-hollywood-studios-asia-dc-idUSSEO35257720070523.

6. Chuan Xu and Nicole Liu, "Hong Kong Disneyland Reports Loss for 2015 as Number of Visitors Drops," *Los Angeles Times*, February 16, 2016, www.latimes.com/entertainment/envelope/cotown/la-et-ct-hong-kong-disneyland-loss-20160216-story.html.

7. "Cuts Cloud Hong Kong Disneyland Expansion," *Financial Times*, March 17, 2009, https://www.ft.com/content/c59c5a72-12bb-11de-9848-0000779fd2ac.

8. "Hong Kong Disneyland's Future Is in Danger," *BusinessWeek*, March 17, 2009, http://www.bloomberg.com/news/articles/2009-03-17/hong-kong-disneylands-future-is-in-danger.

9. Ibid.

10. "Disney Puts Hong Kong Expansion on Hold," *Reuters*, March 16, 2009, www.reuters.com/article/industryNews/idUSTRE52G0I120090317.

11. "Hong Kong Disneyland's Future Is in Danger."

12. Ibid.

13. "Disney, Hong Kong Reach $465m Expansion Deal," *China Daily*, June 30, 2009, www.chinadaily.com.cn/china/2009-06/30/content_8338445.htm.

14. Ricky Brigante, "Mystic Point Grand Opening Celebrated at Hong Kong Disneyland with Debut of Groundbreaking Mystic Manor Dark Ride," *Inside the Magic*, May 16, 2013, www.insidethemagic.net/2013/05/mystic-point-grand-opening-celebrated-at-hong-kong-disneyland-with-debut-of-groundbreaking-mystic-manor-dark-ride/.

15. Lopez, "Disney in Asia, Again?"

16. Tammy Tam, "China's Two Disneylands: Competitors or Complementary Attractions?" *South China Morning Post*, January 31, 2016, www.scmp.com/news/hong-kong/economy/article/1907607/chinas-two-disneylands-competitors-or-complementary.

17. "Disney's Shanghai Park Plan in Doubt: Company Mulls Move to Another Location in China," *NBCNews.com*, December 11, 2006, www.nbcnews.com/id/16153207/ns/business-world_business/t/disneys-shanghai-park-plan-doubt/#.WDJZb-YrKUk.

18. J. T. Areddy and P. Sanders, "Disney's Shanghai Park Plan Advances," *The Wall Street Journal*, January 12, 2009, p. A1.

19. Ibid.

20. "The Speculation Ends—Shanghai Disney Ready to Roll," January 13, 2009, *CN News*, www.china.org.cn/business/news/2009-01/13/content_17101032.htm.

21. "Walt Disney, Shanghai Propose New Theme Park in China (Update 1)," *Bloomberg*, January 9, 2009, www.bloomberg.com/apps/news?pid=20601080&sid=atGa2ymXAMM8&refer=asia.

22. Areddy and Sanders, "Disney's Shanghai Park Plan Advances."

23. Samuel Shen and Sue Zeidler, "Disney Takes China Stride as Shanghai Park Gets Nod," *Reuters*, November 4, 2009, www.reuters.com/article/idUSTRE5A31TC20091104.

24. "Shanghai Disney to Get Approved Land in July," *China Daily*, April 4, 2010, www.chinadaily.com.cn/china/2010–04/14/content_9730662.htm.

25. Thomas Smith, "Shanghai Disney Resort Groundbreaking Ceremony Marks Historic Day," *Disney,*

Exhibit 3 **Walmart International Retail Unit Count (2001–2006)**

Country	2001	2002	2003	2004	2005	2006
Argentina	11	11	11	11	11	11
Brazil	20	22	22	25	149	295
Canada	174	196	213	235	262	278
China	11	19	26	34	43	56
Germany	94	95	94	92	91	88
Japan	0	0	0	0	0	398
Mexico	499	551	597	623	679	774
Puerto Rico	15	17	52	53	54	54
UK	241	250	258	267	282	315
South Korea	6	9	15	15	16	16
Total	1,071	1,170	1,288	1,355	1,587	2,285

Source: Walmart Annual Reports for fiscal years 2001, 2002, 2003, 2004, 2005, 2006.

business represents a solid chunk of Walmart's overall $482 billion in revenue for the fiscal year 2015.[7]

With a market capitalization of more than $200 billion in 2016, Walmart is worth as much as the gross domestic product of Algeria. Four of America's 10 richest individuals are from Walmart's low-profile Walton family, which still owns a 40 percent controlling stake. The company's portfolio ranges from superstores in the U.S. to neighborhood markets in Brazil, bodegas in Mexico, the ASDA supermarket chain in Britain, Japan's nationwide network of Seiyu shops, and a controlling stake in South African retailer Massmart. Walmart sources many of its products from low-cost Chinese suppliers. The pressure group China Labour Watch estimates that if it were a country, Walmart would rank as China's seventh largest trading partner, just ahead of the U.K., spending more than $18 billion annually on Chinese goods.[8]

Walmart Early Internationalization

In venturing beyond its large domestic market, Walmart had a number of regional options, including entering Europe, Asia, or other countries in the Western hemisphere. (See Exhibits 3 and 4.) At the time, however, Walmart lacked the requisite financial, organizational, and managerial resources to pursue multiple countries simultaneously. Instead, it opted for a logically sequenced approach to market entry that would allow it to apply the learning gained from its initial entries to subsequent ones. In the end, during the first five years of its globalization (1991 to 1995), Walmart decided to concentrate heavily on establishing a presence in the Americas: Mexico, Brazil, Argentina, and Canada. Obviously, Canada had the business environment closest to the U.S. and appeared to be the easiest entry destination. The other countries that Walmart chose as its first global points of entry—

Exhibit 4 **Walmart International Retail Unit Count (2006–2015)**

Country	2007	2008	2009	2010	2011	2012	2013	2014	2015
Argentina	13	21	28	43	63	88	94	104	105
Brazil	299	313	345	434	479	512	558	556	557
Canada	289	305	318	317	325	333	379	389	394
Chile	0	0	197	252	279	316	329	380	404
China	73	202	243	279	328	370	393	405	411
Costa Rica	137	149	164	170	180	200	205	214	217
El Salvador	63	70	77	77	78	79	80	83	89
Guatemala	132	145	160	164	175	200	206	209	217
Honduras	41	47	50	53	56	70	72	75	81
India	0	0	0	1	5	15	20	20	20
Japan	392	394	371	371	414	419	438	438	431
Mexico	889	1,023	1,197	1,469	1,730	2,088	2,353	2,199	2,290
Nicaragua	40	46	51	55	60	73	79	80	86
Puerto Rico	54	54	56	56	55	56	55	56	55
UK	335	352	358	371	385	541	565	576	592
Total	2,757	3,121	3,615	4,112	4,612	5,360	5,826	5,784	5,949

Source: Walmart Annual Reports for fiscal years 2007, 2008, 2009, 2010, 2011, 2012, 2013, 2014, 2015.

Mexico (1991), Brazil (1994), and Argentina (1995)—were those with the three largest populations in Latin America.[9]

The European market had certain characteristics that made it less attractive to Walmart as a first point of entry. The European retail industry was mature, implying that a new entrant would have to take market share away from an existing player—a very difficult task. Additionally, there were well-entrenched competitors on the scene (e.g., Carrefour in France and Metro A.G. in Germany) that would likely retaliate vigorously against any new player. Further, as with most newcomers, Walmart's relatively small size and lack of strong local customer relationships would be severe handicaps in the European arena. In addition, the higher growth rates of Latin American and Asian markets would have made a delayed entry into those markets extremely costly in terms of lost opportunities. In contrast, the opportunity costs of delaying acquisition-based entries into European markets appeared to be relatively small.[10]

While the Asian markets had huge potential when Walmart launched its globalization effort in 1991, they were the most distant geographically and different culturally and logistically from the U.S. market. It would have taken considerable financial and managerial resources to establish a presence in Asia.[11] However, by 1996, Walmart felt ready to take on the Asian challenge and it targeted China. This choice made sense in that the lower purchasing power of the Chinese consumer offered huge potential to a low-price retailer like Walmart. Still, China's cultural, linguistic, and geographical distance from the United States presented relatively high entry barriers, so Walmart decided to use two beachheads as learning vehicles for establishing an Asian presence.[12]

During 1992–93, Walmart agreed to sell low-priced products to two Japanese retailers, Ito-Yokado and Yaohan, that would market these products in Japan, Singapore, Hong Kong, Malaysia, Thailand, Indonesia, and the Philippines. Then, in 1994, Walmart entered Hong Kong through a joint venture with the C.P. Pokphand Company, a Thailand-based conglomerate, to open three Value Club membership discount stores in Hong Kong.[13]

Success in Mexico and China

Overall, Walmart has had a very successful experience in Mexico. In 1991 Walmart entered into a joint venture with retail conglomerate Cifra and opened a Sam's Club in Mexico City. In 1997 it gained a majority position in the company and in 2001 changed the store name to Walmart de Mexico, or, more commonly, "Wal-Mex." In addition to its 256 Walmart Supercenters and 161 Sam's Club warehouses, Wal-Mex also operates Bodega food and general merchandise discount stores, Superama supermarkets, and Suburbia apparel stores. The majority of its stores are located in and around Mexico City; however, it does business in over 145 cities throughout Mexico. Opening nearly 100 stores in 2015, Wal-Mex has shown no signs of slowing down. As of 2016, it operated over 2,200 stores in Mexico.[14]

The rapid growth of Wal-Mex over the last decade has not been problem-free. A 2012 report by the *New York Times* uncovered widespread bribery occurring at the Wal-Mex executive level, resulting in a three-year-long corruption investigation by the U.S. Justice Department. According to the *New York Times* report, a senior Walmart lawyer was contacted by a former executive at Walmart de Mexico in September 2005. In the e-mail and follow-up conversations, the former executive (later identified as the lawyer in charge of obtaining construction permits for Walmart de Mexico) indicated that Walmart de Mexico had paid bribes for permits throughout the country to fuel growth prospects. In response, Walmart dispatched investigators to Mexico City. Those investigators found overwhelming evidence of bribery and hundreds of suspect payments totaling more than US$24 million. The investigation also found that Walmart de Mexico's top executives had taken steps to conceal the evidence from Walmart's headquarters.[15] Shortly after the investigation commenced, Walmart warned shareholders that its reputation could be affected by the bribery scandal. Shares dropped by 5 percent in April 2015, representing approximately US$10 billion in value. Walmart noted that inquiries from media and law enforcement could affect the "perception among certain audiences of its role as a corporate citizen."[16] Between 2012 and 2015, roughly two dozen representatives from the U.S. Justice Department, FBI, SEC, and IRS became involved in the investigation.[17] In the wake of the investigation and bribery charges, Walmart has created a new executive position to ensure that all Walmart employees are complying with the U.S. Foreign Corrupt Practices Act.[18]

In late 2006 the company was also approved by Mexico's Finance Ministry to open its own bank. In a country where 75 percent of citizens have never had a bank account due to high fees, "Banco Walmart de Mexico Adelante" added much-needed competition to the financial services industry and offered consumers lower fees than traditional banks.[19] In November 2007, Wal-Mex opened its first consumer bank, Banco Walmart, in Toluca; by December 2014, the company had opened branches in 2,100 stores. Banco Walmart especially targeted the low-income market in a country where just 24 percent of households have savings accounts, compared with 55 percent in Chile. In the short term, this strategy included luring newcomers with easy instructions and entry points, like minimum balances of less than $5 and no commissions, compared with $100 minimums at competing banks. Long term, Wal-Mex's plans included boosting sales via debit cards and easing users into more profitable services like insurance. In 2014 alone, credit card sales

https://www.gfmag.com/magazine/january-2006/milestones--wal-mart-bets-big-on-brazils-market-.

45. Brad Haynes and Nathan Layne, "Insight: Lost in Translation—Wal-Mart Stumbles Hard in Brazil," *Reuters*, February 17, 2016, www.reuters.com/article/us-walmart-brazil-idUSKCN0VQ0EQ.

46. Boyle, "Walmart's Painful Lessons."

47. Ibid.

48. Ibid.

49. Krystina Gustafson and Courtney Reagan, "Wal-Mart to Close 269 Stores as It Retools Fleet," *CNBC*, January 15, 2016, www.cnbc.com/2016/01/15/wal-mart-to-close-269-stores-as-it-retools-fleet.html.

50. Ibid.

51. Laurie Burkitt, "Wal-Mart Says It Will Go Slow in China," *The Wall Street Journal*, April 29, 2015, www.wsj.com/articles/wal-mart-to-open-115-stores-in-china-by-2017-1430270579?cb=logged0.09944356285914002.

52. Ibid.

53. Shashank Bengali, "Wal-Mart, Thwarted by India's Retail Restrictions, Goes Big: Wholesale," *Los Angeles Times*, July 23, 2015, www.latimes.com/world/asia/la-fg-india-walmart-20150723-story.html.

54. Ibid.

55. Shivani Shinde Nadhe, "Walmart Eyes $300-mn Investment by 2020," *Business Standard*, February 17, 2016, www.business-standard.com/article/companies/walmart-chalks-out-expansion-plans-for-india-116021600459_1.html.

56. Kurumi Fukushima, "Wal-mart Renews India Wholesale Expansion, Plans 50 New Stores by 2020," *The Street*, August 12, 2015, www.thestreet.com/story/13253722/1/wal-mart-renews-india-wholesale-expansion-plans-50-new-stores-by-2020.html.

57. Walmart Canada, www.walmartcanada.ca/about-us/.

58. "Walmart Canada Announces Expansion Plans; Retailer Continues to Accelerate Food and E-Commerce Growth," *Walmart*, February 11, 2015, http://corporate.walmart.com/_news_/news-archive/2015/02/11/walmart-canada-announces-expansion-plans-retailer-continues-to-accelerate-food-and-e-commerce-growth.

59. Ibid.

60. Phil Wahba, "Target's Loss Is Wal-Mart's Gain in Canada," *Fortune*, May 8, 2015, http://fortune.com/2015/05/08/walmart-target-canada/.

61. Tiisetso Motsoeneng, "Wal-Mart Makes Slow Progress Navigating Africa's Challenges," *Reuters*, June 2, 2015, www.reuters.com/article/us-wal-mart-stores-africa-idUSKBN0OI12V20150602.

62. "Massmart Announces Plans to Expand to Angola," *Ventures*, April 9, 2014, http://venturesafrica.com/massmart-announces-plans-to-expand-to-angola/.

63. Yomi Kazeem, "Walmart Is Planning to Open Retail Outlets in Nigeria," *Quartz*, July 31, 2015, http://qz.com/469407/walmart-is-planning-to-open-retail-outlets-in-nigeria/.

64. Phil Wahba, "In 2015, Amazon Ate Even More of Walmart's Lunch," *Fortune*, December 22, 2015, http://fortune.com/2015/12/22/retail-ecommerce-2015-amazon-walmart/.

65. Madeline Vuong, "Walmart's E-commerce Growth Slows to 8% as Amazon Soars to Record Sales," *Geek Wire*, February 18, 2016, www.geekwire.com/2016/walmart-and-amazon-face-off-over-online-retail-market/.

66. Mathew Mosk, "Walmart Fires Supplier after Bangladesh Revelation," *ABC News Blotter*, May 15, 2013, http://abcnews.go.com/Blotter/wal-mart-fires-supplier-bangladesh-revelation/story?id=19188673#.Ua3fGEC7Itg.

67. Ulfikar Ali Manik and Jim Yardley, "Another Garment Factory Scare in Bangladesh," *New York Times*, June 14, 2013, p. A11.

68. Steven Greenhouse, "U.S. Retailers Announce Safety Plan," *New York Times*, May 31, 2013, p. B6.

69. Steven Greenhouse, "Obama to Suspend Trade Privileges with Bangladesh," *New York Times*, June 28, 2013, p. B1.

PART THREE

INTERNATIONAL
STRATEGIC
MANAGEMENT

Chapter 8

STRATEGY FORMULATION AND IMPLEMENTATION

OBJECTIVES OF THE CHAPTER

All major MNCs formulate and implement strategies that result from a careful analysis of both external and internal environments. In this process, an MNC will identify the market environment for its goods and services and then evaluate its ability and competitive advantage to capture the market. The success of this strategic planning effort will largely depend on accurate forecasting of the external environment and a realistic appraisal of internal company strengths and weaknesses. In recent years, MNCs have relied on their strategic plans to help refocus their efforts by abandoning old domestic markets and entering new global markets. This strategic global planning process has been critical in their drive to gain market share, increase profitability, and, in some cases, survive. Strategies can be formulated from any level of management, but middle management plays a key role in ensuring that decisions are put into subsequent action.

Chapter 5 addressed overall management across cultures. This chapter focuses on strategic management in the international context, and the basic steps by which a strategic plan is formulated and implemented are examined. The specific objectives of this chapter are

1. **DISCUSS** the meaning, needs, benefits, and approaches of the strategic planning process for today's MNCs.

2. **UNDERSTAND** the tension between pressures for global integration and national responsiveness and the four basic options for international strategies.

3. **IDENTIFY** the basic steps in strategic planning, including environmental scanning, internal resource analysis of the MNC's strengths and weaknesses, and goal formulation.

4. **DESCRIBE** how an MNC implements the strategic plan, such as how it chooses a site for overseas operations.

5. **REVIEW** the three major functions of marketing, production, and finance that are used in implementing a strategic plan.

6. **EXPLAIN** specialized strategies appropriate for emerging markets and international new ventures.

The World of *International Management*

GSK's Prescription for Global Growth

As the world's sixth largest pharmaceutical company, U.K.-based GlaxoSmithKline (GSK) is facing a rapidly changing pharmaceutical environment. The decades of large profit margins built on exclusive "blockbuster" drugs appear to be over. Patents are expiring at an increasing rate, undercutting "Big Pharma's" traditional pricing strategy. Growth in developed markets has slowed significantly, forcing drug companies to refocus their strategy on unfamiliar emerging marketplaces. Even the physical makeup of the pharmaceutical industry has changed as major pharmaceutical companies have acquired other firms from related industries, including generics and biotech companies. These changes mean that GSK's executives, as well as those at other "Big Pharma" companies, must craft a new global strategy to adapt to industry trends.

Pharmerging Markets

Like most other industries, emerging markets hold tremendous growth potential for the pharmaceutical industry. In recent years, GSK has made these markets, which the IMS has coined "pharmerging markets," a central focus of its long-term global sales strategy. By 2014, emerging markets accounted for over a quarter of GSK's revenue.[1]

By the end of 2017, the global market for pharmaceuticals is expected to reach US$1.20 trillion annually, up from US$965 billion five years prior. This sales growth is disproportionately coming from emerging markets. While the market for pharmaceuticals is expected to grow by 14 to 17 percent in China and 11 to 14 percent in India through the end of 2017, Western Europe and the U.S. will experience almost no growth in demand.[2] Furthermore, in developed markets with publicly funded health care plans, pressure by payers to curb drug spending growth will only intensify. To continue to maintain growth, pharmaceutical companies like GSK will have to increasingly depend on consumers in developing economies. The profit margins in the pharmerging markets, however, may be limited. Individuals with lower incomes may not be able to afford expensive medicines and many people do not have access to health insurance. Still, as the standard of living rises in emerging economies, pharmaceutical companies see potential in these markets.

Expanding into emerging markets is often accompanied by difficult growing pains; GSK has not been immune to these challenges. In the summer of 2013, GSK's Chinese operations were rocked by an unprecedented corruption and bribery scandal. Chinese investigations found evidence of widespread bribery of doctors, hospitals, and other medical professionals by GSK representatives. In the wake of the allegations, GSK's third- and fourth-quarter sales in China dropped by 61 and 29 percent respectively.[3] In 2014, the company was fined nearly US$500 million by Chinese authorities. Additionally, four executives were convicted of criminal offenses, with Mark Reilly, head of GSK's Chinese operations at the time, given a three-year suspended prison sentence and fired from the company.[4]

Destination India

For GSK, as well as its competitors, India stands out as a particularly attractive market. In 2014 alone, GSK invested US$1 billion to increase its ownership share of its Indian subsidiary from 50.7 percent to 75 percent.[5] Today, the company employs nearly 5,000 people in the country and holds a 4 percent share of the market.[6]

Though the potential for consumer growth is common to all pharmerging markets, India is also uniquely positioned for manufacturing. Attractive labor costs, along with a skilled workforce, make India perfect for research and development efforts, drug manufacturing, and drug delivery. Moving operations to India has become commonplace in the industry. In 2015, GSK announced plans to build a US$153 million plant near Bangalore. When completed, the facility will be GSK's sixth manufacturing facility in the country and will be capable of manufacturing eight billion tablets and one billion capsules every year.[7]

Today, the Indian pharmaceutical manufacturing industry is the world's third largest by volume.[8] Much of this manufacturing still comes from domestic companies. G.V. Prasad, chief executive of Dr. Reddy's Laboratories, told the *New York Times* that Indian drug makers have the "ability to handle product development on a massive scale at a low cost."[9] Dr. Reddy's diabetes drug has completed Phase 3 clinical trials, the last step before seeking FDA approval.[10] Despite holding a top position in drug manufacturing by volume, the Indian

pharmaceutical market ranks only 14th in revenue, indicating thin margins.[11]

GSK and its competitors in India are not without problems. Pfizer and Sanofi-Aventis both had to recall drugs made by their respective acquired firms in India. Also, the protection of intellectual property rights is an issue. According to *The New York Times:*

> Trying to change its outlaw image as a maker of illegal knock-offs, India toughened its patent laws in 2005. But dozens of intellectual property suits are still being fought between Indian and foreign firms in courts around the world. And big pharmaceutical companies still find securing protection of their intellectual property in India difficult.
>
> . . .
>
> "Cost is one issue, and yes it is important, but there are two other critical factors: intellectual property and quality and safety issues," said Panos Kalaritis, the chief operating officer of Irix Pharmaceuticals, a Florence, S.C., contract research and manufacturing company, which competes with Indian laboratories and factories.[12]

Pricing and profit margins remain a challenge. It was estimated that, in 2016, per capita pharmaceutical spending in the U.S. approached US$900 but stood at only US$33 in India.[13] While one could argue that this shows great potential for future revenue growth in the region, it also highlights the cultural and financial disparity between pharmerging markets, like India, and those in Europe, Japan, and the U.S. Foreign companies like GSK face steep competition from domestic companies. Sun Pharmaceuticals, founded in 1981, still holds a plurality of pharmaceutical sales in India.

A former GSK executive noted that there are large short-term cost-saving gains by outsourcing to India. He asserted, however, that these gains may fall over time. Indian workers' wages may rise substantially and shipping materials to India may become more expensive as the price of oil increases.[14] A good manager assesses all risks from a long-term perspective; therefore, pharmaceutical executives need to take all these factors into consideration.

Patent Expiration; Innovation Still Matters

In addition to market growth shifting to emerging economies, GSK is facing another huge paradigm shift: patents are expiring. In the early 2010s, GSK's asthma drug Advair accounted for 20 percent of its pharmaceutical sales worldwide; today, with the expiration of Advair's patent, generics threaten to significantly undercut its sales. GSK is not alone: In the industry, the sheer volume of imminent patent expiration has been dubbed as a "patent cliff." With many blockbuster drugs introduced in the late 1980s and early 1990s, patent expirations are likely to peak in the coming years.

When companies lose their patent protection, they lose the ability to charge premiums for their products. These premiums are used to fund investments in research and development. Developing a successful drug and achieving approval have become incredibly expensive over the last 15 years; between 2003 and 2014, the average investment needed per successful drug increased from US$800 million to US$2.6 billion.[15] At the same time, governments are putting pressure on pharmaceutical companies to cut prices. As a result of these price pressures, many pharmaceutical companies have chosen to reduce research and development and let go thousands of scientists, especially in the U.S. and the U.K.

Most pharmaceutical companies' strategies have focused on developing and marketing blockbuster drugs targeted at major diseases. During the 1990s, firms profited from their blockbuster drugs, but now they are struggling. As their patents expire, generic competition will decrease their revenues by an estimated hundreds of billions of U.S. dollars.

Research and development, leading to new drugs, is still critical for GSK's long-term success. In the wake of patent expiration of many of GSK's high-grossing drugs, the company has worked to increase its portfolio by introducing new pharmaceuticals to the market. By the end of 2015, GSK had more than 40 experimental drugs in late-stage testing.[16]

New Strategies for New Times

Recent strategic moves by large industry players seem to indicate that, in less developed markets, protecting patents may be an impossible battle to win. For example, GSK has adopted a policy of actually allowing patents to expire and/or licensing patents to generic drug makers for a small royalty. This new approach affects 85 low-income countries.[17]

Other pharmaceutical companies have adopted different strategies, which the companies hope will enable them to thrive in spite of the current challenges. Some companies, such as Pfizer, are looking to enter what is viewed as the cutting edge of biologically derived compounds (versus those that are derived from generally "small" chemical compounds). These companies are moving into the territory in search of heftier margins and better protection from generics. Pfizer, which bought Wyeth in part to acquire biotech experience, is seeking to use biologics to improve aspects of drugs such as Rituxan, a treatment for blood cancers and rheumatoid arthritis, and Enbrel, an arthritis medicine.[18] Roche Holding's purchase of the entirety of biopharmaceutical company Genentech (it has held a majority stake since 1990) may have been driven by a desire to further integrate management and product development and achieve substantial cost savings. And Genzyme, one of the largest biopharma firms, was acquired by French drug maker Sanofi after entertaining offers from various companies.[19]

Others are reemphasizing their vaccine businesses, which had been viewed as relatively low-margin products with little scope for dramatic innovation that could command premium prices. At the same time, these firms are under pressure to provide greater access and cheaper prices for those vaccines, challenging their ability to depend upon these revenues.[20]

Some traditional "branded" companies are linking up with generics in order to lower costs and reach broader markets. In addition to the GSK strategy of licensing patents to generics mentioned above, Pfizer has expanded its licensing agreement with Indian generics maker Aurobindo and has licensed 15 injectable products from Indian generics firm Claris Lifesciences. Sanofi-Aventis has purchased a number of South American generics companies and GSK bought a 16 percent share of its South African generics partner, Aspen Pharmacare.[21] And Teva Pharmaceuticals, an Israeli-based pharma firm, bought Ireland-based Allergan's generic portfolio for US$40 billion in 2015.[22] This mixing of premium and low-cost products was unheard of just a decade ago.

Others are diversifying into a wider range of health care products to generate more predictable income and avoid the gyrations associated with "winner take all" blockbuster drugs. For example, Merck's mergers with Schering-Plough may have been motivated, in part, by a desire to balance the volatility of Merck's drug portfolio with Schering-Plough's extensive human and animal health care product line.[23]

The pharmaceutical industry certainly needs managers who are long-term strategists in order to navigate through the waves of change that it is facing today.

Top Eight Drug Patents That Expired in 2016

Company	Drug Patents Expiring	Revenue in 2015 from Drug (in billions)
AstraZeneca	Crestor	$6.4
Daiichi Sankyo	Benicar	2.6
Merck	Zetia	2.6
AstraZeneca	Seroquel XR	1.3
Eisai	AcipHex Sprinkle	1.2
ViiV Healthcare	Epzicom	1.0
Abbott	Kaletra	1.0
Abbott	Norvir	1.0

Source: Dickson Data, 2016.

Strategic management—the formulation and implementation of a strategy—is a critical function in today's global business environment. GSK and the other large pharmaceutical companies are increasingly drawn to the international markets because of their growth prospects and potential. At the same time, changes in health care markets in the U.S. and Europe, including the expiration of patents and calls for greater cost containment, are exerting pressures on traditional companies to seek alternative income streams but also to reshape their basic business models. The traditional approach to R&D and drug development, which emphasized massive investments in a few potential "blockbusters," may be giving way to alternative strategies, including greater emphasis on what used to be considered "low margin" vaccines, a business line that provides a dependable income stream.

This chapter will examine how multinational corporations use strategic management in their global operations. When formulated and implemented wisely, strategic management sets the course for a company's future. It should answer two simple questions: "Where are we going?" and "How are we going to get there?" Some strategies are consistent across markets, while others must be adapted to regional situations, but in either case, a firm's global strategy should support decision making in all major operations. In the case of large pharma companies, those questions are still being asked as the industry undergoes a dramatic transformation, much of it associated with globalization, competition from new players, changes in regulatory environment, and the implications of these factors for business strategy.

As you read this chapter, think of yourself as a manager in a large pharmaceutical company firm. How might you go about developing a strategic plan to capture greater market share and expand the types of products you are selling? There are some basic steps involved in creating a strategy, but first, let us take a look at what strategic management is and why it is so important.

■ Strategic Management

Strategic management is the process of determining an organization's basic mission and long-term objectives and then implementing a plan of action for pursuing this mission and attaining these objectives. For most companies, regardless of how decentralized, the top management team is responsible for setting the strategy. Middle management has sometimes been viewed as primarily responsible for the strategic implementation process, but now companies are realizing how imperative all levels of management are to the entire process. For example, Volvo discovered that while managers do inform team members of new strategic plans, the most informed, enthusiastic, and effective managers were those who were involved in the entire process.[24]

As companies go international, strategic processes take on added dimensions. A good example is provided by Citibank (a unit of Citicorp), which opened offices in China in 1902 and continued to do business there until 1949, when communists took power. However, in 1984 Citibank quietly returned, and over the last two decades the firm has been slowly increasing its presence in China.[25] Some ways Citibank has done this include opening new branches, expanding the employee base, and increasing stakes in local companies such as Shanghai Pudon Development Bank Co.[26] The Chinese banking environment is closely regulated by the government, and for many years, Citibank's activities were restricted to making local currency loans to foreign multinationals and their joint-venture partners. As a result, the bank does only about 20 percent as much business here as it does in South Korea. However, China's admission into the World Trade Organization (WTO) is changing all of this. Under WTO provisions, local corporations, such as the personal computer maker Legend, electronic goods manufacturer Konda, consumer appliance maker Haier, and telecom service provider China Telecom, will all be able to turn to foreign banks for local currency loans. In 2007, Citibank was one of the first foreign banks to incorporate locally within China. This gives Citibank a major opportunity to expand operations. As of 2016, Citibank China now has branches in 13 Chinese cities and earns roughly US$1 billion in revenue annually.[27]

strategic management
The process of determining an organization's basic mission and long-term objectives, then implementing a plan of action for attaining these goals.

Additionally, under WTO rules, the bank is allowed to offer consumer financial services such as credit cards and home mortgages. Though the Chinese government originally resisted, Citibank was officially given the authorization to offer its own independent credit cards in 2012.[28] Citibank believes that there is a large pent-up demand for credit cards, especially among businesspeople and yuppies who now carry thick wads of currency to pay their bills and make purchases. Another opportunity Citibank sees is in the area of business-to-business (B2B) commerce. As more Chinese firms conduct commerce over the Internet, there will be an increase in Net-related financial services. Citibank has now hooked up with U.S.-based B2B site Commerce One to run its Net-based payment systems, and the bank believes that it can provide this same service for Chinese exporters. Notwithstanding the dramatic losses at Citibank as part of the global financial crisis, and the move to downsize the firm and spin off some units, Citibank remains committed to expansion in Asia. Over 700 branches are currently operating in 14 different Asian markets.[29] In 2014, Citibank hired over 100 bankers to increase its product offerings in the Asia-Pacific region.[30] "We're investing more in Asia now than at any time in our history," said Stephen Bird, co-chief executive officer of Citi Asia Pacific.[31]

While this chapter focuses on the larger picture of strategic planning, it is important to remember that all stages of organizational change incorporate levels of strategy from planning to implementation. This includes innovative ways to improve a product to expanding to international operations.

The Growing Need for Strategic Management

One of the primary reasons that MNCs such as Citibank need strategic management is to keep track of their increasingly diversified operations in a continuously changing international environment. This need is particularly obvious when one considers the amount of foreign direct investment (FDI) that has occurred in recent years. Statistics reveal that FDI has grown three times faster than trade and four times faster than world gross domestic product (GDP).[32] These developments are resulting in a need to coordinate and integrate diverse operations with a unified and agreed-on focus. There are many examples of firms that are doing just this.

One is Ford Motor, which has reentered the market in Thailand and has built a strong sales force to garner market share. The firm's strategic plan here is based on offering the right combination of price and financing to a carefully identified market segment. In particular, Ford is working to keep down the monthly payments so that customers can afford a new vehicle. Despite a coup d'etat in 2014 in Thailand, Ford committed US$186 million in late 2015 to expand its existing Rayong automotive assembly plant. First opened three years prior, the Rayong plant quickly outgrew its original capacity of 180,000 automobiles per year. The new expansion aims to increase production to meet consumer demand for the new Ford Ranger.[33] Additionally, Ford and its Japanese partner Mazda Motor Corp. invested about $1.5 billion in pickup-truck and passenger-car factories in Thailand. Toyota, Honda Motor Co., and General Motors Co. have also built plants in Thailand, Southeast Asia's second-biggest economy, lured by tax incentives and demand amid a domestic population of 70 million. Automakers produced over 1.9 million vehicles in Thailand in 2015, surpassing the United Kingdom to become the 12th-largest automobile manufacturer globally.[34]

General Electric provides another example that reflects the challenge managers face in shedding unprofitable businesses in order to generate capital for expansion into higher-growth product and/or geographic markets. Several years ago, General Electric Co. shed its plastics business, selling it to a Saudi Arabian company for $11.6 billion, and, in 2016, it exited its iconic "white goods" (home appliances) business by selling its operations to Chinese company Haier for US$5.4 billion.[35,36] In its place, GE is aggressively expanding its infrastructure, health care, and environmental technologies businesses, which it sees as providing better growth opportunities in emerging markets. Another example is provided by Genzyme, the large biotech company, which indicated in 2010 that it was pursuing "strategic alternatives" for its genetic-testing, diagnostics, and pharmaceutical intermediates businesses, with potential options including a sale, spin-out, or management buyout because these businesses did not fit with its longer-term strategy.[37] Many thought this strategy could, in part, be in preparation for an eventual sale to a larger pharmaceutical company, as a number of global firms have expressed interest in acquiring the firm.[38] Sure enough, in 2011, Genzyme was acquired by Sanofi, a French MNC, for US$20.1 billion.[39]

Benefits of Strategic Planning

Now that the needs for strategic planning have been explored in our discussion, what are some of the benefits? Many MNCs are convinced that strategic planning is critical to their success, and these efforts are being conducted both at the home office and in the subsidiaries. For example, one study found that 70 percent of the 56 U.S. MNC subsidiaries in Asia and Latin America had comprehensive 5- to 10-year plans.[40] Others found that U.S., European, and Japanese subsidiaries in Brazil were heavily planning-driven[41] and that Australian manufacturing companies use planning systems that are very similar to those of U.S. manufacturing firms.[42]

Do these strategic planning efforts really pay off? To date, the evidence is mixed. Certainly, strategic planning helps an MNC to coordinate and monitor its far-flung operations and deal with political risk (see Chapter 10), competition, and currency instability.

Despite some obvious benefits, there is no definitive evidence that strategic planning in the international arena always results in higher profitability, especially when MNCs try to use home strategies across different cultures (see Chapter 6). Most studies that report favorable results were conducted at least a decade ago. Moreover, many of these findings are tempered with contingency-based recommendations. For example, one study found that when decisions were made mainly at the home office and close coordination between the subsidiary and home office was required, return on investment was negatively affected.[43] Simply put, the home office ends up interfering with the subsidiary, and profitability suffers.

Another study found that planning intensity (the degree to which a firm carries out strategic planning) is an important variable in determining performance.[44] Drawing on results from 22 German MNCs representing 71 percent of Germany's multinational enterprises, the study found that companies with only a few foreign affiliates performed best with medium planning intensity. Those firms with high planning intensity tended to exaggerate the emphasis, and profitability suffered. Companies that earned a high percentage of their total sales in overseas markets, however, did best with a high-intensity planning process and poorly with a low-intensity process. Therefore, although strategic planning usually seems to pay off, as with most other aspects of international management, the specifics of the situation will dictate the success of the process.

Approaches to Formulating and Implementing Strategy

Four common approaches to formulating and implementing strategy are (1) focusing on the economic imperative, (2) addressing the political imperative, (3) emphasizing the quality imperative, and (4) implementing an administrative coordination strategy.

Economic Imperative MNCs that focus on the **economic imperative** employ a worldwide strategy based on cost leadership, differentiation, and segmentation. Middle managers are the key to stimulating profit growth within a company, so expanding those efforts on an international level is a necessary tool to learn for today's new managers.[45] Many of these companies typically sell products for which a large portion of value is added in the upstream activities of the industry's value chain. By the time the product is ready to be sold, much of its value has already been created through research and development, manufacturing, and distribution. Some of the industries in this group include automobiles,

economic imperative
A worldwide strategy based on cost leadership, differentiation, and segmentation.

chemicals, heavy electrical systems, motorcycles, and steel. Because the product is basically homogeneous and requires no alteration to fit the needs of the specific country, management uses a worldwide strategy that is consistent on a country-to-country basis.

The strategy is also used when the product is regarded as a generic good and therefore does not have to be sold based on name brand or support service. A good example is the European PC market. Initially, this market was dominated by such well-known companies as IBM, Apple, and Compaq. However, more recently, clone manufacturers have begun to gain market share. This is because the most influential reasons for buying a PC have changed. A few years ago, the main reasons were brand name, service, and support. Today, price has emerged as a major input into the purchasing decision. Customers now are much more computer literate, and they realize that many PCs offer identical quality performance. Therefore, it does not pay to purchase a high-priced name brand when a lower-priced clone will do the same things. As a result, the economic imperative dominates the strategic plans of computer manufacturers. This process has repeated in many industries as those products become commoditized.

Another economic imperative concept that has gained prominence in recent years is global sourcing, which is proving very useful in formulating and implementing strategy.[46] A good example is provided by the way in which manufacturers are reaching into the supply chain and shortening the buying circle. Li & Fung, Hong Kong's largest export trading company, is one of the world's leading innovators in the development of supply chain management, and the company has managed to use its expertise to whittle costs to the bone. Instead of buying fabric and yarn from one company and letting that firm work on keeping its costs as low as possible, Li & Fung gets actively involved in managing the entire process. How does it keep costs down for orders it receives from The Limited? The chairman of the company explained the firm's economic imperative strategy this way:

> We come in and look at the whole supply chain. We know The Limited is going to order 100,000 garments, but we don't know the style or the colors yet. The buyer will tell us that five weeks before delivery. The trust between us and our supply network means that we can reserve undyed yarn from the yarn supplier. I can lock up capacity at the mills for the weaving and dying with the promise that they'll get an order of a specified size; five weeks before delivery, we will let them know what colors we want. Then I say the same thing to the factories, "I don't know the product specs yet, but I have organized the colors and the fabric and the trim for you, and they'll be delivered to you on this date and you'll have three weeks to produce so many garments."
>
> I've certainly made life harder for myself now. It would be easier to let the factories worry about securing their own fabric and trim. But then the order would take three months, not five weeks. So to shrink the delivery cycle, I go upstream to organize production. And the shorter production time lets the retailer hold off before having to commit to a fashion trend. It's all about flexibility, response time, small production runs, small minimum-order quantities, and the ability to shift direction as the trends move.[47]

Political Imperative   MNCs using the **political imperative** approach to strategic planning are country-responsive; their approach is designed to protect local market niches. The products sold by MNCs often have a large portion of their value added in the downstream activities of the value chain. Industries such as insurance and consumer packaged goods are examples—the success of the product or service generally depends heavily on marketing, sales, and service. Typically, these industries use a country-centered or multi-domestic strategy.

A good example of a country-centered strategy is provided by Thums Up, a local drink that Coca-Cola bought from an Indian bottler in 1993. This drink was created back in the 1970s, shortly after Coca-Cola pulled up stakes and left India. In the ensuing two decades the drink, which is similar in taste to Coke, made major inroads in the Indian market. But when Coca-Cola returned and bought the company, it decided to put Thums Up on the back burner and began pushing its own soft drink. However, local buyers were not interested. They continued to buy Thums Up, and Coca-Cola finally relented. Today

political imperative
Strategic formulation and implementation utilizing strategies that are country-responsive and designed to protect local market niches.

China's Move into Africa

With limited commodities inside of its own borders, China's biggest industries have turned their focus outward to acquire the resources necessary to fuel growth. Africa, in particular, has held a key strategic position for many Chinese companies. Over a million Chinese citizens have moved to various African countries in the last few years, and Chinese-African trade now totals more than US$160 billion in goods every year. In 2016, the Chinese government pledged an additional US$60 billion in loans and other financial assistance to African countries.

China has built a strategy for dealing in Africa that attempts to eliminate political uncertainty and risk. First, China makes it clear that it has no political agenda for the continent. The Chinese government has worked with various African governments, from democracies to dictatorships, and has intentionally steered clear of any involvement in wars and other African foreign affairs. Second, Chinese aid to African countries is not free money, but rather loans and lines of credit that target infrastructure and other capital improvements. In essence, this aid is really an investment; the money is utilized in ways that best suit China's immediate needs on the continent, rather than Africa's needs. Third, China maintains open communication with the governments of the countries where it does business. This is accomplished both on an individual basis, through various cooperation agreements, and on a continent-wide basis, through the Forum on China-Africa Cooperation (FOCAC). The forum, which meets every three years, involves representatives from China and more than 50 African countries. Chinese President Xi Jinping personally attended the 2015 summit, giving him the chance to network with the various country leaders on an individual level.

China's approach to Africa is not without controversy within the international community. In many African countries where China has invested, dictators with various human rights violations still rule. Corruption from these governments has led to extreme poverty and suffering, and some have argued that China's involvement with these dictatorial governments condones their actions. China also faces allegations of trying to "colonize" Africa. While China has portrayed its investments in Africa as a "win-win" situation for the local communities and the Chinese consumers, and Chinese investors have provided many social projects, some have voiced concern that, in realty, China is exploiting Africa's potential future wealth by taking raw materials, manufacturing products from those resources, and then selling finished products back to Africans without transferring the knowledge or skill set required to do the same.

Thums Up is the firm's second-biggest seller in India, just behind Coca-Cola's Sprite, and holds an overall 15 percent market share in the carbonated beverage market.[48] The company spends more money on this soft drink than it does on any of its other product offerings, including Coke.[49] As one observer noted, "In India the 'Real Thing' for Coca-Cola is its Thums Up brand." Recently, Coke has encountered challenges in India, as described in Brief Integrative Case 2.1 at the end of Part Two, but the acknowledgment that Thums Up was the best vehicle for expansion appears to have been validated: In 2015, the company's sales volume grew more than 22 percent and its net profit grew by over 40 percent, partly via a strategy of seeking to penetrate rural consumers, something Thums Up is uniquely qualified to advance.[50,51] Additionally, traditional Coke sales have improved, and it is now one of the fastest-growing soft drinks in the country.[52]

Quality Imperative   A **quality imperative** takes two interdependent paths: (1) a change in attitudes and a raising of expectation for service quality and (2) the implementation of management practices that are designed to make quality improvement an ongoing process.[53] Commonly called total quality management, or simply TQM, the approach takes a wide number of forms, including cross-training personnel to do the jobs of all members in their work group, process reengineering designed to help identify and eliminate redundant tasks and wasteful effort, and reward systems designed to reinforce quality performance.

TQM covers the full gamut, from strategy formulation to implementation. TQM can be summarized as follows:

1. Quality is operationalized by meeting or exceeding customer expectations. Customers include not only the buyer or external user of the product or service but also the support personnel both inside and outside the organization who are associated with the good or service.

quality imperative
Strategic formulation and implementation utilizing strategies of total quality management to meet or exceed customers' expectations and continuously improve products or services.

2. The quality strategy is formulated at the top management level and is diffused throughout the organization. From top executives to hourly employees, everyone operates under a TQM strategy of delivering quality products or services to internal and external customers. Middle managers will better understand and implement these strategies if they are a part of the process.

3. TQM techniques range from traditional inspection and statistical quality control to cutting-edge human resource management techniques, such as self-managing teams and empowerment.[54]

Many MNCs make quality a major part of their overall strategy because they have learned that this is the way to increase market share and profitability. Take the game console industry, for example. In the early 2000s, the success of Sony's PlayStation 2 left Nintendo fighting for market share with its less popular GameCube. A few years later, Nintendo proved to have superior game console quality when it introduced the Wii, leaving Sony scrambling after its less-than-successful launch of the PlayStation 3. By 2016, however, the tables had turned again, as Sony's successful launch of Playstation 4 far outpaced the sales of Nintendo's WiiU and Microsoft's Xbox One.

The auto industry is also a good point of reference. While the U.S. automakers have dramatically increased their overall quality in recent years to close the gap with Japanese auto quality, Japanese firms continued to have fewer safety recalls. Despite recent recalls, Toyota and Honda continue to be ranked very high by American consumers, and Nissan's and Subaru's recent performances were also strong. However, in light of continued improvements by U.S.-based producers, North American–based manufacturers topped many Japanese brands in the J.D. Power and Associates' 2016 Automotive Dependability Study. Half of the top ten brands were U.S. based, with GM producing the leading car for 8 out of the 19 industry segments.[55]

Apple Inc. has experienced rave quality reviews from customers and electronics analysts for its line of Mac products, iPod, iPhone, and iPad. These devices have demonstrated global appeal as Apple's stock soared. Apple introduced the iPhone 6s concurrently in the U.S., U.K., France, Germany, Canada, China, Hong Kong, Singapore, and Japan and made it available in over 70 countries within the first month of its launch, a more aggressive worldwide launch timetable than in the past.[56] More than 13 million phones were sold in the first weekend, setting a new record.[57] In response to several quality-related issues that arose with the iPhone 5s and 6, Apple improved the memory, processor speed, and camera on its iPhone 6s model.[58]

A growing number of MNCs are finding that they must continually revise their strategies and make renewed commitment to the quality imperative because they are being bested by emerging market forces. Motorola, for example, found that its failure to anticipate the industry's switch to digital cell technology was a costly one.[59] In 1998 the company dominated the U.S. handset market, and its StarTAC was popular worldwide. Five years later, the firm's share of the then $160 billion global market for handsets had shrunk from 22 percent to 10 percent and was continuing to fall, while Nokia, Ericsson, and Samsung in particular, with smaller, lighter, and more versatile offerings, were now the dominant players.[60] Motorola's wireless network business also suffered, and in 2011, Motorola partitioned its wireless company from its primary operations. Later that year, Google acquired the new Motorola Mobility wireless division for US$12.5 billion.[61] The quality imperative is never-ending, and MNCs such as Motorola must meet this strategic challenge or pay the price.

Administrative Coordination   An **administrative coordination** approach to formulation and implementation is one in which the MNC makes strategic decisions based on the merits of the individual situation rather than using a predetermined economic or political strategy. A good example is provided by Walmart, which has expanded rapidly into Latin America in recent years. While many of the ideas that worked well in the North American market served as the basis for operations in the Southern Hemisphere,

administrative coordination
Strategic formulation and implementation in which the MNC makes strategic decisions based on the merits of the individual situation rather than using a predetermined economically or politically driven strategy.

the company soon realized that it was doing business in a market where local tastes were different and competition was strong.

Walmart is counting on its international operations to grow 25–30 percent annually, and Latin American operations are critical to this objective. Despite this objective, the company has faced losses in several of its Latin American businesses as it strives to adapt to the local markets. The firm is learning, for example, that the timely delivery of merchandise in places such as São Paulo, where there are continual traffic snarls and the company uses contract truckers for delivery, is often far from ideal. Another challenge is finding suppliers who can produce products to Walmart's specification for easy-to-handle packaging and quality control. A third challenge is learning to adapt to the culture. For example, in Brazil, Walmart brought in stock-handling equipment that did not work with standardized local pallets. It also installed a computerized bookkeeping system that failed to take into account Brazil's wildly complicated tax system. These missteps contributed, in part, to the closing of multiple stores across Brazil in 2016. In-Depth Integrative Case 2.2 at the end of Part Two provides more detail on Walmart's successes and challenges in the international marketplace, including those related to administrative coordination.

Many large MNCs work to combine the economic, political, quality, and administrative approaches to strategic planning. For example, IBM relies on the economic imperative when it has strong market power (especially in less developed countries), the political and quality imperatives when the market requires a calculated response (European countries), and an administrative coordination strategy when rapid, flexible decision making is needed to close the sale. Of the four, however, the first three approaches are much more common because of the firm's desire to coordinate its strategy both regionally and globally.

Global and Regional Strategies

A fundamental tension in international strategic management is the question of when to pursue global or regional (or local) strategies. This is commonly referred to as the globalization vs. national responsiveness conflict. As used here, **global integration** is the production and distribution of products and services of a homogeneous type and quality on a worldwide basis.[62] To a growing extent, the customers of MNCs have homogenized tastes, and this has helped to spread international consumerism. For example, throughout North America, the EU, and Japan, there has been a growing acceptance of standardized, yet increasingly personally, customized goods such as automobiles and computers. This goal of efficient economic performance through a globalization and mass customization strategy, however, has left MNCs open to the charge that they are overlooking the need to address national responsiveness through Internet and intranet technology.

National responsiveness is the need to understand the different consumer tastes in segmented regional markets and respond to different national standards and regulations imposed by autonomous governments and agencies.[63] For example, in designing and building cars, international manufacturers now carefully tailor their offerings in the American market. Toyota's "full-size" T100 pickup proved much too small to attract U.S. buyers. So the firm went back to the drawing board and created a full-size Tundra pickup that is powered by a V-8 engine and has a cabin designed to "accommodate a passenger wearing a 10-gallon cowboy hat."[64] In 2016, more than 15 years after its initial launch, the Tundra was still selling over 100,000 units every year in the U.S.[65] Honda developed its Element SUV with more Americanized features, including enough interior room so that travelers could eat and sleep in the vehicle. Mitsubishi has abandoned its idea of making a global vehicle and has brought out its new Montero Sport SUV in the U.S. market with the features it learned that Americans want: more horsepower, more interior room, more comfort. Meanwhile, for over two decades, U.S. engineers and product designers have been completely responsible for the development of most Nissan vehicles sold in North America. Among other things, they are asking children between the ages

global integration
The production and distribution of products and services of a homogeneous type and quality on a worldwide basis.

national responsiveness
The need to understand the different consumer tastes in segmented regional markets and respond to different national standards and regulations imposed by autonomous governments and agencies.

of 8 and 15, in focus-group sessions, for ideas on storage, cup holders, and other refinements that would make a full-size minivan more attractive to them.[66]

National responsiveness also relates to the need to adapt tools and techniques for managing the local workforce. Sometimes what works well in one country does not work in another, as seen in the following example:

> An American computer company introduced pay-for-performance in both the USA and the Middle East. It worked well in the USA and increased sales briefly in the Middle East before a serious slump occurred. Inquiries showed that indeed the winners among salesmen in the Middle East had done better, but the vast majority had done worse. The wish for their fellows to succeed had been seriously eroded by the contest. Overall morale and sales were down. Ill-will was contagious. When the bosses discovered that certain salespeople were earning more than they did, high individual performances also ceased. But the principal reason for eventually abandoning the system was the discovery that customers were being loaded up with products they could not sell. As A tried to beat B to the bonus, the care of customers began to slip, with serious, if delayed, results.[67]

Global Integration vs. National Responsiveness Matrix The issue of global integration versus national responsiveness can be further analyzed conceptually via a two-dimensional matrix. Figure 8–1 provides an example.

The vertical axis in the figure measures the need for global integration. Movement up the axis results in a greater degree of economic integration. Global integration generates economies of scale (takes advantage of large size) and also capitalizes on further lowering unit costs (through experience curve benefits) as a firm moves into worldwide markets selling its products or services. These economies are captured through centralizing specific activities in the value-added chain. They also occur by reaping the benefits of increased coordination and control of geographically dispersed activities.

The horizontal axis measures the need for multinationals to respond to national responsiveness or differentiation. This suggests that MNCs must address local tastes and

Figure 8–1

Global Integration vs. National Responsiveness

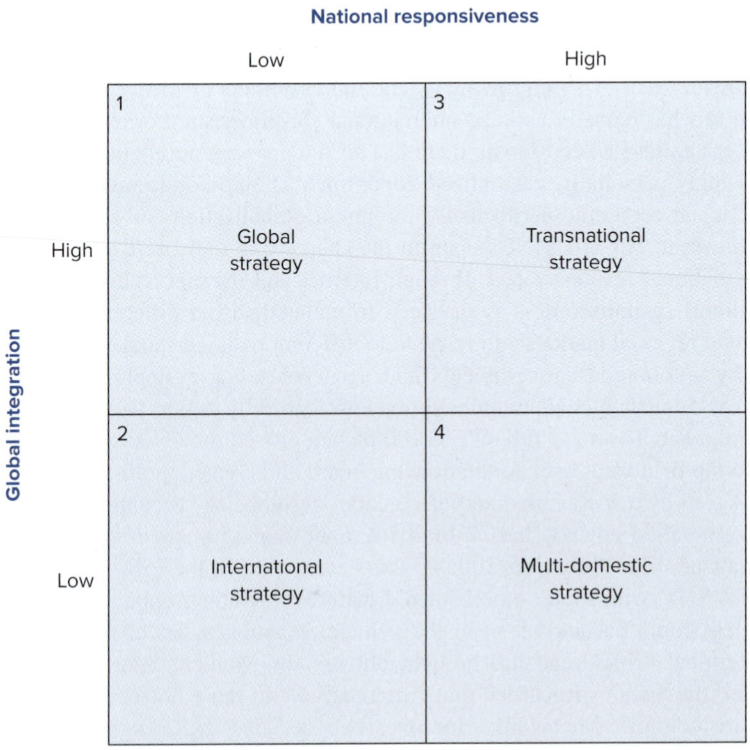

Source: Adapted from information in Christopher A. Bartlett and Sumantra Ghoshal, *Managing Across Borders: The Transnational Solution,* 2nd ed. (Boston: Harvard Business School Press, 1998).

government regulations. The result may be a geographic dispersion of activities or a decentralization of coordination and control for individual MNCs.

Figure 8–1 depicts four basic situations in relation to the degrees of global integration versus national responsiveness. Quadrants 1 and 4 are the simplest cases. In quadrant 1, the need for integration is high and awareness of differentiation is low. In terms of economies of scale, this situation leads to **global strategies** based on price competition. A good example of this is Sony, which has standardized many aspects of its operations and marketing over the years. A few years ago, Sony, along with Hitachi, Panasonic, Philip, and Samsung, among others, worked to standardize the high-definition optical disc industry under the Blu-ray format. Sony's strong distribution network, coupled with its globally popular Playstation 3 gaming console, allowed the company to push the use of the Blu-ray format across markets all over the world. As a result, sales of Blu-ray format discs were able to outpace those of competitor HD-DVD, giving Sony a major advantage in the high-definition disc industry.[68] In this quadrant-1 type of environment, mergers and acquisitions often occur.

> **global strategy**
> Integrated strategy based primarily on price competition.

The opposite situation is represented by quadrant 4, where the need for differentiation is high but the concern for integration low. This quadrant is referred to as **multi-domestic strategy**. In this case, niche companies adapt products to satisfy the high demands of differentiation and ignore economies of scale because integration is not very important. An example of this is Philips, which provides medical equipment to doctors worldwide. As diagnoses become more complex, Philips has to find new innovative ways to simplify the machines used by doctors so that they can spend more time with patients. Yet the medical systems of each country are so different that products must be adapted and adjusted to the particular medical environment. Philips recently sought out opinions from board members, and even asked for participation of fashion designers, to better understand different strategic methods. By using this multidimensional information pool, Philips is moving toward offering even more differentiated products.[69]

> **multi-domestic strategy**
> Differentiated strategy emphasizing local adaptation.

Quadrants 2 and 3 reflect more complex environmental situations. Quadrant 2 incorporates those cases in which both the need for integration and awareness of differentiation are low. Both the potential to obtain economies of scale and the benefits of being sensitive to differentiation are of little value. Typical strategies in quadrant 2 are characterized by increased international standardization of products and services. This mixed approach is often referred to as **international strategy**.

This situation can lead to lower needs for centralized quality control and centralized strategic decision making while eliminating requirements to adapt activities to individual countries. This strategy is decreasingly employed as most industries and products face one or both pressures for global integration and local responsiveness. Nonetheless, companies may experience a very temporary phase in this quadrant, but the standards lie in the other three.

> **international strategy**
> Mixed strategy combining low demand for integration and responsiveness.

In quadrant 3, the needs for integration and differentiation are high. There is a strong need for integration in production along with higher requirements for regional differentiation in marketing. MNCs trying to simultaneously achieve these objectives often refer to them as **transnational strategy**. Quadrant 3 is the most challenging quadrant and the one where successful MNCs seek to operate. The problem for many MNCs, however, is the cultural challenges associated with "localizing" a global focus. One good example of a transnational company is Monsanto. Monsanto offers a very diverse line of hybrid seeds to the agricultural industry. Hybrid seeds are genetically modified seeds which are sterile and must be purchased at the beginning of each season for the specified crop. Monsanto's operations, discussed in Chapter 2, include finding new ways to differentiate its product to best fit the surrounding market. The company offers products which can withstand the various environments and climates of its global customers, from herbicide and insect resistant strains to drought tolerance.[70]

> **transnational strategy**
> Integrated strategy emphasizing both global integration and local responsiveness.

Summary and Implications of the Four Basic Strategies   MNCs can be characterized as using one of four basic international strategies: an international strategy, a multi-domestic strategy, a global strategy, and a transnational strategy. The appropriateness of each strategy depends on pressures for cost reduction and local responsiveness in each country served. Firms that pursue an international strategy have valuable core competencies that host-country competitors do not possess and face minimal pressures for local responsiveness and cost reductions. International firms such as McDonald's, Walmart, and Microsoft have been successful using an international strategy. Organizations pursuing a multi-domestic strategy should do so when there is high pressure for local responsiveness and low pressures for cost reductions. Changing offerings on a localized level increases a firm's overall cost structure but increases the likelihood that its products and services will be responsive to local needs and therefore be successful.[71]

A global strategy is a low-cost strategy. Firms that experience high-cost pressures should use a global strategy in an attempt to benefit from scale economies in production, distribution, and marketing. By offering a standardized product worldwide, firms can leverage their experience and use aggressive pricing schemes. This strategy makes most sense where there are high cost pressures and low demand for localized product offerings. A transnational strategy should be pursued when there are high-cost pressures and high demands for local responsiveness. However, a transnational strategy is very difficult to pursue effectively. Pressures for cost reduction and local responsiveness put contradictory demands on a company because localized product offerings increase cost. Organizations that can find appropriate synergies in global corporate functions are the ones that can leverage a transnational strategy effectively.[72]

Recent analyses of the strategies of MNCs confirm these basic approaches. The globalization–national responsiveness model, which was initially developed from nine in-depth case studies, has been corroborated in large-scale empirical settings. Moreover, it appears as if there are positive performance effects from tailoring the strategy to particular industry and country characteristics.[73]

■ The Basic Steps in Formulating Strategy

The needs, benefits, approaches, and predispositions of strategic planning serve as a point of departure for the basic steps in formulating strategy. In international management, strategic planning can be broken into the following steps: (1) scanning the external environment for opportunities and threats; (2) conducting an internal resource analysis of company strengths and weaknesses; and (3) formulating goals in light of the external scanning and internal analysis. The following sections discuss each step in detail.

Environmental Scanning

environmental scanning
The process of providing management with accurate forecasts of trends related to external changes in geographic areas where the firm currently is doing business or is considering setting up operations.

Environmental scanning attempts to provide management with accurate forecasts of trends that relate to external changes in geographic areas where the firm is currently doing business or considering setting up operations. These changes relate to environmental factors that can affect the company and include the industry or market, technology, regulatory, economic, social, and political aspects.

MNCs observe and evaluate an exorbitant amount of information, and while data are usually collected for all forms of environmental factors, the order in which they approach each factor and the extent to which they are studied depend on the industry and the goals of the MNC.[74] One of the most important foci is the industry or the market. This includes the role of all potential competitors and the relationships surrounding those competitors, such as affiliation with one another or the connection between the company and its customers and suppliers. Monitoring changes in technology will also help keep the company modern and innovative. Some technologic options managers may wish to follow are those that influence business efficiencies or changes in production. From a competitor standpoint, it is good to familiarize oneself with the rise of new products or services and the existing infrastructure.

The regulatory environment can also change at any time, shifting laws or regulatory guidelines. Managers should be aware of ownership or property rights within an area and also what kind of employment practices are exhibited in a region. Minimum wage laws and tax rates should also be considered because they can affect the hiring process and company finances. This is different from the economic environment, which mainly highlights rates, namely, rates of employment, exchange rates, inflation rates, and the level of GNP for a country.

Appropriate observation of the social environment can help the company. Awareness of demographic shifts including age, education, and income, coupled with in-depth knowledge of consumer attitudes, is imperative for a company to assess whether its services would be welcomed or not within a region. Finally, the political environment can impact how a company runs operations. We discussed in Chapter 2 the different political systems that exist across the world, and an understanding of those systems, along with the current state of affairs, can alert MNCs to any warnings that may impede expansion.

After obtaining the information, MNCs then go through an analyzing process that gives rise to the relevant features of the external environment. By performing analyses, the company can discover the risks and opportunities involved in expanding to that region. Typically, managers would communicate the results and then try to formulate the best strategy to take advantage of a ripening market. However, the external environment is not the only aspect to consider, and more information must be reviewed before those steps can be applied.

Environmental scanning is central to discovering if an MNC can survive in a particular region; however, it is only effective if it is done consistently. The environment changes very rapidly, and in order for firms to continually adapt, they must assess the external dynamics that could bolster or hinder future productivity. Each country will have a different perspective as to which factors create the most roadblocks and therefore must be evaluated on a more consistent basis. For example, a recent study showed that while both Malaysian and U.S. managers see competitors and the market as highly important, the U.S. managers considered regulatory issues more relevant than the Malaysians did. In this case, Malaysian MNCs have not been exposed to the sometimes strict directives that U.S. MNCs can face.[75]

Netflix's recent push into Europe provides an example of how this environmental scanning process works. The company analyzed the wireless streaming environment in Europe and concluded that the mobile market was ideal for penetration. As a result, it made a number of strategic positioning moves. First, it signed a deal with Vodafone UK in 2014 to provide new customers with a free six-month subscription to Netflix. The deal includes free 4G streaming for customers over their Vodafone devices, encouraging U.K. customers to use Netflix while on the move. Later in 2014, Netflix rolled-out to six mainland European countries, including France, Germany, and Belgium, to compete directly against existing streaming providers for the more than 100 million potential customers in countries with the highest existing Internet penetration.[76] In 2015, Netflix began to roll out its subscriptions to untapped European regions, with lower levels of penetration by both streaming competitors and high-speed Internet providers. As a result, Netflix took losses in Europe in 2015 and 2016; however, as Internet connectivity and mobile streaming continue to increase in places like Spain, Italy, and eastern Europe, Netflix hopes that its investments will result in large profits and a majority of the market across the European continent.[77]

Another example is Cisco Systems, the world's largest maker of networking equipment, which continues to grow rapidly through acquisitions. For more than 20 years, acquisitions have comprised nearly half of its business activity, with start-up companies key to its strategy. In November 2015, Cisco spent US$700 million to acquire Acano, a British videoconferencing start-up, and in 2016, the company acquired Jasper Technologies, a start-up focused on wireless connections and the "Internet of things," for US$1.4 billion.[78] Cisco's China strategy has resulted from careful scanning of the broad macro political-economic environment as well as of the competitor landscape. Already the world's largest Internet and mobile phone market, China is likely to become even more crucial to the network equipment maker's growth as the country's burgeoning middle class gains access to new technology. Joint ventures and acquisitions have been key to Cisco when conducting business in China and maintaining sales. For example, in 2015, Cisco joined with Chinese start-up Inspur Group to produce computer servers to compete against Huawei Technologies Co. Ltd. and ZTE Corp., two large Chinese rivals. By relying on acquisitions and JVs, Cisco is in a stronger position to work around difficult regulations and government policies, even if overall trade tensions between the United States and China continue.[79,80] In 2015, Cisco committed to invest over US$10 billion in the country over the next several years.[81]

Internal Resource Analysis

When formulating strategy, some firms wait until they have completed their environmental scanning before conducting an internal resource analysis, which is a microeconomic aspect of activity. Others perform these two steps simultaneously. Internal resource analysis helps the firm to evaluate its current managerial, technical, material, and financial resources and capabilities to better assess its strengths and weaknesses. This assessment then is used by the MNC to determine its ability to take advantage of international market opportunities. The primary thrust of this analysis is to match external opportunities (gained through the environmental scan) with internal capabilities (gained through the internal resource analysis). In other words, these evaluations should not be viewed as how the environment creates a barrier to entry, but rather how companies can utilize their resources and capabilities to best take advantage of environmental opportunities.

key success factor (KSF)
A factor necessary for a firm to effectively compete in a market niche.

An internal analysis identifies the key factors for success that will dictate how well the firm is likely to do. A **key success factor (KSF)** is a factor that is necessary for a firm to compete effectively in a market niche. For example, a KSF for an international airline is price. An airline that discounts its prices will gain market share vis-à-vis competitors that do not. A second KSF for the airline is safety, and a third is quality of service in terms of on-time departures and arrivals; convenient schedules; and friendly, helpful personnel. In the automobile industry, quality of products has emerged as the number-one KSF in world markets. Japanese firms have been able to invade the U.S. auto market successfully because they have been able to prove that the quality of their cars is better than that of the average domestically built U.S. car. Toyota and Honda have had a quality edge over the competition in recent years in the eyes of U.S. car buyers. A second KSF is styling. The redesigned Mini-Cooper has been successful, in part, because customers like its unique look.

The key question for the management of an MNC is: Do we have the people and resources that can help us to develop and sustain the necessary KSFs, or can we acquire them? If the answer is yes, the recommendation would be to proceed. If the answer is no, management would begin looking at other markets where it has, or can develop, the necessary KSFs.

The balance between environmental scanning and internal resource analysis can be quite delicate. Managers do not want to spend too much time looking inward; otherwise, they could miss changes in the environment that would alter the company's strengths and weaknesses based on that market. Conversely, managers do not want to appraise the outward view for too long as they could take time away from improving internal systems and taking advantage of opportunities.

Goal Setting for Strategy Formulation

In practice, goal formulation often precedes the first two steps of environmental scanning and internal resource analysis. As used here, however, the more specific goals for the strategic plan come out of external scanning and internal analysis. MNCs pursue a variety of such goals; Table 8–1 provides a list of the most common ones. These goals typically serve as an umbrella beneath which the subsidiaries and other international groups operate.

Table 8–1
Areas for Formulation of MNC Goals

Profitability

Level of profits
Return on assets, investment, equity, sales
Yearly profit growth
Yearly earnings per share growth

Marketing

Total sales volume
Market share—worldwide, region, country
Growth in sales volume
Growth in market share
Integration of country markets for marketing efficiency and effectiveness

Operations

Ratio of foreign to domestic production volume
Economies of scale via international production integration
Quality and cost control
Introduction of cost-efficient production methods

Finance

Financing of foreign affiliates—retained earnings or local borrowing
Taxation—minimizing tax burden globally
Optimum capital structure
Foreign exchange management—minimizing losses from foreign fluctuations

Human Resources

Recruitment and selection
Development of managers with global orientation
Management development of host-country nationals
Compensation and benefits

Profitability and marketing goals almost always dominate the strategic plans of today's MNCs. Profitability, as shown in Table 8–1, is so important because MNCs generally need higher profitability from their overseas operations than they do from their domestic operations. The reason is quite simple: Setting up overseas operations involves greater risk and effort. In addition, a firm that has done well domestically with a product or service usually has done so because the competition is minimal or ineffective. Firms with this advantage often find additional lucrative opportunities outside their borders. Moreover, the more successful a firm is domestically, the more difficult it is to increase market share without strong competitive response. International markets, however, offer an ideal alternative to the desire for increased growth and profitability.

Another reason that profitability and marketing top the list is that these tend to be more externally environmentally responsive, whereas production, finance, and personnel functions tend to be more internally controlled. Thus, for strategic planning, profitability and marketing goals are given higher importance and warrant closer attention. Ford's European operations offer an example. In recent years the automaker had been losing market share in the EU. Starting in 2012, Ford instituted a major overhaul of its European operations, restructuring and streamlining its processes. This included unloading the Land Rover and Jaguar to Tata of India and its share of Volvo to China's Geely. In seeking to improve performance in Europe, Ford also began shipping more cars from its factory in Thailand and, in so doing, saving on costs and increasing margins. Rather than spend money creating European-centric cars, Ford also began selling its more global models within Europe. The restructuring has paid off for the company; after years of losses in the European market, Ford posted profits in 2015 and 2016. Ford's share of the European market, standing at 7.5 percent in 2016, has also increased with its profitability.[82]

Once the strategic goals are set, the MNC will develop specific operational goals and controls, usually through a two-way process at the subsidiary or affiliate level. Home-office management will set certain parameters, and the overseas group will operate within these guidelines. For example, the MNC headquarters may require periodic financial reports, restrict on-site decisions to matters involving less than $100,000, and require that all client contracts be cleared through the home office. These guidelines are designed to ensure that the overseas group's activities support the goals in the strategic plan and that all units operate in a coordinated effort.

■ Strategy Implementation

strategy implementation
The process of providing goods and services in accord with a plan of action.

Once formulated, the strategic plan next must be implemented. **Strategy implementation** provides goods and services in accord with a plan of action. Quite often, this plan will have an overall philosophy or series of guidelines that direct the process. In the case of Japanese electronic-manufacturing firms entering the U.S. market, Chang has found a common approach:

> To reduce the risk of failure, these firms are entering their core businesses and those in which they have stronger competitive advantages over local firms first. The learning from early entry enables firms to launch further entry into areas in which they have the next strongest competitive advantages. As learning accumulates, firms may overcome the disadvantages intrinsic to foreignness. Although primary learning takes place within firms through learning by doing, they may also learn from other firms through the transfer or diffusion of experience. This process is not automatic, however, and it may be enhanced by membership in a corporate network: in firms associated with either horizontal or vertical business, groups were more likely to initiate entries than independent firms. By learning from their own sequential entry experience as well as from other firms in corporate networks, firms build capabilities in foreign entry.[83]

International management must consider three general areas in strategy implementation. First, the MNC must decide where to locate operations. Second, the MNC must carry out entry and ownership strategies (discussed in Chapter 9). Finally, management must implement functional strategies in areas such as marketing, production, and finance.

Location Considerations for Implementation

In choosing a location, today's MNC has two primary considerations: the country and the specific locale within the chosen country. Quite often, the first choice is easier than the second because there are many more alternatives from which to choose a specific locale.

The Country   Traditionally, MNCs have invested in highly industrialized countries, and research reveals that annual investments have been increasing substantially.

In the case of Japan, MNCs are actively engaged in mergers and acquisitions. Intuit Inc. of Menlo Park, California, purchased a financial software specialist in Japan for $52 million in stock and spent $30 million for the Nihon Mikon Company, which sells small business accounting software. Accenture, based in Dublin, Ireland, acquired the Japanese full-service digital agency IMJ in 2016 with the specific aim of gaining traction in the local Japanese market.[84] These purchases point to a new trend in Japan—the acquisition of small firms. However, many larger purchases have also been made.

Foreign investors are also pouring into Mexico, although this investment activity has generated some political controversy in the United States.[85] One reason is that it is a gateway to the American and Canadian markets. A second reason is that Mexico is a very cost-effective place in which to manufacture goods. A third is that the declining value of the peso after Mexico's economic crisis in 1994 and 1995 hit many Mexican businesses hard and left them vulnerable to mergers and acquisitions—an opportunity not lost on many large multinationals. In the period 1996–1997, Britain's B.A.T. Industries PLC took control of Cigarrera La Moderna, Mexico's tobacco giant, in a $1.5 billion deal. A few days earlier, Philip Morris Cos. increased its stake in the second-largest tobacco company, Cigarros La Tabacalera Mexicana SA, to 50 percent from about 29 percent for $400 million. Walmart Stores Inc. announced plans to acquire control of Mexico's largest retailer, Cifra SA, in a deal valued at more than $1 billion, eventually becoming part of Walmex, Walmart's Mexican subsidiary (see In-Depth Integrative Case 2.2). A month later, Procter & Gamble Co. acquired a consumer-products concern, Loreto y Pena Pobre, for $170 million.[86] More recently, acquisitions of Mexican companies have continued, although for more strategic reasons. For example, in April 2015, AT&T acquired Nextel Mexico for US$1.875 billion, citing the rapidly growing middle class. In June 2013, Anheuser-Busch InBev and Grupo Modelo, Mexico's largest brewer, announced completion of their integration in a deal valued at $20.1 billion. In its press release, AB InBev said, "The combination is a natural next step given the successful long-term partnership between AB InBev and Grupo Modelo, which started more than 20 years ago. The combined company will benefit from the significant growth potential that Modelo brands such as Corona have globally outside of the U.S., as well as locally in Mexico, where there will also be opportunities to introduce AB InBev brands through Modelo's distribution network."[87,88]

MNCs often invest in advanced industrialized countries because they offer the largest markets for goods and services. In addition, the established country or geographic locale may have legal restrictions related to imports, encouraging a local presence. Japanese firms, for example, in complying with their voluntary export quotas of cars to the United States as well as responding to dissatisfaction in Washington regarding the continuing trade imbalance with the United States, have established U.S.-based assembly plants. In Europe, because of EU regulations for outsiders, most U.S. and Japanese MNCs have operations in at least one European country, thus ensuring access to the European community at large. In fact, the huge U.S. MNC ITT now operates in each of the original 12 EU countries.

Another consideration in choosing a country is the amount of government control and restrictions on foreign investment. Traditionally, MNCs from around the world resisted anything but very limited business in Eastern European countries with central planning economies. The recent relaxing of the trade rules and move toward free-market economies in the republics of the former Soviet Union and the other Eastern European nations, however, have encouraged MNCs to rethink their positions; more and more are making moves into this largely untapped part of the global market. The same is true in India, although the political climate can be volatile and MNCs must carefully weigh the risks of investing there. Restrictions on foreign investment also play a factor. Countries such as China and India have required that control of the operation be in the hands of local partners. MNCs that are reluctant to accept such conditions will not establish operations there.

In addition to these considerations, MNCs examine the specific benefits offered by host countries, including low tax rates, rent-free land and buildings, low-interest or no-interest loans, subsidized energy and transportation rates, and a well-developed infrastructure that provides many of the services found back home (good roads, communication systems, schools, health care, entertainment, and housing). These benefits will be weighed against any disincentives or performance requirements that must be met by the MNC, such as job-creation quotas, export minimums for generating foreign currency, limits on local market growth, labor regulations, wage and price controls, restrictions on profit repatriation, and controls on the transfer of technology.

Local Issues Once the MNC has selected the country in which to locate, the firm must choose the specific locale. A number of factors influence this choice. Common considerations include access to markets, proximity to competitors, availability of transportation and electric power, and desirability of the location for employees coming in from the outside.

One study found that in selecting U.S. sites, both German and Japanese firms place more importance on accessibility and desirability and less importance on financial considerations.[89] However, financial matters remain important: Many countries attempt to lure MNCs to specific locales by offering special financial packages.

Another common consideration is the nature of the workforce. MNCs prefer to locate near sources of available labor that can be readily trained to do the work. A complementary consideration that often is unspoken is the presence and strength of organized labor. Japanese firms in particular tend to avoid heavily unionized areas.

Still another consideration is the cost of doing business. Manufacturers often set up operations in rural areas, commonly called "greenfield locations," which are much less expensive and do not have the problems of urban areas. Conversely, banks often choose metropolitan areas because they feel they must have a presence in the business district.

Some MNCs opt for locales where the cost of running a small enterprise is significantly lower than that of running a large one. In this way, they spread their risk, setting up many small locations throughout the world rather than one or two large ones. Manufacturing firms are a good example. Some production firms feel that the economies of scale associated with a large-scale plant are more than offset by potential problems that can result should economic or political difficulties develop in the country. These firms' strategy is to spread the risk by opting for a series of small plants throughout a wide geographic region.[90] This location strategy can also be beneficial for stockholders. Research has found that MNCs with a presence in developing countries have significantly higher market values than MNCs that operate only in countries that have advanced economies.[91]

Frontier Markets   Sometimes referred to as pre-emerging, frontier markets are a unique subset of emerging economies. Whereas most traditional emerging markets are financially linked to the economies of their more developed counterparts, frontier markets are less correlated to the ups and downs of the global economy. From an investment point of view, these markets offer potentially high rewards, but with high risk. The most commonly cited frontier markets are located in Africa and Asia.

Business initiatives in frontier markets require careful strategic considerations. One potential approach is to joint-venture with a local company that specializes in the cultural knowledge of the marketplace. The Mara Group, for example, is an African conglomerate that conducts business in a variety of unrelated ventures across the continent. Rather than focus on the financial and technical aspects of the business, the Mara Group provides the marketing, logistical, and bureaucratic assistance to its international partners. The Mara Group also provides a trusted, recognizable brand name to foreign products. Utilizing an office in Dubai, the Mara Group is able to stay well-connected with foreign companies as well as with the African market. IBM is an example of an MNC that has conducted business in frontier markets using a partnership with the Mara Group.[92]

Combining Country and Firm-Specific Factors in International Strategy

International management scholars have developed a simple framework that builds upon the integration-responsiveness framework to help managers understand the interaction between the relative attractiveness of different country locations for a given activity and the firm-level attributes or strengths that can be leveraged in that location.[93] The first set of factors is referred to as CSAs, or country-specific advantages, while the second is referred to as FSAs, or firm-specific advantages. CSAs can be based on natural resource endowments (minerals, energy, forests), the labor force, or less tangible factors that include education and skills, institutional protections of intellectual property, entrepreneurial dynamism, or other factors unique to a given market. FSAs are unique capabilities

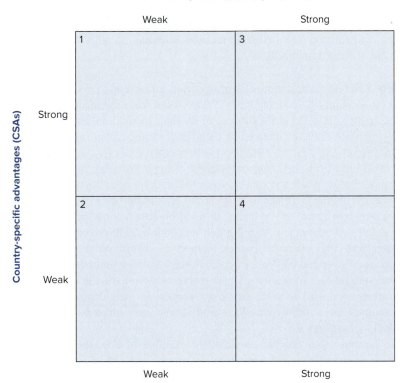

Firm-specific advantages (FSAs)

Source: Alan Rugman and Jonathan P. Doh, *Multinationals and Development*, p. 13. Copyright © 2008. Reprinted by permission of Yale University Press.

Figure 8-2

The CSA-FSA Matrix

proprietary to the organization that may be based on product or process technology, marketing or distributional skills, or managerial know-how.

Managers of MNCs use strategies that build upon the interactions of CSAs and FSAs. Figure 8–2 provides a graphical depiction of this framework. It should be emphasized that the "strength" or "weakness" of FSAs and CSAs is a relative notion that depends on the relevant market and the CSAs and FSAs of potential competitors.

MNCs in quadrants 1, 2, and 3 would be expected to pursue different strategies. Quadrant 1 firms would tend to emphasize cost leadership; they are likely to be resource-based and/or mature, internationally oriented firms producing a commodity-type product. Given these factors, FSAs tend to be less important compared to the CSAs of location and energy costs, which are the main sources of the firm's competitive advantage.

Quadrant 2 firms represent less efficient firms with few intrinsic CSAs or FSAs. Quadrant 2 could also represent domestically based small and medium-sized firms with little global exposure. Firms in quadrant 4 are generally differentiated firms with strong FSAs in marketing and customization. These firms usually have strong brands. In quadrant 4 the FSAs dominate, so in world markets the home-country CSAs are not essential in the long run. Quadrant 3 firms generally can choose either the cost or differentiation strategies, or perhaps combine them because of the strength of both their CSAs and FSAs.

In terms of business strategy, firms in quadrants 2 and 3 can benefit from strategies of both low cost and differentiation. Such a firm is constantly evaluating its production mix. Quadrants 4 and 1 require specific strategies for different types of firms. For instance, a quadrant 4 firm that has strong FSAs in marketing (customization) can operate internationally without reliance on its home-market CSA, or the CSAs of the host nation. For such a firm, in quadrant 4, the CSA is not relevant. In contrast, quadrant 1 has mature multinationals or product divisions determined more by CSAs than by FSAs. By improving potential FSAs in marketing or product innovation and increasing value added through vertical integration, the quadrant 1 firm can move to quadrant 3.

The Role of the Functional Areas in Implementation

To implement strategies, MNCs must tap the primary functional areas of marketing, production, and finance. The following sections examine the roles of these functions in international strategy implementation.

Marketing   The implementation of strategy from a marketing perspective must be determined on a country-by-country basis. What works from the standpoint of marketing in one locale may not necessarily succeed in another. In addition, the specific steps of a marketing approach often are dictated by the overall strategic plan, which in turn is based heavily on market analysis.

German auto firms in Japan are a good example of using marketing analysis to meet customer needs. While automakers from Detriot have been boycotting Japanese auto shows for a decade, the Germans have spent millions of dollars to build dealer, supplier, and service-support networks in Japan, in addition to adapting their cars to Japanese customers' tastes. Volkswagen Audi Nippon has built a $320 million import facility on a deepwater port. This operation, which includes an inspection center and parts warehouse, processed over 100,000 cars in 2015 alone.[94] Daimler and BMW both have introduced lower-priced cars to attract a larger market segment. At the same time, German manufacturers work hard to offer first-class service in their dealerships. As a result, German automakers in recent years have sold almost three times as many cars in Japan as their U.S. competitors do.

The Japanese also provide an excellent example of how the marketing process works. In many cases, Japanese firms have followed a strategy of first building up their market share at home and driving out imported goods. Then, the firms move into newly developed countries, honing their marketing skills as they go along. Finally, the firms move into fully developed countries, ready to compete with the best available. This pattern of implementing strategy has been used in marketing autos, cameras, consumer electronics, home appliances, petrochemicals, steel, and watches. For some products, however, such as computers, the Japanese have moved from their home market directly into fully developed countries and then on to the newly developing nations. Finally, the Japanese have gone directly to developed countries to market products in some cases because the market in Japan was too small. Such products include color TVs, Blu-ray players, and sewing machines. In general, once a firm agrees on the goods it wants to sell in the international marketplace, then the specific marketing strategy is implemented.

The implementation of marketing strategy in the international arena is built around the well-known "four Ps" of marketing—product, price, promotion, and place. As noted in the example of the Japanese, firms often develop and sell a product in local or peripheral markets before expanding to major overseas targets. If the product is designed specifically to meet an overseas demand, however, the process is more direct. Price largely is a function of market demand.[95] For example, the Japanese have found that the U.S. microcomputer market is price-sensitive; by introducing lower-priced clones, the Japanese have been able to make headway, especially in the portable laptop market. The last two Ps, promotion and place, are dictated by local conditions and often left in the hands of those running the subsidiary or affiliate. Local management may implement customer sales incentives, for example, or make arrangements with dealers and salespeople who are helping to move the product locally.

Production   Although marketing usually dominates strategy implementation, the production function also plays a role. If a company is going to export goods to a foreign market, the production process traditionally has been handled through domestic operations. In recent years, however, MNCs have found that whether they are exporting or producing the goods locally in the host country, consideration of worldwide production is important. For example, goods may be produced in foreign countries for export to other nations. Sometimes, a plant will specialize in a particular product and export it to all the MNC's markets; other times, a plant will produce goods only for a specific locale, such as Western Europe or South America. Still other facilities will produce one or more components that are shipped to a larger network of assembly plants. That last option has been widely adopted by pharmaceutical firms and automakers such as Volkswagen and Honda.

As mentioned in the first part of the chapter, if the firm operates production plants in different countries but makes no attempt to integrate its overall operations, the company is known as a multi-domestic. A recent trend has been away from this scattered approach and toward global coordination of operations.

Finally, if the product is labor-intensive, as in the case of microcomputers, then the trend is to farm the product out to low-cost sites such as Mexico or Brazil, where the cost of labor is relatively low and the infrastructure (electric power, communications systems, transportation systems) is sufficient to support production. Sometimes, multiple sources of individual components are used; in other cases, one or two sources are sufficient. In any event, careful coordination of the production function is needed when implementing the strategy, and the result is a product that is truly global in nature.

Finance Use of the finance function to implement strategy normally is developed at the home office and carried out by the overseas affiliate or branch. When a firm went international in the past, the overseas operation commonly relied on the local area for funds, but the rise of global financing has ended this practice. MNCs have learned that transferring funds from one place in the world to another, or borrowing funds in the international money markets, often is less expensive than relying on local sources. Unfortunately, there are problems in these transfers.

Such a problem is representative of those faced by MNCs using the finance function to implement their strategies. One of an MNC's biggest recent headaches when implementing strategies in the financial dimension has been the revaluation of currencies. For example, in the late 1990s, the U.S. dollar increased in value against the Japanese yen. American overseas subsidiaries that held yen found their profits (in terms of dollars) declining. The same was true for those subsidiaries that held Mexican pesos when that government devalued the currency several years ago. When this happens, a subsidiary's profit will decline. After its initial introduction in 1999, the euro declined against the U.S. dollar, but when the dollar subsequently came under pressure, the euro regained strength. One of the more recent examples of financial issues is the expansive U.S. trade deficit with China, where the potentially undervalued yuan has played a role.

When dealing with the inherent risk of volatile monetary exchange rates, some MNCs have bought currency options that (for a price) guarantee convertibility at a specified rate. Others have developed countertrade strategies, whereby they receive products in exchange for currency. For example, PepsiCo received payment in vodka for its products sold in Russia. Countertrade continues to be a popular form of international business, especially in less developed countries and those with nonconvertible currencies.

■ Specialized Strategies

In addition to the basic steps in strategy formulation, the analysis of which strategies may be appropriate based on the globalization vs. national responsiveness framework, and the specific processes in strategy implementation, there are some circumstances that may require specialized strategies. Two that have received considerable attention in recent years are strategies for developing and emerging markets and strategies for international entrepreneurship and new ventures.

Strategies for Emerging Markets

Emerging economies have assumed an increasingly important role in the global economy and are predicted to compose more than half of global economic output by midcentury. Partly in response to this growth, MNCs are directing increasing attention to those markets. Foreign direct investment (FDI) flows into developing countries—one measure of increased integration and business activity between developed and emerging economies—grew from $23.7 billion in 1990 to a projected $850 billion in 2017. In 2015, FDI inflows to developing Asia reached record highs of nearly US$500 billion, matching the total amount received by all developed countries combined. In particular, the "BRIC" economies have been among the largest recipients of FDI. In 2014, Brazil, Russia, India, and China attracted a combined 20 percent of all global FDI inflows.[96]

At the same time, emerging economies pose exceptional risks due to their political and economic volatility and their relatively underdeveloped institutional systems. These risks show up in corruption, failure to enforce contracts, red tape and bureaucratic costs, and general uncertainty in the legal and political environment.[97,98] MNCs must adjust their strategy to respond to these risks. For example, in these risky markets, it may be wise to engage in arm's-length or limited equity investments or to maintain greater control of operations by avoiding joint ventures or other shared ownership structures. In other circumstances, it may be wiser to collaborate with a local partner who can help buffer risks through its political connections. Some of the factors relating to these conditions will be discussed in Chapters 9 and 10. However, two unique types of strategies for emerging markets deserve particular attention here.

First-Mover Strategies   Recent research has suggested that entry order into developing countries may be particularly important given the transitional nature of these markets. In general, in particular industries and economic environments, significant economies are associated with first-mover or early-entry positioning—being the first or one of the first to enter a market. These include capturing learning effects important for increasing market share, achieving scale economies that accrue from opportunities for capturing that greater share, and development of alliances with the most attractive (or in some cases the only) local partner. In emerging economies that are undergoing rapid changes such as privatization and market liberalization, there may be a narrow window of time within which these opportunities can be best exploited. In these conditions, first-mover strategies allow entrants to preempt competition, establish beachhead positions, and influence the evolving competitive environment in a manner conducive to their long-term interests and market position.

One study analyzed these benefits in the case of China, concluding that early entrants have reaped substantial rewards for their efforts, especially when collaborations with governments provided credible commitments that the deals struck in those early years of liberalization would not later be undone. First-mover advantages in some other transitional markets, such as Russia and Eastern Europe, are not so clear. Moreover, there may be substantial risks to premature entry—that is, entry before the basic legal, institutional, and political frameworks for doing business have been established.[99]

Privatization presents a particularly powerful case supporting the competitive effects of first-mover positioning. First movers who succeed in taking over newly privatized state-owned enterprises, such as telecom and energy firms, possess a significant advantage over later entrants, especially when market liberalization is delayed and the host government provides protection to the newly privatized incumbent firms. This was the case in 1998 when the Mexican government accepted a $1.757 billion bid for a minority (20.4 percent) but controlling interest in Telefonos de Mexico (Telmex) from an international consortium composed of Grupo Carso, Southwestern Bell, and France Cable et Radio, an affiliate of France Telecom. Although the Mexican market subsequently opened to competition, Telmex and its foreign partners (the first movers) maintained monopoly control over local networks and were able to bundle local and long-distance service, cross-market, and cross-subsidize, giving Telmex a strong advantage. Moreover, the Mexican government was responsive to providing the Telmex consortium protection and financial support for infrastructure investment, and it did so partly by charging new carriers to help Telmex pay for

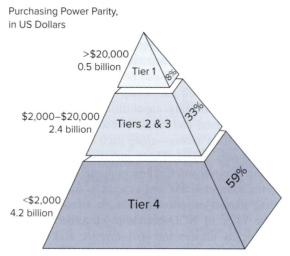

Purchasing Power Parity, in US Dollars

>$20,000
0.5 billion — Tier 1 — 8%

$2,000–$20,000
2.4 billion — Tiers 2 & 3 — 33%

<$2,000
4.2 billion — Tier 4 — 59%

Source: Original graphic by Ben Littell under supervision of Professor Jonathan Doh based on data from the World Bank.

Figure 8–3

The World Population and Income Pyramid in 2016

improvements needed for the long-distance network. In addition, Telmex was able to charge relatively high fees to connect to its network, and the long delay between the initial privatization and market opening allowed these advantages to persist.[100] As of 2016, Telmex still controls 80 percent of all telephone lines in the country and holds a 70 percent share of the wireless market.[101]

Strategies for the "Base of the Pyramid"   Another area of increasing focus for MNCs is the 6 billion or more potential customers around the world who have heretofore been mostly ignored by international business, even within emerging economies, where most MNCs target only the wealthiest consumers. Although FDI in emerging economies has grown rapidly, most has been directed at the big emerging markets previously mentioned—China, India, and Brazil—and even there, most MNC emerging-market strategies have focused exclusively on the elite and emerging middle-class markets, ignoring the vast majority of people considered too poor to be viable customers.[102,103,104] Because of this focus, MNC strategies aimed at tailoring existing practices and products to better fit the needs of emerging-market customers have not succeeded in making products and services available to the mass markets in the developing world—the 4 billion people at the bottom of the economic pyramid who represent over half of the world's population. Figure 8–3 shows the distribution of population and income around the world.

A group of researchers and companies have begun exploring the potentially untapped markets at the base of the pyramid (BOP). They have found that incremental adaptation of existing technologies and products is not effective at the BOP and that the BOP forces MNCs to fundamentally rethink their strategies.[105] Companies must consider smaller-scale strategies and build relationships with local governments, small entrepreneurs, and nonprofits rather than depend on established partners such as central governments and large local companies. Building relationships directly and at the local level contributes to the reputation and fosters the trust necessary to overcome the lack of formal institutions such as intellectual property rights and the rule of law. The BOP may also be an ideal environment for incubating new, leapfrog technologies, including "disruptive" technologies that reduce environmental impacts and increase social benefit such as renewable energy and wireless telecom. Finally, business models forged successfully at the base of the pyramid have the potential to travel profitably to higher-income markets because adding cost and features to a low-cost model may be easier than removing cost and features from high-cost models.[106] This

base of the pyramid strategy
Strategy targeting low-income customers in developing countries.

Can Internet and Mobile Access Transform Poor Economies at the Base of the Pyramid?

Developed countries have experienced dramatic advances in information and communications technology (ICT), notably, sharp increases in penetration of both Internet and wireless phone networks. Developing countries, especially the poorest countries of South Asia and Africa, have not benefited from these trends. Some entrepreneurs, however, see great potential in reaching these "bottom of the pyramid markets," although these efforts have, to date, been challenging. Low literacy rates, poor infrastructure, corruption and other political interference, and incomplete business models have all contributed to stillborn efforts. Yet, these entrepreneurs have persevered.

In terms of wireless service and Internet services, many view Africa as the next great frontier, despite the fact that more than half the population lives on less than $2 a day. From 2000 to 2015, Internet penetration in Africa grew more than 7,000 percent, from just over 4 million in 2000 to 327 million in 2015 (see Table 2–2 in Chapter 2). The total number of mobile subscribers in Africa stood at 386 million in 2015, representing an increase of nearly 40 million in one year. Nearly 90 percent of the continent's population is covered by cellular service.

The increase in the number of mobile cellular subscriptions over the last five years has defied all predictions and Africa remains the region with the highest mobile growth rate. The continent has a high ratio of mobile cellular subscriptions to fixed telephone lines, and the high mobile cellular growth rate suggests that Africa has taken the lead in the shift from fixed to mobile telephony, a trend that can be observed worldwide. The number of Internet users has also grown faster than in other regions, though smartphones, which are the primary method of Internet access for Africans, still remain financially out of reach for many. Data plans are too expensive for the average African consumer, and at several hundred dollars each, the phones themselves are too expensive to purchase.

African countries are facing a number of challenges in increasing ICT levels. These include the lack of full liberalization of markets and the limited availability of infrastructure, such as shortage of international Internet bandwidth. According to a recent report by the U.N.'s ITU agency, the cost of information technology and communication services still far exceeds the average salary. On the question of infrastructure, the report says there are practically no cable networks and many countries face a shortage of international Internet bandwidth. According to the ITU, the figures highlight the acceleration of growth in African mobile and Internet markets outside of South Africa in less than a decade. Growth in Nigeria has been very strong. Kenya, Ghana, Tanzania, and Cote d'Ivoire have also accounted for the change in the distribution of mobile connections.

European companies were among the first to aggressively pursue African cellular markets. Ericsson, Alcatel, and Motorola have pushed into the region, and England's Vodafone Group PLC and France Télécom's Orange unit have set up operations around the region. But other entrepreneurs have identified mobile service and Internet services as a way to make money and empower individuals.

Terracom, an Internet venture started by Greg Wyler, an American tech entrepreneur, entered Rwanda and was granted a contract to connect 300 schools to the Internet. Later, the company bought 99 percent of the shares in Rwandatel, the country's national telecommunications company, for $20 million. Africa's only connection to the network of computers and fiber optic cables that are the Internet's backbone is a $600 million undersea cable running from Portugal down the west coast of Africa. Built in 2002, the cable was supposed to provide cheaper and faster web access, but it didn't deliver. Adding to the problem is that most of the satellites serving Africa were launched nearly 20 years ago and are aging or going out of commission. A satellite set to go into service last year blew up on the launching pad. Power is also an issue, as intermittent power failures in Rwanda hamper efforts to provide a steady electricity source. Meanwhile, Terracom's venture has been plagued by repeated setbacks, with both sides accusing the other of failing to deliver on its promise. "The bottom line is that he promised many things and didn't deliver," said Albert Butare, the country's telecommunications minister.

Africa Online, another venture, was the first Internet service provider in Kenya (1995) and Cote d'Ivoire (1996). It grew to span eight countries across Africa. The company was founded in 1994 by three Kenyans who met each other while students at MIT and Harvard. The idea began as an online news service for Kenyans, which developed from an online community hosted at MIT called KenyaNet, one of several online communities that were among the most fervent virtual communities in the early pre-web 1990s. With the commercialization of the Internet, Africa Online moved its focus away from providing news to connecting Africans on the continent to the Internet. In 1995, the company was bought by International Wireless of Boston, which ultimately became Prodigy. During this period, Africa Online expanded rapidly from its original operation in Kenya to Ghana, Cote d'Ivoire, Tanzania, Uganda, Zambia, Zimbabwe, and Swaziland, with the three Kenyans continuing to manage the operation. Africa Online was the first commercial Internet provider in Kenya and Cote d'Ivoire. In 2007, Africa Online was purchased by South Africa's Telkom.

What makes Africa's mobile and Internet revolution significant is its potential economic impact. The World Bank has been a strong supporter of deploying wireless and Internet communication to improve food production and other development. To some, mobile has become a means to economic empowerment. For example, farmers in Senegal now use their one mobile phone to find eggplant buyers in Dakar willing to pay three times the rate offered by local middlemen. These and other examples suggest the information and communication technology revolution may reap benefits for multinational and local companies, as well as others who may improve

their economic situation by exploiting these new communication opportunities.

Source: Mike Powell, "Culture and the Internet in Africa, a Challenge for Political Economists," *Review of African Political Economy*, June 2001, p. 241; "The Digital Gap," *Economist*, October 20, 2007, p. 64; "The Mobile Revolution in Africa," *Global Finance*, December 2009, p. 49; "Reasons to Cut Off Mr. Mugabe," *Economist*, April 13, 1996, p. 339.

The BOP strategy is challenging to implement. Companies have to offer affordable goods that are highly available in a community that is willing to accept the product. Most importantly, however, is that the company must bring awareness of the product to the general populace. Balancing these is not a simple task because advertising and efficient distribution networks, for example, cost a significant amount, yet the companies cannot add a high price tag. Furthermore, illiteracy issues, poor infrastructure, corruption, and nonexistent distribution channels often associated with poverty-stricken societies deter companies from wanting to invest. Despite the many barriers, companies can be successful. In the early years of cell phone usage, Smart Communications Inc. saw that there was a great opportunity to expand in the Philippines, where about half the population lived in poverty. In 2002, the market forecasted that approximately 30 percent of the population would be using mobile phones by 2008. Smart offered pay-as-you-go phones that could be recharged using a microchip that was already in the cellular phones, making it possible to recharge "over the air." The company then began to offer pricing plans that consisted of extremely small increments, so even the low-income consumer could take advantage of the opportunity. It worked in Smart's favor, as more and more people began using the service daily, and the cellular industry reached a 30 percent margin in 2004, changing forecasts to a shocking 70 percent mobile phone usage rate by 2008. Smart's parent company experienced a more than tenfold increase in profits in 2004 as compared to 2003, due in large part to focusing on the very lucrative market at the base of the pyramid.[113] To learn more about how mobile technology is reaching impoverished countries, see the nearby International Management in Action box.

Entrepreneurial Strategy and New Ventures

In addition to strategies that must be tailored for the particular needs and circumstances in emerging economies, specialized strategies are also required for the international management activities of entrepreneurial and new-venture firms. Most international management activities take place within the context of medium-large MNCs, but, increasingly, small and medium companies, often in the form of new ventures, are getting involved in international management. This has been made possible by advances in telecommunication and Internet technologies and by greater efficiencies and lower costs in shipping, allowing firms that were previously limited to local or national markets to access international customers. These new access channels, however, suggest particular strategies that must be customized and tailored to the unique situations and resource limitations of small, entrepreneurial firms.[114,115]

International Entrepreneurship **International entrepreneurship** has been defined as "a combination of innovative, proactive, and risk-seeking behavior that crosses national borders and is intended to create value in organizations."[116] The internationalization of the marketplace and the increasing number of entrepreneurial firms in the global economy have created new opportunities for small and new-venture firms to accelerate inter-

international entrepreneurship
A combination of innovative, proactive, and risk-seeking behavior that crosses national boundaries and is intended to create value for organizations.

nationalization. This international entrepreneurial activity is being observed in even the smallest and newest organizations. Indeed, one study among 57 privately held Finnish electronics firms during the mid-1990s showed that firms that internationalize after they are established domestically must overcome a number of barriers to that international expansion, such as their domestic orientation, internal domestic political ties, and domestic decision-making inertia. In contrast, firms that internationalize earlier face fewer barriers to learning about the international environment.[117] Thus, the earlier in its existence that an innovative firm internationalizes, the faster it is likely to grow both overall and in foreign markets.

However, despite this new access, there remain limitations to international entrepreneurial activities. In another study, researchers show that deploying a technological learning advantage internationally is no simple process. They studied more than 300 private independent and corporate new ventures based in the United States. Building on past research about the advantages of large, established multinational enterprises, their results from 12 high-technology industries show that greater diversity of national environments is associated with increased technological learning opportunities even for new ventures, whose internationalization is usually thought to be limited.[118] In addition, the breadth, depth, and speed of technological learning from varied international environments is significantly enhanced by formal organizational efforts to integrate knowledge throughout a firm such as cross-functional teams and formal analysis of both successful and failed projects. Further, the research shows that venture performance (growth and return on equity) is improved by technological learning gained from international environments.

International New Ventures and "Born-Global" Firms   Another dimension of the growth of international entrepreneurial activities is the increasing incidence of international new ventures, or **born-global firms**—firms that engage in significant international activity shortly after being established. Building on an empirical study of small firms in Norway and France, researchers found that more than half of the exporting firms established there since 1990 could be classified as "born globals."[119] Examining the differences between newly established firms with high or low export involvement levels revealed that a decision maker's global orientation and market conditions are important factors.

Another study highlighted the critical role of innovative culture, as well as knowledge and capabilities, in this unique breed of international, entrepreneurial firms. An analysis of case studies and surveys revealed key strategies that engender international success among these innovative firms.[120] Successful born-global firms leverage a distinctive mix of orientations and strategies that allow them to succeed in diverse international markets. Their possession of the foundational capabilities of international entrepreneurial orientation and international marketing orientation engender the development of a specific collection of organizational strategies. The most important business strategies employed by born-global firms are global technological competence, unique-products development, quality focus, and leveraging of foreign distributor competences.[121]

There is a difference between born-global firms and born-international firms, as one study showed. Born-international firms tend to export products close to markets, and revenues from these outside markets contribute 25 percent or less of total revenues. Truly born-global firms, however, tend to distribute goods to distant markets in multiple regions, and revenues from international activities tend to surpass 25 percent. It has been found that truly born-global firms tend to survive longer than other seemingly global companies.[122] However, being born global can simply be seen as accelerated internationalization. Another study compared born-global firms to those that sought out joint ventures or acquisitions (see Chapter 9) as a method to expand internationally. Results showed that while the market responds more positively to joint ventures or "partnerships,"

born-global firms
Firms that engage in significant international activities shortly after being established.

the extent to which a born-global is successful greatly depends on how developed the area is that the company is moving into. In other words, while the market appreciates already-established firms because they are familiar, if a start-up does not have the capital to partner with well-known organizations and the international markets are open, then born-global companies may show slightly lower returns in the beginning, but this is not an indicator of survival or ultimate success.[123]

One clear example of a born-global firm is California-based Amazon.com. Like most U.S. Internet firms, Amazon.com has been able to distribute its products and services on an international scale from the outset. Although differing levels of cultural similarities and technological sophistication impact Amazon's potential for success internationally, the Internet as a medium has removed certain entry barriers that have historically restricted quick market entry.[124] Another example is New York–based online trading and investing services E*Trade. The company was able to bring in revenues from 33 countries in only three years, clearly making it a global brand. Allowing customers to actively participate in their investments while offering multilingual technical and professional customer support allowed E*Trade to integrate its services in many countries. The simplified website does not bombard consumers with extraneous information, and allows each person to trade as much or as little as desired, making it inherently customized. It has not been a success story for its entire existence, however. The company was in danger of being left behind when it could not get out of the red, but in 2005, the company was able to become profitable due to the low cost of Internet business and its extremely diverse customer base. Although it had its ups and downs in the following years, it survived the financial crisis with fewer problems than many "bricks and mortar" brokerages.

The Internet clearly provides one of the easiest and most efficient methods of becoming global quickly, but it is important that awareness is brought to the business, or it too can be lost in the digital maze of the World Wide Web. Now more than ever, born-global as a corporate strategy is becoming more attractive and less risky. The opening World of International Management feature of Chapter 11 provides a discussion of the globalization and strategy of two online retailers.

The World of International Management—Revisited

Recall the World of International Management's discussion of the pharmaceutical company GSK that opened this chapter. It is easy to see why pharmaceutical companies are expanding globally and reshaping their business strategies accordingly. Large, traditional pharmaceutical companies are facing pressures from a range of quarters, including new competition from emerging markets. These firms are attempting to lower costs by collaborating with or merging with generic companies, diversifying their product portfolio to provide more consistent revenue streams, investing in newer higher value-added compounds that require biologic expertise, and leveraging their research and development across products and geographies. This is truly an industry in transition, with globalization itself as a major driver of the transformation.

Drawing on your understanding of the need for and the benefits of strategic management, answer these questions: (1) Which imperative is likely to be relatively most important to MNCs in the coming decade: economic, political, or quality? (2) When MNCs scan the environment, what are two key areas for consideration that they must address? (3) Referring to the chapter's opening World of International Management, how would you characterize GSK's strategy within the globalization–national responsiveness framework? (4) Which FSAs and CSAs does it primarily rely upon? To what extent does GSK use a "base of pyramid approach"? How would it affect the company if low-income markets turned out to be a bust?

SUMMARY OF KEY POINTS

1. There is a growing need for strategic management among MNCs. Some of the primary reasons include foreign direct investment is increasing; planning is needed to coordinate and integrate increasingly diverse operations via an overall focus; and emerging international challenges require strategic planning.

2. A strategic plan can take on an economic focus, a political focus, a quality focus, an administrative coordination focus, or some variation of the four. The global integration–national responsiveness framework defines the four basic strategies employed by MNCs: international, global, multi-domestic, and transnational. Although transnational is often the preferred strategy, it is also the most difficult to implement.

3. Strategy formulation consists of several steps. First, the MNC carries out external environmental scanning to identify opportunities and threats. Next, the firm conducts an internal resource analysis of company strengths and weaknesses. Strategic goals then are formulated in light of the results of these external and internal analyses.

4. Strategy implementation is the process of providing goods and services in accord with the predetermined plan of action. This implementation typically involves such considerations as deciding where to locate operations, carrying out an entry and ownership strategy, and using functional strategies to implement the plan. Functional strategies focus on marketing, production, and finance.

5. Strategies for emerging markets and international entrepreneurship/new ventures may require specialized approaches targeted to these unique circumstances.

KEY TERMS

administrative coordination, *298*
base of the pyramid strategy, *313*
born-global firms, *318*
economic imperative, *295*
environmental scanning, *302*
global integration, *299*

global strategy, *301*
international entrepreneurship, *317*
international strategy, *301*
key success factor (KSF), *304*
multi-domestic strategy, *301*
national responsiveness, *299*

political imperative, *296*
quality imperative, *297*
strategic management, *293*
strategy implementation, *306*
transnational strategy, *301*

REVIEW AND DISCUSSION QUESTIONS

1. Of the four imperatives discussed in this chapter—economic, political, quality, and administration—which would be most important to IBM in its efforts to make inroads in the Pacific Rim market? Would this emphasis be the same as that in the United States, or would IBM be giving primary attention to one of the other imperatives? Explain.

2. Define global integration as used in the context of strategic international management. In what way might globalization be a problem for a successful national organization that is intent on going international? In your answer, provide an example of the problem.

3. Some international management experts contend that globalization and national responsiveness are diametrically opposed forces, and that to accommodate one, a multinational must relax its efforts in the other. In what way is this an accurate statement? In what way is it incomplete or inaccurate?

4. Consider that both a retail chain and a manufacturing company want to expand overseas. What environmental factors would have the most impact on these companies? What ratio of environmental scanning to internal analysis should each employ? What key factors of success differentiate the two?

5. Anheuser-Busch is attempting to expand in India, where beer is not widely consumed and liquor dominates the market. What areas should be targeted for strategic goals? What could be some marketing implications in the Indian market?

6. What particular conditions that MNCs face in emerging markets may require specialized strategies? What strategies might be most appropriate in response? How might a company identify opportunities at the "base of the pyramid" (i.e., low-income markets)?

7. What conditions have allowed some firms to be born global? What are some examples of born-global companies?

8. Mercedes changed its U.S. strategy by announcing that it is developing cars for the $30,000 to $45,000 price range (as well as its typical upper-end cars). What might have accounted for this change in strategy? In your answer, include a discussion of the implications from the standpoints of marketing, production, and finance.

INTERNET EXERCISE: INFOSYS'S GLOBAL STRATEGY

Infosys is one of the world's largest IT service providers. It started in India but has rapidly expanded around the world. It offers consulting services, outsourcing, data storage, and other informational management services to all industries. Go to Infosys's website and review the various services it offers. Then answer these questions: How do you think international strategic management is reflected in what you see on the website? What major strategic planning steps would Infosys need to carry out in order to remain a world leader with such diverse offerings? What potential threat, if it occurred, would prove most disastrous for Infosys, and what could the company do to deal with the possibility of this negative development?

ENDNOTES

1. Andrew Ward, "GlaxoSmithKline Sticks with Bet on Emerging Markets," *Financial Times*, February 5, 2014, www.ft.com/cms/s/0/0846f824-8e53-11e3-98c6-00144feab7de.html#axzz44WxDfZQu.

2. "IMS Institute Projects Global Pharma Market of $1.17–1.20 Trillion in 2017," *Pharmaceutical Commerce*, January 20, 2014, www.pharmaceuticalcommerce.com/business_finance?articleid=27085&keyword=IMS%20Institute-global%20pharma-market%20growth.

3. Ward, "GlaxoSmithKline Sticks with Bet on Emerging Markets."

4. Malcolm Moore, "China Fines Glaxo £297m for Bribery, Mark Reilly Sentenced," *The Telegraph*, September 19, 2014, www.telegraph.co.uk/finance/newsbysector/pharmaceuticalsandchemicals/11108376/China-fines-Glaxo-297m-for-bribery-Mark-Reilly-sentenced.html.

5. Ben Hirschler, "GSK Pays $1 Billion to Lift Indian Unit Stake to 75 Percent," *Reuters*, March 10, 2014, www.reuters.com/article/us-glaxosmithkline-india-idUSBREA2909U20140310.

6. GSK India, http://india-pharma.gsk.com/en-in/about-us/.

7. Eric Palmer, "Glaxo Starts $153M Plant in India," *Fierce Pharma Manufacturing*, September 10, 2015, www.fiercepharmamanufacturing.com/story/glaxo-starts-153m-plant-india/2015-09-10.

8. Manish Panchal, Charu Kapoor, and Mansi Mahajan, "Success Strategies for Indian Pharma Industry in an Uncertain World," *Business Standard*, February 17, 2014, www.business-standard.com/content/b2b-chemicals/success-strategies-for-indian-pharma-industry-in-an-uncertain-world-114021701557_1.html.

9. Heather Timmons, "India Expands Role as Drug Producer," *New York Times* online, July 6, 2010, http://www.nytimes.com/2010/07/07/business/global/07indiadrug.html.

10. Ibid.

11. Panchal, Kapoor, and Mahajan, "Success Strategies for Indian Pharma Industry in an Uncertain World."

12. Timmons, "India Expands Role as Drug Producer."

13. IMS Market Prognosis, Economic Intelligence Unit, January 2012.

14. Dr. Derk Bergsma, former vice president of drug discovery group at Glaxosmithkline, personal interview, July 16, 2010.

15. "Cost to Develop and Win Marketing Approval for a New Drug Is $2.6 Billion," *Tufts Center for the Study of Drug Development*, November 18, 2014, http://csdd.tufts.edu/news/complete_story/pr_tufts_csdd_2014_cost_study.

16. Andrew Ward, "GSK Unveils New Drugs to Boost Growth," *Financial Times*, November 3, 2015, www.ft.com/intl/cms/s/0/04375ffa-8229-11e5-84dc-31c8b3b18e5f.html#axzz44WxDfZQu.

17. Julia Kollewe, "GlaxoSmithKline to Lower Drug Prices in Poorer Countries," *The Guardian*, March 31, 2016, www.theguardian.com/business/2016/mar/31/glaxosmithkline-to-lower-drug-prices-to-help-poorer-countries.

18. Jonathan D. Rockoff and Peter Loftus, "Pfizer Pushes on New Biotech Drugs," *The Wall Street Journal*, April 28, 2010, www.wsj.com/articles/SB10001424052748704464704575208580328253618.

19. Jeanne Whalen and Mimosa Spencer, "Sanofi Wins Long-Sought Biotech Deal," *The Wall Street Journal*, February 17, 2011, www.wsj.com/articles/SB10001424052748703373404576147483489656732.

20. Andrew Pollack, "Deal Provides Vaccines to Poor Nations at Lower Cost," *New York Times*, March 24, 2010, p. B2.

21. Matt Wilkinson, "Big Pharma Set for Generics Boost," *Chemistry World*, May 21, 2009, www.rsc.org/chemistryworld/News/2009/May/21050903.asp.

22. Tova Cohen and Steven Scheer, "Teva to Buy Allergan Generic Business for $40.5 Billion, Drops Mylan Bid," *Reuters*, July 27, 2015, www.reuters.com/article/us-allergan-m-a-teva-pharm-ind-idUSKCN0Q10QE20150727.

23. Wilkinson, "Big Pharma Set for Generics Boost."

24. Charlie Nordblom, "Involving Middle Managers in Strategy at Volvo Group," *Strategic Communication Management* 10, no. 2 (February–March 2006), pp. 26–29.

25. Joel Baglole, "Citibank Takes Risk by Issuing Cards in China," *The Wall Street Journal,* March 10, 2004, p. C1.

26. Wang Ming, "Citigroup Sets China Growth," *The Wall Street Journal*, March 15, 2007, p. C7.

27. Julie Steinberg, "Citi to Sell 20% Stake in China Guangfa Bank for $3 Billion," *The Wall Street Journal*, February 29, 2016, www.wsj.com/articles/citi-to-sell-20-stake-in-china-guangfa-bank-for-3-billion-1456739999.

28. Jennifer M. Freedman, "China Nod for Citibank Credit Cards May Show Market Opening," *Bloomberg*, February 6, 2012, www.bloomberg.com/news/2012-02-06/nod-for-citibank-s-credit-cards-may-signal-chinese-banking-market-opening.html.

29. Enoch Yiu, "Citi Continues to Expand Branches to Tap Asia Clients," *South China Morning Post*, September 3, 2012, www.scmp.com/business/banking-finance/article/1028510/citi-continues-expand-branches-tap-asia-clients.

30. Lawrence White, "Citi to Hire 100 Bankers in Asia, Eyes More Business from Smaller Clients," *Reuters*, July 29, 2014, www.reuters.com/article/us-citigroup-asiapac-expansion-idUSK-BN0FY08620140729.

31. Alison Tudor, "Citigroup Eyes More Asian Expansion," *The Wall Street Journal*, July 16, 2010, www.wsj.com/articles/SB10001424052748703722804575368781341607338.

32. *Foreign Investment Restrictions in OECD Countries* (Paris: Organization for Economic Cooperation and Development, June 2003), p. 167.

33. Bahar Karaman, "Ford Thailand to Invest US$186 Million in Rayong Factory," *Thailand Business News*, December 1, 2015, www.thailand-business-news.com/corporate/51708-ford-thailand-invest-us186-million-rayong-factory.html.

34. "Production Statistics," OICA, www.oica.net/category/production-statistics/ (last visited March 21, 2016).

35. "G.E. Acknowledges Plan to Sell Appliance Unit," *Associated Press*, May 17, 2008.

36. Ankit Ajmera, "GE to Sell Appliances Business to China's Haier for $5.4 Billion," *Reuters*, January 15, 2016, www.reuters.com/article/us-ge-divestiture-haier-elec-idUSKCN0UT0AG.

37. Thomas Gryta, "Genzyme Plans Buyback, to Shed Business," *The Wall Street Journal*, May 6, 2010, www.wsj.com/articles/SB1000142405274870368630457522844351267462.

38. Gina Chon and Anupreeta Das, "Genzyme in Talks with Sanofi," *The Wall Street Journal*, August 3, 2010, p. B1.

39. Nina Sovich and Noelle Mennella, "Sanofi to Buy Genzyme for More Than $20 Billion," *Reuters,* February 16, 2011, www.reuters.com/article/2011/02/16/us-genzyme-sanofi-idUSTRE71E4XI20110216.

40. Barry Hopewell, "Strategic Management: A Multiperspective Approach," *Long Range Planning* 36, no. 4 (July 2003), p. 317.

41. Sharon Watson O'Neil, "Managing Foreign Subsidiaries: Agents of Headquarters, or an Independent Network?" *Strategic Management Journal* 21, no. 5 (May 2000), p. 525.

42. Noel Capon, Chris Christodoulou, John U. Farley, and James Hulbert, "A Comparison of Corporate Planning Practice in American and Australian Manufacturing Companies," *Journal of International Business Studies*, Fall 1984, pp. 41–45.

43. Martin K. Welge, "Planning in German Multinational Corporations," *International Studies of Management and Organization*, Spring 1982, pp. 6–37.

44. Martin K. Welge and Michael E. Kenter, "Impact of Planning on Control Effectiveness and Company Performance," *Management International Review* 20, no. 2 (1988), pp. 4–15.

45. Johanna Mair, "Exploring the Determinants of Unit Performance: The Role of Middle Managers in Stimulating Profit Growth," *Group & Organization Management* 30, no. 3 (June 2005), pp. 263–288.

46. See, for example, M. Kotabe and J. Y. Murray, "Global Sourcing Strategy and Sustainable Competitive Advantage," *Industrial Marketing Management* **33** (2004), pp. 7–14.

47. Joan Magretta, "Fast, Global, and Entrepreneurial: Supply Chain Management, Hong Kong Style," *Harvard Business Review*, September–October 1998, p. 108.

48. Ratna Bhushan, "Sprite Topples Thums Up from Numero Uno Position after Three Decades," *Economic Times*, October 8, 2013, http://articles. economictimes.indiatimes.com/2013-10-08/ news/42829160_1_coca-cola-india-thums-up-sprite.

49. Nikhil Deogun, "For Coke in India, Thums Up Is the Real Thing," *The Wall Street Journal*, April 29, 1998, pp. B1, B6.

50. India Knowledge@Wharton, "Coca-Cola India: Winning Hearts and Taste Buds in the Hinterland," *The Wall Street Journal*, May 14, 2010, www.wsj.com/articles/SB1272968140791886501.

51. "Will Emerging Economies Drive Coca-Cola's Growth?" Forbes, December 22, 2015, http:// www.forbes.com/sites/greatspeculations/2015/ 12/22/will-emerging-economies-drive-coca-colas-growth/#2671d52f1be9

52. Ratna Bhushan, "Coca-Cola's Bouquet of Brands Leads Those of PepsiCo in Soft Drinks Market, but Coke Not at the Top," *The Economic Times*, November 2, 2012, http://articles.economictimes. indiatimes.com/2012-11-02/news/34876016_1_ brand-coke-coca-cola-india-drinks-brands.

53. Richard M. Hodgetts, *Measures of Quality and High Performance* (New York: American Management Association, 1998).

54. Sang M. Lee, Fred Luthans, and Richard M. Hodgetts, "Total Quality Management: Implications for Central and Eastern Europe," *Organizational Dynamics*, Spring 1992, pp. 44–45.

55. 55. Greg Gardner, "GM, Toyota Stand Out in J.D. Power Dependability Rankings," *Detroit Free Press*, February 24, 2016, www.freep.com/story/ money/cars/general-motors/2016/02/24/jd-power-dependability-rankings/80806718/.

56. Roger Fingas, "Apple Adds More Launch Locations for iPhone 6s, Apple Watch on Oct. 22 & 23," *Apple Insider*, October 8, 2015, http:// appleinsider.com/articles/15/10/08/apple-adds-more-launch-locations-for-iphone-6s-apple-watch-on-oct-22-23.

57. Sara Ashley O'Brien, "Apple Sells Record 13 Million New iPhones," *CNN Money*, September 28, 2015,

http://money.cnn.com/2015/09/28/technology/apple-13-million-6s-sales/.

58. Jonny Evans, "The Complete iPhone 6S Camera Improvements Guide," *Computer World*, September 14, 2015, www.computerworld.com/ article/2983812/smartphones/the-complete-iphone-6s-camera-improvements-guide.html.

59. Leslie Wayne, "Chief Decided to Step Down at Motorola," *New York Times*, September 20, 2003, p. C1.

60. "Hip Cell," *Chicago Tribune*, June 3, 2004, p. 32.

61. Hayley Tsukayama, "Google Agrees to Acquire Motorola Mobility," *Washington Post*, August 15, 2011, www.washingtonpost.com/blogs/faster-forward/post/google-agrees-to-acquire-motorola-mobility/2011/08/15/gIQABmTkGJ_blog.html.

62. Christopher A. Bartlett and Sumantra Ghoshal, *Managing Across Borders: The Transnational Solution*, updated 2nd ed. (Cambridge, MA: Harvard Business School Press, 2002).

63. Ibid.

64. Royal Ford, "Driven by Demand, Vehicle Buyers Want Versatility and Amenities, Too," *Boston Globe,* February 3, 2004, p. G1.

65. "December 2015 and Year-End Sales Chart," *Toyota*, January 5, 2016, http://pressroom. toyota.com/releases/tms+december+2015+ sales+chart.htm.

66. Royal Ford, "Driven by Demand, Vehicle Buyers Want Versatility and Amenities, Too," *Boston Globe,* February 3, 2004, p. G1.

67. Fons Trompenaars and Charles Hampden-Turner, *Riding the Waves of Culture: Understanding Diversity in Global Business*, 2nd ed. New York: McGraw-Hill, 1998, p. 188.

68. Dan Sabbagh, "How the Blu-ray War Was Won—Sony Outspent, Outsold Toshiba," *The Times*, February 21, 2008, www.thetimes.co.uk/tto/ business/industries/media/article2176487.ece.

69. Kerry Capell, "Thinking Simple at Philips," *BusinessWeek*, December 11, 2006, p. 50.

70. Monsanto, www.monsanto.com.

71. Charles Hill, *Global Business Today*, 3rd ed. (New York: McGraw-Hill, 2004), pp. 376–380.

72. Ibid.

73. See Anne-Wil Harzing, "An Empirical Analysis and Extension of the Bartlett and Ghoshal Typology of Multinational Companies," *Journal of International Business Studies*, First Quarter 2000, pp. 101–120.

74. Kendra S. Albright, "Environmental Scanning: Radar for Success," *Information Management Journal* 38, no. 3 (May–June 2004), pp. 38–44.

75. Manuel Yunggar, "Environment Scanning for Strategic Information: Content Analysis from Malaysia," *Journal of American Academy of Business* 6, no. 2 (March 2005), pp. 324–331.

76. Joan Solsman, "Netflix Invades Europe; Why Expansion beyond the US Is So Critical," *CNET*, September 29, 2014, www.cnet.com/news/netflix-invades-europe-why-international-expansion-is-so-critical/.

77. Sam Schechner, "Netflix Continues European Expansion into Less Connected Markets," *The Wall Street Journal*, June 7, 2015, www.wsj.com/articles/netflix-continues-european-expansion-into-less-connected-markets-1433687654.

78. Jonathan Vanian, "Cisco Just Bought This Hot Startup for Over $1 Billion," *Fortune*, February 3, 2016, http://fortune.com/2016/02/03/cisco-jasper-internet-things/.

79. Eva Dou and Don Clark, "Struggles in China Push Cisco to Strike Deal," *The Wall Street Journal*, September 22, 2015, www.wsj.com/articles/struggles-in-china-push-cisco-to-strike-deal-1442965527.

80. Ritsuko Ando, "Cisco Takes Aim at China Despite Trade Tensions," *Reuters*, April 15, 2010, www.reuters.com/article/us-cisco-china-analysis-idUSTRE63E4RN20100415.

81. Shai Oster and Danielle Muoio, "Cisco Pledges $10 Billion China Investment to Regain Ground," *Bloomberg*, June 17, 2015, www.bloomberg.com/news/articles/2015-06-17/cisco-to-invest-10-billion-in-china-to-create-jobs-promote-r-d.

82. John Rosevear, "Ford's European Sales Jump 18% as Its Turnaround Continues," *Motley Fool*, March 10, 2016, www.fool.com/investing/general/2016/03/10/fords-european-sales-jump-18-as-its-turnaround-con.aspx.

83. Sea Jin Chang, "International Expansion Strategy of Japanese Firms: Capacity Building through Sequential Entry," *Academy of Management Journal*, April 1995, p. 402.

84. Accenture, "Accenture to Acquire Majority Stake in IMJ to Expand Its Digital Capabilities in Japan," press release, April 4, 2016, https://newsroom.accenture.com/news/accenture-to-acquire-majority-stake-in-imj-to-expand-its-digital-capabilities-in-japan.htm.

85. Mary Anastasia O'Grady, "Americas: Teamsters Give NAFTA a Flat Tire," *The Wall Street Journal*, April 16, 2004, p. A15.

86. Joel Millman, "The Economy: Mexican Mergers, Acquisitions Triple from 2001," *The Economist*, December 27, 2002, p. A2.

87. Anheuser-Busch InBev, "Anheuser-Busch InBev Completes Combination with Grupo Modelo," press release, *PR Newswire*, June 4, 2013, www.prnewswire.com/news-releases/anheuser-busch-inbev-completes-combination-with-grupo-modelo-210103631.html.

88. AT&T, "AT&T Completes Acquisition of Nextel Mexico," press release, April 30, 2015, http://about.att.com/story/att_completes_acquisition_of_nextel_mexico.html.

89. Harry I. Chernotsky, "Selecting U.S. Sites: A Case Study of German and Japanese Firms," *Management International Review* 23, no. 2 (1983), pp. 45–55.

90. Also see Roland Calori, Leif Melin, Tugrul Atamer, and Peter Gustavsson, "Innovative International Strategies," *Journal of World Business* 35, no. 4 (2000), pp. 333–354.

91. Christos Pantzalis, "Does Location Matter? An Empirical Analysis of Geographic Scope and MNC Market Valuation," *Journal of International Business Studies*, First Quarter 2001, pp. 133–155.

92. "A Guide in Africa: Why Investors in Frontier Markets Need Someone to Show Them Around," *The Economist*, February 23, 2013, www.economist.com/news/business/21572172-why-investors-frontier-markets-need-someone-show-them-around-guide-africa.

93. This section is adapted from Alan Rugman and Jonathan P. Doh, *Multinationals and Development* (New Haven: Yale University Press, 2008), pp. 12–14.

94. Bertel Schmitt, "How Japan, 'the Most Closed Market in the World,' Managed to Import 360,000 Foreign Cars," *Daily Kanban*, January 12, 2015, http://dailykanban.com/2015/01/japan-closed-market-world-managed-import-360000-foreign-cars/.

95. Das Narayandas, John Quelch, and Gordon Swartz, "Prepare Your Company for Global Pricing," *Sloan Management Review*, Fall 2000, pp. 61–70.

96. UNCTAD, *World Investment Report 2015: Reforming International Investment Governance* (2015), http://unctad.org/en/PublicationsLibrary/wir2015_en.pdf.

97. Jonathan P. Doh and Ravi Ramamurti, "Reassessing Risk in Developing Country Infrastructure," *Long Range Planning* 36, no. 4 (2003), pp. 337–353.

98. Jonathan P. Doh, Peter Rodriguez, Klaus Uhlenbruck, Jamie Collins, and Loraine Eden, "Coping with Corruption in Foreign Markets," *Academy of Management Executive* 17, no. 3 (2003), pp. 114–127.

99. See Yudong Luo and Mike W. Peng, "First Mover Advantages in Investing in Transitional Economies," *Thunderbird International Business Review* 40, no. 2 (March–April 1998), pp. 141–163.

100. For a detailed analysis of first-mover effects of this case, see Jonathan P. Doh, "Entrepreneurial Privatization Strategies: Order of Entry and Local Partner Collaboration as Sources of Competitive Advantage," *Academy of Management Review* 25, no. 3 (2000), pp. 551–571.

101. "Mexican Regulator Requires New Telmex Plan to Open Local Network," *Reuters*, October 11, 2015, www.reuters.com/article/us-mexico-telcoms-idUSKCN0S510120151011.

102. C. K. Prahalad, *The Fortune at the Bottom of the Pyramid: Eradicating Poverty through Profits* (revised and updated 5th Anniversary Edition: *Eradicating Poverty through Profits*) (Philadelphia: Wharton School Publishing, 2009).

103. Stuart Hart and Clayton Christensen, "The Great Leap: Driving Innovation from the Base of the Pyramid," *Sloan Management Review* 44, no. 1 (2002), pp. 51–56.

104. C. K. Prahalad and Stuart L. Hart, "The Fortune at the Bottom of the Pyramid," *Strategy + Business* 26 (2002), pp. 54–67.

105. Joan Enric Ricart, Michael J. Enright, Pankaj Ghemawat, Stuart L. Hart, and Tarun Khanna, "New Frontiers in International Strategy," *Journal of International Business Studies* 35, no. 3 (May 2004), pp. 175–200.

106. Ibid., pp. 194–195.

107. Erik Simanis, "At the Base of the Pyramid," *The Wall Street Journal*, October 26, 2009, p. R7, http://eriksimanis.com/wp-content/uploads/2014/06/Simanis-WSJ-Oct-26-2009.pdf.

108. Nicolas Dahan, Jonathan P. Doh, Jennifer Oetzel, and Michael Yaziji, "Corporate-NGO Collaboration: Creating New Business Models for Developing Markets," *Long Range Planning* 43, no. 2 (2010), pp. 326–342.

109. See http://www.nestlecocoaplan.com/farmer-training-in-cote-divoire/

110. Dimitra Defotis, "Danone: A Less Risky Emerging-Markets Play," *Barron's*, August 8, 2015, http://www.barrons.com/articles/danone-a-less-risky-emerging-markets-play-1439013136

111. Ruth Bender, "Danone Weighs Expansion Opportunities," *The Wall Street Journal*, July 22, 2014, www.wsj.com/articles/danone-weighs-expansion-opportunities-1406050776.

112. Christina Passariello, "Danone Expands Its Pantry to Woo the World's Poor," *The Wall Street Journal*, June 25, 2010, www.wsj.com/articles/SB10001424052748703615104575328943452892722.

113. Jamie Anderson and Niels Billou, "Serving the World's Poor: Innovation at the Base of the Economic Pyramid," *Journal of Business Strategy* 28, no. 2 (2007), pp. 14–21.

114. Benjamin M. Oviatt and Patricia P. McDougall, "The Internationalization of Entrepreneurship," *Journal of International Business Studies* 36 (2005), pp. 2–8;

115. Patricia P. McDougall and Benjamin M. Oviatt, "International Entrepreneurship: The Intersection of Two Research Paths," *Academy of Management Journal* 43 (2000), pp. 902–908.

116. Ibid., p. 902.

117. Erkko Autio, Harry J. Sapienza, and James G. Almeida, "Effects of Age at Entry, Knowledge Intensity, and Irritability on International Growth," *Academy of Management Journal* 43 (2000), pp. 909–924.

118. Shaker A. Zahra, Duane R. Ireland, and Michael A. Hitt, "International Expansion by New Venture Firms: International Diversity, Mode of Market Entry, Technological Learning, and Performance," *Academy of Management Journal* 43 (2000), pp. 925–950.

119. Moen Oystein, "The Born Globals: A New Generation of Small European Exporters," *International Marketing Review* 19, no. 2/3 (2002), pp. 156–175.

120. Gary A. Knight and S. Tamar Cavusgil, "Innovation, Organizational Capabilities, and the Born-Global Firm," *Journal of International Business Studies* 35, no. 2 (2004), pp. 124–141.

121. Ibid.

122. Olli Kuivalainen, Sanna Sundqvist, and Per Servais, "Firms' Degree of Born-Globalness, International Entrepreneurial Orientation and Export Performance," *Journal of World Business* 42 (2007), pp. 253–267.

123. Kimberly C. Gleason and Joan Wiggenhorn, "Born Globals: The Choice of Globalization Strategy, and the Market's Perception of Performance," *Journal of World Business* 42 (2007), pp. 322–335.

124. J. de La Torre and R. W. Moxon, "Electronic Commerce and Global Business: Introduction to

the Symposium," *Journal of International Business* 32, no. 1 (2001), pp. 617–640.

125. CIA, "Saudi Arabia," *The World Factbook* (2016), https://www.cia.gov/library/publications/the-world-factbook/geos/sa.html.

126. Ibid.

127. World Bank, "Saudi Arabia," *World Development Indicators* (2016), http://data.worldbank.org/indicator/NY.GDP.MKTP.KD.ZG/countries/SA?display=graph.

128. CIA, "Saudi Arabia."

129. Ibid.

130. Ibid.

131. Tim Bowler, "Falling Oil Prices: Who Are the Winners and Losers?" *BBC News*, January 19, 2015, www.bbc.com/news/business-29643612.

132. "Saudi Arabia Renews Push for Foreign Investors as Oil Cushion Shrinks," *Bloomberg*, January 25, 2016, www.arabianbusiness.com/saudi-arabia-renews-push-for-foreign-investors-as-oil-cushion-shrinks-619785.html.

Saudi Arabia

Saudi Arabia is a large country in the Middle East covering 856,000 square miles. The country borders the Persian Gulf to the north and the Red Sea to the south. About one-fifth the size of the United States, its natural resources include petroleum and natural gas (among the largest in the world), iron ore, gold, and copper. The two major holy cities of Islam are in Saudi Arabia: Mecca and Medina.[125]

With just over 27 million people, Saudi Arabia is almost entirely Arab Muslim (approximately 90 percent Sunni and 10 percent Shia). The country's population growth rate is estimated at 1.46 percent. Additionally, the country's population is overwhelmingly (approximately 90 percent) younger than 55 years of age. According to U.N. reports, 30 percent of the country's population consists of immigrants.[126]

The country's GDP in 2014 was US$746 billion.[127] From 2011 through 2013, annual GDP growth plummeted from 10 percent to 2.7 percent. With low oil prices worldwide, Saudi Arabia's GDP growth remains stunted at about 3.5 percent.[128]

Saudi Arabia operates its government as a monarchy, wherein the king makes all important official decisions. The king appoints ministers who act as his advisers. In 2011, women were granted the right to vote and run for seats in municipal elections, though gender oppression is still commonplace and integrated into the legal system. The country's laws are based on Islamic law with some Western elements incorporated. For many years, Saudi Arabia has enjoyed favorable relationships with many Western nations. As it is a large exporter of fossil fuel, Western nations are somewhat dependent on maintaining civility with the Saudis despite alleged human rights violations. In recent years, however, the Saudi monarchy and royal family have been suspected of aiding terrorism efforts, leading to somewhat strained relations with countries in Europe and the U.S.[129]

The government maintains strong controls over the country's economy, which is highly reliant on extraction and production of oil and gas. It is the largest exporter of petroleum, is the leader of the Organization of Petroleum Exporting Countries (OPEC), and accounts for approximately 16 percent of proven petroleum reserves. Foreign workers play a vital role in the economy, with more than 6 million expatriates employed in a variety of industries, especially construction and manufacturing. The government is making efforts to diversify its economy by growing the private sector and by seeking to employ more nationals, balancing the workforce.[130]

As oil prices have plummeted in recent years due to a variety of factors, Saudi Arabia and the other OPEC countries have been keeping output levels relatively high, resulting in huge losses. While the country can cover the deficits for the time being, a prolonged period of low oil demand could have devastating effects on the economic health of the country.[131]

You Be the International Management Consultant

As oil prices continue to drop, Saudi Arabia is actively seeking foreign investors to come into the country, especially in sectors such as transportation, health care, tourism, and building materials. The country has also opened the retail sector to companies seeking complete ownership of their business, negating the need for joint venture partnerships. The Saudi officials courting foreign investors say that, despite falling oil prices, the country's other sectors are still growing and provide excellent investment opportunities. Moreover, officials have said they are willing to discuss modifying any rule or regulation that might impede investment by a major foreign company.[132]

Questions

1. Given that the country is actively seeking foreign investors and appears to be creating a pro-business atmosphere, what non-oil businesses do you think would be best suited for expanding into Saudi Arabia?
2. If you were a foreign investor, what concerns would you have about the country? Would you make an investment in the country?

Chapter 9

ENTRY STRATEGIES AND ORGANIZATIONAL STRUCTURES

The success of an international firm can be greatly influenced by how it enters and operates in new markets and by the overall structure and design of its operations. There are a wide variety of entry strategies and organizational structures and designs from which to choose. Selecting the most appropriate strategy and structure depends on a number of factors, such as the desire of the home office for control over its foreign operations and the demands placed on the overseas unit by both the local market and the personnel who work there.

This chapter first discusses some entry strategies and systems of ownership that MNCs may have to choose from when deciding to expand abroad. With regard to the organization itself, the chapter presents and analyzes traditional organizational structures for effective international operations. Then it explores some of the new, nontraditional organizational arrangements stemming from mergers, joint ventures, and the Japanese concept of keiretsu. The specific objectives of this chapter are

1. **DESCRIBE** how an MNC develops and implements entry strategies and ownership structures.

2. **EXAMINE** the major types of entry strategies and organizational structures used in handling international operations.

3. **ANALYZE** the advantages and disadvantages of each type of organizational structure, including the conditions that make one preferable to others.

4. **DESCRIBE** the recent, nontraditional organizational arrangements coming out of mergers, joint ventures, keiretsus, and other new designs including electronic networks and product development structures.

5. **EXPLAIN** how organizational characteristics such as formalization, specialization, and centralization influence how the organization is structured and functions.

The World of *International Management*

Building a Global Brand: Haier's Alignment of Strategy and Structure

Originally founded in 1984 as Qingdao Refrigerator Company, Haier is the largest appliance manufacturer in China. Partially state-owned, the company has expanded its product line over the years to include computers, phones, washers, and other kitchen appliances. Since first offering public shares in the 1990s, Haier has grown tremendously. In 2015, profits reached US$2.7 billion on sales of more than US$32 billion. The company accounts for 10 percent of all appliance sales worldwide.[1] For over five years, Haier has maintained its status as the world leader in large appliance sales.

However, despite this success, most sales have been confined to the Chinese market. This has left Haier particularly susceptible to the volatility of the Chinese economy. For example, in 2015, sales fell for the first time in years due to slowing Chinese economic growth. Furthermore, increasing competition in the domestic appliance marketplace and growing online sales have cut Haier's profit margin, forcing Haier to expand beyond the Chinese market to achieve growth. Expanding into regions around the globe has been a difficult yet necessary transition for the company, requiring careful strategic planning and positioning.

First, foreign acquisitions have enabled Haier to enter new, more profitable markets around the globe. While Haier had found success selling smaller appliances like window air-conditioning units, to consumers in developed economies, the market for large refrigerators and other major appliances has been dominated by domestic brands. In 2012, Haier acquired 90 percent of New Zealand appliance maker Fisher & Paykel for US$770 million. This acquisition provided Haier with access to Fisher & Paykel's patent portfolio while simultaneously opening the Australian, New Zealand, and U.S. markets to Haier's existing product line. In developed economies, consumers tend to purchase more expensive appliances, resulting in greater profit margins than Haier is able to achieve in China.[2] Haier's largest foreign acquisition occurred in 2016, when it purchased GE's appliance division for US$5.4 billion.

This deal was aimed directly at expanding Haier's presence in the U.S. market. Chinese brands, often seen as less reputable by consumers in the United States, have historically struggled to achieve any level of consumer confidence. By acquiring a U.S. brand with a strong domestic reputation, Haier will be able to sell its own products under a trusted brand name. As part of its acquisition deal, Haier will be able to use the GE label for 40 years and will maintain GE's existing appliance division headquarters in Kentucky.[3]

Second, Haier has strategically dispersed its manufacturing facilities around the globe. This has allowed production to match the niche needs of the local market. For example, to meet the demands of the growing smartphone market in southeast Asia, Haier opened a facility specifically for phone production in Indonesia in 2014.[4] In Africa, Haier maintains five manufacturing facilities, tailoring products to best suit the small, but growing, African middle class. In Nigeria, for example, Haier builds and sells air conditioners, refrigerators, and freezers to over half a million people annually, making it the top kitchen appliance producer in the country. To best meet the needs of the Nigerian consumer, Haier has developed refrigerators that can keep food cold for over 100 hours, eliminating food loss during frequent electrical service interruptions.[5] In 2000, Haier became the first Chinese company to open a production facility in the U.S. when it completed its Haier Industrial Park in South Carolina. Spanning over 100 acres and costing US$40 million, the plant focuses on refrigerators for the American market. In 2015, Haier broke ground on a US$72 million expansion to the facility to meet increased U.S. demand. Today, Haier maintains production facilities in over two dozen locations outside of China.

Third, by focusing research and development efforts towards the local market, Haier has been able to better prepare itself for entry to new foreign markets. Using market research and its well-designed distribution network, Haier puts the consumer first by quickly altering its products to suit the feedback it receives. In the U.S., Haier has opened a design center specifically to cater products to the local cultural habits. The company also operates research and development centers in Europe, Australia, and Japan. Additionally, the company actively seeks feedback from salespeople and consumers, often interviewing people while they are shopping in stores.[6] Haier's approach to research and development extends to the Internet, where the company solicits ideas from various users. Haier refers to this strategy as "Open Innovation." By asking open-ended questions on social media platforms—such as "What do you want in air conditioning?"—Haier is able to gain insight from millions of active consumers worldwide, modifying its approach to all aspects of appliance design.[7]

By acquiring reputable foreign brands, opening manufacturing facilities close to consumers, customizing its product line, and reaching out directly to consumers for feedback, Haier best positions itself to achieve success when expanding its product line into new markets.

The World of International Management's discussion of Haier provides a good example of the entry and organizational challenges and options companies face as they do business around the world. Haier localizes its image and product line to best suit its clientele while maintaining the strategies that lead to low costs and strong design. In this chapter, we review the basic entry strategies and organizational structures available to firms as they expand their global reach.

■ Entry Strategies and Ownership Structures

There are a number of common entry strategies and ownership structures in international operations. The most common entry approaches are wholly owned subsidiaries, mergers and acquisitions, alliances and joint ventures, licensing agreements, franchising, and basic export and import operations. Depending on the situation, any one of these can be

Table 9–2
Membership and Market Data for the Largest Airline Alliances (as of December 2015)

	Star Alliance (27 members, Founded 1997)	Sky Team (19 members, Founded 2000)	One World (13 members, Founded 1999)	Rest of Industry (selected major nonaligned carriers)
Passengers per year	654 million	588 million	512 million	
Destinations	1,312	1,052	1,010	
Revenue (billion US$)	177.42	186.33	143.23	
Major airlines	Air Canada (founder)	Aeroflot (2006)	American Airlines (founder)	JetBlue
	Air China (2007)	Aeroméxico (founder)	British Airways (founder)	Southwest
	Air New Zealand (1999)	Air France (founder)	Cathay Pacific (founder)	Aer Lingus
	Air India (2014)	Alitalia (2001)	Iberia (1999)	Icelandair
	ANA (1999)	China Airlines (2011)	Japan Airlines (2007)	Virgin Atlantic
	Avianca (2012)	Delta (founder)	LAN Airlines (2000)	Emirates
	Copa Airlines (2012)	KLM (2004)	Qantas (founder)	Air India
	Lufthansa (founder)	Korean Air (founder)	Qatar (2013)	Gulf Air
	SAS (founder)	Middle East Airlines (2014)	TAM Airlines (2014)	Qantas (founder)
	Singapore Airlines (2000)	Saudia (2012)		China Airlines
	United Airlines (founder)			Jet Airways

Network capacity				
Within North America	23%	28%	15%	34%
Within South America	1	2	14	83
Within Europe	20	16	11	53
Within Middle East	2	0	3	95
Within Africa	23	10	4	63
Within Asia	35	11	9	45
Within Oceania	11	0	32	57
Between N. America and Europe	27	34	21	18
Between N. America and S. America	9	29	40	22
Between Europe and S. America	20	28	22	30
Between N. America and Asia	41	29	10	20
Between Europe and Asia	36	22	19	23

Source: Adapted from Wikipedia, based on airline websites, https://en.wikipedia.org/wiki/Airline_alliance.

JVs, and M&As have been stimulated by a range of factors, including continued overcapacity, emerging markets expansion, and demand for new types of vehicles, including hybrid and electric.[28]

As discussed in Chapter 1, Renault and Nissan maintain a broad-based alliance that includes an equity joint venture arrangement. As a result of Chrysler's bankruptcy, Fiat acquired the U.S. automaker in two transactions over a five-year period, first buying a 20 percent stake in 2009 and later buying all of Chrysler's remaining shares in 2014.[29,30]

GM has long maintained a successful joint venture with China's Shanghai Automotive Industries Corporation (SAIC). Fiat's joint venture with GAC (Guangzhou AutomobileGroup), called GAC Fiat Automobiles Co., Ltd. and headquartered in

Changsha, China, opened a Jeep production facility to meet growing demand for SUVs in China in 2015. The rising power of China and India in the global automotive industry has been made clear by the growth of brands such as Cherry and Tata, and by two major acquisitions a few years ago. In 2010, the Chinese auto company Geely bought Ford's Volvo car unit for $1.8 billion. Reuters declared the deal to be China's "biggest overseas auto purchase," which "underscores China's arrival as a major force in the global auto industry." Two years earlier, another historic deal took place when Indian auto company Tata Motors bought Ford's Land Rover and Jaguar brands. Volvo, Land Rover, and Jaguar are all European brands that Ford had previously purchased.[31,32]

Finally, development of hybrid and electric vehicles has often taken the form of joint ventures because (1) the technologies often do not exist in traditional automotive companies and (2) the market prospect and regulatory uncertainties are high, prompting companies to want to share risks with partners.

All of these collaborations—whether alliances, joint ventures, mergers, or acquisitions—are fueled by opportunities created by integrating some combination of market knowledge and access, technological and managerial capability, scale economies and efficiency, and political and legal imperatives.

Licensing

Another way to gain market entry, which also may be considered a form of alliance, is to acquire the right to a particular product by getting an exclusive license to make or sell the good in a particular geographic locale. A **license** is an agreement that allows one party to use an industrial property right in exchange for payment to the owning party. In a typical arrangement, the party giving the license (the licensor) will allow the other (the licensee) to use a patent, a trademark, or proprietary information in exchange for a fee. The fee usually is based on sales, such as 1 percent of all revenues earned from an industrial motor sold in Asia. The licensor typically restricts licensee sales to a particular geographic locale and limits the time period covered by the arrangement. The firm in this example may have an exclusive right to sell this patented motor in Asia for the next five years. This allows the licensor to seek licensees for other major geographic locales, such as Europe, South America, and Australia.

> **license**
> An agreement that allows one party to use an industrial property right in exchange for payment to the owning party.

Licensing is used under a number of common conditions. For example, the product typically is in the mature stage of the product life cycle, competition is strong, and profit margins are declining. Under these conditions, the licensor is unlikely to want to spend money to enter foreign markets. However, if the company can find an MNC that is already there and willing to add the product to its own current offerings, both sides can benefit from the arrangement. A second common instance of licensing is evident when foreign governments require newly entering firms to make a substantial direct investment in the country. By licensing to a firm already there, the licensee avoids these high entry costs. A third common condition is that the licensor usually is a small firm that lacks financial and managerial resources. Finally, companies that spend a relatively large share of their revenues on research and development (R&D) are likely to be licensors, and those that spend very little on R&D are more likely to be licensees. In fact, some small R&D firms make a handsome profit every year by developing and licensing new products to large firms with diversified product lines.

Some licensors use their industrial property rights to develop and sell goods in certain areas of the world and license others to handle other geographic locales. This provides the licensor with a source of additional revenues, but the license usually is not good for much more than a decade. This is a major disadvantage of licensing. In particular, if the product is very good, the competition will develop improvement patents that allow it to sell similar goods or even new patents that make the current product obsolete. Nevertheless, for the period during which the agreement is in effect, a license can be a very low-cost way of gaining and exploiting foreign markets.

Joint Venturing in Russia

Joint venturing is becoming an increasingly popular strategy for setting up international operations. Russia is particularly interested in these arrangements because of the benefits they offer for attracting foreign capital and helping the country tap its natural resource wealth. However, investors are finding that joint venturing in Russia and the other republics of the former Soviet Union can be fraught with problems. For example, Royal Dutch Shell was recently pressured to give up its majority stake in Sakhalin Island to Gazprom. BP has been forced to renegotiate its contracts with its Russian joint-venture partner, TNK. New laws will require foreign investors interested in Russian energy projects to pair with Kremlin-approved organizations, further empowering the Russian company and government. Kremlin power is not the only problem facing joint-venture investors in Russia. Others include the following:

1. Many Russian partners view a joint venture as an opportunity to travel abroad and gain access to foreign currency; the business itself often is given secondary consideration.

2. Finding a suitable partner, negotiating the deal, and registering the joint venture often take up to a year, mainly because the Russians are unaccustomed to some of the basic steps in putting together business deals.

3. Russian partners typically try to expand joint ventures into unrelated activities.

4. Russians do not like to declare profits because a two-year tax holiday on profits starts from the moment the first profits are declared.

5. The government sometimes allows profits to be repatriated in the form of countertrade. However, much of what can be taken out of the country has limited value because the government keeps control of those resources that are most saleable in the world market.

These representative problems indicate why there is reluctance on the part of some MNCs to enter into joint ventures in Russia. As one of them recently put it, "The country may well turn into an economic sink hole." As a result, many MNCs are wary of potential contracts and are proceeding with caution.

Sources: Keith A. Rosten, "Soviet–U.S. Joint Ventures: Pioneers on a New Frontier," *California Management Review*, Winter 1991, pp. 88–108; Steven Greenhouse, "Chevron to Spend $10 Billion to Seek Oil in Kazakhstan," *New York Times*, May 19, 1992, pp. A1, C9; Louis Uchitelle, "Givebacks by Chevron in Oil Deal," *New York Times*, May 23, 1992, pp. 17, 29; Craig Mellow, "Russia: Making Cash from Chaos," *Fortune*, April 17, 1995, pp. 145–151; Daniel J. McCarthy and Sheila M. Puffer, "Strategic Investment Flexibility for MNE Success in Russia," *Journal of World Business* 32, no. 4 (1997), pp. 293–318; R. Bruce Money and Debra Colton, "The Response of the 'New Consumer' to Promotion in the Transition Economies of the Former Soviet Bloc," *Journal of World Business* 35, no. 2 (2000), pp. 189–206.

Licenses are also common among large firms seeking to acquire technology to bolster an existing product. For example, Microsoft announced it had agreed to a licensing arrangement with ARM Holdings PLC that allows the software giant to design chips based on ARM's technology, a common component in smartphones and tablets.[33]

Franchising

franchise

A business arrangement under which one party (the franchisor) allows another (the franchisee) to operate an enterprise using its trademark, logo, product line, and methods of operation in return for a fee.

Closely related to licensing is franchising. A **franchise** is a business arrangement under which one party (the franchisor) allows another (the franchisee) to operate an enterprise using its trademark, logo, product line, and methods of operation in return for a fee. Franchising is widely used in the fast-food and hotel-motel industries. The concept is very adaptable to the international arena, and with some minor adjustments for the local market, it can result in a highly profitable business. In fast foods, McDonald's, Burger King, and Kentucky Fried Chicken have used franchise arrangements to expand into new markets. In the hotel business, Holiday Inn, among others, has been very successful in gaining worldwide presence through the effective use of franchisees.

Franchise agreements typically require payment of a fee up front and then a percentage of the revenues. In return, the franchisor provides assistance and, in some instances, may require the purchase of goods or supplies to ensure the same quality of goods or services worldwide. Franchising can be beneficial to both groups: It provides the franchisor with a new stream of income and the franchisee with a time-proven concept and products or services that can be quickly brought to market.

■ The Organization Challenge

A natural outgrowth of general international strategy formulation and implementation and specific decisions about how best to enter international markets is the question of how best to structure the organization for international operations. A number of MNCs have recently been rethinking their organizational approaches to international operations.

An excellent illustration of worldwide reorganizing is provided by Coca-Cola, which now delegates a great deal of authority for operations to the local level. This move is designed to increase the ability of the worldwide divisions to respond to their local markets. As a result, decisions related to advertising, products, and packaging are handled by international division managers for their own geographic regions. As an example, in Turkey the regional division has introduced a new pear-flavored drink, while Coke's German operation launched a berry-flavored Fanta. This "local" approach was designed to help Coke improve its international reputation, although Coke's new management is rethinking some aspects of this approach in the face of increasing cost pressures.[34] Even so, Coke continues to diversify its offerings, despite an initial increase in cost. In Brazil, for example, Coke was losing market share as local soda companies were offering low-priced carbonated beverages. Coke offered only three bottle sizes, and simply cutting the price of those did not seem to gain anything for the company. Now, Coke offers 18 different sizes in Brazil, which include many reusable glass bottles that can be returned for credit. While this has not increased market share, it has boosted profits.[35] In India, Coca-Cola has notoriously experienced difficulty gaining market share for its classic Coke brand. Rather than continue to push its signature product in India, Coke purchased the local brand, Thums Up, in 1993. As of 2015, Coca-Cola products (including Thums Up) maintained a 49 percent market share in India, far ahead of rival Pepsi's 30 percent share.[36]

A second example of how firms are meeting international challenges through reorganization is provided by Li & Fung, Hong Kong's largest export trading company and an innovator in the development of supply chain management. The company has global suppliers worldwide that are responsible for providing the firm with a wide range of consumer goods ranging from toys to fashion accessories to luggage. In recent years, Li & Fung reorganized and now manages its day-to-day operations through a group of product managers who are responsible for their individual areas. This new organizational arrangement emerged in a series of steps. In the late 1970s, the company was a regional sourcing agent. Big international buyers would come to Li & Fung for assistance in getting materials and products because the MNC was familiar with the producers throughout Asia and it knew the complex government regulations and how to successfully work through them. The MNC then moved into a more sophisticated stage in which it began developing the entire process for the buyer from concept to prototype to delivery of the goods. By the late 1980s, however, Hong Kong had become a very expensive place to manufacture products, and Li & Fung changed its approach and began organizing around a new concept called "dispersed manufacturing," which draws heavily on dissection of the value chain and coordinating the operations of many suppliers in different geographic locations. For example, when the MNC receives an order from a European retailer to produce a large number of dresses, it has to decide where to buy the yarn in the world market, which companies should get the orders to weave and dye the cloth, where supplemental purchases such as buttons and zippers should be made, and how final shipment must be made to the customer. Commenting on this overall process, the company president noted:

> This is a new type of value added, a truly global product that has never been seen before. The label may say "Made in Thailand," but it's not a Thai product. We dissect the manufacturing process and look for the best solution at each step. We're not asking which country can do the best job overall. Instead, we're pulling apart the value chain and optimizing each step—and we're doing it globally. Not only do the benefits outweigh the costs of logistics and transportation, but the higher value added also lets us charge more for our services. We deliver a sophisticated product and we deliver it fast. If you talk to the big global consumer products companies, they are all moving in this direction—toward being best on a global scale.[37]

the researchers of the comparative study in Taiwan concluded: "Almost 80 percent of Japanese firms and more than 80 percent of American firms in the sample have been operating in Taiwan for about ten years, but they maintain the traits of their distinct cultural origins even though they have been operating in the same (Taiwanese) environment for such a long time."[66]

These findings also reveal that many enterprises view their international operations as extensions of their domestic operations, thus disproving the widely held belief that convergence occurs between overseas operations and local customs. In other words, there is far less of an "international management melting pot" than many people realize. European countries are finding that as they attempt to unify and do business with each other, differing cultures (languages, religions, and values) are very difficult to overcome. A major challenge for the years ahead will be bringing subsidiary organizational characteristics more into line with local customs and cultures.

The World of International Management—Revisited

In this chapter, a number of different entry strategies and organizational arrangements were discussed. Some of these are fairly standard approaches used by MNCs; others represent hybrid or flexible arrangements. Increasingly, entry modes and organizational structures involve collaborative relationships in which control and oversight are shared. Review the chapter opening World of International Management discussion of Haier's integrated approach to global strategy, emphasizing both global and regional aspects. Then think about the major themes of the chapter, forms of entry and organization structure, and answer the following questions: (1) Which organizational structure described in the chapter does Haier's "customer-oriented" structure most closely resemble? (2) How might such a structure help or hinder entry into new markets? (3) Does a matrix or customer-oriented structure lend itself better to forming joint ventures and alliances?

SUMMARY OF KEY POINTS

1. MNCs pursue a range of entry strategies in their international operations. These include wholly owned subsidiaries, mergers and acquisitions, alliances and joint ventures, licensing and franchising, and exporting. In general, the more cooperative forms of entry (alliances, joint ventures, mergers, licensing) are on the rise.

2. A number of different organizational structures are used in international operations. Many MNCs begin by using an export manager or subsidiary to handle overseas business. As the operation grows or the company expands into more markets, the firm often will opt for an international division structure. Further growth may result in adoption of a global structural arrangement, such as a global production division, global area division structure, global functional division, or a mixture of these structures.

3. Although MNCs still use the various structural designs that can be drawn in a hierarchical manner, they recently have begun merging or acquiring other firms or parts of other firms, and the resulting

organizational arrangements are quite different from those of the past. The same is true of the many joint ventures now taking place across the world. One change stems from the Japanese concept of keiretsu, which involves the vertical integration and cooperation of a group of companies. Other examples of new MNC organizational arrangements include the emergence of electronic networks, new approaches to organizing for production development, and the more effective use of IT.

4. A variety of factors help to explain differences in the way that international firms operate. Three organizational characteristics that are of particular importance are formalization, specialization, and centralization. These characteristics often vary from country to country, so that Japanese firms will conduct operations differently from U.S. firms, for example. When MNCs set up international subsidiaries, they often use the same organizational techniques they do at home without necessarily adjusting their approach to better match the local conditions.

KEY TERMS

alliance, *332*

centralization, *352*

decentralization, *352*

formalization, *350*

franchise, *336*

global area division, *342*

global functional division, *343*

global product division, *340*

horizontal specialization, *351*

international division structure, *339*

joint venture (JV), *332*

license, *335*

merger/acquisition, *331*

mixed organization structure, *343*

specialization, *351*

transnational network structure, *344*

vertical specialization, *351*

wholly owned subsidiary, *330*

REVIEW AND DISCUSSION QUESTIONS

1. One of the most common entry strategies for MNCs is the joint venture. Why are so many companies opting for this strategy? Would a fully owned subsidiary be a better choice?

2. A small manufacturing firm believes there is a market for handheld tools that are carefully crafted for local markets. After spending two months in Europe, the president of this firm believes that his company can create a popular line of these tools. What type of organization structure would be of most value to this firm in its initial efforts to go international?

3. If the company in question 2 finds a major market for its products in Europe and decides to expand

into Asia, would you recommend any change in its organization structure? If yes, what would you suggest? If no, why not?

4. If this same company finds after three years of international effort that it is selling 50 percent of its output overseas, what type of organizational structure would you suggest for the future?

5. In what way do the concepts of formalization, specialization, and centralization have an impact on MNC organization structures? In your answer, use a well-known firm such as IBM or Ford to illustrate the practical expressions of these three characteristics.

INTERNET EXERCISE: ORGANIZING FOR EFFECTIVENESS

Every MNC tries to drive down costs by getting its goods and services to the market in the most efficient way. Good examples include auto firms such as Ford Motor and Volkswagen, which have worldwide operations. In recent years Ford has been expanding into Europe and VW has begun setting up operations in Latin America. By building cars closer to the market, these companies hope to reduce their costs and be more responsive to local needs. At the same time this strategy requires a great deal of organization and coordination.

Visit the websites of both firms and examine the scope of their operations. The web address for Ford Motor is www.ford.com, and for Volkswagen it is www.vw.com. Then, based on your findings, answer these questions: What type of organizational arrangement(s) do you see the two firms using in coordinating their worldwide operations? Which of the two companies has the more modern arrangement? Do you think this increases that firm's efficiency, or does it hamper the company's efforts to contain costs and be more competitive? Why?

ENDNOTES

1. "China's Haier Profits Rise 20% in 2015," *China Daily*, January 25, 2016, www.chinadaily.com.cn/business/2016-01/25/content_23227354.htm.

2. Rebecca Howard, "Haier Obtains More Than 90% of Fisher & Paykel Shares," *The Wall Street Journal*, November 5, 2012, www.wsj.com/articles/SB10001424052970204349404578101793819992784?cb=logged0.3215365471907483.

3. Laurie Burkitt, Joann S. Lublin, and Dana Mattioli, "China's Haier to Buy GE Appliance Business for $5.4 Billion," *The Wall Street Journal*, January 15, 2016, www.wsj.com/articles/chinas-haier-to-buy-ge-appliance-business-for-5-4-billion-1452845661.

4. Khoirul Amin, "Haier to Operate First Global Factory in Southeast Asia," *Jakarta Post*, August

32. Foo Yun Chee, "EU Fines Microsoft $731 Million for Broken Promise, Warns Others," *Reuters*, March 6, 2013, www.reuters.com/article/us-eu-microsoft-idUSBRE92500520130306.

33. Prasanta Sahu, Phred Dvorak, and R. Jai Krishna, "India Sets Blackberry Showdown," *The Wall Street Journal*, August 13, 2010, www.wsj.com/articles/SB10001424052748704407804575424750165171256.

34. Jack N. Kondrasuk, "The Effects of 9/11 and Terrorism on Human Resource Management: Recovery, Reconsideration, and Renewal," *Employee Responsibilities and Rights Journal* 16, no. 1 (May 2004), pp. 25–35.

35. J. Hocking, *Beyond Terrorism: The Development of the Australian Security State* (Sydney: Allen & Unwin Pty Ltd, 1993).

36. Kondrasuk, "The Effects of 9/11."

37. Sia Khiun Then and Martin Loosemore, "Terrorism Prevention, Preparedness, and Response in Built Facilities," *Facilities* 24, no. 5–6 (2006), pp. 157–176.

38. David A. Schmidt, "Analyzing Political Risk," *Business Horizons,* July–August 1986, pp. 43–50.

39. Matthew Brzezinski, "Russia Kills Huge Oil Deal with Exxon," *The Wall Street Journal*, August 28, 1997, p. A2.

40. For more, see Thomas A. Pointer, "Political Risk: Managing Government Intervention," in *International Management: Text and Cases*, ed. Paul W. Beamish, J. Peter Killing, Donald J. LeCraw, and Harold Crookell (Homewood, IL: Irwin, 1991), pp. 119–133.

41. See Jonathan P. Doh and Ravi Ramamurti, "Reassessing Risk in Developing Country Infrastructure," *Long Range Planning* 36, no. 4 (2003), pp. 337–353.

42. Tom Arnold, "Saudi Investors Preparing $250M Claim Against Egypt," *The National*, March 18, 2012, www.thenational.ae/business/economy/saudi-investors-preparing-250m-claim-against-egypt.

43. Abde Latif Wahba and Zainab Fattah, "Egypt Seizes Land Valued at $10.6 Billion from Investors," *Bloomberg*, June 6, 2012, www.bloomberg.com/news/articles/2012-06-06/egypt-seized-10-6-billion-of-land-from-firms-minister-says.

44. Nadine Marroushi, "Egypt Post-Mubarak Legal Challenges Test Foreign Investors," *Bloomberg*, October 17, 2012, www.bloomberg.com/news/articles/2012-10-16/egypt-post-mubarak-legal-challenges-testing-foreign-investors.

45. See Jonathan P. Doh and John A. Pearce II, "Corporate Entrepreneurship and Real Options in Transitional Policy Environments: Theory Development," *Journal of Management Studies* 41, no. 4 (2004), pp. 645–664.

46. Doh and Ramamurti, "Reassessing Risk," pp. 344–349.

47. Amy Hillman and Michael A. Hitt, "Corporate Political Strategy Formulation: A Model of Approach, Participation, and Strategy Decisions," *Academy of Management Review* 24, no. 24 (1999), pp. 825–842.

48. Amy Hillman and Gerald Keim, "International Variation in the Business-Government Interface: Institutional and Organizational Considerations," *Academy of Management Review* 20, no. 1 (1995), pp. 193–214.

49. Robert J. Bowman, "Are You Covered?" *World Trade* 8, no. 2 (March 1995), pp. 100–103.

50. Mark A. Hofmann, "Political Risk Market Eases as Supply Outpaces Demand," *Business Insurance* 40, no. 8 (February 20, 2006), pp. 9–10.

51. Jonathan P. Doh and Hildy Teegen, "Nongovernmental Organizations as Institutional Actors in International Business: Theory and Implications," *International Business Review* 11, no. 6 (2002), pp. 665–684.

52. Carlos Tejada, "Truck Maker Volvo Sets Alliance to Enter China," *The Wall Street Journal* online, January 27, 2013, http://online.wsj.com/article/SB10001424127887324039504578264611071184722.html.

53. Siemens, "Factsheet: Siemens in China," 2015, www.siemens.com/press/pool/de/feature/2015/corporate/2015-07-china/factsheet-siemens-china-e.pdf.

54. Siemens, "Siemens and Wasion Establish Joint Venture for Smart Metering Solutions," press release, September 13, 2012, http://www.siemens.com/press/en/pressrelease/?press=/en/pressrelease/2012/infrastructure-cities/smart-grid/icsg201209022.htm&content[]=ICSG&content[]=EM&content[]=EMSG.

55. Siemens, "Siemens and Shanghai Electric Agree on Strategic Wind Power Alliance for China," press release, December 9, 2011, www.siemens.com/press/en/pressrelease/?press=/en/pressrelease/2011/wind-power/ewp201112017.htm.

56. Peter J. Buckley and Mark Casson, "An Economic Model of International Joint Venture Strategy," *Journal of International Business Studies* 27 (1996), pp. 849–876.

57. Farok J. Contractor and Peter Lorange, eds., *Cooperative Strategies in International Business* (Lexington, MA: Lexington Books, 1998).

58. Andrew C. Inkpen, *The Management of International Joint Ventures: An Organizational Learning Perspective* (London: Routledge, 1995).

59. Shige Makino and Andrew Delios, "Local Knowledge Transfer and Performance: Implications for Alliance Formation in Asia," *Journal of International Business Studies* 27 (1996), pp. 905–927.

60. Hildy Teegen and Jonathan P. Doh, "U.S./Mexican Alliance Negotiations: Cultural Impacts on Trust, Authority and Performance," *Thunderbird International Business Review* 44, no. 6 (2002), pp. 749–775.

61. Harry G. Barkema and Freek Vermeulen, "What Differences in the Cultural Backgrounds of Partners Are Detrimental for International Joint Ventures?" *Journal of International Business Studies* 28, no. 4 (1997), pp. 845–864.

62. Dirk Holtbrugge, "Management of International Strategic Business Cooperation: Situation Conditions, Performance Criteria, and Success Factors," *Thunderbird International Business Review* 46, no. 3 (May–June 2004), pp. 255–274.

63. Manuel G. Serapio Jr. and Wayner F. Cascio, "End Games in International Alliances," *Academy of Management Executive* 10, no. 1 (February 1996), pp. 62–73.

64. Julia G. Djarova, "Foreign Investment Strategies and the Attractiveness of Central and Eastern Europe," *International Studies in Management and Organization* 29, no. 1 (Spring 1999), pp. 14–23.

65. Jonathan P. Doh and Hildy Teegen, "Government Mandates and Local Partner Participation in Emerging Markets: Policy and Performance Implications for Government and Business Strategies," paper presented at the annual meeting of the Academy of International Business, Phoenix, AZ, November 20, 2002.

66. Jonathan P. Doh, Peter Rodriguez, Klaus Uhlenbruck, Jamie Collins, and Lorraine Eden, "Coping with Corruption in Foreign Markets," *Academy of Management Executive* 17, no. 3 (2003), pp. 114–127.

67. Serapio and Cascio, "End Games in International Alliances," pp. 71–72.

68. Ford Motor Company, "Ford to Change Stake in Mazda; Both Companies Remain Committed to Strategic Partnership," press release, November 18, 2010, https://media.ford.com/content/fordmedia/fna/us/en/news/2010/11/18/ford-to-change-stake-in-mazda--both-companies-remain-committed-t.html.

69. Edward Norton, "Starbucks in China," *The Economist*, October 4, 2001, pp. 80–82.

70. "Starbucks Acquires Beijing Mei Da Coffee," *Asia Times*, October 27, 2006, www.atimes.com/atimes/China_Business/HJ27Cb02.html.

71. Melissa Allison, "Starbucks Enters Joint Venture in China," *Seattle Times*, July 14, 2011, www.seattletimes.com/business/starbucks-enters-joint-venture-in-china/.

72. Frederick Balfour, "Back on the Radar Screen," *BusinessWeek*, November 2000, p. 27.

73. Henry Gallagher, "A Private Sector Surfaces in Vietnam," *The World & I* 18, no. 11 (November 2003), p. 56.

74. Trien Nguyen, "From Plan to Market: The Economic Transition in Vietnam," *Journal of Economic Literature* 38, no. 3 (September 2000), p. 683.

75. "Vietnam Foreign Direct Investment," *Trading Economics*, 2016, www.tradingeconomics.com/vietnam/foreign-direct-investment.

76. "Ford Delivers Record Sales in ASEAN Region in 2015," *Vietnam Investment Review*, January 26, 2016, www.vir.com.vn/ford-delivers-record-sales-for-asean-region-in-2015.html.

77. CIA, "Brazil," *The World Factbook* (2016), https://www.cia.gov/library/publications/the-world-factbook/geos/br.html.

78. World Bank, "Brazil," *World Development Indicators* (2015), http://data.worldbank.org/country/brazil.

79. CIA. 2016. "The World Factbook," https://www.cia.gov/library/publications/the-world-factbook/geos/br.html.

80. Ibid.

81. Matt Bonesteel, "Brazil Is Melting Down Ahead of the 2016 Rio Olympics," *Washington Post*, September 10, 2015, https://www.washingtonpost.com/news/early-lead/wp/2015/09/10/brazil-is-melting-down-ahead-of-the-2016-rio-olympics/.

Brazil

Brazil is located in eastern South America along the Atlantic Ocean. With a land area just smaller than that of the United States, the country possesses abundant natural resources, including bauxite, gold, iron ore, manganese, nickel, phosphates, platinum, tin, rare earth elements, uranium, petroleum, hydropower, and timber. The country also features a number of globally competitive manufacturing companies. Embraer, one of the world's leading producers of mid-range passenger and military aircraft, and Odebrecht, a diversified conglomerate that develops and installs mass transit systems, sports stadiums, chemical production facilities and other infrastructure projects, are both located in Brazil.[77]

Gaining its independence from Portugal in 1822, Brazil adopted a federative republic system of government. This governmental process includes compulsory voting requirements for those between the ages of 18 and 70. With more than 200 million people and annual growth of about 1 percent, Brazil is one of the most populous countries in the world. The country has moved towards urbanization over the last 50 years; nearly 20 percent of its population now lives in either São Paulo or Rio de Janeiro. Brazil is a diverse place culturally and ethnically. The primary and official language is Portuguese, but Spanish, German, Japanese, and English are also spoken with some regularity. The country is predominantly Christian, with two-thirds of all Brazilians identifying as Roman Catholic. Like most growing developing nations, the vast majority of the population is younger than 55 years old and the median age is only 31.1 years old.[78]

Brazil has the largest economy in all of South America and the eighth largest in the world. That being said, the economy has faced serious challenges both recently and historically, including multiple recessions, high inflation, and currency volatility. In 2014, Brazil's GDP was US$2.347 trillion, but growth has been erratic. After a surging economic expansion of 7.6 percent in 2010, the GDP annual growth rate has been on a steady decline, with just 0.1 percent growth in 2014 and negative growth in 2015. Inflation of nearly 10 percent was a major issue in the country in 2015, as was high unemployment.[79]

The country's main agricultural products include coffee, soybeans, wheat, rice, corn, sugarcane, cocoa, citrus, and beef. Textiles, shoes, chemicals, cement, lumber, iron ore, tin, steel, aircraft, and motor vehicles constitute its main manufactured products. In the global industrial and manufacturing sectors, Brazil has been suffering largely due to its reliance on commodity exports, which have seen demand fall. Brazil is frequently ranked as a difficult place to conduct business (the country finished 116th out of 185 nations in the 2015 "ease of doing business" rankings). In September 2015, Brazil's debt rating was downgraded to "junk," making it even more difficult to find foreign investors and international credit markets.[80]

Brazil was chosen as the host country for both the 2014 World Cup and the 2016 Summer Olympics. Events such as these give a country the chance to grab worldwide attention and showcase the best that their country has to offer. Additionally, if well managed, these types of events can be a net-positive economically due to ticket sales, sponsorship, and television deals. While the 2014 World Cup was held without any major disruptions, the 2016 Olympics faced numerous issues in the months leading up to the event. Negative press over inadequate infrastructure, construction worker safety, and contaminated water causing serious disease dominated news coverage in the spring of 2016. Furthermore, public concern over the spread of the Zika virus resulted in lower-than-expected ticket sales and fewer tourists.[81]

Despite these challenges, Brazil remains the largest and most important economy in South America and one that will continue to exert influence over the greater global environment.

You Be the International Management Consultant

In 2009, Brazil's economy was booming. It was receiving substantial foreign investment from both developed and developing countries, and the country was one of the emerging markets most closely watched for opportunity and growth. All signs suggested that Brazil and its economy were headed in a strong direction. However, in the wake of low oil prices and economic recession in 2015, foreign investors have reason for doubt. In addition, many investors are fleeing from country after a bribery scandal involving the country's state-owned oil company, Petrobras, broke in 2015, ultimately bringing down Brazil's president. Petrobras reported losses of US$2 billion solely as a result of the scandal.

One organization that has pulled out is the Bill and Melinda Gates' Foundation, which has not only decided to cease operations in the country, but is also suing the oil company for its role in the scandal and various investments that the company made. Furthermore, several states in the U.S. invested pension funds in Brazil's economy and are suing for close to $100 billion.

Questions

1. As an international management consultant, what advice would you give to a foreign company looking to move operations into Brazil?
2. Do you think Brazil still holds the potential for future growth?
3. As an investor, do you think that the "buy low" mindset applies to Brazil? If not, what changes would you like to see before making any investment in the country?

Chapter 11

MANAGEMENT DECISION AND CONTROL

Although they are not directly related to internationalization, decision making and control are two management functions that play critical roles in international operations. In *decision making*, a manager chooses a course of action among alternatives. In *controlling*, the manager evaluates results in relation to plans or objectives and decides what action, if any, to take. How these functions are carried out is influenced by the international context. An organization can employ a centralized or decentralized management system depending on such factors as company philosophy or competition. The company also has an array of measures and tools it can use to evaluate firm performance and restructuring options. As with most international operations, culture plays a significant role in what is important in both decision-making processes and control features, and can affect MNC decisions when forming relationships with subsidiaries.

This chapter examines the different decision-making and controlling management functions used by MNCs, notes some of the major factors that account for differences between these functions, and identifies the major challenges of the years ahead. The specific objectives of this chapter are

1. **PROVIDE** comparative examples of decision making in different countries.

2. **PRESENT** some of the major factors affecting the degree of decision-making authority given to overseas units.

3. **COMPARE** and **CONTRAST** direct controls with indirect controls.

4. **DESCRIBE** some of the major differences in the ways that MNCs control operations.

5. **DISCUSS** some of the specific performance measures that are used to control international operations.

The World of *International Management*

Global Online Retail: Amazon v. Alibaba

Over the last two decades, the Internet has revolutionized the way customers around the world shop. According to Forrester Research, U.S. online retail sales alone will reach $523 billion by 2020.[1] Within the U.S., no online merchant has had more success than Amazon. Started in 1995 as a small bookseller, the ecommerce website now sells a variety of products to individuals across North America. While the U.S. has traditionally been the leader in ecommerce, online retail in countries around the world has been growing at a rapid pace.

Perhaps most surprising is the sudden surge of the Alibaba Group, an online Chinese retail conglomerate. Consisting of multiple ecommerce-related websites, the Alibaba Group's combined US$462 billion in transactions in 2015 totaled more than eBay and Amazon combined.[2] And Alibaba's Tmall, the direct competitor to Amazon, is expected to become the largest individual ecommerce site within the decade, surpassing Amazon in total revenue. Despite similar successes in the ecommerce marketplace, managers at Amazon and Alibaba have taken different approaches to the marketplace. What competitive strategies do these two companies use, and which company stands a better shot at long-term success?

Conglomerate versus Specializer

The Alibaba Group is a conglomerate of over a half-dozen individual ecommerce websites, combining business-to-business, business-to-consumer, and consumer-to-consumer transactions under a single ownership umbrella. Through its diverse set of websites, the company can cater to virtually any type of transaction, whether it is a small personal purchase or a multi-million-dollar business transaction. In addition to providing traditional ecommerce services, the Alibaba Group has branched into web-based business solutions. Utilizing its existing infrastructure, Alibaba provides cloud computing and data services to companies of all sizes and has even created its own mobile operating system. Alibaba also operates Alipay, a secure payment transfer service, giving the company control over the entire purchase process. Alipay is now used for over half of all online purchases in the country.[3] Together, the Alibaba Group conglomerate now accounts for 60 percent of all packages shipped within China and 80 percent of all online sales.[4,5]

Amazon, unlike Alibaba, specializes primarily in just business-to-consumer sales. As a result, Amazon's target market is significantly smaller, but more loyal, than Alibaba's. With a primary focus on personal purchases, Amazon has grown into the world's largest online retailer. Recently, however, Amazon has made an effort to expand its offerings. Utilizing the information infrastructure that it established for its traditional business operations, Amazon now offers video streaming, cloud storage, and other web services. And in an attempt to enter the growing tablet market, Amazon released its Kindle Fire. It's seventh edition of the Fire, released in late 2015, retails for under US$50, making it one of the most affordable tablets on the market. The core of Amazon's revenue, however, is still generated from its specialization in business-to-consumer transactions.[6,7]

Merchant versus Facilitator

Amazon not only hosts third-party sellers, but the company also acts as a direct merchant itself. Amazon buys and sells merchandise, ships products, and warehouses inventory. The company currently has over 100 distribution centers strategically spread across the United States, with roughly one million square feet of storage space per center. This direct-seller approach allows Amazon to quickly adapt to changes in demand. The company can directly control the timeliness and quality of most products sold over its interface, giving it the ability to provide unmatched service features, like single-day delivery. By 2016, over 30 percent of the general U.S. population and more than 50 percent of its frequent customers were located with 20 miles of an Amazon warehouse.[8] Furthermore, by hosting third-party merchants, Amazon is able to generate additional revenue on products sold by its users. However, Amazon's merchant strategy, requiring a large investment in fixed assets, has resulted in minimal profits for the company. Though it does not have quite the level of expenses that traditional physical stores have, Amazon's margin is tightened by the other necessary investments, like labor and warehouses.[9]

Alibaba, on the other hand, acts solely as a facilitator for sales between third parties. The company does not carry an inventory, directly sell products, or control distribution. Rather, it simply provides a digital space for those activities to happen. As a result, fixed assets are kept to a minimum. Going forward, the Alibaba Group sees this "efficiency" as a key business strength. While Amazon's scale of operations is capital intensive, Alibaba's approach allows for extra financial flexibility, as it does not need to build, staff, and maintain regional warehouses. One major downside, however, is that Alibaba gives up control over the shipping and distribution operations of its merchants, meaning that mistakes by third-party businesses could reflect negatively on the company as a whole. Furthermore, the company misses out on possible financial gains from direct-to-consumer selling.[10]

Growth Potential

Although both companies are online, and therefore "global," the geographic positioning of Amazon and Alibaba affects their potential future growth. Amazon, founded nearly 20 years ago, grew into the largest online retailer in the world due to its geographic advantages. The North American ecommerce market currently accounts for over 30 percent of all global online sales, and this region is overwhelmingly dominated by Amazon. In fact, Alibaba has not even attempted to enter the North American marketplace due to Amazon's strength. Although Amazon will likely continue to lead business-to-consumer sales in North America, the future growth potential of Amazon is somewhat limited. North America has nearly 90 percent Internet penetration, and the population growth of the region has rapidly slowed. In 2014, online sales totals in Asia-Pacific surpassed North American for the first time. In the coming years, North America's share of global ecommerce will decrease to around 25 percent while Asia-Pacific's share will increase to nearly 40 percent.[11] Unless Amazon actively expands into other regions across the globe, its revenues will likely stagnate.[12]

Alibaba's foothold in Asia holds far more growth potential. Internet penetration in China currently stands at just 50 percent, leaving plenty of room for growth with unreached customers. Furthermore, nearly 40 percent of the world's population resides in Asia, and the population growth rates within Southeast Asia far exceed those of North America. As wealth continues to accumulate in the region, Internet access and ecommerce will likely expand. If the Alibaba Group can maintain its strong standing in Asia, revenue will grow significantly over the next decade.[13]

Whether Amazon's strategy as a specialized direct seller or Alibaba's strategy as a third-party facilitator will lead to greater long-term success is yet to be seen. As Internet usage increases and ecommerce expands beyond North America, managers of companies like Amazon and Alibaba will need to implement new strategies to adapt to the changing marketplace. The advent of online retail has certainly challenged some aspects of managerial decision making for all ecommerce companies.

■ Decision-Making Process and Challenges

decision making
The process of choosing a course of action among alternatives.

The managerial **decision-making** process, choosing a course of action among alternatives, is a common business practice becoming more and more relevant for the international manager as globalization becomes more pervasive. The decision-making process is often linear, though looping back is common, and consists of the general phases outlined in Figure 11–1. The degree to which managers are involved in this procedure depends on the structure of the subsidiaries and the locus of decision making. If decision making is centralized, most important decisions are made at the top; if decision making is decentralized, decisions are delegated to operating personnel. Decision making is used to solve a myriad of issues, including helping the subsidiary respond to economic and political demands of the host country. Decisions that are heavily economic in orientation concentrate on such aspects as return on investment (ROI) for overseas operations. In other instances, cultural differences can both inspire and motivate the process and outcome of decision making.

For example, Ford Motor Company designed and built an inexpensive vehicle, the Ikon, for the Indian market. Engineers took apart the Ford Fiesta and totally rebuilt the car to address buyer needs. Some of the changes that were made included raising the amount of rear headroom to accommodate men in turbans, adjusting doors so that they opened wider in order to avoid catching the flowing saris of women, fitting intake valves

Figure 11–1

Decision-Making Process

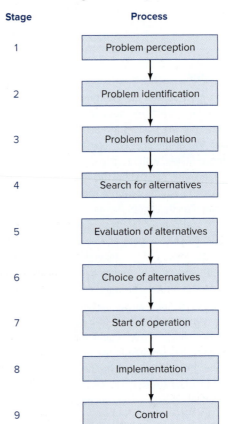

Stage	Process
1	Problem perception
2	Problem identification
3	Problem formulation
4	Search for alternatives
5	Evaluation of alternatives
6	Choice of alternatives
7	Start of operation
8	Implementation
9	Control

Source: Jette Schramm-Nielsen, "Cultural Dimensions of Decision Making: Denmark and France Compared," *Journal of Managerial Psychology* 16, no. 6 (2001), p. 408.

to avoid auto flooding during the monsoon season, toughening shock absorbers to handle the pockmarked city streets, and adjusting the air-conditioning system to deal with the intense summer heat.[14] As a result of these decisions, the car sold very well in India. Ford replicated that same strategy with the Ikon's successor, the Fiesta Mark VI. Santander, the largest bank in Europe by market capitalization, is vesting more autonomy in its subsidiaries by listing subsidiaries in its principal foreign markets and thereby strengthening their independence and autonomy from the Spanish headquarters. A number of European banks, including Santander and HSBC Holdings PLC (see In-Depth Integrative Case 4.1 at the end of Part Four), establish foreign subsidiaries as opposed to direct branches. Santander Chief Executive Officer Alfredo Saenz said, "We also believe it's good for the local management teams, because having local minority shareholders breathing down their neck keeps them on their toes, and it's a good way of identifying the franchise as local, instead of foreign." In addition, the IPO boosted the visibility of the bank in Brazil, resulted in greater access to local capital, and put a higher value on the franchise than what analysts were giving it before the float. When Santander sold 15 percent of its Brazilian unit, the unit alone was valued at €34 billion, more than European rivals Deutsche Bank or Société Générale.[15]

The way in which decision making is carried out will be influenced by a number of factors. We will first look at some of the factors, then provide some comparative examples in order to illustrate some of the differences.

Factors Affecting Decision-Making Authority

A number of factors influence international managers' conclusions about retaining authority or delegating decision making to a subsidiary. Table 11–1 lists some of the most important situational factors, and the following discussion evaluates the influential aspects.

One of the major concerns for organizations is how efficient the processes are that are put in place. The size of a company can have great importance in this realm. Larger organizations may choose to centralize authority for critical decisions in order to ensure efficiency through greater coordination and integration of operations. The same holds true for companies that have a high degree of interdependence because there is a greater need for coordination. This is especially relevant when organizations provide a large investment because they prefer to keep track of progress. It is quite common for the

Table 11–1
Factors That Influence Centralization or Decentralization of Decision Making in Subsidiary Operations

Encourage Centralization	Encourage Decentralization
Large size	Small size
Large capital investment	Small capital investment
Relatively high importance to MNC	Relatively low importance to MNC
Highly competitive environment	Stable environment
Strong volume-to-unit-cost relationship	Weak volume-to-unit-cost relationship
High degree of technology	Moderate to low degree of technology
Strong importance attached to brand name, patent rights, etc.	Little importance attached to brand name, patent rights, etc.
Low level of product diversification	High level of product diversification
Homogeneous product lines	Heterogeneous product lines
Small geographic distance between home office and subsidiary	Large geographic distance between home office and subsidiary
High interdependence between the units	Low interdependence between the units
Fewer highly competent managers in host country	More highly competent managers in host country
Much experience in international business	Little experience in international business

investing company to send home-office personnel to the subsidiary and report on the situation, and for subsidiary managers to submit periodic reports. Both of the above scenarios imply that the subsidiary is of great importance to the MNC, and it is customary in these situations for subsidiary managers to clear any decisions with the home office before implementation. In fact, MNCs often will hire someone who they know will respond to their directives and will regard this individual as an extension of the central management staff.

Another efficiency checkpoint arises when competition is high. In domestic situations, when competition increases, management will decentralize authority and give the local manager greater decision-making authority. This reduces the time that is needed for responding to competitive threats. In the international arena, however, sometimes the opposite approach is used. As competition increases and profit margins are driven down, home-office management often seeks to standardize product and marketing decisions to reduce cost and maintain profitability. Many upper-level operating decisions are made by central management and merely implemented by the subsidiary, although, in some instances, companies still opt to decentralize operations if product diversification is necessary. Kraft Heinz Company provides an example of a recent effort to centralize operations to improve efficiency and competitiveness. Following H. J. Heinz's 2015 acquisition of the Kraft Foods Group, seven manufacturing facilities were closed to consolidate processes. Roughly 2,600 manufacturing jobs, representing 6 percent of the company's workforce, were eliminated by the closures. Additionally, 2,500 office jobs were eliminated to remove redundancy in management positions. The consolidation aims to increase global growth while decreasing costs, resulting in US$1.5 billion in savings. Kraft Heinz plans to invest millions in upgrading the remaining manufacturing facilities to meet increasing product demand, strengthening the acquired company and making the combined firm leaner and better positioned globally.[16] Firms that are able to produce large quantities will have a lower cost per unit than those that produce at smaller amounts, and home-office management will often take the initiative to oversee sourcing, marketing, and overall strategy to keep costs down.

Efficient processes become increasingly important as diversification or differences between the parent and subsidiary increase. This refers not only to specific products and services that may need to be tailored to geographic areas, but also to the socioeconomic, political, legal, and cultural environments in which the subsidiary exists. In this case, the subsidiary would have superior staff and resources that would only become increasingly skilled in manufacturing and marketing products at the local level over time. Decentralization is emphasized here, and there exists a direct relationship between the physical distance and different environments between the parent and subsidiary and the level of decentralization. In other words, the farther apart the two units are in either geographical area or cultural beliefs, the higher the level of decentralization.

Experience proves to be a simple indicator of efficiency. For example, if the subsidiary has highly competent local managers, the chances for decentralization are increased because the home office has more confidence in delegating to the local level and less to gain by making all the important decisions. Conversely, if the local managers are inexperienced or not highly effective, the MNC likely will centralize decision making and make many of the major decisions at headquarters. Furthermore, if the firm itself has a great deal of international experience, its operations will likely be more centralized as it has already exhibited a high efficiency level and increasing management decision making at the local level may slow processes.

Protection of goods and services is also important to an MNC. It would not be a very lucrative experience to spend valuable time and money on R&D processes only to have competitors successfully mimic products and essentially take away market share. For this reason and many others, it is common for MNCs to centralize operations when dealing with sophisticated levels of technology. This is particularly true for high-tech, research-intensive firms such as computer and pharmaceutical companies, which do not want their technology controlled at the local level. Furthermore, a company is likely to centralize decision-making processes when there are important brand names or patent rights involved as it wants to create as much protection as possible.

In some areas of operation, MNCs tend to retain decision making at the top (centralization); other areas fall within the domain of subsidiary management (decentralization). It is most common to find finance, R&D, and strategic planning decisions being made at MNC headquarters with the subsidiaries working within the parameters established by the home office. In addition, when the subsidiary is selling new products in growing markets, centralized decision making is more likely. As the product line matures and the subsidiary managers gain experience, however, the company will start to rely more on decentralized decision making. These decisions involve planning and budgeting systems, performance evaluations, assignment of managers to the subsidiary, and use of coordinating committees to mesh the operations of the subsidiary with the worldwide operations of the MNC. The right degree of centralized or decentralized decision making can be critical to the success of the MNC.

Deloitte, the accounting and management consulting firm, describes some of the challenges associated with postmerger integration in the area of centralization and decentralization:

> The union of two European engineering companies is a prime example of a merger that brought together companies with very different structures—a business unit of a much larger corporation and a stand-alone company. The business unit had a more decentralized management approach with responsibilities delegated within functional areas such as procurement and IT. In contrast, the stand-alone company had a more centralized approach with a strong corporate headquarters retaining control over IT, finance, procurement and HR. Bringing these two disparate structures together without reconciling these differences almost destroyed the new company. Sales plummeted and key people left, unable to adjust to the new corporate structure. Within three years the company collapsed, to be swiftly scooped up by a competitor.[17]

Cultural Differences and Comparative Examples of Decision Making

Culture, whether outside or within the organization (see Chapters 4 and 6, respectively), has an effect on how individuals and businesses perceive situations and subsequently react. This knowledge raises the question: Do decision-making philosophies and practices differ from country to country? Research shows that to some extent they do, although there also is evidence that many international operations, regardless of foreign or domestic ownership, use similar decision-making norms.

One study showed that French and Danish managers do not approach the decision-making process in the same manner.[18] The French managers tend to spend ample time on searching for and evaluating alternatives (see Figure 11–1), exhibiting rationality and intelligence in each option. While the French approach each opportunity with a sense of creativity and logic, they tend to become quite emotionally charged rather quickly if challenged. Middle managers report to higher-level managers, who ultimately make the final decision. Therefore, the individualistic nature of the French creates an environment in which middle managers vie for the recognition and praise of the upper management. Furthermore, middle-management implementation of ideas tends to be lacking because that stage is often seen as boring, practical work that lacks the prestige managers strive to achieve. Control, discussed later in the chapter, is quite high in the French firms at every level, so where implementation fails, control will compensate.

Danish managers tend to emphasize different stages in the decision-making process (see Figure 11–1). They do not spend as much time searching or analyzing alternatives to optimize production but instead choose the option that can be started and implemented quickly and still bring about the relative desired results. They are less emotionally responsive and tend to take a straightforward approach. Danes do not emphasize control in operations because it tends to be a sign that management lacks confidence in the areas that "require" high control. The cooperative as opposed to individualistic emphasis in Danish corporations, coupled with a results-oriented environment, breeds a situation in which decisions are made quickly and middle managers are given autonomy.

Overall, the pragmatic nature of the Danes and the French need for intellectual prowess mark why each is more adept at different stages of the decision-making process.

The French tend to be better at stages 4, 5, and 9, while the Danes are more adept at stages 6, 7, and 8 (see Figure 11–1). As one Danish manager in France says:

> They [Danes and Frenchmen] do not analyze and synthesize the same way. The French tend to think that the Danes are not thorough enough, and the Danes tend to think that the French are too complicated. At his desk, the Frenchman tends to keep on working on the case. He seems to agree neither with his surroundings nor with himself. This means that when he has analyzed a case and has come to a conclusion, then he would like to go over it once more. I think that Frenchmen think in a more synthetic way . . . and he has a tendency to say: "well, yes, but what if it can still be done in another maybe smarter way." This means that in fact he is wasting time instead of making improvements.[19]

codetermination
A legal system that requires workers and their managers to discuss major decisions.

In Germany, managers focus more on productivity and quality of goods and services than on managing subordinates, which often translates into companies pursuing long-term approaches. In addition, management education is highly technical, and a legal system called **codetermination** requires workers and their managers to discuss major decisions. As a result, German MNCs tend to be fairly centralized, autocratic, and hierarchical. Scandinavian countries also have codetermination, but the Swedes focus much more on quality of work life and the importance of the individual in the organization. As a result, decision making in Sweden is decentralized and participative.

ringisei
A Japanese term that means "decision making by consensus."

The Japanese are somewhat different from the Europeans, though they still employ a long-term focus. They make heavy use of a decision-making process called **ringisei**, or decision making by consensus. Under this system, any changes in procedures and routines, tactics, and even strategies of a firm are organized by those directly concerned with those changes. The final decision is made at the top level after an elaborate examination of the proposal through successively higher levels in the management hierarchy, and results in acceptance or rejection of a decision only through consensus at every echelon of the management structure.[20]

tatemae
A Japanese term that means "doing the right thing" according to the norm.

honne
A Japanese term that means "what one really wants to do."

Sometimes Japanese consensus decision making can be very time-consuming. However, in practice most Japanese managers know how to respond to "suggestions" from the top and to act accordingly—thus saving a great deal of time. Many outsiders misunderstand how Japanese managers make such decisions. In Japan, what should be done is called **tatemae**, whereas what one really feels, which may be quite different, is **honne**. Because it is vital to do what others expect in a given context, situations arise that often strike Westerners as a game of charades. Nevertheless, it is very important in Japan to play out the situation according to what each person believes others expect to happen.

Another cultural difference is how managers view time in the decision-making process. As we saw from the French-Danish example earlier, the French do not value time as much as their counterparts. The French want to ensure that the best alternative was put into action, whereas the Danes want to act first and take advantage of opportunities. This is key in many international decision-making processes, as globalization has opened the door to extreme competition, and all players need to be able to both identify and make the most of profitable prospects.

total quality management (TQM)
An organizational strategy and the accompanying techniques that result in the delivery of high-quality products or services to customers.

In another study of decision making in teams composed of Swedes, Germans, and combinations of the two, researchers found Swedish teams featured higher team orientation, flatter organizational hierarchies, and more open-minded and informal work attitudes. In this study, German team members were perceived to be faster in decision making, to have clearer responsibilities for the individual, and to be more willing to accept a changed or unpopular decision. In Swedish teams, decision making appeared more transparent and less formal. On German teams, the process is largely dominated by the decision authority of an expert in the field. This is in contrast to the group decision-making style used in Swedish teams.[21]

Total Quality Management Decisions

To achieve world-class competitiveness, MNCs are finding that a commitment to total quality management is critical. **Total quality management (TQM)** is an organizational strategy and accompanying techniques that result in delivery of high-quality products or services to customers.[22] The concept and techniques of TQM, which were introduced in Chapter 8 in relation to strategic planning, also are relevant to decision making and controlling.

One of the primary areas where TQM is having a big impact is in manufacturing. A number of TQM techniques have been successfully applied to improve the quality of manufactured goods. One is the use of concurrent engineering/interfunctional teams in which designers, engineers, production specialists, and customers work together to develop new products. This approach involves all the necessary parties and overcomes what used to be an all-too-common procedure: The design people would tell the manufacturing group what to produce, and the latter would send the finished product to retail stores for sale to the customer. Today, MNCs taking a TQM approach are customer-driven. They use TQM techniques to tailor their output to customer needs, and they require the same approach from their own suppliers.[23] Recently, Lenovo has transformed its design process from an engineer-driven one to a customer-driven one. In 2016, the company developed and began using an application that pulls together unstructured customer feedback from a variety of sources, including YouTube comments, online forums, and traditional call centers, and organizes the data in a useful way so that Lenovo can design tablets and products that best meet consumer demands.[24]

A particularly critical issue is how much decision making to delegate to subordinates. TQM uses employee **empowerment**. Individuals and teams are encouraged to generate and implement ideas for improving quality and are given the decision-making authority and necessary resources and information to implement them. Many MNCs have had outstanding success with empowerment. For example, General Electric credits employee empowerment for cutting in half the time needed to change product-mix production of its dishwashers in response to market demand.

Another TQM technique that is successfully employed by MNCs is rewards and recognition. These range from increases in pay and benefits to the use of merit pay, discretionary bonuses, pay-for-skills and knowledge plans, plaques, and public recognition. The important thing to realize is that the rewards and recognition approaches that work well in one country may be ineffective in another. For example, individual recognition in the U.S. may be appropriate and valued by workers, but in Japan, group rewards are more appropriate as Japanese do not like to be singled out for personal praise. Similarly, although putting a picture or plaque on the wall to honor an individual is common practice in the United States, these rewards are frowned on in Finland, for they remind the workers that their neighbors, the Russians, used this system to encourage people to increase output (but not necessarily quality), and while the Russian economy is beginning to make headway, it was once in shambles in part due to poor decision making.

Still another technique associated with TQM is the use of ongoing training to achieve continual improvement. This training takes a wide variety of forms, ranging from statistical quality control techniques to team meetings designed to generate ideas for streamlining operations and eliminating waste. In all cases, the objective is to apply what the Japanese call **kaizen**, or continuous improvement. By adopting a TQM perspective and applying the techniques discussed earlier, MNCs find that they can both develop and maintain a worldwide competitive edge. A good example is provided by Herman Miller, the American office furniture company. Herman Miller manufactures some of the best-selling office task chairs worldwide. Over the last 15 years, the company has used the kaizen mindset to improve quality by 1,000 percent and productivity by 500 percent. Originally, it took approximately 82 seconds for Herman Miller to produce a single chair from its production line. Today, it only takes 17 seconds.[25] Table 11–2 provides some examples of the new thinking that is now emerging regarding quality.

Ford Motor Company has been able to thrive in the post-global recession environment due in part to its implementation of kaizen principles. As a former vice president at Boeing, Ford CEO Alan Mulally brought the philosophy with him when he came to

empowerment
The process of giving individuals and teams the resources, information, and authority they need to develop ideas and effectively implement them.

kaizen
A Japanese term that means "continuous improvement."

Table 11–2
The Emergence of New Beliefs Regarding Quality

Old Myth	New Truth
Quality is the responsibility of the people in the Quality Control Department.	Quality is everyone's job.
Training is costly.	Training does not cost; it saves.
New quality programs have high initial costs.	The best quality programs do not have up-front costs.
Better quality will cost the company a lot of money.	As quality goes up, costs come down.
The measurement of data should be kept to a minimum.	An organization cannot have too much relevant data on hand.
It is human to make mistakes.	Perfection—total customer satisfaction—is a standard that should be vigorously pursued.
Some defects are major and should be addressed, but many are minor and can be ignored.	No defects are acceptable, regardless of whether they are major or minor.
Quality improvements are made in small, continuous steps.	In improving quality, both small and large improvements are necessary.
Quality improvement takes time.	Quality does not take time; it saves time.
Haste makes waste.	Thoughtful speed improves quality.
Quality programs are best oriented toward areas such as products and manufacturing.	Quality is important in all areas, including administration and service.
After a number of quality improvements, customers are no longer able to see additional improvements.	Customers are able to see all improvements, including those in price, delivery, and performance.
Good ideas can be found throughout the organization.	Good ideas can be found everywhere, including in the operations of competitors and organizations providing similar goods and services.
Suppliers need to be price competitive.	Suppliers need to be quality competitive.

Source: Reported in Richard M. Hodgetts, *Measures of Quality and High Performance* (New York: American Management Association, 1998), p. 14.

the company in 2006. By focusing on implementing more efficient procedures, Ford was able to create 5,000 new jobs in the United States in 2014.[26]

Indirectly related to TQM is ISO 9000, International Standards Organization (ISO) certification, to ensure quality products and services. Areas that are examined by the ISO certification team include design (product or service specifications), process control (instruction for manufacturing or service functions), purchasing, service (e.g., instructions for conducting after-sales service), inspection and testing, and training. ISO 9000 certification is becoming a necessary prerequisite to doing business in the EU, but it also is increasingly used as a screening criterion for bidding on contracts or getting business in the United States and other parts of the world.

Decisions for Attacking the Competition

Another series of key decisions relates to MNC actions that are designed to attack the competition and gain a foothold in world markets. An example is Ford Motor Company's decision to challenge other automakers, like Tata, and to be a major player in developing markets, such as Asia and Africa. As a result of this decision, Ford has been shifting production closer to the local consumer and away from its stagnant U.S. home market. In 2015, Ford announced plans to open a manufacturing plant for its pickup truck, the Ranger, in Lagos, Nigeria. As Ford's first plant in Africa outside of South Africa, the new Lagos facility aims to provide Ford with the infrastructure and manufacturing capacity necessary for future growth.[27] Ford has also opened plants in China and Thailand in recent years, with the ability to produce more than 100,000 vehicles every year for the local Asian market.[28]

Another example of decision making for attacking the competition is provided by the global luxury car industry. While German automakers Audi, Mercedes-Benz, and BMW all share the same goal of leading the international luxury vehicle market, the companies are taking different approaches to beat the competition. Audi has made the decision to target younger professionals in established markets. This strategy is reflected in the company's new, trendy body designs. Though the demographics of the luxury vehicle market favors older consumers, Audi's approach has been fairly successful. More than 90,000 units are now sold annually in the U.S., vaulting Audi into fourth place in the local market. Conversely, BMW has attempted to undermine the competition by focusing on providing more options and personalization for its consumers. With a variety of engine and body options, the company offers more than 100 different combinations for its luxury vehicles in the U.S. And Mercedes, which holds the largest share of the luxury vehicle market, has taken a lowest-cost strategy. With its CLA 250 starting at under US$30,000, the luxury sedan offers high value for a price that is less than that of the average car sale in the U.S.[29]

■ Decision and Control Linkages

controlling
The process of evaluating results in relation to plans or objectives and deciding what action, if any, to take.

Decision making and **controlling** are two vital and often interlinked functions of international management. As an example of a company that struggled with control issues, Canadian company Blackberry Limited (formerly Research in Motion) ultimately failed in the smartphone industry due to its slow market response. Over the course of just six years, Blackberry evolved from the most promising phone producer to just a footnote. In 2009, Blackberry was one of the fastest-growing companies in the world, with an 84 percent increase in earnings.[30] Blackberry held an estimated 41 percent share of the smartphone market in the U.S. by 2010, making it more popular than Apple's iPhone. However, as Apple and Samsung introduced touchscreens and innovated to meet customer demands, Blackberry continued producing phones with full keyboards. In the high-tech sector, where the pace of change is incredibly fast, Blackberry's resistance to meet customer expectations led to a rapid decline in market share. By the time Blackberry finally adapted to the evolving mobile market, it was too late; by 2015, Blackberry's market share dropped to just 1 percent.[31,32]

Another example of how the control function plays out is Universal Studios Japan. To attract visitors to the Osaka location, this new theme park was specially built based on feedback from Japanese tourists at Universal parks in Orlando and Los Angeles. The company wanted to learn what these visitors liked and disliked and then use this information in its Osaka park. One theme clearly emerged: The Japanese wanted an authentic American experience but also expected the park to cater to their own cultural preferences. In the process of controlling the creation of the new park, thousands of decisions were made regarding what to include and what to leave out. For example, seafood pizza and gumbo-style soup were put on the menu, but a fried-shrimp concoction with colored rice crackers was rejected. It was decided that in a musical number based on the movie *Beetlejuice*, the main character should talk in Japanese and his sidekicks would speak and sing in English. The decision to put in a restaurant called Shakin's, based on the 1906 San Francisco earthquake, turned out to be not a good idea because Osaka has had terrible earthquakes that killed thousands of people.

Other decisions were made to give the "American" park a uniquely Japanese flavor. The nation's penchant for buying edible souvenirs inspired a 6,000-square-foot confection shop packed with Japanese sweets such as dinosaur-shaped bean cakes. Restrooms include Japanese-style squat toilets. Even the park layout caters to the tendency of Japanese crowds to flow clockwise in an orderly manner, contrary to more chaotic U.S.

crowds that steer right. And millions of dollars were spent on the Jurassic Park water slide to widen the landing pond, redesign boat hulls, and install underwater wave-damping panels to reduce spray. Why? Many fastidious Japanese don't like to get wet, even on what's billed as one of the world's biggest water slides.[33]

The efforts to design a uniquely Japanese theme park with an American feel seem to be paying off. Fifteen years after first opening, Universal Studios Japan is now the fifth-most-visited amusement park worldwide, attracting over 13 million visitors in 2015.[34] Universal Studios Japan is the only non-Disney park to make the top-ten attendance list.[35] The company has discovered that creating an emotional connection between the consumer and the park, instead of focusing on the power of Hollywood, encourages people to frequent the park. The success that Universal has had in integrating Japanese and American culture has encouraged the company to expand further into the Asian market; in fact, plans are already in place to open Universal Studios in Moscow, Beijing, and South Korea between 2020 and 2022.[36,37] (See related discussion in In-Depth Integrative Case 2.1b on Disney in Asia at end of Part Two.)

■ The Controlling Process

As we've stated, controlling involves evaluating results in relation to plans or objectives and deciding what action to take next. An excellent illustration of this process can be seen through ConocoPhillips' recent strategic changes to its investments in Russia. Over two decades ago, shortly after the collapse of the Soviet Union, the U.S.-based company joined with Russian-based Rosneft to form the Polar Lights Company. The investment looked like a wise decision initially; teaming with Rosneft would allow ConocoPhillips access to Russia's massive oil and gas fields, and the deal made ConocoPhillips one of the largest foreign players inside of Russia. By the early 2000s, however, high taxes and unrealized returns worried executives and shareholders. After years of losses, ConocoPhillips sold its 50 percent stake in the joint venture in December 2015, freeing up capital for investments in more lucrative markets and projects.[38]

The control process is of course crucial for MNCs in the fast-moving personal computer (PC) business. Until the mid-1990s, PCs were built using the traditional model shown in Figure 11–2. Today the direct-sales model and the hybrid model are the most common. PC firms are finding that they must keep on the cutting edge more than any other industry because of the relentless pace of technological change. This is where the control function becomes especially critical for success. For example, stringent controls keep the inventory in the system as small as possible. PCs are manufactured using a just-in-time approach (a customer orders the unit and has it made to specifications) or an almost just-in-time approach (a retailer orders 30 units and sells them all within a few weeks). Because technology in the PC industry changes so quickly, any units that are not sold in retail outlets within 60 days may be outdated and must be severely discounted and sold for whatever the market will bear. In turn, these costs are often assumed by the manufacturer. As a result, PC manufacturers are very much inclined to build to order or to ship in quantities that can be sold quickly. In this way the firm's control system helps ensure that inventory moves through the system profitably.[39]

Of particular interest is how companies attempt to control their overseas operations to become integrated, coordinated units. A number of control problems may arise: (1) The objectives of the overseas operation and the corporation conflict. (2) The objectives of joint-venture partners and corporate management are not in accord. (3) Degrees of experience and competence in planning vary widely among managers running the various overseas units. (4) Finally, there may be basic philosophic disagreements about the objectives and policies of international operations, largely because of cultural differences between home- and host-country managers. The following discussion examines the various types of control that are used in international operations and the approaches that are often employed in dealing with typical problems.

| Figure 11–2 | Models of PC Manufacturing |

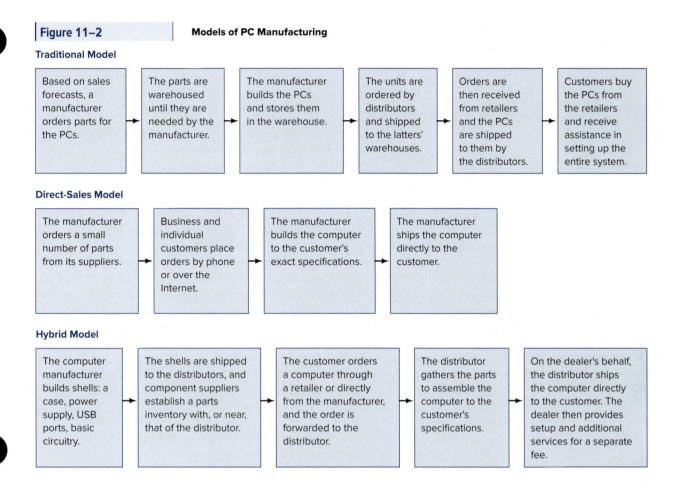

Traditional Model

| Based on sales forecasts, a manufacturer orders parts for the PCs. | → | The parts are warehoused until they are needed by the manufacturer. | → | The manufacturer builds the PCs and stores them in the warehouse. | → | The units are ordered by distributors and shipped to the latters' warehouses. | → | Orders are then received from retailers and the PCs are shipped to them by the distributors. | → | Customers buy the PCs from the retailers and receive assistance in setting up the entire system. |

Direct-Sales Model

| The manufacturer orders a small number of parts from its suppliers. | → | Business and individual customers place orders by phone or over the Internet. | → | The manufacturer builds the computer to the customer's exact specifications. | → | The manufacturer ships the computer directly to the customer. |

Hybrid Model

| The computer manufacturer builds shells: a case, power supply, USB ports, basic circuitry. | → | The shells are shipped to the distributors, and component suppliers establish a parts inventory with, or near, that of the distributor. | → | The customer orders a computer through a retailer or directly from the manufacturer, and the order is forwarded to the distributor. | → | The distributor gathers the parts to assemble the computer to the customer's specifications. | → | On the dealer's behalf, the distributor ships the computer directly to the customer. The dealer then provides setup and additional services for a separate fee. |

Types of Control

There are two common, complementary ways of looking at how MNCs control operations. One way is by determining whether the enterprise chooses to use internal or external control in devising its overall strategy. The other is by looking at the ways in which the organization uses direct and indirect controls.

Internal and External Control   From an internal control standpoint, an MNC will focus on the things that it does best. At the same time, of course, management wants to ensure that there is a market for the goods and services that it is offering. So the company first needs to find out what the customers want and be prepared to respond appropriately. This requires an external control focus. Naturally, every MNC will give consideration to both internal and external perspectives on control. However, one is often given more attention than the other. In explaining this idea, Trompenaars and Hampden-Turner set forth four management views regarding how a control strategy should be devised and implemented:

1. No one dealing with customers is without a strategy of sorts. Our task is to find out which of these strategies work, which don't, and why. Devising our own strategy in the abstract and imposing it downwards only spreads confusion.

2. No one dealing with customers is without a strategy of sorts. Our task is to find out which of these strategies work and then create a master strategy from proven successful initiatives by encouraging and combining the best.

3. To be a leader is to be the chief deviser of strategy. Using all the experience, information, and intelligence we can mobilize, we need to devise an innovative strategy and then cascade it down the hierarchy.

4. To be a leader is to be the chief deviser of strategy. Using all the experience, information, and intelligence we can mobilize, we must create a broad thrust, while leaving it to subordinates to fit these to customer needs.

Trompenaars and Hampden-Turner ask managers to rank each of these four statements by placing a "1" next to the one they feel would most likely be used in their company, a "2" next to the second most likely, on down to a "4" next to the one that would be the last choice. This ranking helps managers better see whether they use an external or an internal control approach. Answer 1 focuses most strongly on an external-directed approach and rejects the internal control option. Answer 3 represents the opposite. Answer 2 affirms a connection between an external-directed strategy and an inner-directed one, whereas answer 4 does the opposite.[40]

Cultures differ in the control approach they use. For example, among U.S. MNCs it is common to find managers using an internal control approach. Among Asian firms an external control approach is more typical. Table 11–3 provides some contrasts between the two.

direct controls
The use of face-to-face or personal meetings for the purpose of monitoring operations.

Direct Controls   **Direct controls** involve the use of face-to-face or personal meetings to monitor operations. A good example is how International Telephone and Telegraph (ITT) holds monthly management meetings at its New York headquarters. These meetings are run by the CEO of the company, and reports are submitted by each ITT unit manager throughout the world. Problems are discussed, goals set, evaluations made, and actions taken that will help the unit improve its effectiveness.

Another common form of direct control is visits by top executives to overseas affiliates or subsidiaries. During these visits, top managers can learn firsthand the problems and challenges facing the unit and offer assistance.

A third form is the staffing practices of MNCs. By determining whom to send overseas to run the unit, the corporation can directly control how the operation will be run. The company will want the manager to make operating decisions and handle

---

Table 11–3
The Impact of Internal- and External-Oriented Cultures on the Control Process

Key Differences Between . . .

Internal Control	External Control
Often dominating attitude bordering on aggressiveness toward the environment.	Often flexible attitude, willing to compromise and keep the peace.
Conflict and resistance mean that a person has convictions.	Harmony, responsiveness, and sensibility are encouraged.
The focus is on self, function, one's own group, and one's own organization.	The focus is on others such as customers, partners, and colleagues.
There is discomfort when the environment seems "out of control" or changeable.	There is comfort with waves, shifts, and cycles, which are regarded as "natural."

Tips for Doing Business with . . .

Internally Controlled (for externals)	Externally Controlled (for internals)
Playing "hardball" is legitimate to test the resilience of an opponent.	Softness, persistence, politeness, and long patience will get rewards.
It is most important to "win your objective."	It is most important to maintain one's relationships with others.
Win some, lose some.	Win together, lose apart.

Source: Adapted from Fons Trompenaars and Charles Hampden-Turner, *Riding the Waves of Culture: Understanding Diversity in Global Business*, 2nd ed. (New York: McGraw-Hill, 1998), pp. 160–161.

day-to-day matters, but the individual also will know which decisions should be cleared with the home office. In fact, this approach to direct control sometimes results in a manager who is more responsive to central management than to the needs of the local unit.

And finally, a fourth form is the organizational structure itself. By designing a structure that makes the unit highly responsive to home-office requests and communications, the MNC ensures that all overseas operations are run in accord with central management's desires. This structure can be established through formal reporting relationships and chain of command (who reports to whom).

Indirect Controls   **Indirect controls** involve the use of reports and other written forms of communication to control operations. One of the most common examples is the use of monthly operating reports that are sent to the home office. Other examples, which typically are used to supplement the operating report, include financial statements, such as balance sheets, income statements, cash budgets, and financial ratios that provide insights into the unit's financial health. The home office will use these operating and financial data to evaluate how well things are going and make decisions regarding necessary changes. Three sets of financial statements usually are required from subsidiaries: (1) statements prepared to meet the national accounting standards and procedures prescribed by law and other professional organizations in the host country, (2) statements prepared to comply with the accounting principles and standards required by the home country, and (3) statements prepared to meet the financial consolidation requirements of the home country.

Indirect controls are particularly important in international management because of the great expense associated with direct methods of control. Typically, MNCs will use indirect controls to monitor performance on a monthly basis, whereas direct controls are used semiannually or annually. This dual approach often provides the company with effective control of its operations at a price that also is cost-effective.

indirect controls
The use of reports and other written forms of communication to control operations.

Approaches to Control

International managers can employ many different approaches to control. These approaches typically are dictated by the MNC's philosophy of control, the economic environment in which the overseas unit is operating, and the needs and desires of the managerial personnel who staff the unit. Working within control parameters, MNCs will structure their processes so that they are as efficient and effective as possible. Typically, the tools used will give the unit manager the autonomy needed to adapt to changes in the market as well as to attract competent local personnel. These tools will also provide for coordination of operations with the home office, so that the overseas unit operates in harmony with the MNC's overall strategic plan.

Some control tools are universal. For example, all MNCs use financial tools in monitoring overseas units. This was true as long as four decades ago, when the following was reported:

> The cross-cultural homogeneity in financial control is in marked contrast to the heterogeneity exercised over the areas of international operations. American subsidiaries of Italian and Scandinavian firms are virtually independent operationally from their parents in functions pertaining to marketing, production, and research and development; whereas, the subsidiaries of German and British firms have limited freedom in these areas. Almost no autonomy on financial matters is given by any nationality to the subsidiaries.[41]

Some Major Differences   MNCs control operations in many different ways, and these often vary considerably from country to country. For example, how British firms monitor their overseas operations often is different from how German or French firms do. Similarly, U.S. MNCs tend to have their own approach to controlling, and it differs from both European and Japanese approaches. When Horovitz examined the key characteristics of top management control in Great Britain, Germany, and France, he found that British controls had four common characteristics: (1) Financial records were sophisticated and heavily emphasized. (2) Top management tended to focus its attention on major problem areas and did not get involved in specific, detailed matters of control. (3) Control was used more for general guidance than for surveillance. (4) Operating units had a large amount of marketing autonomy.[42]

This model was in marked contrast to that of German managers, who employed very detailed control and focused attention on all variances large and small. These managers also placed heavy control on the production area and stressed operational efficiency. In achieving this centralized control, managers used a large central staff for measuring performance, analyzing variances, and compiling quantitative reports for senior executives. Overall, the control process in the German firms was used as a policing and surveillance instrument. French managers employed a control system that was closer to that of the Germans than to the British. Control was used more for surveillance than for guiding operations, and the process was centrally administered. Even so, the French system was less systematic and sophisticated.[43]

How do U.S. MNCs differ from their European counterparts? One comparative study found that a major difference is that U.S. firms tend to rely much more heavily on reports and other performance-related data. Americans make greater use of output control, and Europeans rely more heavily on behavioral control. Commenting on the differences between these two groups, the researcher noted: "This pattern appears to be quite robust and continues to exist even when a number of common factors that seem to influence control are taken into account."[44] Some specific findings from this study include

1. Control in U.S. MNCs focuses more on the quantifiable, objective aspects of a foreign subsidiary, whereas control in European MNCs tends to be used to measure more qualitative aspects. The U.S. approach allows comparative analyses between other foreign operations as well as domestic units; the European measures are more flexible and allow control to be exercised on a unit-by-unit basis.

2. Control in U.S. MNCs requires more precise plans and budgets in generating suitable standards for comparison. Control in European MNCs requires a high level of companywide understanding and agreement regarding what constitutes appropriate behavior and how such behavior supports the goals of both the subsidiary and the parent firm.

3. Control in U.S. MNCs requires large central staffs and centralized information-processing capability. Control in European MNCs requires a larger cadre of capable expatriate managers who are willing to spend long periods of time abroad. This control characteristic is reflected in the career approaches used in the various MNCs. Although U.S. multinationals do not encourage lengthy stays in foreign management positions, European MNCs often regard these positions as stepping-stones to higher offices.

4. Control in European MNCs requires more decentralization of operating decision making than does control in U.S. MNCs.

5. Control in European MNCs favors short vertical spans or reporting channels from the foreign subsidiary to responsible positions in the parent.[45]

As noted in the discussion of decision making, these differences help explain why many researchers have found European subsidiaries to be more decentralized than U.S. subsidiaries. Europeans rely on the managerial personnel they assign from headquarters to run the unit properly. Americans tend to hire a greater percentage of local management people and control operations through reports and other objective, performance-related data. The difference results in Europeans' relying more on socio-emotional control systems and Americans' opting for task-oriented, objective control systems.

Evaluating Approaches to Control   Is one control approach any better than the other? The answer is that each seems to work best for its respective group. Some studies predict that as MNCs increase in size, they likely will move toward the objective orientation of the U.S. MNCs. Commenting on the data gathered from large German and U.S. MNCs, two researchers concluded:

> Control mechanisms have to be harmonized with the main characteristics of management corporate structure to become an integrated part of the global organization concept and to meet situational needs. Trying to explain the differences in concepts of control, we have to consider that the companies of the U.S. sample were much larger and more diversified. Accordingly, they use different corporate structures, combining operational units into larger units and integrating these through primarily centralized, indirect, and task-oriented control. The German companies have not (yet) reached this size and complexity, so a behavioral model of control seems to be fitting.[46]

So in deciding which form of control to use, MNCs must determine whether they want a more bureaucratic or a more cultural control approach; and from the cultural perspective, it must be remembered that this control will vary across subsidiaries.

■ Performance Evaluation as a Mechanism of Control

A number of performance measures are used for control purposes. Three of the most common evaluate financial performance, quality performance, and personnel performance.

Financial Performance

Financial performance evaluation of a foreign subsidiary or affiliate is usually based on profit and loss and return on investment. **Profit** and loss (P&L) is the amount remaining after all expenses are deducted from total revenues. **Return on investment (ROI)** is measured by dividing profit by assets; some firms use profit divided by owners' equity (return on owners' investment, or ROOI) in referring to the return-on-investment performance measure. In any case, the most important part of the ROI calculation is profits, which often can be manipulated by management. Thus, the amount of profit directly relates to how well or how poorly a unit is judged to perform. For example, if an MNC has an operation in both country A and country B and taxes are lower in country A, the MNC may be able to benefit if the two units have occasion to do business with each other. This benefit can be accomplished by having the unit in country A charge higher prices than usual to the unit in country B, thus providing greater net profits to the MNC. Simply put, sometimes differences in tax rates can be used to maximize overall MNC profits. This same basic form of manipulation can be used in transferring money from one country to another, which can be explained as follows:

profit
The amount remaining after all expenses are deducted from total revenues.

return on investment (ROI)
Return measured by dividing profit by assets.

> Transfer prices are manipulated upward or downward depending on whether the parent company wishes to inject or remove cash into or from a subsidiary. Prices on imports by a subsidiary from a related subsidiary are raised if the multinational company wishes to move funds from the receiver to the seller, but they are lowered if the objective is to keep the funds in the importing subsidiary. . . . Multinational companies have been known to use transfer pricing for moving excess cash from subsidiaries located in countries with weak currencies to countries with strong currencies in order to protect the value of their current assets.[47]

The so-called bottom-line (i.e., profit or loss) performance of subsidiaries also can be affected by a devaluation or revaluation of local currency. For example, if a country devalues its currency, then subsidiary export sales will increase because the price of these goods will be lower for foreign buyers, whose currencies now have greater purchasing power. If the country revalues its currency, then export sales will decline because the price of goods for foreign buyers will rise because their currencies now have less purchasing power in the subsidiary's country. Likewise, a devaluation of the currency will increase the cost of imported materials and supplies for the subsidiary, and a revaluation will decrease these costs because of the relative changes in the purchasing power of local currency. Because devaluation and revaluation of local currency are outside the control of the overseas unit, bottom-line performance sometimes will be a result of external conditions that do not accurately reflect how well the operation actually is being run, which should be considered when evaluating a subsidiary's performance.

Of course, not all bottom-line financial performance is a result of manipulation or external economic conditions. Frequently, other forces account for the problem. For example, Volkswagen has long struggled to meet profit margin goals in recent years. One reason for this poor performance is that labor costs in Lower Saxony, where approximately half its workforce is located and workers are strongly unionized, are very high. Workers here produce only 40 vehicles per employee annually, in contrast to the VW plant in Navarra, Spain, which turns out 79 vehicles per employee per year. Why doesn't VW move work to lower-cost production sites? The major reason is that the state of Lower Saxony owns 19 percent of the company's voting stock, so the workers' jobs are protected. As recently as 2014, Volkswagen management proposed massive cost-cutting measures to increase profitability, but union representatives in Lower Saxony have fought back fearing local job losses.[48,49] Simply put, relying solely on financial results to evaluate performance can result in misleading conclusions.

Quality Performance

Just as quality has become a major focus in decision making, it also is a major dimension of the modern control process of MNCs. The term *quality control* (QC) has been around for a long time, and it is a major function of production and operations management. Besides the TQM techniques of concurrent engineering/interfunctional teams, employee empowerment, reward/recognition systems, and training, discussed earlier in this chapter in the context of decision making, another technique more directly associated with the control function is the use of quality circles, which have been popularized by the Japanese. A **quality control circle (QCC)** is a group of workers who meet on a regular basis to discuss ways of improving the quality of work. This approach has helped many MNCs improve the quality of their goods and services dramatically.

> **quality control circle (QCC)**
> A group of workers who meet on a regular basis to discuss ways of improving the quality of work.

Why are Japanese-made goods of higher quality than the goods of many other countries? The answer cannot rest solely on technology because many MNCs have the same or superior technology, or the financial ability to purchase it. There must be other causal factors. The nearby International Management in Action box "How the Japanese Do Things Differently" gives some details about these factors. One study attempted to answer the question by examining the differences between Japanese and U.S. manufacturers of air conditioners.[50] In this analysis, many of the commonly cited reasons for superior Japanese quality were discovered to be inaccurate. So what were the reasons for the quality differences?

One reason was the focus on keeping the workplace clean and ensuring that all machinery and equipment were properly maintained. The Japanese firms were more careful in handling incoming parts and materials, work-in-process, and finished products than their U.S. counterparts. Japanese companies also employed equipment fixtures to a greater extent than did U.S. manufacturers in ensuring proper alignment of parts during final assembly.

The Japanese minimized worker error by assigning new employees to existing work teams or pairing them with supervisors. In this way, the new workers gained important experience under the watchful eye of someone who could correct their mistakes.

Another interesting finding was that the Japanese made effective use of QCCs. Quality targets were set, and responsibility for their attainment then fell on the circle while management provided support assistance. This was stated by the researcher as follows:

> In supporting the activities of their QCCs, the Japanese firms in this industry routinely collected extensive quality data. Information on defects was compiled daily, and analyzed for trends. Perhaps most important, the data were made easily accessible to line workers, often in the form of publicly posted charts. More detailed data were available to QCCs on request.[51]

How the Japanese Do Things Differently

Japanese firms do a number of things extremely well. One is to train their people carefully, a strategy that many successful U.S. firms also employ. Another is to try to remain on the technological cutting edge. A third, increasingly important because of its uniqueness to the Japanese, is to keep a keen focus on developing and bringing to market goods that are competitively priced.

In contrast to Western firms, many Japanese companies use a "target cost" approach. Like other multinational firms, Japanese companies begin the new product development process by conducting marketing research and examining the characteristics of the product to be produced. At this point, however, the Japanese take a different approach. The traditional approach used by MNCs around the world is next to go into designing, engineering, and supplier pricing and then to determine if the cost is sufficiently competitive to move ahead with manufacturing. Japanese manufacturers, in contrast, first determine the price that the consumer most likely will accept, and then they work with design, engineering, and supply people to ensure that the product can be produced at this price. The other major difference is that after most firms manufacture a product, they will engage in periodic cost reductions. The Japanese, however, use a kaizen approach, which fosters continuous cost-reduction efforts.

The critical difference between the two systems is that the Japanese get costs out of the product during the planning and design stage. Additionally, they look at profit in terms of product lines rather than just individual goods, so a consumer product that would be rejected for production by a U.S. or European firm because its projected profitability is too low may be accepted by a Japanese firm because the product will attract additional customers to other offerings in the line. A good example is Sony, which decided to build a smaller version of its compact personal stereo system and market it to older consumers. Sony knew that the profitability of the unit would not be as high as usual, but it went ahead because the product would provide another market niche for the firm and strengthen its reputation. Also, a side benefit is that once a product is out there, it may appeal to an unanticipated market. This was the case with Sony's compact personal stereo system. The unit caught on with young people, and Sony's sales were 50 percent greater than anticipated. Had Sony based its manufacturing decision solely on "stand-alone" profitability, the unit never would have been produced.

These approaches are not unique to Japanese firms. Foreign companies operating in Japan are catching on and using them as well. Coca-Cola Japan is the leading company in the Japanese soft drink market, which sees the introduction of more than 1,000 new products each year. Most offerings do not last very long, and a cost accountant might well argue that it is not worth the effort to produce them. However, Coca-Cola introduces one new product a month. Most of these sodas, soft drinks, and cold coffees survive less than 90 days, but Coke does not let the short-term bottom line dictate the decision. The firm goes beyond quick profitability and looks at the overall picture. Result: Coca-Cola continues to be the leading soft drink firm in Japan despite competition that often is more vigorous than that in the United States.

Sources: Ford S. Worthy, "Japan's Smart Secret Weapon," *Fortune*, August 12, 1991, pp. 72–75; Brenton R. Schlender, "Hard Times for High Tech," *Fortune*, March 22, 1993, p. 98; Ronald Henkoff, "Companies That Train Best," *Fortune*, March 22, 1993; Jim Carlton, "Sega Leaps Ahead by Shipping New Player Early," *The Wall Street Journal*, May 11, 1995, pp. B1, B3; Jeffrey K. Liker and Yen-Chun Wu, "Japanese Automakers, U.S. Suppliers and Supply-Chain Superiority," *Sloan Management Review*, Fall 2000, pp. 81–93.

This finding pointed out an important difference between Americans and Japanese. The Japanese pushed data on quality down to the operating employees in the quality circles, whereas Americans tended to aggregate the quality data into summary reports aimed at middle and upper management.

Another important difference is that the Japanese tend to build in early warning systems so that they know when something is going wrong. Incoming field data, for example, are reviewed immediately by the quality department, and problems are assigned to one of two categories: routine or emergency. Special efforts then are made to resolve the emergency problems as quickly as possible. High failure rates attributable to a single persistent problem are identified and handled much faster than they would be in U.S. firms. Still another reason is that the Japanese work closely with their suppliers so that the latter's quality increases. In fact, research shows that among suppliers that have contracts with both American and Japanese auto plants in the United States, the Japanese plants get higher performance from their suppliers than do the American.[52] The Japanese are able to accomplish this because they work closely with their suppliers and help them develop lean manufacturing capabilities. Some of the steps that Japanese manufacturers

at the time, like Yahoo and AOL, but it was indisputable that Google offered the best search services. The innovative PageRank algorithm was combined with a minimalist homepage that focused on its search tool and reminded the user of its chief focus while helping to reinforce confidence in its best feature. Having secured a solid foothold in America, Google continued to seek more ways to expand. Visionaries from the very beginning, Page and Brin created Google to have "simplicity in our user interface and the scalability in our back-end systems [that] enables us to expand very quickly."[13]

By anticipating the need to be flexible in order to expand, Google was set to go global. And as Larry Page remarked: "Google's search engine has always had strong global appeal. We attribute this success to the site's simplicity of design, ease of use, and highly relevant results. By localizing our search services to new international communities, Google will open up a host of new revenue, sales, and partnership channels."[14]

Unfortunately, Asian countries in general had always been more difficult to penetrate because of competition from well-established local search engines. As recently as 2015, local search engine Naver had a market share of 49.8 percent in South Korea, while Google had 36.9 percent.[15] Furthermore, China posed the greatest roadblock with censorship and competition from Baidu. However, with a population of one billion people and Internet usage on a steady climb, Google was determined to establish a stronger foothold in China.

China's Internet Users and Population

	Users (millions)	Population (millions)	Percent
2004	96	1,310	7.3
2005	112	1,318	8.5
2006	140	1,326	10.5
2007	213	1,334	16.0
2008	303	1,343	22.6
2009	391	1,351	28.9
2010	466	1,360	34.3
2011	524	1,368	38.3
2012	564	1,377	41.0
2013	618	1,386	44.6
2014	642	1,394	46.0

Source: "China Internet Users," *Internet Live Stats*, www.internetlivestats.com/internet-users/china/.

Google vs. Baidu

China's policies have directly influenced the competitive landscape for search firms in China. In the space of Internet search, Baidu is usually referred to as China's Google. But in reality, Baidu holds a strong market share lead over Google.[16] Prior to the launch of Google.cn in 2006 in China, Google held 33.3 percent of the search engine market share between Shanghai, Beijing, and Guangzhou while Baidu held 47.9 percent.[17] Google was optimistic

about the close margin in market share and considered the possibility of perhaps buying out Baidu in competition. But instead, in mid-2006, Google made a fatal mistake, selling its 2.6 percent stake of more than $60 million in Baidu shares and introducing Google.cn to China.[18]

Nevertheless, Google.cn was launched with the promise that it would agree to block certain websites in return for the opportunity to run local Chinese services.[19] Google promised to notify Chinese users when their search results would be censored and also promised not to maintain any services that involved personal or confidential data, like Gmail or Blogger, on the mainland. Google.cn was a response to improve the poor service Google believed it was providing in China. As senior policy counsel Andrew McLaughlin put it, "Google users in China today struggle with a service that, to be blunt, isn't very good . . . the website is slow, and sometimes produces results that when clicked on, stall out the user's browser. Our Google News service is never available; Google Images is accessible only half the time . . . the level of service we've been able to provide in China is not something we're proud of."[20]

Fundamentally, Google's strategic move to create a local presence with Google.cn was driven by its desire to follow its mission of creating the most organized and efficient search engine. However, while Google thought it had the flexibility to set up a better search engine in China, Baidu CEO Robin Li was already ahead of the curve. While PageRank was being developed by Page and Brin, Robin Li was simultaneously working on a similar strategy for site-ranking called RankDex. As a result, this similar search concept was brought to Baidu. In the end, Google had erroneously presumed that it could overtake Baidu by maximizing its core competencies within China.[21]

Not only did Baidu have a strong competing search engine against Google, but it also provided several innovative search features customized for more local tastes. It introduced community-oriented services, including information-exchanging bulletin boards and instant messaging. These extra services appealed strongly to Chinese Internet users and put Baidu ahead of a foreign Google that did not seem to understand the Chinese market as well.

In addition, Baidu also took an extra step that Google missed by setting up "a national network of advertising resellers in 200 Chinese cities to educate businesses about the power of online advertising."[22] By specifically targeting the business market segment, Baidu aimed to secure the Shanghai business sector. To secure the more general student population in Beijing, Baidu also offered a search engine that provided easy access to pirated film and music downloads.[23]

While Baidu strategically offered services that targeted specific market segments, Google was at a loss because of its slow comprehension of the Chinese market. Among one of the failures Google made was its attempt to rebrand

Google.cn to Guge, which was Chinese for Harvest Song. Six months after the launch of Guge, "72.6 percent (62.8 percent of the users whose first choice was Google) of the interviewed users still weren't able to [recall] the Chinese name of Google."[24] The lack of brand loyalty was reflected in the insignificant number of Google users who were willing to convert from using the Chinese version of Google.com to Guge. Most users still preferred to use the original Google.com that was only censored by the People's Republic of China.[25]

Google seemed to be fighting a losing battle, while Baidu continued to receive positive press coverage during its 2005 IPO on NASDAQ. Consequently, in just one year, Baidu gained 14 percent of the search engine market share while Google lost 8 percent.[26]

In the following year, 2007, Google fought hard to hold onto its piece of the China market, increasing its total market share from 19.2 percent to 22.8 percent while Baidu fell from 63.7 percent to 58.1 percent. Google increased its efforts by "hiring Chinese employees and . . . partnering with Chinese technology firms . . . [and establishing] two research centers, one in Beijing and one in Shanghai."[27]

The small victory was short-lived as Google was soon met with conflict from both China's and the U.S.'s governments.

The Challenge of Censorship: Google under Fire

Shortly after Google.cn received its license from the Chinese government in 2007, Google proceeded to sign a set of guidelines, designed to reduce the risk that their actions would lead to human rights abuses in China and other countries.[28] By promising to comply with censorship when the government filed a formal request, this effectively removed Google's presence from the majority of human rights activities.

From this point forward, Google was fiercely criticized for running advertisements from nonlicensed medical websites in 2008, launching free music services, scanning books without proper copyright laws, and making pornographic content easily available multiple times in 2009.[29] What has unfolded in the most recent years has been the climax of this drama between country and company.

On January 13, 2010, in response to an attack on the Gmail accounts of human rights activists by the Chinese government, Google released an initial statement saying that it was ready to end censorship of its search service.[30] The announcement caused a stir, with speculations that Google would pull out of China completely.

Soon afterwards, however, CEO Eric Schmidt released a counterstatement stating that Google was planning to stay in China, even if it was forced to close down its local search services and just carry through with its other range of services.[31] In the same month, Hillary Clinton, the U.S.

Secretary of State, called upon Beijing to carry out a thorough and transparent investigation regarding the cyber hacks of human rights activists' e-mail accounts. Ultimately, she threw her weight behind Google's threat to pull out of China unless Beijing permitted an "unfiltered search engine."[32]

Following the conflict in January, Google formally announced in March that all Google.cn users would be directed to the uncensored Google.com.hk website instead. According to Google, the decision reflected a legal move that still allowed mainland users access to their search engine.[33] The move to stop offering a local search engine and battling with China over censorship reflected a shift in Google's attitude, giving up competing with Baidu for Internet usage. In April, Google's share of Chinese Internet searches dropped from 35.6 percent to 30.9 percent and Baidu's rose from 58.4 percent to 64 percent.[34] Despite no longer providing Google.cn to China, Google still cannot escape the censorship battles and attacks on its server. In 2014, China restricted access to nearly all of Google's auxiliary services.[35] Almost instantly, Google's market share in China dropped to less than 2 percent.

But criticisms of Google have not always been from China. On March 22, 2011, New York Judge Denny Chin rejected a settlement between Google and both the Authors Guild and the Association of American Publishers (AAP). The original settlement had included an annual payment of $125 million in royalties to the copyright owners in order for Google to continue its project of scanning and selling online access to 150 million books.[36] But copyright concerns persisted because no one could establish ownership of the digitized and scanned pages. It was concluded that Google's current pact would simply give the company an unfair advantage over its competitors while rewarding it for engaging in wholesale copying of copyrighted works without permission.

In October 2012, the AAP announced a new, yet controversial, settlement deal with Google. For each book already scanned by Google, publishers could choose to contact Google for removal. Moving forward, every digitized book catalog would first require an express opt-in from publishers. None of the financial terms of the deal were released. The Authors Guild, on the other hand, still remains in litigation, leading a class-action lawsuit criticizing Google for its opt-out approach.[37] In 2014, legal appeals were filed challenging the validity of the financial settlement.

Google's Future: Innovation & Alphabet Inc.

The challenges of censorship in China have forced Google to look beyond the appeal of China's gargantuan search market. Instead, Google has shifted its focus to the operating systems of smartphones. At the end of 2015, Google's Android operating system enjoyed a market share of nearly 75 percent. Android is closely held by Google; so closely, in fact, that Google had been unwilling to share the most recent versions of code with Chinese smartphone developers. A recent example of this is when Google forced the delayed release of a smartphone manufactured by Acer Inc., which ran an operating system called Aliyun. This operating system was allegedly created by taking Android's software and making unapproved changes that were headed by the Chinese ecommerce organization Alibaba.[38]

Relationships are extremely hostile between Google and China, and the options for China are quickly disappearing. The only course of action left for China is to build its own Chinese mobile-OS for Chinese mobile devices.[39] Mobile continues to dominate a large portion of Google's strategy. When Google purchased Motorola Mobility in May 2012, it had hoped that the accompanying treasure trove of over 17,000 patents would yield innumerable benefits. But this has not been the case. After the $12.4 billion purchase, Google still has yet to win a decisive legal case with a big payoff.[40] As a result, Google sold Motorola Mobility in January 2014, though it retained most of the patents as part of the deal.

Regardless of the challenges, Google still has accumulated a powerful tool by acquiring Motorola Mobility's patents. Google now possesses among the best IPR for designing devices, and Google has the software to supplement those devices and integrate them vertically into its online systems.[41] Despite selling most of the hardware business to Lenovo in 2014, this purchase was ultimately consistent with Google's hope to reposition itself as a bigger player in the space of mobile technology.

The rate at which technology is becoming even more integrated into our lives is astounding, and Google is on the forefront of that mission. With its app for Android users, called "Google Keep," it hopes to target early software adopters looking for another way to manage all of their sticky notes, photos, and lists. But yet again, a central component to this new advancement is trust. While some users are easily giving up more private ground in the routine of their daily lives, others are questioning whether or not the free services are worth it, especially because similar projects like Google Reader or iGoogle have been terminated.[42]

For Google, these privacy issues have taken off internationally. In April 2013, Germany prosecuted Google for "scooping up sensitive personal information in the Street View mapping project." The total fine added up to $189,225, which is a drop in the bucket compared to Google's profits of $10.7 billion in 2012. Such fees are usually already factored into the business expenses of large data-mining corporations like Google. But these fines are not uncommon. Rather, it is the opposite, and often considered regular behavior. Google has accumulated several violations over the years. In 2014, the French regulatory body CNIL forced Google to pay a large fine. Additionally, the CNIL ruled that if an individual asks for search results based on his or her name to be removed from Google's search engine, Google must comply. In 2012, Google paid $7 million to settle with 38 states that had filed against the company. In

a separate case related to the Safari browser, the Federal Trade Commission penalized Google $22.5 million, "the largest civil penalty ever levied."[43] Future lawsuits are likely to follow in the U.K. following a 2015 British Court of Appeals ruling that citizens have the right to sue Google for any misuse of private information.[44]

Google's extensive reach in data is only growing in size. At around the same time that Germany was bringing its charges against Google, Google cemented its Global Human Trafficking Hotline Network, committing $3 million to bring together three NGOs: Polaris Project, Liberty Asia, and La Strada International. But one question still remains, even in the face of Google's good intentions: Can this company be trusted with sensitive information now regarding potentially trafficked victims? Have we gone too far by giving Google so much credit and by painting Google with a philanthropic stroke? In response to these questions, head of philanthropy at Palantir Technologies Jason Payne points out, "Just because someone's human rights have been eviscerated, doesn't mean that their civil liberties and electronic rights can be eviscerated."[45] Regardless of Google's legal efforts and privacy challenges, it is still pressing on with several innovative projects.

The most imaginative of Google's upcoming projects is a wearable beta technology device called Google Glass. The thrust of this new device is in the power of voice command for queries such as the weather, a built-in GPS, and the ability to take point-of-view photos and videos from an intimate perspective. All of this self-generated media is then directly uploaded to a user's Google+ account in private mode by default.[46]

Google is also considering several other projects including Android@Home, Google's attempt at home automation, connecting light bulbs, coffee pots, and alarm clocks.[47] Another project is Google Fiber, which focuses on delivering Internet speeds "100 times faster than the average Internet connection in the United States."[48] Driverless cars are also another ambitious goal for the company, which would go nicely with its current database of road maps. Google's strategy is clear: With billions of dollars spent on research and development, Google knows that it has a responsibility to push out products that no other company would dare to dream about, all the while pursuing high-tech inventions that integrate with our daily lives.

To better structure the company for future innovation and diversification, Google reorganized itself under a newly formed umbrella company, called Alphabet Inc., in 2015. Alphabet Inc. consists of multiple subsidiaries, each with a distinct focus. Under this new corporate structure, the Google Inc. brand continues to operate Google.com, Google Maps, and YouTube, but the tasks associated with other company goals are spread to newly created Alphabet Inc. subsidiaries. Calico, incorporated in 2013, is centered around biotech research and development, with a specific focus on disease and aging. Google Capital and GV (formerly Google Ventures) function as the venture capital arms of Alphabet Inc., targeting both tech startups and growth-stage companies. Perhaps the most interesting subsidiary is Google X (known simply as "X"), which functions as the heart of innovation at Alphabet Inc. As a secret research and development lab, Google X is responsible for developing the driverless car and Google Glass. Another exciting project, called "Project Loon," involves the deployment of atmospheric balloons to increase Internet access worldwide.

As Google expands, and its presence permeates developing markets, its opportunities are abundant. This is especially true because most of the newly connected Internet users are living in areas of conflict and could potentially experience drastic changes to their social structures as a result of interacting with Google. A company such as Google could extend its influence beyond that of a nation-state by empowering desperate citizens with the ideas or information they need to incite a revolution. New innovative Google projects, like "Project Loon," will connect the developing world with access to information and communication in ways that were previously impossible.

Ultimately, Google's international strategy will continue to align itself with its information strategy, continually leveraging the opportunities of both computational science and human ingenuity. At the same time, Google will continue to face political threats of censorship and information restriction and challenges to its privacy policies and practices. But the reverberations from its new technology will continue to generate commotion in the markets and challenges to governments and their information policies.

Questions for Review

1. How would you characterize China's market for online search and related services?
2. Why was Google initially attracted to China? What changed its perspective?
3. Should companies like Google conform to the Chinese government's expectation regarding privacy, censorship, and distribution of information?
4. What advantages does Baidu have over Google in the Chinese marketplace? How might Google overcome those advantages?
5. What recommendations would you make for Google in China going forward?

Source: This case was prepared by Karl Li and Pin-Pin Liao of Villanova University under the supervision of Professor Jonathan Doh as the basis for class discussion. Additional research assistance was provided by Ben Littell. It is not intended to illustrate either effective or ineffective managerial capability or administrative responsibility.

ENDNOTES

1. "Wife & Son of Well-Known Political Prisoner & Christian, Guo Quan Arrive in US," *ChinaAid.org*, January 24, 2012, www.chinaaid.org/2012/01/wife-son-of-well-known-political.html.
2. Ibid.
3. "About Google," *Google.com*, May 7, 2013. www.google.com/about/.
4. Justine Lau, "A History of Google in China," Financial Times Online, July 9, 2010, HYPERLINK "http://www.ft.com/cms/s/0/faf86fbc-0009-11df-8626-00144feabdc0.html?ft_site=falcon" \l "axzz4S04lPr4a" www.ft.com/cms/s/0/faf86fbc-0009-11df-8626-00144feabdc0.html?ft_site=falcon#axzz4S04lPr4a.
5. Ibid.
6. John Battelle, "The Birth of Google," *Wired.com*, August 2005, www.wired.com/wired/archive/13.08/battelle.html?tw=wn_tophead_4.
7. Lawrence Page, Sergey Brin, Rajeev Motwani, and Terry Winograd, "The PageRank Citation Ranking: Bringing Order to the Web," *Stanford Digital Library Project*, September 16, 1997, http://ilpubs.stanford.edu:8090/422/1/1999-66.pdf.
8. "BackRub," *Google Web Archives*, December 4, 1997, http://web.archive.org/web/19971210065425/backrub.stanford.edu/backrub.html.
9. "Google: Our History in Depth," *Google.com*, May 7, 2013, www.google.com/about/company/history.
10. "If the Check Says 'Google Inc.,' We're 'Google Inc.,'" *Wired.com*, September 7, 2007, www.wired.com/science/discoveries/news/2007/09/dayintech_0907.
11. "Google Receives $25 million in Equity Funding," *Google Web Archives*, June 7, 1997, http://web.archive.org/web/20000309205910/http://www.google.com/pressrel/pressrelease1.html.
12. "Google Goes Global with Addition of 10 Languages," *Google.com*, May 9, 2000, http://googlepress.blogspot.com/2000/05/google-goes-global-with-addition-of-10.html.
13. "Internet and Search Engine Usage by Country," *Internet World Stats*, http://ptgmedia.pearsoncmg.com/images/9780789747884/supplements/9780789747884_appC.pdf.
14. "Google: Our History in Depth."
15. Maureen Gleeson, "Why Google Can't Dominate Search in South Korea," *Oban Digital*, January 30, 2015, www.obandigital.com/gb/blog/2015/01/30/why-google-cant-dominate-search-in-south-korea/.
16. Ginny Marvin, "Google Still Dominant, but Baidu Benefitting from Google Ban in China Says eMarketer," March 31, 2015, http://searchengineland.

com/google-still-dominant-but-baidu-benefitting-from-google-ban-in-china-says-emarketer-217745.

17. "Google Losing Market Share in China," *Search Engine Journal,* September 21, 2006, www.searchenginejournal.com/google-losing-market-share-in-china/3816.

18. Rebecca Fannin, "Why Google Is Quitting China," *Forbes.com,* January 15, 2010, www.forbes.com/2010/01/15/baidu-china-search-intelligent-technology-google.html.

19. "Google: Our History in Depth."

20. Andrew McLaughlin, "Google in China," *Google's Official Blog,* January 27, 2006, https://googleblog.blogspot.com/2006/01/google-in-china.html.

21. Fannin, "Why Google Is Quitting China."

22. Ibid.

23. "Google Losing Market Share in China."

24. Ibid.

25. Ibid.

26. Ibid.

27. "Web History of China," *Timetoast.com,* 2010, www.timetoast.com/timelines/web-history-of-china.

28. Justine Lau, "A History of Google in China," *Financial Times Online,* July 9, 2010, www.ft.com/cms/s/0/faf86fbc-0009-11df-8626-00144feabdc0.html#axzz2MmJQVW1J.

29. Ibid.

30. Ibid.

31. "Google Aims to Stay in China Despite Censorship Clash," *Financial Times,* January 22, 2010, www.ft.com/intl/cms/s/2/f9ff5bcc-06ce-11df-b058-00144feabdc0.html#axzz2RynyO1Rd.

32. Chris McGreal and Bobbie Johnson, "Hillary Clinton Criticises Beijing over Internet Censorship," *The Guardian,* January 21, 2010, https://www.theguardian.com/world/2010/jan/21/hillary-clinton-china-internet-censorship.

33. "A New Approach to China: An Update," *Google's Official Blog*, March 22, 2010, http://googleblog.blogspot.com/2010/03/new-approach-to-china-update.html.

34. Loretta Chao, "Google Loses Chinese Market Share," *The Wall Street Journal*, April 27, 2010, http://online.wsj.com/article/SB10001424052748703465204575207833281993688.html.

35. Charles Riley, "The Great Firewall of China Is Nearly Complete," *CNN Money,* December 30, 2014, http://money.cnn.com/2014/12/30/technology/china-internet-firewall-google/.

36. Dominic Rushe, "US Judge Writes Unhappy Ending for Google's Online Library Plans," *The Guardian,* March 22, 2011, www.guardian.co.uk/technology/2011/mar/23/google-online-library-plans-thwarted.

37. Julianne Pepitone, "Google Strikes Deal with Publishers over Universal Library," *CNNMoney.com,* October 4, 2012, http://money.cnn.com/2012/10/04/technology/google-books-settlement/index.html.

38. Paul Mozur, "China Criticizes Android's Dominance," *The Wall Street Journal,* March 5, 2013, http://online.wsj.com/article/SB10001424127887324539404578342132324098420.html.

39. J. O'Dell, "China: Google's Too Controlling. We Should Create Our Own Damn Smartphone OS," *Venturebeat.com,* March 5, 2013, http://venturebeat.com/2013/03/05/china-google-android-drama/.

40. Susan Decker and Brian Womack, "Motorola Buyout Fails to Yield Patent Jackpot for Google," *Business Report*, April 30, 2013, www.iol.co.za/business/international/motorola-buyout-fails-to-yield-patent-jackpot-for-google-1.1508190#.UYQPdrXqnoI.

41. Google, "Facts about Google's Acquisition of Motorola," press release, 2013, www.google.com/press/motorola/.

42. Ezra Klein, "Google's Trust Problem," *Washington Post,* March 21, 2013, www.washingtonpost.com/blogs/wonkblog/wp/2013/03/21/googles-trust-problem/.

43. Claire Cain Miller, "Stern Words, and a Pea-Size Punishment, for Google," *New York Times,* April 22, 2013, www.nytimes.com/2013/04/23/business/global/stern-words-and-pea-size-punishment-for-google.html.

44. Kevin Cahill, "Google Appeal Ruling Should Send Shivers through US Tech Companies," *Computer Weekly,* March 30, 2015, www.computerweekly.com/news/4500243342/Google-appeal-ruling-should-sent-shivers-through-US-tech-companies.

45. Liat Clark, "Google Launches Global Human Trafficking Helpline and Data Network," *Arstechnica,* April 10, 2013, http://arstechnica.com/tech-policy/2013/04/google-launches-global-human-trafficking-helpline-and-data-network/.

46. Lance Ulanoff, "This Is Why Google Glass Is the Future," *Mashable,* April 30, 2013, http://mashable.com/2013/04/30/google-glass-future/.

47. Eric Mack, "Google Future Tech: 10 Coolest Google R&D Projects," *CIO.com,* 2013, www.cio.com/article/694854/Google_Future_Tech_10_Coolest_Google_R_D_Projects?page5 11#slideshow.

48. Chris Ciaccia, "Google's Future: Doing the Impossible," *BGR,* April 19, 2013, http://bgr.com/2013/04/19/google-earnings-analysis-q1-2013-449971/.

Tata "Nano": The People's Car

In January 2008 during India's main auto show in New Delhi, Tata Motors introduced to the Indian public its ultra-cheap car "Nano" that was expected to retail for as little as the equivalent of $2,500, or about the price of the optional DVD player on the Lexus LX 470 sport utility vehicle.[1] This event had driven unprecedented public attention because Tata's new vehicle was projected to revolutionize the auto industry.[2]

The emergence of Tata Motors on the global auto scene marks the advent of India as a global center for small-car production and represents a victory for those who advocate making cheap goods for potential customers at the "bottom of the pyramid" in emerging markets. Most of all, the car could give millions of people now relegated to lesser means of transportation the chance to drive cars.[3] In India, there were an estimated 18 cars for every thousand people in 2009, compared with 47 per thousand in China and 802 in the U.S. Far more middle-class Indians bought and transported their entire families on scooters.[4]

According to some analysts, Tata Motor's Chairman Ratan Tata hopes to use the Nano to become the Henry Ford of emerging India, in part by offering a car at a fraction of the price of rival products. The company is gambling that its tiny price tag will make it appealing to Indians who now drive motorcycles and scooters.

While India's population is more than 1 billion people, only around 1 million passenger cars were sold in the country in 2007, one-tenth as many as in China. By contrast, more than 7 million motorcycles and scooters were sold. Mr. Tata said the tiny car is aimed at keeping the families of India's growing middle class from having to travel with as many as four people on a scooter.[5]

Speaking at the unveiling ceremony at the 9th Auto Expo in New Delhi, Ratan Tata said, "I observed families riding on two-wheelers—the father driving the scooter, his young kid standing in front of him, his wife seated behind him holding a little baby. It led me to wonder whether one could conceive of a safe, affordable, all-weather form of transport for such a family. Tata Motors' engineers and designers gave their all for about four years to realize this goal. Today, we indeed have a People's Car, which is affordable and yet built to meet safety requirements and emission norms, to be fuel efficient and low on emissions. We are happy to present the People's Car to India and we hope it brings the joy, pride and utility of owning a car to many families who need personal mobility."[6]

Middle-class household incomes in India start at roughly $6,000 a year, so a $3,000 car is the kind of innovation that could create millions of new drivers. Eight million Indians currently own cars, according to the Mumbai-based credit-rating agency Crisil. Another 18 million have the means to buy one. However, the Nano could increase that pool of potential auto owners by as much as 65 percent, to 30 million. "This goes beyond economics and class," says Ravi Kant, managing director of Tata Motors. "This crosses the urban-rural divide. Now a car is within the reach of people who never imagined they would own a car. It's a triumph for our company. And for India."[7]

Designed with a Family in Mind

Though Nano's design triggered different comments from the public—some people called it handsome;[8] others called it egg shaped[9]—overall Tata Motors was very proud of the design, which was developed with a family in mind.[10] From Tata's perspective, the new Nano addresses several key characteristics that Indian families would prize in a car: low price, adequate comfort, fuel efficiency, and safety.

According to Tata, Nano has a roomy passenger compartment with generous leg space and head room, and it can comfortably seat four people. Four doors with high seating position make ingress and egress easy. With a snub nose and a sloping roof, the world's cheapest car can hold five people—if they squeeze.[11] Nano's dimensions are as follows: length of 3.1 meters, width of 1.5 meters, and height of 1.6 meters. Tata suggests these compact dimensions should allow the car to effortlessly maneuver on busy roads in cities as well as in rural areas. Its mono-volume design, with wheels at the corners and the power train at the rear, enables it to combine both space and maneuverability.[12] At 10 feet long, the Nano is about 2 feet shorter than a Mini Cooper.[13]

The car is available in both standard and deluxe versions. According to the company, both versions offer a wide range of body colors and other accessories so that the car can be customized to an individual's preferences.[14] But reviewers called the basic version spare: It has no radio, no air bags, no passenger-side mirror, and only one windshield wiper. If you want air conditioning to cope with India's brutal summers, you need to get the deluxe version.

According to the company, Nano has a fuel-efficient engine powered by the lean design strategy that has helped minimize weight, maximize performance per unit of energy consumed, and deliver higher fuel efficiency.[15] The final design stands at 1,322 pounds, 528 pounds lighter than the flyweight Honda Insight. To power it, the engineers settled on a 33-horsepower, 623-cc, two-cylinder engine housed in the rear; to service it, the mechanic must remove a set of bolts in the 5.4-cubic-foot trunk. The payoff: an uncommonly efficient 47 miles per gallon running at top speed (65 mph). But that doesn't mean Nano owners won't spend a lot of time pumping gas—the minuscule tank holds just 3.9 gallons.[16]

According to the company, the People's Car's safety performance exceeds current Indian regulatory requirements. With an all-sheet-metal body, it has a strong passenger compartment, with safety features such as crumple zones, intrusion-resistant doors, seat belts, strong seats and anchorages, and the rear tailgate glass bonded to the body. Tubeless tires further enhance safety. Tata also placed emphasis on environmental friendliness. According to a corporate press release, the People's Car's tailpipe emission performance exceeds regulatory requirements. In terms of overall pollutants, it has a lower pollution level than two-wheelers being manufactured in India today.[17]

About Tata Motors

Tata Motors is a part of the Tata Group. The Tata Group is considered the General Electric of India, a sprawling conglomerate with a commanding presence in media, telecom, outsourcing, retailing, and real estate. Started in 1868 as a textile wholesaler, the company branched out into luxury hotels after, as legend has it, founder Jamsetji Tata was turned away from a posh establishment because of his skin color. In 1945, a few years before the British left India, Tata created Tata Motors and started producing locomotives and, eventually, autos. In 1998, Tata Motors introduced the country's first indigenously designed car. The homegrown Indica, which now sells for around $6,000, became ubiquitous as a taxi.[18]

Meanwhile, the Tata Group has been expanding globally. It bought the tea company Tetley in 2000 and acquired Anglo-Dutch steel giant Corus in 2007. It maintains Tata Consultancy Services offices in 54 countries and owns hotels in Boston, New York, and San Francisco. In March 2008, Tata Motors bought Jaguar and Land Rover from the financially strangled Ford Motors.[19]

Tata Motors listed on the New York Stock Exchange in 2004. After thousands of changes, in the quarter ending December 2006 Tata earned $116 million on revenue of $1.55 billion. Annual revenue grew to $5.2 billion for the fiscal year ending in March 2006.[20] Now Tata Motors Limited is India's largest automobile company, with consolidated revenues of US$39 billion in 2015. It is the leader in commercial vehicles in each segment, and among the top three in passenger vehicles with winning products in the compact, midsize car, and utility vehicle segments. The company is the world's fifth largest truck manufacturer and the world's second largest bus manufacturer. The company's 60,000 employees are guided by the vision to be "best in the manner in which we operate, best in the products we deliver, and best in our value system and ethics."[21]

Established in 1945, Tata Motors' presence cuts across the length and breadth of India. Over 4 million Tata vehicles ply on Indian roads since they first rolled out in 1954. The company's manufacturing base in India is spread across Jamshedpur (Jharkhand), Pune (Maharashtra), Lucknow (Uttar Pradesh), Pantnagar (Uttarakhand), and Dharwad (Karnataka). Following a strategic alliance with Fiat in 2005, it has set up an industrial joint venture with Fiat Group Automobiles at Ranjangaon (Maharashtra) to produce both Fiat and Tata cars and Fiat powertrains. The company is establishing a new plant at Sanand (Gujarat). The company's dealership, sales, services, and spare parts network comprises over 3,500 touch points; Tata Motors also distributes and markets Fiat-branded cars in India.[22]

Tata Motors has also emerged as an international automobile company. Through subsidiaries and associate companies, Tata Motors has operations in the U.K., South Korea, Thailand, and Spain. Among them is Jaguar Land Rover, a business comprising the two iconic British brands that was acquired in 2008. In 2004, it acquired the Daewoo Commercial Vehicles Company, South Korea's second largest truck maker. The rechristened Tata Daewoo Commercial Vehicles Company has launched several new products in the Korean market, while also exporting these products to several international markets. Today two-thirds of heavy commercial vehicle exports out of South Korea are from Tata Daewoo.[23]

In 2005, Tata Motors acquired a 21 percent stake in Hispano Carrocera, a well-regarded Spanish bus and coach manufacturer, and subsequently the remaining stake in 2009. Hispano's presence is being expanded in other markets. In 2006, Tata Motors formed a joint venture with the Brazil-based Marcopolo, a global leader in body building for buses and coaches, to manufacture fully built buses and coaches for India and select international markets. In 2006, Tata Motors entered into a joint venture with Thonburi Automotive Assembly Plant Company of Thailand to manufacture and market the company's pickup vehicles in Thailand. The new plant of Tata Motors (Thailand) has begun production of the Xenon pickup truck, with the Xenon having been launched in Thailand in 2008.[24]

Tata Motors is also expanding its international footprint, established through exports since 1961. The company's commercial and passenger vehicles are already being marketed in several countries in Europe, Africa, the Middle East, South East Asia, South Asia, and South America. It has franchisee/joint venture assembly operations in Kenya, Bangladesh, Ukraine, Russia, Senegal, and South Africa. Through its subsidiaries, the company is engaged in engineering and automotive solutions, construction equipment manufacturing, automotive vehicle components manufacturing and supply chain activities, machine tools and factory automation solutions, high-precision tooling and plastic and electronic components for automotive and computer applications, and automotive retailing and service operations.[25]

The foundation of the company's growth over the last 50 years is a deep understanding of economic stimuli and customer needs, and the ability to translate them into customer-desired offerings through leading-edge R&D. With over 3,000 engineers and scientists, the company's Engineering Research Centre, established in 1966, has enabled pioneering technologies and products. The company today has R&D centers in Pune, Jamshedpur, Lucknow, and Dharwad in India, and in South Korea, Spain, and the U.K. It was Tata Motors that developed the first indigenously developed light commercial vehicle, India's first sports utility vehicle, and, in 1998, the Tata Indica, India's first fully indigenous passenger car. Within two years of launch, Tata Indica became India's largest-selling car in its segment. In 2005, Tata Motors created a new segment by launching the Tata Ace, India's first indigenously developed mini-truck. In January 2008, Tata Motors unveiled its People's Car, the Tata Nano, which was launched in India in March 2009.[26]

Tata Motors is equally focused on environment-friendly technologies in emissions and alternative fuels. It has developed electric and hybrid vehicles for both personal and public transportation. It has also been implementing several environment-friendly technologies in manufacturing processes, significantly enhancing resource conservation.[27]

Tata Motors is committed to improving the quality of life of communities by working on four thrust areas: employability, education, health, and environment. The firm's activities touch the lives of more than a million citizens. Its support for education and employability is focused on youth and women, ranging from schools to technical education institutes, to actual facilitation of income generation. In health, Tata's intervention is in both preventive and curative health care. The goal of environment protection is achieved through planting tree, conserving water and creating new water bodies, and, last but not least, introducing appropriate technologies in Tata vehicles and operations for constantly enhancing environment care.[28]

Tata Motors Milestones

It has been a long and accelerating journey for Tata Motors until it became India's leading automobile manufacturer. Here are some significant milestones in the company's journey toward excellence and leadership:[29]

1945 • Tata Engineering and Locomotive Co. Ltd. was established to manufacture locomotives and other engineering products.

1948 • Steam road roller introduced in collaboration with Marshall Sons (U.K.).

1954 • Collaboration with Daimler Benz AG, West Germany, for manufacture of medium commercial vehicles. The first vehicle rolled out within 6 months of the contract.

1959 • Research and Development Centre set up at Jamshedpur.

1961 • Exports begin with the first truck being shipped to Ceylon, now Sri Lanka.

1966 • Setting up of the Engineering Research Centre at Pune to provide impetus to automobile Research and Development.

1971 • Introduction of DI engines.

1977 • First commercial vehicle manufactured in Pune.

1983 • Manufacture of heavy commercial vehicle commences.

1985 • First hydraulic excavator produced with Hitachi collaboration.

1986 • Production of first light commercial vehicle, Tata 407, indigenously designed, followed by Tata 608.

1989 • Introduction of the Tatamobile 206—3rd LCV model.

1991 • Launch of the 1st indigenous passenger car, Tata Sierra.
  • TAC 20 crane produced.
  • One millionth vehicle rolled out.

1992 • Launch of the Tata Estate.

1993 • Joint venture agreement signed with Cummins Engine Co. Inc. for the manufacture of high-horsepower and emission-friendly diesel engines.

1994 • Launch of Tata Sumo—the multi-utility vehicle.
  • Launch of LPT 709—a full-forward-control, light commercial vehicle.
  • Joint venture agreement signed with M/s Daimler-Benz/Mercedes-Benz for manufacture of Mercedes Benz passenger cars in India.
  • Joint venture agreement signed with Tata Holset Ltd., U.K., for manufacturing turbochargers to be used on Cummins engines.

1995 • Mercedes Benz car E220 launched.

1996 • Tata Sumo deluxe launched.

1997 • Tata Sierra Turbo launched.
  • 100,000th Tata Sumo rolled out.

1998 • Tata Safari—India's first sports utility vehicle launched.
  • Two millionth vehicle rolled out.
  • Indica, India's first fully indigenous passenger car, launched.

1999 • 115,000 bookings for Indica registered against full payment within a week.
  • Commercial production of Indica commences in full swing.

2000 • First consignment of 160 Indicas shipped to Malta.
  • Indica with Bharat Stage 2 (Euro II)—compliant diesel engine launched.
  • Utility vehicles with Bharat 2 (Euro II)—compliant engine launched.
  • Indica 2000 (Euro II) with multipoint fuel-injection petrol engine launched.
  • Launch of CNG buses.
  • Launch of 1109 vehicle—an intermediate commercial vehicle.

2001
- Indica V2 launched—2nd generation Indica.
- 100,000th Indica wheeled out.
- Launch of CNG Indica.
- Launch of the Tata Safari EX.
- Indica V2 becomes India's number one car in its segment.
- Exits joint venture with Daimler Chrysler.

2002
- Unveiling of the Tata Sedan at Auto Expo 2002.
- Petrol version of Indica V2 launched.
- Launch of the EX series in commercial vehicles.
- Launch of the Tata 207 DI.
- 200,000th Indica rolled out.
- 500,000th passenger vehicle rolled out.
- Launch of the Tata Sumo '1' Series.
- Launch of the Tata Indigo.
- Tata Engineering signed a product agreement with MG Rover of the U.K.

2003
- Launch of the Tata Safari Limited Edition.
- The Tata Indigo Station Wagon unveiled at the Geneva Motor Show.
- On July 29, J. R. D. Tata's birth anniversary, Tata Engineering becomes Tata Motors Limited.
- Three millionth vehicle produced.
- First CityRover rolled out.
- 135 PS Tata Safari EXi Petrol launched.
- Tata SFC 407 EX Turbo launched.

2004
- Tata Motors unveils new product range at Auto Expo '04.
- New Tata Indica V2 launched.
- Tata Motors and Daewoo Commercial Vehicle Co. Ltd. sign investment agreement.
- Indigo Advent unveiled at Geneva Motor Show.
- Tata Motors completes acquisition of Daewoo Commercial Vehicle Company.
- Tata LPT 909 EX launched.
- Tata Daewoo Commercial Vehicle Co. Ltd. (TDCV) launches the heavy-duty truck NOVUS, in Korea.
- Sumo Victa launched.
- Indigo Marina launched.
- Tata Motors lists on the NYSE.

2005
- Tata Motors rolls out the 500,000th passenger car from its car plant facility in Pune.
- The Tata Xover unveiled at the 75th Geneva Motor Show.
- Branded buses and coaches—Starbus and Globus—launched.
- Tata Motors acquires 21% stake in Hispano Carrocera SA, Spanish bus manufacturing company.
- Tata Ace, India's first mini truck, launched.
- Tata Motors wins JRD QV award for business excellence.
- The power-packed Safari Dicor is launched.
- Introduction of Indigo SX series, luxury variant of Tata Indigo.
- Tata Motors launches Indica V2 Turbo Diesel.
- One millionth passenger car produced and sold.
- Inauguration of new factory at Jamshedpur for Novus.
- Tata TL 4×4, India's first sports utility truck (SUT), is launched.
- Launch of Tata Novus.
- Launch of Novus range of medium trucks in Korea, by Tata Daewoo Commercial Vehicle Co. (TDCV).

2006
- Tata Motors vehicle sales in India cross four million mark.
- Tata Motors unveils new long wheel base premium Indigo & X-over concept at Auto Expo 2006.
- Indica V2 Xeta launched.
- Passenger vehicle sales in India cross one million mark.
- Tata Motors and Marcopolo, Brazil, announce joint venture to manufacture fully built buses and coaches for India and markets abroad.
- Tata Motors' first plant for small cars to come up in West Bengal.
- Tata Motors extends CNG options on its hatchback and estate range.
- TDCV develops South Korea's first LNG-powered tractor-trailer.
- Tata Motors and Fiat Group announce three additional cooperation agreements.
- Tata Motors introduces a new Indigo range.

2007
- Construction of small car plant at Singur, West Bengal, begins on January 21.
- New 2007 Indica V2 range is launched.
- Tata Motors launches the longwheel base Indigo XL, India's first stretch limousine.
- Common rail diesel (DICOR) engine extended to Indigo sedan and estate range.
- Tata Motors and Thonburi Automotive Assembly Plant Co. (Thonburi) announce formation of a joint venture company in Thailand to manufacture, assemble, and market pickup trucks.
- Rollout of 100,000th Ace.
- Tata-Fiat plant at Ranjangaon inaugurated.
- Launch of a new upgraded range of its entry-level utility vehicle offering, the Tata Spacio.
- CRM-DMS initiative crosses the 1,000th location milestone.
- Launch of Magic, a comfortable, safe, four-wheeler public transportation mode, developed on the Ace platform.
- Launch of Winger, India's only maxi-van.
- Fiat Group and Tata Motors announce establishment of joint venture in India.
- Launch of the Sumo Victa Turbo DI, the new upgraded range of its entry-level utility vehicle, the Sumo Spacio.
- Tata Motors launches Indica V2 Turbo with dual air-bags and ABS.
- Launch of new Safari DICOR 2.2 VTT range, powered by a new 2.2 L Direct Injection Common Rail (DICOR) engine.
- Rollout of the one millionth passenger car off the Indica platform.

2008
- Ace plant at Pantnagar (Uttarakhand) begins production.
- Indica Vista, the new generation Indica, is launched.
- Tata Motors' new plant for Nano to come up in Gujarat.
- Latest common rail diesel offering, the Indica V2 DICOR, launched.
- Indigo CS (Compact Sedan), world's first sub-four-meter sedan, launched.
- Launch of the new Sumo—Sumo Grande, which combines the looks of an SUV with the comforts of a family car.

- Tata Motors unveils its People's Car, Nano, at the ninth Auto Expo.
- Xenon, one-ton pickup truck, launched in Thailand.
- Tata Motors signs definitive agreement with Ford Motor Company to purchase Jaguar and Land Rover.
- Tata Motors completes acquisition of Jaguar Land Rover.
- Tata Motors introduces new Super Milo range of buses.
- Tata Motors is Official Vehicle Provider to Youth Baton Relay for The III Commonwealth Youth Games, Pune 2008.
- Indica Vista, the second generation Indica, is launched.
- Tata Motors launches passenger cars and the new pickup in D.R. Congo.

2009
- Tata Motors begins distribution of Prima World truck.
- Tata Motors launches the next generation all-new Indigo MANZA.
- FREELANDER 2 launched in India.
- Tata Marcopolo Motors' Dharwad plant begins production.
- Tata Motors launches Nano—The People's Car.
- Introduction of new world standard truck range.
- Launch of premium luxury vehicles Jaguar XF, XFR, and XKR and Land Rover Discovery 3, Range Rover Sport, and Range Rover from Jaguar and Land Rover in India.

Secrets behind the Low Price

How could Tata Motors make a car so inexpensively? It started by looking at everything from scratch, applying what some analysts have described as "Gandhian engineering" principles—deep frugality with a willingness to challenge conventional wisdom. A lot of features that Western consumers take for granted—air conditioning, power brakes, radios, etc.—are missing from the entry-level model.[30]

In order to succeed with building a low-cost affordable car, Tata Motors began by studying and trying to understand the customer. What do the customers need? What do they really want? What can they afford? The customer was ever-present in the development of the Nano. Tata didn't set the price of the Nano by calculating the cost of production and then adding a margin. Rather, it set $2,500 as the price that it thought customers could pay and then worked backward, with the help of partners willing to take on a challenge, to build a $2,500 car that would reward all involved with a small profit.[31]

More fundamentally, the engineers worked to do more with less. Tata has been able to slash the price by asking his engineers and suppliers to redesign the many components to cut costs. The speedometer, for example, is in the center of the dashboard over the air vents, not behind the steering wheel, so the dashboard can be built with fewer parts.[32] To save $10, Tata engineers redesigned the suspension to eliminate actuators in the headlights, the levelers that adjust the angle of the beam depending on how

the car is loaded, according to Mr. Chaturvedi of Lumax. In lieu of the solid steel beam that typically connects steering wheels to axles, one supplier, Sona Koyo Steering Systems, used a hollow tube, said Kiran Deshmukh, the chief operating officer of the company, which is based in Delhi.[33]

Also, Nano is smaller in overall dimensions than the Suzuki Maruti, a similar but higher-priced low-cost competitor assembled in India, but it offers about 20 percent more seating capacity as a result of design choices such as putting the wheels at the extreme edges of the car. The Nano is also much lighter than comparable models as a result of a reduction in the amount of steel in the car (including the use of an aluminum engine) and the use of lightweight steel where possible.[34]

However, Nano engineers and partners didn't simply strip features out of an existing car to create a new low-cost model, which most other manufacturers have done when making affordable cars. Instead, they looked at their target customers' lives for cost-cutting ideas. So, for instance, the Nano has a smaller engine than other cars because more horsepower would be wasted in India's jam-packed cities, where the average speed is 10 to 20 miles per hour.[35] The car currently meets all Indian emission, pollution, and safety standards, although it only attains a maximum speed of about 65 mph. The fuel efficiency is also attractive to economy-driven consumers—nearly 50 miles to the gallon.[36]

Nano ultimately became a triumph of creativity and innovation. For example, Tata Motors has filed for 34 patents associated with the design of the Nano, although some suggest that measuring progress solely by patent creation misses a key dimension of innovation. Some of the most valuable innovations take existing, patented components and remix them in ways that more effectively serve the needs of large numbers of customers. The most innovative aspect of the Nano is its modular design. The Nano is constructed of components that can be built and shipped separately to be assembled in a variety of locations. In effect, the Nano is being sold in kits that are distributed, assembled, and serviced by local entrepreneurs.[37]

As Ratan Tata, chair of the Tata group of companies, observed in an interview with *The Times of London*: "A bunch of entrepreneurs could establish an assembly operation and Tata Motors would train their people, would oversee their quality assurance and they would become satellite assembly operations for us. So we would create entrepreneurs across the country that would produce the car. We would produce the mass items and ship it to them as kits. That is my idea of dispersing wealth. The service person would be like an insurance agent who would be trained, have a cell phone and scooter and would be assigned to a set of customers."[38]

This is part of a broader pattern of innovation emerging in India in a variety of markets, ranging from diesel

34. Hagel and Brown, "Learning from Tata's Nano."

35. Scanlon, "What Can Tata's Nano Teach Detroit?"

36. Hagel and Brown, "Learning from Tata's Nano."

37. Ibid.

38. Ibid.

39. Ibid.

40. "Villagers Raise Slogans against Car Company," *The Hindu,* May 26, 2006, www.thehindu.com/todays-paper/tp-national/villagers-raise-slogans-against-car-company/article3138420.ece.

41. Nick Kurczewski, "Tata Motors Shuts Down Nano Factory," September 3, 2008.

42. Stephanie Grimmett, "Tata Motors Makes Its Move Out of Singur," *Seeking Alpha,* September 5, 2008, http://seekingalpha.com/article/94106–tata-motors-makes-its-move-out-of-singur.

43. Ibid.

44. Rina Chandran and Sujoy Dhar, "Tata Motors Says Looking for Alternative Nano Site," *Reuters,* September 2, 2008, www.reuters.com/article/idUSDEL24564.

45. Kurczewski, "Tata Motors Shuts Down Nano Factory."

46. Malini Hariharan, "INSIGHT: Singur Dispute Could Hurt India Projects," *ICIS News,* September 1, 2008, www.icis.com/resources/news/2008/09/01/9153231/insight-singur-dispute-could-hurt-india-projects/.

47. Ibid.

48. Ibid.

49. Chandran and Dhar, "Tata Motors Says Looking for Alternative Nano Site."

50. Nick Kurczewski, "Tough Times for the Tata Nano," *New York Times,* December 26, 2008, http://wheels.blogs.nytimes.com/2008/12/26/tough-times-for-the-tata-nano/.

51. A memorandum of understanding (MOU or MoU) is a document describing a bilateral or multilateral agreement between parties. It expresses a convergence of will between the parties, indicating an intended common line of action. It is often used in cases where parties either do not imply a legal commitment or in situations where the parties cannot create a legally enforceable agreement. (Source: http://en.wikipedia.org/wiki/Memorandum_of_understanding.)

52. During a bandh, a major political party or a large chunk of a community declares a general strike, usually lasting one day. Often bandh means that the community or political party declaring a bandh expects the general public to stay in their homes and strike work. (Source: http://en.wikipedia.org/wiki/Bandh.)

53. "Buddha's Loss Is Modi's Gain as Nano Goes to Gujarat," *NDTV,* October 7, 2008.

54. "Nano Car Project: Third Petition Filed in Gujarat High Court," *Economic Times,* December 18, 2008, http://economictimes.indiatimes.com/News/News_By_Industry/Auto/Automobiles/Nano_Car_Project_Third_petition_filed_in_Gujarat_High_Court/articleshow/3857739.cms.

55. Kurczewski, "Tough Times for the Tata Nano."

56. Nair, "Tata Motors Gets 203,000 Orders for Nano, World's Cheapest Car."

57. Ibid.

58. Ibid.

59. Ibid.

60. Ibid.

61. "Tata's Nano: Stuck in Low Gear," *The Economist,* August 20, 2011, www.economist.com/node/21526374.

62. Adam Werbach, "Fizzling Sales in India for the Tata Nano, 'The Peoples's Car,'" *The Atlantic,* December 3, 2010, www.theatlantic.com/business/archive/2010/12/fizzling-sales-in-india-for-the-tata-nano-the-peoples-car/67435/.

63. "Tata's Nano: Stuck in Low Gear."

64. Tim Pollard, "Tata Ramps Up Production of Nano to Boost Slow Sales," *Automotive and Motoring News,* November 25, 2010, www.carmagazine.co.uk/car-news/industry-news/tata/tata-ramps-up-production-of-nano-to-boost-slow-sales/.

65. Sumant Banerji, "Tata Nano Turns Three; Life Has Just Begun for the World's Cheapest Car," *Hindustan Times,* July 16, 2012, www.hindustan-times.com/autos/tata-nano-turns-three-life-has-just-begun-for-the-world-s-cheapest-car/story-gff1uCmNHh0HryvSACvLL.html.

66. Tata Motors, *Directors Report, FY 2015,* www.tatamotors.com/investors/financials/70-ar-html/directors-report.html.

67. Bellman, "Tata's High-Stakes Bet on Low-Cost Car."

68. Carney, "India's 50-MPG Tata Nano: Auto Solution or Pollution?"

69. Ibid.

70. Bellman, "Tata's High-Stakes Bet on Low-Cost Car."

71. Ibid.

72. Anil K. Gupta and Haiyan Wang, "Tata Nano: Not Just a Car but Also a Platform," *BusinessWeek,* January 29, 2010.

73. Giridharadas, "Four Wheels for the Masses: The $2,500 Car."

74. Matthew DeBord, "Is the Tata Nano America's Good Enough Car?" *The Big Money,* January 21, 2010.

75. Ibid.

PART FOUR

ORGANIZATIONAL
BEHAVIOR AND
HUMAN RESOURCE
MANAGEMENT

Chapter 12

MOTIVATION ACROSS CULTURES

OBJECTIVES OF THE CHAPTER

Motivation is closely related to the performance of human resources in modern organizations. Although the motivation process may be similar across cultures, there are clear differences in motivation that are culturally based. What motivates employees in the United States may be only moderately effective in Japan, France, or Nigeria. Therefore, although motivation in the workplace is related to stimulating and encouraging employee performance in many situations and environments, an international context requires country-by-country, or at least regional, examination of differences in motivation and its sources.

This chapter examines motivation as a psychological process and explores how motivation can be used to understand and improve employee performance. It also identifies and describes internationally researched work-motivation theories and discusses their relevance for international human resource management. The specific objectives of this chapter are

1. **DEFINE** *motivation*, and explain it as a psychological process.

2. **EXAMINE** the hierarchy-of-needs, two-factor, and achievement motivation theories, and assess their value to international human resource management.

3. **DISCUSS** how an understanding of employee satisfaction can be useful in human resource management throughout the world.

4. **EXAMINE** the value of process theories in motivating employees worldwide.

5. **UNDERSTAND** the importance of job design, work centrality, and rewards in motivating employees in an international context.

The World of *International Management*

Motivating Employees in a Multicultural Context: Insights from Emerging Markets

According to Patricia Odell of *PROMO* magazine, "As U.S. companies continue to expand globally, currently employing more than 60 million overseas workers, motivating and rewarding these diverse workforces is a significant challenge to organizations." Bob Nelson, Ph.D., author of *1001 Ways to Reward Employees*, told *PROMO* magazine, "One size doesn't fit all when it comes to employee motivation—rewards that motivate best are those that are most valued by the person you are trying to thank."[1]

According to *BusinessWeek*, numerous well-known firms have enlisted the help of Globoforce, an Irish company, to design their corporate recognition programs. Globoforce's program lets employees choose a reward they want, such as tickets to a concert or a $50 gift card to their favorite store. In this way, Globoforce tailors rewards to specific employee preferences.[2] This personalized approach to motivation appears to work well; a 2016 study found that employees who received recognition rewards were more likely to feel engaged in their jobs and proud of their work.[3]

These employee preferences are often correlated with culture. For example, in a certain Australian company, recognizing specific employees through programs like "Employee of the Month" effectively work as a strong motivator. Australian employees, with an individualistic culture, tend to feel comfortable when specific key performers are rewarded for their individual contributions, and many will work harder to achieve this recognition. In a certain Chinese company, however, this same approach may actually demotivate employees. Chinese employees, who tend to be collectivist, may view an individual award or bonus to be embarrassing. In this type of culture, recognition of the entire workgroup might be more effective, stengthening the entire team rather than causing division.[4]

Furthermore, managers must be aware that a reward in one culture may be viewed differently in another culture. Bob Nelson shares a story of how a pharmaceutical company decided to give customized watches bearing the company logo to all 44,000 employees around the world. When Nelson told this story to Taiwanese employees of a different company, they remarked that such a gift would never work in their culture. Timepieces are associated with death in Taiwan and China.[5]

So, as a manager, how does one motivate employees? There are general management principles that can be applied to most cultural settings. But also, there are specific considerations for each individual culture. Next, we mention some general concepts that have proved useful and then discuss motivating Chinese employees in particular.

Motivating Employees: General Principles

In its guide on how to motivate employees, *The Wall Street Journal* suggests that motivation involves "creat[ing] conditions that make people want to offer maximum effort, [having] employees harness self-direction and self-control in pursuit of common objectives, . . . [r]ewarding people for achievement," providing responsibility that allows them to rise to the challenge, and "[u]nleashing their imagination, ingenuity and creativity. . . ."[6]

In addition, Bob Nelson notes that today employees "expect work to be an integrated part of their lives—not their entire lives."[7] Thus, managers can likely increase employee motivation by offering more flexible working hours. With technology, it has become much easier for employees to work from home. Nelson also emphasizes that discussing career options in the organization and providing learning and development opportunities often motivates employees.[8]

Frequently, managers focus on extrinsic rewards, such as pay, to motivate employees, while ignoring intrinsic rewards. Kenneth Thomas told *BusinessWeek*, "Research shows that managers underestimate the importance of intrinsic rewards." *BusinessWeek* describes intrinsic rewards as "the psychological lift that employees get from doing work that matters to them."[9] Intrinsic rewards include the personal feeling of accomplishment that employees have when completing work. In a collectivistic culture, such as Argentina, an intrinsic reward may be the satisfaction of helping the group complete a project. In an individualistic country, like the United Kingdom, an intrinsic reward may be the satisfaction of personally exceeding sales goals or efficiency.

Motivating Employees in China

A WorkChina™ employee opinion survey, consisting of 10,000 employees from 67 companies in China, found that compensation had a limited role in motivating Chinese employees. Jim Leininger of Watson Wyatt Beijing wrote:

> Increasing employee satisfaction by raising salaries may result in short-term retention, but employees who stay in your organization because of high salaries may also leave for higher salaries. Thus, compensation is sometimes called a "hygiene issue." It is something that is not noticed until it is missing. A noncompetitive compensation system is easily "noticed" by employees and can lead to turnover. However, having high salary levels does not necessarily lead to highly committed employees or lower turnover. Other things become the distinguishing factors once average compensation levels are satisfied.[10]

The following factors were found to be strong drivers of employee commitment:

- *Management effectiveness.* Employees are motivated when their managers have sound decision-making ability, successfully engage their employees, and value their employees.

- *Positive work environment.* To be productive, employees need a healthy, safe workplace with access to information needed to do their jobs.

- *Objective performance management system.* Watson Wyatt's 2003 compensation survey demonstrated that, for the typical employee, at least one month's salary will be tied to a performance measure—either for the employee personally or for the company itself. Managers must ensure that the performance management system is objective, fair, and clearly communicated to employees.

- *Clear communication.* Managers can increase commitment by making sure employees understand their company's goals, their own job, and the link between their job and the customer.[11]

In contrast, Fisher and Yuan's case study of Chinese employees of a major hotel in Shanghai found that good wages and good working conditions were the most important motivating factors. They discovered that employees' intrinsic needs for interesting work, personal growth, and involvement tended to be lower, especially among older Chinese workers, as compared with employees in Western cultures. According to Fisher and Yuan, managers of MNCs with ventures in China should take note that Chinese employees appreciate wage raises, increased housing subsidies, and employee share ownership. Chinese

Figure 12-7

Selected Countries on the Uncertainty-Avoidance and Masculinity Scales

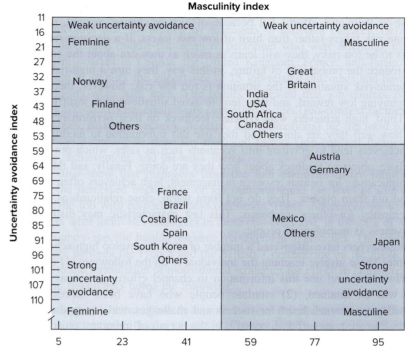

Source: Adapted from Geert Hofstede, "The Cultural Relativity of Organizational Practices and Theories," *Journal of International Business Studies*, Fall 1983, p. 86.

or to live with ambiguity. These societies also tend to have moderate-to-high masculinity, as measured by the high importance they assign to the acquisition of money and other physical assets and the low value they give to caring for others and for the quality of work life. This combination (see the upper right quadrant of Figure 12–7) is found almost exclusively in Anglo countries or in nations that have been closely associated with them through colonization or treaty, such as India, Singapore, and Hong Kong (countries associated with Great Britain) and the Philippines (associated with the United States).

Countries that fall into one of the other three quadrants of Figure 12–7 will not be very supportive of the high need for achievement. MNCs in these geographic regions, therefore, would be wise to formulate a human resource management strategy for either changing the situation or adjusting to it. If they decide to change the situation, they must design jobs to fit the needs of their people or put people through an achievement motivation training program to create high-achieving managers and entrepreneurs.

A number of years ago, McClelland was able to demonstrate the success of such achievement motivation training programs with underdeveloped countries. For example, in India, he conducted such a program with considerable success. In following up these Indian trainees over the subsequent 6 to 10 months, he found that two-thirds were unusually active in achievement-oriented activities. They had started new businesses, investigated new product lines, increased profits, or expanded their present organizations. For example, the owner of a small radio store opened a paint and varnish factory after completing the program. McClelland concluded that this training appeared to have doubled the natural rate of unusual achievement-oriented activity in the group studied.[49]

If international human resource managers cannot change the situation or train the participants, then they must adjust to the specific conditions of the country and formulate a motivation strategy that is based on those conditions. In many cases, this requires consideration of a need-hierarchy approach blended with an achievement approach. Hofstede offers such advice in dealing with the countries in the various quadrants of Figure 12–7:

> The countries on the feminine side . . . distinguish themselves by focusing on quality of life rather than on performance and on relationships between people rather than on money and things. This means social motivation: quality of life plus security and quality of life plus risk.[50]

In the case of countries that are attempting to introduce changes that incorporate values from one of the other quadrants in Figure 12–7, the challenge can be even greater.

In summary, achievement motivation theory provides additional insights into the motivation of personnel around the world. Like the need-hierarchy and two-factor theories, however, achievement motivation theory must be modified to meet the specific needs of the local culture. The culture of many countries does not support high achievement. However, the cultures of Anglo countries and those that reward entrepreneurial effort do support achievement motivation, and their human resources should probably be managed accordingly.

■ Select Process Theories

While content theories are useful in explaining motivation for managing international personnel, process theories can also lead to better understanding. As noted earlier, the process theories explain how employee behavior is initiated, redirected, and halted; and some of these theories have been used to examine motivation in the international arena. Among the most widely recognized are equity theory, goal-setting theory, and expectancy theory. The following briefly examines each of these three and their relevance to international human resource management.

Equity Theory

Equity theory focuses on how motivation is affected by people's perception of how fairly they are being treated. The theory holds that if people perceive that they are being treated equitably, this perception will have a positive effect on their job performance and satisfaction, and there is no need to strive for equity. Conversely, if they believe they are not being treated fairly, especially in relation to relevant others, they will be dissatisfied, and this belief will have a negative effect on their job performance and they will strive to restore equity.

equity theory
A process theory that focuses on how motivation is affected by people's perception of how fairly they are being treated.

There is considerable research to support the fundamental equity principle in Western work groups.[51] However, when the theory is examined on an international basis, the results are mixed. Yuchtman, for example, studied equity perceptions among managers and nonmanagers in an Israeli kibbutz production unit.[52] In this setting everyone was treated the same, but the managers reported lower satisfaction levels than the workers. The managers perceived their contributions to be greater than those of any other group in the kibbutz. As a result of this perception, they felt that they were undercompensated for their value and effort. These findings support the basic concepts of equity theory.

One study, which assumed that Western thought was synonymous with individualism and Eastern thought with collectivism, indicated that there are both similarities and differences between how cultures view the equity model. The model consists of employee inputs, subsequent outcomes, areas employees choose to compare the self to, and the motivation to change any perceived inequity that may exist between the self and the point of comparison (such as co-workers or employees in similar industries and positions).[53] A summary comparison is provided in Table 12–6.

On the other hand, a number of studies cast doubt on the relevance of equity theory in explaining motivation in an international setting. Perhaps the biggest shortcoming is that the theory appears to be culture-bound. For example, equity theory postulates that when people are not treated fairly, they will take steps to reduce the inequity by, for example, doing less work, filing a grievance, or getting a transfer to another department. In Asia and the Middle East, however, employees often readily accept inequitable treatment in order to preserve group harmony. Additionally, in countries such as Japan and Korea, men and women typically receive different pay for doing the same work, yet because of years of cultural conditioning, women may not feel they are being treated inequitably.[54,55] Some researchers have explained this finding by suggesting that these women compare themselves only to other women and in this comparison feel they are

Table 12–6
Individualistic and Collectivist Approaches to Equity Model

	Western (Individualistic) Cultures	Eastern (Collectivist) Cultures
Inputs	Effort	Loyalty
	Intelligence	Support
	Education	Respect
	Experience	Organizational tenure
	Skill	Organizational status
	Social status	Group member
Outcomes	Pay	Harmony
	Autonomy	Social status
	Seniority status	Acceptance
	Fringe benefits	Solidarity
	Job status	Cohesion
	Status symbol	
Comparisons	*Situation*	*Organizational Group*
	Physical proximity	Similar industry
	Job facet	Similar product/service
	Personal	*In-Group*
	Gender	Status
	Age	Job
	Position	Tenure
	Professionalism	Age
		Position
Motivation to Reduce Inequity	Change personal inputs	*Organizational Group*
	Provoke alternate outcomes	Change points of comparison
	Psychologically distort inputs and outcomes	Psychologically distort inputs and outcomes
	Leave the field	*In-Group*
	Change points of comparison	Alter inputs of self
		Psychologically distort inputs and outcomes

Source: Adapted from Paul A. Fadil et al., "Equity or Equality?. . .," *Cross-Cultural Management* 12, no. 4 (2005), p. 23.

being treated equitably. While this may be true, the results still point to the fact that equity theory is not universally applicable in explaining motivation and job satisfaction. In short, although the theory may help explain why "equal pay for equal work" is a guiding motivation principle in countries such as the United States and Canada, it may have limited value in other areas of the world, including Asia and Latin America, where compensation differences based on gender, at least traditionally, have been culturally acceptable.

Goal-Setting Theory

goal-setting theory
A process theory that focuses on how individuals go about setting goals and responding to them and the overall impact of this process on motivation.

Goal-setting theory focuses on how individuals go about setting goals and responding to them and the overall impact of this process on motivation. Specific areas that are given attention in goal-setting theory include the level of participation in setting goals, goal difficulty, goal specificity, and the importance of objective, timely feedback to progress toward goals. Unlike many theories of motivation, goal setting has been continually refined and developed.[56] There is considerable research evidence showing that employees perform extremely well when they are assigned specific and challenging goals that they have had a hand in setting.[57] But most of these studies have been conducted in the United States, while few of them have been carried out in other cultures.[58] One study that did examine goal setting in an international setting looked at Norwegian employee participation in goal setting.[59] The researchers found that the Norwegian employees shunned participation and preferred to have their union representatives work with management in determining work goals. This led the researchers to conclude that individual participation in goal setting was seen as inconsistent with the prevailing philosophy of participation through union representatives. Unlike the United States, where employee participation in setting goals is motivational, it had no value for the Norwegian employees in this study.

Similar results to the Norwegian study have been reported by Earley, who found that workers in the U.K. responded more favorably to a goal-setting program sponsored by the union stewards than to one sponsored by management. This led Earley to conclude that the transferability across cultural settings of management concepts such as participation in goal setting may well be affected by the prevailing work norms.[60] In order to further test this proposition, Erez and Earley studied American and Israeli subjects and found that participative strategies led to higher levels of goal acceptance and performance in both cultures than did strategies in which objectives were assigned by higher-level management.[61] In other words, the value of goal-setting theory may well be determined by culture. In the case, for example, of Asian and Latin work groups, where collectivism is very high, the theory may have limited value for MNC managers in selected countries.

Expectancy Theory

Expectancy theory postulates that motivation is largely influenced by a multiplicative combination of a person's belief that (a) effort will lead to performance, (b) performance will lead to specific outcomes, and (c) the outcomes will be of value to the individual.[62] In addition, the theory predicts that high performance followed by high rewards will lead to high satisfaction.[63] Does this theory have universal application? Eden used it in studying workers in an Israeli kibbutz and found some support;[64] and Matsui and colleagues reported that the theory could be applied successfully in Japan.[65] On the other hand, it is important to remember that expectancy theory is based on employees having considerable control over their environment, a condition that does not exist in many cultures (e.g., Asia). In particular, in societies where people believe that much of what happens is beyond their control, this theory may have less value. It would seem that expectancy theory is best able to explain worker motivation in cultures where there is a strong internal locus of control (e.g., in the United States). In short, the theory seems culture-bound, and international managers must be aware of this limitation in their efforts to apply this theory to motivate human resources.

> **expectancy theory**
> A process theory that postulates that motivation is influenced by a person's belief that (a) effort will lead to performance, (b) performance will lead to specific outcomes, and (c) the outcomes will be of value to the individual.

■ Motivation Applied: Job Design, Work Centrality, and Rewards

Content and process theories provide important insights into and understanding of ways to motivate human resources in international management. So, too, do applied concepts such as job design, work centrality, and rewards.

Job Design

Job design consists of a job's content, the methods that are used on the job, and the way in which the job relates to other jobs in the organization. Job design typically is a function of the work to be done and the way in which management wants it to be carried out. These factors help explain why the same type of work may have a different impact on the motivation of human resources in various parts of the world and result in differing qualities of work life.

> **job design**
> A job's content, the methods that are used on the job, and the way the job relates to other jobs in the organization.

Table 12–7
Cultural Dimensions in Japan, Sweden, and the United States

Cultural Dimension	Degree of Dimension		
	High/Strong X ←	Moderate — X —	Low/Weak → X
Uncertainty avoidance	J		USA S
Individualism	USA	S	J
Power distance		J USA	S
Masculinity	J	USA	S

Source: From Geert Hofstede, "The Cultural Relativity of the Quality of Life Concept," *Academy of Management Review,* July 1984, pp. 391, 393.

Quality of Work Life: The Impact of Culture   Quality of work life (QWL) is not the same throughout the world. For example, assembly-line employees in Japan work at a rapid pace for hours and have very little control over their work activities. In Sweden, assembly-line employees work at a more relaxed pace and have a great deal of control over their work activities. U.S. assembly-line employees are somewhere in between; they typically work at a pace that is less demanding than that in Japan but more structured than that in Sweden.

What accounts for these differences? One answer is found in the culture of the country. QWL is directly related to culture. Table 12–7 compares the United States, Japan, and Sweden along the four cultural dimensions described in Chapter 4. A brief look shows that each country has a different cultural profile, helping explain why similar jobs may be designed quite differently from country to country. Assembly-line work provides a good basis for comparison.

In Japan, there is strong uncertainty avoidance. The Japanese like to structure tasks so there is no doubt regarding what is to be done and how it is to be done. Individualism is low, so there is strong emphasis on security, and individual risk taking is discouraged. The power-distance index is high, so Japanese workers are accustomed to taking orders from those above them. The masculinity index for the Japanese is high, which shows that they put a great deal of importance on money and other material symbols of success. In designing jobs, the Japanese structure tasks so that the work is performed within these cultural constraints. Japanese managers work their employees extremely hard. Although Japanese workers contribute many ideas through the extensive use of quality circles, Japanese managers give them very little say in what actually goes on in the organization (in contrast to the erroneous picture often portrayed by the media, which presents Japanese firms as highly democratic and managed from the bottom up)[66] and depend heavily on monetary rewards, as reflected by the fact that the Japanese rate money as an important motivator more than the workers in any other industrialized country do.

In Sweden, uncertainty avoidance is low, so job descriptions, policy manuals, and similar work-related materials are more open-ended or general in contrast with the detailed procedural materials developed by the Japanese. In addition, Swedish workers are encouraged to make decisions and to take risks. Swedes exhibit a moderate-to-high degree of individualism, which is reflected in their emphasis on individual decision making (in contrast to the collective or group decision making of the Japanese). They have a weak power-distance index, which means that Swedish managers use participative approaches in leading their people. Swedes score low on masculinity, which means that interpersonal relations and the ability to interact with other workers and discuss job-related matters are important. These cultural dimensions result in job designs that are markedly different from those in Japan.

Cultural dimensions in the United States are closer to those of Sweden than to those of Japan. In addition, except for individualism, the U.S. profile is between that of

Sweden and Japan (again see Table 12–7). This means that job design in U.S. assembly plants tends to be more flexible or unstructured than that of the Japanese but more rigid than that of the Swedes.

This same pattern holds for many other jobs in these three countries. All job designs tend to reflect the cultural values of the country. The challenge for MNCs is to adjust job design to meet the needs of the host country's culture. For example, when Japanese firms enter the United States, they often are surprised to learn that people resent close control. In fact, there is evidence that the most profitable Japanese-owned companies in the United States are those that delegate a high degree of authority to their U.S. managers.[67] Similarly, Japanese firms operating in Sweden find that quality of work life is a central concern for the personnel and that a less structured, highly participative management style is needed for success. Some of the best examples of efforts to integrate job designs with culture and personality are provided by sociotechnical job designs.

Sociotechnical Job Designs

Sociotechnical designs are job designs that blend personnel and technology. The objective of these designs is to integrate new technology into the workplace so that workers accept and use it to increase overall productivity. Because new technology often requires people to learn new methods and, in some cases, work faster, employee resistance is common. Effective sociotechnical design can overcome these problems. There are a number of good examples, and perhaps the most famous is that of Volvo, the Swedish automaker.

sociotechnical designs
Job designs that blend personnel and technology.

Sociotechnical changes reflective of the cultural values of the workers were introduced at Volvo's Kalmar plant. Autonomous work groups were formed and given the authority to elect their own supervisors as well as to schedule, assign, and inspect their own work. Each group was allowed to work at its own pace, although there was an overall output objective for the week, and each group was expected to attain this goal.[68] The outcome was very positive and resulted in Volvo building another plant that employed even more sophisticated sociotechnical job-design concepts. Volvo's plant layout, however, did not prevent the firm from having some problems. Both Japanese and North American automakers were able to produce cars in far less time, putting Volvo at a cost disadvantage. As a result, stagnant economies in Asia, coupled with weakening demand for Volvo's product lines in both Europe and the United States, resulted in the firm laying off workers and taking steps to increase its efficiency.[69,70]

Without sacrificing efficiency, other firms have introduced sociotechnical designs for better blending of their personnel and technology. A well-known U.S. example is General Foods, which set up autonomous groups at its Topeka, Kansas, plant to produce Gaines pet food. Patterned after the Volvo example, the General Foods project allowed workers to share responsibility and work in a highly democratic environment. Other U.S. firms also have opted for a self-managed team approach. In fact, research reports that the concept of multifunctional teams with autonomy for generating successful product innovation is more widely used by successful U.S., Japanese, and European firms than any other teamwork concept.[71] Its use must be tempered by the cultural situation, however. And even the widely publicized General Foods project at Topeka had some problems. Some former employees indicate that the approach steadily eroded and that some managers were openly hostile because it undermined their power, authority, and decision-making flexibility. The most effective job design will be a result of both the job to be done and the cultural values that support a particular approach.[72] For MNCs, the challenge will be to make the fit between the design and the culture.

At the same time, it is important to realize that functional job descriptions now are being phased out in many MNCs and replaced by more of a process approach. The result is a more horizontal network that relies on communication and teamwork. This approach also is useful in helping create and sustain partnerships with other firms.

Work Centrality

work centrality
The importance of work in an individual's life relative to other areas of interest.

Work centrality, which can be defined as the importance of work in an individual's life relative to his or her other areas of interest (family, church, leisure), provides important insights into how to motivate human resources in different cultures.[73] After conducting a review of the literature, Bhagat and associates found that Japan has the highest level of work centrality, followed by moderately high levels for Israel, average levels for the United States and Belgium, moderately low levels for the Netherlands and Germany, and low levels for Britain.[74] These findings indicate that successful multinationals in Japan must realize that although work is an integral part of the Japanese lifestyle, work in the United States must be more balanced with a concern for other interests. Unfortunately, this is likely to become increasingly more difficult for Japanese firms in Japan because stagnant population growth is creating a shortage of personnel. As a result, growing numbers of Japanese firms are now trying to push the mandatory retirement age to 65 from 60 and, except for workers in the United States, Japanese workers put in the most hours.[75,76]

Value of Work   Although work is an important part of the lifestyles of most people, this emphasis can be attributed to a variety of conditions. For example, one reason that Americans and Japanese work such long hours is that the cost of living is high, and hourly employees cannot afford to pass up the opportunity for extra money. Among salaried employees who are not paid extra, most Japanese managers expect their subordinates to stay late at work, and overtime has become a requirement of the job. Moreover, there is recent evidence that Japanese workers may do far less work in a business day than outsiders would suspect.

Many people are unaware of these facts and have misperceptions of why the Japanese and Americans work so hard and the importance of work to them. The same is true of Germans and Americans. In recent years, the number of hours worked annually by German workers has been declining, while the number for Americans has been on the rise. What accounts for this trend? Some observers have explained it in cultural terms, noting that Germans place high value on lifestyle and often prefer leisure to work, while their American counterparts are just the opposite. In fact, research reveals that culture may have little to do with it. A study by the National Bureau of Economic Research (NBER) found a far wider range of wages within American companies than in German firms, and this large pay disparity has created incentives for American employees to work harder. For instance, Table 12–8 compares U.S. and German salaries based on a "Step 1" or entry-level pay scale. In particular, many U.S. workers believe that if they work harder, their chances of getting pay hikes and promotions will increase, and there are historical data to support this belief. An analysis of worker histories in the United States and Germany led NBER researchers to estimate that American workers who increase their working time by 10 percent, for example, from 2,000 to 2,200 hours annually, will raise their future earnings by about 1 percent for each year in which they put in extra hours.

Obviously, factors other than culture—such as gender, industry, and organizational characteristics—influence the degree and type of work centrality within a country. These factors, in turn, interact with national cultural characteristics. One study of work centrality examined the effect of parenthood on men and on women regarding the centrality of and investment in work and family in the bicultural context of the Israeli high-tech industry (i.e., the family-centered Israeli society on the one hand and the masculine work-centered high-tech industry on the other hand). This study found a contrasting parenthood effect on men and women. Fathers showed higher relative work centrality than childless men, whereas mothers showed lower relative work centrality than women without children. Fathers invested more weekly hours in paid work than childless men, whereas mothers invested fewer weekly hours in paid work than women without children. In the parents' sub-sample, mothers evinced higher relative family centrality than fathers. Mothers also invested more weekly hours in child care and core housework tasks than fathers. A key finding was that the contrasting parenthood effect prevails even in the

Table 12–8
2016 Annual Salaries: U.S. and Germany

Grade	U.S. Salary (Annual, in US$)	German Salary (Annual, in US$)
1	$ 18,343	$25,405
2	20,623	25,405
3	22,502	26,268
4	25,261	27,448
5	28,282	29,260
6	31,504	30,518
7	35,009	31,072
8	38,771	33,114
9	42,823	35,318
10	47,158	39,794
11	51,811	41,295
12	62,101	42,701
13	73,846	51,571
14	87,263	56,966
15	102,646	71,691

Source: https://www.opm.gov/policy-data-oversight/pay-leave/salaries-wages/salary-tables/pdf/2016/GS.pdf and calculated from http://oeffentlicher-dienst.info/beamte/land/.

demanding high-tech sector, in which women are expected to work long hours and play down their care-giving activities.[77]

Another important area of consideration is the importance of work as a part of overall lifestyle. In the case of Japanese workers, in particular, there has been a growing interest in the impact of overwork on the physical condition of employees. A report by the Japanese government noted that one-third of the working-age population suffers from chronic fatigue, and a recent survey by the Japanese prime minister's office found that a majority of those who were surveyed complained of being chronically tired and feeling emotionally stressed and some complained about abusive conditions in the workplace.[78,79] Fortunately, as seen in the International Management in Action box "Karoshi: Stressed Out in Japan," the effects of overwork or job burnout—**karoshi** in Japanese—are beginning to be recognized as a real social problem. Other Asian countries that are subject to accelerated development are also experiencing job stress. Chinese workers, for example, are exhibiting classic Western signs of stress and overwork. Burnout, substance abuse, eating disorders, and depression abound, not to mention time away from the family. The culture is such that employees will not seek counseling, as it is a sign of weakness and embarrassment. However, like the Japanese, the Chinese are seeing the issue and attempting to approach a solution that will alleviate stress and save face.[80]

karoshi
A Japanese term that means "overwork" or "job burnout."

Job Satisfaction　In addition to the implications that value of work has for motivating human resources across cultures, another interesting contrast is job satisfaction. For example, one study found that Japanese office workers may be much less satisfied with their jobs than their U.S., Canadian, and EU counterparts are. The Americans, who reported the highest level of satisfaction in this study, were pleased with job challenges, opportunities for teamwork, and ability to make a significant contribution at work. Japanese workers were least pleased with these three factors.[81] Similar findings were uncovered by Luthans and his associates, who reported that U.S. employees had higher organizational commitment than Japanese or Korean workers in their cross-cultural study. What makes these findings particularly interesting is that a large percentage of the Japanese and Korean workers were supervisory employees, who

Karoshi: Stressed Out in Japan

Doing business in Japan can be a real killer. Overwork, or *karoshi*, as it is called in Japan, claims 10,000 lives annually in this hard-driving, competitive economic society according to Hiroshi Kawahito, a lawyer who founded the National Defense Council for Victims of Karoshi.

One of the cases is Jun Ishii of Mitsui & Company. Ishii was one of the firm's only speakers of Russian. In the year before his death, Ishii made 10 trips to Russia, totaling 115 days. No sooner would he arrive home from one trip than the company would send him out again. The grueling pace took its toll. While on a trip, Ishii collapsed and died of a heart attack. His widow filed a lawsuit against Mitsui & Company, charging that her husband had been worked to death. Tokyo labor regulators ruled that Ishii had indeed died of karoshi, and the government now is paying annual worker's compensation to the widow. The company also cooperated and agreed to make a one-time payment of $240,000.

The reason that the case received so much publicity is that this is one of the few instances in which the government ruled that a person died from overwork. Now regulators are expanding karoshi compensation to salaried as well as hourly workers. This development is receiving the attention of the top management of many Japanese multinationals, and some Japanese MNCs are beginning to take steps to prevent the likelihood of overwork. For example, Mitsui & Company now assesses its managers based on how well they set overtime hours, keep subordinates healthy, and encourage workers to take vacations. Matsushita Electric has extended vacations from 16 days annually to 23 days and now requires all workers to take this time off. One branch of Nippon Telegraph & Telephone found that stress made some workers irritable and ill, so the company initiated periods of silent meditation. Other companies are following suit, although there still are many Japanese who work well over 2,500 hours a year and feel both frustrated and burned out by job demands.

On the positive side, the Ishii case likely will bring about some improvements in working conditions for many Japanese employees. Experts admit, however, that it is difficult to determine if karoshi is caused by work demands or by private, late-night socializing that may be work-related. Other possible causes include high stress, lack of exercise, and fatty diets, but whatever the cause, one thing is clear: More and more Japanese families no longer are willing to accept the belief that karoshi is a risk that all employees must accept. Work may be a killer, but this outcome can be prevented through more carefully implemented job designs and work processes.

At the same time, recent reports show that there is still a long way to go. In Saku, Japan, for example, the city's main hospital has found that 32 percent of the patients hospitalized in the internal medicine and psychiatric wards are being treated for chronic fatigue syndrome, a diagnosis that is made only after six months of severe, continuous fatigue in the absence of any organic illness. Japanese doctors attribute this explosion of chronic fatigue syndrome to stress. Moreover, during the prolonged economic downturn, a growing number of businesspeople found themselves suffering from these symptoms. And to make matters worse, there is growing concern about alcoholism among workers. Over the past four decades, per capita alcohol consumption in most countries has declined, but in Japan it has risen fourfold. The per capita consumption of alcohol in Japan is equal to that in the United States. Even this comparison is misleading because researchers have found that most Japanese women do not drink at all, but Japanese men in their 50s drink more than twice as much as their American counterparts. Additionally, young Japanese employees find that drinking is considered necessary, and some of them have raised complaints about *alru-hara*, or alcohol harassment (forced/pressured alcohol consumption).

Dealing with overwork will continue to be a challenge both for Japanese firms and for the government. The same is true of the growing problems associated with alcohol that are being brought on by stress and business cultures that have long supported alcohol consumption as a way of doing business and fitting into the social structure.

Sources: Michael Zielenziger, "Alcohol Consumption a Rising Problem in Japan," *Miami Herald*, December 28, 2000, p. 10A; Howard K. French, "A Postmodern Plague Ravages Japan's Workers," *New York Times*, February 21, 2000, p. A4; William S. Brown, Rebecca E. Lubove, and James Kwalwasser, "Karoshi: Alternative Perspectives of Japanese Management Styles," *Business Horizons*, March–April 1994, pp. 58–60; Karen Lowry Miller, "Now, Japan Is Admitting It: Work Kills Executives," *BusinessWeek*, August 3, 1992, p. 35.

could be expected to be more committed to their organization than nonsupervisory employees, and a significant percentage of these employees also had lifetime guarantees.[82] This study also showed that findings related to job satisfaction in the international arena often are different from expected.[83]

Conventional wisdom not always being substantiated has been reinforced by cross-cultural studies that found Japanese workers who already were highly paid, and then received even higher wages, experienced decreased job satisfaction, morale, commitment, and intention to remain with the firm. This contrasts sharply with U.S. workers, who did not experience these negative feelings.[84] These findings show that the motivation approaches used in one culture may have limited value in another.[85]

Research by Kakabadse and Myers also has brought to light findings that are contradictory to commonly accepted beliefs. These researchers examined job satisfaction among managers from the United Kingdom, France, Belgium, Sweden, and Finland. It has long been assumed that satisfaction is highest at the upper levels of organizations; however, this study found varying degrees of satisfaction among managers, depending on the country. The researchers reported that senior managers from France and Finland display greater job dissatisfaction than the managers from the remaining countries. In terms of satisfaction with and commitment to the organization, British, German, and Swedish managers display the highest levels of commitment. Equally, British and German managers highlight that they feel stretched in their job, but senior managers from French organizations suggest that their jobs lack sufficient challenge and stimulus. In keeping with the job-related views displayed by French managers, they equally indicate their desire to leave their job because of their unsatisfactory work-related circumstances.[86]

On the other hand, research also reveals that some of the conditions that help create organizational commitment among U.S. workers also have value in other cultures. For example, a large study of Korean employees ($n = 1,192$ in 27 companies in 8 major industries) found that consistent with U.S. studies, Korean employees' position in the hierarchy, tenure in their current position, and age all related significantly to organizational commitment. Also, as in previous studies in the United States, as the size of the Korean organizations increased, commitment decreased, and the more positive the climate perceptions, the greater was the commitment.[87] In other words, there is at least beginning evidence that the theoretic constructs predicting organizational commitment may hold across cultures.

Also related to motivation are job attitudes toward quality of work life. Recent research reports that EU workers see a strong relationship between how well they do their jobs and the ability to get what they want out of life. U.S. workers were not as supportive of this relationship, and Japanese workers were least likely to see any connection.

This finding raises an interesting motivation-related issue regarding how well, for example, American, European, and Japanese employees can work together effectively. Some researchers have recently raised the question of how Japanese firms will be able to have effective strategic alliances with American and European companies if the work values of the partners are so different. Tornvall, after conducting a detailed examination of the work practices of five companies—Fuji-Kiku, a spare-parts firm in Japan; Toyota Motor Ltd. of Japan; Volvo Automobile AB of Sweden; SAAB Automobile AB, Sweden; and the General Motors plant in Saginaw, Michigan—concluded that there were benefits from the approaches used by each. This led him to recommend what he calls a "balance in the synergy" between the partners.[88] Some of his suggestions included the following:

Moving away from	Moving toward
Logical and reason-centered, individualistic thinking	A more holistic, idealistic, and group thinking approach to problem solving
Viewing work as a necessary burden	Viewing work as a challenging and development activity
The avoidance of risk taking and the feeling of distrust of others	An emphasis on cooperation, trust, and personal concern for others
The habit of analyzing things in such great depth that it results in "paralysis through analysis"	Cooperation built on intuition and pragmatism
An emphasis on control	An emphasis on flexibility

In large degree, this balance will require all three groups—Americans, Europeans, and Asians—to make changes in the way they approach work.

In conclusion, it should be remembered that work is important in every society. The extent of importance varies, however, and much of what is "known" about work as

introductory wages, but they need to consider the costs involved in retaining (or losing) valuable talent. Until recently, awareness of the needs of employees in the international context was reflected simply in wage incentives, but more and more organizations are realizing that the less tangible values of work environment, recognition of intertwined work/family relationships, and the opportunity to continue education are highly regarded in many cultures. Identifying specific cultural viewpoints early can help MNCs in any country to grow and may be the key to continued survival.

The challenge for international managers is to put together a motivational package that addresses the specific needs of the employee or group in each region where an MNC serves. Applying the ideas presented in this chapter, answer the following questions: (1) What are some of the things that successful MNCs do to effectively motivate European employees? Chinese employees? Southeast-Asian (Indonesian) employees? (2) What kinds of incentives do scientific and technical employees respond to that might not be as meaningful to other categories of employees? (3) What advantages might employees see in working for a truly global company (as opposed to a North American MNC)?

SUMMARY OF KEY POINTS

1. Two basic types of theories explain motivation: content and process. Content theories of motivation have received much more attention in international management research because they provide the opportunity to create a composite picture of the motivation of human resources in a particular country or region. In addition, content theories more directly provide ways for managers to improve the performance of their human resources.

2. Maslow's hierarchy-of-needs theory has been studied in a number of different countries. Researchers have found that regardless of the country, managers have to be concerned with the satisfaction of these needs for their human resources.

3. Some researchers have suggested that satisfaction profiles are not very useful for studying motivation in an international setting because there are so many different subcultures within any country or even at different levels of a given organization. These researchers have suggested that job categories are more effective for examining motivation because job level (managers versus operating employees) and the need hierarchy have established correspondences.

4. Like Maslow's theory, Herzberg's two-factor theory has received considerable attention in the international arena, and Herzberg's original findings from the United States have been replicated in other countries. Cross-cultural studies related to job satisfaction also have been conducted. The data show that job content is more important than job context to job satisfaction.

5. The third content theory of motivation that has received a great amount of attention in the international arena is the need for achievement. Some current findings show that this need is not as widely held across cultures as was previously believed. In some parts of the world, however, such as Anglo countries, cultural values encourage people to be high achievers. In particular, Dutch researcher Geert Hofstede suggested that an analysis of two cultural dimensions, uncertainty avoidance and masculinity, helps to identify high-achieving societies. Once again, it can be concluded that different cultures will support different motivational needs, and that international managers developing strategies to motivate their human resources for improved performance must recognize cultural differences.

6. Process theories have also contributed to the understanding of motivation in the international arena. Equity theory focuses on how motivation is affected by people's perception of how fairly they are being treated, and there is considerable research to support the fundamental equity principle in Western work groups. However, when the theory is examined on an international basis, the results are mixed. Perhaps the biggest shortcoming of the theory is that it appears to be culture-bound. For example, in Japan and Korea, men and women typically receive different pay for doing precisely the same work, and this is at least traditionally not perceived as inequitable to women.

7. Goal-setting theory focuses on how individuals go about setting goals and responding to them and the overall impact of this process on motivation. There is evidence showing that employees

perform extremely well when they are assigned specific and challenging goals that they had a hand in setting. However, most of these goal-setting studies have been conducted in the United States; few of them have been carried out in other cultures. Additionally, research results on the effects of goal setting at the individual level are very limited, and culture may well account for these outcomes.

8. Expectancy theory postulates that motivation is largely influenced by a multiplicative combination of a person's belief that effort will lead to performance, that performance will lead to specific outcomes, and that these outcomes are valued by the individual. There is mixed support for this theory. Many researchers believe that the theory best explains motivation in countries characterized by an internal locus of control.

9. Although content and process theories provide important insights into the motivation of human resources, three additional areas that have received a great deal of recent attention in the application of motivation theory are job design, work centrality, and reward systems. Job design is influenced by culture as well as the specific methods that are used to bring together the people and the work. Work centrality helps to explain the importance of work in an individual's life relative to other areas

of interest. In recent years, work has become a relatively greater part of the average U.S. employee's life and perhaps less a part of the average Japanese worker's life. Research also indicates that Japanese office workers are less satisfied with their jobs than are U.S., Canadian, and EU workers, suggesting once again that MNCs need to design motivation packages that address the specific needs of different cultures. This is also true for rewards. Research shows that the relative motivational value of monetary and nonmonetary rewards is influenced by culture. Countries with high individualism, such as the United States and the U.K., tend to make wide use of individual incentives, while collectivistic countries such as those in Asia prefer group-oriented incentives.

10. A central point of the chapter is that some motivational practices may have universal appeal, but more often they need tailoring to fit to the culture in which an MNC may be working. Research shows that some motivational approaches in the United States have been successfully transferred to Russia. More often creative modification to familiar approaches is necessary. The importance for international managers of focusing on employee motivation is unquestioned. The challenge lies in finding the appropriate applications of motivational theory to the specific culture at hand.

KEY TERMS

achievement motivation theory, 446

content theories of motivation, 436

equity theory, 449

esteem needs, 437

expectancy theory, 451

extrinsic, 434

goal-setting theory, 450

hygiene factors, 442

intrinsic, 434

job-content factors, 446

job-context factors, 446

job design, 451

karoshi, 455

motivation, 434

motivators, 442

physiological needs, 437

process theories of motivation, 436

safety needs, 437

self-actualization needs, 437

social needs, 437

sociotechnical designs, 453

two-factor theory of motivation, 442

work centrality, 454

REVIEW AND DISCUSSION QUESTIONS

1. Do people throughout the world have needs similar to those described in Maslow's need hierarchy? What does your answer reveal about using universal assumptions regarding motivation?

2. Is Herzberg's two-factor theory universally applicable to human resource management, or is its value limited to Anglo countries?

3. What are the dominant characteristics of high achievers? Using Figure 12–7 as your point of reference, determine which countries likely will have the greatest percentage of high achievers. Why is this so? Of what value is your answer to the study of international management?

4. A U.S. manufacturer is planning to open a plant in Sweden. What should this firm know about the quality of work life in Sweden that would have a direct effect on job design in the plant? Give an example.

5. What does a U.S. firm setting up operations in Japan need to know about work centrality in that country? How would this information be of value to the multinational? Conversely, what would a Japanese firm need to know about work centrality in the United States? Explain.

6. In managing operations in Europe, which process theory—equity theory, goal-setting theory, or expectancy theory—would be of most value to an American manager? Why?

7. What do international managers need to know about the use of reward incentives to motivate personnel? What role does culture play in this process?

INTERNET EXERCISE: MOTIVATING POTENTIAL EMPLOYEES

In order for multinationals to continue expanding their operations, they must be able to attract and retain highly qualified personnel in many countries. Much of their success in doing this will be tied to the motivational package that they offer, including financial opportunities, benefits and perquisites, meaningful work, and an environment that promotes productivity and worker creativity. Automotive firms, in particular, are a good example of MNCs that are trying very hard to increase their worldwide market share. So for them, employee motivation is an area that is getting a lot of attention.

Go to the web and look at the career opportunities that are currently being offered by Nestlé, Unilever, and Procter & Gamble (websites: nestle.com, unilever.com, us.pg.com). All three of these companies provide information about the career opportunities they offer. Based on this information, answer these questions: (1) What are some of the things that all three firms offer to motivate new employees? (2) Which of the three has the best motivational package? Why? (3) Are there any major differences between P&G and European-based rivals? What conclusion can you draw from this?

ENDNOTES

1. Patricia Odell, "Motivating Employees on a Global Scale: Author Bob Nelson," *PROMO*, November 9, 2005, www.chiefmarketer.com/motivating-employees-on-a-global-scale-author-bob-nelson/.

2. Matthew Boyle, "Motivating without Money," *BusinessWeek,* April 24, 2009, https://www.bloomberg.com/news/articles/2009-04-24/motivating-without-money.

3. "New Globoforce Survey Shows Recognition Creates More Human-Focused Workplaces," *Business Wire*, March 24, 2016, www.businesswire.com/news/home/20160324005325/en/Globoforce-Survey-Shows-Recognition-Creates-Human-Focused-Workplaces.

4. Matthew MacLachlan, "Management Tips: How to Motivate Your International Workforce," *Communicaid*, May 18, 2016, https://www.communicaid.com/cross-cultural-training/blog/motivating-international-workforce/.

5. Odell, "Motivating Employees on a Global Scale."

6. "Motivating Employees," How-To Guide: Managing Your People, *The Wall Street Journal*, http://guides.wsj.com/management/managing-your-people/how-to-motivate-employees/.

7. Odell, "Motivating Employees on a Global Scale."

8. Patricia Odell, "Motivating Employees on a Global Scale: Author Bob Nelson," *PROMO Magazine,* November 9, 2005, http://promomagazine.com/incentives/motivating_empolyees_110905.

9. Boyle, "Motivating without Money."

10. Jim Leininger, "The Key to Retention: Committed Employees," December 26, 2008, https://vinhnguyen.wordpress.com/2008/12/26/the-key-to-retention-committed-employees/.

11. Ibid.

12. Cynthia D. Fisher and Anne Xue Ya Yuan, "What Motivates Employees? A Comparison of U.S. and Chinese Employees," *The International Journal of Human Resource Management* 9, no. 3 (June 1998), pp. 516–528.

13. Sondra Thiederman, "Motivating Employees from Other Cultures," *Monster.com*, https://www.monster.com/career-advice/article/Motivating-Employees-from-Other-Cultures.

14. Ibid.

15. David Beswick, "Management Implications of the Interaction between Intrinsic Motivation and Extrinsic Rewards," Seminar notes, February 16, 2007.

16. Abbass F. Alkhafaji, *Competitive Global Management* (Delray Beach, FL: St. Lucie Press, 1995), p. 118.

17. Dianne H. B. Welsh, Fred Luthans, and Steven Sommer, "Managing Russian Factory Workers: The Impact of U.S.-Based Behavioral and Participative Techniques," *Academy of Management Journal*, February 1993, p. 75.

18. Andrew Sergeant and Stephen Frenkel, "Managing People in China: Perceptions of Expatriate Managers," *Journal of World Business* 33, no. 1 (1998), p. 21.

19. "Economic Tonic: Japan's Economy," *The Economist*, May 22, 2004, p. 87.

20. Michael H. Lubatkin, Momar Ndiaye, and Richard Vengroff, "The Nature of Managerial Work in Developing Countries: A Limited Test of the Universalist Hypothesis," *Journal of International Business Studies* 28 (1997), pp. 711–733.

21. For a more detailed discussion, see Fred Luthans, *Organizational Behavior*, 12th ed. (New York: Irwin/McGraw-Hill, 2010), chapter 6.

22. A. H. Maslow, "A Theory of Human Motivation," *Psychological Review*, July 1943, pp. 390–396.

23. For more information on this topic, see Richard Mead, *International Management: Cross-Cultural Dimensions* (Cambridge, MA: Blackwell, 1994), pp. 209–212.

24. See Richard M. Hodgetts, *Modern Human Relations at Work*, 8th ed. (Hinsdale, IL: Dryden Press, 2002), chapter 2.

25. Mason Haire, Edwin E. Ghiselli, and Lyman W. Porter, *Managerial Thinking: An International Study* (New York: Wiley, 1966).

26. Ibid., p. 75.

27. Edwin C. Nevis, "Cultural Assumption and Productivity: The United States and China," *Sloan Management Review*, Spring 1983, pp. 17–29.

28. Geert H. Hofstede, "The Colors of Collars," *Columbia Journal of World Business*, September 1972, pp. 72–78.

29. Ibid., p. 72.

30. George H. Hines, "Cross-Cultural Differences in Two-Factor Motivation Theory," *Journal of Applied Psychology*, December 1973, p. 376.

31. Donald D. White and Julio Leon, "The Two-Factor Theory: New Questions, New Answers," *National Academy of Management Proceedings*, 1976, p. 358.

32. D. Macarov, "Work Patterns and Satisfactions in an Israeli Kibbutz: A Test of the Herzberg Hypothesis," *Personnel Psychology*, Autumn 1972, p. 492.

33. Peter D. Machungwa and Neal Schmitt, "Work Motivation in a Developing Country," *Journal of Applied Psychology*, February 1983, pp. 31–42.

34. Farhad Analoui, "What Motivates Senior Managers? The Case of Romania," *Journal of Managerial Psychology* 15, no. 4 (2000).

35. G. E. Popp, H. J. Davis, and T. T. Herbert, "An International Study of Intrinsic Motivation Composition," *Management International Review* 26, no. 3 (1986), pp. 28–35.

36. Also see Rabi S. Bhagat et al., "Cross-Cultural Issues in Organizational Psychology: Emergent Trends and Directions for Research in the 1990s," in *International Review of Industrial and Organizational Psychology*, ed. C. L. Cooper and I. Robertson (New York: Wiley, 1990), p. 76.

37. Rabindra N. Kanungo and Richard W. Wright, "A Cross-Cultural Comparative Study of Managerial Job Attitudes," *Journal of International Business Studies*, Fall 1983, pp. 115–129.

38. Ibid., pp. 127–128.

39. Fred Luthans, "A Paradigm Shift in Eastern Europe: Some Helpful Management Development Techniques," *Journal of Management Development* 12, no. 8 (1993), pp. 53–60.

40. For more information on the characteristics of high achievers, see David C. McClelland, "Business Drive and National Achievement," *Harvard Business Review*, July–August 1962, pp. 99–112.

41. Luthans, *Organizational Behavior*, pp. 253–256.

42. S. Iwawaki and R. Lynn, "Measuring Achievement Motivation in Japan and Great Britain," *Journal of Cross-Cultural Psychology* 3 (1999), pp. 219–220.

43. For more on this, see J. C. Abegglen and G. Stalk, *Kaisha: The Japanese Corporation* (New York: Basic Books, 1985).

44. See also R. M. Steers, Y. K. Shin, and G. R. Ungson, *The Chaebol: Korea's New Industrial Might* (New York: McGraw-Hill, 1989).

45. Fred Luthans, Brooke R. Envick, and Mary F. Sully, "Characteristics of Successful Entrepreneurs: Do They Fit the Cultures of Developing Countries?" *Proceedings of the Pan Pacific Conference*, 1995, pp. 25–27.

46. These data were reported in David C. McClelland, *The Achieving Society* (Princeton, NJ: Van Nostrand, 1961), p. 294.

47. E. J. Murray, *Motivation and Emotion* (Englewood Cliffs, NJ: Prentice Hall, 1964), p. 101.

48. David J. Krus and Jane A. Rysberg, "Industrial Managers and nAch: Comparable and Compatible?" *Journal of Cross-Cultural Psychology*, December 1976, pp. 491–496.

49. David C. McClelland, "Achievement Motivation Can Be Developed," *Harvard Business Review*, November–December 1965, p. 20.

50. Geert Hofstede, "Motivation, Leadership, and Organization: Do American Theories Apply Abroad?" *Organizational Dynamics*, Summer 1980, pp. 55–56.

51. For more on this, see Richard M. Steers and Carlos J. Sanchez-Runde, "Culture, Motivation, and Work Behavior," in *Handbook of Cross-Cultural Management*, ed. Martin J. Gannon and Karen L. Newman (London: Basil Blackwell, 2002).

52. E. Yuchtman, "Reward Distribution and Work-Role Attractiveness in the Kibbutz: Reflections on Equity Theory," *American Sociological Review* 37 (1972), pp. 581–595.

53. Paul A. Fadil, Robert J. Williams, Wanthanee Limpaphayom, and Cindi Smatt, "Equity or Equality? A Conceptual Examination of the Influence of Individualism/Collectivism on the Cross-Cultural Application of the Equity Theory," *Cross Cultural Management* 12, no. 4 (2005), pp. 17–35.

54. R. M. Steers, S. J. Bischoff, and L. H. Higgins, "Cross-Cultural Management Research: The Fish and the Fisherman," *Journal of Management Inquiry* 1 (1992), pp. 321–330.

55. Ken I. Kim, Hun-Joon Park, and Nori Suzuki, "Reward Allocations in the U.S., Japan, and Korea: A Comparison of Individualistic and Collectivistic Cultures," *Academy of Management Journal*, March 1990, pp. 188–198.

56. Luthans, *Organizational Behavior*, p. 520.

57. Edwin A. Locke and Gary P. Latham, *A Theory of Goal-Setting and Task Performance* (Englewood Cliffs, NJ: Prentice Hall, 1990).

58. M. Erez, "The Congruence of Goal-Setting Strategies with Socio-Cultural Values and Its Effect on Performance," *Journal of Management* 12 (1986), pp. 585–592.

59. J. P. French, J. Israel, and D. As, "An Experiment in a Norwegian Factory: Interpersonal Dimension in Decision-Making," *Human Relations* 13 (1960), pp. 3–19.

60. P. C. Earley, "Supervisors and Shop Stewards as Sources of Contextual Information in Goal-Setting," *Journal of Applied Psychology* 71 (1986), pp. 111–118.

61. M. Erez and P. C. Earley, "Comparative Analysis of Goal-Setting Strategies across Cultures," *Journal of Applied Psychology* 72, no. 4 (1987), pp. 658–665.

62. Victor Vroom, *Work and Motivation* (New York: Wiley, 1964).

63. Lyman W. Porter and Edward E. Lawler III, *Managerial Attitudes and Performance* (Homewood, IL: Irwin, 1968).

64. Dov Eden, "Intrinsic and Extrinsic Rewards and Motives: Replication and Extension with Kibbutz Workers," *Journal of Applied Social Psychology* 5 (1975), pp. 348–361.

65. T. Matsui, T. Kakuyama, and M. L. Onglatco, "Effects of Goals and Feedback on Performance in Groups," *Journal of Applied Psychology* 72 (1987), pp. 407–415.

66. For a systematic analysis of this and other myths of Japanese management, see Richard M. Hodgetts and Fred Luthans, "Japanese HR Management Practices," *Personnel*, April 1989, pp. 42–45.

67. David Nicklaus, "Labor's Pains," *St. Louis Post-Dispatch*, September 2, 2002, p. A1.

68. For more on this topic, see Noel M. Tichy and Thore Sandstrom, "Organizational Innovations in Sweden," *Columbia Journal of World Business*, Summer 1974, pp. 18–28.

69. "Automotive Brief—Volvo AB: Profit Rose 80% in 4th Period, Bolstered by Truck Division," *The Wall Street Journal*, February 4, 2004, p. A1.

70. "Cars Brief: Volvo," *The Wall Street Journal*, March 16, 2004, p. A1.

71. Edward McDonough, "Market-Oriented Product Innovation," *R&D Management*, June 2004, p. 335.

72. Eric Sundstrom, Kenneth P. DeMeuse, and David Futrell, "Work Teams: Application and Effectiveness," *American Psychologist*, February 1990, pp. 120–133.

73. See Lillian H. Chaney and Jeanette S. Martin, *Intercultural Business Communication* (Englewood Cliffs, NJ: Prentice Hall, 1995), pp. 46–47.

74. Bhagat et al., "Cross-Cultural Issues," p. 72.

75. Jonathan Watts, "Japan's Old Shy Away from Retiring," *The Guardian*, August 5, 2002, p. 12.

76. "U.S. Workers Most Productive; but Study Says Europeans Have More Output per Hour," *Houston Chronicle*, September 1, 2003, p. 27.

77. Raphael Snir, Itzhak Harpaz, and Dorit Ben-Baruch, "Centrality of and Investment in Work and Family among Israeli High-Tech Workers: A Bicultural Perspective," *Cross-Cultural Research* 43, no. 4 (2009), pp. 366–385.

78. Howard W. French, "A Postmodern Plague Ravages Japan's Workers," *New York Times*, February 21, 2000, p. A4.

79. "Japanese Workers See Abuses by Bosses," *Los Angeles Times*, June 30, 2003, p. C5.

80. Michelle Conlin, "Go-Go-Going to Pieces in China," *BusinessWeek*, April 23, 2007, p. 88.

81. "Satisfaction in the USA, Unhappiness in Japanese Offices," *Personnel*, January 1992, p. 8.

82. Fred Luthans, Harriette S. McCaul, and Nancy G. Dodd, "Organizational Commitment: A Comparison of American, Japanese, and Korean Employees," *Academy of Management Journal*, March 1985, pp. 213–219.

83. For other research on this topic, see Shahid N. Bhuian, Eid S. Al-Shammari, and Omar A. Jefri, "Work-Related Attitudes and Job Characteristics of Expatriates in Saudi Arabia," *Thunderbird International Business Review*, January–February 2001, pp. 21–31.

84. David I. Levine, "What Do Wages Buy?" *Administrative Science Quarterly*, September 1993, pp. 462–483.

85. David Heming, "What Wages Buy in the U.S. and Japan," *Academy of Management Executive*, November 1994, pp. 88–89.

86. Andrew Kakabadse and Andrew Myers, "Qualities of Top Management: Comparisons of European Manufacturers," *Journal of Management Development* 14, no. 1 (1995), p. 6.

87. Steven M. Sommer, Seung-Hyun Bae, and Fred Luthans, "Organizational Commitment across Cultures: The Impact of Antecedents on Korean Employees," *Human Relations* 49, no. 7 (1996), pp. 977–993.

88. Anders Tornvall, "Work-Values in Japan: Work and Work Motivation in a Comparative Setting," in *Managing Across Cultures: Issues and Perspectives*, ed. Pat Joynt and Malcolm Warner (London: International Thomson Business Press, 1996), p. 256.

89. Stephen Kerr, "Practical, Cost-Neutral Alternatives That You May Know, but Don't Practice," *Organizational Dynamics*, Summer 1999, pp. 61–70.

90. "U.S. Workers Most Productive."

91. Matthew O. Hughes and Andrew Pirnie, "Retirement Reform Worldwide," *LIMRA's MarketFacts Quarterly* 22, no. 2 (Spring 2003), p. 12.

92. In the case of money, for example, see Swee Hoon Ang, "The Power of Money: A Cross-Cultural Analysis of Business-Related Beliefs," *Journal of World Business* 35, no. 1 (2000), pp. 43–60.

93. J. Milliman, S. Nason, M. A. von Glinow, P. Hou, K. B. Lowe, and N. Kim, "In Search of 'Best' Strategies Pay Practices: An Exploratory Study of Japan, Korea, Taiwan, and the United States," in *Advances in International Comparative Management*, ed. S. B. Prasad (Greenwich, CT: JAI Press, 1995), pp. 227–252.

94. "Equilar 200 Highest-Paid CEO Rankings," *New York Times & Equilar*, 2015, www.equilar.com/reports/18-200-highest-paid-CEO-rankings-2015.html.

95. S. C. Schneider, S. A. Wittenberg-Cox, and L. Hansen, *Honeywell Europe* (Insead, 1991).

96. C. M. Vance, S. R. McClaine, D. M. Boje, and H. D. Stage, "An Examination of the Transferability of Traditional Performance Appraisal Principles across Cultural Boundaries," *Management International Review* 32, no. 4 (1992), pp. 313–326.

97. David Sirota and J. Michael Greenwood, "Understand Your Overseas Workforce," *Harvard Business Review*, January–February 1971, pp. 53–60.

98. D. E. Sanger, "Performance Related Pay in Japan," *International Herald Tribune*, October 5, 1993, p. 20.

99. S. H. Nam, "Culture, Control, and Commitment in International Joint Ventures," *International Journal of Human Resource Management* 6 (1995), pp. 553–567.

100. Dianne H. B. Welsh, Fred Luthans, and Steven Sommer, "Managing Russian Factory Workers: The Impact of U.S.-Based Behavioral and

Participative Techniques," *Academy of Management Journal*, February 1993, pp. 58–79.

101. Anita Raghavan and G. Thomas Sims, "'Golden Parachutes' Emerge in European Deals," *The Wall Street Journal*, February 14, 2000, pp. A17, A18.

102. Susan C. Schneider and Jean-Louis Barsoux, *Managing Across Cultures*, 2nd ed. (London: Prentice Hall, 2003).

103. CIA, "Indonesia," *The World Factbook* (2016), https://www.cia.gov/library/publications/the-world-factbook/geos/id.html.

104. Ibid.

105. World Bank, "Indonesia," *World Development Indicators* (2016), http://data.worldbank.org/country/indonesia.

106. Michelle Davidson, "IBM and Indosat Ooredoo Partner to Bring Cloud Services to Indonesia," *Silicon Angle*, March 11, 2016, http://siliconangle.com/blog/2016/03/11/ibm-and-indosat-ooredo-partner-to-bring-cloud-services-to-indonesia/.

107. Ibid.

Indonesia

The island nation of Indonesia is located along the Equator in southeast Asia, straddling the border between the Indian and Pacific oceans. The country is tropical and volcanic, and includes more than 14,000 individual islands. Over 60 percent of the country is covered by rainforest. The combined land area of Indonesia is fairly large, at about three times the size of Texas. Second only to Brazil in terms of biodiversity, Indonesia's natural resources include petroleum, tin, natural gas, nickel, timber, bauxite, copper, fertile soils, coal, gold, and silver.[103]

The fourth most populous country in the world, Indonesia has more than 250 million residents and has a steady annual population growth rate of about 1 percent. The country is young, with more than a quarter of Indonesians under the age of 14. There is a great amount of ethnic and cultural diversity throughout the various islands and population centers. Religiously, nearly 90 percent of Indonesians practice Islam, making the country the largest Muslim population in the world.[104]

The Dutch colonized Indonesia in the early 17th century, retaining control until World War II, when the Japanese occupied the country. It is estimated that as many as 4 million Indonesians died during the occupation. After World War II, the Dutch retained control of the islands until 1949, when sovereignty was finally granted to Indonesia. From 1949 until 1968, the country was essentially under authoritarian rule under President Sukamo. A successful coup by General Suharto led to his "New Order" administration, which opened trade between Indonesia and the West but was also steeped in corruption. In the wake of the Asian financial crisis, Suharto resigned in 1998, giving way to democratic elections in 1999. A direct presidential election was held for the first time in 2004. Indonesia's GDP stood at US$888.5 billion in 2014, and GDP per capita was US$3,475. The Indonesian economy has expanded by about 5 percent annually over the last several years.[105]

You Be the International Management Consultant

Indosat Ooredoo, Indonesia's largest telecommunications company, partnered with IBM in 2016 to develop software services specifically designed for the needs of Indonesian businesses. The five-year agreement, worth $200 million, has the ultimate goals of helping the country's businesses streamline their operations, increase productivity, and encourage innovation. Modern technology has become more pervasive in Indonesia in the last 20 years, and this partnership is aimed at continuing that growth. Prior to partnering with IBM, Indosat Ooredoo had attempted to develop and implement its own version of cloud services without much success.[106]

Indosat Ooredoo, as a member of Qatar Ooredoo Group, reported 69 million subscribers at the end of the third quarter of 2015. Data usage by its customers increased by 155 percent year over year. Revenue grew 10.5 percent over the same period. Partnering with IBM will allow Indosat Ooredoo to leverage IBM's infrastructure to support this growth. For example, IBM Global Technology Services offers end-to-end IT consulting and business services supported by an unparalleled global delivery network.[107]

Questions

1. As an international management consultant, how do you view this partnership for Indosat Ooredoo?

2. How does this partnership help IBM? If you were a consultant for an unrelated company, does this deal increase your interest in expanding into Indonesia?

Chapter 13

LEADERSHIP ACROSS CULTURES

Leadership is often credited (or blamed) for the success (or failure) of international operations. As with other aspects of management, leadership styles and practices that work well in one culture are not necessarily effective in another. The leadership approach commonly used by U.S. managers would not necessarily be the same as that employed in other parts of the world. Even within the same country, effective leadership tends to be very situation-specific. However, as with the other areas of international management you have studied in this text, certain leadership styles and practices may be more or less universally applicable and transcend international boundaries. This chapter examines some differences and similarities in leadership styles across cultures.

First, we review the basic foundation for the study of leadership. Next, we examine leadership in various parts of the world, Europe, East Asia, and the Middle East, including some developing countries. Finally, we'll analyze specific types of leadership, drawing from recent research on leadership across cultures. The specific objectives of this chapter are

1. **DESCRIBE** the basic philosophic foundation and styles of managerial leadership.

2. **EXAMINE** the attitudes of European managers toward leadership practices.

3. **COMPARE** and **CONTRAST** leadership styles in Japan with those in the United States.

4. **REVIEW** leadership approaches in China, the Middle East, and developing countries.

5. **EXAMINE** recent research and findings regarding leadership across cultures.

6. **DISCUSS** the relationship of culture clusters and leader behavior on effective leadership practices, including increasing calls for more responsible global leadership.

The World of *International Management*

Global Leadership Development: An Emerging Need

Firms are currently bolstering their leadership development programs to prevent a future shortage of managers. As reported in *The Wall Street Journal* in August 2010, the number of potential managers has decreased as a result of layoffs and cuts in training during the economic downturn. Larry Looker, Amway Corp.'s manager of global leadership development, told *The Wall Street Journal*, "We're finding times when we want to open a new market but don't have anyone with the capabilities to do it. It's a real weakness."[1] When Amway needed country managers for an expansion in Latin America, it could not find qualified candidates in its local operations. During the recession, Amway put on hold two leadership development programs. In 2011, it restarted these programs with the hope of training future managers. It's a positive sign that companies are growing their global leadership development programs.[2] What does a global leadership development program look like? What qualities are companies looking for in candidates for these programs? What are the benefits to the individual in participating in such a program? To answer these questions, one MNC will be examined in detail.

Spotlight on Roche

The worldwide health care company Roche has extensive global leadership development programs. Roche has 81,507 employees and is active in 150 countries. Roche's training for employees includes language courses, interpersonal skills training, and individual coaching and programs on leadership and change management.[3]

According to Roche's website, "Every Roche site has its own training and development programs geared to local needs and resources, and in line with local legal and regulatory requirements."[4] One such program is Shanghai Roche Pharma's "People & Leadership Development Program." Shanghai Roche has a specific training program for managers to reinforce leadership skills, such as strategic leadership. Furthermore, each employee has an individualized development plan. Based on the Roche 3E (Experience, Education, and Exposure) development model, each employee works with his or her manager to work out a customized development plan together.[5]

To prepare its future leaders, Roche offers two distinct leadership programs, especially designed for managers:

1. *Leadership Impact.* Through this program, managers can build their

   - People management skills (developing, coaching, etc.).
   - Functional management skills (process knowledge and compliance).
   - Leadership skills (creating a vision, guiding a team, etc.).

2. *Leadership Excellence.* Through this program, senior-level managers can

   - Remain honest and transparent regarding the realities of their roles.
   - Provide each other with support through peer networking.
   - Increase their collective competencies while sharing common challenges.[6]

Moreover, Roche has a special global leadership development program in its home country, Switzerland. One of Roche's programs has been highlighted on LinkedIn. The following is adapted from a description of the Perspectives Global Accelerated Talent Development Program at Roche:

> Our success is built on innovation, curiosity, and diversity, and on seeing each other's differences as an advantage. The headquarters in Basel is one of Roche's largest sites; over 8,000 people from approximately 80 countries work at Roche Basel.
>
> The Perspectives Global Accelerated Talent Development Program is a Roche Corporate program designed to provide a "rapid fire" induction experience to one of the two divisions of Roche (Pharmaceuticals/Diagnostics). It is targeted at talented individuals who are at a very early stage of their career and are seeking to make significant contributions to the industry. Roche is looking for highly energetic and globally mobile future business leaders from around the globe.[7]

Recognizing the central importance of experiential learning and development, Perspectives provides a unique opportunity to build a broad global network, experience different areas of the business, and gain skills that will be necessary for a career in general management in an accelerated timeframe.

Features of the Perspectives program include

- Two years (temporary contract), four assignments of six months (three or four are typically international assignments).

- Completely tailored to your development needs and areas of interest in line with Roche needs.
- Diverse experience: different areas of the business, functions, countries, sites, markets, leadership styles, business and ethnic cultures.
- Training targeted at accelerating your leadership capabilities.
- Personal Development Coach: dedicated senior management support throughout the program and beyond.[8]

For this program, Roche is looking for candidates with master's degrees, fluency in two languages, global mindset and mobility, strong leadership potential and business acumen, and excellent communication skills.[9]

Employee Development Yields Results

Two Roche employees' experiences demonstrate the results of Roche's training programs.

At age 24, Luciana, an employee at the Roche Diagnostics affiliate in São Paolo, Brazil, participated in one of Roche's programs. As part of the program, she had the opportunity to work at Roche Diagnostics in Rotkreuz, Switzerland, and the Roche Diagnostics affiliate in Burgess Hill, U.K. Those at Roche believe, "Experiencing new ways of working and thinking inspires creativity in employees, advancing their careers and the company."[10]

This appears to have been the case for Luciana. As a result of her experience, Luciana said, "I have no words to describe how it changes your point of view of life. In two and a half years at Roche, I feel I've gained five years' growth. I have opportunities to grow every day, with challenging projects, good professionals around me, and space to express myself and to learn how to express myself better."[11]

Tuygan Goeker has been at Roche for 30 years. His career "has scarcely stood still, punctuated by a change in responsibilities or a country move every three to four years." He has worked in Roche Istanbul, in Roche Indonesia, and at the Roche headquarters in Switzerland. Today, he is head of the Central and Eastern Europe, Middle East, Africa, and Indian subcontinent region. He is currently working on developing strategies for maximizing market potential in Brazil, Russia, India, China, South Korea, Mexico, and his native Turkey. As an international manager, Tuygan has learned adaptability. Tuygan said, "Along the way I've had to expand the way I define success. Sometimes the scope or budget of a new role has been

Table 13–3
Clusters of Countries in the Haire, Ghiselli, and Porter Study

Nordic-European Countries	Anglo-American Countries
Denmark	England
Germany	United States
Norway	
Sweden	**Developing Countries**
	Argentina
	Chile
Latin-European Countries	India
Belgium	
France	
Italy	**Japan**
Spain	

Overall Results of Research on Attitudes of European Managers   Responses by managers to the four areas covered in the Haire, Ghiselli, and Porter study, as noted in Chapter 12, are quite dated but remain the most comprehensive available and are relevant to the current discussion of leadership similarities and differences. The specifics by country may have changed somewhat over the years, but the leadership processes revealed should not be out of date. The clusters of countries studied by these researchers are shown in Table 13–3. Results indicate that none of the leaders from various parts of the world, on average, were very supportive of the belief that individuals have a capacity for leadership and initiative. The researchers put it this way: "In each country, in each group of countries, in all of the countries taken together, there is a relatively low opinion of the capabilities of the average person, coupled with a relatively positive belief in the necessity for democratic-type supervisory practices."[46]

An analysis of standard scores compared each cluster of countries against the others, and it revealed that Anglo leaders tend to have more faith in the capacity of their people for leadership and initiative than do the other clusters. They also believe that sharing information and objectives is important; however, when it comes to participation and internal control, the Anglo group tends to give relatively more autocratic responses than all the other clusters except developing countries. Interestingly, Anglo leaders reported a much stronger belief in the value of external rewards (pay, promotion, etc.) than did any of the other clusters except that of the developing countries. These findings clearly illustrate that attitudes toward leadership practices tend to be quite different in various parts of the world.

The Role of Level, Size, and Age on European Managers' Attitudes toward Leadership
The research of Haire and associates provided important additional details within each cluster of European countries. These findings indicated that in some countries, higher-level managers tended to express more democratic values than lower-level managers; however, in other countries, the opposite was true. For example, in England, higher-level managers responded with more democratic attitudes on all four leadership dimensions, whereas in the United States, lower-level managers gave more democratically oriented responses on all four. In the Scandinavian countries, higher-level managers tended to respond more democratically; in Germany, lower-level managers tended to have more democratic attitudes.

Company size also tended to influence the degree of participative-autocratic attitudes. There was more support among managers in small firms than in large ones regarding the belief that individuals have a capacity for leadership and initiative; however, respondents from large firms were more supportive of sharing information and objectives, participation, and use of internal control.

There were findings that age also had some influence on participative attitudes. Younger managers were more likely to have democratic values when it came to capacity for leadership and initiative and to sharing information and objectives, although on the other two areas of leadership practices older and younger managers differed little. In specific countries, some important differences were found. For example, younger managers in both the United States and Sweden espoused more democratic values than did their older counterparts; in Belgium, the opposite was true.

Japanese Leadership Approaches

Japan is well known for its paternalistic approach to leadership. As noted in Figure 12–7, Japanese culture promotes a high safety or security need, which is present among home country-based employees as well as MNC expatriates. For example, one study examined the cultural orientations of 522 employees of 28 Japanese-owned firms in the United States and found that the native Japanese employees were more likely than their U.S. counterparts to value paternalistic company behavior.[47,48] Another study found that Koreans also value such paternalism.[49] However, major differences appear in leadership approaches used by the Japanese and those in other locales.

For example, the comprehensive Haire, Ghiselli, and Porter study found that Japanese managers have much greater belief in the capacity of subordinates for leadership and initiative than do managers in most other countries.[50] In fact, in the study, only managers in Anglo-American countries had stronger feelings in this area. The Japanese also expressed attitudes toward the use of participation to a greater degree than others. In the other two leadership areas, sharing information and objectives and using internal control, the Japanese respondents were above average but not distinctive. Overall, however, this study found that the Japanese respondents scored highest on the four areas of leadership combined. In other words, these findings provide evidence that Japanese leaders have considerable confidence in the overall ability of their subordinates and use a style that allows their people to actively participate in decisions.

In addition, the leadership process used by Japanese managers places a strong emphasis on ambiguous goals. Subordinates are typically unsure of what their manager wants them to do. As a result, they spend a great deal of time overpreparing their assignments. Some observers believe that this leadership approach is time-consuming and wasteful. However, it has a number of important benefits. One is that the leader is able to maintain stronger control of the followers because the latter do not know with certainty what is expected of them. So they prepare themselves for every eventuality. Second, by placing the subordinates in a position where they must examine a great deal of information, the manager ensures that the personnel are well prepared to deal with the situation and all its ramifications. Third, the approach helps the leader maintain order and provide guidance, even when the leader is not as knowledgeable as the followers.

Two experts on the behavior of Japanese management have noted that salarymen (middle managers) survive in the organization by anticipating contingencies and being prepared to deal with them. So when the manager asks a question and the salaryman shows that he has done the research needed to answer the question, the middle manager also shows himself to be a reliable person. The leader does not have to tell the salaryman to be prepared; the individual knows what is expected of him.

Japanese managers operate this way because they usually have less expertise in a division's day-to-day business than their subordinates do. It is the manager's job to maintain harmony, not to be a technical expert. Consequently, a senior manager doesn't necessarily realize that E, F, G, and H are important to know. He gives ambiguous directions to his subordinates so they can use their superior expertise to go beyond A, B, C, and D. One salaryman explained it this way: "When my boss asks me to write a report, I infer what he wants to know and what he needs to know without being told what he wants." Another interviewee added that subordinates who receive high performance evaluations are those who know what the boss wants without needing to be told. What frustrates Japanese managers about non-Japanese employees is the feeling that, if they tell such a person they want A through D, they will never extract E through H; instead, they'll get exactly what they asked for. Inferring what the boss would have wanted had he only known to ask is a tough game, but it is the one salarymen must play.[51]

Some researchers believe that this paternalistic approach may have impeded and constrained Toyota's ability to respond quickly to vehicle quality safety problems, resulting in major recalls in 2010, 2012, and 2014. The *Financial Times* reported that, in response, Toyota has shifted more responsibility to non-Japanese managers by promoting North Americans and Europeans to run factories outside Japan. Toyota officials concluded that poor communication between local managers and their bosses in Japan contributed to the crisis. In the U.S. especially, warnings from local managers about the outcry were either passed on too slowly or not at all.[52]

Differences between Japanese and U.S. Leadership Styles

In a number of ways, Japanese leadership styles differ from those in the United States. For example, the Haire and associates study found that except for internal control, large U.S. firms tend to be more democratic than small ones, whereas in Japan, the profile is quite different.[53] A second difference is that younger U.S. managers appear to express more democratic attitudes than their older counterparts on all four leadership dimensions, but younger Japanese fall into this category only for sharing information and objectives and in the use of internal control.[54] Simply put, evidence points to some similarities between U.S. and Japanese leadership styles, but major differences also exist.

A number of reasons have been cited for these differences. One of the most common is that Japanese and U.S. managers have a basically different philosophy of managing people. Table 13–4 provides a comparison of seven key characteristics that come from Ouchi's *Theory Z*, which combines Japanese and U.S. assumptions and approaches. Note in the table that the Japanese leadership approach is heavily group-oriented, paternalistic, and concerned with the employee's work and personal life. The U.S. leadership approach is almost the opposite.[55]

Another difference between Japanese and U.S. leadership styles is how senior-level managers process information and learn. Japanese executives are taught and tend to use **variety amplification**, which is the creation of uncertainty and the analysis of many alternatives regarding future action. By contrast, U.S. executives are taught and tend to use **variety reduction**, which is the limiting of uncertainty and the focusing of action on a limited number of alternatives.[56] Through acculturation, patterning, and mentoring, as well as formal training, U.S. managers tend to limit the scope of questions and issues

variety amplification
The creation of uncertainty and the analysis of many alternatives regarding future action.

variety reduction
The limiting of uncertainty and the focusing of action on a limited number of alternatives.

Table 13–4
Japanese vs. U.S. Leadership Styles

Philosophical Dimension	Japanese Approach	U.S. Approach
Employment	Often for life; layoffs are rare	Usually short term; layoffs are common
Evaluation and promotion	Very slow; big promotions may not come for the first 10 years	Very fast; those not quickly promoted often seek employment elsewhere
Career paths	Very general; people rotate from one area to another and become familiar with all areas of operations	Very specialized; people tend to stay in one area (accounting, sales, etc.) for their entire careers
Decision making	Carried out via group decision making	Carried out by the individual manager
Control mechanism	Very implicit and informal; people rely heavily on trust and goodwill	Very explicit; people know exactly what to control and how to do it
Responsibility	Shared collectively	Assigned to individuals
Concern for employees	Management's concern extends to the whole life, business and social, of the worker	Management concerned basically with the individual's work life only

Source: Adapted from William Ouchi, *Theory Z: How American Business Can Meet the Japanese Challenge* (Reading, MA: Addison-Wesley, 1981).

before them, emphasize one or two central aspects of that topic, identify specific employees to respond to it, and focus on a goal or objective that is attainable. Japanese managers, in contrast, tend to be inclusive in their consideration of issues or problems, seek a large quantity of information to inform the problem, encourage all employees to engage in solutions, and aim for goals that are distant in the future.

Further, this research found that the Japanese focused very heavily on problems, while the U.S. managers focused on opportunities.[57] The Japanese were more willing to allow poor performance to continue for a time so that those who were involved would learn from their mistakes, but the Americans worked to stop poor performance as quickly as possible. Finally, the Japanese sought creative approaches to managing projects and tried to avoid relying on experience, but the Americans sought to build on their experiences.

Still another major reason accounting for differences in leadership styles is that the Japanese tend to be more ethnocentric than their U.S. counterparts. The Japanese think of themselves as Japanese managers who are operating overseas; most do not view themselves as international managers. As a result, even if they do adapt their leadership approach on the surface to that of the country in which they are operating, they still believe in the Japanese way of doing things and are reluctant to abandon it.

Despite these differences, managerial practices indicate that there may be more similarities than once believed. For example, at Google, located in the United States, employees are given freedom to innovate and take the lead in developing new products. The company adopted a policy of "20 percent time," which gives employees the opportunity to spend a portion of their work day dedicated to projects that most interest them. Management allows employees to e-mail them directly for any reason, and cross-functional teams are encouraged to interact and build relationships outside of project work.[58] Japanese firms such as Sony use a similar approach, encouraging personnel to assume authority, use initiative, and work as a team. Major emphasis also is given to developing communication links between management and the employees and to encouraging people to do their best.

Another common trend is the movement toward team orientation and away from individualism. The International Management in Action box "Global Teams" illustrates this point.

Leadership in China

In the past few years a growing amount of attention has been focused on leadership in China. In particular, international researchers are interested in learning if the country's economic progress is creating a new cadre of leaders whose styles are different from the styles of leaders of the past. In one of the most comprehensive studies to date, Ralston and his colleagues found that, indeed, a new generation of Chinese leaders is emerging and they are somewhat different from past leaders in work values.[59]

The researchers gathered data from a large number of managers and professionals ($n = 869$) who were about to take part in management development programs. These individuals were part of what the researchers called the "New Generation" of Chinese organizational leaders. The researchers wanted to determine if this new generation of managers had the same work values as those of the "Current Generation" and "Older Generation" groups. In their investigation, the researchers focused their attention on the importance that the respondents assigned to three areas: individualism, collectivism, and Confucianism. Individualism was measured by the importance assigned to self-sufficiency and personal accomplishments. Collectivism was measured by the person's willingness to subordinate personal goals to those of the work group with an emphasis on sharing and group harmony. Confucianism was measured by the importance the respondent assigned to societal harmony, virtuous interpersonal behavior, and personal and interpersonal harmony.

The researchers found that the new generation group scored significantly higher on individualism than did the current and older generation groups. In addition, the new generation leaders scored significantly lower than the other two groups on collectivism and Confucianism. These values appear to reflect the period of relative openness and

Global Teams

Institutional productivity used to involve a cavalcade of employees manning factory floors, where meetings with international subsidiaries had to be carefully planned. As technology continues to evolve and the window for decision-making periods quickly closes, the need to instantly connect and coordinate with regional and transnational offices becomes imperative to stay competitive. But how is this implemented? International leaders now put increasing focus on developing global teams that are capable of overcoming cultural barriers and working together in an efficient, harmonious manner. At Dallas-based Maxus Energy (a wholly owned subsidiary of YPF, the largest Argentinean corporation), teams consist of Americans, Dutch, British, and Indonesians who have been brought together to pursue a common goal: maximize oil and gas production. Capitalizing on the technical expertise of the members and their willingness to work together, the team has helped the company to achieve its objective and add oil reserves to its stockpiles—an almost unprecedented achievement. This story is only one of many that help illustrate the way in which global teams are being created and used to achieve difficult international objectives.

In developing effective global teams, companies are finding there are four phases in the process. In phase one, the team members come together with their own expectations, culture, and values. In phase two, members go through a self-awareness period, during which they learn to respect the cultures of the other team members. Phase three is characterized by a developing trust among members, and in phase four, team members begin working in a collaborative way.

How are MNCs able to create the environment that is needed for this metamorphosis? Several specific steps are implemented by management, including

1. The objectives of the group are carefully identified and communicated to the members.

2. Team members are carefully chosen so that the group has the necessary skills and personnel to reinforce and complement each other.

3. Each person learns what he or she is to contribute to the group, thus promoting a feeling of self-importance and interdependency.

4. Cultural differences between the members are discussed so that members can achieve a better understanding of how they may work together effectively.

5. Measurable outcomes are identified so that the team can chart its progress and determine how well it is doing. Management also continually stresses the team's purpose and its measurable outcomes so that the group does not lose sight of its goals.

6. Specially designed training programs are used to help the team members develop interpersonal, intercultural skills.

7. Lines of communication are spelled out so that everyone understands how to communicate with other members of the group.

8. Members are continually praised and rewarded for innovative ideas and actions.

MNCs now find that global teams are critical to their ability to compete successfully in the world market. As a result, leaders who are able to create and lead interdisciplinary, culturally diverse groups are finding themselves in increasing demand by MNCs.

Sources: Jitao Li, Katherine R. Xin, Anne Tsui, and Donald C. Hambrick, "Building Effective International Joint Venture Leadership Teams in China," *Journal of World Business* 34, no. 1 (1999), pp. 52–68; Charlene Marmer Solomon, "Global Teams: The Ultimate Collaboration," *Personnel Journal*, September 1995, pp. 49–58; Andrew Kakabdse and Andrew Myers, "Qualities of Top Management: Comparison of European Manufacturers," *Journal of Management Development* 14, no. 1 (1995), pp. 5–15; Noel M. Tichy, Michael I. Brimm, Ram Chran, and Hiroraka Takeuchi, "Leadership Development as a Lever for Global Transformation," in *Globalizing Management: Creating and Leading the Competitive Organization*, ed. Vladimir Pucik, Noel M. Tichy, and Carole K. Barnett (New York: Wiley, 1993), pp. 47–60; Gloria Barczak and Edward F. McDonough III, "Leading Global Product Development Teams," *Research Technology Management* 46, no. 6 (November/December 2003), pp. 14–18; Michael J. Marquard and Lisa Horvath, *Global Teams* (Palo Alto, CA: Davies-Black, 2001).

freedom, often called the "Social Reform Era," during which these new managers grew up. They have had greater exposure to Western societal influences, and this may well be resulting in leadership styles similar to those of Western managers.

These research findings show that leadership is culturally influenced, but as the economy of China continues to change and the country moves more and more toward capitalism, the work values of managers may also change. As a result, the new generation of leaders may well use leadership styles similar to those in the West, something that has also occurred in Japan, as seen in Figures 13–3 and 13–4.

Table 13–5
Differences between Middle Eastern and Western Management

Management Dimensions	Middle Eastern Management	Western Management
Leadership	Highly authoritarian tone, rigid instructions. Too many management directives.	Less emphasis on leader's personality, considerable weight on leader's style and performance.
Organizational structures	Highly bureaucratic, overcentralized, with power and authority at the top. Vague relationships. Ambiguous and unpredictable organization environments.	Less bureaucratic, more delegation of authority. Relatively decentralized structure.
Decision making	Ad hoc planning, decisions made at the highest level of management. Unwillingness to take high risk inherent in decision making.	Sophisticated planning techniques, modern tools of decision making, elaborate management information systems.
Performance evaluation and control	Informal control mechanisms, routine checks on performance. Lack of vigorous performance evaluation systems.	Fairly advanced control systems focusing on cost reduction and organizational effectiveness.
Personnel policies	Heavy reliance on personal contacts and getting individuals from the "right social origin" to fill major positions.	Sound personnel management policies. Candidates' qualifications are usually the basis for selection decisions.
Communication	The tone depends on the communicants. Social position, power, and family influence are ever-present factors. Chain of command must be followed rigidly. People relate to each other tightly and specifically. Friendships are intense and binding.	Stress usually on equality and a minimization of difference. People relate to each other loosely and generally. Friendships not intense and binding.

Source: From M. K. Badawy, "Styles of Mideastern Managers," *California Management Review* 22, no. 3 (Spring 1980), pp. 51–58.

Leadership in the Middle East

Research also has been conducted on Middle East countries to determine the similarities and differences in managerial attitudes toward leadership practices. For example, in a follow-up study to that of Haire and associates, midlevel managers from Arab countries were surveyed and found to have higher attitude scores for capacity for leadership and initiative than those from any of the other countries or clusters reported in Table 13–3.[60] The Arab managers' scores for sharing information and objectives, participation, and internal control, however, all were significantly lower than the scores of managers in the other countries and clusters reported in Table 13–3. The researcher concluded that the results were accounted for by the culture of the Middle East region. Table 13–5 summarizes not only the leadership differences between Middle Eastern and Western managers but also other areas of organization and management.

More recent research provides some evidence that there may be much greater similarity between Middle Eastern leadership styles and those of Western countries.[61] In particular, the observation was made that Western management practices are very evident in the Arabian Gulf region because of the close business ties between the West and this oil-rich area and the increasing educational attainment, often in Western universities, of Middle Eastern managers. A study on decision-making styles in the United Arab Emirates showed that organizational culture, level of technology, level of education, and management responsibility were good predictors of decision-making styles in such an environment.[62] These findings were consistent with similar studies in Western environments. Also, results indicated a tendency toward participative leadership styles among young Arab middle management, as well as among highly educated managers of all ages.[63]

Leadership Approaches in India

India is developing at a rapid rate as MNCs increase investment. India's workforce is quite knowledgeable in the high-tech industry, and society as a whole is moving toward higher education. However, India is still bound by old traditions. This raises the question, What kind of leadership style does India need to satisfy its traditional roots while heading into a high-tech future? One study showed that Indian workers were more productive when managers took a high-people and high-task approach (participative). Meanwhile, the less productive workers were managed by individuals who showed high-people orientation, but low focus on task-related objectives.[64] These findings may indicate that it is important in India to focus on the individual, but in order to be efficient and produce results, managers need to maintain awareness of the tasks that need to be completed.

Because of India's long affiliation with Great Britain, leadership styles in India would seem more likely to be participative than those in the Middle East or in other developing countries. Haire and associates found some degree of similarity between leadership styles in India and Anglo-American countries, but it was not significant. The study found Indians to be similar to the Anglo-Americans in managerial attitudes toward capacity for leadership and initiative, participation, and internal control. The difference is in sharing information and objectives. The Indian managers' responses tended to be quite similar to those of managers in other developing countries.[65] These findings from India show that a participative leadership style may be more common and more effective in developing countries than has been reported previously. Over time, developing countries (as also shown in the case of the Persian Gulf nations) may be moving toward a more participative leadership style. Recently, researchers have suggested there may be some unique management and leadership styles that emerge from the polyglot nature of India's population and some of the unique challenges of doing business there. For example, some suggest that Indian leaders can improvise quickly to overcome hurdles, a concept sometimes referred to here as *jugaad*.[66]

Leadership Approaches in Latin America

Research pertaining to leadership styles in Latin America has indicated that as globalization increases, so does the transitional nature of managers within these regions. One study that compared Latin American leadership styles reviewed past research indicating an initial universality among the countries.[67] In Mexico, leaders tended to have a combination of authoritarian and participative behaviors, while Chile, Argentina, and Bolivia also showed signs of authoritarian behaviors. Typically, Mexican managers who welcomed input from subordinates were viewed as incompetent and weak. This may be the reason that in Mexico, as well as in Chile, managers tend to be socially distant from those working below them. Romero found that Mexican managers who worked close to the U.S. border, however, exhibited even more participative behavior, and that trend enhanced as globalization increased.[68] Overall, the study found that Mexico is moving toward a modern leadership style, while other Latin American countries continue to lead based on tradition. However, this is not the only viewpoint.

Haire and associates originally found quite different results for Chile and Argentina, and one can only assume that Peru would be similar to the aforementioned countries due to their geographic and cultural similarities. The results from the study for those two developing countries were similar to those for India.[69] Additional research, however, has found that leadership styles in Peru may be much closer to those in the United States than was previously assumed.

As in the case of Middle Eastern managers, these findings in South America indicate there indeed may be more similarities in international leadership styles than previously assumed. As countries become more economically advanced, participative styles may well gain in importance. Of course, this does not mean that MNCs can use the same leadership styles in their various locations around the world. There still must be careful contingency application of leadership styles (different styles for different situations); however, many of the more enlightened participative leadership styles used in the United States and other economically advanced countries, such as Japan, also may have value in managing international operations even in developing countries as well as in the emerging Eastern European countries.

■ Recent Findings and Insights about Leadership

In recent years researchers have begun raising the question of universality of leadership behavior. Do effective leaders, regardless of their country culture or job, act similarly? A second, and somewhat linked, research inquiry has focused on the question, Are there a host of specific behaviors, attitudes, and values that leaders in the 21st century will need in order to be successful? Thus far the findings have been mixed. Some investigators have found that there is a trend toward universalism for leadership; others have concluded that culture continues to be a determining factor and that an effective leader, for example, in Sweden will not be as effective in Italy if he or she employs the same approach, most likely due to motivational factors being different (see Chapter 12). One of the most interesting recent efforts has been conducted by Bass and his associates, and has focused on the universality and effectiveness of both transformational and transactional leadership.

Transformational, Transactional, and Charismatic Leadership

Transformational leaders are visionary agents with a sense of mission who are capable of motivating their followers to accept new goals and new ways of doing things. One recent variant on transformational leadership focuses on the individual's charismatic traits and abilities. This research stream, known as the study of **charismatic leaders**, has explored how the individual abilities of an executive work to inspire and motivate her or his subordinates.[70] **Transactional leaders** are individuals who exchange rewards for effort and performance and work on a "something for something" basis.[71] Do these types of leaders exist worldwide, and is their effectiveness consistent in terms of performance? Drawing on an analysis of studies conducted in Canada, India, Italy, Japan, New Zealand, Singapore, and Sweden, as well as in the United States, Bass discovered that very little of the variance in leadership behavior could be attributed to culture. In fact, in many cases he found that national differences accounted for less than 10 percent of the results. This led him to create a model of leadership and conclude that "although this model . . . may require adjustments and fine-tuning as we move across cultures, particularly into non-Western cultures, overall, it holds up as having considerable universal potential."[72]

Simply stated, Bass discovered that there was far more universalism in leadership than had been believed previously. Additionally, after studying thousands of international cases, he found that the most effective managers were transformational leaders and they were characterized by four interrelated factors. For convenience, the factors are referred to as the "4 I's," and they can be described this way:

1. *Idealized influence.* Transformational leaders are a source of charisma and enjoy the admiration of their followers. They enhance pride, loyalty, and confidence in their people, and they align these followers by providing a common purpose or vision that the latter willingly accept.

2. *Inspirational motivation.* These leaders are extremely effective in articulating their vision, mission, and beliefs in clear-cut ways, thus providing an easy-to-understand sense of purpose regarding what needs to be done.

3. *Intellectual stimulation.* Transformational leaders are able to get their followers to question old paradigms and to accept new views of the world regarding how things now need to be done.

4. *Individualized consideration.* These leaders are able to diagnose and elevate the needs of each of their followers through individualized consideration, thus furthering the development of these people.[73]

Bass also discovered that there were four other types of leaders. All of these are less effective than the transformational leader, although the degree of their effectiveness (or ineffectiveness) will vary. The most effective of the remaining four types was labeled the *contingent reward (CR) leader* by Bass. This leader clarifies what needs to be done and provides both psychic and material rewards to those who comply with his or

transformational leaders
Leaders who are visionary agents with a sense of mission and who are capable of motivating their followers to accept new goals and new ways of doing things.

charismatic leaders
Leaders who inspire and motivate employees through their charismatic traits and abilities.

transactional leaders
Individuals who exchange rewards for effort and performance and work on a "something for something" basis.

Figure 13–5

An Optimal Profile of Universal Leadership Behaviors

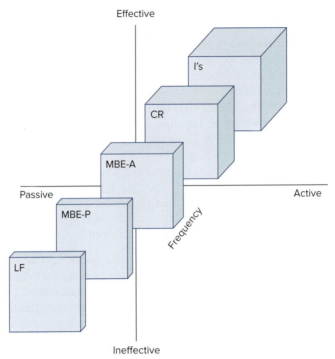

Source: Adapted from Bernard M. Bass, "Is There Universality in the Full Range Model of Leadership?" *International Journal of Public Administration* 16, no. 6 (1996), p. 738.

her directives. The next most effective manager is the *active management-by-exception (MBE-A) leader.* This individual monitors follower performance and takes corrective action when deviations from standards occur. The next manager in terms of effectiveness is the *passive management-by-exception (MBE-P) leader.* This leader takes action or intervenes in situations only when standards are not met. Finally, there is the *laissez-faire (LF) leader.* This person avoids intervening or accepting responsibility for follower actions.

Bass found that through the use of higher-order factor analysis, it is possible to develop a leadership model that illustrates the effectiveness of all five types of leaders: I's (transformational), CR, MBE-A, MBE-P, and LF. Figure 13–5 presents this model. The higher the box in the figure and the farther to the right on the shaded base area, the more effective and active is the leader. Notice that the 4 I's box is taller than any of the others in the figure and is located more to the right than any of the others. The CR box is second tallest and second closest to the right, on down to the LF box, which is the shortest and farthest from the right margin.

Bass also found that the 4 I's were positively correlated with each other, but less so with contingent reward. Moreover, there was a near zero correlation between the 4 I's and management-by-exception styles, and there was an inverse correlation between these four factors and the laissez-faire leadership style.

Does this mean that effective leader behaviors are the same regardless of country? Bass concluded that this statement is not quite true—but there is far more universalism than people believed previously. In putting his findings in perspective, he concluded that there certainly would be differences in leadership behavior from country to country.[74] For example, he noted that transformational leaders in Honduras would have to be more directive than their counterparts in Norway. Moreover, culture can create some problems in using universal leadership concepts in countries such as Japan, where the use of contingent reward systems is not as widespread as in the West. These reward systems can also become meaningless in Arab and Turkish cultures, where there is a strong belief that things will happen "if God wills" and not because a leader has decided to carry them out. Yet even after taking these differences into consideration, Bass contends that universal leadership behavior is far more common than many people realize.[75]

Qualities for Successful Leaders

Another recent research approach that has been used to address the issue of international leadership is that of examining the characteristics that companies are looking for in their new executive hires. Are all firms seeking the same types of behaviors or qualities or, for example, are companies in Sweden looking for executives with qualities that are quite different from those being sought by Italian firms? The answer to this type of question can help shed light on international leadership because it helps focus attention on the behaviors that organizations believe are important in their managerial workforce. It also helps examine the impact, if any, of culture on leadership style.

Tollgerdt-Andersson examined thousands of advertisements for executives in the European Union (EU). She began by studying ads in Swedish newspapers and journals, noting the qualities, characteristics, and behaviors that were being sought. She then expanded her focus to publications in other European countries including Denmark, Norway, Germany, Great Britain, France, Italy, and Spain. The results are reported in Table 13–6. Based on this analysis, she concluded:

> Generally, there seem to be great differences between the European countries regarding their leadership requirements. Different characteristics are stressed in the various countries. There are also differences concerning how frequently various characteristics are demanded in each country. Some kind of personal or social quality is mentioned much more often in the Scandinavian countries than in the other European countries. In the Scandinavian advertisements, you often see many qualities mentioned in a single advertisement. This can be seen in other European countries too, but it is much more rare. Generally, the characteristics mentioned in a single advertisement do not exceed three and fairly often, especially in Mediterranean countries (in 46–48% of the advertisements) no personal or social characteristics are mentioned at all.[76]

At the same time, Tollgerdt-Andersson did find that there were similarities between nations. For example, Italy and Spain had common patterns regarding desirable leadership characteristics. Between 52 and 54 percent of the ads she reviewed in these two countries stated specific personal and social abilities that were needed by the job applicant. The same pattern was true for Germany and Great Britain, where between 64 and 68 percent of the advertisements set forth the personal and social abilities required for the job. In the Scandinavian countries, these percentages ranged between 80 and 85.

Admittedly, it may be difficult to determine the degree of similarity between ads in different countries (or cultural clusters) because there may be implied meanings in the messages or it may be the custom in a country not to mention certain abilities but simply to assume that applicants know that these will be assessed in making the final hiring decision. Additionally, Tollgerdt-Andersson did find that all countries expected executive applicants to have good social and personal qualities. So some degree of universalism in leadership behaviors was uncovered. On the other hand, the requirements differed from country to country, showing that effective leaders in northern Europe may not be able to transfer their skills to the southern part of the continent with equal results. This led Tollgerdt-Andersson to conclude that multicultural understanding will continue to be a requirement for effective leadership in the 21st century. She put it this way: "If tomorrow's leaders possess international competence and understanding of other cultures it will, hopefully, result in the increased competitive cooperation which is essential if European commerce and industry is to compete with, for example, the USA and Asia."[77]

Culture Clusters and Leader Effectiveness

Although the foregoing discussion indicates there is research to support universalism in leadership behavior, recent findings also show that effective leader behaviors tend to vary by cultural cluster. Brodbeck and his associates conducted a large survey of middle

respect for the other person. Latin American managers, meanwhile, vary their tone of voice continually, and this form of exaggeration is viewed by them as showing that they are very interested in what they are saying and committed to their point of view. Knowing how to communicate can greatly influence leadership across cultures. Here is an example:

> A British manager posted to Nigeria found that it was very effective to raise his voice for important issues. His Nigerian subordinates viewed that unexpected explosion by a normally self-controlled manager as a sign of extra concern. After success in Nigeria he was posted to Malaysia. Shouting there was a sign of loss of face; his colleagues did not take him seriously and he was transferred.[79]

One of the keys to successful global leadership is knowing which style and which behavior work best in a given culture and adapting appropriately. In the case of affective and neutral cultures, for example, Trompenaars and Hampden-Turner have offered the specific tips provided in Table 13–8.

Table 13–8
Leadership Tips for Doing Business in Affective and Neutral Cultures

When Managing or Being Managed in . . .

Affective Cultures	Neutral Cultures
Avoid a detached, ambiguous, and cool demeanor because this will be interpreted as negative behavior.	Avoid warm, excessive, or enthusiastic behaviors because these will be interpreted as a lack of personal control over one's feelings and be viewed as inconsistent with one's high status.
Find out whose work and enthusiasm are being directed into which projects, so you are able to appreciate the vigor and commitment they have for these efforts.	Extensively prepare the things you have to do and then stick tenaciously to the issues.
Let people be emotional without personally becoming intimidated or coerced by their behavior.	Look for cues regarding whether people are pleased or angry and then amplify their importance.

When Doing Business with Individuals in . . .

Affective Cultures (for Those from Neutral Cultures)	Neutral Cultures (for Those from Affective Cultures)
Do not be put off stride when others create scenes and get histrionic; take time-outs for sober reflection and hard assessments.	Ask for time-outs from meetings and negotiations where you can patch each other up and rest between games of poker with the "impassive ones."
When others are expressing goodwill, respond warmly.	Put down as much as you can on paper before beginning the negotiation.
Remember that the other person's enthusiasm and readiness to agree or disagree do not mean that the individual has made up his or her mind.	Remember that the other person's lack of emotional tone does not mean that the individual is uninterested or bored, only that the person does not like to show his or her hand.
Keep in mind that the entire negotiation is typically focused on you as a person and not so much on the object or proposition that is being discussed.	Keep in mind that the entire negotiation is typically focused on the object or proposition that is being discussed and not on you as a person.

Recognize the Way in Which People Behave in . . .

Affective Cultures	Neutral Cultures
They reveal their thoughts and feelings both verbally and nonverbally.	They often do not reveal what they are thinking or feeling.
Emotions flow easily, vehemently, and without inhibition.	Emotions are often dammed up, although they may occasionally explode.
Heated, vital, and animated expressions are admired.	Cool and self-possessed conduct is admired.
Touching, gesturing, and strong facial expressions are common.	Physical contact, gesturing, or strong facial expressions are not used.
Statements are made fluently and dramatically.	Statements are often read out in a monotone voice.

Source: Adapted from Fons Trompenaars and Charles Hampden-Turner, *Riding the Waves of Culture: Understanding Diversity in Global Business*, 2nd ed. (New York: McGraw-Hill, 1998), pp. 80–82.

Cross-Cultural Leadership: Insights from the GLOBE Study

As discussed in Chapter 4, the GLOBE (Global Leadership and Organizational Behavior Effectiveness) research program, a 20-year, multimethod, three-phased study, is examining the relationships among societal and organizational culture, societal and organizational effectiveness, and leadership. In addition to the identification of nine major dimensions of culture described in Chapter 4, the GLOBE program also includes the classification of leadership behaviors. Through a qualitative and quantitative analysis, GLOBE researchers determined that leadership behaviors can be summarized into six culturally endorsed implicit leadership (CLT) dimensions:

- **Charismatic/Value-Based** leadership captures the ability of leaders to inspire, motivate, and encourage high performance outcomes from others based on a foundation of core values.
- **Team-Oriented** leadership places emphasis on effective team building and implementation of a common goal among team members.
- **Participative** leadership reflects the extent to which leaders involve others in decisions and their implementation.
- **Humane-Oriented** leadership comprises supportive and considerate leadership.
- **Autonomous** leadership refers to independent and individualistic leadership behaviors.
- **Self-Protective** leadership "focuses on ensuring the safety and security of the individual and group through status-enhancement and face-saving."[80]

As is the case in the classification of culture dimensions, these categories build on and extend classifications of leadership styles described earlier in this chapter.

Phases 1 and 2 of the GLOBE study, like earlier research, found that certain attributes of leadership were universally endorsed, while others were viewed as effective only in certain cultures. Among the leadership attributes found to be effective across cultures are being trustworthy, just, and honest (having integrity); having foresight and planning ahead; being positive, dynamic, encouraging, and motivating and building confidence; and being communicative and informed and being a coordinator and a team integrator.[81] Several attributes were also found to be universally undesirable in leadership. Traits such as irritable, malevolent, and ruthless were rated as inhibitors of strong leadership across all cultures.[82]

In linking the cultural dimensions of the GLOBE study with the leadership styles described above, the GLOBE researchers investigated the association between cultural values and leadership attributes, and cultural practices and leadership attributes. With regard to the relationship between cultural values and leadership attributes, the GLOBE researchers concluded the following:

- Collectivism I values, as found in Sweden and other Nordic and Scandinavian countries, were likely to view Participative and Self-Protective leadership behaviors favorably while viewing Autonomous leadership behaviors negatively.[83]
- In-Group Collectivism II values, as found in societies such as the Philippines and other East Asian countries, were positively related to Charismatic/Value-Based leadership and Team-Oriented leadership.[84]
- Gender Egalitarian values, as found in countries such as Hungary, Russia, and Poland, were positively associated with Participative and Charismatic/Value-Based leader attributes.[85]
- Performance Orientation values, as found in countries such as Switzerland, Singapore, and Hong Kong, were positively associated with Participative and Charismatic/Value-Based leader attributes.[86]
- Future Orientation values, as found in societies such as Singapore, were positively associated with Self-Protective and Humane-Oriented leader attributes.[87]

Culture and Leadership," *Journal of World Business* 47, (2012), pp. 504–518.

94. Ibid.

95. Narda Quigley, Mary Sully De Luque, and Robert J. House, "Responsible Leadership and Governance in a Global Context: Insights from the GLOBE Study," in *Handbook of Responsible Leadership and Governance in Global Business*, ed. Jonathan P. Doh and Stephen A. Stumpf (London: Edward Elgar Publishing, 2005), pp. 352–379.

96. Lori D. Paris, Jon P. Howell, Peter W. Dorfman, and Paul J. Hanges, "Preferred Leadership Prototypes of Male and Female Leaders in 27 Countries," *Journal of International Business Studies* 40, no. 8 (2009), pp. 1396–1405.

97. Kim S. Cameron, Jane E. Dutton, and Robert E. Quinn, *Positive Organizational Scholarship* (San Francisco: Berrett-Koehler, 2003), p. 3.

98. Ibid.

99. C. Cooper, T. A. Scandura, and C. A. Schriesheim, "Looking Forward but Learning from Our Past: Potential Challenges to Developing Authentic Leadership Theory and Authentic Leaders," *The Leadership Quarterly* 16, no. 3 (2005), pp. 475–493.

100. B. Avolio, F. Luthans, and F. O. Walumba, *Authentic Leadership: Theory Building for Veritable Sustained Performance* (Gallup Leadership Institute, University of Nebraska–Lincoln, 2004), p. 4.

101. B. Shamir and G. Eilam, "What's Your Story? A Life-Stories Approach to Authentic Leadership Development," *The Leadership Quarterly* 16, no. 3 (2005), pp. 395–417.

102. William L. Gardner, Bruce J. Avolio, Fred Luthans, Douglas R. May, and Fred Walumbwa, "Can You See the Real Me? A Self-Based Model of Authentic Leader and Follower Development," *The Leadership Quarterly* 16 (2005), pp. 343–372.

103. Ibid.

104. Bruce J. Avolio and William L. Gardner, "Authentic Leadership Development: Getting to the Root of Positive Forms of Leadership," *The Leadership Quarterly* 16 (2005), pp. 315–338.

105. Ibid.

106. World Economic Forum, "Declining Public Trust Foremost a Leadership Problem," press release, January 14, 2003.

107. Ibid.

108. David Waldman, Donald Siegel, and Mansour Javidan, "Transformational Leadership and Corporate Social Responsibility," in *Handbook of Responsible Leadership and Governance in Global Business*, ed. Doh and Stumpf.

109. Jonathan P. Doh and Stephen A. Stumpf, "Toward a Framework of Responsible Leadership and Governance," in *Handbook of Responsible Leadership and Governance in Global Business*, ed. Doh and Stumpf.

110. Allen Morrison, "Integrity and Global Leadership," *Journal of Business Ethics* 31, no. 1 (May 2001), p. 65.

111. Lao Tzu, *Tao Te Ching*, trans. John C. H. Wu (Boston, MA: Shambhala, 2006), p. 35.

112. Robert Greenleaf, *Servant Leadership: A Journey into the Nature of Legitimate Power and Greatness*, 25th anniversary ed. (Mahwah, NJ: Paulist Press, 2002).

113. Stephen A. Stumpf, "Career Goal: Entrepreneur?" *International Journal of Career Management* 4, no. 2 (1992), pp. 26–32.

114. T. K. Maloy, "Entrepreneurs Need Moms," United Press International, March 11, 2004.

115. Dominic Rushe, "Tim Cook Apologises after Chinese Media Rounds on Apple," *The Guardian*, April 1, 2013, https://www.theguardian.com/technology/2013/apr/01/apple-tim-cook-china-apology.

116. CIA, "Germany," *The World Factbook* (2016), https://www.cia.gov/library/publications/the-world-factbook/geos/gm.html.

117. Ibid.

118. World Bank, "Germany," *Country at a Glance* (2016), www.worldbank.org/en/country/germany.

119. Don Clark, "Cisco Steps Up Investments in Germany and Its Own Slack Competitor," *The Wall Street Journal*, March 9, 2016, www.wsj.com/articles/cisco-steps-up-investments-in-germany-slack-competitor-1457463551.

120. Cisco Systems, "Cisco Announces $500 Million Investment to Accelerate Country Digitization in Germany," press release, March 8, 2016, http://investor.cisco.com/investor-relations/news-and-events/news/news-details/2016/Cisco-Announces-500-Million-Investment-to-Accelerate-Country-Digitization-in-Germany/default.aspx.

Germany

Situated in the heart of central Europe, Germany straddles the border of Western and Eastern Europe. Neighboring countries include the Netherlands, Austria, Belgium, France, Luxembourg, Switzerland, Denmark, Poland, and the Czech Republic. Slightly smaller than the state of Montana, the country maintains shipping routes through its access to the North and Baltic Seas. Major natural resources include coal, lignite, natural gas, iron ore, copper, nickel, uranium, potash, salt, construction materials, timber, and arable land.[116]

Germany, with a population of 80,854,408, is the second largest nation in Europe, behind only Russia. Like most of Western Europe, its population is slowly declining at 0.17 percent annually. The country is quickly aging; in 2015, median age reached 46.5 years old. The two largest age segments of the population are 25–54 year olds (42 percent) and 65 or older (21.5 percent). The country is not very ethnically or religiously diverse. Over 90 percent of the population is of German descent, and the country is primarily Protestant or Roman Catholic. Only 4 percent of the population identifies as Muslim.[117]

European power struggles immersed Germany in two devastating World Wars in the first half of the 20th century, leaving the country occupied by the Allied powers of the U.S., U.K., France, and the Soviet Union in 1945. Tensions between the Soviet Union and the other Allied powers resulted in the division of Germany in 1949 into two states: the western Federal Republic of Germany (FRG) and the eastern German Democratic Republic (GDR). The democratic FRG embedded itself into key Western economic and security organizations, the European Commission, and NATO, while the communist GDR was the front line of the Soviet-led Warsaw Pact. The decline of the Soviet Union in the 1980s allowed for German reunification in 1990. Although 40 years of economic isolation left the former East Germany with significant deficits in education, productivity, and wages, unified Germany has expended considerable funds to raise the entire country to Western standards.

In the wake of World War II and its fairly recent unification, Germany has emerged as the largest economy in Europe and fifth largest in the world. The country's GDP stood at US$3.868 trillion in 2014, resulting in a high GDP per capita of US$46,268. Despite stagnant economic growth across much of Europe, Germany's GDP is expected to expand at 1.5 percent over the next several years. Germany is a leading exporter of machinery, vehicles, chemicals, and household equipment and benefits from a highly skilled labor force.[118]

You Be the International Management Consultant

In a March 2016 announcement, U.S.-based Cisco Systems Inc., one of the largest computer-networking equipment manufacturers worldwide, disclosed plans for major future investments in Germany. According to the company, it would spend a half billion U.S. dollars in the country between 2016 and 2018, with goals of "accelerating its 'digitization'" and investing in startups. Additionally, Cisco stated a desire to work together with the German government on various future technology initiatives.[119]

With its highly educated workforce, Germany offers a unique appeal for tech companies. In recent years, the country has served as a hotbed for companies focusing on digital security. Cisco, with extensive experience in networking security innovations, plans to take advantage of this specialized market niche by creating a "Security Center of Excellence" in the country. The center will focus on bringing customers, academics, small businesses, and Cisco's employees together to solve larger security challenges. Additionally, the company will offer training programs to build skills for potential future employees.[120]

Questions

1. As a management consultant, what opportunities do you see for Cisco in Germany?
2. What are some potential benefits that companies, like Cisco, can gain by partnering with public sector entities and foreign governments of developed nations as opposed to ones in emerging nations?

Chapter 14

HUMAN RESOURCE SELECTION AND DEVELOPMENT ACROSS CULTURES

Firms conducting international business need to be particularly concerned with human resource management issues—including selection, training, and development—to better prepare their personnel for overseas assignments. This chapter focuses on potential sources of human resources that can be employed for overseas assignments, procedures that are used in their selection process, and compensation issues. In this chapter we discuss training and development and the various types of training that are commonly offered. The specific objectives of this chapter are

1. **IDENTIFY** the three basic sources that MNCs can tap when filling management vacancies in overseas operations in addition to options of subcontracting and outsourcing.

2. **DESCRIBE** the selection criteria and procedures used by organizations and individual managers when making final decisions.

3. **DISCUSS** the reasons why people return from overseas assignments, and present some of the strategies used to ensure a smooth transition back into the home-market operation.

4. **DESCRIBE** the training process, the most common reasons for training, and the types of training that often are provided.

5. **EXPLAIN** how cultural assimilators work and why they are so highly regarded.

OBJECTIVES OF THE CHAPTER

The World of *International Management*

The Challenge of Talent Retention in India

Retaining talented employees is a challenge for managers around the world. Somewhat to the surprise of MNCs, this challenge has become particularly acute in India. According to a 2015 study by Ernst & Young, only 6 percent of Indian firms felt that they had best-in-class capability for recruitment activities, and only 4 percent stated that they had best-in-class capability for hiring employees with scarce or critical skills.[1]

The same study found that employee turnover was particularly high for customer-facing employees, with a fifth of all firms seeing annual turnover greater than 20 percent.[2] Such high employee turnover has a cost. Shyamal Majumdar of India's *Business Standard* explained that frontline employees in a top company cost 40 percent of their salaries to replace and top managers cost 150–200 percent of their salaries to replace.[3]

Right Management's Executive Overview described the business implications of high Indian employee turnover:

> In IT, for example, it is important for clients to develop close relationships with employees working on projects. Frequent turnover means continually building new relationships with replacements, thereby slowing down projects and harming both efficiency and client trust. In manufacturing, high attrition results in the expensive and time-consuming exercise of training recent hires about new technologies.[4]

Because of the cost of hiring and retraining employees, MNCs in India may not be able to secure the cost savings that led them to India in the first place.

More Than Money

Discussing retaining talent in India, Elena Groznaya points out that MNCs sometimes mistakenly use the same methods to try to retain employees in India as in the home country. These methods are often compensation driven. In India's relationship-oriented culture, however, employees are primarily motivated not by compensation, but by a sense of "family" in their companies. Groznaya states: "Traditional Indian companies often play the role of a family extension for their staff" and give employees a feeling of belonging.[5]

A comprehensive talent management and HR practices study in India supported the conclusion that compensation is not the main factor in retaining Indian employees. Villanova School of Business and Right Management conducted a survey of 4,811 individuals from 28 Indian companies in five industries. According to Right Management's Executive Overview, the researchers found:

> While the common perception is that pay is the key element in attracting and retaining talent in India, as well as other emerging countries, our results showed a more complex array of factors played a significant role. Most notably, they included the value of intrinsic rewards—the employees' sense of progress, competence, influence/choice, and opportunity to do meaningful work. Compensation was not the most significant factor in either retention or engagement, a phenomenon that held true across all industries. Among respondents who indicated an intent to stay, only 30 percent were "very satisfied" with their compensation.[6]

The key to high retention is keeping employees engaged. The researchers discovered that "lack of engagement was by far the strongest single factor leading to intent to leave an organization. The lesson is clear: The more engaged an employee, the likelier he or she will stay."[7]

Four Factors Correlated to Employee Engagement

What steps can managers take to keep employees engaged? The researchers identified four HR practices that are correlated with employee engagement, as measured by employees' feelings of pride and satisfaction in the organization. These factors were performance management, professional development, manager support, and an organizational commitment to a larger social purpose.[8]

> *Performance Management* The researchers found a significant relationship between retention and a favorable assessment of a firm's performance management system. Of employees who were in the top third of those who rated their company's performance management practices highly, "56.1 percent had strong pride in the

organization, 65.9 percent had strong satisfaction with the organization, and only 23.5 percent indicated a strong intention to leave." In contrast, of the bottom third, "only 17.3 percent had strong pride in the organization, 11.1 percent had strong satisfaction, and 48.8 percent expressed a strong intention to leave."[9]

When setting up performance management systems at Indian firms, managers need to be coached on how to provide constructive feedback. Indian managers are often hesitant to criticize their employees, but with coaching, they can learn how to use criticism to help employees improve their performance.[10]

Professional Development Employees who are satisfied with their firm's professional development opportunities are more likely to remain at the firm. For instance, the researchers found that of those respondents who did not like the professional development practices at their companies, "52.3 percent indicated intent to leave within 12 months vs. 18.7 percent in organizations that strongly supported those practices." Employees are more engaged when they have clear opportunities for growth in their career. A typical career path may involve the opportunity to work on different projects, participate in overseas assignments, and eventually take on a managerial role.[11]

Employee assessments should be an important part of the development process. These assessments "can ensure that companies hire the right people for the right jobs and . . . will also help to pinpoint those people with the potential to move into management roles."[12]

Management Support From the study, the researchers found that "Due to the urgent need for managerial level personnel, employees in India are often promoted to supervisory roles before they're ready to assume such responsibilities." Furthermore, many respondents in the study were dissatisfied with their manager's ability to engage with their team: "Only 47 percent of respondents agreed that their immediate supervisor was able to provide support and develop his or her team effectively." This gap in management skills has a negative impact on employee retention. If employees are working

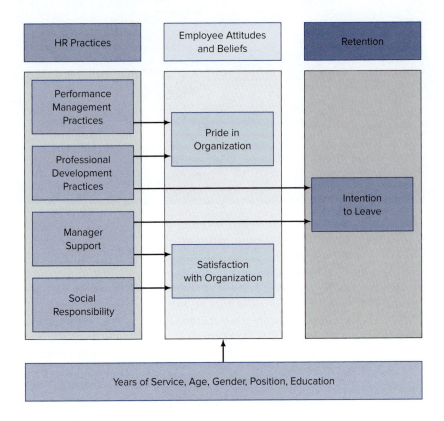

for a supervisor who lacks management skills, they are more likely to leave the company.[13]

Thus, Indian firms need to train new managers in the basics of management, such as how to reach team objectives and how to mentor employees. Mentoring is an essential management skill in India, where leaders often act as personal advisers. Having effective managers to support their employees is critical to increasing employee retention.[14]

Social Responsibility Many Indian employees highly value commitment to the community. Firms can engage employees by providing them with opportunities to participate in initiatives to help social causes, such as alleviating poverty. These initiatives should be highlighted in annual reports.[15]

Start on the First Day

The highlights of the research study mentioned were published in an article in *MIT Sloan Management Review*. According to the article, "The best companies drive employee satisfaction and pride by providing management support, training, and professional opportunities early on. . . . Employers should start an employee's professional development plan on his or her *first day*."[16]

One of the researchers in the study, Dr. Jonathan Doh, told the *MIT Sloan Management Review*, "Our findings suggest that even six months from the start date is probably too late. [At that point] the employee is already making decisions about whether to stay around or not." MNCs can make the decision to stay an easy one by offering employees effective professional development, performance management systems, and manager support.[17]

Once, India was seen as a source of never-ending talent. Today, India poses some of the same challenges in attracting, hiring, and retaining talent as do many developed countries, with some issues that are particular to the Indian context. Originally, MNCs searched overseas for inexpensive labor, but as countries become more developed and education levels increase, and as employers in home countries worry about a diminishing labor force, the search has shifted. As more highly skilled workers become available in other countries, MNCs have a growing number of sources for their human resources; however, as more MNCs and local firms vie for this talent, a "talent war" may ensue. MNCs may also be able to access foreign human resources by hiring them on a temporary or permanent basis in the home country. Often, they will subcontract or outsource work to foreign employees in home and host countries. This complex web of relationships creates significant managerial challenges and opportunities and suggests that there will always be a need for highly skilled, culturally sensitive, and geographically mobile managerial talent.

In this chapter, we explore the procedure of international human resource (HR) selection and training and examine the difficulties of developing a global human resource management process in the presence of dissimilar cultural norms. At the same time, we survey emerging trends in international human resource management, including the increasing use of temporary and contingent staffing to fill the growing global HR needs of MNCs. We also review training and development programs designed to help employees prepare for and succeed in their foreign assignments and adjust to conditions once they return home.

■ The Importance of International Human Resources

Human resources is an essential part of any organization because it provides the human capital that keeps operations running. Human resource management is also key to an efficient, productive workplace. We discussed in Chapter 12 how financial compensation can motivate employees, but creative human resource management can play an even more important role. By focusing on the employees, or the human resources themselves, organizations have found that positive organizational structure leads to company success in the market.[18] Sometimes this is recognized through compensation, such as competitive salaries, good benefits, promotions, training, education opportunities, and so forth, which has been known to motivate employees and reduce turnover because there are further incentives to strive for. Other times, companies will provide employees with daily comforts such as meals where an employee's family is welcome to attend, fitness centers, laundry rooms, or even services such as oil changes while at work. Showing the employees that they are not simply cogs in a machine, but that their time is valued and they are thanked for it, often builds morale and can increase company sales through a shared drive to succeed. Furthermore, recognizing the potential in employees and encouraging teamwork can lead to greater risk taking and innovations.[19]

Getting the Employee Perspective

Whether managers are trying to increase productivity or decrease turnover rates, it is good to get a sense of how the employees feel they are being treated. Times continue to change, and while employees in the past could be considered one unit, today people are realizing their individual talents and their need to be recognized. For instance, global companies are experiencing a labor shortage as skilled workers are in high demand.[20] In essence, skilled workers can almost walk in and request the kind of compensation they desire, and companies may be willing to accept the terms. Even outside this context of labor shortages, firms are restructuring how they look at employees for many good reasons. By segmenting the workforce into categories (but avoiding differentiation based on age or gender because that may imply a form of discrimination) and by offering choices, flexibility, and a personal touch to each employee package, employers are able to provide an underlying sense of commitment because the employee is getting what he or she wants. In other words, by focusing on employees and tailoring human resource management to the individual, people are naturally influenced to stay longer and be more committed to the organization they have joined.[21] However, before a company can keep the employee, it must first hire.

Employees as Critical Resources

Attracting the most qualified employees and matching them to the jobs for which they are best suited are important for the success of any organization. For international organizations, the selection and development of human resources are especially challenging and vitally important. As prevalent and useful as e-mail and web- and teleconferencing have become, and despite the increasing incidence of subcontracting and outsourcing, face-to-face human contact will remain an important means of communication and transferring "tacit" knowledge—knowledge that cannot be formalized in manuals or written guidelines. Hence, most companies continue to deploy human resources around the world as they are needed, although the range of options for filling human resource needs is expanding.

Investing in International Assignments

MNCs must send expatriate ("expat") managers overseas, no matter how good "virtual" communications become. There are quite a few costs involved, including pre-assignment training, and potential costs due to failure. According to a recent study, expatriate employees cost roughly 2.5 times that of a domestic employee. Furthermore, 10 percent of expatriate projects fail, adding to the overall cost of doing business.[22] Given these high costs, many MNCs are turning to locally engaged employees or third-country nationals.[23] In addition, the improved education of many populations around the world gives MNCs more options when considering international human resource needs. The emergence of highly trained technical and scientific employees in emerging markets and the increased prevalence of MBA-type training in many developed and developing countries have dramatically expanded the pool of talent from which MNCs can draw. Yet some companies are still having difficulty in winning the "war for talent." A recent report from China noted that despite much greater levels of advanced education, there is still a shortage of skilled management. "We need a lot more people than we have now, and we need a higher caliber of people," said Guo Ming, Coca-Cola's human resource director for Greater China.[24]

Adjustment problems of expats undertaking international assignments can be reduced through careful selection and training. Language training and cross-cultural training are especially important, but they are often neglected by MNCs in a hurry to deploy resources to meet critical needs.[25] The demand for globally adept managers will likely grow, and MNCs will need to continue to invest in recruiting and training the best future leaders.

MNCs are also under increasing pressure to keep jobs at home, and their international HR practices have come under close scrutiny. In particular, the "importing" of programmers from India at a fraction of domestic wages, combined with the offshore outsourcing of work to high-tech employees in lower-cost countries, has created political and social challenges for MNCs seeking to manage their international human resources efficiently and effectively. All of this suggests an ongoing need for attention to and investment in this challenging area.

Economic Pressures

It is important to note that the human resources function within MNCs is itself changing as a result of ongoing pressures for reduced costs and increased efficiencies. There was a time when human resources departments handled every staffing need at a company, from hiring and firing to administering benefits and determining salaries. According to a 2015 study by Bloomberg BNA, HR personnel-to-staff ratios dipped from 1.3 per 100 in 2014 to 1.1 per 100 in 2015. At large companies, defined as having 2,500 employees or more, the ratio of HR personnel-to-staff drops to just 0.6 per 100. Further, some of what in-house HR departments oversaw is now being outsourced, due to increased scrutiny of the costs associated with these "staff" (versus revenue-generating "line") functions. The 2015 Bloomberg BNA study found that two-thirds of employers outsourced at least one HR activity.[26]

The actions that companies take during an economic recession, in regards to employee compensation and benefits, vary based on a multitude of factors. However, looking back to the 2009–2010 global recession can provide some clues as to how companies may react during future economic downturns. Pay freezes or reductions, along with hiring freezes, were quite common during the global recession. A survey taken during the global recession by Towers Perrin (now Willis Towers Watson) found that 42 percent of organizations were planning hiring freezes and reductions as well as pay cuts. Another survey, an update to ECA International's Salary Trends Survey, conducted annually for more than 50 countries, found that 40 percent of companies planned to freeze pay. On average, salary increases were half as high as anticipated before the economic crisis set in. In Canada, increases dropped from 4 percent to 1 percent. Salary increases in Western Europe averaged around 2 percent, according to the survey, while those in Eastern Europe were just under 5 percent. Russia, Romania, and Latvia saw the greatest increases, while workers in Lithuania, the Irish Republic, and Switzerland were expected to receive the smallest pay raises in the region.

Likely due in part to the pay and hiring freezes utilized by many companies to improve financial metrics, employers expressed concern over long-term talent retention during the global recession. Sixty-two percent of companies in the Towers Perrin survey stated that they were worried about the potential impact on their ability to keep high-performing talent or those in pivotal roles. In response, organizations reserved their salary increases and cash rewards for their most talented and top-performing employees, even while pay is cut for the rest of the workforce.

■ Sources of Human Resources

MNCs can tap four basic sources for positions: (1) home-country nationals, (2) host-country nationals, (3) third-country nationals, and (4) inpatriates. In addition, many MNCs are outsourcing aspects of their global operations and in so doing are engaging temporary or contingent employees. The following sections analyze each of these major sources.

Home-Country Nationals

Home-country nationals are managers who are citizens of the country where the MNC is headquartered. In fact, sometimes the term *headquarters nationals* is used. These managers commonly are called **expatriates**, or simply "expats," which refers to those who live and work outside their home country. Historically, MNCs have staffed key positions in their foreign affiliates with home-country nationals or expatriates. For many companies and for the most senior positions, that trend persists. Major U.S. and European companies such as Cisco Systems and IBM have been sending expats to India. According to a 2015 estimate, about 30,000 expat managers are there now, with that number expected to grow by 10 to 15 percent per year.[27] However, some research has shown that in many instances, host-country nationals may be better suited for the job. Richards, for example, investigated staffing practices for the purpose of determining when companies are more likely to use an expatriate rather than a local manager. She conducted interviews with senior-level headquarters managers at 24 U.S. multinational manufacturing firms and with managers at their U.K. and Thai subsidiaries. This study found that local managers were most effective in subsidiaries located in developing countries or those that relied on a local customer base. In contrast, expatriates were most effective when they were in charge of larger subsidiaries or those with a marketing theme similar to that at headquarters.[28]

There are a variety of reasons for using home-country nationals. One of the most common is to start up operations. Another is to provide technical expertise. A third is to help the MNC maintain financial control over the operation.[29] Other commonly cited reasons include the desire to provide the company's more promising managers with international experience to equip them better for more responsible positions; the need to maintain and facilitate organizational coordination and control; the unavailability of managerial talent in the host country; the company's view of the foreign operation as short lived; the host country's multiracial population, which might mean that selecting a manager of either race would result in political or social problems; the company's conviction that it must maintain a foreign image in the host country; and the belief of some companies that a home-country manager is the best person for the job.[30]

home-country nationals
Expatriate managers who are citizens of the country where the multinational corporation is headquartered.

expatriates
Managers who live and work outside their home country. They are citizens of the country where the multinational corporation is headquartered.

In recent years, there has been a trend away from using home-country nationals, given the costs, somewhat uncertain returns, and increasing availability of host-country and third-country nationals and inpatriates.

Host-Country Nationals

host-country nationals
Local managers who are hired by the MNC.

Host-country nationals are local managers who are hired by the MNC. For a number of reasons, many MNCs use host-country managers at the middle- and lower-level ranks. One reason in particular is that many countries expect the MNC to hire local talent, and the use of host-country nationals is a good way to meet this expectation. Also, even if an MNC wanted to staff all management positions with home-country personnel, it would be unlikely to have this many available managers, and the cost of transferring and maintaining them in the host country would be prohibitive.

In some cases government regulations dictate selection practices and mandate at least some degree of "nativization." In Brazil, for example, two-thirds of the employees in any foreign subsidiary traditionally have to be Brazilian nationals. Additionally, the Brazilian Labor Code states that pay to foreigners must not exceed one-third of the company's total payroll. Brazil is not alone; many countries exert real and subtle pressures to staff the upper-management ranks with nationals. In the past, these pressures by host countries have led companies such as Standard Oil to change their approach to selecting managers. These regulations have substantial costs in that shielding local employees from international competition may create a sense of entitlement and result in low productivity.

Sony is trying the host-country approach in the United States. Employees are encouraged to accept or decline styles that emerge from Japanese headquarters, depending on American tastes. Furthermore, innovative creations are birthed at the U.S. site, all with an American flavor. Sony believes that local citizens are the best qualified for the job, as opposed to Japanese managers, because they already have a working knowledge of the language and culture, and it may be difficult for Sony to understand preferred styles otherwise.[31] The International Management in Action box "Important Tips on Working for Foreigners" gives examples of how Americans can better adapt to foreign bosses.

Third-Country Nationals

third-country nationals (TCNs)
Managers who are citizens of countries other than the country in which the MNC is headquartered or the one in which the managers are assigned to work by the MNC.

Third-country nationals (TCNs) are managers who are citizens of countries other than the country in which the MNC is headquartered or the one in which they are assigned to work by the MNC. Available data on third-country nationals are not as extensive as those on home- or host-country nationals.

A number of advantages have been cited for using TCNs. One is that the salary and benefit package usually is less than that of a home-country national, although in recent years, the salary gap between the two has begun to diminish. A second reason is that the TCN may have a very good working knowledge of the region or speak the same language as the local people. This helps explain why many U.S. MNCs hire English or Scottish managers for top positions at subsidiaries in former British colonies such as Jamaica, India, the West Indies, and Kenya. It also explains why successful MNCs such as Gillette, Coca-Cola, and IBM recruit local managers and train them to run overseas subsidiaries. Other cited benefits of using TCNs include

1. TCN managers, particularly those who have had assignments in the headquarters country, can often achieve corporate objectives more effectively than expatriates or local nationals. In particular, they frequently have a deep understanding of the corporation's policies from the perspective of a foreigner and can communicate and implement those policies more effectively to others than can expats.

2. During periods of rapid expansion, TCNs can not only substitute for expatriates in new and growing operations but also offer different perspectives that can complement and expand on the sometimes narrowly focused viewpoints of both local nationals and headquarters personnel.

Important Tips on Working for Foreigners

As the Japanese, South Koreans, and Europeans continue to expand their economic horizons, increased employment opportunities will be available worldwide. Is it a good idea to work for foreigners? Those who have done so have learned that there are both rewards and penalties associated with this career choice. Following are some useful tips that have been drawn from the experiences of those who have worked for foreign MNCs.

First, most U.S. managers are taught to make fast decisions, but most foreign managers take more time and view rapid decision making as unnecessary and sometimes bad. In the United States, we hear the cliché, "The effective manager is right 51 percent of the time." In Europe, this percentage is perceived as much too low, which helps explain why European managers analyze situations in much more depth than most U.S. managers do. Americans working for foreign-owned firms have to focus on making slower and more accurate decisions.

Second, most Americans are taught to operate without much direction. In Latin countries, managers are accustomed to giving a great deal of direction, and in East Asian firms, there is little structure and direction. Americans have to learn to adjust to the decision-making process of the particular company.

Third, most Americans go home around 5 p.m. If there is more paperwork to do, they take it with them. Japanese managers, in contrast, stay late at the office and often view those who leave early as being lazy. Americans either have to adapt or have to convince the manager that they are working as hard as their peers but in a different physical location.

Fourth, many international firms say that their official language is English. However, important conversations always are carried out in the home country's language, so it is important to learn that language.

Fifth, many foreign MNCs make use of fear to motivate their people. This is particularly true in manufacturing work, where personnel are under continuous pressure to maintain high output and quality. For instance, those who do not like to work under intense conditions would have a very difficult time succeeding in Chinese auto assembly plants. Americans have to understand that humanistic climates of work may be the exception rather than the rule.

Finally, despite the fact that discrimination in employment is outlawed in the United States, it is practiced by many MNCs, including those operating in the United States. Women seldom are given the same opportunities as men, and top-level jobs almost always are reserved for home-office personnel. In many cases, Americans have accepted or accommodated to this ethnocentric (nationalistic) approach.

Nevertheless, as Chapter 3 discussed, ethics and social responsibility are becoming a major issue in the international arena, and these moral challenges must be met now and in the future.

Sources: Martin J. Gannon, *Understanding Global Cultures*, 2nd ed. (Thousand Oaks, CA: Sage, 2001); Richard D. Lewis, *When Cultures Collide* (London: Nicholas Brealey, 1999); Roger E. Axtell, ed., *Do's and Taboos around the World* (New York: Wiley, 1990); John Holusha, "No Utopia but to Workers It's a Job," *New York Times*, January 29, 1989, sec. 3, pp. 1, 10; Faye Rice, "Should You Work for a Foreigner?" *Fortune*, August 1, 1988, pp. 123–124; Jeanne Whalen, "American Finds Himself Atop Russian Oil Giant in Turmoil," *The Wall Street Journal*, October 30, 2003, p. B1.

3. In joint ventures, TCNs can demonstrate a global or transnational image and bring unique cross-cultural skills to the relationship.[32]

In recent years, a new term has emerged in international management—inpatriates. An **inpatriate**, or inpat, is an individual from a host country or a third-country national who is assigned to work in the home country. Even Japanese MNCs are now beginning to rely on inpatriates to help them meet their international challenges. Harvey and Buckley report:

inpatriates
Individuals from a host country or third-country nationals who are assigned to work in the home country.

> The Japanese are reducing their unicultural orientation in their global businesses. Yoichi Morishita, president of Matsushita, has ordered that top management must reflect the cultural diversity of the countries where Matsushita does business. Sony sells 80 percent of its products overseas and recently recognized the need to become multicultural. It has appointed two foreigners to its board of directors and has plans to hire host-country nationals who are to be integrated into the top management of the parent organization. At the same time, the Chairman of Sony has stated that in five years the board of directors of Sony will reflect the diversity of countries that are important to the future of the company. Similarly, Toshiba plans to have a more representative top management and board of directors to facilitate long-run global strategies.[33]

This growing use of inpats is helping MNCs better develop their global core competencies. As a result, today a new breed of multilingual, multiexperienced, so-called global managers or transnational managers is truly emerging.[34] These new managers are part of a growing group of international executives who can manage across borders and do not fit the traditional third-country nationals mold. With a unified Europe and other such developments in North America and Asia, these global managers are in great demand. Additionally, with labor shortages developing in certain regions, there is a wave of migration from regions with an abundance of personnel to those where the demand is strongest.

Subcontracting and Outsourcing

Other potential sources of international management talent are subcontracting and offshore outsourcing (introduced in Chapter 1). Offshore outsourcing is made possible by the increasing organizational and technological capacity of companies to separate, coordinate, and integrate geographically dispersed human resources—whether employed directly by the firm or contracted out—across distant geographic borders. The development of this capacity can be traced to the earlier growth of international subcontracting as well as to the international diffusion of lean production systems (which originated with Japanese auto manufacturers) to other manufacturing and service sectors. In particular, service industries are exploiting inexpensive telecommunications to transmit engineering, medical, legal, and accounting services to be performed in locations previously viewed as remote. Rising levels of educational attainment in developing countries such as China, India, and the Philippines, especially in the scientific and technical fields, make offshoring increasingly attractive for a range of international human resource needs.

These developments are not without controversy, however. On the one hand, offshore outsourcing, as well as the hiring of temporary workers from abroad on special visas, similar to inpatriates, presents significant opportunities for cost savings and lower overhead. On the other hand, the recent wave of media attention has focused on widespread concern that in an age of cheap telecommunications, almost any job—professional or blue collar—can be performed in India for a fraction of U.S. wages. In particular, as discussed in Chapter 1, union groups, politicians, and NGOs have challenged MNCs' right to engage in labor "arbitrage."

Offshoring is reaching a new era, and while the top reason that MNCs look to other countries for labor is still to save money, there has been a decline all around in qualified personnel, which has brought about an emerging focus on other factors, notably access to qualified personnel.

Moreover, although the cost for a computer programmer or a middle manager in India remains a small fraction of the cost for a similar employee in the United States (a programmer with three to five years' experience makes about $25,000 in India but about $65,000 in the United States), the wage savings do not necessarily translate directly into overall savings because the typical outsourcing contract between an American company and an Indian vendor saves less than half as much as the wage differences would imply.[35] Microsoft faced this challenge when it hired two Indian outsourcing companies, Infosys and Satyam, to provide skilled software architects for its projects. In this case, the work of software architects and developers was being done by employees of the Indian companies working at Microsoft facilities in the United States. Although the actual employees were paid much less than U.S. counterparts ($30,000 to $40,000), Microsoft was billed $90 an hour for software architects, or at a yearly rate of more than $180,000. The onsite work was done by Indian software engineers who came to the United States on H-1B visas, which allow foreign workers to be employed in the United States for up to six years. Microsoft also contracted work in India through the firms, with billing rates of $23 to $36 an hour.[36]

Though politically controversial, outsourcing can save companies significant costs and is very profitable for firms that specialize in providing these services on a contract basis. U.S.-based firms such as EDS, IBM, and Deloitte have developed specific competencies in global production and HR coordination, including managing the HR functions that must support it. These firms combine low labor costs, specialized technical capabilities, and coordination expertise.

Outsourcing can also create quality control problems for some companies, as demonstrated by British telecom giant BT's decision in 2016 to repatriate some of its call-center staff from India to the U.K. due to quality control problems. The move, costing

BT roughly £80 million, aims to improve customer satisfaction by increasing the number of customer calls answered in the U.K. from 50 percent to 80 percent. Roughly 1,000 positions will ultimately be transferred back to the U.K.[37]

Despite the limitations, offshore subcontracting will remain an important tool for managing and deploying international human resources. A recent study by the Hackett Group estimated that U.S. and European companies sent an average of 150,000 jobs offshore every year between 2002 and 2016.[38] Although subcontracting provides important flexibility in the human resource practices of MNCs operating globally, it also requires skilled international managers to coordinate and oversee the complex relationships that arise from it.

This is especially true as offshoring begins a new generation. In a survey by Duke University's Offshoring Research Network, significant differences were found in the perspectives of home (source) and host (destination) countries. Specifically, individuals in home countries were often worried about losing jobs to host countries, exacerbated by the fact that higher-end jobs are now being shipped overseas.[39] This is not the case from the organizations' point of view. It is becoming increasingly difficult for managers to find the appropriate talent. More and more, companies are looking overseas in areas such as R&D and procurement to supplement the lack of experts in the home country. This does not take jobs away from home countries; it simply opens jobs globally as managers attempt to fit the skills of the worker to the job itself.[40] Furthermore, companies are very specific about which country they search when looking to fill particular job functions. Figure 14–1 provides a graphical depiction of this reality. Overall, offshoring is a trend that does not appear to be on its way out, but instead is evolving through alternative motivators and continuing to innovatively help the company grow.

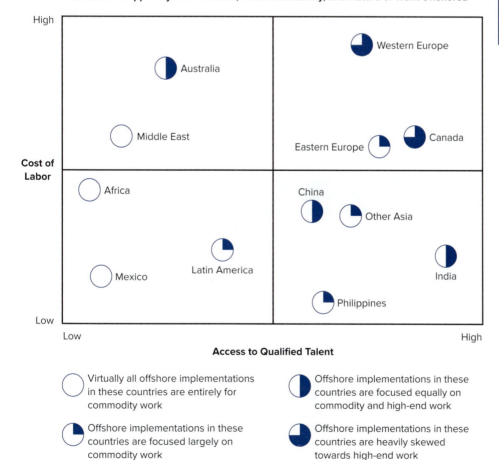

Figure 14–1

Skills MNCs Seek within Countries

Source: Arie Y. Lewin and Vinay Couto, *Next Generation Offshoring: The Globalization of Innovation, 2006 Survey Report* (Durham: Duke Center for International Business Education and Research, 2007).

■ Selection Criteria for International Assignments

international selection criteria
Factors used to choose personnel for international assignments.

Making an effective selection decision for an overseas assignment can prove to be a major problem. Typically, this decision is based on **international selection criteria**, which are factors used to choose international managers. These selections are influenced by the MNC's experience and often are culturally based. Sometimes as many as a dozen criteria are used, although most MNCs give serious consideration to only five or six.[41] Table 14–1 reports the importance of some of these criteria as ranked by Australian, expatriate, and Asian managers from 60 leading Australian, New Zealand, British, and U.S. MNCs with operations in South Asia.[42]

General Criteria

Some selection criteria are given a great deal of weight; others receive, at best, only lip service. A company sending people overseas for the first time often will have a much longer list of criteria than will an experienced MNC that has developed a "short list."

Typically, both technical and human criteria are considered. Firms that fail to consider both often find that their rate of failure is quite high. For example, Peterson, Napier, and Shul-Shim investigated the primary criteria that MNCs use when choosing personnel for overseas assignments and found that the Japanese and American MNCs in their survey ranked both technical expertise and interpersonal skills as very important.[43] The following sections examine some of the most commonly used selection criteria for overseas assignments in more depth.

Adaptability to Cultural Change

Overseas managers must be able to adapt to change. They also need a degree of cultural toughness. Research shows that many managers are exhilarated at the beginning of their overseas assignment. After a few months, however, a form of culture shock creeps in, and they begin to encounter frustration and feel confused in their new environment. This may be a good sign because it shows that the expatriate manager is becoming involved in the new culture and not just isolating himself or herself from the environment.

As this initial and trying period comes to an end, expatriates tend to identify more with the host-country culture, which only increases as managers become more adept at

Table 14–1
Rank of Criteria in Expatriate Selection

	Australian Managers (*n* = 47)	Expatriate Managers* (*n* = 52)	Asian Managers (*n* = 15)
1. Ability to adapt	1	1	2
2. Technical competence	2	3	1
3. Spouse and family adaptability	3	2	4
4. Human relations skill	4	4	3
5. Desire to serve overseas	5	5	5
6. Previous overseas experience	6	7	7
7. Understanding of host-country culture	7	6	6
8. Academic qualifications	8	8	8
9. Knowledge of language of country	9	9	9
10. Understanding of home-country culture	10	10	10

*U.S., British, Canadian, French, New Zealand, or Australian managers working for an MNC outside their home countries.
Source: From Raymond J. Stone, "Expatriate Selection and Failure," *Human Resource Planning* 14, no. 1 (1991).

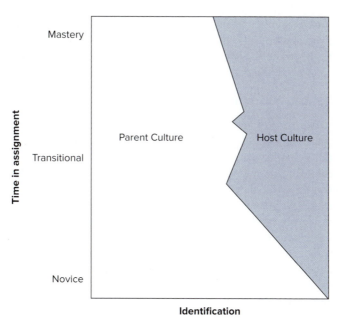

Figure 14–2

Evolution of Parent and Host Culture Identification

Source: Juan Sanchez, Paul Spector, and Cary Cooper, "Adapting to a Boundaryless World: A Developmental Expatriate Model," *Academy of Management Executive* 14, no. 2 (2000), p. 100.

the position. As seen in Figure 14–2, upon first arrival, the expatriates identify almost wholly with the home country. Over time, they become more familiar with their surroundings and become more of an integral part of the environment. This integration can lead to a higher sense of satisfaction with the job and a lessening of stress and alienation.[44]

Organizations examine a number of characteristics to determine whether an individual is sufficiently adaptable. Examples include work experiences with cultures other than one's own, previous overseas travel, knowledge of foreign languages (fluency generally is not necessary), and recent immigration background or heritage. Others include (1) the ability to integrate with different people, cultures, and types of business organizations; (2) the ability to sense developments in the host country and accurately evaluate them; (3) the ability to solve problems within different frameworks and from different perspectives; (4) sensitivity to the fine print of differences of culture, politics, religion, and ethics, in addition to individual differences; and (5) flexibility in managing operations on a continuous basis despite lack of assistance and gaps in information.

In research conducted among expatriates in China, Selmar found that those who were best able to deal with their new situation had developed coping strategies characterized by sociocultural and psychological adjustments including (1) feeling comfortable that their work challenges can be met, (2) being able to adjust to their new living conditions, (3) learning how to interact well with host-country nationals outside of work, and (4) feeling reasonably happy and being able to enjoy day-to-day activities.[45] And Caligiuri, after examining how host nationals help expatriates adjust, reported that certain types of personality characteristics are important in this process. In particular, her findings suggest that greater contact with host nationals helps with cross-cultural adjustment when the person also possesses the personality trait of openness. She also found that sociability was directly related to effective adjustment.[46]

Physical and Emotional Health

Most organizations require that their overseas managers have good physical and emotional health. Some examples are fairly obvious. An employee with a heart condition or a nervous disorder would not be considered. The psychological ability of individuals to withstand culture shock, if this could be discerned, would be an issue, as would the current marital status as it affected an individual's ability to cope in a foreign environment.

For example, one U.S. oil company operating in the Middle East considers middle-aged men with grown children to be the best able to cope with culture shock, and for some locations in the desert, considers people from Texas or southern California to be a better fit than those from New England.

Age, Experience, and Education

Most MNCs strive for a balance between age and experience. There is evidence that younger managers are more eager for international assignments. These managers tend to be more "worldly" and have a greater appreciation of other cultures than older managers do. By the same token, young people often are the least developed in management experience and technical skills; they lack real-world experience. To gain the desired balance, many firms send both young and seasoned personnel to the same overseas post. Many companies consider an academic degree, preferably a graduate degree, to be of critical importance to an international executive; however, universal agreement regarding the ideal type of degree is nonexistent. MNCs, of course, use formal education only as a point of departure for their own training and development efforts. For example, Siemens of Germany gives members of its international management team specific training designed to help them deal more effectively with the types of problems they will face on the job.

Language Training

The ability to speak the language of the country in which a manager is doing business can be extremely valuable. One recognized weakness of many MNCs is that they do not give sufficient attention to the importance of language training. English is the primary language of international business, and most expatriates from all countries can converse in English. Those who can speak only English are at a distinct disadvantage when doing business in non-English-speaking countries, however. In other words, language can be a very critical factor.

Traditionally, managers from English-speaking countries have done very poorly in the language area. However, in recent years, expatriates have made an effort to improve their conversational skills. According to the 2015 HSBC Expat Explorer, 63 percent of employees on an international assignment ultimately learned the local language. The level of development within the host country appears to significantly impact whether or not expatriates work to improve their speaking skills; in developed countries, 67 percent of expatriates made an attempt to learn the host country's language, while only 51 percent of those in developing nations made an attempt.[47]

For many expatriates, being able to speak with locals in their own language is a major milestone in finally feeling connected to the foreign country. This is especially important for countries like Russia, where successful integration is heavily dependent on being able to converse in Russian; of expatriates surveyed there, more than 70 percent were making an effort to improve their speech skills.[48]

Motivation for a Foreign Assignment

Although individuals being sent overseas should have a desire to work abroad, this usually is not sufficient motivation. International management experts contend that the candidate also must believe in the importance of the job and even have something of an element of idealism or a sense of mission. Applicants who are unhappy with their current situation at home and are looking to get away seldom make effective overseas managers.

Some experts believe that a desire for adventure or a pioneering spirit is an acceptable reason for wanting to go overseas. Other motivators that often are cited include the desire to increase one's chances for promotion and the opportunity to improve one's economic status. For example, many U.S. MNCs regard international experience as being critical for promotion to the upper ranks. In addition, thanks to the supplemental wage and benefit package, U.S. managers sometimes find that they can make, and especially save, more money than if they remained stateside.

And while many may romanticize the expatriate life, it is clear that the travel mystique continues to motivate professionals to desire and seek an assignment abroad. A recent survey found that at least 40 percent of Britons say that they would like to work or retire abroad. And according to a report in the British *Daily Telegraph*:

> And it's not just about the sunshine. Becoming an expatriate is an adventure, a new beginning, a fresh start, and it is in human nature to want to explore. Global mobility is as old as humankind itself. The ancient migration routes of our earliest ancestors are well documented and the distances travelled by primitive man still continue to amaze. There were even expatriates in the Bible—consider the exodus from Egypt for example. Indeed, the forced expatriation of Adam and Eve from the garden of Eden is the starting point for the entire Biblical narrative. Was Eve the very first "trailing spouse"? In more recent times entire civilizations have been influenced by explorers such as Marco Polo, Christopher Columbus, Captain Cook and the Pilgrim Fathers. So moving across continents is nothing new but its continued rise has been underpinned by the drive towards globalization aided by the revolution in communication throughout the 20th century. Technologies have allowed companies to globalize in ways which were simply unimaginable in earlier times. Indeed such is the commitment to globalization, that many major companies now structure their reporting lines along global delivery lines rather than local geographic control.[49]

Spouses and Dependents or Work-Family Issues

Spouses and dependents are another important consideration when a person is to be chosen for an overseas assignment. If the family is not happy, the manager often performs poorly and may either be terminated or simply decide to leave the organization. Shaffer and her associates recently collected multisource data from 324 expatriates in 46 countries and found that the amount of organizational support that an expatriate feels he or she is receiving and the interplay between the person's work and family domains have a direct and unique influence on the individual's intentions regarding staying with or leaving the enterprise.[50] For this reason, some firms interview both the spouse and the manager before deciding whether to approve the assignment. This can be a very important decision for the firm because it focuses on the importance of family as a critical issue to a successful assignment. One popular approach in appraising the family's suitability for an overseas assignment is called **adaptability screening**. This process evaluates how well the family is likely to stand up to the rigors and stress of overseas life. The company will look for a number of things in this screening, including how closely knit the family is, how well it can withstand stress, and how well it can adjust to a new culture and climate. The reason this family criterion receives so much attention is that MNCs have learned that an unhappy executive will be unproductive on the job and the individual will want to transfer home long before the tour of duty is complete. These findings were affirmed and extended by Borstorff and her associates, who examined the factors associated with employee willingness to work overseas and concluded that

adaptability screening
The process of evaluating how well a family is likely to stand up to the stress of overseas life.

1. Unmarried employees are more willing than any other group to accept expat assignments.
2. Married couples without children at home or those with non-teenage children are probably the most willing to move.
3. Prior international experience appears associated with willingness to work as an expatriate.
4. Individuals most committed to their professional careers and to their employing organizations are prone to be more willing to work as expatriates.
5. Careers and attitudes of spouses will likely have a significant impact on employee willingness to move overseas.
6. Employee and spouse perceptions of organizational support for expatriates are critical to employee willingness to work overseas.[51]

Table 14–2
Activities That Are Important for Expatriate Spouses
(scale: 1–5, 5 = Very important)

Mean Score	Activity
Average from All Respondents	
4.33	Company help in obtaining necessary paperwork (permits, etc.) for spouse
4.28	Adequate notice of relocation
4.24	Predeparture training for spouse and children
4.23	Counseling for spouse regarding work/activity opportunities in foreign location
4.05	Employment networks coordinated with other international networks
3.97	Help with spouse's reentry into home country
3.93	Financial support for education
3.76	Compensation for spouse's lost wages and/or benefits
3.71	Creation of a job for spouse
3.58	Development of support groups for spouses
3.24	Administrative support (office space, secretarial services, etc.) for spouse
3.11	Financial support for research
3.01	Financial support for volunteer activities
2.90	Financial support for creative activities
Average from Male Spouses	
4.86	Employment networks coordinated with other international organizations
4.71	Help with spouse's reentry into home country
4.71	Administrative support (office space, secretarial services, etc.) for spouse
4.57	Compensation for spouse's lost wages and/or benefits
4.29	Adequate notice of relocation
4.29	Counseling for spouse regarding work/activity opportunities in foreign location
3.86	Predeparture training for spouse and children
3.71	Creation of a job for spouse
3.71	Financial support for volunteer activities
3.43	Financial support for education
3.14	Financial support for research
3.14	Financial support for creative activities
3.00	Development of support groups for spouses

Source: Adapted from Betty Jane Punnett, "Towards Effective Management of Expatriate Spouses," *Journal of World Business* 33, no. 3 (1997), p. 249.

These findings indicate that organizations cannot afford to overlook the role of the spouse in the expat selection decision process. What, in particular, can be done to address their concerns?[52] Table 14–2 provides some insights into this answer. Additionally, the table adds a factor often overlooked in this process—situations in which the wife is being assigned overseas and the husband is the "other" spouse. Although many of the concerns of the male spouse are similar to those of spouses in general, a close look at Table 14–2 shows that some of the concerns of the males are different in their rank ordering.

Leadership Ability

The ability to influence people to act in a particular way—leadership—is another important criterion in selecting managers for an international assignment. Determining whether a person who is an effective leader in the home country will be equally effective in an overseas environment can be difficult, however. When determining whether an applicant has the desired leadership ability, many firms look for specific characteristics, such as maturity, emotional stability, the ability to communicate well, independence, initiative, creativity, and good health. If these characteristics are present and the person has been an effective leader in the home country, MNCs assume that the individual also will do well overseas.

Other Considerations

Applicants also can take certain steps to prepare themselves better for international assignments. Tu and Sullivan suggest the applicant can carry out a number of different phases of preparation.[53] In phase one, they suggest focusing on self-evaluation and general awareness. This includes answering the question, Is an international assignment really for me? Other questions in the first phase include finding out if one's spouse and family support the decision to go international and collecting general information on the available job opportunities.

Phase two is characterized by a concentration on activities that should be completed before a person is selected. Some of these include (1) conducting a technical skills match to ensure that one's skills are in line with those that are required for the job; (2) starting to learn the language, customs, and etiquette of the region where one will be posted; (3) developing an awareness of the culture and value systems of this geographic area; and (4) making one's superior aware of this interest in an international assignment.

The third phase consists of activities to be completed after being selected for an overseas assignment. Some of these include (1) attending training sessions provided by the company; (2) conferring with colleagues who have had experience in the assigned region; (3) speaking with expatriates and foreign nationals about the assigned country; and (4) if possible, visiting the host country with one's spouse before the formally scheduled departure.

■ Economic Pressures and Trends in Expat Assignments

Despite the economic stagnation in many markets across the globe, most MNCs continue to make overseas assignments. A 2015 survey of 143 MNCs, conducted by Brookfield Global Relocation Services, found that 95 percent of all international assignments were successful. Additionally, the companies surveyed appeared optimistic about their global business outlook, with nearly 90 percent stating that they anticipated increasing or holding steady their number of international assignments. The most commonly cited objective of expatriate assignments was filling a managerial or technical gap (49 percent), though career development and local relationship building were also mentioned by many employers as intended goals. Employees also reported strong benefits from international assignments, including faster promotions, higher pay, stronger performance ratings, and more mobility within the company upon assignment completion.[54]

Despite the relatively high reported success rate, international assignments can fail. More often, employees reject expatriate opportunities when they arise. Not surprisingly, issues relating to employees' families were cited as the most common reasons for assignment refusal. In total, 38 percent of those surveyed stated that family concerns were their primary reason for assignment refusal. Another 17 percent indicated that their spouse's career was their number one reason to reject an overseas assignment. When asked about overcoming the challenges that their expatriate programs faced, 40 percent of employers responded that helping employees overcome family adjustment issues was "very critical." Overcoming educational challenges faced by employees' children was rated equally as high. If employers are aiming to decrease assignment rejection due to family concerns, they may need to improve the familial benefits that they provide. For example, of the employers surveyed, only eight percent provided assistance to help support elderly family members while employees were away on assignment. Additionally, less than half of the companies surveyed offered any kind of spousal support in the areas of obtaining a work permit, providing employment search services, assisting with education, or identifying local support networks.[55]

International assignments can be incredibly expensive. Three-quarters of the companies survey in 2015 stated that they were facing increasing pressure to reduce the overall cost of their expatriate programs. Part of this pressure may be due to the fact that traditional financial metrics, such as return on investment, are not utilized by the overwhelming majority of companies when evaluating the success or failure of their overseas program. The primary objectives of most international assignments are not directly profit-based, and more than half of the employers surveyed indicated that return on investment would be difficult to quantify. Other findings from the survey included

- 19 percent of expatriates were women.
- 71 percent of expatriates were 30 to 49 years old.
- 74 percent of expatriates were married, higher than the 66 percent historical average.
- 52 percent of expatriates had children accompanying them.
- Spouses and partners accompanied 80 percent of expatriates, representing a slight decrease over the last decade.
- Nearly half of the spouses were employed before an assignment but not during it. Only four percent were employed during an assignment but not before; 11 percent were employed both before and during the assignment.
- 56 percent of expatriates were relocated to or from the headquarters country, and nearly two-thirds were relocated to a country outside of their region.
- The United States, China, and the United Kingdom were the most frequently cited locations for expatriate assignments.
- Brazil, China, and the U.A.E. were the primary emerging destinations.
- China, India, and the United Kingdom were cited as the locations with the highest assignment failure rates.[56]

■ International Human Resource Selection Procedures

MNCs use a number of selection procedures. The two most common are tests and interviews. Some international firms use one; a smaller percentage employ both. Theoretical models containing the variables that are important for adjusting to an overseas assignment have been developed. These adjustment models can help contribute to more effective selection of expatriates. The following sections examine traditional testing and interviewing procedures and then present an adjustment model.

Testing and Interviewing Procedures

Some evidence suggests that although some firms use testing, it is not extremely popular. For example, an early study found that almost 80 percent of the 127 foreign operations managers who were surveyed reported that their companies used no tests in the selection process.[57] This contrasts with the more widespread testing that these firms use when selecting domestic managers. Many MNCs report that the costs, questionable accuracy, and poor predictive record make testing of limited value.

Many firms do use interviews to screen people for overseas assignments. One expert notes: "It is generally agreed that extensive interviews of candidates (and their spouses) by senior executives still ultimately provide the best method of selection."[58] Tung's research supports these comments. For example, 52 percent of the U.S. MNCs she surveyed reported that in the case of managerial candidates, MNCs conducted interviews with both the manager and his or her spouse, and 47 percent conducted interviews with the candidate alone. Concerning these findings, Tung concluded:

> These figures suggest that in management-type positions which involve more extensive contact with the local community, as compared to technically oriented positions, the adaptability of the spouse to living in a foreign environment was perceived as important for successful performance abroad. However, even for technically oriented positions, a sizable proportion of the firms did conduct interviews with both candidate and spouse. This lends support to the contention of other researchers that MNCs are becoming increasingly cognizant of the importance of this factor to effective performance abroad.[59]

The Adjustment Process

In recent years, international human resource management specialists have developed models that help to explain the factors involved in effectively adjusting to overseas assignments.[60,61] These adjustment models help to identify the underpinnings of the effective selection of expatriates.

There are two major types of adjustments that an expatriate must make when going on an overseas assignment: anticipatory and in-country adjustments. Anticipatory adjustment is carried out before the expat leaves for the assignment and is influenced by a number of important factors. One factor is the pre-departure training that is provided. This often takes the form of cross-cultural seminars or workshops, and it is designed to acquaint expats with the culture and work life of the country to which they will be posted. Another factor affecting anticipatory adjustment is the previous experience the expat may have had with the assigned country or with countries with similar cultures. The organizational input into anticipatory adjustment is most directly related and concerned with the selection process. Traditionally, MNCs relied on only one important selection criterion for overseas assignments: technical competence. Obviously, technical competence is important, but it is only one of a number of skills that will be needed. If the MNC concentrates only on technical competence as a selection criterion, then it is not properly preparing the expatriate managers for successful adjustment in overseas assignments. As a result, expats are going to go abroad believing that they are prepared to deal with the challenges awaiting them, and they will be wrong.

In-country adjustment takes place once the expatriate is on site, and a number of factors will influence his or her ability to adjust effectively. One factor is the expat's ability to maintain a positive outlook in the face of a high-pressure situation, to interact well with host nationals, and to perceive and evaluate the host country's cultural values and norms correctly. A second factor is the job itself, as reflected by the clarity of the role the expat plays in the host management team, the authority the expat has to make decisions, the newness of the work-related challenges, and the amount of role conflict that exists. A third factor is the organizational culture and how easily the expat can adjust to it. A fourth is nonwork matters, such as the toughness with which the expatriate faces a whole new cultural experience and how well his or her family can adjust to the rigors of the new assignment. A fifth and final factor identified in the adjustment model is the expat's ability to develop effective socialization tactics and to understand "what's what" and "who's who" in the host organization.

Another model of expatriate adjustment emphasized the formation of network ties in the host country to obtain critical informational and emotional support resources, proposing a five-stage process model that delineates how expatriates form adjustment-facilitating support ties in a culturally unfamiliar context. These include

- Stage 1: Factors influencing expatriates' motivation to seek support from actors in the host country.
- Stage 2: Factors influencing expatriates' selection of and support seeking toward actors.
- Stage 3: Factors influencing contacted actors' ability and willingness to provide support.
- Stage 4: Factors influencing expatriates' utilization of received support.
- Stage 5: Factors influencing expatriates' addition of actors to network.[62]

These anticipatory and in-country factors will influence the expatriate's mode and degree of adjustment to an overseas assignment. They can help to explain why effective selection of expatriates is multifaceted and can be very difficult and challenging. But if all works out well, the individual can become a very important part of the organization's overseas operations. McCormick and Chapman illustrated this by showing the changes

Figure 14–3

The Relocation Transition Curve

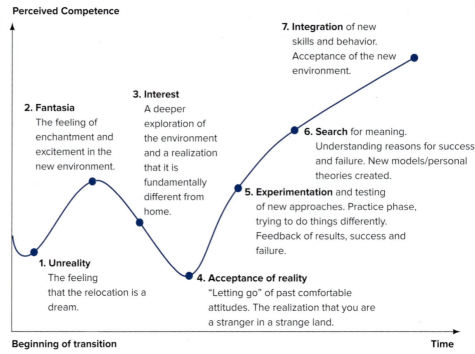

Perceived Competence

7. Integration of new skills and behavior. Acceptance of the new environment.

2. Fantasia
The feeling of enchantment and excitement in the new environment.

3. Interest
A deeper exploration of the environment and a realization that it is fundamentally different from home.

6. Search for meaning. Understanding reasons for success and failure. New models/personal theories created.

5. Experimentation and testing of new approaches. Practice phase, trying to do things differently. Feedback of results, success and failure.

1. Unreality
The feeling that the relocation is a dream.

4. Acceptance of reality
"Letting go" of past comfortable attitudes. The realization that you are a stranger in a strange land.

Beginning of transition   **Time**

Source: Adapted from Iain McCormick and Tony Chapman, "Executive Relocation: Personal and Organizational Tactics," in *Managing Across Cultures: Issues and Perspectives*, ed. Pat Joynt and Malcolm Warner (London: International Thomson Business Press, 1996), p. 368.

that an expat goes through as he or she seeks to adjust to the new assignment.[63] As seen in Figure 14–3, early enthusiasm often gives way to cold reality, and the expat typically ends up in a search to balance personal and work demands with the new environment. In many cases, fortunately, everything works out well. Additionally, one of the ways in which MNCs often try to put potential expats at ease about their new assignment is by presenting an attractive compensation package.

■ Compensation

One of the reasons there has been a decline in the number of expats in recent years is that MNCs have found that the expense can be prohibitive. Reynolds estimated that, on average, "expats cost employers two to five times as much as home-country counterparts and frequently ten or more times as much as local nationals in the country to which they are assigned."[64] As seen in Figure 14–4, the cost of living in some of the major cities is extremely high, and these expenses must be included somewhere in the compensation package.

The recession of the late 2000s placed additional pressure on firms to control costs associated with expatriate assignments. Mercer reported in 2009 that nearly 40 percent of MNCs were planning on revising their current international assignment policy in the face of declining corporate growth and profitability, as well as an uncertain economic environment. The increasing trend toward localization reflects companies' efforts to either tap into the local talents or to offer less generous packages to locally hired foreign workers. This localization approach was quite consistent among regions and countries around the world, including for companies operating in emerging markets (such as China, India, and Vietnam), where the local compensation and benefits packages are less generous than home-country plans. In terms of expatriate benefits and allowances, the elements that are least likely to be eliminated for localized employees are housing allowances and education benefits. Mercer did find that localization is practiced in Europe and in

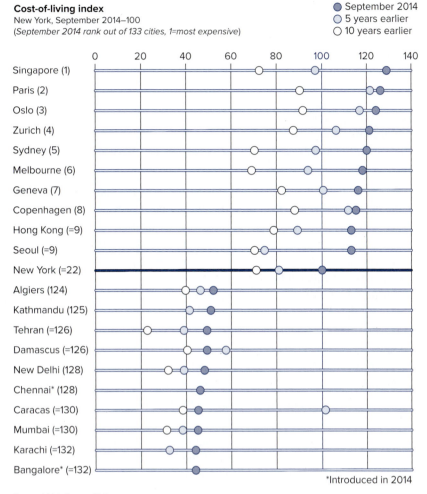

Cost-of-living index
New York, September 2014–100
(*September 2014 rank out of 133 cities, 1=most expensive*)

● September 2014
○ 5 years earlier
○ 10 years earlier

Figure 14–4

Cost-of-Living Index

*Introduced in 2014

Source: Economist Intelligence Unit.

North America more than in Latin America and Asia Pacific. In recent years, however, localization has picked up in the Asia Pacific region, particularly as companies want to tap into the regional talent pool and contain costs.[65]

Common Elements of Compensation Packages

The overall compensation package often varies from country to country. As Bailey noted:

> Compensation programs implemented in a global organization will not mirror an organization's domestic plan because of differences in legally mandated benefits, tax laws, cultures, and employee expectation based on local practices. The additional challenge in compensation design is the requirement that excessive costs be avoided and at the same time employee morale be maintained at high levels.[66]

There are five common elements in the typical expatriate compensation package: base salary, benefits, allowances, incentives, and taxes.

Base Salary   Base salary is the amount of money that an expatriate normally receives in the home country. In the United States, this has often been in the range of $200,000–$300,000 for upper-middle managers in recent years, and this rate is similar to that paid to managers in both Japan and Germany. The exchange rates, of course, also affect the real wages.

Expatriate salaries typically are set according to the base pay of the home countries. Therefore, a German manager working for a U.S. MNC and assigned to Spain would have a base salary that reflects the salary structure in Germany. U.S. expatriates have salaries tied to U.S. levels. The salaries usually are paid in home currency, local currency, or a combination of the two. The base pay also serves as the benchmark against which bonuses and benefits are calculated.

Benefits Approximately one-third of compensation for regular employees is benefits. These benefits compose a similar, or even larger, portion of expat compensation. A number of thorny issues surround compensation for expatriates, however. These include

1. Whether MNCs should maintain expatriates in home-country benefit programs, particularly if these programs are not tax-deductible.
2. Whether MNCs have the option of enrolling expatriates in host-country benefit programs or making up any difference in coverage.
3. Whether host-country legislation regarding termination of employment affects employee benefits entitlements.
4. Whether the home or host country is responsible for the expatriates' social security benefits.
5. Whether benefits should be subject to the requirements of the home or host country.
6. Which country should pay for the benefits.
7. Whether other benefits should be used to offset any shortfall in coverage.
8. Whether home-country benefits programs should be available to local nationals.

Most U.S.-based MNCs include expatriate managers in their home-office benefits program at no additional cost to the expats. If the host country requires expats to contribute to their social security program, the MNC typically picks up the tab. Fortunately, several international agreements between countries recently have eliminated such dual coverage and expenses.

Additionally, MNCs often provide expatriates with extra vacation and with special leaves. The MNC typically will pay the airfare for expats and their families to make an annual visit home, for emergency leave, and for expenses when a relative in the home country is ill or dies.

Allowances Allowances are an expensive feature of expatriate compensation packages. One of the most common parts is a cost-of-living allowance—a payment for differences between the home country and the overseas assignment. This allowance is designed to provide the expat with the same standard of living that he or she enjoyed in the home country, and it may cover a variety of expenses, including relocation, housing, education, and hardship.

Relocation expenses typically involve moving, shipping, and storage charges that are associated with personal furniture, clothing, and other items that the expatriate and his or her family are (or are not) taking to the new assignment. Related expenses also may include cars and club memberships in the host country, although these perks commonly are provided only to senior-level expats.

Housing allowances cover a wide range. Some firms provide the expat with a residence during the assignment and pay all associated expenses. Others give a predetermined housing allotment each month and let expats choose their own residence. Additionally, some MNCs help those going on assignment with the sale or lease of the house they are leaving behind; if the house is sold, the company usually pays closing costs and other associated expenses.

Education allowances for the expat's children are another integral part of the compensation package. These expenses cover costs such as tuition, enrollment fees, books, supplies, transportation, room, board, and school uniforms. In some cases, expenses to attend postsecondary schools also are covered.

Hardship allowances are designed to induce expats to work in hazardous areas or in an area with a poor quality of life. Those who are assigned to Eastern Europe, China, and some Middle Eastern countries sometimes are granted a hardship premium. These payments may be in the form of a lump sum ($10,000 to $50,000) or a percentage (15 to 50 percent) of the expat's base compensation.

Incentives In recent years, some MNCs have also been designing special incentive programs for keeping expats motivated. In the process, a growing number of firms have dropped the ongoing premium for overseas assignments and replaced it with a one-time, lump-sum premium. For example, in the early 1990s, over 60 percent of MNCs gave ongoing premiums to their expats. Today that percentage is under 50 percent and continuing to decline. Peterson and his colleagues, for example, examined the human resource policies of 24 U.S., British, German, and Japanese subsidiaries and found that in only 10 of the cases did the multinational have a policy of paying expatriates higher compensation than they would have received if they had stayed in their home country.[67]

The lump-sum payment has a number of benefits. One is that expats realize that they will be given this payment just once—when they move to the international locale. So the payment tends to retain its value as an incentive. A second is that the costs to the company are less because there is only one payment and no future financial commitment. A third is that because it is a separate payment, distinguishable from regular pay, it is more readily available for saving or spending.

The specific incentive program that is used will vary, and expats like this. Researchers, for example, have found that some of the factors that influence the type and amount of incentive include whether the person is moving within or between continents and where the person is being stationed. Table 14–3 provides some of the latest survey information related to worldwide employer incentive practices.

Finally, it is important to recognize that growing numbers of MNCs are beginning to phase out incentive premiums. Instead, they are focusing on creating a cadre of expats who are motivated by nonfinancial incentives.

Taxes Another major component of expatriate compensation is tax equalization. For example, an expat may have two tax bills, one from the host country and one from the

---

Table 14–3
Employer Incentive Practices around the World

Percent of MNCs Paying for Moves within Continents				
Type of Premium	**Asia**	**Europe**	**North America**	**Total**
Ongoing	62%	46%	29%	42%
Lump sum	21	20	25	23
None	16	27	42	32
Percent of MNCs Paying for Moves between Continents				
Type of Premium	**Asia**	**Europe**	**North America**	**Total**
Ongoing	63%	54%	39%	49%
Lump sum	24	18	30	26
None	13	21	27	22

Source: Derived from Geoffrey W. Latta, "Expatriate Incentives: Beyond Tradition," *HR Focus*, March 1998, p. S4.

U.S. Internal Revenue Service, for the same pay. IRS Code Section 911 permits a deduction of up to $100,800 on foreign-earned income. Top-level expats often earn far more than this, however; thus, they may pay two tax bills for the amount by which their pay exceeds $100,800.

Usually, MNCs pay the extra tax burden. The most common way is by determining the base salary and other extras (e.g., bonuses) that the expat would make if based in the home country. Taxes on this income then are computed and compared with the taxes due on the expat's income. Any taxes that exceed what would have been imposed in the home country are paid by the MNC, and any windfall is kept by the expat as a reward for taking the assignment.

Tailoring the Package

Working within the five common elements just described, MNCs will tailor compensation packages to fit the specific situation. For example, senior-level managers in Japan are paid only around four times as much as junior staff members. This is in sharp contrast to the United States, where the multiple is much higher. A similar situation exists in Europe, where many senior-level managers make far less than their U.S. counterparts and stockholders, politicians, and the general public oppose U.S.-style affluence. Can a senior-level U.S. expat be paid a salary that is significantly higher than local senior-level managers in the overseas subsidiary, or would the disparity create morale problems? This is a difficult question to answer and must be given careful consideration. One solution is to link pay and performance to attract and retain outstanding personnel.

In formulating the compensation package, a number of approaches can be used. The most common is the **balance-sheet approach**, which involves ensuring that the expat is "made whole" and does not lose money by taking the assignment. A second and often complementary approach is negotiation, which involves working out a special, ad hoc arrangement that is acceptable to both the company and the expat. A third approach, **localization**, involves paying the expat a salary that is comparable to the salaries of local nationals. This approach most commonly is used with individuals early in their careers who are being given a long-term overseas assignment. A fourth approach is the **lump-sum method**, which involves giving the expat a predetermined amount of money and letting the individual make his or her own decisions regarding how to spend it. A fifth is the **cafeteria approach**, which entails giving expats a series of options and letting them decide how to spend the available funds. For example, expats who have children may opt for private schooling; expats who have no children may choose a chauffeur-driven car or an upscale apartment. A sixth method is the **regional system**, under which the MNC sets a compensation system for all expats who are assigned to a particular region, so that (for example) everyone going to Europe falls under one particular system and everyone being assigned to South America is covered by a different system.[68,69] The most important thing to remember about global compensation is that the package must be cost-effective and fair. If it meets these two criteria, it likely will be acceptable to all parties.

As a result of the 2008–2010 recession, many companies are making changes to their expatriate staffing and compensation practices. While many companies have developed short-term assignment and business-travel policies to more efficiently fill their staffing needs, more comprehensive measures, such as shifting home-country employees working in foreign locations from expatriate to "local plus" packages, are becoming more common.[70] Participants in two surveys by HR consultancy ORC Worldwide—Survey on Local-Plus Packages in Hong Kong and Singapore and Survey on Local-Plus Packages for Expatriates in China—report a growing trend toward expatriate "light" or "local-plus" packages. "These alternative packages often base the assignee's salary on host country pay structures," says Phil Stanley, managing director of ORC Worldwide's Asia-Pacific region, "but then tack on a few expatriate type benefits, such as some form of housing assistance and possibly an allowance to partially cover children's education."[71]

balance-sheet approach
An approach to developing an expatriate compensation package that ensures the expat is "made whole" and does not lose money by taking the assignment.

localization
An approach to developing an expatriate compensation package that involves paying the expat a salary comparable to that of local nationals.

lump-sum method
An approach to developing an expatriate compensation package that involves giving the expat a predetermined amount of money and letting the individual make his or her own decisions regarding how to spend it.

cafeteria approach
An approach to developing an expatriate compensation package that entails giving the individual a series of options and letting the person decide how to spend the available funds.

regional system
An approach to developing an expatriate compensation package that involves setting a compensation system for all expats who are assigned to a particular region and paying everyone in accord with that system.

■ Individual and Host-Country Viewpoints

Until now, we have examined the selection process mostly from the standpoint of the MNC: What will be best for the company? However, two additional perspectives for selection warrant consideration: (1) that of the individual who is being selected and (2) that of the country to which the candidate will be sent. Research shows that each has specific desires and motivations regarding the expatriate selection process.

Candidate Motivations

Why do individuals accept foreign assignments? One answer is a greater demand for their talents abroad than at home. For example, a growing number of senior U.S. managers have moved to Mexico because of Mexico's growing need for experienced executives. The findings of one early study grouped the participating countries into clusters: Anglo (Australia, Austria, Canada, India, New Zealand, South Africa, Switzerland, United Kingdom, and United States); Northern European (Denmark, Finland, Norway); French (Belgium and France); Northern South American (Colombia, Mexico, and Peru); Southern South American (Argentina and Chile); and Independent (Brazil, Germany, Israel, Japan, Sweden, and Venezuela).[72] Within these groupings, researchers were able to identify major motivational differences. Some of their findings included

1. The Anglo cluster was more interested in individual achievement and less interested in the desire for security than any other cluster.

2. The French cluster was similar to the Anglo cluster, except that less importance was given to individual achievement and more to security.

3. Countries in the Northern European cluster were more oriented to job accomplishment and less to getting ahead; considerable importance was assigned to jobs not interfering with personal lives.

4. In South American clusters, individual achievement goals were less important than in most other clusters. Fringe benefits were particularly important to South American groups.

5. Germans were similar to those in the South American clusters, except that they placed a greater emphasis on advancement and earnings.

6. The Japanese were unique in their mix of desires. They placed high value on earnings opportunities but low value on advancement. They were high on challenge but low on autonomy. At the same time, they placed strong emphasis on working in a friendly, efficient department and having good physical working conditions.

Another interesting focus of attention has been on those countries that expatriates like best. A study conducted by Ingemar Torbiorn found that the 1,100 Swedish expatriates surveyed were at least fairly well satisfied with their host country and in some cases were very satisfied. Five of the countries that they liked very much were Switzerland, Belgium, England, the United States, and Portugal.[73] These countries are still popular today, which makes sense because they are included in the top tier of countries with the highest quality of life. The criteria include such things as family life, economic life, unemployment rates, political stability, and so forth to determine how safe or attractive the country is.

Host-Country Desires

Although many MNCs try to choose people who fit in well, little attention has been paid to the host country's point of view. Whom would it like to see put in managerial positions? One study that compared U.S., Indonesian, and Mexican managers found that

Figure 14–5

Comparative Positive Managerial Behavior by Country

Source: Original graphic by Ben Littell under supervision of Professor Jonathan Doh based on data from Charles M. Vance and Yongsun Paik, "One Size Fits All in Expatriate Pre-departure Training? Comparing the Host Country Voices of Mexican, Indonesian and U.S. Workers," *Journal of Management Development* 21, No. 7–8 (2002), p. 566.

behaviors can distinguish them from one another and that host countries would prefer a managerial style similar to that of their country.[74] For example, positive managerial behaviors, such as honesty and follow-through with employees, distinguish Indonesian and U.S. managers from Mexican managers. As seen in Chapter 4, this could partially be due to the power distance suggested by Hofstede. Furthermore, negative managerial behaviors, such as public criticism and discipline toward employees, also distinguish Indonesian and U.S. managers from Mexican managers. It has been suggested that the dynamic in the workplace has to do with the familial structure, namely that Mexican workers place a higher value on family over work than do their U.S. or Indonesian counterparts. This can be a factor in how the positive and negative behaviors are expressed in each country, as outlined in Figures 14–5 and 14–6. Overall, it is important for managers to take the host-country perspectives into consideration, or it could result in an ineffectual endeavor.

Figure 14–6

Comparative Negative Managerial Behavior by Country

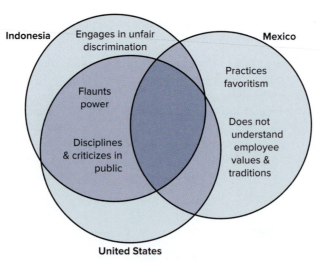

Source: Original graphic by Ben Littell under supervision of Professor Jonathan Doh based on data from Charles M. Vance and Yongsun Paik, "One Size Fits All in Expatriate Pre-departure Training? Comparing the Host Country Vices of Mexican, Indonesian and U.S. Workers," *Journal of Management Development* 21, No. 7–8 (2002), p. 566.

■ Repatriation of Expatriates

For most overseas managers, **repatriation**, the return to one's home country, occurs within five years of the time they leave. Few expatriates remain overseas for the duration of their stay with the firm.[75] When they return, these expatriates often find themselves facing readjustment problems, and some MNCs are trying to deal with these problems through use of transition strategies.

repatriation
The return to one's home country from an overseas management assignment.

Reasons for Returning

The most common reason that expatriates return home from overseas assignments is that their formally agreed-on tour of duty is over. Before they left, the expatriates were told that they would be posted overseas for a predetermined period, often two to three years, and they are returning as planned. This is considered a successfully completed assignment. According to a 2015 study by Brookfield Global Relocation Services, 94 percent of all expatriate assignments were completed as intended.[76]

Though infrequent, early returns do occur. The most common reason, accounting for 23 percent of all terminated assignments, is family concerns. This encompasses a variety of issues common to many expatriate families, including spouses who have difficulty acclimating to a new culture and expatriates who want their children educated in a home-country school.[77] The second most common reason for expatriates to return early is due to company restructuring. Business opportunities change rapidly, and the usefulness of an overseas assignment might decline if a company changes strategy. In these instances, the expatriate may have had every intent on staying and completing his or her full assignment. Per Brookfield Global Relocation Services, this accounts for about 19 percent of all early returns.[78]

Common fears that many expatriates and their families have before embarking on an overseas assignment rarely pose an issue once the expatriate arrives in the host country. For example, only 3 percent of all failed assignments were due to security concerns, and just 5 percent of expatriates faced cultural challenges that resulted in an early leave. Over the last several decades, MNCs have continually improved their selection process of suitable employees for expatriate experiences; as a result, the overwhelming majority of international assignments succeed.[79]

Readjustment Problems

Many companies that say they want their people to have international experience often seem unsure of what to do with these managers when they return. One recent survey of midsize and large firms found that 80 percent of these companies send people abroad and more than half of them intend to increase the number they have on assignment overseas. However, responses from returning expats point to problems. Three-quarters of the respondents said that they felt their permanent position upon returning home was a demotion. Over 60 percent said that they lacked the opportunities to put their foreign experience to work, and 60 percent said that their company had not communicated clearly about what would happen to them when they returned. Perhaps worst of all, within a year of returning, 25 percent of the managers had left the company.[80] These statistics are not surprising to those who have been studying repatriation problems. In fact, one researcher reported the following expatriate comments about their experiences:

> My colleagues react indifferently to my international assignment. . . . They view me as doing a job I did in the past; they don't see me as having gained anything while overseas.
>
> I had no specific reentry job to return to. I wanted to leave international and return to domestic. Working abroad magnifies problems while isolating effects. You deal with more problems, but the home office doesn't know the details of the good or bad effects. Managerially, I'm out of touch.
>
> I'm bored at work. . . . I run upstairs to see what [another returning colleague] is doing. He says, "Nothing." Me, too.[81]

Other readjustment problems are more personal in nature. Many expatriates find that the salary and fringe benefits to which they have become accustomed in the foreign assignment now are lost, and adjusting to this lower standard of living is difficult. In addition, those who sold their houses and now must buy new ones find that the monthly cost often is much higher than when they left. The children often are placed in public schools, where classes are much larger than in the overseas private schools. Many also miss the cultural lifestyles, as in the case of an executive who is transferred from Paris, France, to a medium-sized city in the United States, or from any developed country to an underdeveloped country. Additionally, many returning expatriates have learned that their international experiences are not viewed as important. Many Japanese expatriates, for example, report that when they return, their experiences should be downplayed if they want to "fit in" with the organization. In fact, reports one recent *New York Times* article, a substantial number of Japanese expatriates "are happier overseas than they are back home."[82]

Other research supports the findings noted here and offers operative recommendations for action. Based on questionnaires completed by 174 respondents who had been repatriated from four large U.S. MNCs, Black found the following:

1. With few exceptions, individuals whose expectations were met had the most positive levels of repatriation adjustment and job performance.

2. In the case of high-level managers in particular, expatriates whose job demands were greater, rather than less, than expected reported high levels of repatriation adjustment and job performance. Those having greater job demands may have put in more effort and had better adjustment and performance.

3. Job performance and repatriation adjustment were greater for individuals whose job constraint expectations were undermet than for those individuals whose expectations were overmet. In other words, job constraints were viewed as an undesirable aspect of the job, and having them turn out to be less than expected was a pleasant surprise that helped adjustment and performance.

4. When living and housing conditions turned out to be better than expected, general repatriation adjustment and job performance were better.

5. Individuals whose general expectations were met or overmet had job evaluations that placed them 10 percent higher than those whose general expectations were unmet.[83]

Transition Strategies

To help smooth the adjustment from an overseas to a stateside assignment, some MNCs have developed **transition strategies**, which can take a number of different forms. One is the use of **repatriation agreements**, whereby the firm tells an individual how long she or he will be posted overseas and promises to give the individual, on return, a job that is mutually acceptable. This agreement typically does not promise a specific position or salary, but the agreement may state that the person will be given a job that is equal to, if not better than, the one held before leaving.[84]

Some firms also rent or otherwise maintain expatriates' homes until they return. The Aluminum Company of America and Union Carbide both have such plans for managers going overseas. This plan helps reduce the financial shock that often accompanies home shopping by returning expatriates. A third strategy is to use senior executives as sponsors of managers abroad.

Still another approach is to keep expatriate managers apprised of what is going on at corporate headquarters and to plug these managers into projects at the home office whenever they are on leave in the home country. This helps maintain the person's visibility and ensures the individual is looked on as a regular member of the management staff.

One study surveyed 99 employees and managers with international experience in 21 corporations.[85] The findings reveal that cultural reentry, financial implications, and the nature of job assignments are three major areas of expatriate concern. In particular, some of the main problems of repatriation identified in this study include (1) adjusting to life back home, (2) facing a financial package that is not as good as that overseas, (3) having less autonomy in the stateside job than in the overseas position, and (4) not receiving any career counseling from the company. To the extent that the MNC can address these types of problems, the transition will be smooth, and the expatriate's performance effectiveness once home will increase quickly. Some additional steps suggested by experts in this area include

1. Arrange an event to welcome and recognize the employee and family, either formally or informally.
2. Establish support to facilitate family reintegration.
3. Offer repatriation counseling or workshops to ease the adjustment.
4. Assist the spouse with job counseling, résumé writing, and interviewing techniques.
5. Provide educational counseling for the children.
6. Provide the employee with a thorough debriefing by a facilitator to identify new knowledge, insights, and skills and to provide a forum to showcase new competencies.
7. Offer international outplacement to the employee and reentry counseling to the entire family if no positions are possible.
8. Arrange a postassignment interview with the expatriate and spouse to review their view of the assignment and address any repatriation issues.[86]

Hammer and his associates echo these types of recommendations. Based on research that they conducted in two multinational corporations among expats and their spouses, they concluded:

> The findings from the present study suggest that one of the key transitional activities for returning expatriates and their spouses from a corporate context should involve targeted communication from the home environment concerning the expectations of the home office toward the return of the repatriate executive and his/her family (role relationships). Further, reentry training should focus primarily on helping the repatriate manager and spouse align their expectations with the actual situation that will be encountered upon arrival in the home culture both within the organizational context as well as more broadly within the social milieu. To the degree that corporate communication and reentry training activities help the returning executive and spouse in expectation alignment, the executive's level of reentry satisfaction should be higher and the degree of reentry difficulties less.[87]

Additionally, in recent years many MNCs have begun using inpatriates to supplement their home-office staff and some of the same issues discussed here with repatriation come into play.

■ Training in International Management

Training is the process of altering employee behavior and attitudes in a way that increases the probability of goal attainment. Training is particularly important in preparing employees for overseas assignments because it helps ensure that their full potential will be tapped.[88,89,90] One of the things that training can do is to help expat managers better understand the customs, cultures, and work habits of the local culture. The simplest training, in terms of preparation time, is to place a cultural integrator in each foreign operation. This individual is responsible for ensuring that the operation's business systems are in accord with those of the local culture. The integrator advises, guides, and recommends actions needed to ensure this synchronization.[91]

Unfortunately, although using an integrator can help, it is seldom sufficient. Recent experience clearly reveals that in creating an effective global team, the MNC must

training
The process of altering employee behavior and attitudes in a way that increases the probability of goal attainment.

designed for the target audience. Some of the specific steps that well-designed cultural training programs follow include

1. Local instructors and a translator, typically someone who is bicultural, observe the pilot training program or examine written training materials.
2. The educational designer then debriefs the observation with the translator, curriculum writer, and local instructors.
3. Together, the group examines the structure and sequence, ice breaker, and other materials that will be used in the training.
4. The group then collectively identifies stories, metaphors, experiences, and examples in the culture that will fit into the new training program.
5. The educational designer and curriculum writer make the necessary changes in the training materials.
6. The local instructors are trained to use the newly developed materials.
7. After the designer, translator, and native-language trainers are satisfied, the materials are printed.
8. The language and content of the training materials are tested with a pilot group.[112]

In developing the instructional materials, culturally specific guidelines are carefully followed so that the training does not lose any of its effectiveness.[113] For example, inappropriate pictures or scenarios that might prove to be offensive to the audience must be screened out. Handouts and other instructional materials that are designed to enhance the learning process are provided for all participants. If the trainees are learning a second language, generous use of visuals and live demonstrations will be employed. Despite all these efforts, however, errors sometimes occur.

■ Cultural Assimilators

cultural assimilator
A programmed learning technique designed to expose members of one culture to some of the basic concepts, attitudes, role perceptions, customs, and values of another culture.

The cultural assimilator has become one of the most effective approaches to cross-cultural training. A **cultural assimilator** is a programmed learning technique that is designed to expose members of one culture to some of the basic concepts, attitudes, role perceptions, customs, and values of another culture. These assimilators are developed for each pair of cultures. For example, if an MNC is going to send three U.S. managers from Chicago to Caracas, a cultural assimilator would be developed to familiarize the three Americans with Venezuelan customs and cultures. If three Venezuelan managers from Caracas were to be transferred to Singapore, another assimilator would be developed to familiarize the managers with Singapore customs and cultures.

In most cases, these assimilators require the trainee to read a short episode of a cultural encounter and choose an interpretation of what has happened and why. If the trainee's choice is correct, he or she goes on to the next episode. If the response is incorrect, the trainee is asked to reread the episode and choose another response.

Choice of Content of the Assimilators   One of the major problems in constructing an effective cultural assimilator is deciding what is important enough to include. Some assimilators use critical incidents that are identified as being important. To be classified as a critical incident, a situation must meet at least one of the following conditions:

1. An expatriate and a host national interact in the situation.
2. The situation is puzzling or likely to be misinterpreted by the expatriate.
3. The situation can be interpreted accurately if sufficient knowledge about the culture is available.
4. The situation is relevant to the expatriate's task or mission requirements.[114]

These incidents typically are obtained by asking expatriates and host nationals with whom they come in contact to describe specific intercultural occurrences or events that made a major difference in their attitudes or behavior toward members of the other culture. These incidents can be pleasant, unpleasant, or simply nonunderstandable occurrences.

Validation of the Assimilator   The term **validity** refers to the quality of being effective, of producing the desired results. It means that an instrument—in this case, the cultural assimilator—measures what it is intended to measure. After the cultural assimilator's critical incidents are constructed and the alternative responses are written, the process is validated. Making sure that the assimilator is valid is the crux of its effectiveness. One way to test an assimilator is to draw a sample from the target culture and ask these people to read the scenarios that have been written, choosing the alternative they feel is most appropriate. If a large percentage of the group agrees that one of the alternatives is preferable, this scenario is used in the assimilator. If more than one of the four alternatives receives strong support, however, either the scenario or the alternatives are revised until there is general agreement or the scenario is dropped.

After the final incidents are chosen, they are sequenced in the assimilator booklet and can be put online to be taken electronically. Similar cultural concepts are placed together and presented, beginning with simple situations and progressing to more complex ones. Most cultural assimilator programs start out with 150 to 200 incidents, of which 75 to 100 eventually are included in the final product.

The Cost-Benefit Analysis of Assimilators   The assimilator approach to training can be quite expensive. A typical 75- to 100-incident program often requires approximately 800 hours to develop. Assuming that a training specialist is costing the company $50 an hour including benefits, the cost is around $40,000 per assimilator. This cost can be spread over many trainees, and the program may not need to be changed every year. An MNC that sends 40 people a year to a foreign country for which an assimilator has been constructed is paying only $200 per person for this programmed training. In the long run, the costs often are more than justified. In addition, the concept can be applied to nearly all cultures. Many different assimilators have been constructed, including Arab, Thai, Honduran, and Greek, to name but four. Most importantly, research shows that these assimilators improve the effectiveness and satisfaction of individuals being trained as compared with other training methods.

Positive Organizational Behavior

We discussed in Chapter 13 how leaders can increase motivation and morale if they focus on the positives, or strengths, of individuals. The positive internal traits of the leader, along with the other factors, tend to lead to consistent positive behaviors. Luthans has done extensive research on **positive organizational behavior (POB)**. He defines it as

> The study and application of positively oriented human resource strengths and psychological capacities that can be measured, developed, and effectively managed for performance improvement in today's workplace.[115]

Positivity in the workplace has been connected to employee satisfaction. The positive environment, however, consists of many layers. Luthans and Youssef postulated that in order for an organization to be the most efficient and innovative, it must have positive traits, states, and systems in order to promote positive behavior. The positive traits were covered in Chapter 13 and consist of conscientiousness, emotional stability, extroversion, agreeableness, openness to experience, core self-evaluations, and positive psychological traits. A positive state is domain-specific, and reactions and behaviors may change depending on the environment. Research has shown that other "states" are self-efficacy, hope, optimism, resiliency, and psychological capital.[116]

Finally, positive organizations focus on the selection, development, and management of human resources. This positive approach attempts to match employee skills and talents with organizational goals and expectations. When employees are treated well, they will be motivated to give back to the institution. Therefore, when these individual traits, internal and external states, and organizations all focus on the positive, the resulting organizational citizenship behavior (OCB) also will be positive. Furthermore, altruism, conscientiousness, and courtesy will be inadvertently emphasized.[117]

validity
The quality of being effective, of producing the desired results. A valid test or selection technique measures what it is intended to measure.

positive organizational behavior (POB)
The study and application of positively oriented human resource strengths and psychological capacities that can be measured, developed, and effectively managed for performance improvement in today's workplace.

As with most examples, the description above is culturally specific. That is, what seem to be positive internal or external factors in one country may not be the same in another. However, human resources are essential to an organization no matter its location, and MNCs should do all they can to focus on the power of human capital to drive organizational success.

■ Future Trends

The coming decades will be important and transformational ones for international human resources. The 2015 Brookfield Global Relocation Services survey concluded that several issues will emerge as critical for managing a global workforce. At the top of the list, according to Brookfield, will be the localization of expatriates. As the nature of temporary assignments evolves, companies and employees will be more closely scrutinizing the costs and benefits of the assignments.

Some companies are questioning the basic decision of supporting expensive international assignments. Employees are also questioning the personal and professional value of an overseas assignment, especially if such assignments have little influence in helping them to advance in their careers. Current industry estimates indicate that between 25 and 45 percent of employees leave the company within just one year of repatriation. "This is a key issue for global organizations, since this is a population of employees that they have invested so heavily in," Sullivan said. "Losing these employees represents a significant loss of experience and talent. Many of the companies we surveyed are beginning to see the integration of talent management and international assignment mobility as a strategy to turn this loss into a competitive gain."

Another trend is the emergence of "cross-border" commuters, employees who regularly move back and forth between countries. Commuter assignments, as an alternative to short-term (and even long-term) assignments, have begun to take a larger role, especially in Europe, given the deepening integration of the European Union and the resultant cross-border employee mobility. The report suggests this trend is likely to continue and accelerate.[118]

One of the most profound trends, first explored in Chapter 1 of this book, is the dramatic rise and growth of emerging markets. Brookfield's survey notes that emerging locations run the spectrum of countries from those that are long-time assignment destinations to those that are just this year appearing as locations for expatriate assignments. To some degree, this trend may offset the effects of the other trends, suggesting that although the particular structure and duration may evolve, expatriate assignments are likely to continue as part of the arsenal of MNCs seeking to leverage talent for global success.

The World of International Management—Revisited

The World of International Management that opened this chapter illustrated how the desire to source and retain talent has become a global phenomenon, affecting most major markets, including India. In a time of increased globalization, firms must be able to source talent from a range of locations. Given the increasing presence of foreign MNCs in India—and the dramatic growth of India's domestic offshore outsourcing sector—employee retention has become a critical issue. One interesting observation is that employees are motivated by intrinsic rewards that go beyond financial compensation. Attracting and retaining talent turns out be a complex process in which both financial and nonfinancial issues come into play.

As outlined in this chapter, MNCs are realizing the intense challenges associated with the selection, development, and training of international human resources. MNCs have a range of options when selecting employees for overseas assignments, and increasing numbers of tools and resources are available to help develop, train, and deploy those individuals. Human resource selection and development across cultures cannot be taken lightly. Firms that do not invest in their human resource processes will face additional costs related to poor labor relations, quality control, and other issues. Now that you have read the chapter and reflected back on the chapter's opening World of International Management about

Lessons in Global Leadership Development: The PWC Ulysses Program

PricewaterhouseCoopers (PwC), one of the "Final 4" global accounting firms, has for several years sent top midcareer talent to the developing world for eight-week service projects under its "Ulysses" Program. After the merger of Price Waterhouse and Coopers Lybrand in 1998, the combined firm decided it needed a new model for a global professional services organization. Executives recognized that global problems were not increasing or decreasing, but changing and reshaping, the way business is done. In response, the firm created "Project Ulysses" in 2001, which sends a number of emerging leaders each year to a developing nation for two and a half months to work on service projects and programs. The purpose is not only to aid those in need, but to develop leadership skills on an individual level by taking executives out of their comfort zone, on a team level by pairing two to three partners together from different nations, and on the organizational level by creating stakeholder networks on a much broader level. For a relatively modest investment—about $15,000 per person, plus salaries—Ulysses both tests the talent and expands the world view of the accounting firm's future leaders. Since the company started the program in 2000, it has attracted the attention of Johnson & Johnson, Cisco Systems, and other big companies considering their own programs.

The projects, which range from helping an ecotourism collective in Belize to AIDS work in Namibia and organic farming in Zambia, take the participants out of their comfort zone and force them to build upon their leadership skills in a new and challenging environment. The benefit of pairing partners from three different places is that they draw on their own cultures to make decisions. As one participant noted, "You realize that perhaps the way you see things isn't necessarily the best way." In 2003, PwC partner Tahir Ayub was assigned a consulting gig unlike anything he had done before. His job was helping village leaders in the Namibian outback grapple with their community's growing AIDS crisis. Faced with language barriers, cultural differences, and scant access to electricity, Ayub, 39, and two colleagues had to scrap their PowerPoint presentations in favor of a more low-tech approach: face-to-face discussion. The village chiefs learned that they needed to garner community support for programs to combat the disease, and Ayub learned an important lesson as well: Technology isn't always the answer. "You better put your beliefs and biases to one side and figure out new ways to look at things," he said.

Although traditional business education and training have historically focused on helping firms improve financial performance, increasingly, B-schools and training programs are adding social responsibility to their curriculum. Further, graduates are increasingly signaling they want to work for firms with a positive reputation for social responsibility and service. According to a *Wall Street Journal* article, top corporate executives are now pairing with MBA programs across the country to help students gain a better understanding of responsible global leadership. In fact, a recent study showed that 75 percent of Americans consider a company's commitment to social issues when deciding where to work, and that six out of ten employees wish their companies did more

to help globally. According to Liz Maw, executive director of Net Impact, a corporate nonprofit dedicated to social responsibility, "The companies most involved in corporate social responsibility are the ones that have already seen their bottom line and brand awareness increase."

While results are hard to quantify, PwC is convinced that the program works. All two dozen of the initial graduates are still working at the company. Half of them have been promoted, and most have new responsibilities. Just as important, all 24 people say they have a stronger commitment to PwC—in part because of the commitment the firm made to them and in part because of their new vision of the firm's values. Says global managing partner Willem Bröcker: "We get better partners from this exercise." The Ulysses Program is PwC's answer to one of the biggest challenges confronting professional services companies: identifying and training up-and-coming leaders who can find unconventional answers to intractable problems. By tradition and necessity, new PwC leaders are nurtured from within. With 8,000 partners, identifying those with the necessary business savvy and relationship-building skills isn't easy. But just as the program gives partners a new view of PwC, it also gives PwC a new view of them, particularly their ability to hold up under pressure.

PwC says the program, now in its third cycle, gives participants a broad, international perspective that's crucial for a company that does business around the world. Traditional executive education programs turn out men and women who have specific job skills but little familiarity with issues outside their narrow specialty, according to Douglas Ready, director of the International Consortium for Executive Development Research. PwC says Ulysses helps prepare participants for challenges that go beyond the strict confines of accounting or consulting and instills values such as community involvement that are essential to success in any field.

Ulysses has also given PwC a very positive name in the accounting and broader professional services community. The project has taught the partners to understand risks more holistically, to consider all stakeholders that are involved, and to realize that doing business is not about one goal, but many.

Sources: Alina Dizik, "Sustainability Is a Growing Theme," *The Wall Street Journal*, March 4, 2010, http://online.wsj.com/article/SB1000142405274 8704541304575099514203847820.html?KEYWORDS=social+responsibility (accessed October 21, 2010); Global Giving Matters, "PricewaterhouseCoopers' Project Ulysses—Linking Global Leadership Training to a Community Development," *Synergos*, September/October 2004, www.synergos.org/globalgivingmatters/features/0409ulysses.htm (accessed October 21, 2010); Jessi Hempel and Seth Porges, "It Takes a Village—and a Consultant; PricewaterhouseCoopers Tests Partners by Sending Them to Work in Poor Nations," *Businessweek*, September 6, 2004, https://www.bloomberg.com/news/articles/2004-09-05/it-takes-a-village-and-a-consultant (accessed October 21, 2010); Jessica Marquez, "Companies Send Employees on Volunteer Projects Abroad to Cultivate Leadership Skills," *Workforce Management*, November 21, 2005, pp. 50–51, www.workforce.com/2005/12/02/companies-send-employees-on-volunteer-projects-abroad-to-cultivate-leadership-skills/ (accessed October 21, 2010); Nicola M. Pless, Thomas Maak, and Günter K. Stahl, "Developing Responsible Global Leaders through International Service Learning Programs: The Ulysses Experience," *Academy of Management Learning and Education* 10, no. 2 (2011), pp. 237–260.

employee retention in India, answer the following questions: (1) What are the costs and benefits of hiring home-, host-, and third-country nationals for overseas assignments? (2) What skill sets are important for international assignments, and how can employees be prepared for such assignments? (3) What are the implications of offshore outsourcing for the management of human resources globally and in India in particular?

SUMMARY OF KEY POINTS

1. MNCs can use four basic sources for filling overseas positions: home-country nationals (expatriates), host-country nationals, third-country nationals, and inpatriates. The most common reason for using home-country nationals, or expatriates, is to get the overseas operation under way. Once this is done, many MNCs turn the top management job over to a host-country national who is familiar with the culture and language and who often commands a lower salary than the home-country national. The primary reason for using third-country nationals is that these people have the necessary expertise for the job. The use of inpatriates (a host-country or third-country national assigned to the home office) recognizes the need for diversity at the home office. This movement builds a transnational core competency for MNCs. In addition, MNCs can subcontract or outsource to take advantage of lower human resource costs and increase flexibility.

2. Many criteria are used in selecting managers for overseas assignments. Some of these include adaptability, independence, self-reliance, physical and emotional health, age, experience, education, knowledge of the local language, motivation, the support of spouse and children, and leadership.

3. Individuals who meet selection criteria are given some form of screening. Some firms use psychological testing, but this approach has lost popularity in recent years. More commonly, candidates are given interviews. Theoretical models that identify important anticipatory and in-country dimensions of adjustment offer help in effective selection.

4. Compensating expatriates can be a difficult problem because there are many variables to consider. However, most compensation packages are designed around five common elements: base salary, benefits, allowances, incentives, and taxes. Working within these elements, the MNC will tailor the package to fit the specific situation. In doing so, there are five different approaches that can be used: balance-sheet approach, localization, lump-sum method, cafeteria approach, and regional method. Whichever one (or combination) is used, the package must be both cost-effective and fair.

5. A manager might be willing to take an international assignment for a number of reasons: increased pay, promotion potential, the opportunity for greater responsibility, the chance to travel, and the ability to use his or her talents and skills. Research shows that most home countries prefer that the individual who is selected to head the affiliate or subsidiary be a local manager, even though this often does not occur.

6. At some time, most expatriates return home, usually when their predetermined tour is over. Sometimes, managers return because they want to leave early; at other times, they return because of poor performance on their part. In any event, readjustment problems can arise back home, and the longer a manager has been gone, the bigger the problems usually are. Some firms are developing transition strategies to help expatriates adjust to their new environments.

7. Training is the process of altering employee behavior and attitudes to increase the probability of goal attainment. Many expatriates need training before (as well as during) their overseas stay. A number of factors will influence a company's approach to training. One is the basic type of MNC: ethnocentric, polycentric, regiocentric, or geocentric. Another factor is the learning style of the trainees.

8. There are two primary reasons for training: organizational and personal. Organizational reasons include overcoming ethnocentrism, improving communication, and validating the effectiveness of training programs. Personal reasons include improving the ability of expatriates to interact locally and increasing the effectiveness of leadership styles. There are two types of training programs: standard and tailor-made. Research shows that small firms usually rely on standard programs and larger MNCs tailor their training. Common approaches to training include elements such as cultural orientation, cultural assimilators, language training, sensitivity training, and field experience.

9. A cultural assimilator is a programmed learning approach that is designed to expose members of one culture to some of the basic concepts, attitudes, role perceptions, customs, and values of another. Assimilators have been developed for many different cultures. Their validity has resulted in the improved effectiveness and satisfaction of those being trained as compared with other training methods.

KEY TERMS

adaptability screening, 521

balance-sheet approach, 530

cafeteria approach, 530

cultural assimilator, 544

ethnocentric MNC, 537

ethnocentrism, 539

expatriates, 513

geocentric MNC, 538

home-country nationals, 513

host-country nationals, 514

inpatriates, 515

international selection criteria, 518

learning, 538

localization, 530

lump-sum method, 530

polycentric MNC, 538

positive organizational behavior (POB), 545

regiocentric MNC, 538

regional system, 530

repatriation, 533

repatriation agreements, 534

third-country nationals (TCNs), 514

training, 535

transition strategies, 534

validity, 545

REVIEW AND DISCUSSION QUESTIONS

1. A New York-based MNC is in the process of staffing a subsidiary in New Delhi, India. Why would it consider using expatriate managers in the unit? Local managers? Third-country managers?

2. What selection criteria are most important in choosing people for an overseas assignment? Identify and describe the four that you judge to be of most universal importance, and defend your choice.

3. What are the major common elements in an expat's compensation package? Besides base pay, which would be most important to you? Why?

4. Why are individuals motivated to accept international assignments? Which of these motivations would you rank as positive reasons? Which would you regard as negative reasons?

5. Why do expatriates return early? What can MNCs do to prevent this from happening? Identify and discuss three steps they can take.

6. What kinds of problems do expatriates face when returning home? Identify and describe four of the most important. What can MNCs do to deal with these repatriation problems effectively?

7. How do the following types of MNCs differ: ethnocentric, polycentric, regiocentric, and geocentric? Which type is most likely to provide international management training to its people? Which is least likely to provide international management training to its people?

8. IBM is planning on sending three managers to its Zurich office, two to Madrid, and two to Tokyo. None of these individuals has any international experience. Would you expect the company to use a standard training program or a tailor-made program for each group?

9. Zygen Inc., a medium-sized manufacturing firm, is planning to enter into a joint venture in China. Would training be of any value to those managers who will be part of this venture? If so, what types of training would you recommend?

10. Hofstadt & Hoerr, a German-based insurance firm, is planning on expanding out of the EU and opening offices in Chicago and Buenos Aires. How would a cultural assimilator be of value in training the MNC's expatriates? Is the assimilator a valid training tool?

11. Ford is in the process of training managers for overseas assignments. Would a global leadership program be a useful approach? Why or why not?

12. Microsoft is weighing setting up an R&D facility in India to develop new software applications. Should it staff the new facility with Microsoft employees? Indian employees? Or should it subcontract with an Indian firm? Explain your answer and some of the potential challenges in implementing it.

INTERNET EXERCISE: COKE GOES WORLDWIDE

As seen in this chapter, the recruiting and selecting of managers is critical to effective international management. This is particularly true in the case of firms that are expanding their international operations or currently do business in a large number of countries. These MNCs are continually having to replace managers who are retiring or moving to other companies. Coca-Cola is an excellent example. Go to the company's website at www.coke.com and look at the career opportunities that it offers overseas. In particular, pay close attention to current opportunities in Europe, Africa, and Asia. Read what the company has to say, and then contact one of the individuals whose e-mail address is provided.

Ask this company representative about the opportunities and challenges of working in that country or geographic area. Then, using this information, coupled with the chapter material, answer these questions: (1) From what you have learned from the Coca-Cola inquiry, what types of education or experience would you need to be hired by the company? (2) What kinds of international career opportunities does Coke offer?

(3) If you were hired by Coke, what type of financial package could you expect? (4) In what areas of the world is Coke focusing more of its attention? (5) What kinds of management and leadership training programs does Coke offer?

ENDNOTES

1. Ernst & Young, "Talent Trends in India, 2015: People and Organization," www.ey.com/Publication/vwLUAssets/ey-talent-trends-in-india-2015/$FILE/ey-talent-trends-in-india-2015.pdf.

2. Ibid.

3. Shyamal Majumdar, "Retaining Talent: Are Companies Doing Enough?" *Business Standard*, March 19, 2010, http://business.rediff.com/column/2010/mar/19/guest-retaining-talent-are-companies-doing-enough.htm.

4. "Stemming the Tide of Attrition in India: Keys to Increasing Retention," *Executive Overview*, *Right Management*, Executive Summary of a paper by Jonathan P. Doh, Steven A. Stumpf, Walter Tymon, and Michael Haid, 2008.

5. Elena Groznaya, "Attrition and Motivation: Retaining Staff in India," *tcWorld*, July 2009, www.tcworld.info/e-magazine/business-culture/article/attrition-and-motivation-retaining-staff-in-india/.

6. "Stemming the Tide of Attrition in India."

7. Ibid.

8. Ibid.

9. Ibid.

10. Ibid.

11. Ibid.

12. Ibid.

13. Ibid.

14. Ibid.

15. Ibid.

16. Elaine Appleton Grant, "How to Retain Talent in India," Synopsis of a paper by Jonathan P. Doh, Steven A. Stumpf, Walter Tymon, and Michael Haid, *MIT Sloan Management Review* 50, no. 1 (Fall 2008).

17. Ibid.

18. "How HR Contributes at Best Small and Midsize Companies to Work For," *Human Resource Department Management Report*, August 2004, p. 2.

19. Ann Pomeroy, "Cooking Up Innovation," *HR Magazine*, November 2004, pp. 46–53.

20. Peter Coy and Jack Ewing, "Where Are All the Workers?" *Businessweek*, April 9, 2007, pp. 28–31.

21. Susan Cantrell, "The Work Force of One," *The Wall Street Journal*, June 16, 2007, p. R10.

22. Declan Mulkeen, "Reducing the Cost of Global Mobility," *Communicaid*, August 29, 2014, https://www.communicaid.com/cross-cultural-training/blog/reducing-the-cost-of-global-mobility/.

23. Also see Kenneth Groh and Mark Allen, "Global Staffing: Are Expatriates the Only Answer?" *HR Focus*, March 1998, pp. S1–S2.

24. Leslie Chang, "China's Grads Find Jobs Scarce," *The Wall Street Journal*, June 22, 2004, p. A17.

25. Nick Forster, "Expatriates and the Impact of Cross-Cultural Training," *Human Resource Management Journal* 10, no. 3 (2000), pp. 63–78.

26. Bloomberg BNA, "HR Department Benchmarks and Analysis 2015–2016," October 2015.

27. Sulekha Nair, "Boom Time Again: Expats Make a Beeline for India as Economy Reviving, Start-ups Buzzing," *F. Business*, July 3, 2015, www.firstpost.com/business/boom-time-again-expats-make-a-beeline-to-india-as-economy-reviving-start-ups-buzzing-2322942.html.

28. Malika Richards, "U.S. Multinational Staffing Practices and Implications for Subsidiary Performance in the U.K. and Thailand," *Thunderbird International Business Review*, March–April 2001, pp. 225–242.

29. Richard B. Peterson, Nancy K. Napier, and Won Shul-Shim, "Expatriate Management: A Comparison of MNCs Across Four Parent Countries," *Thunderbird International Business Review*, March–April 2000, p. 150.

30. Arvind V. Phatak, *International Dimensions of Management*, 2nd ed. (Boston: PWS-Kent Publishing, 1989), p. 106.

31. Cliff Edwards and Kenji Hall, "Remade in the USA," *BusinessWeek*, May 7, 2007, pp. 44–45.

32. Calvin Reynolds, "Strategic Employment of Third Country Nationals," *HR Planning* 20, no. 1 (1997), p. 38.

33. Michael G. Harvey and M. Ronald Buckley, "Managing Inpatriates: Building a Global Core Competency," *Journal of World Business* 32, no. 1 (1997), p. 36.

34. For some additional insights about inpatriates and worldwide staffing, see Michael Harvey and Milorad M. Novicevic, "Staffing Global Marketing Positions: What We Don't Know Can Make a Difference," *Journal of World Business* 35, no. 1 (2000), pp. 80–94.

35. Noam Scheiber, "As a Center for Outsourcing, India Could Be Losing Its Edge," *New York Times*, May 9, 2004, p. 3.

36. Steve Lohr, "Evidence of High-Skill Work Going Abroad," *New York Times*, June 16, 2004, p. C2.

37. Kate Palmer, "BT Hires 1,000 UK Call-Centre Staff in Pledge to Improve Poor Customer Service," *The Telegraph*, January 18, 2016, www.telegraph.co.uk/finance/newsbysector/mediatechnologyandtelecoms/telecoms/12105305/BT-to-create-1000-UK-jobs-as-it-bolsters-call-centres-amid-poor-service-levels.html.

38. "Shape Up," *The Economist*, January 19, 2013, www.economist.com/news/special-report/21569568-offshored-jobs-return-rich-countries-must-prove-they-have-what-it-takes-shape.

39. Arie Lewin and Vinay Couto, *Next Generation Offshoring: The Globalization of Innovation, 2006 Survey Report* (Durham: Duke Center for International Business Education and Research, 2007), pp. 7–10.

40. Ibid.

41. Winfred Arthur Jr. and Winston Bennett Jr., "The International Assignee: The Relative Importance of Factors Perceived to Contribute to Success," *Personnel Psychology*, Spring 1995, pp. 99–114.

42. Also see Michael G. Harvey, Milorad M. Novicevic, and Cheri Speier, "An Innovative Global Management Staffing System: A Competency-Based Perspective," *Human Resource Management*, Winter 2000, pp. 381–394.

43. Peterson, Napier, and Shul-Shim, "Expatriate Management," p. 151.

44. Juan Sanchez, Paul Spector, and Cary Cooper, "Adapting to a Boundaryless World: A Developmental Expatriate Model," *Academy of Management Executive* 14, no. 2 (2000), pp. 96–106.

45. Jan Selmar, "Effects of Coping Strategies on Sociocultural and Psychological Adjustment of Western Expatriate Managers in the PRC," *Journal of World Business* 34, no. 1 (1999), pp. 41–51.

46. Paula M. Caligiuri, "Selecting Expatriates for Personality Characteristics: A Moderating Effect of Personality on the Relationship between Host National Contact and Cross-Cultural Adjustment," *Management International Review* 40, no. 1 (2000), pp. 61–80.

47. HSBC Expat, *Expat Explorer: Balancing Life Abroad* (2015), https://www.expatexplorer.hsbc.com/survey/files/pdfs/overall-reports/2015/HSBC_Expat_Explorer_2015_report.pdf.

48. Ibid.

49. Brian Friedman, "How to Move and Manage the Best People around the World; An Assignment Overseas Is Often Now Seen as a Vital Career Move," *The Daily Telegraph*, May 15, 2010, p. 8.

50. Margaret A. Shaffer, David A. Harrison, K. Matthew Gilley, and Dora M. Luk, "Struggling for Balance amid Turbulence on International Assignments: Work-Family Conflict, Support, and Commitment," *Journal of Management* 27 (2001), pp. 99–121.

51. Patricia C. Borstorff, Stanley G. Harris, Hubert S. Field, and William F. Giles, "Who'll Go? A Review of Factors Associated with Employee Willingness to Work Overseas," *Human Resource Planning* 20, no. 3 (1997), p. 38.

52. See Betty Jane Punnett, "Towards Effective Management of Expatriate Spouses," *Journal of World Business* 33, no. 3 (1997), pp. 243–256.

53. Howard Tu and Sherry E. Sullivan, "Preparing Yourself for an International Assignment," *Business Horizons*, January–February 1994, p. 68.

54. "2015 Global Mobility Trends," *Brookfield Global Relocation Services*, http://globalmobilitytrends.brookfieldgrs.com/#/collapse8?q=58.

55. Ibid.

56. Ibid.

57. James C. Baker and John M. Ivancevich, "The Assignment of American Executives Abroad: Systematic, Haphazard or Chaotic?" *California Management Review*, Spring 1971, p. 41.

58. Jean E. Heller, "Criteria for Selecting an International Manager," *Personnel*, May–June 1980, p. 53.

59. Rosalie L. Tung, "U.S. Multinationals: A Study of Their Selection and Training Procedures for Overseas Assignments," *National Academy of Management Proceedings* (Atlanta, 1979), p. 65.

60. This section is based on J. Stewart Black, Mark Mendenhall, and Gary Oddou, "Toward a Comprehensive Model of International Adjustment: An Integration of Multiple Theoretical Perspectives," *Academy of Management Review*, April 1991, pp. 291–317.

61. For more on this area, see Jaime Bonache, Chris Brewster, and Vesa Suutari, "Expatriation: A Developing Research Agenda," *Thunderbird International Business Review*, January–February 2001, pp. 3–20.

62. Crystal I. C. Farh, Kathryn M. Bartol, Debra L. Shapiro, and Jiseon Shin, "Networking Abroad: A Process Model of How Expatriates Form Support Ties to Facilitate Adjustment," *Academy of Management Review* 35, no. 3 (2010), pp. 434–454.

63. Iain McCormick and Tony Chapman, "Executive Relocation: Personal and Organizational Tactics," in *Managing Across Cultures: Issues and Perspectives*, ed. Pat Joynt and Malcolm Warner (London: International Thomson Business Press, 1996), pp. 326–337.

64. Calvin Reynolds, "Expatriate Compensation in Historical Perspective," *Journal of World Business* 32, no. 2 (1997), p. 127.

65. Cathy Loose, "Home and Away," *China Staff* 16, no. 3, pp. 24–26.

66. Elaine K. Bailey, "International Compensation," in *Global Perspectives of Human Resource Management*, ed. Oded Shenkar (Englewood Cliffs, NJ: Prentice Hall, 1995), p. 148.

67. Peterson, Napier, and Shul-Shim, "Expatriate Management," p. 155.

68. See Dennis R. Briscoe, Randall S. Schuler, and Lisbeth Claus, *International Human Resource Management* (Global HRM) (Routledge, 2008).

69. See also Ute Krudewagen and Susan Eandi, "Designing Employee Policies for an International Workforce," *Workspan* 53, no. 6 (2010), p. 74.

70. Cheryl Spielman and Gerald A. Tammaro, "8 Action Items for Expatriate Planning in an Economic Downturn," *Workspan* 52, no. 10 (2009), p. 58.

71. "Pay Variations in Asia," *HR Magazine*, 2010, p. 6.

72. David Sirota and J. Michael Greenwood, "Understand Your Overseas Workforce," *Harvard Business Review*, January–February 1971, pp. 53–60.

73. Ingemar Torbiorn, *Living Abroad* (New York: Wiley, 1982), p. 127.

74. Charles Vance and Yongsun Paik, "One Size Fits All in Expatriate Pre-departure Training? Comparing the Host Country Voices of Mexican, Indonesian and U.S. Workers," *Journal of Management Development* 21, no. 7–8 (2002), pp. 557–572.

75. Chi-Sum Wong and Kenneth S. Law, "Managing Localization of Human Resources in the PRC: A Practical Model," *Journal of World Business* 34, no. 1 (1999), pp. 28–29.

76. "2015 Global Mobility Trends."

77. Ibid.

78. Ibid.

79. Ibid.

80. Jobert E. Abueva, "Return of the Native Executive," *New York Times*, May 17, 2000, p. C1.

81. Nancy J. Adler, *International Dimensions of Organizational Behavior*, 2nd ed. (Boston: PWS-Kent Publishing, 1991), p. 236.

82. Howard W. French, "Japan Unsettles Returnees, Who Yearn to Leave Again," *New York Times*, May 2, 2000, p. A12.

83. J. Stewart Black, "Coming Home: The Relationship of Expatriate Expectations with Repatriate Adjustment and Job Performance," *Human Relations* 45, no. 2 (1992), p. 188.

84. Wong and Law, "Managing Localization of Human Resources," p. 36.

85. Nancy K. Napier and Richard B. Peterson, "Expatriate Reentry: What Do Expatriates Have to Say?" *Human Resource Planning* 14, no. 1 (1991), pp. 19–28.

86. Charlene Marmer Solomon, "Repatriation: Up, Down or Out?" *Personnel Journal*, January 1995, p. 32.

87. Mitchell R. Hammer, William Hart, and Randall Rogan, "Can You Go Home Again? An Analysis of the Repatriation of Corporate Managers and Spouses," *Management International Review* 38, no. 1 (1998), p. 81.

88. Karen Roberts, Ellen Ernst Kossek, and Cynthia Ozeki, "Managing the Global Workforce: Challenges and Strategies," *Academy of Management Executive*, November 1998, pp. 93–106.

89. See also Mark C. Blino and Daniel C. Feldman, "Increasing the Skill Utilization of Expatriates," *Human Resource Management* 39, no. 4 (Winter 2000), pp. 367–379.

90. See also Ben L. Kedia and Ananda Mukherji, "Global Managers: Developing a Mindset for Global Competitiveness," *Journal of World Business* 34, no. 3 (1999), pp. 230–251.

91. Robert C. Maddox and Douglas Short, "The Cultural Integrator," *Business Horizons*, November–December 1988, pp. 57–59.

92. Michael Hickins, "Creating a Global Team," *Management Review*, September 1998, p. 6.

93. Charlene Marmer Solomon, "Global Operations Demand That HR Rethink Diversity," *Personnel Journal*, July 1994, p. 50.

94. Paul R. Sparrow and Pawan S. Budhwar, "Competition and Change: Mapping the Indian HRM Recipe Against Worldwide Patterns," *Journal of World Business* 32, no. 3 (1997), p. 231.

95. See also Wong and Law, "Managing Localization of Human Resources," pp. 32–33.

96. Bodil Jones, "What Future European Recruits Want," *Management Review*, January 1998, p. 6.

97. Filiz Tabak, Janet Stern Solomon, and Christine Nielsen, "Managerial Success: A Profile of Future Managers in China," *SAM Advanced Management Journal*, Autumn 1998, pp. 18–26.

98. Also see Allan Bird, Sully Taylor, and Schon Beechler, "A Typology of International Human Resource Management in Japanese Multinational Corporations: Organizational Implications," *Human Resource Management*, Summer 1998, pp. 159–176.

99. Fred Luthans, *Organizational Behavior*, 10th ed. (New York: McGraw-Hill/Irwin, 2004), chapter 16.

100. Noel M. Tichy and Eli Cohen, "The Teaching Organization," *Training and Development Journal*, July 1998, p. 27.

101. Peter Prud'homme van Reine and Fons Trompenaars, "Invited Reaction: Developing Expatriates for the Asia-Pacific Region," *Human Resource Development Quarterly* 11, no. 3 (Fall 2000), p. 238.

102. J. Hayes and C. W. Allinson, "Cultural Differences in the Learning Styles of Managers," *Management International Review* 28, no. 3 (1988), p. 76.

103. See, for example, Jennifer Smith, "Southeast Asia's Search for Managers," *Management Review*, June 1998, p. 9.

104. Also see Schon Beechler and John Zhuang Yang, "The Transfer of Japanese-Style Management to American Subsidiaries: Contingencies, Constraints, and Competencies," *Journal of International Business Studies*, Third Quarter 1994, pp. 467–491.

105. Allan Bird and Schon Beechler, "Links between Business Strategy and Human Resource Management Strategy in U.S.-Based Japanese Subsidiaries: An Empirical Investigation," *Journal of International Business Studies*, First Quarter 1995, p. 40.

106. Linda K. Stroh and Paula M. Caligiuri, "Increasing Global Competitiveness through Effective People Management," *Journal of World Business* 33, no. 1 (1998), p. 10.

107. For more on this, see Tomoko Yoshida and Richard W. Breslin, "Intercultural Skills and Recommended Behaviors," in *Global Perspectives of Human Resource Management*, ed. Shenkar, pp. 112–131.

108. Alan M. Barrett, "Training and Development of Expatriates and Home Country Nationals," in *Global Perspectives of Human Resource Management*, ed. Shenkar, p. 135.

109. Yukimo Ono, "Japanese Firms Don't Let Masters Rule," *The Wall Street Journal*, May 4, 1992, p. B1.

110. See Wong and Law, "Managing Localization of Human Resources," pp. 32–33.

111. See Andrew Sergeant and Stephen Frenkel, "Managing People in China: Perceptions of Expatriate Managers," *Journal of World Business* 33, no. 1 (1998), pp. 17–34.

112. Michael J. Marquardt and Dean W. Engel, *Global Human Resource Management* (Englewood Cliffs, NJ: Prentice Hall, 1995), p. 44.

113. Ingmar Bjorkman and Yuan Lu, "A Corporate Perspective on the Management of Human Resources in China," *Journal of World Business* 34, no. 1 (1999), pp. 20–21.

114. Fred E. Fiedler, Terence Mitchell, and Harry C. Triandis, "The Culture Assimilator: An Approach to Cross-Cultural Training," *Journal of Applied Psychology*, April 1971, p. 97.

115. Fred Luthans, "Positive Organizational Behavior: Developing and Managing Psychological Strengths," *Academy of Management Executive* 16, no. 1 (2002), p. 59.

116. Fred Luthans and Carolyn M. Youssef, "Emerging Positive Organizational Behavior," *Journal of Management* 33, no. 3 (June 2007), pp. 321–349.

117. Ibid.

118. "What Are Companies' Top Concerns for Relocating Employees over the Next Decade?" *Business Wire*, June 28, 2010.

119. CIA, "Russia," *The World Factbook* (2016), https://www.cia.gov/library/publications/the-world-factbook/geos/rs.html.

120. Ibid.

121. World Bank, "Russian Federation," *World Development Indicators* (2016), http://data.worldbank.org/country/russian-federation.

122. Kira Zavyalova, "Russia GDP Seen Down 3.8 Percent in 2015, Minus 0.3 Percent in 2016," *Reuters*, December 24, 2015, www.reuters.com/article/us-russia-economy-idUSKBN0U70ZO20151224.

123. "From Bad to Worse," *The Economist*, April 16, 2014, www.economist.com/news/business/21601006-domestic-and-foreign-firms-wonder-how-serious-things-might-get-bad-worse.

124. Stephanie Baker, "BP's Dudley Relives Russian Nightmare Alongside Rosneft Boss," *Bloomberg*, December 18, 2014, www.bloomberg.com/news/articles/2014-12-18/bp-s-dudley-relives-russian-nightmare-alongside-rosneft-boss.

Russia

Straddling the European and Asian continents, Russia stretches from Belarus in the west to the Pacific Ocean in the east. Russia is rich in various natural resources including oil, natural gas, coal, strategic minerals, reserves of rare earth elements, and timber. For the last 15 years, the Russian economy has been disproportionately dependent on oil and natural gas.[119]

Russia's population is currently estimated at over 142 million people. Over three-quarters of the residents are of Russian descent, though there are sizable populations of Tatars, Ukrainians, and Bashkirs as well. Russia's population growth is fairly stable. Organized religion is not heavily practiced, with just 15–20 percent identifying as Russian Orthodox, 10–15 percent identifying as Muslim, and approximately 2 percent identifying as Christian. The population is concentrated in the age group of 25–54 years old, representing slightly less than half of the total population.[120]

Russia's estimated GDP in 2014 was US$1.861 trillion.[121] The Russian economy contracted in 2014 and 2015, and strong growth is not predicted to return until energy prices increase.[122] Russia's economic issues go beyond just the decline in oil prices. The government is one of the biggest barriers to any sustainable growth to the Russian economy. Russia's legal system is largely inefficient and difficult to maneuver, and the government itself becomes intertwined in the private sector through its closely managed state-owned enterprises and varying levels of corruption. Worsening its already sluggish economy, Russia made a large and costly financial commitment to its annexation of Crimea in 2014. This action resulted in a further worsening of already-strained relations with the West, including the United States and the European Union.

Russia's government is a federation. Vladimir Putin has held most executive power since his first presidential election in 2000. While Russia has certainly evolved from its days as a purely communist society, the state is still deeply intertwined in all aspects of the economy. After the Crimea invasion, the United States imposed sanctions on dealings with its own companies and certain Russian individuals and companies. These sanctions have added to the already-deteriorating consumer confidence and have prompted Russia to redirect its efforts to Asia to attract foreign investment.[123]

You Be the International Management Consultant

Bob Dudley, currently British Petroleum's CEO, had to flee from Russia in 2008 when he headed a joint venture between BP and a group of Russian billionaires. During that time, he faced a number of lawsuits from other businessmen in the oil industry and tax probes from the government. Now, as BP CEO, he is watching his company's bet in Russia suffer from declining oil prices and from the U.S.-imposed sanctions. BP is the largest foreign investor in the country's oil industry and holds a 20 percent stake in a state-owned oil company. Surrounding all of these factors affecting BP's stake is also the threat that the government may impose capital controls on state-owned oil companies—and therefore restricting the dividends that BP could receive from its investment.[124]

Questions

1. Given the Russian government's history of interfering with private business, would you make as large of an investment in Russia as BP has done?
2. What are the pros and cons of this investment?
3. Does the fact that BP's investment is suffering from Ukraine-related sanctions affect your decision to invest in the country in any sense?

IKEA's Global Renovations

In September 2015, Swedish furniture retailer IKEA announced record revenue of $36 billion for 2015 and an 8.9 percent increase in profit over 2014. Despite many highly publicized setbacks over the years, including a scandal regarding use of horse meat in its iconic meatballs in 2013 and accusations of forced labor in the 1980s, IKEA continues to prosper in markets around the world. Since expanding outside of Europe over 30 years ago, IKEA has attempted to balance its unique approach to both the retail shopping experience and its own expansion as it has sought to achieve a reputation for social responsibility and sustainability.

IKEA's Humble Beginnings

The idea of IKEA began in 1935 in the small province of southern Sweden, Smaland, where the people are known for their hard work and for making the most from very little means. Ingvar Kamprad, a nine-year-old boy with a strong entrepreneurial spirit, began by selling fish and Christmas decorations to those in the local community. By age 17, using a gift of money from his father, Kamprad established the company IKEA. Kamprad created the name IKEA by combining his initials, the initials of his hometown farm, and the initials of a nearby village. During that period he sold everything from pens to gadgets to stockings, and within a short time he was able to put together a mail-order catalog. By 1947 Kamprad decided to introduce home furnishings to the product mix and by 1951 eliminated all other products lines, focusing solely on the home furniture market.

Kamprad built his empire on the foundation of offering a "wide range of home furnishings of good design and functionality at a price low enough to be affordable to most people."[1] With this idea in hand, he set out to build a business that met the needs of the Swedish people, showing no differentiation between rich and poor.

Around this time, he was seeing a great deal of pressure from other furniture providers in his direct market. In 1956, with his suppliers facing pressure to boycott due to increased competition, Kamprad decided to design his own furniture and have a manufacturer produce it. This seemingly small decision led IKEA to offer low prices and efficient packaging, which are still the capstones of the business today.

It is universally believed that IKEA's growth and success are a direct result of Kamprad's vision, values, and culture, which he cultivated in all aspects of IKEA's business model. His openness to change, his drive for innovation, and his focus on his stakeholders have made IKEA what it is today: the largest and most successful furniture retailer in the world.

Growth and Expansion

The first IKEA store opened in Almhult, Sweden, in 1958. In 1963 IKEA opened its first international store in Oslo, Norway, and two years after that opened a flagship store near Stockholm. In 1973 IKEA spread to mainland Europe, opening stores in Switzerland and Germany. Germany, to this day, remains IKEA's largest market. Following these markets, a store was opened in Australia in 1977 and in the Netherlands in 1979. The first store in the United States did not arrive until 1985, which is surprising given IKEA's record-breaking $5 billion in revenue in the U.S. in 2015. The U.S. opening was quickly followed by the first one in the United Kingdom. See Table 1 for a more detailed timeline of IKEA's expansion.

IKEA now operates over 384 stores in 48 countries, with 155,000 employees as of 2016. The fast growth was primarily organic, with IKEA maintaining full control over the company, as it still does today. Several "business format franchises" currently exist, where local entrepreneurs took on the capital investment and the management, and left the merchandising and marketing to IKEA. Since 1982, IKEA has been owned by a foundation, and remaining private is a keystone of success to ensure that the culture and values remain intact.

Specifically, the Netherlands-based company Inter IKEA Systems BV owns the franchise, and Ingka holding company, of which Kamprad is the senior advisor, operates over 300 stores worldwide. In addition, a separate company, Ikano, manages the Kamprad fortune and owns several other IKEA stores in its own right.

IKEA's success cannot be ignored in today's turbulent market, with IKEA being commended for entering and remaining in traditionally difficult markets. What keeps the IKEA group going strong is its corporate initiatives embedded in Swedish heritage. These corporate initiatives are visually apparent throughout the stores and have been considered a "significant force of competitive advantage."[2]

The Swedish lifestyle incorporates a "fresh, healthy way of life" with bright colors and textiles even though Sweden does not see a great amount of sunlight. The high quality, stress-free furniture and the caring employees represent a

Table 1   **Timeline of Major Events in IKEA's History**

1926	Founder Ingvar Kamprad is born in Smaland, Sweden.
1931	Kamprad begins selling matches to nearby neighbors.
1933–1935	Kamprad uses his bicycle to expand territory, and begins selling flower seeds, greeting cards, Christmas tree decorations.
1943	Using money from his father, Kamprad founds IKEA, selling pens, wallets, picture frames, table runners, watches, jewelry, and nylon stockings.
1945	First IKEA advertisement is in a local newspaper.
1948	IKEA begins selling furniture.
1951	The first IKEA catalog is published and Kamprad decides to focus solely on selling furniture.
1953	First showroom opens in Almhult, Sweden.
1956	IKEA decides to design its own furniture and flat pack it for self-assembly.
1958	First IKEA opens in Sweden.
1960	First IKEA restaurant opens at the Almhult location.
1963	IKEA enters Oslo, Norway.
1969	IKEA enters Copenhagen, Denmark.
1973	IKEA enters Zurich, Switzerland.
1975	IKEA enters Sydney, Australia.
1976	IKEA enters Vancouver, Canada.
1977	IKEA enters Vienna, Austria.
1979	IKEA enters Rotterdam, Netherlands.
1981	IKEA enters Paris, France.
1982	The IKEA Group is formed.
1984	IKEA enters Brussels, Belgium.
1985	IKEA enters Philadelphia, USA.
1986	A new president and CEO, Anders Moberg, takes over.
1987	IKEA enters Manchester, UK.
1989	IKEA enters Milan, Italy.
1990	The IKEA Group develops its first environmental policy.
1990	IKEA enters Budapest, Hungary.
1991	IKEA enters Prague, Czech Republic, and Poznan, Poland.
1993	IKEA Group becomes a member of the global forest certification organization Forest Stewardship Council (FSC).
1996	IKEA enters Madrid, Spain.
1997	Global website is launched.
1997	IKEA's sustainable approach to shipping, titled "IKEA, Transport and the Environment," is created.
1998	IKEA enters Shanghai, China.
1999	New president and CEO, Anders Dahlvig, is named.
2000	IKEA enters Moscow, Russia, Kamprad's "last big hobby."
2000	IKEA code of conduct, IWAY, is launched.
2000	Online shopping begins.
June 2004	IKEA enters Lisbon, Portugal.
July 2004	The 200th store opens.
December 2004	Opening ceremonies in Moscow are cancelled due to protracted disputes with government over corruption.
May 2006	IKEA enters Tokyo, Japan.
January 2006	IKEA Food is launched.
June 2009	IKEA halts further investment in Russia.
October 2012	IKEA is criticized for removing women from Saudi Arabia ads.
November 2012	IKEA publicly apologizes for forced labor practices in East Germany 25–30 years prior.
February 2013	IKEA is under attack for horsemeat found in European meatballs.
March 2013	IKEA now admits to contamination of chocolate cake in China.
March 2013	IKEA announces future partnership with Marriott for budget hotel chains in Europe.
July 2015	IKEA issues a warning regarding its popular "Malm" line of dressers after it is revealed that dressers had a tendency to tip over, killing two infants.
September 2015	IKEA announces record-high global revenue of US$35.7 billion for the fiscal year.

Swedish tradition where "rich and poor alike were well looked after."[3] Food stands with Swedish snacks are prominent in every store. Also, the do-it-yourself requirement of customers to perform some of the work by putting together and/or transporting the furniture facilitates low prices.

Every IKEA store is built fundamentally similar, but each has a distinct local flare. Within any IKEA there are "free pushchairs, supervised childcare and sometimes children's playgrounds as well as wheelchairs for the disabled."[4] In addition, a receptionist's desk holds catalogs, tape measures, and pens and pencils, and a wide range of staff members are always throughout the store to aid any customer in need of help.

One of the biggest reasons for IKEA's success on a global level has been its ability to enter new international markets yet keep its core values and brand image consistent.

This is something that other companies have not been able to tackle as successfully, and a brief look into IKEA's international strategy will provide a strong understanding of why the company has been so successful with global expansion while at the same time maintaining a positive corporate image.

Global Expansion

IKEA is a unique case, not only because its founder wrote a vision and a set of core values over 60 years ago that are still in use today, but also because the founder is still a part of everyday management. Ingvar Kamprad, now Sweden's richest man at over 90 years old, created these core values that have driven business growth, shaped culture, and ultimately built a brand image that has propelled IKEA to huge success. In fact, some believe that the culture, embedded deep in every store, transcends the actual products.

Vision, Core Values, Brand

Kamprad began with his vision to offer "a wide range of well-designed, functional home furnishing products at prices so low that as many people as possible will be able to afford them."[5] From this vision came a set of corporate values that are still followed today. The three defining values that drive operations to this day are "common sense and simplicity," "dare to be different," and "working together."[6]

Common sense and simplicity, created as a value in 1943, follows the belief that "complicated rules paralyze!" The principle that simplicity prevails both internally and externally has been a major driving force in operations since IKEA's inception. Simplicity can be seen in large warehouse stores; in interactions between management, suppliers, and customers; and in cost cutting.

Cost cutting is seen throughout the business, especially at the management level. One will not find management flying first class or staying in luxury hotels. Cost-saving techniques are seen at every level, allowing IKEA to not just verbalize its commitment to low prices, but to physically have significantly lower prices than the competition.

Dare to be different, also created in 1943, is about always finding a new path by asking the question, "why?" By constantly questioning the status quo, IKEA has found success in innovation and in its ability to continually change and evolve. For instance, Ingvar Kamprad, when conceiving IKEA, asked himself, "Why must well-designed furniture always be so expensive? Why do the most famous designers always fail to reach the majority of people with their ideas?"[7]

That simple question has led IKEA to create what it is known for today, and will continue to guide the company moving forward. Kamprad believes that it is more difficult now than ever before to find new ways to solve problems and, in the face of strong competition, will allow IKEA to differentiate even further from the competition.

Working together was added to IKEA's values in 1956 when the furniture was recreated for self-assembly by customers. IKEA even released this statement in 1999: "You (the customer) do your part. We (IKEA) do our part. Together we save money."[8] It is very representative of its belief to work together in every aspect of the business and help each other along the way.

According to Tarnovskaya et al., the vision, values, and culture, taken together with systems and networks, form the "value proposition for customers."[9] In other words, how these values permeate into the business will be apparent to customers, allowing them to form their own opinion on the brand. The customers and stakeholders of IKEA, therefore, ultimately define the brand essence.

Corporate brand is a construct of "intangible nature," built through relationships, perceptions, and behaviors. It involves all stakeholders, including "customers, competitors, employees, and other business actors."[10] By taking the values created by Ingvar Kamprad years ago and embedding them in all company stakeholders, IKEA has developed strong corporate brand values that have led them to success both domestically and internationally.

Internationalization Strategies

As the number of stakeholders increases, especially across country borders, the more difficult it is to maintain a uniform brand image and goals. IKEA has found success when expanding internationally by staying consistent with the global values described while still allowing some room for a unique local flare.

"Employees become the ambassadors of the brand values," as they are the salesmen of the firm. If employees do not believe in the values and live them, the customers surely won't either. IKEA succeeds by bringing in a staff of experienced IKEA employees, traditionally Swedish, to train and reshape the culture in each new market. For instance, IKEA trains all new staff members on the core competencies seen as most important to support brand vision and values, and the success of this lies not only in training, but also in recruitment.

An IKEA HR corporate manager was quoted as saying, "Our goal is to employ co-workers who understand and embrace our core values and will reflect and reinforce those."[11] By focusing heavily on the recruitment process, IKEA is able to ensure it hires the right type of employee who can potentially change his or her own personal traditional values and become a believer and salesperson of the IKEA brand. Edvardsson et al. even argued that values are coproduced with customers, and given that employees are communicating the brand to the customer, communication becomes a value in itself.[12]

Another important stakeholder that plays a strong role in internationalization is the supplier. The global supplier plays a large role because it needs to act as a firm base for the company when entering new markets, to continually support IKEA in order to avoid the necessity of constantly forming new relationships. Just as important, though, is the need for local suppliers, who are very beneficial and most often necessary within each market, but who typically hold views contradictory to Swedish values.

In 2000, IKEA created a code called "The IKEA Way," or "IWAY," that puts forth standards of acceptable working conditions for suppliers. The code touches on many aspects such as child labor, forestry, and corruption, with the main goal to make "sustainable development the core business value."[13]

With nearly 1,000 suppliers in 50 countries, IKEA focuses on long-term relationships with suppliers who not only produce low-cost, high-quality goods, but who positively impact working conditions, the commodities, and the environment as well. "On a global scale, IKEA has more than 1,000 employees involved in purchasing. Purchasing is divided into 16 regional 'trading areas,' encompassing 43 trading service offices in 33 countries."[14]

Every supplier is chosen based on his or her ability to meet predetermined standards set forth in the IWAY, focusing specifically around management style, financial situation, sourcing of materials, equipment, impact on the environment, and location. The IWAY is made up of 19 areas containing over 90 issues that must be met. It is revised every two years and IKEA has a staff of internal auditors selected to research the suppliers' ability to meet the IWAY requirements. Once a supplier makes it to the final stage of approval, goals and plans are set in place to further improve working conditions.

When entering a new market, IKEA chooses and trains local suppliers similarly to its processes for recruiting and hiring employees. For instance, when entering Russia, IKEA's strategy was to build a local supplier base through "active cooperation in the Russian wood industry."[15] IKEA's proactive strategy was difficult, given that IKEA bases its strategy for long-term commitments on feelings of trust, which was very uncommon for Russians, who "operate under great uncertainty and are reluctant to enter into long-term commitments."[16] However, IKEA took the time to understand the Russian positions and invested heavily to change their opinions and behaviors.

Global expansion has proven historically difficult, yet IKEA has found a way to not only balance the entire customer experience, but also achieve a reputation for social responsibility and sustainability in the process. One of its greatest impacts thus far has been on the environment. In 1997, before the IWAY was even finalized, IKEA sought to increase the efficiency of transportation by writing "IKEA, transport and the environment."[17] Its purpose was to limit pollution from travel and strategically place all stakeholders geographically. Based on responses gathered by a University of Bari study, 60 percent of stakeholders lived less than 20 km from the store. According to one author, "IKEA's intuition was not so much to involve some vendors in this

program, but more to formalize this synergy through the sharing of an ethical code. A code whose purpose is not only practical in terms of production, but also symbolic of the ability of the Swedish corporation to use its brand as a means to ensure the work of all those with whom it collaborates."[18]

The goal is to limit manpower and trips by using flatpacks, and ultimately limit CO_2 emissions through decreased travel. In 2001, with 170 carriers, IKEA asked its suppliers to meet certain requirements—". . . IKEA recommended they update transport vehicles to more modern models. The company also required a switch to less polluting fuels as well as the establishment of environmental protection policies and action plans to control pollution."[19] By 2010, results in Italy, for example, showed a decrease from 75 percent to 65 percent of road transport as well as CO_2 emissions reductions.

According to chief sustainability officer Steve Howard, IKEA has also installed 700,000 solar panels across its stores as of 2016 and plans to invest US$600 million more into renewable energy for its stores by 2020. IKEA also now owns wind farms in six countries and has committed to use 100 percent renewable energy sources by 2020.[20]

IKEA's dedication to the environment and strong network of stakeholders has been yet another point of success when entering international markets. A look into a few internationalization examples will provide further information on IKEA's global practices.

IKEA's Internationalization Journey

China Entry and Expansion

IKEA entered China in 1998 and moved slower than it had in other locations. By 2006, it had opened three stores, and there were a total of 19 stores by 2016. The Beijing location, which opened in 2006, has been tagged as IKEA's largest-volume store globally with over 6 million visitors annually.

IKEA originally entered China as a joint venture with the Chinese government. In 2004, China entered the World Trade Organization and, as a result, the third location in Quangzhou was able to be wholly owned by IKEA, as well as all subsequent openings.

Asia has been a difficult market for IKEA, notably because of the extreme cultural differences between Asia and Sweden. It has not been an easy road for IKEA, yet even in difficult times, Asia cannot be ignored given its sheer size.

Asia makes up 30 percent of IKEA's sourcing, and the large population results in daily visitors, for instance, on a Saturday in Beijing equaling the number of weekly visitors to a store in the West. The size and population, though, also come at a price for the company that created a successful business based on principles of standardization with local adaptation.

China is vastly different from all Western markets in size, culture, and tastes, and has forced IKEA to alter its marketing strategies to meet demand. The core strategy of the company is to offer low-cost, high-quality furniture, meaning the cost must be low in comparison to other furniture providers in the country. Other businesses in China, though, are traditionally providing the lowest cost options. Therefore, IKEA, faced with extreme competition and copycats, had to alter its emphasis to the higher-income population, who see its furniture as more of a luxury purchase.

IKEA has also seen challenges in the open-showroom-selling environment, which is designed to allow customers to envision the design of a room and touch the furniture. The Chinese are not accustomed to this and view it as a hangout. Customers can often be found reading, lounging, and napping on the furniture, or gathering around looking for freebies. In fact, during a 2015 heat wave, IKEA had to issue a formal policy prohibiting customers from sleeping in the air-conditioned bed section of the store. Furthermore, several China locations have now become hotspots for senior citizen romance.

The seniors show up in groups, sit for hours in the cafeteria, and bring their own food and tea. To deal with these groups taking up all the space without actually making a purchase, IKEA has added guards and created special seating areas for those patrons who only want to sit and not shop. Because of these situations, IKEA had to adapt each store to its unique surroundings and cultural differences in order to successfully meet the needs of the Chinese economy.

Although it has been a difficult undertaking, China has become the most important growth market for IKEA. In 2015, despite a slowing Chinese economy, sales grew over 20 percent.

Russia Entry and Setbacks

IKEA entered Russia in 2000 as a "last big hobby" for founder Ingvar Kamprad, then age 81. Amid large changes in culture and a great deal of training, IKEA was a huge success with its "mega-mall" business model. The first store in Russia drew 40,000 shoppers on the first day, and as of 2016 IKEA operates 14 stores with approximately 200 million visitors each year.

Although IKEA has seen success in Russia, the road to get there was not always easy. Like China, Russia's culture is extremely different from Sweden's, and changing a culture without changing the IKEA brand values proved to be extremely difficult. For instance, when hiring, IKEA wants its employees to have a personality that lends to the IKEA business model rather than a comprehensive resume, whereas Russians place a great deal of emphasis on education and experience.

Training was also an issue for the Russian employees, who value academic training and had a negative perception of the "shop floor training" provided by IKEA trainers. However, the IKEA trainers stuck to the IKEA model and began reaching their new Russian counterparts by altering the Russians' previously held views.

In 1998, after the currency devaluation and economic collapse seen throughout Russia, IKEA stood by its side, refusing to abandon the country IKEA worked so hard to enter. This dedication created a strong outlook among the Russian population. However, IKEA's challenges in Russia did not diminish following this symbol of perseverance.

After entering Russia in 2000, IKEA invested $4 billion in ten years. This amount would seem to be a plan that would pay in dividends, when looking at the original statistics, but, according to Kamprad, IKEA "had been 'cheated' out of $190 million" due to the rampant corruption running through Russia. According to the 2015 Corruption Perception Index, Russia ranked 119th out of 167 countries as the most corrupt, whereas Sweden ranked 3rd[21]. In addition, Transparency International's most recent Bribe Payer Index ranked Russia last out of the 28 countries evaluated, making it the most likely place for bribes to be paid out of the largest economies globally[22].

What is a company dedicated to fair business practices supposed to do in an opportunistic market flooded with corruption? IKEA played fair, and dealt with blow after blow from the Russian government. In 2004, the opening ceremonies of a new store in Moscow were cancelled at the last minute due to the location being too near a gas pipeline. Following that, in 2007, the company planned on opening a Samara, Russia, location, which a year and a half later still remained closed.

In June 2009, IKEA announced it would suspend all further investment in the country due to the troubles it previously faced with the government. And in 2010, the company announced that two expatriate executives were fired for taking part in bribes involving the Russian utility company, Lenenergo, in the prior year.

IKEA took a great deal of heat for taking bribes during an anticorruption campaign put forth by the company during the Russian turbulence. Although it is never acceptable to participate in corruption in any way, even turning a blind eye to it, anticorruption experts were quoted as saying: "How to reconcile tough antibribery corporate policies back home with the corrupt rules of the game in Russia is a nigh-impossible task."[23]

It has been pointed out that, given IKEA's role as one of Russia's largest foreign investors, the fact that the company has always previously performed business ethically as proven by Sweden's place on the Corruption Perception Index shows just how difficult it is to perform business, and perform it well, in Russia.

Although IKEA is driven by a positive social mission and proactively seeks out stakeholders who support its core values, it does not always work out ideally. IKEA has recently been in the negative media spotlight as a result of a few cases that go against its code of conduct. It is important to mention, though, that IKEA was not acting in haste, but rather these examples should highlight why the company must stay on its toes in the midst of ubiquitous information, social networks, and media and governments eager to take advantage of companies in general.

Exhibit 1   **Location of New Stores by IKEA**

Year	City/Country
1958	Almhult, Sweden
1963	Oslo, Norway
1969	Copenhagen, Denmark
1973	Zurich, Switzerland
1975	Sydney, Australia
1976	Vancouver, Canada
1977	Vienna, Austria
1979	Rotterdam, Netherlands
1981	Paris, France
1984	Brussels, Belgium
1985	Philadelphia, USA
1987	Manchester, UK
1989	Milan, Italy
1990	Budapest, Hungary
1991	Prague, Czech Republic
1991	Poznan, Poland
1996	Madrid, Spain
1998	Shanghai, China
2000	Moscow, Russia
2004	Lisbon, Portugal
2005	Istanbul, Turkey
2007	Bucharest, Romania
2009	Dublin, Ireland
2013	Cairo, Egypt
2013	Doha, Qatar
2014	Tangerang, Indonesia
2014	Gwangmyeong, South Korea
2015	Casablanca, Morocco

Recent Challenges and Opportunities

Delayed Expansion into India

Despite plans to expand into India for a decade, IKEA still has yet to open a store in the country. In the wake of an economic slowdown in China and Russia, IKEA has attempted to expedite its entry into the Indian market, only to face red tape and limiting bureaucracy.

In 2007, when IKEA first tried to expand into India, the company sought to bypass the legal regulations that require foreign companies to work with a local company in a joint venture. IKEA believed that it would be far more successful operating on its own, and the company believed that it could lobby the Indian government into agreeing. Unfortunately for IKEA, the lobbying efforts took over five years until the government finally waived the joint venture requirements, significantly delaying IKEA's proposed timeline.

In 2016, IKEA ran into further problems after failing to find suitable local suppliers that meet IKEA's standards. Per Indian law and IKEA's agreement with the government, one-third of all products sold in India must be produced in India. After an extensive search across the country for local products that the company could add to its Indian catalog, IKEA came up empty-handed. Local rugs were discovered to have been woven by child labor, tables contained unsafe levels of toxic materials, and plates were found to leak chemicals into food.

In total, IKEA plans to open approximately 25 stores. With the success that IKEA has achieved in other emerging markets, India holds great potential for the company, if IKEA is able to successfully navigate the country's infamous red tape to begin opening stores.

Images in Saudi Arabia

IKEA came under attack in October 2012 for removing pictures of women from catalogs destined for Saudi Arabia. That year alone, IKEA planned to produce over 200 million copies of its catalog in 62 different versions. However, it admitted to tailoring the images "to suit fashion-related tastes of local markets."[24]

IKEA publicly apologized for altering the Saudi images in a statement, noting that such self-censorship was inconsistent with its values. "We're deeply sorry for what has happened,"[25] Ulrika Englesson Sandman said, "It's not the local franchisee that has removed the photos. The error has occurred in the process of producing the proposal to Saudi Arabia, and that is ultimately our responsibility."[26]

Catalogs still remain the primary source of marketing for IKEA, and it comes at a time when Saudi Arabia is in a political firestorm over its treatment of women. The same photographs had been published in 27 languages for 37 countries with the women present, leaving many to wonder about IKEA's stance on gender equality.

Forced Labor Practices

IKEA publicly apologized in November 2012 for having profited by the use of prisoners in East Germany 25 to 30 years prior. The issue was publicized when, earlier in the year, the media began reporting on the connection. In response to the accusation, IKEA hired Ernst & Young, which researched 20,000 pages of internal records and 80,000 pages of state and federal documents in addition to interviews of 90 former employees and witnesses.

It was realized that political prisoners were in fact used in the production of IKEA merchandise during that time, even though IKEA initially questioned the use of prisoners by suppliers. Jeanette Skjelmose, sustainability manager, showed her remorse in a public statement: "We deeply regret that this could happen. . . . The use of political prisoners in production has never been acceptable to the IKEA Group. At the time, we didn't have today's well-developed control systems and obviously didn't do enough to prevent such production conditions among our former G.D.P. suppliers."[27]

When speaking of their current control systems, Skjelmose was probably referring to the previously mentioned IWAY code of conduct standards. In addition to placing provisions on working conditions, touched on in the code, IKEA also conducts audits on suppliers over 1,000 times every year just to ensure a situation like this will not arise again.

This news comes as a large surprise to those who follow IKEA and its traditionally positive social impact. IKEA has even been commended many times over the years for its strong stance on social issues, such as child labor. Susan Bissell of UNICEF (the United Nations Children's Fund) in South Asia was quoted as saying,

> The risk of falling into disrepute and becoming the victim of consumer boycotts has driven many companies to move production from South Asia to areas which are easier to control. Those companies which stay on do everything they can to conceal their presence. I wish more companies had the courage to follow IKEA's example: stay on and actively work on the problems and take genuine social responsibility. IKEA is a sponsor of UNICEF [...] but we regard IKEA as a cooperation partner rather than a contributor [...].[28]

Many even commended IKEA for how it handled this situation. IKEA took on the responsibility of hiring Ernst & Young to investigate the situation at the first mention of forced labor. It is not the only company to have profited from such actions, but one of the few that took action against its prior role. In fact, Christian Sachse, a Berlin historian, spoke of how common this act was, and said it would "take years of research to properly understand the field."[29]

For now, IKEA has accepted its wrongdoing and is moving forward while trying to make things right. The company has vowed its commitment to donate funds and provide an effort to research the issue of forced labor in East Germany, and stands as one of the only companies that is coming forward and taking action to turn the negative into a positive.

Horsemeat Scandal

In light of the horsemeat scandal raging across Europe, inspectors from the Czech Republic found traces of the meat in IKEA's European signature meatballs in February 2013. Although the United States' supply remained unaffected, customer morale is likely to have been impacted. One customer was even quoted as saying, "I am more trusting of Swedish companies and it makes me wonder about corporate integrity in a way I never have questioned Swedes before."[30]

In a public statement, IKEA reassured communities and supporters across the world that they are committed to high-quality, safe food and will not stand for any ingredients other than those listed in the recipe. The company guaranteed the public that it is taking all concerns very seriously, and assured all that no product is actually harmful if eaten. The real issue is the discrepancy in labeling.

Five percent of IKEA's total revenue comes from food, and currently meatballs in 13 countries have been removed. It is a situation affecting many of Europe's leading food companies, including Nestlé SA and ABP Food Group's Silvercrest Food. As IKEA's private investigation continues, it will need to continue to ease the nerves of the disheartened public.

Cake Contamination

Just one month after the horsemeat scandal took place, IKEA again found itself in the news for chocolate cake that was discovered to contain traces of coliform bacteria, a contaminant found in the environment and in the feces of humans and warm-blooded animals, according to *The Wall Street Journal*.[31] Although the cakes posed no true health hazards, as the issue was caught before the cakes hit stores, it came at a bad time publicly.

The Shanghai quarantine bureau destroyed two tons of the cake, and IKEA performed a formal investigation and removed the cakes from restaurants in 23 countries. The company has released a formal apology for all concerns raised regarding the issue.

Budget Hotel Chain

IKEA, in a more positive light, announced a new partnership with Marriott to open a budget-friendly hotel chain called "Moxy," targeted toward next-generation travelers in Europe. The partnership aims to sneak into the economy sector of the European travel market, which represents half of the largest travel market worldwide.

The hope was to secure locations of 50 hotels in the next five years, as well as 150 hotels in the next 10 years. The first opened in Milan, Italy, in 2014. All rooms are designed to be the same size with the same décor, typically contemporary with large wall art, a flat-screen TV, and USB ports. The hotel stay also includes a continental breakfast, bars, and public spaces for the low price of 60 to 85 euros a night.

This comes as a new initiative for the largest furniture retailer, as well as for Marriott, who currently owns over 3,700 properties in 74 countries but is now seeking a spot in the economy segment. The brand will be operated by a franchise and will stay in line with IKEA's low-cost, high-quality mentality.

Amid IKEA's international success, president of the U.S. IKEA, Mike Ward, believes this is just the beginning. In addition to entering new markets, as seen in its partnership with Marriott, IKEA is also placing a strong focus on making its current line of business even better. The company is investing heavily in core products, particularly in the U.S. market, to battle the predisposition that the product line is primarily for those in their "starting-up phase." IKEA has also begun offering delivery service in some markets and plans on putting other strategies into place throughout 2013 to further highlight itself as a quality brand that not only acts responsibly, but also listens to its customers.

There will also be a shift in leadership structure moving forward, as CEO Mikael Ohlsson plans to leave IKEA by early September 2013. Although there has been much speculation as to succession plans for Ingvar Kamprad, he does plan on providing his three sons with larger ownership roles moving forward, while Kamprad himself will continue his role as senior advisor to the Ingka holding company. He plans on staying with the company for years to come as its key decision maker.

Questions for Review

1. How would you describe IKEA's overall approach to international expansion? What were some of the important successes and challenges it experienced along the way?

2. What macro- and micro-political risks did IKEA face when it first considered entry into Russia? What kinds of preemptive and/or proactive political strategies might it have pursued to mitigate these risks?

3. How should IKEA respond to some of the recent scandals concerning product

contamination, sourcing, working conditions, and product safety?

4. What motivation, leadership, and international HR approaches has IKEA pursued to achieve its international success? What additional steps might it consider given its expanding global reach and impending change in leadership?

Source: This case was prepared by Deborah Zachar of Villanova University under the supervision of Professor Jonathan Doh as the basis for class discussion. Additional research assistance was provided by Ben Littell. It is not intended to illustrate either effective or ineffective managerial capability or administrative responsibility.

ENDNOTES

1. Bo Edvardsson, Bo Enquist, and Michael Hay, "Values-Based Service Brands: Narratives from IKEA," *Managing Service Quality* 16, no. 3 (2006), pp. 230–246.

2. Jens Hansegard and Sven Grundberg, "IKEA Chief Executive to Step Down," *The Wall Street Journal Online*, September 17, 2012, www.wsj.com/articles/SB10000872396390443816804578001922463079746.

3. "Our Swedish Origins," *IKEA*, 2013, www.ikea.com/ms/en_JP/about_ikea/the_ikea_way/swedish_heritage/index.html.

4. "The Story of IKEA," *Management Practice*, no. 8 (1997), pp. 33–34.

5. Veronika Tarnovskaya, Ulf Elg, and Steve Burt, "The Role of Corporate Branding in a Market Driving Strategy," *International Journal of Retail & Distribution Management* 36, no. 11 (2008), pp. 941–965.

6. Mats Urde, "Uncovering the Corporate Brand's Core Values," *Management Decision* 47, no. 4 (2009), pp. 616–638.

7. Edvardsson, Enquist, and Hay, "Values-Based Service Brands."

8. Urde, "Uncovering the Corporate Brand's Core Values."

9. Tarnovskaya, Elg, and Burt, "The Role of Corporate Branding in a Market Driving Strategy."

10. Ibid.

11. Ibid.

12. Edvardsson, Enquist, and Hay, "Values-Based Service Brands."

13. Dario A. Schirone and Germano Torkan, "New Transport Organization by IKEA. An Example of Social Responsibility in Corporate Strategy," *Advances in Management & Applied Economics* 2, no. 3 (2012), pp. 181–193.

14. "Welcome Inside Our Company," *IKEA*, www.ikea.com/ms/en_US/this-is-ikea/company-information/.

15. Tarnovskaya, Elg, and Burt, "The Role of Corporate Branding in a Market Driving Strategy."

16. Ibid.

17. Schirone and Torkan, "New Transport Organization by IKEA."

18. Ibid.

19. Ibid.

20. Kowitt, Beth. "Can Ikea turn its blond world green?" *Fortune*, March 10, 2015. turhttp://fortune.com/2015/03/10/can-ikea-turn-green/

21. Transparency International, Corruption Perceptions Index 2015. https://www.transparency.org/cpi2015/

22. Ibid.

23. Oleg Nikishenkov, "IKEA Case Exposes Bribe Culture in Russia," *Moscow News*, February 23, 2010, http://www.news.rin.ru/eng/news///14152/all//.

24. Anna Molin, "IKEA Regrets Cutting Women from Saudi Ad," *The Wall Street Journal*, October 1, 2012, www.wsj.com/articles/SB10000872396390444592404578030274200387136.

25. Ibid.

26. Ibid.

27. Tiffany Hsu, "Ikea: 'We Deeply Regret' Use of Forced Labor in East Germany," *Los Angeles Times*, November 16, 2012, http://articles.latimes.com/2012/nov/16/business/la-fi-mo-ikea-forced-labor-germany-20121116.

28. Edvardsson, Enquist, and Hay, "Values-Based Service Brands."

29. Nicholas Kulish and Julia Werdigier, "Ikea Admits Forced Labor Was Used in 1980s," *New York Times*, November 16, 2012, www.nytimes.com/2012/11/17/business/global/ikea-to-report-on-allegations-of-using-forced-labor-during-cold-war.html.

30. Anna Molin and John Stoll, "IKEA's Iconic Meatball Drawn into Horse-Meat Scandal," *The Wall Street Journal*, February 25, 2013, www.wsj.com/articles/SB10001424127887323384604578325864020138732.

31. Jens Hansegard, "IKEA: Chinese Officials Find Coliform Bacteria in IKEA Cakes," *The Wall Street Journal*, March 5, 2013.

HSBC in China

Introduction

After years of negotiations, China finally acceded to the World Trade Organization (WTO) in December 2001 (see Exhibit 1). This development was a significant milestone in China's integration with the global economy. One of the most important and far-reaching consequences was the transformation of China's financial sector. China's banking, insurance, and securities industries were long due for a major overhaul, and the WTO requirements guaranteed that the liberalization of China's economy would extend to the important financial sector. China's banking sector had become a casualty of the state. Banks and other financial institutions haphazardly extended loans to state-owned enterprises (SOEs) based not on sound credit analysis but favoritism and government-directed policy. As a consequence, crippling debt from bad and underperforming loans mounted, with no effective market disciplines to rein it in.

China recognized that opening up the banking sector could bolster its financial system. Foreign management would help overhaul the banking sector and put the focus on returns, instead of promoting a social agenda. This fiscal agenda would ultimately lead to a stronger and more stable economy. Yet after years of direction from the state,

Chinese bank managers did not have the necessary skills to transform the banks on their own. Guo Shuqing, shortly after being promoted to chairman of China Construction Bank, admitted that "more than 90 percent of the bank's risk managers are unqualified."[1]

Immediately upon accession to the WTO, China's banking sector began to open to foreign banks. Initially, foreign banks were allowed to conduct foreign currency business without any market access restrictions and conduct local currency business with foreign-invested enterprises and foreign individuals. In addition, the liberalization of foreign investment rules made Chinese banks attractive targets for foreign financial institutions. Sweeping domestic changes have followed. Strong emphasis has been placed on interest rate liberalization and clearer and more consistent regulation, and a frenzy of IPOs of state-owned banks has followed. It was in this context that HSBC rapidly expanded its presence in China.

HSBC, known for its international scope and careful, judicious strategy, made a series of key investments in the early 2000s that arguably gave it the most extensive position in China of any foreign financial group. These

Exhibit 1   **China's WTO Commitments**

General Cross-Sector Commitments

- Reforms to lower trade barriers in every sector of the economy, opening its markets to foreign companies and their exports from the first day of accession.
- Provide national treatment and improved market access to goods and services from other WTO members.
- Special rules regarding subsidies and the operation of state-owned enterprises, in light of the state's large role in China's economy.
- Undertake important changes to its legal framework, designed to add transparency and predictability to business dealings and improve the process of foreign market entry.
- Agreement to assume the obligations of more than 20 *existing* multilateral WTO agreements, covering all areas of trade.
- Under the acquired rights commitment, agreed that the conditions of ownership, operation, and scope of activities for a foreign company under any existing agreement would not be made more restrictive than they were on the date of China's accession to the WTO.
- Licensing procedures that were streamlined, transparent, and more predictable.

Commitments Specific to the Financial Services Industry

- Allow foreign banks to conduct *foreign currency business* without any market access or national treatment limitations.
- Allow foreign banks to conduct *local currency business* with foreign-invested enterprises and foreign individuals (subject to geographic restrictions).
- Banking services (with a five-year transitional plan) by foreign banks:

    Within two years after accession, foreign banks would be able to conduct *domestic* currency business with Chinese enterprises (subject to geographic restrictions).

    Within five years after accession, foreign banks would be able to conduct domestic currency business with Chinese individuals, and all geographic restrictions will be lifted.

    Foreign banks also would be permitted to provide financial leasing services at the same time that Chinese banks are permitted to do so.

investments included two separate transactions that resulted in a 19.9 percent stake in both Ping An insurance and Bank of Communications, the fifth largest bank in China. HSBC had a long history in Asia and was uniquely positioned to take advantage of China's vast population and mushrooming middle class, high savings rates (in the range of 40 percent), and huge capital investments. HSBC recognized that the current banking system was not capitalizing on this vast opportunity and sought to get in on the ground floor in this new environment. Perhaps, with further liberalization, however, China would allow future investors to establish even greater claims to Chinese banks. Citigroup's successful effort to gain a controlling stake in Guandgong Development Bank appeared to undermine earlier investors who had been limited by China's rule that allowed foreigners to own no more than 19.9 percent of domestic financial institutions. Did the huge potential rewards of being an early mover in China mitigate the promise of uncertainty and risks of doing business in an emerging market? After being burned in Argentina, could HSBC relax its conservative philosophy in its China strategy? If the economy took a turn for the worse, HSBC could face heavy losses. On the other hand, could HSBC afford not to be an early mover in a region where it had a longstanding presence?

Background on HSBC

History

Thomas Sutherland founded the Hongkong and Shanghai Banking Corporation (Hongkong Bank) in 1865 to finance the growing trade between Europe, India, and China. Sutherland, a Scot, was working for the Peninsular and Oriental Steam Navigation Company when he recognized a considerable demand for local banking facilities in Hong Kong and on the China coast. Hongkong Bank opened in Hong Kong in March 1865 and in Shanghai a month later.

The bank rapidly expanded by opening agencies and branches across the globe, reaching as far as Europe and North America, but maintained a distinct focus on China and the Asia-Pacific region. Hongkong Bank helped pioneer modern banking during this time in a number of countries, such as Japan, where it opened a branch in 1866 and advised the government on banking and currency, and Thailand, where it opened the country's first bank in 1888 and printed the country's first banknotes. By the 1880s, the bank issued banknotes and held government funds in Hong Kong, and also helped manage British government accounts in China, Japan, Penang, and Singapore. In 1876, the bank handled China's first public loan, and thereafter issued most of China's public loans. Hongkong Bank had become the foremost financial institution in Asia by the close of the 19th century.

After the First World War, the Hongkong Bank anticipated an expansion in its Asian markets and took a leading role in stabilizing the Chinese national currency. The tumultuous Second World War, for its part, saw most of the bank's European staff become prisoners of war to the advancing Japanese.

The Postwar Years

In the postwar years, Hongkong Bank turned to dramatic expansion through acquisitions and alliances in order to diversify. The acquisitions began with the British Bank of the Middle East (Persia and the Gulf states) and the Mercantile Bank (India and Malaya) in 1959, and were followed by acquiring a majority interest in Hong Kong's Hang Seng Bank in 1965. The 51 percent controlling interest in Hang Seng Bank was acquired during a local banking crisis for $12.4 million. As of 2016, HSBC's interest in the bank was 62 percent and was over US$20 billion. Hang Seng, which retained its name and management, has been a consistently strong performer. The bank made further acquisitions in the United Kingdom and Europe (from 1973), North America (from 1980), and Latin America (from 1997), as well as other Asian markets.

Under Chairman Michael Sandberg, Hongkong Bank entered the North American market with a $314 million, 51 percent acquisition of Marine Midland, a regional bank in upstate New York. In 1987, the bank purchased the remaining 49 percent, doubling Hongkong Bank's investment and providing the bank a significant U.S. presence. As a condition of the acquisition, however, Marine Midland retained its senior management.

Move to London and Acquisitions

In 1991, Hongkong Bank reorganized as HSBC Holdings and moved its headquarters in 1993 to London from Hong Kong. Sandberg's successor, William Purves, led HSBC's purchase of the U.K.'s Midland Bank in 1992. This acquisition fortified HSBC's European presence and doubled its assets. The move also enhanced HSBC's global presence and advanced the bank's reputation as a global financial services company.

Other major acquisitions of the 1990s included Republic Bank and Safra Holdings in the United States, which doubled HSBC's private banking business; investment moves in Brazil and Argentina in 1997; and acquisition of Mexico's Bital in 2002. In 2000, HSBC acquired CCF in France. By 2006, HSBC had assets exceeding $1,860 billion, customers numbering close to 100 million, and operations on six continents. In recent years, HSBC has made a major commitment to emerging markets, especially China and Mexico, but also Brazil, India, and smaller developing economies.

Expansion, Acquisition, and Succession

Early 1990s: The World's Local Bank

HSBC Holding Company set up a group policy in 1991 that established 11 quasi-independent banks, each a separate subsidiary with its own balance sheet. The head office provided essential functions, such as strategic planning, human resource management, and legal, administrative, and financial planning and control. This setup promoted prompter decision making at a local level and greater accountability. HSBC portrayed itself as "the world's local bank," recognizing the importance of globalization, flexibility, and local responsiveness.

HSBC established distinct customer groups or lines of business that overlaid existing geographic designations. This encouraged maximizing the benefits of its universal scope, such as sharing best practices of product development, management, and marketing. The geographic perspective was melded closely with a customer group perspective, demanding both global and local thinking. Traditionally, HSBC's culture embraced caution, thrift, discipline, and risk avoidance. The bank looked at long-term survival and considered markets in 50-year views. Thrift manifested through the company, and even the chairman flew economy class on flights less than three hours.

Late 1990s: Bond's Rein and Move to "HSBC"

Sir John Bond became CEO of HSBC in 1993 and chairman in 1998, bringing with him a hands-on entrepreneurial style and exceptionally ambitious goals. He pursued acquisitions beyond HSBC's traditional core, in pursuit of such attractive financial segments as wealth management, investment banking, online retail financing, and consumer finance. Bond considered shareholder value and economic profit in deciding when acquisition premiums were in order, which was in contrast to his predecessor's "three times book value" rule. By 2001, Bond had authorized investments of over $21 billion on acquisitions and new ventures.

In 1998, Bond adopted the HSBC brand and preserved "The Hongkong & Shanghai Banking Corp." name only for its bank based in Hong Kong. HSBC branded its subsidiary banks across the world with the parent bank's acronym and greatly expanded marketing efforts in 2000. In March 2002, HSBC's marketing message became "the world's local bank," which would help the brand become one of the world's top 50 most recognizable brands by 2003.

2000s: Household Acquisition

In 2003, a US$15.5 billion acquisition of Household International, the U.S. consumer lending business, became the basis of HSBC's Consumer Finance customer group. Household utilized a unique system to forecast the likelihood that customers would repay debt, which used a 13-year database of consumer behavior. Household was controversial and yet presented great opportunity. HSBC desired to leverage this new skill in developing countries, yet was unable to find all demographic and credit data that Household normally relies on in the United States. HSBC particularly looked to extend the Household model into China and Mexico. However, the subprime mortgage crisis hit the United States hard in 2007–2008 and had a major impact on Household operations.

Six years after acquiring Household International, HSBC effectively conceded that the deal was a mistake. In March 2009 HSBC made public that it would close all 800 remaining branches of HSBC Finance Corp., the former Household Financial, resulting in 6,100 job cuts nationwide. HSBC had already closed about 600 HFC and Beneficial branches over the past two years. "High levels of delinquency, given rising levels of unemployment, mean that the business model for subprime home equity refinancing is not sustainable,"[2] said Niall Booker, HSBC Finance chief executive during one of the media conferences. HSBC Finance said it would retain its credit card business, and HSBC Holdings would keep its New York–based HSBC Bank USA. HSBC officials also said that the bank would continue to help mortgage customers with loan repayments and foreclosure-prevention efforts.

The HSBC Finance (Household) executives pointed out that it was hard to predict in 2003 that the global financial crisis and the recession would occur. When the crisis hit hard in 2008, the subprime mortgage market led to more than $1.15 trillion of credit losses and write-downs at financial institutions and government bailouts of companies ranging from Citigroup Inc. to Royal Bank of Scotland Group Plc of Edinburgh, as noted by Bloomberg analysts. HSBC was one of the first banks to acknowledge the possibility of upcoming subprime mortgage problems and set aside about $53 billion to cover bad loans during the past three years.

2008–2009: Economic Crisis and Financial Performance

The consequences of global economic crisis were severe for the world's banking system, prompting thousands of banks to seek financial assistance from their local government. Many banks were burdened with highly overvalued "bad loans" and suffered huge losses. Unlike many global players, HSBC reported a profit for 2008, but it still took a hit: Its pretax profit of $9.3 billion was 62 percent below the $24.2 billion reported for 2007. The bank also cut its dividend for the full year by 29 percent to 64 cents per share. The slide in profits was largely the result of a goodwill impairment charge of $10.6 billion in the United States. In spite of the bitter loss in North America, HSBC performed much better in the other parts of the world. For example, in Europe, pretax profit rose to $10.9 billion from $8.6 billion. Profit from Hong Kong fell to $5.46 billion from $7.34 billion, while earnings from the rest of Asia rose to $6.47 billion from $6.01 billion. HSBC is still considered one of the world's strongest banks by some measures. The bank's market value of $68.2 billion in early 2009 ranked it behind only Industrial & Commercial Bank of China Ltd., China Construction Bank Corp., Bank of China Ltd., and JPMorgan Chase & Co.

To the credit of HSBC management, the bank avoided taking U.K. government "bailout" funding, unlike other big banks. Instead, HSBC made plans to raise £12.5 billion ($17.9 billion) in capital to prepare for further deterioration of the global economy. Also, responding to growing public anger over the scale of bonuses paid to many senior bankers, HSBC said no performance share awards would be made for 2008 and that no executive director would receive a cash bonus.

2010s: Refocused Strategy & Divestment

In the wake of the financial crisis, HSBC took a fresh look at its expansion and operational strategies. As part of this refocusing, the company promoted Stuart Gulliver to CEO in 2011. Within months, Gulliver announced plans to decrease overhead by US$3.5 billion, primarily through cuts to its retail banking operations in developed markets. The company formally abandoned its "World's Local Bank" philosophy, announced plans to withdraw from 20 countries, and indicated that 25,000 jobs would be cut within two years. Nearly 200 local banking branches in the U.S. were sold to First Niagara Financial Group Inc., halving HSBC's retail operations in the country. Additionally, HSBC's U.S. credit card business was sold to Capital One Financial Corp. for US$2.6 billion. Though most downscaling of operations occurred in developed countries, targeted divestment has occurred in some emerging markets; in 2015, HSBC sold its Brazilian operations to Banco Bradesco after several years of poor performance

Managing for Growth

HSBC's strategic plan, "Managing for Growth," was launched in the early 2000s. This strategy builds on HSBC's global, international scope and seeks to grow by focusing on the key customer groups of personal financial services; consumer finance; commercial banking; corporate, investment banking, and markets; and private banking. "Managing for Growth" is intended to be "evolutionary, not revolutionary," and aims to vault HSBC to the world's leading financial services company. HSBC seeks to grow earnings over the long term, using its peers as a benchmark. It also plans to invest in delivery platforms, technology, its people, and its brand name to prop

up the future value of HSBC's stock market rating and total shareholder return. HSBC retains its core values of communication, long-term focus, ethical relationships, teamwork, prudence, creativity, high standards, ambition, customer-focused marketing, and corporate social responsibility, all with an international outlook.

Strategic Pillars

As part of the growth strategy, HSBC identified eight strategic pillars:

> *Brand:* continue to establish HSBC and its hexagon symbol as one of the top global brands for customer experience and corporate social responsibility.
> *Personal Financial Services:* drive growth in key markets and through appropriate channels; emerging markets are essential markets with a burgeoning demand.
> *Consumer Finance:* offer both a wider product range and penetrate new markets, such as the emerging country markets.
> *Commercial Banking:* leverage HSBC's international reach through effective relationship management and improved product offerings.
> *Corporate, Investment Banking, and Markets:* accelerate growth by enhancing capital markets and advisory capabilities.
> *Private Banking:* a focus on serving the highest value personal clients.
> *People:* draw in, develop and motivate HSBC's people.
> *TSR:* fulfill HSBC's TSR target by achieving strong competitive performances in earnings per share growth and efficiency.[3]

Focus on Emerging Markets

Back in 2000, HSBC had half of its assets in developing countries. Most earnings, however, stemmed from mature markets, such as Hong Kong and Britain. All but 5 percent of group profits came from five economies, while India and Latin America each added only 1 percent to group profit. By 2005, however, HSBC executives recognized the earnings potential of emerging markets. As then-Chairman Stephen Green noted, "There is a general rule of thumb that says the emerging markets grow faster than mature markets as economies and the financial services sector grows faster than the real economy in emerging markets because you are starting from very low penetration of financial services in general."[4]

Though cost-cutting measures enacted in the 2010s have stagnated HSBC's overall net profit before tax, the proportion of net profit earned in emerging markets has soared (see Exhibit 2). Across the board, HSBC's pretax profits in emerging markets have increased from US$2.4 billion in 2004 to $6.0 billion in 2014. The largest growth, by far, has come from China. Between 2004 and 2014, HSBC's profit in China jumped from

Exhibit 2 HSBC Emerging Markets

Pretax Profits 2004 vs. 2014

Country	2004 (US$ mil)	2014 (US$ mil)	% Change 2004–2014
Argentina	154	384	149.4
Brazil	281	(247)	(187.9)
China	32	2,951	9,121.9
India	178	700	293.3
Indonesia	76	198	160.5
Malaysia	214	496	131.8
Mexico	774	51	(93.4)
Saudi Arabia	122	486	298.4
South Korea	89	180	102.2
Taiwan	107	221	106.5
Turkey	142	(64)	(145.1)
UAE	192	662	244.8
Total	**2,361**	**6,018**	154.9
Total profit before tax (all countries)	18,943	18,680	(1.4)

US$32 million to nearly US$3 billion, and the Chinese market now accounts for more than 15 percent of HSBC's total net profit before tax. Strong gains in India are also noteworthy, with profits increasing by more than 200 percent.

Liberalization of China's Banking Sector

China's Banking Sector Pre-WTO

Before the WTO accession negotiations, China's banking industry operated as a cog in China's centrally planned economy. The state commercial banks performed a social function, during China's post-Mao drive to industrialize, instead of operating for economic return. Consequently, the banks adhered to directed lending practices from the government and in turn created some of China's most successful enterprises, but also supported thousands of other inefficient and unprofitable state-owned enterprises. This practice left state commercial banks with massive amounts of debt that were largely unrecoverable and hordes of non-performing loans.

In addition to widespread losses, instability ensued in the banking system overall. To make matters worse, corruption and mismanagement ran rampant throughout the sector, sapping away consumer and investor confidence.

WTO Accession

Following 15 years of negotiation and two decades of economic reform in China, December 11, 2001, marked China's accession to the World Trade Organization. The main objective of the WTO agreement was to open China's market up to foreign competition. The deadline for complete implementation was December 11, 2006.

China made a number of implementations immediately. To begin with, foreign banks were allowed to conduct foreign currency business without any market access restrictions. Also, foreign banks were allowed to conduct local currency business with foreign-invested enterprises and foreign individuals (with geographic restrictions). Within two years of accession, China agreed to allow foreign banks to conduct domestic currency business with Chinese enterprises (geographic restrictions). Within five years, foreign banks could conduct domestic currency business with Chinese individuals (no geographic restrictions); and foreign banks were able to provide financial leasing services at the same time as Chinese banks. Under the WTO investment provisions, China agreed to allow foreign ownership of Chinese banks (up to 25 percent), with no single foreign investor permitted to own more than 20 percent.

"Bank reform has become the most crucial task for the government in pushing forward economic reforms,"[5] said Yi Xianrong, an economist at the Chinese Academy of Social Sciences in Beijing. Indeed, bank reform is critical to stabilizing and advancing the Chinese economy.

Domestic Reform

China has undertaken a number of domestic reforms in order to overhaul the banking industry. China has engaged in interest rate liberalization by removing certain interest rate and price controls. Instead of being pegged to the U.S. dollar, as it once was, China's currency exchange rate is now pegged to within 0.3 percent of a basket of currencies, dominated by a group including the U.S. dollar, euro, Japanese yen, South Korean won, British pound, Thai baht, and Russian ruble. Throughout the 2000s, analysts estimated that the yuan was undervalued, leading to complaints from the international community. However, most experts believed that the currency was no longer undervalued by mid-2015.

Regulation has long been a concern in the Chinese banking industry. China has made major progress by creating regulatory agencies. In 2003, China created a central regulator, the China Banking Regulatory Commission (CBRC), out of the central bank. The regulator's 20,000 staff members endeavor to shift the banks' focus from senseless loans and growth mind-sets to a goal of preserving capital and generating returns.

Concurrently, China is striving to make regulatory and reporting requirements more clear because they have often proved confusing barriers to foreign investment. Since 1998, China has intensified accounting, prudential, and regulatory standards. Prior to 1998, the banks booked interest income for up to three years even if it was not being paid. Now, the banks can do so for only 90 days, which is the international norm. Still, it has been all too common for Chinese banks to ignore regulations and not monitor loans. As a result of poor accounting, the banks themselves are sometimes unsure of their bad loans. Lai Xiaomin, head of the CBRC's Beijing office, admits that "when our banks disclose information, they don't always do so in a totally honest manner."[6] Indeed, the lack of reliable accounting can hamper investment. As one Hong Kong investor put it, "When you take a state-owned enterprise that has had weak internal controls, it can be enormously labor-intensive to come up with financials we can work with."[7] In 2006, regulators overhauled the system in which almost one-third of a company's shares were "nontradable." Fixing this problem has helped energize the market and welcome in individual investors.

New regulations, it is hoped, will address China's history of dishonesty and embezzlement. With the tight connection of Chinese banks with local governments, corruption has choked the Chinese banking system. As of 2016, most of China's commercial banks have introduced better governance, shareholding, and incentive structures, while also adding independent directors to their boards. Foreign management and knowledge are intended to flush the Chinese banking system with managerial talent. To help encourage foreign banks, China is relaxing some foreign bank restrictions. The Chinese government has also taken steps to eliminate bad loans by bailing out banks.

IPO Explosion

Over the last 15 years, China has aggressively pursued IPOs of state-owned banks, a policy that has been met with a strong response from investors eager to tap into the populous country and seize first-mover advantages (see Exhibit 3). HSBC's purchase of a 19.9 percent stake in Bank of Communications (BoCOM) in June 2004 was the pioneering, substantial foreign bank investment in China. In 2005, the listing of the Industrial and Commercial Bank of China on the Shanghai and Hong Kong Stock Exchanges resulted in the then-largest IPO in history. Bank of America invested heavily in China Construction Bank between 2005 and 2013, and the Royal Bank of Scotland, Temasek, and UBS all made significant investments in the Bank of China. In 2010, the IPO of the Agricultural Bank of China raised over US$22 billion, surpassing the record set by the Industrial and Commercial Bank of China.

The central bank expects foreigners to bring much-needed improvements to the state banks' risk-management and internal control systems, including credit-risk assessment and more transparent reporting. With capital

Exhibit 3   Early Foreign Bank Investments in China

PRC Bank	Foreign Partner	% Stake	Price	Date
Bank of Shanghai	HSBC	8.00	$62.6 m	12/2001
	IFC	7.00	$25.0 m	
	Shanghai Commercial Bank (HK)	3.00	$15.7 m	
Shanghai Pudong Dev. Bank	Citigroup	4.62	$72.0 m	12/2003
Fujian Asian Bank	HSBC	50.00	Less than $20 m	12/2003
Bank of Communications	HSBC	19.90	$1.75 b	6/2004
Xian CCB	Scotia Bank	12.4	$3.2 m	10/2004
Jinan City CCB	Commonwealth Bank of Australia	11.0	$17 m[1]	11/2004
Shenzhen Dev. Bank	Newbridge Capital	17.9	$1.23 b	12/2004
Minsheng Bank	Temasek	4.9		1/2005
Hangzhou CCB	Commonwealth Bank of Australia	19.90	$78.0 m	4/2005
China Construction Bank	Bank of America	9.00	$3.0 b	6/2005
	Temasek	5.1	$1.5 m[2]	
Bank of China	Royal Bank of Scotland	5.00	$3.1 b	8/2005
	UBS	1.6	$500 m[3]	9/2005
	Temasek	10.00	$3.1 b[4]	9/2005
Industrial Commercial BOC	Goldman, Allianz, AmEx			8/2005
Nanjing CCB	BNP Paribas	19.20	$27.0 m	10/2005
Hua Xia Bank	Deutsche Bank	9.9	$329 m[5]	10/2005
	Sal. Oppenheim Jr.	4.1		10/2005
Bank of Beijing	ING	19.90	$214 m	3/2005

[1]Guonan Ma, "Sharing China's Bank Restructuring," *China and World Economy* 14, no. 3 (2006), p. 8.

[2]David Lague and Donald Greenlees, "China's Troubled Banks Lure Investors," *International Herald Tribune*, September 9, 2005.

[3]"UBS to Invest $500 Million in Bank of China," *NBC News*, September 27, 2005, http://www.nbcnews.com/id/9501208/ns/business-world_business/., assessed October 4, 2006.

[4]Luo Jun and Xiao Yu, "Temasek to Buy 10% of China Bank," *International Herald Tribune*, September 1, 2005.

[5]"Deutsche Bank Seals Chinese Deal," *BBC News*, October 17, 2005, news.bbc.co.uk/2/hi/business/4348560.stm, accessed October 4, 2006.

allocated more efficiently, a more stable financial system will follow, and the economy will become more open to foreign competition.

Two Steps Forward

Pulling back from some of its commitments, China indirectly delayed the implementation of its WTO commitments. On February 1, 2002, the People's Bank of China (PBOC) issued regulations and implementation rules governing foreign-funded banks. While these measures met the commitments of the WTO agreement, the PBOC was taking a very conservative approach in opening up the banking sector. For example, foreign-funded banks could open only one branch every 12 months.

In the wake of these early obstacles, there have been positive changes. Capital requirements were reduced, additional cities were opened up to foreign banking, and the "one branch every 12 months" restriction was lifted. Central bank officials have indicated willingness to eventually elevate the foreign ownership limit above the current 25 percent, but experts doubt it will ever go beyond 50 percent. In January 2007, China opened its financial sector to foreign investors, which was one of its last WTO membership commitments. Under the new rules, foreign banks in China finally have the opportunity to offer services in the local currency—yuan—which was previously prohibited.

Capital is still mostly allocated to state-owned enterprises even though private companies have been China's growth engine. Private companies produce 52 percent of GDP in China, but only account for 27 percent of outstanding loans. By sinking money into state-owned enterprises, China's banks are dragging the economy. China's banks had difficulty lending to private companies in the past because of challenges related to gathering and processing the necessary information on them. As a response, China launched its first national credit bureau in early 2006. By 2014, more than 60 percent of China's population had credit history records maintained by the national credit bureau. China's banks have been satisfying a social role but now must allocate capital efficiently in order to generate positive economic return.

Investments in Ping An and BoCOM

With its longstanding presence in China, HSBC was among the best-positioned financial institutions to take advantage of China's market opening.

Ping An Insurance: 2002–2013

In October 2002, HSBC announced that it had taken a 10 percent stake in Ping An Insurance, China's second largest insurer, for $600 million, and in May 2005, HSBC indicated it was investing an additional HK$8.1 billion (US$1.04 billion) for an additional 9.91 percent stake in Ping An, doubling its holding in the number-two life insurer. HSBC paid HK$13.20 a share for the stakes held by investment banks Goldman Sachs and Morgan Stanley, lifting HSBC's holding to 19.9 percent, the maximum stake allowed by a single foreign investor.

"This is good news for Ping An," said Kenneth Lee, an analyst at Daiwa Institute of Research. "HSBC is buying at a premium and is replacing Goldman Sachs and Morgan Stanley, which are venture capital investors. HSBC is a long-term investor and will help Ping An to develop its insurance platform," he said.

The investments proved to be rewarding for HSBC. In 2011, China's insurance market reported an 18.5 percent increase in premium income as compared to 2010. Total premium income in China experienced a 5.3 percent increase during this same time period. In 2013, HSBC sold its stake in Ping An for a US$2.6 billion profit.

The BoCOM Deal

HSBC invested $1.8 billion for a 19.9 percent stake in BoCOM in June 2004. HSBC's chairman at the time, Sir John Bond, commented on the company's long-term perspective: "[I]t is inevitable that China will become a superpower. And indeed, desirable. And we are positioning our business for the decades ahead accordingly."[8] HSBC wanted a piece of the alluring Chinese market, which Goldman Sachs predicts will overtake the United States as the number-one economy in the world by 2040, and wanted to deepen its international scope in line with the "Managing for Growth" strategy.

Speaking one month after HSBC's big move, then-CEO and future chair Stephen Green expounded upon China: "[T]he potential in China's domestic market is the largest in history." China is the "world's manufacturer," and as the population continues to urbanize and industrialize, it increasingly has more disposable income, the workers become greater consumers, and the middle class expands. China has one of the world's highest savings rates, at around 40 percent, and already has around one-third of the $1.2 trillion of central bank foreign exchange reserves sitting in Asia. Further, access to capital is not a problem, as foreign direct investment (FDI) floods the country. The challenge facing China is to recycle and invest its pool of savings efficiently.

HSBC recognized the huge potential in the market for banking services, as well as credit cards. As part of its emerging market strategy, HSBC wanted to feed the demand for credit cards in these markets. Green commented: "[O]ur joint venture with Bank of Communications for credit cards is one which we think has a lot of exciting prospects. Bank of Communications has over 30 million debit cards in issue. Over time, a proportion of those is going to convert to credit cards. And we are issuing co-branded credit cards with the Bank of Communications."[9] HSBC saw an opportunity to shepherd millions of new people into the banking system.

HSBC's Green acquiesced that emerging markets do carry risk. This risk was starkly evident during the HSBC debacle in Argentina during the country's economic crisis. China's epic turnaround could conceivably flop, and heavily invested banks could pay dearly. The banking system in China was and is very fragile. Would China's banks be able to break away from state-directed lending and its lasting effects? The banks further rely on the continued acceleration of the economy, and many rely on volatile real estate loans. HSBC recognized other challenges for China, including the need to strengthen regulations, build social security, stem corruption, and fortify the financial system.

HSBC's holdings in BoCOM, which are among the largest by a foreign bank in China, have posted mixed results over the last ten years. In 2015, BoCOM's listings on the Hong Kong stock exchange dropped more than 11 percent. In reaction, BoCOM announced that it would allow HSBC greater control in decision making, including the appointment of a new vice chair.

Recent Developments and Future Competitive Conditions

Current Strategies in China

Foreign banks that operate in China have different strategies. Some of them have purchased smaller stakes of Chinese financial institutions, while some prefer to buy a bigger stake of a small bank. Nevertheless, they all want to be in China. The best strategy, in theory, has turned out to be with a local partner. Bob Edgar, senior managing director at Australia and New Zealand Banking Group Ltd., said that "it would be very difficult to go into a market like that and undertake the cost of establishing a branch network, getting a customer base of hundreds of thousands if not millions of customers. That already exists, so why would we want to set it up again?"[10]

Many foreign banks, however, experience difficulties when working with a local partner. The credit standards are not as strict as they should be, and there is still endemic corruption at different levels. In addition, the partners gain influence in the foreign bank. This is the reason why HSBC has decided to invest "outside the Big Four": so it would have bigger control in operations. Peter Wong, executive director of HSBC's Hong Kong and Mainland China operations, has commented: "[T]he state-owned banks would be too big." So only the future will tell what is the best strategy.

The competition in China's banking industry is continuing to grow. Recently, foreign banks have increasingly turned to joint ventures as a strategy for increasing investment in China. In 2011, Morgan Stanley formed a joint venture with Huaxin Securities Co. Ltd. to facilitate expansion into China. Morgan Stanley owns a third of the venture, while Huaxin Securities maintains two-thirds control. The deal gives Morgan Stanley the ability to underwrite and trade bonds. UBS, Goldman Sachs, Royal Bank of Scotland, and Deutsche Bank have formed similar joint ventures in recent years, with the foreign bank maintaining a minority share while the domestic partner holds the majority position.

When it comes to utilizing joint ventures as a way to increase investment in mainland China, HSBC has lagged behind its peers. In 2015, HSBC finally announced its first securities joint venture in China, with Shenzhen Qianhai Financial Holdings as its local partner. The delay, however, may have proved beneficial; unlike most other foreign banks with joint ventures in China, HSBC was able to secure a majority share of the deal.

Shifting towards Asian Operations

Despite the mixed performance results over the last several years with its BoCOM joint venture, HSBC shows no signs of scaling back its operations in China. In fact, CEO Stuart Gulliver announced plans to do just the opposite in 2015. While the abandonment of the "World's Local Bank" strategy resulted in job cuts and branch closings in many developed markets, Gulliver stated that HSBC was planning to hire more than 25,000 new employees in the Asian region in the coming years.

Much of HSBC's future profitability appears to hinge on China and other Asian markets. In 2015, European and North American holdings accounted for 30 percent and 15 percent of HSBC's assets, respectively, but only 3 percent and 8 percent of net profits before tax. Additionally, future growth prospects in those regions appear bleak. In both Europe and the United States, revenues have remained stagnated for several years. Conversely, 40 percent of HSBC's assets were located in Asian markets by 2015. These markets, growing at 7 percent annually, accounted for 78 percent of net profits before tax.

While HSBC only had 200 branches and a deposit base of US$40 billion in mainland China as of 2015, GDP growth projections indicate that the Guangdong province will be the largest banking center worldwide by 2025. HSBC's strategy for future investment in the Guangdong area, and specifically in Shenzhen, is dependent on increasingly liberal banking reforms by the Chinese government. As of 2015, China was still heavily regulating the opening of new branches, which, if it remains unchanged, could hinder HSBC's expansion plans.

HSBC's Expansion in Vietnam and Taiwan

HSBC has found success in other Asian markets over the last decade. In 2009, HSBC won approval from the Vietnamese government to become the first foreign bank to set up a locally incorporated entity. New laws that have helped open Vietnam's banking sector to foreign companies were introduced as part of the communist country's inclusion in the World Trade Organization. The change in legal status in Vietnam has made it easier for HSBC's local operations to set up branches across the country. That year, HSBC hired more than 400 additional staff in Vietnam in anticipation of its expansion. This has brought the number of staff members there to more than 1,000. In Vietnam, HSBC also owns 10 percent of Bao Viet Holdings, an insurance company, and 20 percent of Vietnam Technological & Commercial Joint Stock Bank, or Techcombank. In 2015, HSBC was named both Best Foreign Investment Bank in Vietnam and Best Foreign Commercial Bank in Vietnam by FinanceAsia.

Similarly, in 2009 HSBC was the first bank to incorporate locally within Taiwan. Growth has been slow but steady; by 2015, HSBC was operating 40 branches throughout the island, with half of those located in Taipei. HSBC has incorpated various corporate sustainability initiatives into its Taiwan operations, including donating to various educational and environmental charities. In 2015, HSBC received Taiwan's Excellence in Corporate Social Responsibility award for its efforts.

Future Competitive Conditions

Despite the economic crisis, there were several geographical regions that did not fall into economic recession in the 2008–2010 period. China, foremost, experienced strong economic growth throughout this period. China's gross domestic product expanded 10.7 percent in the fourth quarter of 2009, bringing full-year growth to 8.7 percent. That came in above the government's targeted 8 percent growth and well above many economists' estimates. China officially surpassed Japan as the world's second-largest economy in mid 2010. The growth numbers demonstrate that Beijing's stimulus program—a response to the global economic slowdown that focused on massive bank lending and public investments in infrastructure—helped avert an economic slowdown. However, as the developed world has begun to recover and economies like the United States, Germany, and the United Kingdom have seen modest gain in GDP growth, China has shown signs of a significant slowdown. By 2015, China's growth rate had slipped to less than 7 percent.

In 2014, China surpassed the United States to become the largest recipient of FDI worldwide. More than US$128 billion in investments flowed into China in 2014 alone. Despite the economic slowdown that China is experiencing, FDI inflows continue to increase year over year.

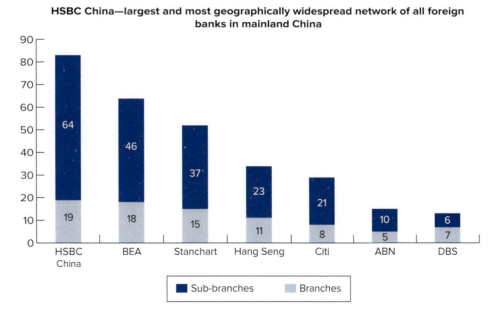

Locally incorporated foreign banks by network

HSBC China—largest and most geographically widespread network of all foreign banks in mainland China

Note: As of end-April 2009 (excluding representative offices, administrative offices, etc.)

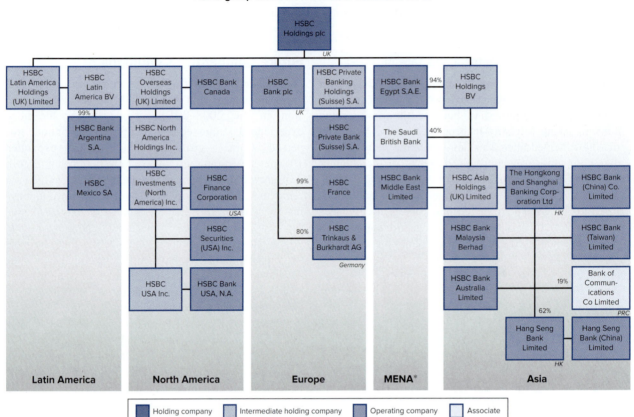

HSBC group structure chart as of December 2015

*Middle East and North Africa

Source: "Simplified Structure Chart: Principal Entities," *The HSBC Group,* http://www.hsbc.com/about-hsbc/structure-and-network.

Exhibit 4   **Top 10 Banks in China, Ranked by Tier 1 Capital in 2014**

Rank	Bank	Tier 1 Capital	Assets	Rank (by Assets)	Foreign Bank Shareholder
1	ICBC	207,614	3,100,254	1	
2	China Construction Bank	173,992	2,517,734	2	
3	Bank of China	149,729	2,273,730	4	
4	Agricultural Bank of China	137,410	2,386,447	3	
5	Bank of Communications	68,333	976,882	5	**HSBC**
6	China Merchants Bank	41,690	658,210	7	
7	China Citic Bank	37,427	596,721	10	BBVA
8	Shanghai Pudong Development Bank	34,042	603,101	8	
9	China Minsheng Bank	33,232	528,714	11	
10	Industrial Bank	32,965	602,661	9	Hang Seng Bank

Source: Ernst & Young, *Future Directions for Foreign Banks in China* (2014), Appendix C.

HSBC's future development will depend heavily on two things. First, the competition will play a major role in HSBC's strategy. HSBC competitors are aggressively seeking opportunities in China, and HSBC has to constantly work to maintain and expand its market position. Second, HSBC's success will depend on the opportunities that the company sees in the other emerging markets of the world.

HSBC's Current China Strategy

HSBC's strategy in China is carried out by its 100 percent subsidiary HSBC Bank (China) Company Limited. As of 2016 HSBC Bank (China) was a network of more than 170 bank outlets (branches and sub-branches) with 6,000 employees spread across 50 cities. At this time HSBC had the largest and most geographically widespread network of banks in mainland China compared to other foreign banks operating in China.

In its attempt to mitigate the negative impact of economic crisis and strengthen its competitive position, HSBC took several measures to redefine and clarify its strategies for the nearest future. China was identified to be the center of the Group's emerging markets strategy. HSBC has formally defined its strategy for China as follows: "To be the leading foreign bank in China in terms of market share and profitability, and deliver significant offshore China-related business to the Group."

HSBC has identified key priorities aimed at achieving its strategic goals for China:

1. *International connectivity*—Connect its Chinese operations with the rest of HSBC Group's operations. This includes maintaining Chinese-dedicated desks in overseas offices and creating foreign representative positions within China.

2. *RMB internationalization*—Become the leading bank for RMB globally. Currently, more than 150 countries are doing business with RMB, with France, Singapore, and the U.K. leading the way.

3. *Network and presence*—Use network leadership to maintain a strong presence in the market.

4. *Capabilities and licenses*—Maintain product leadership in China, when compared to other foreign banks operating in the country.

5. *People*—Hire and retain the best employees, and leverage those employees as a resource for business growth and organizational effectiveness.

6. *Strategic partners*—Maintain and build strong strategic partnerships and facilitate business cooperation.

HSBC Group's Overall Current Strategy

HSBC Group's overall international strategy has evolved in the years since the global recession. As of 2016, the overall company strategy is currently designed around two global trends:

First, HSBC plans to focus on growing markets in Asia, Latin America, Africa, and the Middle East. Due to demographic shifts and increasing urbanization, those emerging markets are predicted to increase by 400 percent by 2050, providing a large consumer base that could potentially become retail banking customers. To maximize return, HSBC plans to focus on wealth management across these regions, but only enter retail banking in locations where there are enough middle-class consumers to return a profit.

Second, HSBC plans to take advantage of increasing international trade and cross-border capital flows. To acheive this, HSBC aims to reach small- to medium-sized multinational enterprises from a variety of home countries, build loyalty with these companies, and then continue to serve these companies as they grow from smaller startups to large conglomerates.

To decide where to expand and invest, HSBC has developed a decision-making framework. The framework evaluates the relevance, the quality of the returns, and the risk of financial crime to determine whether HSBC should increase investment, improve its operations, or withdraw from the market.

2016 and Beyond

Despite HSBC's slimming of operations around the globe in an effort to cut costs, HSBC has reaffirmed its future plans for growth in the Chinese market. In late 2015, HSBC announced plans to add over 3,000 employees to the Pearl River Delta region in an effort to increase its retail banking business. The boost is aimed at increasing HSBC's pretax profits in the region by a factor of 10 by the year 2020. The Pearl River Delta, which includes the cities of Shenzhen and Foshan, includes a rapidly expanding middle-class population that could serve as future HSBC retail banking customers.

Using the six filters in decision-making

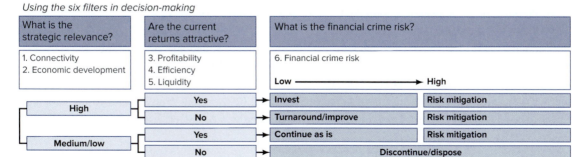

HSBC Decision-Making Framework

Source: HSBC, *Strategic Report 2014* (February 2015), http://www.hsbc.com/our-approach/reports-and-documentation.

The bank is also working toward being one of mainland China's first foreign-listed companies to tap into the country's liquidity and to raise its overall profile there. Credit card usage has been increasing rapidly within the country, with nearly 500 million credit cards issued by the end of 2015. HSBC has moved to grab a larger share of this growing market. Between 2004 and 2016, HSBC and Bank of Communications co-issued over 40 million co-branded credit cards in China. In early 2016, HSBC was granted approval to begin issuing credit cards on its own, effectively ending the credit card portion of its joint venture and allowing HSBC to take complete control over its credit card operations.

HSBC's China experience has been one of steady and consistent expansion and success. While there have been some setbacks, its overall approach, emphasizing close collaboration with the Chinese government and local partners, reliance on local staff and talent, and its overall shift in global strategy from developed to emerging markets, has served it well.

Questions for Review

1. How has HSBC adapted its global strategy to operate in China, both before and after China's WTO accession?

2. Discuss HSBC's strategy for entering and operating in other emerging markets. Where has it found success, and where has it faced setbacks? Why?

3. What are the pros and cons of HSBC's "Managing for Growth" strategy?

4. How did HSBC withstand the world economic crisis? Was HSBC's position weakened or strengthened as result of the crisis? How did HSBC alter its strategy in the wake of the recession?

5. What are some changing economic factors that HSBC will need to take into consideration in the coming years?

Exercise

HSBC is considering asking the government of China (China Banking Regulatory Commission—CBRC) to allow it to increase its stake in BoCom above the limit currently in place (25% total foreign ownership; 20% for an individual foreign investor). Break into four groups:

1. HSBC
2. BoCom
3. Citibank
4. CBRC

Groups 1–3 should prepare a 5-minute presentation on whether the government of China should grant the request and, if so, what the ownership limit should be (30%? 50%?) and whether it should be extended to other foreign financial institutions (e.g., Citibank). Then, Group 4 should discuss the question and report its decision.

Source: This case was prepared by Jonathan Doh of Villanova University as the basis for class discussion. Additional research assistance was provided by Courtney Asher, Elizabeth Stewart, Tetyana Azarova, and Ben Littell. It is not intended to illustrate either effective or ineffective managerial capability or administrative responsibility.

ENDNOTES

1. "China's Banking Industry: A Great Big Banking Gamble," *The Economist*, October 25, 2005.

2. Becky Yerak, "HSBC Plans to Close Household Financial, Beneficial Consumer Loan Units," *Chicago Tribune*, March 3, 2009, http://articles. chicagotribune.com/2009-03-03/news/0903021009_ 1_hsbc-holdings-plc-hsbc-bank-usa-household-international.

3. "Our Strategy," *HSBC*, www.hsbc.com/about-hsbc/our-strategy.

4. Carrick Mollenkamp, "HSBC CEO Discusses the Bank's Expansion Plans," *The Wall Street Journal*, October 23, 2005.

5. Peter S. Goodman, "China Approves Plan for Huge Bank IPO," *Washington Post*, July 20, 2006, p. D5.

6. "China's Banking Industry: A Great Big Banking Gamble."

7. Barney Jopson, "China Struggles to Overcome Shortage of Good Accountants," *Financial Times*, June 6, 2006, p. 11.

8. Sir John Bond, "China: The Re-emergence of the Middle Kingdom," *Speech*, July 19, 2005.

9. Carrick Mollenkamp, "HSBC Plans Push in Emerging Markets," *The Wall Street Journal*, October 24, 2005.

10. K. C. Swanson, "Buying into China's Banks," *Corporate Dealmaker*, September–October 2006, p. 18.

Chiquita's Global Turnaround

On January 12, 2004, Chiquita named Fernando Aguirre as the company's new president and CEO, replacing Cyrus Freidhem, who had held the position since the company's emergence from bankruptcy in March 2002. In his 23 years with Cincinnati-based Procter & Gamble (P&G), Aguirre served in a variety of positions, including president of P&G Brazil and president of P&G Mexico. In his first remarks to Chiquita employees and investors, Aguirre reiterated the importance of corporate responsibility: "In terms of managing businesses and people, while I am profit-conscious, I make decisions first and foremost based on values and principles. In that respect, I'm proud to be joining a company with Core Values that guide day-to-day operations and one where corporate responsibility is an important part of our company culture."[1]

Over the past several years, social responsibility has become the watchword of this traditional company with midwestern roots but a checkered history. In 2004, Chiquita scarcely resembled the company that once held a reputation as cold, uncaring, and indifferent, frustrated with mediocre returns, a lack of innovation, and a demoralized workforce. Throughout the 20th century, hostile relationships with its labor unions and employees and a reputation for immorality solidified by the actions of its predecessor company, United Fruit, helped to slow Chiquita's growth. In addition, by the late 1990s, consumption of bananas had declined in major markets, and Chiquita's position in Europe had been compromised by the European Union's preferential import relationships with its members' former colonies in the Caribbean, Africa, and the Pacific. These factors helped push Chiquita to seek Chapter 11 bankruptcy protection in November 2001.

Through a serious and dedicated internal analysis, a thorough reevaluation of its core mission and business principles, and a concerted effort to reach out to some of its primary stakeholders—such as employees—who had become disenchanted and alienated, by early 2003, Chiquita had engineered the beginnings of a turnaround. One of the most impressive aspects of this recovery was Chiquita's success in redirecting and redefining its reputation through a more open and transparent approach to its global operations and to the various stakeholder groups with which it interacted. In addition, Chiquita had substantially reformed its labor practices and relations and initiated a set of projects in sustainable development and community action in its various locations around the world. Both labor unions and nongovernmental organizations (NGOs) lauded these steps.

Yet despite Chiquita's apparent turnaround, lingering problems remained in financial performance, organizational efficiency, and a strategy for the future. How could Chiquita sustain the positive momentum from its turnaround in reputation and employee relations to deliver improved and sustainable business performance in a global industry environment plagued by low margins and intense competition?

Chiquita's Background

Chiquita Brands International Inc. is a multinational producer, distributor, and marketer of bananas and other fresh produce. The company also distributes and markets fresh-cut fruit and other branded, value-added fruit products. Approximately 60 percent of its 2003 revenues of $2.6 billion came from bananas. Since adding new products and acquiring Fresh Express, the U.S. market leader in fresh salads, in 2005, bananas have totaled 43 percent of Chiquita's net sales. In 2003, the banana division consisted of 19,000 employees, mainly working on more than 100 banana farms in countries throughout Latin America, including Guatemala, Honduras, Nicaragua, Ecuador, Costa Rica, Panama, and Colombia. Approximately 45 percent of all bananas sold by Chiquita are from Chiquita-owned farms; independent suppliers in Latin America produce the remainder. Chiquita is one of the global market leaders in banana supply and production (see Table 1). Because Chiquita's exports are often a substantial part of the foreign trade of the Latin American countries in which the company operates, relationships with suppliers, workers' unions, and communities are critical elements for success.

Chiquita sources bananas from many developing Latin American countries, countries that historically have struggled with poverty, literacy, access to affordable health care,

Table 1 **Banana World Market Share Leaders, 1999, 2002, and 2005**

	2005	2002	1999
Chiquita	25%	23%	25%
Dole	25	25	25
Del Monte	15	16	15
Fyfess	8	8	8
Noboa	11	11	11

Source: Banana Link.

and limited infrastructure. The image of the banana industry has long been tarnished by its historical support of the failed U.S. invasion of Cuba in 1961, child labor, unsafe working conditions, sexual discrimination, low wages, and accusations of serious brutality against unionizing workers. Chiquita's reputation was damaged by past events, notably those associated with its predecessor company, United Fruit. These included allegations of the company's participation in labor rights suppression in Colombia in the 1920s, the use of company ships in the U.S. government–backed overthrow of the Guatemalan government in 1954, and involvement in a bribery scandal in Honduras in 1975. In the 1980s and 1990s, Chiquita clearly projected a defensive and protective culture, conveying a closed-door impression of its policies and practices.

Because bananas are produced all year long, local communities are closely tied together by the performance of farms. Many employees live in houses owned by the company, most of which are located on the farms themselves. In many areas, Chiquita provides electricity, potable water, medical facilities, and other basic services. However, labor relations remained strained throughout the 1980s and 1990s.

Chiquita's Downward Spiral

Although Chiquita improved its environmental procedures throughout the 1990s, many human rights groups, including Banana Link and US/Labor Education in the Americas, organized an outspoken campaign against all banana companies to improve social conditions on their plantations. One morning in early 1998, executives at Chiquita were devastated to see their company splashed all over the newspapers after an undercover investigation into "dangerous and illegal business practices" throughout Chiquita's Latin American operations. This was a watershed moment for the company.

The *Cincinnati Enquirer*, a paper based in the same town as Chiquita's corporate headquarters, printed an exposé contending that Chiquita was guilty of "labor, human rights, environmental and political violations in Central America."[2] Although the newspaper was later forced to retract the series after it was discovered that a reporter had illegally penetrated Chiquita's voicemail system, the damage was done.

Corporate image was further damaged when the firm emphasized the violation of its privacy instead of addressing the possible validity of the claims made. According to Jeff Zalla, current corporate responsibility officer at Chiquita, the strategy backfired. "It left some people with an unsavory impression of our company,"[3] he said.

Damaging media coverage and a renewed desire to evaluate its own ethics performance and gain support for a common set of values and standards for environmental and social performance served as catalysts for the institution of corporate social responsibility policies at Chiquita. After recognizing the need for a complete corporate makeover, Chiquita's then-CEO Steve Warshaw declared his commitment to leading in the area of corporate responsibility and pledged that the company would do much more than just repair previous damage. Four years later, despite changes in the executive management group, Chiquita's corporate social responsibility programs were a positive example of leading responsibility change in today's multinational business environment.

In January 2001, Chiquita announced that it could no longer pay the interest on its $862 million debt. The fiercely competitive banana industry, downward trends in prices due to excess supply, EU restrictive trade quotas, poor labor-union relations, and the market view of bananas as a low-margin commodity all contributed to Chiquita's bankruptcy filing. Chiquita attributed much of the responsibility to the European Union. In 1993, the EU imposed quotas that gave preferential treatment to banana imports from ACP (Africa, Caribbean, and Pacific) countries that were former European colonies, ostensibly to help these former European colonies boost their international trade and commerce. Before the 1993 act, 70 percent of the bananas sold in Europe came from Latin America, and Chiquita had a 22 percent share of the world's banana market. After the quotas were imposed, Chiquita claimed that its European market share was cut in half, costing $200 million a year in lost earnings.

Although many of its difficulties were intensified by the EU policy, Chiquita's problems had begun to develop before the 1993 decision. Most important, miscalculations of increases in European demand in the 1990s resulted in an oversupply, leading to depressed banana prices worldwide. Although prices recovered somewhat (see Table 2),

Table 2   **Banana Prices: Regional Year-over-Year Percentage Change, 2003 vs. 2002**

Region	Q1, 03	Q2, 03	Q3, 03	Q4, 03	Year
North America	3%	24%	1%	22%	21%
European core markets—US$	11	12	5	18	12
European core markets—local currency	29	210	29	0	27
Central & E. Europe/Mediterranean—US$	4	23	4	2	22
Central & E. Europe/Mediterranean—local currency	215	222	210	214	219
Asia—US$	27	0	3	12	0
Asia—local currency	218	27	3	6	25

Source: Company reports.

Table 3   **Key Developments in Chiquita's History**

1899	United Fruit Company is created through a merger of fruit companies.
1903	The company is listed on the New York Stock Exchange; it builds refrigerated ships.
1918	Thirteen banana ships are lost after being commissioned by Allied forces in World War I.
1941	Allied forces in World War II commission company ships, and the banana industry nearly shuts down.
1945	Twenty-seven ships and 275 men on company ships are lost serving Allied forces.
1950	The company starts massive postwar banana-planting projects.
1961	Company ships provide support for failed U.S. invasion of Cuba.
1964	The company begins a large-scale branding program for produce and starts using banana stickers bearing the Chiquita name.
1970	United Fruit merges with AMK Corp. and becomes United Brands Company.
1975	United Brands is involved in Honduran bribery scandal, which leads to enactment of U.S. Foreign Corrupt Practices Act. Company stocks plunge, and CEO Eli Black commits suicide.
1990	United Brands changes name to Chiquita Brands International.
1993	EU banana regulations cut Chiquita's market share by more than 50 percent. Chiquita begins working with Rainforest Alliance and Better Banana Project.
1994	Start of the "banana wars" between the EU and WTO. Follows complaints by Chiquita that EU favors Caribbean banana suppliers over Latin American importers.
1998	Chiquita becomes largest U.S. private-label fruit canner. Becomes first large company to meet with COLSIBA, an affiliation of Latin American banana unions.
1999	Faces possible auction proposed by large shareholder American Financial Group.
2000	Adopts expanded code of conduct. All 115 Chiquita-owned farms achieve Better Banana certification.
2001	Restructures debt after stopping payments on $862 million loan; cites prejudiced trade pacts by EU.
2001	Files for Chapter 11 bankruptcy protection.
2001	Issues first (2000) corporate responsibility report.
2002	Chiquita shareholders and bondholders support reorganization plan.
2002	Issues 2001 corporate responsibility report.
2003	Chiquita reports positive net income under reorganized company.
2003	SustainableBusiness.com names Chiquita one of the top 20 sustainable stock picks for the second year in a row.
2004	Maintained market leadership in the growing EU.
2005	Chiquita acquires Fresh Express, U.S. market leader in fresh salads.
2006	Awarded the Contribution to the Community Award by the American-Costa Rican Chamber of Commerce for its Nature & Community Project in Costa Rica.
2007	Chiquita faces a $25 million fine from the U.S. Department of Justice for payments made to Colombian paramilitary groups for the protection of its employees.

CEO Keith Linder blamed $284 million in losses in 2001 on a "decline in product quality resulting from an extraordinary outbreak of disease and unusual weather patterns."[4] At the end of 2006, Chiquita still faced financial difficulties as a result of a "perfect storm" of higher tariffs, increased competition in the EU banana market, U.S. consumer concerns about the safety of fresh spinach (another Chiquita product), and higher industry costs overall. While the company expressed dissatisfaction with 2006 results, it also stated that "we firmly believe our 2006 results are not indicative of the underlying strengths of Chiquita's business or our long-term potential."[5] Table 3 provides a comprehensive summary of key developments in Chiquita's history.

Dispute over Access to European Banana Markets

Chiquita has long claimed that its recent struggles are a direct result of the 1993 EU decision to put restrictive quotas on imports from Latin American suppliers. Immediately after the decision by the EU in 1993 to extend preferential quotas to its former Caribbean and African colonies, Chiquita took the issue to the U.S. trade representative, suggesting violations of free trade. In 1994, a General Agreement on Tariffs and Trade (GATT) panel ruled that the new regime violates GATT obligations, but the EU blocked adoption of the ruling by the full GATT. In 1996, the United States, along with Ecuador, Guatemala, Honduras, and Mexico, challenged the new regime under the new World Trade Organization (WTO) dispute-settlement mechanism, which came into force after the Uruguay Round of GATT negotiations.

In May 1997, a WTO panel ruled that the EU's banana import regime violated WTO obligations under the General Agreement on Trade in Services and the Agreement on Import Licensing Procedures. In September 1997, the WTO Appellate Body upheld the panel ruling, granting the EU 15 months, until January 1, 1999, to comply with the ruling. In January 1999, the deadline for EU compliance expired, and the United States sought WTO authorization to impose retaliatory tariffs. In April 1999, the WTO Dispute Settlement Body authorized U.S. retaliatory tariffs amounting to $191.4 million a year—the level of damage to U.S. companies calculated by arbitrators— and the United States immediately began steps to withhold liquidation of European imports, the first step in the imposition of the tariffs.

In April 2001, the United States and the European Commission announced that they had reached agreement resolving their dispute. The agreement took effect on July 1, 2001, at which time the United States suspended the retaliatory sanctions imposed on EU imports in 1999. Import volumes of bananas were returned to levels comparable to those prior to 1993, and the EU committed to moving to a tariff-only system in 2006 as part of its overall WTO obligations.

The dispute has taken its toll on the banana trade by creating uncertainty for smaller producers reliant on EU markets under the quota system and for large producers such as Chiquita that were forced to expend considerable financial and other resources in the course of the dispute. High tariffs in the EU continue to be a financial burden for Chiquita.

Corporate Responsibility

Chiquita had begun to initiate corporate responsibility projects in 1992 when it adopted Better Banana Project standards designed to improve environmental and worker conditions on its farms. Then, after the 1998 exposé in the *Cincinnati Enquirer*, Chiquita management began to conduct a series of broader companywide reviews of its conduct, policies, and internal and external operations and relationships, all designed to integrate corporate responsibility throughout the company's operations.

In 1998, Chiquita initiated several projects aimed at implementing its corporate responsibility efforts worldwide. Two internal groups were formed: the Senior Management Group and the Corporate Responsibility Steering Committee. The former consists of eight top managers of Chiquita's global businesses, including the president/CEO and COO of banana operations. The Senior Management Group is ultimately responsible for providing strategic vision and leadership for corporate responsibility. The Steering Committee, also consisting of eight members, was constructed to help streamline corporate social responsibility policies throughout each operational area of the firm.

In August 1999, Chiquita adopted the four key values that now guide all strategic business decision making worldwide. After a year of discussions, interviews, and debates on the merits of an internal corporate social responsibility policy, Chiquita defined the following four core values:

> *Integrity:* We live by our Core Values. We communicate in an open, honest and straightforward manner. We conduct our business ethically and lawfully.
> *Respect:* We treat people fairly and respectfully. We recognize the importance of family in the lives of our employees. We value and benefit from individual and cultural differences. We foster individual expression, open dialogue and a sense of belonging.

> *Opportunity:* We believe the continuous growth and development of our employees is key to our success. We encourage teamwork. We recognize employees for their contributions to the company's success.
> *Responsibility:* We take pride in our work, in our products and in satisfying our customers. We act responsibly in the communities and environments in which we live and work. We are accountable for the careful use of all resources entrusted to us and for providing appropriate returns to our shareholders.[6]

In support of the four core values, Chiquita undertook reforms to link its corporate governance and corporate responsibility policies. These reforms included expanding the role of the board's Audit Committee to oversee the firm's corporate responsibility (CR) mission and to evaluate whether the firm had the right people, policies, and programs in place to properly advance the CR agenda. In addition, in May 2000, Chiquita appointed a full-time vice president and CR officer responsible for all aspects of corporate social responsibility. According to Chiquita, the four core values, supported by the senior management group and CR committee, have helped drive responsible change throughout the entire organization. Each business decision must be evaluated through the lens of CR policies.

Chiquita also began to realize that a corporate social responsibility platform could mean a competitive advantage in the banana market. Dennis Christou, vice president of marketing-Europe, explained: "Bananas are, by definition, a commodity and U.K. consumers do not generally see fruit as branded. Chiquita is trying to change this. We have a brand because we own certain values and a relationship with consumers. And we communicate with them. They have expectations about Chiquita."[7] In particular, environmental and social performance are of keen interest to some leading European customers. In 2002, 56 percent of Chiquita's sales in northern European markets were to customers who had either inspected farms or formally asked questions about environmental and social performance. This was a 5 percent increase—about 13,000 forty-pound boxes per week—over the prior year.

Chiquita also strengthened its commitment to the Better Bananas Project. Under this program, external auditors audit all Chiquita farms annually. Chiquita has made an important partnership with Rainforest Alliance, which has been integral in assessing Chiquita's environmental practices, especially related to deforestation. The Rainforest Alliance, which claims that the world's rainforests are being deforested at a rate of 1 percent per year (or two U.S. football fields every second), has annually accredited every Chiquita farm since 2000. Chiquita also encourages its independent producers, which supply Chiquita with about 50 percent of its bananas, to achieve Rainforest Alliance certification. In 2002, the volume of bananas purchased from certified farms rose from 33 to 46 percent,

Table 4 Better Banana Project Principles

1. **Ecosystem Conservation.** Protect existing ecosystems; recovery of damaged ecosystems in plantation area.

2. **Wildlife Conservation.** Protect biodiversity, especially endangered species.

3. **Fair Treatment and Good Conditions for Workers.** Comply with local and international labor laws/norms; maintain policy of nondiscrimination; support freedom of association.

4. **Community Relations.** Be a "good neighbor," contributing to the social and economic development of local communities.

5. **Integrated Pest Management.** Reduction in use of pesticides; training for workers in pesticide use/management/risks.

6. **Integrated Waste Management.** Reduction of the production of wastes that contaminate the environment and harm human health; institute recycling.

7. **Conservation of Water Resources.** Reduce and reuse the water used in production; establish buffer zones of vegetation around waterways; protect water from contamination.

8. **Soil Conservation.** Control erosion; promote soil conservation and replenishment.

9. **Planning and Monitoring.** Plan and monitor banana cultivation activities according to environmental, social, and economic measures.

Source: Adapted from Rainforest Alliance, Normas Generales Para la Certificación del Cultivo de Banano, May 2002, www.rainforest-alliance.org.

and farms certified through June 2003 brought the total to 65 percent. As of August 2006, all of the farms owned by the Chiquita Company are certified by the Rainforest Alliance. Along with all of Chiquita's farms, the Rainforest Alliance has also certified the majority of the independent farms connected to Chiquita. TreeHugger.com also contends that "Chiquita now recycles 100 percent of its plastic bags into paving stones and has reduced pesticide use by 26 percent."[8] Table 4 presents the nine principles of the Better Banana Project. According to insiders, the adoption of third-party standards has helped Chiquita drive a stronger internal commitment to achieving excellence—and to cut costs. In 2003, the Rainforest Alliance estimated that Chiquita reduced production spending by $100 million as a result of a $20 million investment to reduce agrochemical use. In a more recent effort to increase its corporate responsibility profile, Chiquita Bananas pledged to boycott oil from Canada's tar sands in November 2011.

Chiquita is receiving increasing recognition for its efforts. In 2005, SustainableBusiness.com, publisher of *The Progressive Investor* newsletter, named Chiquita to its list of the world's top 20 sustainable stock picks, known as the SB20, for the fourth year in a row. SustainableBusiness.com identifies its picks by asking leading investment advisers to recommend companies that stand out as world leaders in both sustainability and financial strength. In April 2004, the Trust for the Americas, a division of the Organization of Americas, selected Chiquita Brands as the winner of the 2004 Corporate Citizen of the Americas

Award for Chiquita's Nuevo San Juan Home-Ownership Project in Honduras. Also in 2004, Chiquita earned the Ethic Award from the AGEPE Editorial Group and KPMG in Italy for its initiatives in the field of ethics, environmental protection, and workplace improvements.

One recent setback for Chiquita's corporate responsibility profile involved its banana-producing subsidiary in Colombia. After a 2003 probe into the company's finances, Chiquita self-reported to the U.S. Department of Justice (DOJ) that it had made payments to left- and right-wing paramilitary groups in Colombia such as the AUC, ELN, and FARC. These payments, beginning in 1997, were made in order to protect the lives of its employees. Colombia has one of the highest kidnapping rates in the world and a murder rate 11 times that of the United States. "It's certainly a common understanding that in order to do business in Colombia, payments have to be made for at best security, or at worst extortion," explained Ron Oswald, general secretary of the International Union of Foodworkers, which represents Chiquita workers in Latin America (including many in Colombia).

The U.S. 1996 Anti-Terrorism Act makes it illegal to support any organizations identified as a terrorist threat. As of September 2001, the list of terrorist threats included the Colombian paramilitary groups. In a company press release, Chiquita chairman and CEO Fernando Aguirre explained, "The payments . . . were always motivated by our good faith concern for the safety of our employees. Nevertheless, we recognized—and acted upon—our legal obligation to inform the DOJ of this admittedly difficult situation."[9] Officially announced in 2007, Chiquita faced a $25 million fine for the payments it made in Colombia. In anticipation of the decision, the company set aside funds in 2006 to pay the fine. Chiquita does not believe the fines will hurt its operations. Perhaps as a result of the pending DOJ investigation and decision, Chiquita sold its Colombian subsidiary in 2004.

Global Codes of Conduct, Standards, and Labor Practices

In late 2001, Ron Oswald, general secretary of the International Union of Food Workers, was asked if he had seen improvements in Chiquita's internal and external corporate policies. He responded, "Yes. It is a company that is totally unrecognizable from five years ago."[10] Clearly Chiquita had come a long way.

Traditionally, relations between Chiquita and labor unions in Latin America were mired in conflict and mistrust. In 1998, after recognizing the need for change in the way it deals with its line, Chiquita began striving to adhere to SA8000, the widely accepted international labor rights standard. Management struggled with the decision of whether to adopt an outside standard or to develop an internal measurement gauge for corporate responsibility.

After much deliberation, management concluded that adopting the SA8000 standard would yield the most credibility with external stakeholders because SA8000 gives detailed requirements for adequacy of management systems for implementation. Having an external standard forces Chiquita to push CR change down through each organizational level so that the firm is able to meet third-party requirements.

In May 2000 Chiquita expanded its code of conduct to include SA8000. Standards now included areas such as food safety, labor standards, employee health and safety, environmental protection, and legal compliance. Recognizing the importance of labor support and its resounding effect on corporate image, Chiquita began an open dialogue with the International Union of Food Workers and the Coalition of Latin American Banana Workers' Unions (COLSIBA). By June 2001, the firm had reached an agreement with both organizations, pledging to respect worker rights as elaborated in ILO conventions, address long-standing health and safety concerns for workers, and ensure that its independent suppliers did likewise. This made Chiquita the first multinational corporation in the agricultural sector to sign a worker rights agreement. Management credits this agreement as having helped to build a positive image, improving relations with both internal and external stakeholders. In mid-2001, Chiquita published its first corporate responsibility report detailing the firm's future CR strategies and goals. Both stakeholders and media outlets have been impressed with the complete turnaround in the transparency of Chiquita's corporate agenda, which has led to a much more favorable impression of the company.

In order to adhere to the organization's own core values and to the SA8000 labor standard, Chiquita routinely performs internal audits in all of its Latin American operations. NGOs also conduct external audits. After the audits are completed, each local management team plans corrective actions using the firm's code of conduct and core values as decision-making guides. At year-end 2003, independent auditors certified Chiquita's operations in Costa Rica, Colombia, and Panama to the SA8000 standard. Chiquita's operations were the first ever to earn SA8000 certification in each of these countries. In its 2006 corporate responsibility report, Chiquita announced that it has maintained 100 percent certification of its banana farms in Latin America in accordance with the Rainforest Alliance, Social Accountability 8000, and EurepGAP standards (environmental, labor, and human rights and food safety standards, respectively).

Marketing the Message

Although it would seem advantageous for Chiquita to communicate and leverage the great strides it has made through its corporate responsibility effort, management seems reluctant to promote its achievements through the typical mass communication vehicles. Indeed, when Chiquita attempted to advertise its certification process with commercials in Denmark that equated its Central American banana farms with a "glorious rainforest," the ads were met with skepticism and thought to be unrealistic.

Instead of mass advertising, the firm has opted for a longer-term marketing strategy based on educating leading opinion makers and critics alike. According to Dennis Christou, vice president of marketing–Europe, there is a natural suspicion among consumers about commercially driven messages. He believes that customers feel more trust in the message if it's delivered by an external body rather than by the company or by a paid advocate of the business. That is a main reason why the firm is relying on viral marketing tactics and third-party testimonials as the means of spreading its message. Retailers are treated differently: They must be exposed to improvements at Chiquita because they determine which exclusive brand to carry on an annual basis. However, Christou believes that creating brand recognition with consumers is possible through nonobtrusive, reputable means.

Defining and conveying a brand's differences in a commodities marketplace is difficult. Nevertheless, Chiquita believes it can carve out its own niche by distinguishing itself as a leader in corporate responsibility. Instead of positioning itself solely on the basis of price, Chiquita is hoping that its distinctive competency in CR will help it stand out from the pack. The company got a boost in this regard in April 2003, when Chiquita, along with Ben and Jerry's, received the first Award for Outstanding Sustainability Reporting presented by the Coalition for Environmentally Responsible Economies (CERES) and the Association of Chartered Certified Accountants. In 2006, Chiquita won Costa Rica's Contribution to the Community Award for its Nature and Community Project, which preserves biodiversity and promotes nature conservation awareness.

Recent Performance, Acquisition, and Future Path

Chiquita drastically shifted its strategic decision-making models and broader corporate operating principles in the wake of its reorganization. Debt repayments and other reorganization costs resulted in significant losses. Chiquita made great strides in improving its financial performance by cutting costs and streamlining its local and global operations. In 2003, the year after it filed for bankruptcy, Chiquita's net sales were $2.6 billion, up from $1.6 billion the year before. In 2006, net sales reached a record $4.5 billion (due in part to the acquisition of Fresh Express).

In 2011 the Chiquita Company celebrated its fourth consecutive year of increasing profitability. Chair and CEO Fernando Aguirre stated that Chiquita "had a much better

Table 5 **Chiquita Brands Balance Sheet as of December 31, 2014, 2013, 2012, 2011 (in thousands)**

	2014	2013	2012	2011
Assets				
Cash and equivalents	$ 47,160	$ 54,017	$ 2,601	$ —
Other current assets	535,904	575,178	987	266
Total current assets	583,064	629,195	3,588	266
Investments in and accounts with subsidiaries	110,220	108,077	647,471	1,071,132
Other assets	918,754	921,866	18,919	23,332
Total assets	$1,612,038	$1,659,138	$669,978	$1,094,730
Liabilities and Shareholders' Equity				
Accounts payable and accrued liabilities	$ 374,241	$ 406,307	$ 15,363	$ 15,354
Total current liabilities	378,944	408,578	15,363	15,354
Long-term debt	637,518	629,353	259,520	249,805
Total liabilities	1,288,704	1,284,700	299,576	294,660
Shareholders' equity	323,334	374,438	370,402	800,070
Total liabilities and shareholders' equity	$1,612,038	$1,659,138	$669,978	$1,094,730

Source: Company reports.

Table 6 **Chiquita Brands International Income Statement, 2012–2014 (in thousands)**

	Year Ended 12/31/2014	Year Ended 12/31/2013	Year Ended 12/31/2012
Net sales	$3,090,224	$3,057,482	$3,078,337
Cost of sales	2,735,117	2,708,428	2,743,040
SG&A	218,061	233,706	275,231
Equity in earnings of subsidiaries (loss)	(2,750)	(258)	33,433
Operating income (loss)	27,404	49,845	(253,834)
Interest expense	(61,896)	(61,144)	(45,299)
Interest income	2,715	2,856	3,131
Loss on debt extinguishment	(521)	(6,275)	—
Other income (expense), net	(9,906)	3,522	(1,793)
Income (loss) before income taxes	(42,204)	(11,196)	(297,795)
Income tax (expense) benefit	(20,332)	(4,619)	(105,239)
Net income (loss)	(62,536)	(15,815)	(405,017)

Source: Company reports.

year in bananas driven by higher pricing and volume in North America, and initial recovery in Europe. Our salads business did not perform as well as expected and we've taken a number of corrective actions and adapted our structure and strategy to be more successful and profitable."[11]

Beginning in 2012, however, Chiquita's sales and profitability began to stall. With global banana sales decreasing, Chiquita's revenue fell to US$3 billion, and the company posted losses for three consecutive years (see Tables 5 and 6). In 2014, following three years of flat sales, Chiquita's management began looking externally for new solutions for cutting costs and increasing revenue.

In early 2014, Chiquita reached a preliminary merger agreement with Ireland-based fruit and produce company Fyffes. The deal would have created the largest banana distributor in the world, with an estimated 160 million boxes of bananas sold annually. Around the same time, Brazilian holding company Cutrale-Safra offered Chiquita shareholders a buyout deal worth around US$14 per share. In October 2014, shareholders for Chiquita unexpectedly rejected the merger with Fyffes and accepted a slightly revised takeover bid by Cutrale-Safra. With the close of the deal, Chiquita became a privately held Brazilian company.

Chiquita's new ownership faces a challenging task of bringing financial success back to the company. Future financial stability depends, in part, on external market factors such as steady or rising international banana prices and consumer demand. Internally, the company's performance will result from the effectiveness of financial controls on the cost side, and successful marketing, emphasizing differentiation and value-added production, on the revenue side. Although Chiquita has gone to impressive lengths to turn around its reputation and performance, it continues to face a challenging and competitive international business environment and must make continuous progress in its management and operations in order to achieve a healthy and sustainable financial future.

Questions for Review

1. How would you characterize Chiquita's historical approach to global management?

2. Describe Chiquita's approach to human resource management in its global supply chain. What particular human resource challenges does Chiquita face as the purchaser, producer, and supplier of a commodity?

3. Does Chiquita's global corporate responsibility (CR) program create a conflict between owners and other stakeholders? Who are Chiquita's main stakeholders in the United States and around the world, and how are they affected by Chiquita's CR program?

4. How would you characterize Chiquita's past and present leadership? How does leadership affect a company's overall reputation?

5. Do you believe Chiquita would have changed its policies without the presence of damaging stories in the media? If not, what does this say about Chiquita's old management style?

6. What challenges does Chiquita's new ownership face in continuing to turn the company around and bring profitability back to its operations?

Exercise

Chiquita's management, represented by the CEO, is considering input from various groups about its strategic direction and continued reorganization. Your group represents one of the following interests:

1. Shareholders of the previous company who lost most of the value of the shares after the company declared bankruptcy.

2. Shareholders in the Safra Group.

3. Employees and union representatives of North American operations.

4. Employees and union representatives of South American operations.

5. Representatives of the nongovernmental organization Rainforest Action Network.

Spend five minutes preparing two or three requests to the management team about your group's interests and priorities for the company. Then conduct an open forum in which you discuss these requests among the different groups.

Source: This case was prepared by Professor Jonathan Doh and Erik Holt of Villanova University as the basis for class discussion. Additional research assistance was provided by Courtney Asher and Benjamin Littell. It is not intended to illustrate either effective or ineffective managerial capability or administrative responsibility. We appreciate assistance from Sherrie Terry and Michael Mitchell of Chiquita International. Any errors remain those of the authors.

ENDNOTES

1. "Chiquita Names New CEO," *Cincinnati Business Courier*, January 12, 2004.

2. Geert de Lombaerde, "Chiquita Outlook Improves Following EU Deal," *Cincinnati Business Courier*, April 20, 2001.

3. Nicholas Stein, "Yes, We Have No Profits," *Fortune*, November 26, 2001, pp. 182–196.

4. Ibid.

5. Chiquita Brands International, Inc., *2006 Annual Report*, http://investors.chiquita.com/phoenix.zhtml?c=119836&p=irol-reportsAnnual.

6. "Ethics & Code of Conduct," *Chiquita*, www.chiquita.com/The-Chiquita-Difference/Ethics-Codes-of-Conduct.aspx.

7. Marco Werre, "Implementing Corporate Responsibility: The Chiquita Case," *Journal of Business Ethics* 44, no. 2 (May 2003), pp. 247–260.

8. Collin Dunn, "Chiquita Cleans Up Its Act," *TreeHugger.com*, August 10, 2006, www.treehugger.com/green-food/chiquita-cleans-up-its-act.html.

9. Chiquita Brands International, Inc., "Chiquita Statement on Agreement with U.S. Department of Justice," press release, March 14, 2007, http://investors.chiquita.com/phoenix.zhtml?c=119836&p=irol-newsArticle&ID=974081.

10. Stein, "Yes, We Have No Profits."

11. "Chiquita Brands International, Inc.: Chiquita Reports Fourth Quarter and Full-Year 2011 Results," *Chiquita*, February 21, 2012, http://investors.chiquita.com/phoenix.zhtml?c=119836&p=irol-newsArticle&id=1663424.

SKILL-BUILDING
AND EXPERIENTIAL
EXERCISES

- **Personal Skill-Building Exercises**
- **In-Class Simulations (Available in Connect, connect.mheducation.com)**

1. The Culture Quiz

Objectives

- To stimulate awareness of cultural differences
- To promote consideration of the impact of cultural differences in a global economy
- To stimulate dialogue between domestic and international students
- To explore issues raised by culturally diverse workforces

Background

Few, if any, traditions and values are universally held. Many business dealings have succeeded or failed because of a manager's awareness or lack of understanding of the traditions and values of his/her foreign counterparts. With the world business community so closely intertwined and interdependent, it is critical that managers today become increasingly aware of the differences that exist.

How culturally aware are you? Try the questions below.

Instructions

Working alone or with a small group, answer the questions (without peeking at the answers). When you do look at the answers, be sure to read the explanations. If you are taking the quiz with students from countries other than your own, explore what the answer might be in your country and theirs.

1. In Japan, loudly slurping your soup is considered to be
   a. rude and obnoxious.
   b. a sign that you like the soup.
   c. okay at home but not in public.
   d. something only foreigners do.

2. In Korea, business leaders tend to
   a. encourage strong commitment to teamwork and cooperation.
   b. encourage competition among subordinates.
   c. discourage subordinates from reporting directly, preferring information to come through well-defined channels.
   d. encourage close relationships with their subordinates.

3. In Japan, virtually every kind of drink is sold in public vending machines except for
   a. beer.
   b. diet drinks with saccharine.
   c. already sweetened coffee.
   d. soft drinks from U.S. companies.

4. In Latin America, managers
   a. are most likely to hire members of their own families.
   b. consider hiring members of their own families to be inappropriate.
   c. stress the importance of hiring members of minority groups.
   d. usually hire more people than are actually needed to do a job.

5. In Ethiopia, when a woman opens the front door of her home, it means
   a. she is ready to receive guests for a meal.
   b. only family members may enter.
   c. religious spirits may move freely in and out of the home.
   d. she has agreed to have sex with any man who enters.

6. In Latin America, businesspeople
   a. consider it impolite to make eye contact while talking to one another.
   b. always wait until the other person is finished speaking before starting to speak.
   c. touch each other more than North Americans do under similar circumstances.
   d. avoid touching one another as it is considered an invasion of privacy.

7. The principal religion in Malaysia is
   a. Buddhism.
   b. Judaism.
   c. Christianity.
   d. Islam.

8. In Thailand
   a. it is common to see men walking along holding hands.
   b. it is common to see a man and a woman holding hands in public.
   c. it is rude for men and women to walk together.
   d. men and women traditionally kiss each other on meeting in the street.

9. When eating in India, it is appropriate to
   a. take food with your right hand and eat with your left.
   b. take food with your left hand and eat with your right.
   c. take food and eat it with your left hand.
   d. take food and eat it with your right hand.

10. Pointing your toes at someone in Thailand is
   a. a symbol of respect, much like the Japanese bow.
   b. considered rude even if it is done by accident.
   c. an invitation to dance.
   d. the standard public greeting.

11. American managers tend to base the performance appraisals of their subordinates on performance, while in Iran, managers are more likely to base their performance appraisals on
   a. religion.
   b. seniority.
   c. friendship.
   d. ability.

12. In China, the status of every business negotiation is
   a. reported daily in the press.
   b. private, and details are not discussed publicly.
   c. subjected to scrutiny by a public tribunal on a regular basis.
   d. directed by the elders of every commune.

13. When rewarding a Hispanic worker for a job well done, it is best not to
   a. praise him or her publicly.
   b. say "thank you."
   c. offer a raise.
   d. offer a promotion.

14. In some South American countries, it is considered normal and acceptable to show up for a social appointment
   a. ten to fifteen minutes early.
   b. ten to fifteen minutes late.
   c. fifteen minutes to an hour late.
   d. one to two hours late.

15. In France, when friends talk to one another
   a. they generally stand about three feet apart.
   b. it is typical to shout.
   c. they stand closer to one another than Americans do.
   d. it is always with a third party present.

16. When giving flowers as gifts in Western Europe, be careful not to give
   a. tulips and jonquils.
   b. daisies and lilacs.
   c. chrysanthemums and calla lilies.
   d. lilacs and apple blossoms.

17. The appropriate gift-giving protocol for a male executive doing business in Saudi Arabia is to
   a. give a man a gift from you to his wife.
   b. present gifts to the wife or wives in person.

   c. give gifts only to the eldest wife.
   d. not give a gift to the wife at all.

18. If you want to give a necktie or a scarf to a Latin American, it is best to avoid the color
   a. red.
   b. purple.
   c. green.
   d. black.

19. The doors in German offices and homes are generally kept
   a. wide open to symbolize an acceptance and welcome of friends and strangers.
   b. slightly ajar to suggest that people should knock before entering.
   c. half-opened, suggesting that some people are welcome and others are not.
   d. tightly shut to preserve privacy and personal space.

20. In the area that was formerly West Germany, leaders who display charisma are
   a. not among the most desired.
   b. the ones most respected and sought after.
   c. invited frequently to serve on boards of cultural organizations.
   d. pushed to get involved in political activities.

21. American managers running businesses in Mexico have found that by increasing the salaries of Mexican workers, they
   a. increased the number of hours the workers were willing to work.
   b. enticed more workers to work night shifts.
   c. decreased the number of hours workers would agree to work.
   d. decreased production rates.

22. Chinese culture teaches people
   a. to seek psychiatric help for personal problems.
   b. to avoid conflict and internalize personal problems.
   c. to deal with conflict with immediate confrontation.
   d. to seek help from authorities whenever conflict arises.

23. One wedding gift that should not be given to a Chinese couple would be
   a. a jade bowl.
   b. a clock.
   c. a basket of oranges.
   d. shifts embroidered with dragon patterns.

24. In Venezuela, New Year's Eve is generally spent
    a. in quiet family gatherings.
    b. at wild neighborhood street parties.
    c. in restaurants with horns, hats, and live music and dancing.
    d. at pig roasts on the beach.

25. If you order "bubble and squeak" in a London pub, you will get
    a. two goldfish fried in olive oil.
    b. a very cold beer in a chilled glass, rather than the usual warm beer.
    c. Alka Seltzer and a glass of water.
    d. chopped cabbage and mashed potatoes fried together.

26. When a stranger in India wants to know what you do for a living and how much you earn, he will
    a. ask your guide.
    b. invite you to his home and, after getting to know you, will ask.
    c. come over and ask you directly, without introduction.
    d. respect your privacy above all.

27. When you feel you are being taken advantage of in a business exchange in Vietnam, it is important to
    a. let the anger show in your face but not in your words.
    b. say that you are angry, but keep your facial expression neutral.
    c. not show any anger in any way.
    d. end the business dealings immediately, and walk away.

28. When a taxi driver in India shakes his head from side to side, it probably means
    a. he thinks your price is too high.
    b. he isn't going in your direction.
    c. he will take you where you want to go.
    d. he doesn't understand what you're asking.

29. In England, holding your index and middle fingers up in a V with the back of your hand facing another person is seen as
    a. a gesture of peace.
    b. a gesture of victory.
    c. a signal that you want two of something.
    d. a vulgar gesture.

Answers to the Culture Quiz

1. *b.* Slurping your soup or noodles in Japan is good manners in both public and private. It indicates enjoyment and appreciation of the quality. [Source: Eiji Kanno and Constance O'Keefe, *New Japan Solo* (Tokyo: Japan National Tourist Organization, 1990), p. 20.]

2. *b.* Korean managers use a "divide-and-rule" method of leadership that encourages competition among subordinates. They do this to ensure that they can exercise maximum control. In addition, they stay informed by having individuals report directly to them. This way, they can know more than anyone else. [Source: Richard M. Castaldi and Tjipyanto Soerjanto, "Contrasts in East Asian Management Practices," *Journal of Management in Practice* 2, no. 1 (1990), pp. 25–27.]

3. *b.* Saccharine-sweetened drinks may not be sold in Japan by law. On the other hand, beer, a wide variety of Japanese and international soft drinks, and so forth, are widely available from vending machines along the streets and in buildings. You're supposed to be at least 18 to buy the alcoholic ones, however. [Source: Eiji Kanno and Constance O'Keefe, *New Japan Solo* (Tokyo: Japan National Tourist Organization, 1990), p. 20.]

4. *a.* Family is considered to be very important in Latin America, so managers are likely to hire their relatives more quickly than hiring strangers. [Source: Nancy J. Adler, *International Dimensions of Organizational Behavior*, 2nd ed. (Boston: PWS-Kent, 1991).]

5. *d.* The act, by a woman, of opening the front door signifies that she has agreed to have sex with any man who enters. [Source: Adam Pertman, "Wandering No More," *Boston Globe Magazine*, June 30, 1991, pp. 10ff.]

6. *c.* Touching one another during business negotiations is common practice. [Source: Nancy J. Adler, *International Dimensions of Organizational Behavior*, 2nd ed. (Boston: PWS-Kent, 1991).]

7. *d.* Approximately 45 percent of the people in Malaysia follow Islam, the country's "official" religion. [Source: Hans Johannes Hoefer, ed., *Malaysia* (Englewood Cliffs, NJ: Prentice Hall, 1984).]

8. *a.* Men holding hands is considered a sign of friendship. Public displays of affection between men and women, however, are unacceptable. [Source: William Warren, Star Black, and M. R. Priya Rangsit, eds., *Thailand* (Englewood Cliffs, NJ: Prentice Hall, 1985).]

9. *d.* In India, as in many Asian countries, toilet paper is not used. Instead, water and the left hand are used, after which the left hand is thoroughly cleaned. Still, the left hand is considered to be polluted and therefore inappropriate for use during eating or touching another person. [Source: Gitanjali Kolanad, *Culture Shock! India* (Portland, OR: Graphic Arts Center Publishing Company, 1996), p. 117.]

10. *b.* This is especially an insult if it is done deliberately because the feet are the lowest part of the body. [Source: William Warren, Star Black, and M. R. Priya Rangsit, eds., *Thailand* (Englewood Cliffs, NJ: Prentice Hall, 1985).]

11. *c.* Adler suggests that friendship is valued over task competence in Iran. [Source: Nancy J. Adler, *International Dimensions of Organizational Behavior*, 2nd ed. (Boston: PWS-Kent, 1991).]

12. *b.* Public discussion of business dealings is considered inappropriate. Kaplan et al. report that "the Chinese may even have used a premature announcement to extract better terms from executives" who were too embarrassed to admit that there was never really a contract. [Source: Frederic Kaplan, Julian Sobin, and Arne de Keijzer, *The China Guidebook* (Boston: Houghton Mifflin, 1987).]

13. *a.* Public praise for Hispanics and Asians is generally embarrassing because modesty is an important cultural value. [Source: Jim Braham, "No, You Don't Manage Everyone the Same," *Industry Week*, February 6, 1989.] In Japan, being singled out for praise is also an embarrassment. A common saying in that country is, "The nail that sticks up gets hammered down."

14. *d.* Though being late is frowned upon in the United States, being late is not only accepted but expected in some South American countries. [Source: Lloyd S. Baird, James E. Post, and John F. Mahon, *Management: Functions and Responsibilities* (New York: Harper & Row, 1990).]

15. *c.* Personal space in most European countries is much smaller than in the United States. Americans generally like at least two feet of space around themselves, while it is not unusual for Europeans to be virtually touching. [Source: Lloyd S. Baird, James E. Post, and John F. Mahon, *Management: Functions and Responsibilities* (New York: Harper & Row, 1990).]

16. *c.* Chrysanthemums and calla lilies are both associated with funerals. [Source: Theodore Fischer, *Pinnacle: International Issue*, March–April 1991, p. 4.]

17. *d.* In Arab cultures, it is considered inappropriate for wives to accept gifts or even attention from other men. [Source: Theodore Fischer, *Pinnacle: International Issue*, March–April 1991, p. 4.]

18. *b.* In Argentina and other Latin American countries, purple is associated with the serious fasting period of Lent. [Source: Theodore Fischer, *Pinnacle: International Issue*, March–April 1991, p. 4.]

19. *d.* Private space is considered so important in Germany that partitions are erected to separate people from one another. Privacy screens and walled gardens are the norm. [Source: Julius Fast,

Subtext: Making Body Language Work (New York: Viking Penguin Books, 1991), p. 207.]

20. *a.* Though political leaders in the United States are increasingly selected on their ability to inspire, charisma is a suspect trait in what was West Germany, where Hitler's charisma is still associated with evil intent and harmful outcomes. [Source: Nancy J. Adler, *International Dimensions of Organizational Behavior*, 2nd ed. (Boston: PWS-Kent, 1991), p. 149.]

21. *c.* Paying Mexican workers more means, in the eyes of the workers, that they can make the same amount of money in fewer hours and thus have more time for enjoying life. [Source: Nancy J. Adler, *International Dimensions of Organizational Behavior*, 2nd ed. (Boston: PWS-Kent, 1991), pp. 30 and 159.]

22. *b.* Psychological therapy is not an accepted concept in China. In addition, communism has kept most Chinese from expressing opinions openly. [Source: James McGregor, "Burma Road Heroin Breeds Addicts, AIDS Along China's Border," *The Wall Street Journal*, September 29, 1992, p. 1.]

23. *b.* The Chinese regard a clock as a bad omen because the word for clock, pronounced *zhong*, is phonetically similar to another Chinese word that means "the end." Jade is highly valued as symbolizing superior virtues, and oranges and dragon patterns are also auspicious symbols. [Source: Dr. Evelyn Lip, "Culture and Customs," *Silver Kris*, February 1994, p. 84.]

24. *a.* Venezuelans do the reverse of what most people in other countries do on Christmas and New Year's. On Christmas, they socialize. While fireworks are shot off on both nights, most restaurants are closed and the streets are quiet. [Source: Tony Perrottet, ed., *Venezuela* (Boston: Houghton Mifflin, 1994), p. 97.]

25. *d.* Other popular pub food includes bangers and mash (sausages and mashed potatoes), ploughman's lunch (bread, cheese, and pickled onions), and cottage pie (baked minced meat with onions and topped with mashed potatoes). [Source: Ravi Desai, ed., *Let's Go: The Budget Guide to Britain and Ireland* (London: Pan Books, 1990), p. 83.]

26. *c.* Indians are generally uninhibited about staring at strangers and asking them about personal details in their lives. Social distance and personal privacy are not common social conventions in India. [Source: Frank Kusy, *India* (Chester, CT: The Globe Pequot Press, 1989), p. 27.]

27. *c.* Vernon Weitzel of the Australian National University advises never to show anger when dealing with Vietnamese officials or businesspeople. Showing anger causes you to lose face and is considered rude. Weitzel also recommends always smiling, not complaining or criticizing anyone, and not being inquisitive about personal matters. [Source: Daniel Robinson and Joe Cummings, *Vietnam, Laos & Cambodia* (Australia: Lonely Planet Publications, 1991), p. 96.]

28. *c.* What looks to Westerners like a refusal is really an Indian way of saying "yes." It can also express general agreement with what you're saying or suggest that an individual is interested in what you have to say. [Source: Gitanjali Kolanad, *Culture Shock! India* (Portland, OR: Graphic Arts Center Publishing Company, 1996), p. 114.]

29. *d.* In England, this simple hand gesture is considered vulgar and obscene. In a report to *The Boston Globe,* an American who had been working in London wrote, "I wish someone had told me before I emphatically explained to one of the draftsmen at work why I needed two complete sets of drawings." [Source: "Finger Gestures Can Spell Trouble," *The Berkshire Eagle,* January 26, 1997, p. E5.]

Source: Exercises 1, 3, 4, and 5 are from Janet W. Wohlberg, Gail E. Gilmore, and Steven B. Wolff, *OB in Action,* 5th ed. (Boston: Houghton Mifflin, 1998).

2. "When in Bogotá . . ."

As Jim Reynolds looked out the small window of the Boeing 757, he saw the glimmer of lights in the distance. After a five-hour flight, he arrived in Bogotá, Colombia, at 9:35 p.m. on a clear Friday evening. It had been nearly five years since Jim had seen his best friend, Rodrigo Cardozo. The two had met in college and kept in touch over the years. During their school years, Rodrigo would often accompany Jim when he went home to Chicago for the holidays.

Entering the main terminal, Jim found himself in what looked like a recently bombed building. Piles of debris were everywhere. Lights hung from the ceiling by exposed electrical wires, and the walls and floors were rough, unfinished concrete. "Certainly, aesthetics are not a major concern at the Bogotá International Airport," Jim thought.

As he came to the end of the long, dimly lit corridor, an expressionless customs official reached out his hand and gestured for Jim's travel documents.

"Passaporte, por favor. Bienvenidos a Bogotá, Señor Reynolds. Estás en vacacciones?"

"Sí," Jim replied.

After a few routine questions, Jim was allowed to pass through customs feeling relatively unscathed.

"Loquillo! Loquillo! Estamos aquí! Jim, Jim," a voice shouted.

Trying to find the origin of the voice among the dense crowd, Jim finally spotted Rodrigo. "Hey, man. How've you been? You look great!"

"Jim, it's so good to see you. How've you been? I would like you to meet my wife, Eva. Eva, this is my best friend, Jim. He's the one in all those pictures I've shown you."

Late Night Begins the Day

Close to an hour later, Jim, Rodrigo, and Eva arrived at Rodrigo's parents' house on the other side of Bogotá from the airport. As Jim was aware, it is customary for couples to live with their parents for a number of years after their marriage, and Rodrigo and Eva were following that custom.

Darío, Rodrigo's father, owned an import/export business in Bogotá. He was a knowledgeable and educated man and, from what Jim knew, a master of business negotiations. Over the years, Darío had conducted business with people in nearly every country in Central and South America, the United States, Europe, Hong Kong, and some parts of Africa. Jim had first met Darío with Rodrigo in Boston in 1989.

"Jim, welcome to my house," Darío boomed effusively as the group walked in. "I am so pleased that you're finally in Bogotá. Would you like something to drink—whiskey, bourbon, Aguardiente?"

"Aguardiente!" Rodrigo urged.

"Yes, Jim would like some Aguardiente. I understand you're going to Bahía tonight," Darío added.

"Where?" Jim asked, looking around. "I didn't know we were going anywhere tonight."

"Don't worry, Jim, todo bien, todo bien," Rodrigo assured him. "We're going dancing, so get dressed. Let's go."

The reality of being in Colombia hit Jim at about 11:15 that night when he and his friends entered Bahía, a Bogotá nightclub. The rhythms of salsa and merengue filled the club. Jim's mind flashed back to the Latin dance parties he and Rodrigo had had in Boston with their friends from Central and South America.

"Jim, this is my cousin, Diana. She'll be your partner tonight," Rodrigo said. "You'll get to practice your Spanish too; she doesn't speak a word of English. Have fun."

For the next six hours, they danced and drank. This is the Colombian way. At 5:30 the next morning, Rodrigo decided it was time to leave to get something to eat. On the drive home, they stopped at an outdoor grill in the mountains where many people had congregated for the same reason. Everyone was eating arepas con queso and mazorca, and drinking Aguardiente.

Next, they continued to an outdoor party just down the street. Here, they danced and drank until the sun crested over the mountains of Bogotá. It was about 7:00 a.m. when they decided to conclude the celebration—for now.

Saturday was spent recovering from the previous evening and also touring some local spots in the country. However, Saturday night was a repeat of Friday. After being in Colombia for three days, Jim had slept a total of about four hours. Fortunately, Monday was a national holiday.

Business before Pleasure before Business?

Although Jim was having a great time, he had also scheduled a series of business meetings with directors of business schools at various Bogotá universities for the week to come. Jim worked as an acquisitions editor for Academia Press, a major publisher of college-level business textbooks. The purpose of the meetings was to establish business contacts in the Colombian market. It was hoped that these initial contacts would lead to others in Latin America.

At Academia Press headquarters in New York, Jim and Caroline Evans, his boss, had discussed the opportunities in Latin America. Although Academia Press routinely published international editions of its texts, total international sales never represented more than 15 percent of their gross. Consequently, international

589

markets had never been pursued aggressively. Caroline, however, saw the Latin American markets as having a lot of potential within the next three to five years. She envisioned this market alone, in time, representing 15 to 20 percent of gross sales. Moreover, she felt that within the next ten years, international sales could reach 40 percent if developed properly. With numbers like that, it was evident to Jim that this deal was important, not only to the company but to his career as well. If Jim was able to open these markets, he might receive a promotion and be able to continue to work in Central and South America.

Jim's first meeting was scheduled for 11:00 a.m. on Tuesday, the second on Wednesday at 11:00 a.m., and the third on Friday at 3:00 p.m. At precisely 11:00 a.m. on Tuesday, Jim arrived at Javeriana University, where he was to meet with Professors Emilio Muñoz, Diana Espitia, and Enrique Ronderos. When he arrived, Professor Muñoz was waiting for him in the conference room.

"Señor Reynolds, I am delighted to meet you. How was your flight?"

"Wonderful," Jim replied.

"And how do you like Bogotá so far? Have you been able to sightsee?"

"No, I haven't had the chance to get around the city yet. I hope to see some things later in the week."

"Well, before you leave, you must visit *El Museo de Oro*. It is the finest collection of gold artifacts from the various indigenous Indian tribes in Colombia. Although much of the gold was stolen by the Spanish, many pieces have survived." For the next 30 minutes, Professor Muñoz spoke of everything from the upcoming presidential elections to World Cup soccer.

Jim looked at his watch, concerned about the other professors who had not yet arrived and about the meeting for which he had prepared.

"Is there something wrong, Señor Reynolds?"

"No, no, I was just wondering about the others; it's 11:30."

"Don't worry. They'll be here shortly. Traffic in Bogotá at this hour is terrible. They're probably caught in a traffic jam."

Just then, Professors Espitia and Ronderos walked in.

"Muy buenas, Señor Reynolds," Professor Espitia said warmly. "Please forgive us for the delay. Traffic is simply awful at this time of day."

"Oh, that's not necessary. I understand. Traffic in New York can be absolutely horrendous as well," Jim replied. "Sometimes it takes two hours to get from one end of the city to the other."

"Have you had lunch yet, Señor Reynolds?" asked Professor Ronderos.

Jim shook his head.

"Why don't we go to lunch, and we can talk there?" Professor Ronderos suggested.

After discussing the restaurants in the area, the professors decided on El Club Ejecutivo. It was nearly 12:30 p.m. when they arrived.

"It's been an hour and a half, and we haven't discussed anything," Jim thought. He was concerned that the Colombians were not very interested in what he had to offer. Throughout lunch, Jim grew increasingly concerned that the professors were more interested in his trying typical Colombian dishes and visiting the sights in Bogotá than in Academia's textbooks. They were fascinated that Jim knew how to dance salsa and merengue and impressed that he spoke Spanish with a slight Colombian accent; Señorita Espitia said she found it amusing. That seemed much more important than his knowledge of business textbooks and publishing in general.

By the end of lunch, Jim was nearly beside himself. It was now after 2:30 p.m. and nothing had been accomplished.

"Why don't we all go to Monserate tomorrow? It's absolutely beautiful up there, Señor Reynolds," Professor Ronderos suggested, going on to describe the mountain that overlooks Bogotá and the myths and traditions that surround it.

"That's a wonderful idea," Professor Espitia added.

"Monserate it is then. Jim, it has been a pleasure. I look forward to our meeting tomorrow," Professor Ronderos said with a slight bow.

"Señor Reynolds, would you like a ride home?" Professor Muñoz asked.

"Yes, if it's not too much trouble."

On the way home, Jim was relatively quiet.

"Do you feel okay?"

"It must be jet lag catching up to me. I'm sure it's nothing," Jim responded. Concerned about the way the meeting had gone, Jim realized that he had never even had a chance to mention Academia Press's various titles and how these texts could be used to create a new curriculum or supplement an existing curriculum at the professors' business school.

When in Bogotá

On arriving at the house, Jim went upstairs and sat in the living room glumly sipping a cup of aguapanela. "I just don't get it," he thought. "The Colombians couldn't have been happier with the way the meeting turned out, but we didn't do anything. We didn't even talk about one book. I just don't understand what went wrong."

In a short time, Darío arrived. "Muy buenas, Jim. How did your meetings go today with the directors?" he asked.

"I don't know. I don't know what to think. We didn't do anything. We didn't talk about business at all. We talked more about the sights I should see and the places I should visit before I leave Colombia. I'm supposed to call my boss this afternoon and tell her how the initial meeting went. What am I going to tell her? 'Sorry, we just decided to plan my vacation in Colombia instead of discussing business.' I can't afford to have this deal fall through."

Darío laughed.

"Señor, I'm serious."

"Jim, I understand. Believe me. Tell me about your meeting today."

Jim recounted every detail of the meeting to Darío, who smiled and nodded his head as he listened.

"Jim, you have to understand one thing before you continue negotiating with the directors."

"What's that?"

"You're in Colombia now," Darío said simply.

Jim stared at him with a puzzled look. "And?"

"And what, Jim?"

"Is there something else I should know?"

"That's where you need to start. You let the directors set the tone of the meeting. It's obvious they felt very comfortable with you, or they wouldn't have invited you to Monserate. Here in Colombia, Jim, we do business differently. Right now, you're building friendship. You're building their trust in you. This is very important in doing business in all of Latin America."

After a moment's pause, "Jim," Darío continued, "would you rather do business with a friend or someone you hardly know?"

As Darío went on to analyze the meeting, Jim realized that his perception of the situation had been formed by his experiences in the United States. "When in Bogotá," he thought, "I guess I had better think like the Colombians."

"Jim, you've gained the respect and the trust of the directors. In my opinion, your first meeting was a complete success."

"What should I expect in the meetings to come?" Jim asked.

"Don't worry," he responded. "Just let the directors worry about that. You'll come to an agreement before the end of the week. I guarantee it."

Questions for Discussion

1. What differences does Jim notice between life in the United States and life in Colombia?

2. What differences does Jim notice between doing business in the United States and doing business in Colombia? How might these same factors differ in other countries?

3. What advice would you give Jim for closing his deals? Why?

Source: Written by Matthew C. Shull, twitter.com/Matthew_Shull. All rights reserved. Used with permission.

3. The International Cola Alliances

Objectives

- To introduce some of the complexities involved in doing business across international borders
- To examine what happens when countries seek to do business with one another without the benefit of a common language and customs

Background

Even with a common language, communication can break down, and interpretations of words and actions often can confound understanding and incur negative attributions of purpose. Add to this the differences of personal needs that exist from individual to individual, as well as national and cultural needs that exist from country to country. These limitless variables make cooperation across borders even more complex.

The Story

You are a delegation from a country that would like to enter into a large cooperative effort with a number of other countries for the production and distribution of a popular soft drink produced by the American company International Cola. In the past, countries in your region of the world have been resistant to allowing foreign soft drinks into their markets, despite consumer demands. However, recent thinking is that the advantages of allowing this competition outweigh the disadvantages.

International Cola has expressed an interest in setting up a bottling plant, a regional corporate headquarters, and four distribution depots. Their goal, of course, is to do this in the most economically efficient way possible to maximize profits. However, because the executives at International Cola believe this area to be a rich new market with outstanding potential and are therefore eager to get in, they have ceded to the demands of the various governments in the proposed alliance. These require International Cola to allow for local control of the facilities; to maintain only 49 percent interest in the facilities with local partners holding 51 percent ownership; and to allow the participating governments to work out among themselves the details of where the facilities will be located.

For the countries involved, having one or more of these facilities located within their borders will bring jobs, revenue, and a certain amount of prestige. (It is possible for a single country to have all six of the facilities: regional headquarters, bottling plant, distribution depots.)

Each of the countries involved shares at least two borders with the other countries. This has not always been the most peaceful area. Border skirmishes are frequent, most stemming from minor misunderstandings that became inflated by vast cultural and religious differences.

These distinct cultural differences between your country and your neighbors will likely become even more evident as you pursue the negotiation. It will be up to you to decide how to respond to them. While it is important for you to retain your own cultural integrity—for example, when you first meet a delegate from another country you will likely greet him or her in the cultural style of your country—you understand the importance of being sensitive to one another. If you understand, for example, that the cultural style of another country is to bow on meeting, whereas you shake hands, you may wish to bow instead.

Because you are negotiating the venture across borders, and each country has a different primary language, you have agreed to negotiate in English, but none of you are entirely fluent. Therefore, a few phrases will creep in from your own languages.

Wear your country's flag in a visible place at all times.

Instructions

Step 1 *(30–40 minutes—may be done before class)* Working in small groups (5–7), develop a profile of your country and its people based on profile sheets 1 and 2.

After you have completed profile sheets 1 and 2, briefly discuss them to be sure there is mutual understanding of what the group's behavior and negotiating stance are to be during the negotiation.

Step 2 *(20 minutes—may be done before class)* Based on the profile sheets, decide which International Cola facilities you believe you should have in your country and why you believe they should be in your country rather than one of the others that will be represented. For example, if you have a highly educated population, you may argue that you should be the home of the regional corporate headquarters; be aware, however, that another country might argue that you should not have bottling and distribution facilities because these do not require a highly educated or skilled labor force.

On the negotiation sheet, make a list of the facilities you believe your country should have and some notes as to what your arguments will be for having them. Also, make some notes on what you believe the other countries' counterarguments will be and how you expect to respond to them.

Step 3 *(30–45 minutes—in class)* Everyone in your group should pin a copy of your country's flag and motto on himself or herself in a visible place. One to three representatives from your group (delegation) should nego-tiate the arrangements for International Cola's facilities with the representatives from the other delegations. Be sure to use the cultural norms of your country during the negotiation, but *do not tell* the others what your social norms are.

Representatives should introduce themselves to one another on an individual basis. After personal introductions, representatives should form a circle in the center of the room with their delegations behind them, briefly describe their countries, state their positions, and begin negotiations. During negotiations, representatives should make an effort to use their new language at least three times. They should not use English for any of the six phrases listed.

Delegation representatives and the other members of their groups may communicate with one another at any point during the negotiation, but only in writing. Group members may also communicate among themselves, but only in writing during the negotiation.

Any group or representative may ask for a side meeting with one or more of the other groups during the negotiation. Side meetings may not last more than five minutes.

At any time in the negotiation, the delegation may change its representative. When such a change is made, the new representative and the other delegates must reintroduce themselves and greet one another.

Those members of each delegation who are not directly negotiating should be active observers. Use the observer sheet to record situations in which other groups insulted them, shamed them, or were otherwise offensive.

At the end of 45 minutes, the negotiation should be concluded whether or not an agreement has been reached.

Questions for Discussion

1. What role did cultural differences play in the various phases of the negotiation process? Be careful not to overlook the introductory phase. Was the negotiation frustrating? Satisfying? Other? Why?

2. At any time, did delegations recognize the cultural differences between themselves and the others? If so, was any attempt made to try to adapt to another country's norms? Why? Why not? Would there have been a benefit in doing so? Why?

3. What role did language differences play during the negotiation? What was the effect of lack of understanding or miscommunication on the process?

4. Did the delegations from various countries attempt to find mutual goals and interests despite their differences? In what ways were the best interests of the overall plan subjugated to the individual interests of each country? What rhetoric was used to justify the personal interests?

5. To what degree did groups construct their countries to best justify their position? In situations where this happened, did it work? Why? Why not?

Profile Sheet 1

1. Select a name for your country:

_____

Be sure that the name of your country appears on or around the flag (see below).

2. In the space below, design your country's flag or emblem. Make enough copies so that each member of your group has one to wear.

3. Write a slogan for your country that best embodies your country's ideals and goals. Include the slogan on or around the flag.

_____

_____

4. Make up a partial language with a vocabulary of up to twenty-five (25) words into which you should translate the following phrases for use during negotiations:

Phrase	Translation
I agree.	_____
I disagree.	_____
This is unacceptable.	_____
I don't understand your point.	_____
You have insulted me.	_____
Please repeat that.	_____

5. Briefly describe how people in your country react when they have been insulted.

_____

_____

_____

_____

_____

Profile Sheet 2

Describe your country by selecting one element from each of the following lists. After you have made your selections, list the elements that make up your country's description on a separate piece of paper and add any additional elements you wish.

Population Density

_____ high density with overpopulation a problem

_____ moderate density—high end

_____ moderate density—average

_____ moderate density—low end

_____ low density

Average Educational Level

_____ less than 3 years—large percent totally illiterate

_____ 3–6 years—widespread functional illiteracy

_____ 6–9 years—functional illiteracy a problem in scattered areas

_____ 9–12 years—most read and write at functional levels

_____ 12+ years—a highly educated and functioning population

Per Capita Income

_____ under $1,000 per year

_____ $1,000–5,000 per year

_____ $5,000–10,000 per year

_____ $10,000–20,000 per year

_____ $20,000–30,000 per year

_____ $30,000–40,000 per year

_____ $40,000+ per year

Climate

_____ tropical

_____ arctic

_____ mixed in different areas

_____ runs range from season to season

Form of Government

_____ socialist

_____ democratic

_____ communist

_____ monarchy

_____ dictatorship

_____ other (specify)

Dominant Racial-Ethnic Group

_____ Asian

_____ black

_____ white

_____ other (specify)

Dominant Religion

_____ animist

_____ atheist/agnostic

_____ Buddhist

_____ Catholic

_____ Hindu

_____ Islam

_____ Jewish

_____ Mormon

_____ Protestant (specify) _____

_____ other (specify) _____

Negotiation Sheet

1. What facilities do you believe your country should have?

_____
_____
_____
_____

2. What facilities of those listed above are you willing to relinquish to reach agreement?

_____
_____
_____

3. On what bases will you justify your need or desire for having the facilities you have listed?

_____
_____
_____
_____
_____
_____
_____
_____

Observer Sheet

1. List actions taken by members of other delegations that were insulting, created shame for you and your delegation, or were otherwise offensive based on your country's norms. Include notes on the context in which the actions were taken.

_____
_____
_____
_____

2. Based on the above list, what happened to your interest in forming an alliance and your belief that a mutual agreement could be reached?

4. Whom to Hire?

Objectives

- To explore participants' cultural biases and expectations
- To examine cultural differences
- To consider the impact culture has on hiring decisions

Instructions

Step 1 (10–15 minutes) Read the background information and descriptions of each of the applicants. Consider the job and the cultures within which the individual to be hired will be operating. Rank the candidates from 1 to 5, with 1 being your first choice, and enter your rankings on the ranking sheet in the column marked "My Ranking." Briefly, list the reasons for each of your rankings.

Do not discuss your rankings with your classmates until told to do so.

Step 2 (30–40 minutes) Working with three to four of your classmates, discuss the applicants and rank them in the order of group preference. Do not vote.

Rank the candidates from 1 to 5, with 1 being the group's first choice, and enter your group rankings on the ranking sheet in the column marked "Group Ranking." Briefly list the reasons for each of the group's rankings.

If your group represents more than one culture, explore the ways in which each person's cultural background may have influenced his or her individual decisions.

Step 3 (open-ended) Report your rankings to the class, and discuss the areas of difference that emerged within your group while you were trying to reach consensus.

Questions for Discussion

1. Was your group able to explore openly any culturally based biases that came up—for example, feelings about homosexuality, religion, personality traits, politics?

2. Did you make any comments or observations that you feel would have been fully acceptable in your own culture but were not accepted by the group? Explain.

3. If the answer to question 2 was yes, how did the reaction of the group make you feel about your membership in it? How did you handle the situation?

4. What implications do you believe these cultural differences would have in business dealings?

Background

You are a member of the management committee of a multinational company that does business in 23 countries. While your company's headquarters are in Holland, your offices are scattered fairly evenly throughout the four hemispheres. Primary markets have been in Europe and North America; the strongest emerging market is the Pacific Rim. Company executives would like to develop what they see as a powerful potential market in the Middle East. Sales in all areas except the Pacific Rim have shown slow growth over the past two years.

At present, your company is seeking to restructure and revitalize its worldwide marketing efforts. To accomplish this, you have determined that you need to hire a key marketing person to introduce fresh ideas and a new perspective. There is no one currently in your company who is qualified to do this, and so you have decided to look outside. The job title is "vice president for international marketing"; it carries with it a salary well into six figures (US$), plus elaborate benefits, an unlimited expense account, a car, and the use of the corporate jet. The person you hire will be based at the company's headquarters and will travel frequently.

A lengthy search has turned up five people with good potential. It is now up to you to decide whom to hire. Although all the applicants have expressed a sincere interest in the position, it is possible that they may change their minds once the job is offered. Therefore, you must rank them in order of preference so that if your first choice declines the position, you can go on to the second, and so on.

Applicants: Park L., age 41, Married with Three Children

Park L. is currently senior vice president for marketing at a major Korean high-technology firm. You have been told by the head of your Seoul office that his reputation as an expert in international marketing is outstanding. The market share of his company's products has consistently increased since he joined the company just over 15 years ago. His company's market share is now well ahead of that of competing producers in the Pacific Rim.

Park started with his present company immediately after his graduation from the University of Seoul and has worked his way up through the ranks. He does not have a graduate degree. You sense that Park has a keen understanding of organizational politics and knows how to play them. He recognizes that because the company he works for now is family controlled, it is unlikely that he will ever move much higher than his present situation. Park has told you that he is interested in the growth potential offered at your company.

In addition to his native tongue, Park is able to carry on a reasonably fluent conversation in English and has a minimal working knowledge of German and French. His wife, who appears quiet and quite traditional, and his children speak only Korean.

Kiran K., age 50, Widow with One Adult Child

Kiran K. is a Sikh woman living in Malaysia. She began her teaching career while finishing her DBA (doctorate in business administration) at the Harvard Business School and published her first book on international marketing ten months after graduation. Her doctoral dissertation was based on the international marketing of pharmaceuticals, but she has also done research and published on other areas of international marketing.

Two months after the publication of her book, Kiran went to work in the international marketing department of a Fortune 500 company, where she stayed for the next ten years. She returned to teaching when Maura University offered her a full professorship with tenure, and she has been there since that time. Her academic position has allowed her to pursue a number of research interests and to write authoritative books and papers in her field. At present, she is well published and internationally recognized as an expert on international marketing. In addition, she has an active consulting practice throughout Southeast Asia.

You have learned through your office in Kuala Lumpur that Kiran's only child, a 23-year-old son, is severely mentally and physically disabled. You sense that part of her interest in the job with your company is to have the income to guarantee his care should anything happen to her. Her son would go with her to Holland, should she be given the job, where he will need to be enrolled in special support programs.

In addition to fluency in Malay, English, and Hindi, Kiran speaks and writes German and Spanish and is able to converse in Japanese and Mandarin.

Peter V., age 44, Single

Peter is a white South African. He had worked in a key position in the international marketing division of an American Fortune 100 company until the company pulled out of his country eight months ago. While the company wanted to keep him on, offering to move him from Johannesburg to its New York headquarters, Peter decided that it was time to look elsewhere. He had begun to feel somewhat dead-ended in his position and apparently sees the position at your company as an opportunity to try out new territory. Like your other candidates for the position, Peter

has a long list of accomplishments and is widely recognized as outstanding in his field. People in your company who have had contacts with him say that Peter is creative, hardworking, and loyal. In addition, you have been told that Peter is a top-flight manager of people who is able to push his employees to the highest levels of performance. And, you are told, he is very organized.

Peter has a PhD in computer science from a leading South African university and an MBA from Purdue's Krannert School of Business.

Peter had been a vehement opponent of apartheid and is still very much a social activist. His high political visibility within South Africa had made his life there difficult, and even now, with the end of apartheid, he would like to get out. His constant male companion, P. K. Kahn, would be coming with him to Holland, and Peter would like your personnel office to help P. K. find an appropriate position.

Peter speaks and reads English, Dutch, Afrikaans, and Swahili and can converse in German.

Tex P., age 36, Divorced with One Child

Tex is currently job hunting. His former job as head of marketing for a single-product, high-technology firm—highly specialized workstations for sophisticated artificial intelligence applications—ended when the company was bought out by Texas Instruments. Tex had been with his previous company virtually from the time the company was started six years earlier. Having to leave his job was an irony to Tex as it was largely due to the success of his efforts that the company was bought out. You sense that he is a little bitter, and he tells you that jobs offered to him by TI were beneath him and not worthy of consideration.

Tex has both his undergraduate and MBA degrees from Stanford University. In addition, he was a Rhodes Scholar and won a Fulbright scholarship, which he used to support himself while he undertook a two-year research project on the marketing of high-technology equipment to Third World countries.

You have learned through your New York office that Tex has a reputation for being aggressive and hard driving. Apparently he is a workaholic who has been known to work 18 to 20 hours a day, seven days a week. He seems to have little time for his personal life.

In addition to his native English, Tex has a minimal command of French—which he admits he hasn't used since his college days.

Zvi C., age 40, Married with Five Children

Zvi began his career after receiving his MBA from the Sloan School of Management at the Massachusetts Institute of Technology (MIT). His first job was as marketing manager for a German company doing business in Israel.

Subject Index

A page number with an *e* indicates an exhibit; an *f* a figure; an *n,* a source note or footnote; a *t,* a table.